P9-ARM-549

Textiles: FIBER TO FABRIC

FOURTH EDITION

Textiles

FIBER

GREGG DIVISION/McGRAW-HILL

M. DAVID POTTER

Professor of Business
San Francisco State College
San Francisco, California

BERNARD P. CORBMAN

Dean of Faculty and
Professor, Department of
Business and Commerce
Bronx Community College
Bronx, New York

TO FABRIC

New York
St. Louis
Dallas
San Francisco
Toronto
BOOK COMPANY London
Sydney

BOOK DESIGN BY BARBARA DUPREE KNOWLES

TEXTILES: FIBER TO FABRIC, Fourth Edition

Copyright © 1967, 1959 by McGraw-Hill, Inc.
All Rights Reserved. Copyright 1954, 1945 by
McGraw-Hill, Inc. All Rights Reserved. Printed
in the United States of America. No part of this
publication may be reproduced, stored in a retrieval
system, or transmitted, in any form or by any
means, electronic, mechanical, photocopying, recording, or otherwise, without the prior written
permission of the publisher.
Library of Congress Catalog Card Number: 66-21868

ISBN 07-050542-X
67890 HDBP 76543

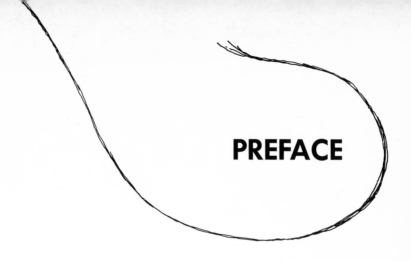

PREFACE

Textiles: Fiber to Fabric, Fourth Edition, a successor to *Fiber to Fabric,* first published in 1945, is a comprehensive blending of both the revolutionary new developments in the textile field and the traditional background information necessary for a full understanding of this huge, complex, and fast-moving industry. In addition, this enriched edition provides the basic information needed by (1) students who are preparing for careers in the textile industry—in manufacturing, retailing, purchasing, or promoting; (2) beginning workers engaged in some phase of the textile complex; (3) consumers and home economists who need sound guidance in the selection and care of textile products; (4) teachers who need a complete basic text on textiles, adaptable to a variety of curricula and student needs; and (5) established specialists who need an up-to-date reference book.

SCOPE OF COVERAGE ■ *Textiles: Fiber to Fabric,* Fourth Edition, places stress on the comparison, selection, usage, and care of fabrics and merchandise items as well as on the theory and processes underlying their manufacture and development. Wherever possible, topics have been expanded so that the book may continue to serve as a comprehensive survey of the textile field.

New methods of finishing, such as improved wash and wear for cottons, permanent press for all-cottons and cotton blends, durable press for wools, fabric bonding, and foam laminating, are surveyed. The wide application of "stretch" in fabrics is given considerable attention through discussions of stretch fibers, yarns, finishes, and the resultant stretch fabrics. New dyes and optical brighteners are also considered.

The newer strains of cotton fibers recently introduced on the market are explained, evaluated, and compared, as are the new and improved forms of rayons, nylons, acrylics, polyesters, sarans, and glass fibers. New in this edition are the chapters on modacrylic, spandex, and polypropylene olefin fibers, as well as on textured yarns.

Special attention is given to the growing acceptance of fabric constructions other than weaving. Knitting, for example, is treated independently and in great detail. Nonwovens, tufting, and the new mali constructions are also covered.

In this edition the authors compare fabrics of all types in reference to their performance, durability, care requirements, and related characteristics. Thus the student has an opportunity to develop an ability to select goods wisely and with discrimination.

Detailed descriptions and information are provided on home furnishings, such as rugs, and on personal garments, such as sweaters and hosiery. The detailed discussions of hosiery, for example, cover evaluations of various knitted constructions, gauge, and denier.

PLAN OF BOOK ■ The plan of *Textiles: Fiber to Fabric,* while following a distinct line of development, is by no means rigid. Each chapter is an entity unto itself, so that the instructor may adapt the text to an outline that seems more appropriate for his particular textile course of study or group of students.

The sequence of chapters of the previous edition, which was based on many years of teaching experience and was helpful to students and teachers in the past, has been changed slightly to provide a presentation better suited to the numerous developments in this field.

The book opens with an introduction to the various fibers and tells how to identify them. Then the reader is taken through the logical, related sequence of chapters from fiber to finished fabric. As an example, a chapter is devoted to spinning the fiber into various types of yarn. This is followed by treatment of fabric construction in a chapter on weaving, an expanded chapter on knitting, and a separate chapter on the less predominant, but growing, minor fabric constructions.

Subsequent chapters review the many types of finishes, dyes and dyeing methods, and decorating techniques.

Also included are the history of textile development, the methods of manufacture, and the characteristics, evaluations, and care of each type of textile. Comparative characteristics of all fibers are presented in a summary chapter. Subsequent chapters of the book cover minor textile fibers, rugs and carpets, and care of fabrics, thus rounding out the reader's acquaintance with the field of textiles.

LEARNING AIDS ■ The text has been written and presented in a manner that facilitates understanding and, therefore, learning of the basic aspects of the textile field.

Teachability. *Textiles: Fiber to Fabric* does not require a previous knowledge of textiles or a background in science. Its vocabulary is simple and direct. Technical theory and concepts and methods are intermingled with practical information that the layman needs and understands readily. Where physical or chemical terminology is necessary, it is presented clearly and in an understandable manner. The student is also provided with trade names of fibers and finishes and with glossaries for significant fabrics.

Specific facts to be considered when purchasing items such as sheets, towels, and hosiery are organized and presented for ready reference. The general care of fabrics is fully discussed, including detailed information on stain removal.

Visual Aids. Illustrations help to make the more technical material understandable. Photographs and diagrams are used by the authors to clarify new materials and to simplify complex industrial processes. Summary charts quickly identify and review the principal points covered and compare the specific items discussed.

Cross-References. Information in the text is organized so that the book can be used as a reference source as well as a classroom text. Although each topic is treated independently, cross-reference notations minimize repetition and enable the reader to find specific information, such as properties of fibers, description of fabrics, new finishes, and the like.

End-of-Chapter Material. There are two kinds of end-of-chapter activities. (1) Review Questions provide an opportunity for classroom discussion and review and are based on the text material. (2) Suggested Activities are provided for selected chapters as appropriate. They give the student direction for enriching activities that will further increase his understanding of the subject.

Bibliography. An extensive bibliography provides reading and reference sources for independent study. Listed are current books, periodicals, trade journals, and brochures covering the wide area of textiles. Names and addresses of textile companies and other organizations that have educational material available are also provided.

Instructor's Key. The answers to all Review Questions are derived from the text. Therefore, the instructor can base his evaluation and grading of the students' work on the text assigned.

ACKNOWLEDGMENTS

This fourth edition has entailed much research. Special thanks are extended to Robert Pinault, Associate Editor, *Textile World*, for his assistance in the revision of the chapter on Dyeing as well as for other helpful suggestions. The gathering and evaluation of material for other chapters in this edition has been greatly facilitated by the kind cooperation of a great many companies and organizations, and by the officers and personnel acting in their behalf. Grateful acknowledgments are made to the following:

Hanna Cohen, Promotion Department, Abaco Fabrics Corporation; R. J. Richardson, Manager, Product Technical Information, Allied Chemical Corporation; Ruth Holman, Public Relations, American Carpet Institute; John J. Whalen and Arthur Niedleman, Public Relations, and Lynn Waplington, Product Publicity Supervisor, American Cyanamid Company; J. R. Heyward, Technical Publications Coordinator, American Enka Corporation; A. A. Cook, Technical Director, Arkansas Company, Inc.; John W. Lane, President, and William W. Lane, Vice-President, Atlas Electric Devices Company.

James E. Ryan, Product Manager, Polyester Products, Beaunit Fibers; Bibb Manufacturing Company; Clifford W. Birch, P.E., President, Birch Brothers, Inc.; Denise Hynes McMahon, Manager, Consumer Relations, and Virginia E. Meyer, Technical Information Section, Celanese Fibers Company; Yvette Neier, Merchandising Coordinator, and Ettagale Blauer, Public Relations Specialist, Chemstrand Company; Edward R. Rogers, Marketing Services, Ciba Chemical & Dye Company; Jerome D. Gelula, Executive Vice-President, Marketing/Merchandising, Coin Sales Corporation.

John H. Sasson, Quality Control Director, Compax Corporation; Shirley Institute: Cotton, Silk, & Manmade Fibres Research Assn., Manchester, England; Frank M. Soling, Director of Merchandising, Courtaulds North America, Inc.; Howell R. Geib, Jr., Sales Manager, Cranston Print Works Company; Fred Barbaro, Vice-President and General Manager, Cravenette Company; Klaus W. Bahlo, Vice-President, and Ralph A. Huey, Assistant Advertising Manager,

Crompton & Knowles Corporation; Raymond A. Pingree, Technical Director, Crown Chemical Corporation; J. R. Schurz, Sales Engineer, Curlator Corporation.

Robert M. Gardiner, Director of Community Relations, Dan River Mills, Inc; H. William Petry, Deering Milliken Research Corporation; Harold A. Cook, Publicity Manager, Dow Corning Corporation; E. G. Dearborn, Advertising Dept., James Adshead, Jr. and Alexander L. Murphy, Public Relations Department, E. I. du Pont de Nemours & Company; Robert E. Webb, Technical Editor, Fibers Division, Eastman Chemical Products, Inc.; Herbert A. Briggs, Vice-President, Fibers Control Corporation; Charles L. Cohen, Fiber Industries, Inc.; A. E. Martin, Jr., Director of Technical Services, Firestone Synthetic Fibers Company.

John L. Kelly, Advertising Manager, Apparel and Home Furnishings, and Judith H. Smeltzer, Product Information Services, Fibers Operations, FMC Corporation, American Viscose Division; Richard Morrow, Franklin Process Company; J. L. Powell, Technical Director, Globe Manufacturing Company; D. J. Fraser, Fiber and Film Department, and Susan Foster, R. B. Teeple, Jr., E. T. Shell, Hercules Powder Company; Les Rossi, Public Relations Department, and C. E. Sigler, J. P. Stevens & Co., Inc.; James Hunder Machine Company; George A. Billingsley, Group Leader, Chemical Section, Licensing Division, and J. Gorman Walsh, Director, Bancroft Marketing Division, Joseph Bancroft & Sons Co.

Ronald W. Kostka, Senior Division Publicist, and Joseph M. Franey, Product Publicity, 3M Company; Arthur N. Tingley, Vice-President, Technical Service and Development, and J. S. Campbell, Madison Throwing Company, Inc.; Joseph A. Curry, Advertising Manager, McGregor-Doniger Inc.; Leon E. Seidel, Vice-President, Metlon Corporation; Jerome Campbell, Editor, Modern Textiles Magazine; Donald A. Yeskoo, Manager, Plastics-Industrial Advertising, Nopco Chemical Company; F. A. Mennerich, Manager, Testing Division, and James E. Murphy, Supervisor of Public Relations, and John W. Dougherty, Advertising Manager, Owens-Corning Fiberglas Corporation.

Anne Cain, Public Relations, and Albert W. Metzger, Merchandising Manager, Decorative Fabrics, Pittsburgh Plate Glass Company; Carl Horowitz, President, Polymer Research Corporation of America; Philip M. Salaff, Printex Corporation; Dr. Victor Ehrlich, Division of Research, Reeves Brothers, Inc.; Clinton Reynolds, Reynolds Advertising Agency; E. E. Rettberg, Jr., President, Scholler Brothers, Inc.; T. Bennett, Fabrics Machine Division, Scott & Williams, Incorporated; M. McCord, Spring Mills, Inc.; Marshall Goree, Sales Manager, Standard-Coosa-Thatcher Company.

Steel Heddle Manufacturing Company; James Allan, Sales Manager, Taylor, Stiles & Company; E. W. Harris, Applications, Textile Development, The Dow Badische Company; Herbert H. Stadtlander, The Kenyon Piece Dyeworks, Inc.; Paul Askew, Sales Department, The Singer Company; Adeline A. Dembeck, Advertising & Promotion Director, The United Piece Dye Works; William N. Schwarze, Turbo Machine Company; R. K. Kennedy, Union Carbide Corporation; Dr. Wilson A. Reeves, Chief, Cotton Finishes Laboratory, and Vernon R. Bourdette, Public Information Officer, Southern Utilization Research and Development Division, and Harold P. Lundgren, Chief, Wool and Mohair Laboratory, United States Department of Agriculture.

Thomas S. Healey, and L. M. Boulware, Sales Manager, Vyrene and Lastex Yarns, Textile Division, and R. C. Hunt, Product Application Supervisor, Polypropylene, and Evelyn V. Sulser, Development Department, Polypropylene, and Doris Tarrant, Public Relations, United States Rubber Company; Richard MacKenzie, Technical Service Manager, The Vectra Company; F. Donald Spencer, Vogt Manufacturing Corporation; J. Longenecker, Advertising Manager, Textile Machinery Division, The Warner & Swasey Co.; C. F. Fitzgerald, Assistant Sales Manager, Wildman Jacquard Co.

M. David Potter
Bernard P. Corbman

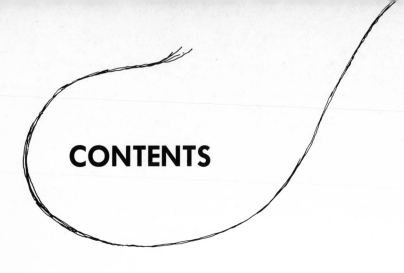

CONTENTS

Textiles: **FIBER TO FABRIC**

UNDER THE MICROSCOPE

1

TEXTILE FIBERS

Textiles have such an important bearing on our daily lives that everyone needs to know something about them. From earliest times, man has used textiles of various types for covering, warmth, personal adornment, and even to display personal wealth. Today, textiles are still used for these purposes and everyone is an ultimate consumer. You use textiles in some form even if you are not the direct purchaser. Included among consumers are merchandisers of many types, from the wholesale textile manufacturer and merchant to the retail-store sales force. Many of the industries—for example, the automobile industry—are important consumers of textiles in various forms. Other consumers are homemakers, dressmakers, interior decorators, and retail-store customers, as well as students who are studying for these and various other occupations and professions in which a knowledge of textiles is of major importance.

The merchant, particularly, and all those who work for him must be thoroughly familiar with the merchandise they are handling if they wish to be successful. Only thorough knowledge will prevent the mistakes that are too often made in buying and selling.

REASONS FOR STUDYING TEXTILES

A study of textiles will show, for example, why certain fabrics are more durable and therefore more serviceable for specific purposes. It will explain why certain fabrics make cool wearing apparel as well as give an impression of coolness when used as decoration. The quality of cleanliness, also, must be estimated before purchasing, when that is an important factor.

Complete knowledge of textiles will facilitate an intelligent appraisal of standards and brands of merchandise and will develop the ability to distinguish quality in fabrics and, in turn, to appreciate the proper uses for the different qualities. As a result, the consumer merchant and the consumer customer will know how to buy and what to buy, and salespeople will know how to render good service to those consumers who have not had the advantage of a formal course in textiles.

In recent years, giant strides have been made in the textile industry that have greatly influenced our general economic growth. The prosperity and growth of related industries, such as petroleum and chemistry, and dependent industries, such as retail apparel stores, have produced broader employment opportunities. Competition for the consumer's dollar has fostered the creation of new textile fibers with specific qualities to compete with well-established fibers. New fiber blends have been created to combine many of these qualities into new types of yarns with new trade names. There are also new names for the fabrics made of these new fibers and yarns. New finishes have been developed to add new and interesting characteristics to fibers, yarns, and fabrics.

This welter of creativity and the myriad of trade names present a challenge to the consumer, who is sometimes knowledgeable but frequently confused. Yet he need not be. Without being overly technical, this information can be easily understood and consequently very useful to the consumer in his business and personal life. All of this information can be adopted for such utilitarian benefits as economy, durability, serviceability, and comfort as well as for such aesthetic values as hand (or feel), texture, design, and color.

In the study of textiles, the initial interest of the student will become an absorbing one when he discovers the natural fascination of fabrics and their cultural associations, particularly when factual study is supplemented by the handling of actual textile materials. The subject will seem worthwhile as you become familiar with illustrative specimens and fabrics and handle and compare the raw materials of which fabrics are made as well as the finished consumers' goods.

SEQUENCE OF FABRIC CONSTRUCTION

In beginning the study of textiles, you should have in your hand a sample of a *woven* fabric. Note that it is constructed by interlacing sets of yarns that run lengthwise and crosswise. It is from the interlacing, or weaving, of yarns that such textile materials are made. A close examination of any one of these yarns will reveal the fibrous substance from which the yarn is made. Such yarns comprise a multitude of fine, hairlike fibers or filaments that have been separated, made parallel, overlapped, and twisted together by various processes.

There is a logical development of raw material into finished consumers' goods. Studying textile materials in the interesting sequence of "fiber to yarn to fabric" will help you understand the construction and ultimate qualities of the fabrics with which you will become familiar. Here are the steps in the manufacture of fabrics from raw material to finished goods.

1. Fiber, which is spun (or twisted) into yarn or directly compressed into fabric.
2. Yarn, which is woven, knitted, or otherwise made into fabric.
3. Fabric, which by various finishing processes becomes finished consumers' goods.

KINDS OF FIBERS

The textile industry uses many different kinds of fibers as its raw materials. Some of these fibers were known and used by mankind in the earlier years of civilization, as well as in modern times. Other fibers have acquired varied degrees of importance in recent years. New fibers are being produced and tested daily. The factors influencing the development and utilization of all these fibers include their ability to be spun, their availability in sufficient quantity, the cost or economy of production, and the desirability of their properties to consumers.

Natural fibers that occur in nature in fiber form can be classified as *vegetable, animal,* and *mineral.* Vegetable fibers, found in the cell walls of plants, are cellulosic in composition. Animal fibers, produced by animals or insects, are protein in composition. The mineral fiber, asbestos, is mined from certain types of rock.

Man-made fibers are derived from various sources. For instance, man has taken the natural material of cellulose from cotton linters and wood pulp, processed it chemically, and changed its form and several other characteristics into fibers of various lengths. These are classified as *man-made cellulosic fibers.* He has also taken the protein out of such products as corn, processed it chemically, and converted it into *man-made protein fibers.*

Man-made fibers created from other sources are *mineral fibers, metallic fibers,* and *rubber fibers.* Glass fibers are produced by combining silica sand, limestone, and certain other minerals. Metallic fibers are produced by mining and refining such metals as aluminum, silver, and gold. Man has also tapped the sap from the rubber tree and developed rubber fibers (as well as certain chemical compositions for synthetic rubber fibers).

Newer types of fibers have been and are still being created by research chemists as companies strive to imitate properties of other fibers, to develop other characteristics, or to combine certain properties. These fibers are synthesized by combining carbon, oxygen, hydrogen, and other simple chemical elements into large complex molecular combinations or structures called *polymers.* Chemists, in fact, discover new chemical compositions and invent new substances that they form into fibers having certain desired characteristics.

Before 1960, the development of new fibers caused difficulty in the textile industry in terms of nomenclature, classification, and identification. The confusion was compounded by the trend of manufacturers to identify each of their fibers with a different trade name. Consumers became confused by these names and found it difficult and sometimes impossible to identify the fiber content of the products they saw in the stores. Often they did not know whether an identifying name represented a particular kind of fiber or a trade name for some kind of newly created fiber. Subsequently, the United States Congress enacted the Textile Fiber Products Identification Act, which became effective on March 3, 1960. This Act requires that the labels of all textile products must show the fiber contents for amounts above 5 percent, both by fiber name and generic (or family) name, and that all fibers must be listed in descending order of their predominence with the amount of each fiber indicated in percent by weight of the total fiber content. (The label must also indicate the name or registered number of the person or company marketing or retailing the product and, if the product is imported, the name of the country where it was manufactured.) To standardize this identification procedure, the Federal Trade Commission assigned 18 generic groups of man-made fibers according to chemical composition.

While this arrangement has brought about some standardization, clarification, and easier identification of fibers, the generic types do not provide for related groupings. Indeed, it has been found difficult by many authorities to arrange them into logical groupings by characteristics of types. One such grouping, as suggested by the Man-Made Fiber Producers Association, Inc., is cellulosic, synthetic long-chain polymers, and nonfibrous natural substances.

The following table identifies all fibers by type, name, and source or classification. It includes the authors' suggested extension or modification of the Association's grouping of nonfibrous natural substances into their derivations.

CLASSIFICATION OF FIBERS

TYPE	NAME OF FIBER	SOURCE OR COMPOSITION
Natural Fibers:		
Vegetable	Cotton	Cotton boll (cellulose)
	Linen	Flax stalk (cellulose)
	Jute	Jute stalk (cellulose)
	Hemp	Hemp or abaca stalk (cellulose)
	Sisal	Agave leaf (cellulose)
	Kapok	Kapok tree (cellulose)
	Ramie	Rhea or China grass (cellulose)
	Coir	Coconut husk (cellulose)
	Pina	Pineapple leaf (cellulose)
Animal	Wool	Sheep (protein)
	Silk	Silkworm (protein)
	Hair	Hair-bearing animals (protein)
Mineral	Asbestos	Varieties of rock (silicate of magnesium and calcuim)
Man-Made Fibers:		
Cellulosic	Rayon	Cotton linters or wood
	Acetate	Cotton linters or wood
	Triacetate	Cotton linters or wood
Synthetic Long-Chain Polymers	Nylon	Polyamide
	Polyester	Dihydric alcohol and terephthalic acid
	Acrylic	Acrylonitrile (at least 85%)
	Modacrylic	Acrylonitrile (35%–84%)
	Spandex	Polyurethane (at least 85%)
	Olefin	Ethylene or propylene (at least 85%)
	Saran	Vinylidene chloride (at least 80%)
	Vinyon	Vinyl chloride (at least 85%)
	Vinal*	Vinyl alcohol (at least 50%)
	Nytril*	Vinylidene dinitrile (at least 85%)
	Fluorocarbon	Tetrafluoroethylene
	Lastrile	Acrylonitrile (10%–50%) and a diene
	Alginate*	Calcium alginate
Mineral	Glass	Silica sand, limestone, and other minerals
	Ceramic	Minerals
Metallic	Metal	Aluminum, silver, gold, stainless steel
Rubber	Rubber	Natural or synthetic rubber
Protein	Azlon*	Corn, soybean, etc.

* Not presently in commercial production in United States.

COMPOSITION AND STRUCTURE OF FIBERS

Each textile fiber has its own distinctive structural shape and markings that, under a microscope with a magnification of at least 100, supply an absolute identification of the fiber. Certain general observations also help to identify fibers without the use of a microscope. These differences in structure determine the various characteristics of the different fibers and explain why some fibers are to be preferred to others for certain uses. The illustrations in this chapter show cross-sectional and longitudinal photomicrographs of the various fibers.

THE NATURAL FIBERS

VEGETABLE FIBERS ■ Of the several vegetable fibers, each derived from a different plant, two are recognized as major textile fibers. They are *cotton,* which grows in the seedpod, or boll, of the cotton plant, and *linen,* which grows in the stalk of the flax plant. (The minor vegetable fibers are discussed in Chapter 26.)

Cotton. Unlike other fibers obtained from plants, the cotton fiber is a single elongated cell. Under the microscope, it resembles a collapsed, spirally twisted tube with a rough surface. The thin cell wall of the fiber has from 200 to 400 turns of natural twist, or convolutions, to the inch. The fiber appears flat, twisted, and ribbonlike, with a wide inner canal (the lumen) and a granular effect. Chemically, the fiber contains about 90 percent cellulose and about 6 percent moisture; the remainder consists of natural impurities. The outer surface of the fiber is covered with a protective waxlike coating, which gives the fiber a somewhat adhesive quality.

Because of the natural twist in cotton fiber, it may be spun easily into yarn. Some cotton fibers, however, look different under the microscope and do not have this natural twist. Such fibers have been subjected to the commercially important process of mercerization, which causes the naturally flat, twisted cotton fiber to swell and become straight, smooth, and round. The straightness of the fiber causes light to be reflected on the smooth surface and produces a lustrous effect that is commercially valuable. The resultant fabric is called *mercerized cotton.*

Flax. Under the microscope, the hairlike flax fiber shows several-sided cylindrical filaments with fine pointed ends. The filaments are cemented together at intervals in the form of markings, or nodes, by a gummy substance called *pectin.* The long flax filaments contain a lumen, or inner canal, which appears as a narrow line. The fiber somewhat resembles a straight, smooth bamboo stick, with its joints producing a slight natural unevenness that cannot be eliminated. Chemically, the flax fiber is composed of about 70 percent cellulose and about 25 percent pectin; the remainder consists of woody tissue and ash. From such fibers, linen yarns are produced. To the naked eye, linen yarns appear smooth, straight, compact, and lustrous. Flax fibers are more brittle and less flexible than cotton fibers.

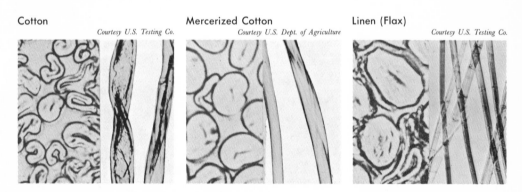

Cotton
Courtesy U.S. Testing Co.

Mercerized Cotton
Courtesy U.S. Dept. of Agriculture

Linen (Flax)
Courtesy U.S. Testing Co.

ANIMAL FIBERS ■ There are several animal fibers, each obtained from a different source, but only two are recognized as major textile fibers. They are *wool,* which grows from the skin of sheep, and *silk,* which is unwound from the cocoon of a moth caterpillar, known as the silkworm. (The minor *hair* fibers, such as camel, llama, alpaca, mohair, cashmere, vicuna, guanaco, and rabbit, are discussed in Chapter 13.)

Wool. Wool fiber is irregular and roughly cylindrical, tapered at the end, and multicellular in structure. Under the microscope, a cross section shows three fundamental layers—the epidermis, the cortex, and the medulla. The epidermis, or outer layer, consists of scales or flattened plates, ranging from 1,000 to 4,000 to an inch. These scales give the fiber its cohesive quality. They vary in type, from those having smaller, finer scales with smoother edges to those having coarser scales with irregular edges. The finer, softer, warmer fibers have more numerous and smoother scales. The thicker, coarser, less-warm fibers have fewer and rougher scales. The better fibers with more and finer scales are duller in appearance than the poorer quality wool fibers with fewer scales.

The second layer, the cortex, is the main fiber body. It gives the fiber strength and elasticity and consists of intermediate cells that hold the color pigment.

The innermost layer is the medulla, which consists of large spiral-shaped, air-filled cells. The medulla is discernible only in coarse and medium wools and only under high magnification. It is the central canal, varying in appearance from a narrow to a broad line or from a continuous to an interrupted line. Some wool fibers that have no cortical layer are compensated with a larger proportion of medullary cells. This fact lessens the affinity for dyes, because the medulla has more fat than has the rest of the fiber. The finer wools, having no medulla, absorb dyes more readily.

Two striking characteristics of wool fiber are its susceptibility to heat and its felting property, which is caused by the horny epidermal scales. Because of this felting property, only pressure, heat, and moisture are required to make wool fibers into the type of fabric called *felt.*

Chemically, wool is the only natural fiber that contains sulfur. It is composed of the following basic elements in these approximate proportions: carbon, 49 percent; oxygen, 24 percent; nitrogen, 16 percent; hydrogen, 7 percent; sulfur, 4 percent. These elements combine to form a protein known as *keratin.*

Silk. Raw silk fiber as it comes from the cultivated cocoon is called *bave.* Under the microscope, this bave appears somewhat elliptical. It is composed of

Wool   Silk   Wild, or Tussah, Silk

Courtesy American Woolen Co.   *Courtesy U.S. Testing Co.*   *Courtesy U.S. Dept. of Agriculture*

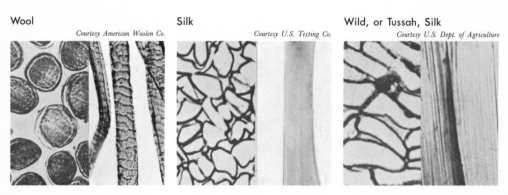

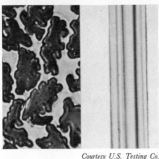
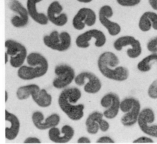

Courtesy U.S. Testing Co.

Courtesy American Viscose Corp.

Courtesy American Enka Corp.

Viscose Rayon

Avron Viscose Rayon

Krispglo Viscose Rayon

the *fibroin,* consisting of two filaments, each of which is called a *brin,* held together by *sericin,* a gummy substance that gives the bave a rather uneven surface. As the sericin is removed by hot water, the two brin filaments appear clearly as fine, lustrous, somewhat triangularly shaped transparent rods.

Wild silk, or tussah silk, may be distinguished from cultivated silk by its coarse thick form, which appears flattened. Cultivated silk is a narrow fiber with no markings. Wild silk is a broader fiber with fine, wavy longitudinal lines running across its surface, giving it a dark hue under the microscope.

Chemically, the silk fibroin and sericin are composed of approximately 95 percent protein and about 5 percent wax, fat, salts, and ash.

THE MAN-MADE FIBERS

CELLULOSIC FIBERS ■ The three types of man-made cellulosic fibers—*rayon, acetate,* and *triacetate*— are derived either from the cellulose of the cell walls of short cotton fibers (called linters) or from, more frequently, pine wood. Pure cellulose appears as a formless white substance that is converted by chemical treatment and produced into fiber form. Paper, for instance, is almost pure cellulose.

Rayons. Until recently, there were only three basic varieties of rayon: *viscose, cuprammonium,* and *nitrocellulose.* In the history of man-made fibers, nitrocellulose rayon is important because it was the first to be produced. However, it has been superseded by two others: *high wet-modulus* and *saponified* rayon. Both these fibers have a glasslike luster under the microscope and appear to have a uniform diameter when viewed longitudinally. (The appearance of fine pepperlike particles on a cross-sectional view is an indication that the rayon has been delustered.) The rayon filaments differ in appearance according to the process used in their manufacture.

Viscose rayon, although produced in several forms, basically has a crosssectional view under the microscope that is very irregular. These irregularities or wrinkles run the length of the fiber and appear as striations or fine lines in the longitudinal view on an otherwise glossy surface.

Viscose rayon is also produced in modified forms. A *high-tenacity* rayon fiber is produced by causing the cellulose to coagulate rapidly, thereby forming a tough skin and making the fiber stronger. One such fiber is sold under the trade name of *Avron.*

Other methods of modifying viscose rayon produce crimp in the fibers when they are treated chemically. *Crimped Fibro* is a trade name for one of these.

Cuprammonium rayon shows no markings; it is a fine, smooth, glossy fiber. The cross-sectional appearance is nearly round.

High wet-modulus rayon is another form of rayon. This type does not weaken significantly when wet, as ordinary viscose rayon does. This process is done by controlling the molecular structure to give maximum chain length and regularity in a fibril structure. There are several of these rayons under such trade names as *Avril, Lirelle, Zantrel Polynosic,* and the more recent (1966) *Nupron* and *Xena.*

Under the microscope, Avril more closely resembles cuprammonium rayon than any of the other rayons. The fiber is relatively smooth, and its cross section is almost round. Lirelle is more irregularly shaped with an occasional indentation and protrusion on its surface. Zantrel is almost round to oval in cross section with dark flecks that give it a duller appearance.

Saponified rayon is a fiber of pure cellulose. It has been regenerated from cellulose acetate that has been treated by saponification (removal of the acetyl groups) and stretched. The stretching orients the molecular structure of the fiber, which gives it superior strength. It is sold under the trade name of *Fortisan.* The fiber somewhat resembles acetate and has a lustrous appearance. Its cross-sectional view is irregular and lobar; in its longitudinal view, the indentations (caused by the lobes) show up as fine, lengthwise lines.

Acetate. This fiber consists of a cellulose compound identified as an acetylated cellulose—a cellulose salt. Consequently, it possesses different qualities from the rayons. The fiber comes in bright, semidull, and dull forms. Generally, the cross-sectional view of acetate is less irregular than viscose rayon, and it has a rather bulbous appearance with indentations. These indentations appear as occasional line markings or striations in the longitudinal view. The cross section can be regulated during the manufacturing process to produce flat or "Y" shapes. These changes vary the appearance and hand of the fiber.

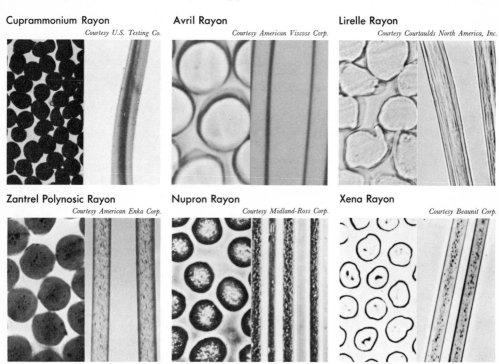

Cuprammonium Rayon
Courtesy U.S. Testing Co.

Avril Rayon
Courtesy American Viscose Corp.

Lirelle Rayon
Courtesy Courtaulds North America, Inc.

Zantrel Polynosic Rayon
Courtesy American Enka Corp.

Nupron Rayon
Courtesy Midland-Ross Corp.

Xena Rayon
Courtesy Beaunit Corp.

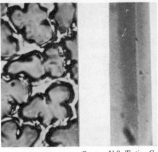
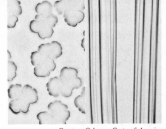

Left: Acetate. Right: Triacetate (Arnel).

Courtesy U.S. Testing Co.   Courtesy Celanese Corp. of America

Triacetate. This fiber consists of an acetylated cellulose that retains acetic groupings when it is being produced as triacetate cellulose. Its qualities are therefore different from those of acetate. The cross-sectional view is much like that of the acetate fiber—bulbous with indentations. The longitudinal view appears straight and smooth, but it has heavy lines caused by the grooves in the surface. The fiber comes in both bright and dull forms.

SYNTHETIC LONG-CHAIN POLYMERS ■ This group of fibers is distinguished by being synthesized or created by man from various elements into large molecules called *linear polymers* because they are connected in linklike fashion. The molecules of each particular compound are arranged in parallel lines or rows in the fiber, similar to the way fibers are arranged in yarn. This arrangement of molecules is called *molecular orientation*. The properties of such fibers are dependent upon their chemical compositions and kinds of molecular orientation. There are ten distinct varieties of synthetic long-chain polymers. The fiber definitions that follow were set forth by the Federal Trade Commission in accordance with the Textile Fiber Products Identification Act.

Courtesy American Enka Corp.   Courtesy American Enka Corp.

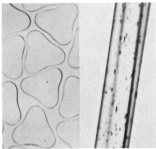

Top left to right: Enkatron Nylon; Enkalure Nylon. Bottom left to right: Nylon; Nylon Semidull; Antron Nylon.

Courtesy E. I. duPont de Nemours & Co.   Courtesy E. I. duPont de Nemours & Co.   Courtesy E. I. duPont de Nemours & Co.

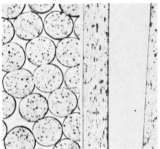

Nylon. Nylon is a manufactured fiber in which the fiber-forming substance is any long-chain synthetic polyamide having recurring amide groups as an integral part of the polymer chain. The elements of carbon, oxygen, nitrogen, and hydrogen are combined by chemical processes into compounds which react to form long-chain molecules, known chemically as polyamides, and are formed into fibers. While there are variations in production of the fiber, the microscopic appearance is basically fine, round, smooth, and translucent. One type, *Cantrece,* is a bicomponent in which two fibers adhere as one. It can be highly lustrous, semidull, or dull.

Polyester. Polyester is a manufactured fiber in which the fiber-forming substance is any long-chain synthetic polymer composed of at least 85 percent by weight of an ester of a dihydric alcohol and terephthalic acid. In producing such fibers the basic elements of carbon, oxygen, and hydrogen are polymerized. Variations are possible in the methods of production, in the combination of ingredients, and in the ultimate molecular structures of the fiber-forming substance. Each of the seven varieties of polyesters is identified by its own trade name: *Dacron, Fortrel, Kodel, Vycron, Blue C, Enka,* and *Phoenix.* An eighth, *Trevira* polyester fiber, is expected to be introduced late in 1967.

Dacron polyester fiber in regular form is straight, smooth, and almost perfectly round. It has a characteristic speckled appearance that is visible both in the longitudinal and cross-sectional views. Other types of Dacron have different shapes. They may be ribbonlike or trilobal, providing variation in hand and appearance.

Fortrel polyester fiber has a round cross section and is somewhat cloudy in appearance.

Kodel polyester fiber looks very much like Dacron. It is speckled and has a semidull appearance. Its cross-sectional view is relatively round, and its longitudinal view is straight.

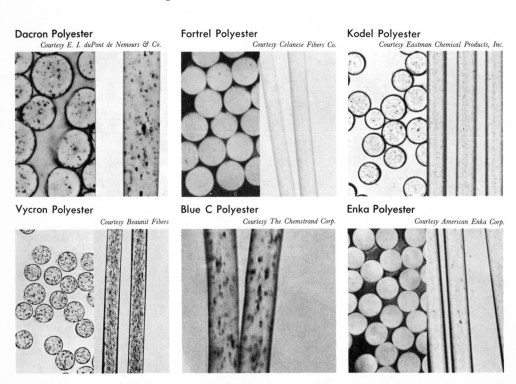

Dacron Polyester
Courtesy E. I. duPont de Nemours & Co.

Fortrel Polyester
Courtesy Celanese Fibers Co.

Kodel Polyester
Courtesy Eastman Chemical Products, Inc.

Vycron Polyester
Courtesy Beaunit Fibers

Blue C Polyester
Courtesy The Chemstrand Corp.

Enka Polyester
Courtesy American Enka Corp.

Vycron polyester fiber closely resembles Kodel. It, too, is speckled and semi-dull with a longitudinal view that is relatively round, straight, and smooth.

Blue C polyester fiber is also speckled and semidull. Its cross section is relatively round and its longitudinal view is straight and smooth.

Enka polyester fiber has a round cross section and is clear. Its longitudinal view is straight and smooth.

Acrylic. Acrylic is a manufactured fiber in which the fiber-forming substance is any long-chain synthetic polymer composed of at least 85 percent by weight of acrylonitrile units. By complicated processes, the basic elements of carbon, hydrogen, and nitrogen are usually synthesized with small amounts of other chemicals (to improve the fiber's ability to absorb dyes) into large polymer combinations. Variations are possible in the methods of production, in the combination of ingredients, and in the ultimate molecular structures of the fiber-forming substance. Five varieties of acrylics are identified by the trade names *Acrilan, Creslan, Orlon, Zefran,* and *Zefkrome.* Each of these has its own modifications, which have special properties to suit particular purposes.

Acrilan has a bean-shaped cross section; its longitudinal appearance is straight and smooth. It may be bright or semidull with speckles.

Orlon has a somewhat flat, dog-bone cross section; its longitudinal view is rather flat and smooth. One type, *Sayelle,* is a bicomponent in which two fibers adhere as one. Orlon is a semidull fiber.

Creslan acrylic fiber has an almost round cross section; its longitudinal appearance is straight and smooth. It may be bright or semidull with speckles.

Zefran is classified as an acrylic because it is composed primarily of acrylonitrile with a copolymer. Its cross section is almost round; its longitudinal appearance is smooth and straight. It may be bright or semidull with speckles.

Zefkrome is a variant of Zefran. Its primary difference in appearance is that the fiber has been impregnated with a predetermined color.

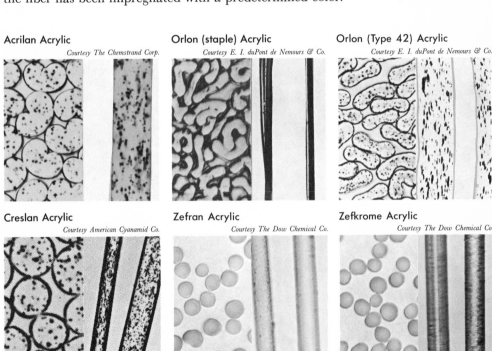

Acrilan Acrylic
Courtesy The Chemstrand Corp.

Orlon (staple) Acrylic
Courtesy E. I. duPont de Nemours & Co.

Orlon (Type 42) Acrylic
Courtesy E. I. duPont de Nemours & Co.

Creslan Acrylic
Courtesy American Cyanamid Co.

Zefran Acrylic
Courtesy The Dow Chemical Co.

Zefkrome Acrylic
Courtesy The Dow Chemical Co.

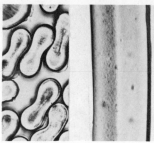
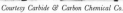
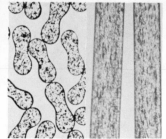

Left to right: Dynel Polyester; Verel Polyester.

Courtesy Carbide & Carbon Chemical Co.

Courtesy Eastman Chemical Products, Inc.

Modacrylic. Modacrylic is a manufactured fiber in which the fiber-forming substance is any long-chain synthetic polymer composed of less than 85 percent but at least 35 percent by weight of acrylonitrile units. As the definition indicates, variations are possible in producing this type of fiber. Modacrylics are made from resins that are copolymers or combinations of acrylonitrile and other compounds, such as vinyl chloride, vinylidene chloride, or vinylidene dicyanide. These chemicals are made of such elements as carbon, hydrogen, nitrogen, and chlorine, which are obtained from natural gas, coal air, salt, and water. Trade names of two varieties are *Dynel* and *Verel*, which, in turn, have modifications.

Dynel modacrylic fiber is partly an acrylic and partly a vinyl chloride. The fibers are produced in several types and may vary slightly in shape from flat to dog-bone and oval; the surface is smooth. The fiber is semidull.

Verel modacrylic fiber is partly an acrylic and partly an undisclosed copolymer. It is produced in several types. The cross section is dog-bone, and the longitudinal view is straight and smooth. The fiber may be bright or dull.

Spandex. Spandex is a manufactured fiber in which the fiber-forming substance is a long-chain synthetic polymer comprised of at least 85 percent of a segmented polyurethane. As the definition indicates, variations are possible in producing this type of fiber. The basic elements of nitrogen, hydrogen, carbon, and oxygen are synthesized with other substances to ethyl ester compounds in polymer chains of soft segments or sections that provide stretch and hard segments that hold the chains together. Trade names of five varieties are

Courtesy The Chemstrand Corp.

Courtesy Globe Manufacturing Co.

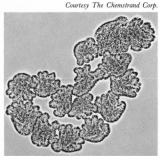

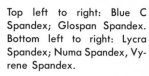

Top left to right: Blue C Spandex; Glospan Spandex. Bottom left to right: Lycra Spandex; Numa Spandex, Vyrene Spandex.

Courtesy E. I. duPont de Nemours & Co.

Courtesy American Cyanamid Co.

Courtesy U.S. Rubber Co.

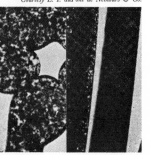

Left to right: Herculon Polypropylene; Polycrest Olefin
Polypropylene.

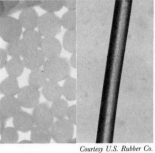

Courtesy Hercules Powder Co., Inc.   Courtesy U.S. Rubber Co.

Blue C, Glospan, Lycra, Numa, and *Vyrene.* All the fibers are white and opaque. Two more recently announced spandex fibers not yet in commercial production are *Duraspun* and *Unel.*

Blue C spandex in cross section is a group of irregular-shaped speckled filaments that are fused together at points of contact, which gives it a spongelike appearance. In longitudinal view, the fused multifilaments appear as a single straight fiber.

Glospan spandex looks similar to Blue C except that the multifilaments are more compactly fused, which gives a more solid appearance.

Lycra spandex also appears in cross section to be fused multifilaments. However, the individual filaments are speckled and dog-bone in shape. The longitudinal view is straight.

Numa spandex has a cross section showing fused, irregular-shaped filaments. These filaments tend to have minimal contact with each other, giving a more open appearance between them than exists in the other spandex fibers.

Vyrene is unique among the spandex fibers insofar as it is the only monofilament. In cross section it is somewhat round and speckled; its longitudinal appearance is straight, smooth, and opaque.

Olefin. Olefin is a manufactured fiber in which the fiber-forming substance is any long-chain synthetic polymer composed of at least 85 percent by weight of ethylene, propylene, or other olefin units. As the definition indicates, variations are possible in producing this type of fiber. The carbon-hydrogen chains polymerized to produce this fiber are obtained from the cracking of petroleum. Polyethylene, the original olefin fiber, has been superseded by polypropylene.

Several types of polypropylene fibers are produced under different trade names. Under the microscope, they are quite similar in basic appearance. The usual cross section of the fiber is relatively round, and the longitudinal view is straight and smooth. Some types may have speckles in both views, which indicates a delusterant. The cross section may be altered to give a desired appearance and hand to the fiber.

Saran. Saran is a manufactured fiber in which the fiber-forming substance is any long-chain synthetic polymer composed of at least 80 percent by weight of vinylidene chloride units. As the definition indicates, variations are possible in producing this fiber. Originally, it was produced as a copolymer of vinylidene chloride and vinyl chloride synthesized from ethylene (from petroleum) and chlorine (from the salt of seawater). The fiber is smooth, round, and translucent.

Vinyon. Vinyon is a manufactured fiber in which the fiber-forming substance is any long-chain synthetic polymer composed of at least 85 percent by weight of vinyl chloride units. This fiber is produced through the synthesis of the basic

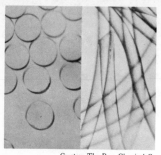

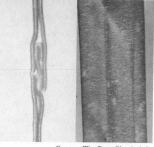

Left to right: Saran; Rovana Saran.

Courtesy The Dow Chemical Co.   *Courtesy The Dow Chemical Co.*

materials of chlorine, carbon, and hydrogen that are derived from saltwater and petroleum. Variations are produced from copolymers.

Because this fiber has a very low melting point, it is limited to industrial use and to certain bonded fabric applications for consumer use. It is consequently not treated in any detail in this text.

Nytril. Nytril is a manufactured fiber containing at least 85 percent of a long-chain polymer of vinylidene dinitrile where the vinylidene dinitrile content is no less than any other unit in the polymer chain. The raw materials for the production of this fiber are natural gas and ammonia from which carbon, oxygen, hydrogen, and nitrogen are synthesized into monomers and copolymerized. The fiber has a cross-sectional shape that is flat, with a slightly irregular surface and rounded ends.

This fiber was originally marketed in the United States under the trade name of *Darvan.* It is presently produced only in Europe in limited quantity under the trade name of *Travis.*

Fluorocarbon. This fiber is polymerized from fluorspar and chloroform and is sold under Du Pont's trademark, *Teflon.* It is extremely difficult to dye and has excellent resistance to chemicals, mildew, bacteria, and insects. For these reasons it is used primarily for industrial applications rather than for consumer fabric uses. Consequently, it is not defined under the Textile Fiber Products Identification Act and is not discussed further in this text.

Lastrile. This fiber is a manufactured fiber in which the fiber-forming substance is a copolymer of acrylonitrile and a diene composed of not more than 50 percent but at least 10 percent by weight of acrylonitrile units. Lastrile is in the early developmental stage. It is an elastic fiber. The first such fiber to be announced is *Orofil.* No other specific information regarding its production or properties is yet available.

MINERAL FIBER ■ Man has taken such natural minerals as silica sand, limestone, soda ash, borax, boric acid, feldspar, and fluorspar and has fused them under very high temperatures into glass which can be processed into fiber.

Glass. Glass is a manufactured fiber in which the fiber-forming substance is glass. The fiber is smooth, round, translucent, highly lustrous, quite flexible.

Ceramic. A new group of fibers not classified by the F.T.C. is that of ceramic fibers. Most information regarding production and specific properties is lacking. The fibers are multifilament, are highly heat resistant, and show excellent promise for aerospace applications. Two trade names are *Avceram* and *Fiberfrax.*

METALLIC FIBER ■ Metallic fiber is a manufactured fiber composed of metal, plastic-coated metal, metal-coated plastic, or a core completely covered

Left to right: Glass Fiber; Lurex, with cross section showing metal layer sandwiched between two layers of Mylar film.

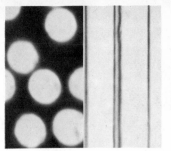 

Courtesy Owens-Corning Fiberglas Corp.   *Courtesy The Dow Chemical Co.*

by metal. This fiber is usually produced in flat, narrow, smooth strips with a gleaming luster.

RUBBER FIBER ■ Rubber fiber is a manufactured fiber in which the fiber-forming substance is comprised of natural or synthetic rubber. The treated rubber is produced in cylindrical form, so that the cross-sectional view is round and the longitudinal surface is relatively smooth.

AZLON ■ Azlon is a manufactured fiber in which the fiber-forming substance is composed of any regenerated naturally occurring proteins. The production of this fiber remains in the experimental stage. *Vicara* was the last protein fiber produced commercially in this country from the zein of corn, but it has subsequently been discontinued. It had a round cross-sectional appearance and a smooth longitudinal surface.

REVIEW QUESTIONS

1 Name five industries that are dependent upon or related to the textile industry, and indicate how they are related.

2 Name five areas of employment in the textile industry.

3 How can good knowledge of textiles be of value to the consumer?

4 (a) What are the two major groups of natural fibers? (b) Identify the fibers and their sources in each group.

5 What is meant by *generic fiber name?*

6 (a) Group the man-made fibers according to basic composition. (b) Identify the fibers in each group.

7 What is the difference between man-made fibers of natural nonfibrous substances and natural fibers?

8 How does the composition of man-made fibers of natural nonfibrous substances differ from man-made synthetic fibers?

9 (a) What are the basic provisions of the Textile Fiber Products Identification Act? (b) Who administers the law?

SUGGESTED ACTIVITY

Prepare a chart with drawings of the microscopic views of each of the man-made fibers.

The Textile Fiber Products Identification Act requires that the manufacturers of cloth garments and household textiles attach labels to their products specifying the fiber content. These manufacturers are expected to know this information since it is they who tell the fabric producers the requirements for the fabrics they intend to purchase. Should a product manufacturer want to identify or verify the fiber content himself, he must be in a position either to make the appropriate technical analysis or to refer samples to a testing laboratory.

The retailer, in turn, is held responsible under the Act to see that labels or hangtags are attached to the textile products before he sells them. He must therefore rely on his vendor to provide him with properly labeled merchandise. Sometimes imported merchandise arrives unlabeled or sometimes labels become detached and lost. It is then the merchant's responsibility to have appropriate labels made and to attach them to the merchandise. Ready recognition and identification of fiber content in fabrics has become extremely difficult even for knowledgeable and experienced merchants because of the growing variety of types of fibers, the blending techniques in yarn and fabric construction, and the finishes that affect the appearance and hand of the fabrics. If the fabric producer cannot provide the merchant with reliable information, he must either rely upon certain tests (performed readily, in some instances), send samples to his own testing bureau, or utilize the services of a testing company.

The consumer has the greatest handicap in identifying fiber content of fabrics. Should he lose the label from a textile product, he may not know the composition of the fabric and therefore not know what to expect of it or how to care for it. Because he is usually not in a position to make a laboratory analysis, he must rely, insofar as he can, upon certain nontechnical tests.

THE NONTECHNICAL TESTS

There are several methods that do not require any special equipment for identifying textile fibers. Although they have certain limitations, they are useful because they are simple to perform and, under certain circumstances, provide ready identification.

FEELING TEST ■ The feeling test requires perception if it is to be of any value. Skilled perception is acquired only after handling many different fabrics over a period of time. To understand what is meant by "feeling" a fabric, place your finger on a sample of wool. The heat generated by the finger remains in the area because wool is a nonconductor of heat. Consequently, wool fabric "feels warm to the touch." If your finger is placed on a sample composed of the vegetable fibers—that is, cotton, linen, or even rayon—the heat of the finger passes off because such fibers are conductors of heat. These fabrics, therefore, "feel cool to the touch." Limitations of this test become apparent as we examine and compare fabrics of different fiber contents.

Cotton. Cotton is cool to the touch and feels soft and inelastic.

Linen. Linen is cold and smooth and has a leathery feel.

Wool. Wool is warm to the touch and feels elastic and springy.

Silk. Silk feels warm, smooth, and elastic.

Rayon. Rayon filament fabrics feel cool, smooth, inelastic, and generally lack the body of silk. The staple fabrics may be given various textural qualities of the natural fibers but they generally lack their "life."

Acetate. Acetate filament fabrics feel smoother, a little warmer, more elastic, and more resilient than rayon. They also have more body and draping quality. The staple fabrics feel very much like rayon but may have a little more warmth and resilience.

Triacetate. Triacetate fabrics have the feel of acetate but are more resilient.

Nylon. Nylon filament fabrics feel very smooth, lightweight, elastic, quite resilient. Draping quality is good. Staple fabrics have a woollike hand.

Polyesters. Polyester filament fabrics feel very much like nylon but tend to be stiffer and, therefore, have less draping quality. The staple fabrics may have either a cottonlike or woollike texture. The cottonlike texture is smoother and a bit more slippery than fine cotton, and it is very resilient.

Acrylics. Acrylic fibers have the feel of wool but are much lighter in weight. Depending upon the manner of spinning the yarn, they may feel as soft as cashmere. Generally, they have a slippery or slick feeling that the natural fibers do not have.

Modacrylics. Although modacrylic fibers may be slightly stiffer than acrylics, they are actually very difficult to distinguish by feel.

Spandex. Since fabrics containing spandex fiber are usually made with other fibers, the fabric may have the feel of any of the other fibers. Such fabrics will have the additional characteristic of elasticity in the direction that the spandex fiber is running.

Olefin. Olefin fibers are extremely lightweight and very resilient. The hand of the polypropylene fiber is similar to that of the polyesters.

Saran. Saran fabrics are heavy, smooth, flexible, with a typical plastic feel.

Vinyon. Vinyon fabrics feel somewhat like saran fabrics.

Nytril. Nytril fabrics are lightweight and have a soft, warm, pleasant hand somewhat like the acrylics.

Glass. Glass fabrics made of filament fibers are heavy, smooth, and somewhat lustrous. Fabrics made of staple have a soft, cottonlike hand.

Metal. Metal fibers have the obvious metallic luster and are smooth, flat, ribbonlike, and very flexible.

Rubber. Rubber fiber may be readily confused with spandex, depending on how it is made into yarn. However, rubber is much heavier.

BURNING TEST ■ To recognize the composition of fabrics by the burning test, the sample of fiber, yarn, or fabric should be moved slowly toward a small flame and the reaction to the heat carefully observed. One end of the sample should then be put directly into the flame to determine its burning rate and characteristics. After it is removed from the flame, the burning characteristics should continue to be observed and the burning odor noted. After the sample has cooled, the ash should be examined for characteristics such as amount, form, hardness, and color.

If both the lengthwise and the crosswise yarns in a fabric are known to be of the same substance, the sample may be tested as a whole. More than one kind of yarn, however, is sometimes used in a fabric. When the presence of different yarns is suspected, the lengthwise yarns should be separated from the crosswise yarns and each set should be tested separately. When it is believed that more than one fiber has been blended into a single yarn, the yarn should be untwisted and, with the aid of a magnifying glass and tweezers, the individual fibers separated.

One should also be alert to the possibility that finishing agents may have been used on the fabrics. These finishes can change the burning characteristics of the sample.

Cotton. Cotton yarn blazes quickly when it comes in contact with the flame because the cellulose ingredient is highly inflammable. The ash is light and feathery and has a vegetable odor similar to that of burned paper; mercerized cotton produces a black ash. Because cotton is highly inflammable, do not use cotton where its proximity to flame becomes a fire hazard; for example, pot holders should be made of wool, never of cotton.

Linen. Linen, when burned, produces an ash similar to cotton ash because both fabrics are of vegetable substance. Linen ash is also light and feathery and has the odor of burned paper. Although linen fabric burns somewhat more slowly than cotton because linen yarns are heavier, the pace of burning is not sufficiently different to aid in distinguishing linen from cotton.

Wool. Wool is slow to ignite and has a characteristic small, slow, flickering flame that sizzles and curls. It can be extinguished easily, as the fabric ceases flaming when the fire is withdrawn. Wool ash is dark and crisp, and it falls into an irregular shape that can be crushed easily. The ash has a strong animal odor resembling burning feathers or hair, which indicates the presence of an animal substance or of a fiber obtained from an animal. The characteristic odor of burned wool is due to the sulfur ingredient.

Silk. Pure silk also burns slowly and ceases flaming when the fire is withdrawn. The ash of silk appears in the form of round, crisp, shiny black beads that, like the ash of wool, can be crushed easily with the fingers. The ash has an animal odor less pronounced than that of wool, as silk does not contain sulfur.

In manufacturing, additional body is given to silk fabrics by weighting them with metallic fillers. Weighted silk burns without showing a visible flame. The burned part becomes incandescent; it chars and gradually smolders away, leaving a coherent ash that is a screenlike skeleton of the original fabric. The odor of the ash of weighted silk is similar to that of pure silk.

Rayons. Like cottons, the rayons ignite quickly. They burn with a bright yellow flame, sometimes more rapidly than cotton because rayons are essentially purified cellulose. The odor of burning *viscose, cuprammonium,* and *high wet-modulus*

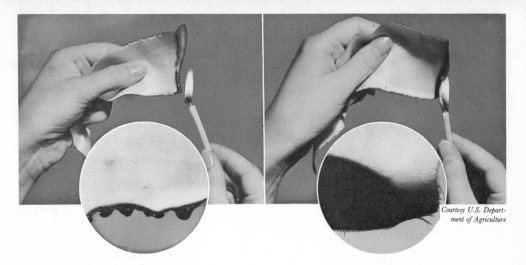

*Courtesy U.S. Depart-
ment of Agriculture*

Pure-dye silk burns (left) with a small flame that soon dies, leaving an ash in the form of small, brittle, shiny black balls along the edge of the fabric. Weighted silk burns (right) without showing a visible flame. It chars and leaves a coherent ash, a skeleton of the original fabric.

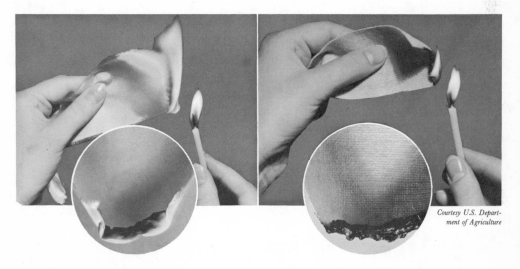

*Courtesy U.S. Depart-
ment of Agriculture*

Acetate blazes (left) as it burns. The fabric puckers, curls, and fuses into an irregular black residue that hardens when cooled. Wool burns slowly (right) with a small flickering flame. The fabric sizzles and curls. The ash is black, irregular, and crisp.

rayons is like that of burning paper, also a cellulosic product; the odor of *saponified* rayon (such as Fortisan) is not as strong. The ash disintegrates unless the fiber has been chemically dulled.

Acetate. Acetate blazes as it burns. The edge of the fabric puckers and curls as the material fuses and melts into a hard mass. Acetate sputters and drips like tar. The ash of acetate is hard and brittle, and is difficult to crush between the fingers. Because of the acetic acid used in the manufacture of acetate, the ash has an acid odor similar to that of vinegar.

BURNING TESTS

Fiber	Approaching Flame	In Flame	Removed from Flame	Odor	Ash
NATURAL FIBERS					
COTTON	Scorches; ignites readily	Burns quickly; yellow flame	Continues to burn rapidly; has afterglow	Burning paper	Light, feathery, gray-ish; black ash denotes mercerized cotton
LINEN	Scorches; ignites easily	Yellow flame; burns slower than cotton if yarns are heavier	Continues to burn	Burning paper	Feathery, gray ash
SILK (pure-dye)	Smolders	Burns; melts slowly; sputters	Supports combustion with difficulty; ceases flaming	Like burning feathers or hair, but less pronounced than wool	Round, crisp, shiny black beads; easily crushed
SILK (weighted)	Smolders	Burns with a glow	Burned part becomes briefly incandescent; then chars	Like burning feathers or hair	Screenlike skeleton of original sample
WOOL	Smolders	Small, slow flickering flame; sizzles and curls	Ceases flaming	Like burning feathers or hair	Crisp dark ash; irregular shape; crushes easily
MAN-MADE FIBERS					
ACETATE	Fuses away from flame; turns black	Flames quickly; fabric puckers, sputters, melts, drips like burning tar	Continues to burn and melt	Like vinegar	Brittle, hard, irregular black ash, difficult to crush
ACRYLICS Orlon	Fuses and shrinks away from flame	Flames rapidly; fabric puckers, sputters, melts	Continues to burn and melt	Faintly like burning meat	Brittle, hard irregular, black bead
Acrilan	Fuses and shrinks away from flame	Flames rapidly and melts	Continues to burn and melt	Burning steak	Brittle, hard, irregular, black bead
Creslan	Fuses and shrinks away from flame	Flames and melts	Continues to burn and melt	Sharp sweet	Brittle, hard, irregular, black bead
Zefran	Fuses and melts	Sputters slightly; flames	Continues to burn and melt	Turmeric-like	Irregular black ash that crushes easily
Zefkrome	Fuses and melts	Sputters slightly; flames	Continues to burn and melt	Turmeric-like	Irregular black ash that crushes easily

MODACRYLICS Dynel	Fuses away from flame	Burns very slowly with melting	Self-extinguishing	Sharp-sweet	Brittle, hard, irregular, black bead
Verel	Fuses away from flame	Burns very slowly with melting	Self-extinguishing	Sharp, similar to burning gun powder	Brittle, hard, irregular, black bead
NYLON	Fuses and shrinks away from flame	Burns slowly with melting	Flame diminishes and tends to die out	Somewhat like celery	Hard, round, tough, gray bead
OLEFIN Polypropylene	Fuses, shrinks, and curls away from flame	Melts; burns slowly	Burns slowly with difficulty	Faintly like burning asphalt	Hard, round, light tan bead
POLYESTERS Dacron	Fuses and shrinks away from flame	Burns slowly with melting	Burns with difficulty	Slightly sweetish	Hard, round, brittle black bead
Kodel	Fuses and shrinks away from flame	Burns slowly with melting	Burns with difficulty; produces soot	Faintly like burning pine tar	Hard, round, black bead
RAYONS Cuprammonium High Wet-Modulus Viscose	Scorches; ignites quickly	Burns quickly; yellow flame	Continues to burn; no afterglow as with cotton	Burning paper	Light, gray, feathery
Saponified	Scorches; ignites quickly	Burns quickly; yellow flame	Continues to burn; no afterglow	Burning paper, but not as strong as other rayons	No ash unless dull type
RUBBER	Smolders	Melts and shrivels away from flame	Self-extinguishing	Very disagreeable and pungent	Hard, brittle, black, irregular bead
SARAN	Fuses and shrinks away from flame	Burns very slowly with melting	Self-extinguishing	Acrid, sweet	Hard, black, irregular bead
SPANDEX	Fuses but does not shrink away from flame	Burns with melting	Continues to burn with melting	Acrid	Soft, fluffy, black
TRIACETATE Arnel	Fuses away from flame; turns black	Flames quickly; fabric puckers, sputters, melts, drips like burning tar	Continues to burn and melt	Like vinegar	Brittle, hard, irregular black ash, difficult to crush
VINYON	Fuses and shrinks away from flame	Burns very slowly with melting	Self-extinguishing	Sweet	Hard, black, irregular bead

Triacetate. Triacetate is similar to acetate in both its chemical composition and its reaction to heat and flame. It flames quickly and then melts into a hard mass. As triacetate burns, it drips like burning tar. The ash is hard and brittle and has an acid odor like that of vinegar.

Nylon. Nylon melts before it burns. As it burns, it shrinks from the flame and forms a hard round bead that cannot be crushed between the fingers. While burning, it has a pungent odor.

Polyesters. The polyesters, *Dacron, Kodel, Fortrel,* and *Vycron,* fuse and shrink from the flame. They melt and burn slowly in the flame; when they are removed, they burn with difficulty. Kodel produces a slight soot. Dacron has a slightly sweetish odor; Kodel smells faintly like burning pine tar. The ashes of these four polyesters are hard, round, black, and beady.

Acrylics. The acrylic fibers *Orlon, Acrilan,* and *Creslan* melt, shrink away from the flame, fuse, and burn leaving a brittle, black, irregular-shaped bead. Their rate of burning is between that of cotton and acetate. Orlon gives off an odor that faintly resembles burning flesh; Acrilan smells a little stronger, like burning steak; Creslan has a sharp, sweet odor. The acrylic fibers *Zefran* and *Zefkrome* flame rapidly and sputter slightly. The edges curl as the fabrics blaze, leaving a black ash that can be crushed easily between the fingers. The odor is somewhat like turmeric.

Modacrylics. The modacrylic fibers, *Dynel* and *Verel,* will not support combustion and do not flame. They melt, shrink away from the flame, and harden into a brittle ash. Dynel gives off a sharp, sweet odor; Verel has a sharp odor similar to that of burning condite or gunpowder.

Spandex. Elastic yarns are usually combined with yarns of other fibers or are encased in a layer of other fibers. In both instances, the spandex fiber must be separated. *Lycra, Glospan,* and *Vyrene* spandex fibers melt, fuse, and burn without shrinking away from the flame; they leave a soft, fluffy, black ash and give off an acrid odor.

Olefins. The olefins that are *polypropylene,* such as *Herculon* and *Marvess,* also shrink, fuse, and curl away from the flame. They melt and burn slowly, giving off an odor that faintly resembles burning asphalt. They have a hard, round, light tan bead.

Saran. Saran fiber burns very slowly. It melts, fuses, and shrinks away from the flame, leaving a hard, black, irregular bead. It stops burning when it is removed from the flame. The odor is like that of slightly pungent melting paraffin.

Vinyon. Vinyon fiber fuses and shrinks away from the flame. It melts and burns slowly in the flame and extinguishes when it is removed. It gives off a sweet odor. The ash is a hard, black, irregular bead.

Nytril. Nytril fiber fuses and melts before it reaches the flame. In the flame, it melts and burns readily, leaving a hard, black, irregular bead and giving off a sweet, nitrogenous odor.

Glass. Glass fiber does not burn; it melts, however, at temperatures above 1500 degrees Fahrenheit.

Metal. Metallic fibers do not burn. However, the film that covers the metal will melt and burn with a slightly sweetish odor, leaving a brittle, beady ash.

Rubber. Rubber fibers are usually covered with another fiber that must be removed for this test. Rubber melts, shrivels away from the flame, and is self-extinguishing. It leaves a hard, irregular ash and a very disagreeable, pungent odor.

Azlon. Azlon fibers burn somewhat like wool with a small, slow flame that sizzles. It curls away from the flame and leaves a small black bead that crushes easily. It has the odor of burning chicken feathers or hair.

Limitation of Burning Test. It is apparent that many fibers have similar burning reactions that might cause doubt and occassional confusion. Nevertheless, the burning test provides a means of preliminary examination and elimination. It will separate and identify certain types or groups of fibers for technical testing when this is necessary.

BREAKING TEST ■ The breaking test is also nontechnical, yet it affords a convenient means of identifying fabrics. Recognition of a yarn by this test requires close observation of the fiber ends when the yarn is broken apart. A piece of yarn about 12 inches long is required for this test. The yarn must be untwisted very gently to restore the natural formation that the fiber had before twist was inserted by the spinning operation. When two or more strands have been combined in a single yarn, the yarns must be untwisted gently until a single strand is obtained. Care must also be used when pulling a yarn apart; otherwise, the broken fiber ends will not take their characteristic pattern.

Cotton. Because cotton yarns are made from short-staple fiber, the breaking of a cotton yarn will show fiber ends that are short, even, fuzzy, and brushlike. There is a characteristic curl to the ends, caused by the natural twist of the fiber. The inelasticity of cotton yarn causes it to snap when pulled apart.

Linen. When it is suspected that a yarn is composed of linen fiber, a long piece of yarn is needed for testing because long staple may be anticipated. If a break does not occur readily when the yarn is untwisted and gently pulled apart,

To examine the breaking pattern of cotton, linen, or rayon yarn, untwist the yarn (top left) and tear it apart (top right). Rayon yarn will show lustrous, inelastic filaments (bottom left). Cotton yarn will show brushlike ends that are short, even, and fuzzy (bottom center). Linen yarn will break unevenly, showing long, pointed ends that are inelastic and lustrous (bottom right).

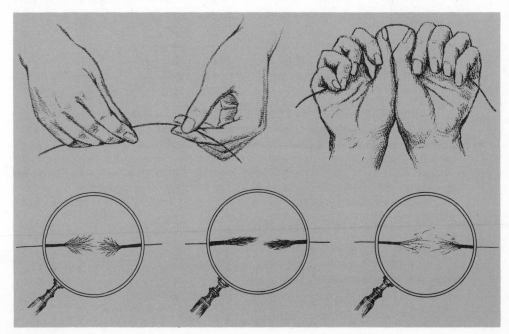

the span must be increased to exert tension on a longer staple. Untwisting should be continued along the span, and the yarn again pulled gently. If necessary, the span should be increased again. The breaking pattern of a linen yarn shows long, straight, lustrous fiber ends that are pointed and uneven at the tips. The fiber ends never curl. They point outward with marked stiffness, which indicates a lack of flexibility.

Wool. A wool yarn has a characteristic fuzzy surface. When the yarn is pulled gently for the breaking test, it stretches easily because of its elasticity. The breaking pattern shows fiber ends that are wavy and spiral.

Silk. A silk yarn stretches easily when pulled, and silk ranks close to wool in elasticity. Because of its strength, the silk yarn stretches a considerable degree and breaks apart finally with a snap, but only after it has exceeded its limit of stretch. The broken fiber ends appear fine and lustrous.

Rayon. If tension is exerted on a dry rayon yarn, the yarn appears to be comparatively strong, though inelastic, and does not break easily. When a rayon yarn is moistened with the tongue, a slight pull breaks the yarn easily. The broken fiber ends create a pattern similar to that of a tree with numerous stiff branches, produced by the bursting of the separate filaments. The effectiveness of this test will vary, however, with the type of rayon; high-tenacity rayon, for example, breaks with much greater difficulty.

Spandex. Because spandex yarns will stretch as much as 700 percent when one tries to break them, there may be difficulty in distinguishing it from rubber.

Limitation of Breaking Test. As has been indicated, there are many limitations to this test. One limitation is indicated in testing spun rayon. As spun rayon can easily simulate wool, linen, or even cotton, its breaking pattern can be similar to the characteristic pattern of wool, cotton, or linen. The characteristic loss of strength that wet viscose rayon shows is not evident when other forms, such as high wet-modulus rayon, exist.

Spun rayon is only one example of the limitation of this test. It would be difficult to determine accurately whether a yarn is composed of nylon, polyester, or any of the other stronger synthetic fibers. These fibers are relatively strong, and the degree of tension used in trying to break these yarns by hand cannot be measured accurately. Furthermore, the broken ends of these yarns may look like each other, or like wool, cotton, or some other fiber, depending on whether filament or a form of staple fiber, such as artificially crimped staple, were used in the manufacture of the yarn.

DISTINGUISHING LINEN FROM COTTON ■ The identification of linen and cotton fabrics has always been of special interest to the analytical consumer. Because cotton can be made to simulate linen, additional nontechnical tests for distinguishing linen from cotton are evaluated here. Some of these tests are adequate. Others are not recommended because finishing substances commonly used in the manufacturing process interfere with the expected reaction.

Squeezing Test. A simple method of distinguishing linen from cotton is to pull a yarn through two tightly compressed fingertips. If the yarn emerges stiff and straight, it is linen; if limp and drooping, it is cotton.

Curl Test. If the end of a single filament turns in a clockwise direction when squeezed between the moistened thumb and finger, the fabric is linen. If the tip turns counterclockwise, the fabric is cotton.

Tearing Test. Linen fabrics do not tear readily, but they do tend to slip apart when subjected to strain. A sample can be identified as cotton if it tears readily with a characteristic shrill sound.

Reaction to Oil. If lightweight oil or glycerine is dropped on a linen fabric, a translucent area appears; if dropped on cotton, the area is opaque.

Ink Test. If a drop of ink is placed on a linen fabric, the ink spreads evenly in a circular form. In contrast, a drop of ink on a cotton fabric tends to spread outward with a fading density toward the outer edge, which makes a slightly irregular outer rim that is more oval than circular. The ink test is not considered reliable because finishing substances may interfere with this reaction.

Moisture Test. A common practice is to attempt to identify linen by noting the pace of absorption when a drop of saliva is placed on the undersurface of the fabric. As linen absorbs water quickly, it is believed that this test will identify the linen fiber. But finishing substances in linen interfere with this test, and it is not recommended. Also, sheer cotton fabrics absorb a drop of saliva even more quickly than fine linen.

THE TECHNICAL TESTS

Where laboratory equipment is available, much more reliable testing techniques may be employed. However, these require technical knowledge and skill, particularly in handling many of the chemicals.

MICROSCOPE TEST ■ Identification by microscope, as studied in Chapter 1, is a reliable test that can be used to distinguish the fibers. Knowing what the fibers look like under the microscope will also help you understand other identification tests. Certain manufacturing and finishing processes, such as mercerizing and delustering, affect the appearance of a fiber under the microscope. In addition, a dark-colored fabric cannot be identified under the microscope because the light necessary for identification cannot pass through a dark substance. The dyestuff must be removed, or "stripped," by the use of a bleaching chemical, which is determined by the composition of the fabric. When stripping is essential and there is considerable doubt as to the composition of fiber, chemical tests are advisable.

CHEMICAL TESTS ■ In addition to the microscope, chemical tests are another means of identifying fibers. But chemical tests are not intended for the general consumer. Their value is demonstrated, however, by the fact that some consumer magazines and retail stores have their own laboratories for testing fabrics.

This method of identification has also become increasingly difficult as new fibers that are chemically very similar are developed and more fibers are blended and mixed in fabrics. There is no individual solvent or chemical identification for each fiber and no single solvent procedure for separating and identifying fibers in combinations. However, testing by solvents is very effective when it is used as a technique for eliminating and cross-checking.

In order to obtain accurate results, the fabrics to be tested should be thoroughly cleaned and the finishing agents should be removed. The fabric should be unraveled, yarns untwisted, and the fibers put in as loose a form as possible.

Distinguishing Animal from Vegetable Fibers with an Alkali. As strong alkalies destroy animal substances, a 5 percent solution of lye in water (½ teaspoon of lye in a glass of water) can be used to eliminate wool and silk fibers from a sample that contains a mixture of fibers. The action of this chemical (also known as caustic soda or sodium hydroxide) is hastened by boiling the solution before the sample is immersed. The wool and silk fibers will be completely dissolved. The vegetable fibers will not be affected. Another test is necessary to identify those fibers.

Distinguishing Vegetable from Animal Fibers with an Acid. As dilute acids destroy vegetable fibers, a 2 percent solution of sulfuric acid may be used to distinguish vegetable from animal fibers. A drop of the solution is placed on a sample of the fabric, which is then placed between two blotters and pressed with a hot iron. The spotted area will become charred if the fabric is cotton, linen, or rayon.

Distinguishing Silk from Wool. If the fibers in a sample are known to consist of silk and wool, and identification of each is desired, the use of concentrated cold hydrochloric acid will dissolve the silk and cause the wool fiber to swell.

Distinguishing Linen from Cotton. Before any chemical test is made to distinguish linen from cotton, all surface dressings should be removed from the samples by boiling them for a few minutes in a solution of dilute sodium hydroxide, about ½ percent. Then any of the following tests can be made.

Immersing cotton and linen samples in a 1 percent solution of fuchsin in alcohol produces a rose-red color in both samples. After the samples have been washed and then immersed in ammonia, linen retains the red coloration, but cotton does not. This test is sometimes made with a 1 percent solution of magenta, a red dyestuff.

Cotton fibers are weakened more than linen fibers if samples are immersed in concentrated sulfuric acid for two minutes. After the samples are rinsed and immersed in weak ammonia, the cotton fibers dissolve, leaving the linen fibers unaffected. When cotton and linen samples are immersed in a solution of iodine and zinc chloride (Herzberg's stain), cotton is stained reddish purple and linen is stained blue to purple. When samples are immersed in a caustic soda solution, cotton remains white and linen turns yellowish.

Distinguishing Rayons from Acetate. A solution containing equal parts of concentrated sulfuric acid and iodine (crystals) may be used to distinguish each of the different fibers. When samples are immersed in this solution, a dark-blue coloration indicates viscose; a light-blue coloration indicates cuprammonium; a yellow coloration indicates acetate. Another test to distinguish acetate from rayon, when both types are known to be used in a fabric, is to immerse the sample in a 50 percent solution of acetic acid. The acetate dissolves; the rayons are not affected. All rayons will dissolve in a 60 percent solution of sulfuric acid or a concentrated solution of hydrochloric acid.

Distinguishing Acetate from Other Fibers. If a sample of acetate is immersed in an 80 percent solution of acetone (a chemical used in nail polish removers), the acetate fibers will dissolve but Arnel, Dynel, and Verel will swell.

Distinguishing Arnel from Other Fibers. When a specimen of fabric or a blend of fibers is immersed at room temperature for one hour in a mixture of 90 percent methylene chloride and 10 percent ethanol (or methanol), Arnel and acetate will be dissolved, but other commonly used fibers will be virtually unaffected. (Dynel, however, is softened and gains weight when similarly treated.) Arnel can be differentiated from acetate by immersing a sample of fabric or fibers in benzyl alcohol at 50 degrees centigrade for one hour. Arnel is virtually unaffected, but the acetate completely dissolves.

Distinguishing Nylon from Other Fibers. Nylon can be distinguished from acetate by attempting to dissolve it in acetone. Nylon will not dissolve in acetone. If the yarn or fabric is thought to contain wool and/or nylon, the fabric may be immersed in a boiling solution of sodium hydroxide. The nylon is insoluble in such a solution, but wool will dissolve. In fact, nylon's insolubility in boiling sodium hydroxide makes it easily distinguishable from most other fibers. The only common solvents in which nylon is soluble are concentrated formic acid, phenol, and cresol.

Distinguishing Dacron from Other Fibers. Like acetate and nylon, Dacron is soluble in hot metacresol; however, unlike acetate it is not soluble in acetone, and unlike nylon it is not soluble in concentrated formic acid. Dacron is soluble in dimethylformamide after ten minutes at temperatures of 135–140 degrees centigrade.

Distinguishing Kodel from Other Fibers. Kodel will dissolve when boiled in methyl salicylate for ten minutes. However, since acetates, Arnel, and Dacron are also affected by this reagent, the specimen should first be tested for these fibers as a means of elimination.

Distinguishing Orlon from Other Fibers. Orlon is often blended with wool, cotton, silk, rayon, acetate, nylon, and Dacron. Even when not blended, Orlon may be mistaken for one of the other fibers. If the fiber is Orlon, it will not be affected by these common solvents: glacial acetic acid, chloroform, acetone, and 88 percent formic acid.

Distinguishing Acrilan from Other Fibers. Acrilan is insoluble in acetone, formic acid, 70 percent sulfuric acid, and sodium hypochlorite. It will dissolve in dimethylformamide.

Distinguishing Creslan from Other Fibers. Creslan may be differentiated from other fibers with which it may be blended because it will not be affected by glacial acetic acid, chloroform, acetone, or 88 percent formic acid. But this is also true for Orlon; therefore, to determine whether the remaining fibers are Creslan or Orlon, place the sample in a solution of nitric acid. A 2.5 to 1 nitric acid solution will dissolve Creslan; a 3 to 1 solution must be used to dissolve Orlon.

Distinguishing Zefran and Zefkrome from Other Fibers. Zefran and Zefkrome are so similar in composition that the prime differentiation between the two is whether the fiber has been solution-dyed. A strong bleach will remove the dye from Zefran, but Zefkrome, which is solution-dyed, will retain its color.

Since both fibers are in the acrylic group, their reactions to some of the solvents for the other acrylics are similar. However, Zefran and Zefkrome will dissolve more readily than the others in dimethylformamide at 100 degrees centigrade.

Distinguishing Dynel from Other Fibers. Although Dynel is often used alone, it may be blended with other fibers. It is easily distinguishable, however, from other fibers by chemical tests. It is highly resistant to a wide variety of inorganic acids, bases, salts, hydrocarbons, and most organic solvents. A 100 percent solution of acetone, cyclohexanone, and dimethylformamide are each solvents in varying degrees. Other cyclic ketones and certain amines cause some solvent or swelling action at high temperatures.

Distinguishing Verel from Other Fibers. When placed in pyridene and heated, Verel turns reddish brown but does not dissolve. It will dissolve in 100 percent solutions of acetone, cyclohexanone, or dimethylformamide.

Distinguishing Spandex from Other Fibers. The characteristics and appearance of spandex fibers should make them readily identifiable. However, there is sometimes some confusion with the stretch yarns, including those made from rubber. In this case, a test for spandex fiber is to heat the specimen in dimethylformamide. Spandex fiber will dissolve in the solution at 200 degrees Fahrenheit.

Distinguishing Saran from Other Fibers. A 100 percent solution of acetone will not affect saran. At elevated temperatures, saran will dissolve in dioxan and cyclohexanone. Saran is also soluble in ammonium hydroxide.

Distinguishing Olefins from Other Fibers. Olefin and saran fibers are soluble in metaxylene at 282 degrees Fahrenheit at the boil. To differentiate between these fibers, saran fibers are soluble in dimethylformamide but olefin fibers are not. Olefin and saran fibers can also be separated by dissolving the saran in a solution of dioxane 1,4 at 200 degrees Fahrenheit; olefin fibers will not dissolve in this solution.

Distinguishing Polyethylene Olefins from Polypropylene Olefins. Both polypropylene and polyethylene fibers will dissolve in decalin after a few minutes at the boiling point; however, polypropylene will not dissolve in cyclohexane as polyethylene will after ten minutes at the boiling point.

Distinguishing Vinyon from Other Fibers. Solvents for Vinyon HH are a 100 percent solution of acetone, a 50 to 50 solution of acetone-carbon disulfide, chloroform, chlorobenzene, or cyclohexanone. Since these reagents are also used to identify other fibers, Vinyon HH can be distinguished only by elimination.

Distinguishing Nytril Fiber from Other Fibers. Nytril fibers will dissolve in dimethylformamide at room temperature after five minutes. However, since acrylics and modacrylics also dissolve in dimethylformamide, it should be observed that nytril fibers partly disintegrate in metacresol, but acrylics do not. Also, nytril fibers dissolve in 60 percent nitric acid at 75 degrees Fahrenheit, but modacrylic fibers do not.

Distinguishing Glass Fibers from Other Fibers. Two specific solvents for quick identification of glass fibers are hydrofluoric acid and hot phosphoric acid.

REVIEW QUESTIONS

1 Why is the identification of fibers by labeling according to their substance important?

2 List the advantages and the limitations of the burning test when it is used to differentiate cotton, linen, wool, silk, rayon, and acetate.

3 Describe three tests used to differentiate cotton and linen.

4 Describe the breaking test as applied to cotton, linen, wool, silk.

5 Describe the differences between cotton and wool in the burning test.

6 What chemical processes would you use to distinguish (a) the animal fibers from the vegetable fibers, (b) cotton from linen?

7 Why is spun rayon difficult to identify by the feeling test or the breaking test?

8 What two positive tests permit identification of rayon and acetate?

9 What three tests differentiate silk from rayon?

10 Compare the effect of burning on acetate and on rayon in regard to flame, odor, and ash.

11 Compare the results of the breaking test on viscose and on linen yarn.

12 Why would you choose a woolen instead of a cotton blanket to put out a flame?

13 Why could the moisture test fail to determine whether sheets were linen or cotton? What other tests would you suggest?

14 What chemical test differentiates acetate and Arnel triacetate?

15 What chemical tests differentiate nylon from other fibers? Describe results.

16 How can acrylic fibers be differentiated from modacrylic fibers?

17 What chemical tests would identify the polyesters?

18 What chemical tests would identify the polypropylene fibers?

19 How would you differentiate spandex from rubber and stretch nylon?

20 What will dissolve glass fiber?

21 What are some serious limitations of (a) the nontechnical and (b) the technical tests?

SUGGESTED ACTIVITIES

1 Prepare a chart of the burning characteristics of the man-made fibers.

2 As a consumer, which tests do you consider to be useful to you? Make several tests to prove your point.

SPINNING

3

FIBER TO YARN

The formation of yarn becomes possible when fibers have surfaces capable of cohesiveness. This quality is exemplified by the scales of the wool fiber, the convolutions of the cotton fiber, and the roughness of the flax fiber. Elasticity or flexibility permits the fibers to be twisted around one another.

Primitive man discovered that a succession of fibers could be twisted into a continuous yarn. This was probably accomplished slowly and laboriously at first, but the greater strength thus produced and the many uses soon found for articles made from continuous yarns led to the invention of hand implements to aid and improve the process of twisting and spinning. Many such implements and methods are still used by the more primitive peoples in various parts of the world as well as by persons who are interested in reviving artistic handicraft. At the same time, it was necessary to invent simple methods of disentangling, separating, and arranging the fibers according to their length, other than by just using the fingers. Thus, crude methods of carding were invented to separate the fibers according to their length of staple. Uniformity of staple gives yarns a required evenness and improves the quality of the yarn.

BASIC PROCESSES

The value and character of a yarn are determined by (1) kind and quality of fiber; (2) amount of processing necessary to produce fineness; and (3) amount of twist, which increases tensile strength in the finished yarn. The purpose of the yarn must be anticipated, as this determines the number and kind of manufacturing operations.

Because the production of cotton yarn lends itself to a simple description of the manufacturing operations that make fiber into yarn, cotton fiber has been used in this chapter to illustrate the spinning process. It must be remembered, however, that all other raw fibers pass through similar spinning operations, although, of course, there are differences that will be explained in the chapters dealing with the various fibers. One such difference occurs when long strands or filaments, such as silk, are used rather than staple. In such instances, the required number of filaments are simply twisted together in a ropelike fashion as described in the paragraphs on the manufacture of silk yarns in Chapter 14.

The development of short fibers, or staple, into yarn, when stated in terms of basic manufacturing processes, is as follows: carding, combing, drawing out, twisting, and winding. As the raw fiber passes through these processes, it is successively called *lap, sliver, roving,* and finally *yarn.* Here are the manufacturing operations in which these stages occur.

1. Lap to card sliver by the carding process
2. Card sliver to comb sliver by the combing process (if the fiber is to be combed)
3. Sliver to roving by the drawing-out process
4. Roving to yarn by the drawing and twisting process
5. Reeled on bobbins, spools, or cones by the winding process

OPENING AND BLENDING ■ When bales are opened at the mill, the compressed masses of raw fiber are loosened and exposed to the atmosphere. Variation in the raw material is eliminated by mixing together parts of several bales and feeding the material into the opening machines. This blending of the raw material results in greater uniformity. Hard lumps in the fibers are loosened, and the heavier impurities—such as dirt, leaves, burs, and any remaining seeds—are removed by three machines known as pickers: breaker, intermediate, and finisher. These machines clean and form the cotton into *laps,* or rolls; the laps are 40 inches wide and 1 inch thick and weigh about 40 pounds each.

In recent years, another technique has been developed that replaces the pickers. A carousel revolves twelve bales of cotton in a circular path above four beaters that pluck the cotton from the bales. The cotton is moved by air pressure to an automixer where it is blended and then passed directly to the carding machine. It is not formed into laps.

Automatic opening and blending of cotton fiber.

Courtesy James Hunter Machine Company

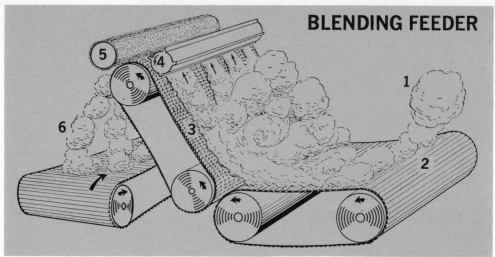

BLENDING FEEDER

Illustrations and copy on this page Courtesy of Bibb Manufacturing Co.

Cotton is thrown from bales (1) onto apron (2). Apron moves cotton to blending apron (3). Blending apron has sharp spikes that raise cotton until part of it is knocked off by roll (4). Some of the cotton stays on apron. The cotton knocked back by roll (4) continues to churn and blend until picked up again by apron. Another roll (5) strips off cotton that was not knocked back by previous roll (4). Cotton falls on conveyor belt (6) and is carried to next process.

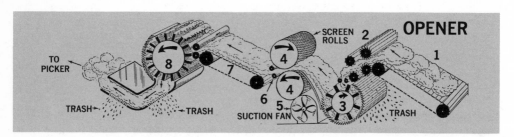

OPENER

Lint cotton falls on apron (1) and passes between feeder rolls (2) to beater cylinder (3). The rapidly whirling beater blades take off small tufts of cotton, knock out trash, and loosen up the mass. The two screen rolls (4) are made of screen material and air is sucked out of them by fan (5). This draws the cotton from beater and condenses it on the surface of the screen rolls from which it is taken and passed on by the small rolls (6). Air suction through cotton takes out dirt and trash. Conveyor belt (7) passes cotton to another type of beater (8). (Beaters shown are typical of the many types used.) From beater, the cotton passes to a conveyor and is carried to picker.

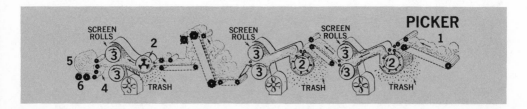

PICKER

Cotton in a loose mass enters picker, which is a series of beaters (2), and screen rolls (3) similar to those described under "opening" but progressively more refined. At the final output of beater and screen system (4), cotton has again been formed into a sheet or "lap." At this point the "evener" operates to feed more or less cotton to make lap perfectly uniform as it is wound up into a "lap roll" (5) on winding rolls (6). Lap roll is then taken to the carding process.

CARDING

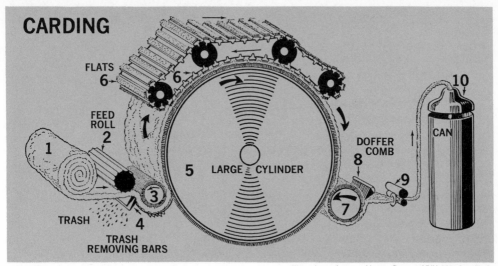

FLATS
6

FEED ROLL
2

1

3

TRASH

4

TRASH REMOVING BARS

6

6

5   LARGE   CYLINDER

DOFFER COMB

8

7

9

10

CAN

Illustrations and copy on this page Courtesy of Bibb Manufacturing Co.

The lap (1) from picker unrolls and feed roll (2) passes cotton to the "lickerin" roll (3) (covered with sawtoothlike wire). The lickerin roll passes fiber against cleaner bars (4) and gives it up to large cylinder (5), which passes between the thousands of fine wires on surface of cylinder and on flats (6). The cotton follows large cylinder to doffer cylinder (7), which removes lint from large cylinder. The doffer comb (8) vibrates against doffer cylinder and takes lint off in a filmy web that passes through condenser rolls (9), coiler head (10), and then into can. The sliver may be passed from can to *combing* for further removal of foreign matter and parallelization of fiber or directly to *drawing*.

DRAWING

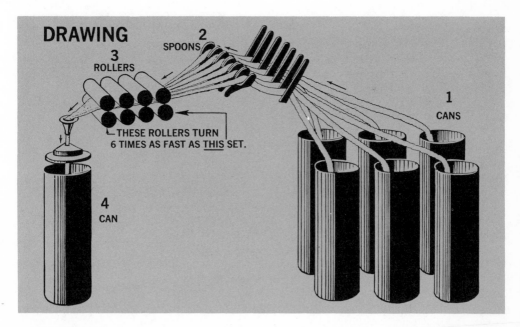

2
SPOONS

3
ROLLERS

← THESE ROLLERS TURN 6 TIMES AS FAST AS THIS SET.

4
CAN

1
CANS

Six cans (1) that were filled at cards feed each drawing frame delivery. The spoons (2) are connected so that if any one of the six slivers from can should break, the machine automatically stops. This prevents making uneven yarn later. Each of four sets of rolls (3) runs successively faster than preceding set. The last set runs approximately six times as fast as the first set; consequently, sliver coming out is the same size as each one of six going in but it comes out six times as many yards per minute. The sliver is neatly coiled again in roving can (4) by coiler head. The sliver is now much more uniform and fibers are much more nearly parallel. The sliver is now ready for roving frames. In actual practice, drawing is usually repeated.

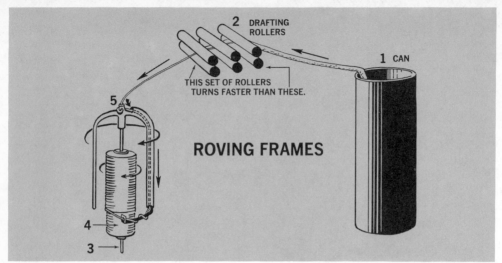

ROVING FRAMES

2 DRAFTING ROLLERS

THIS SET OF ROLLERS TURNS FASTER THAN THESE.

1 CAN

5

4

3

Illustrations and copy on this page Courtesy of Bibb Manufacturing Co.

The can of sliver (1) from drawing frames is fed between three sets of drafting rolls (2). Each following set of rolls runs faster than preceding set. This pulls sliver and thins it down, making fibers more nearly parallel. The spindle (3) turns flyer (5) and is driven at a constant speed. The front rolls (nearest flyer) are set at a speed that gives strand coming out of rolls a definite number of turns of twist per inch as it moves along between rolls and flyer. The bobbin (4) is driven by a source separate from gear that drives spindle and flyer. The bobbin is regulated to turn automatically at a speed sufficiently faster than flyer, which causes roving to wind on bobbin at same rate it is delivered by front roll.

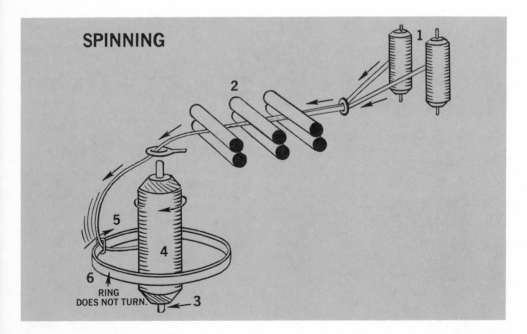

SPINNING

1

2

5

4

6

RING DOES NOT TURN.

3

The principle for spinning is the same as that used for roving except that the operation is more refined and a ring and traveler are used instead of the flyer. From bobbin (1) roving is fed between sets of drafting rolls (2) to draw strand down to its final desired size. The spindle (3) turns bobbin (4) at a constant speed. The front set of rolls is adjusted to deliver yarn at a speed sufficient to insert desired amount of twist as strand moves along. The traveler (5) glides freely around ring (6). The tension caused by drag of traveler causes yarn to wind on bobbin at same rate of speed as it is delivered by rolls.

CARDING ■ In the lap stage, the fibers are still in a tangled condition and contain waste material. Before this raw stock can be made into yarn, these impurities must be removed and the fibers must be straightened. Such straightening or smoothing is necessary for all natural staple fibers; otherwise, it would be impossible to produce fine yarns from what is originally a tangled mass. This initial process of arranging the fibers in a parallel fashion is known as *carding*. The work is done on a carding machine, where the lap is unrolled and drawn on a revolving cylinder covered with very fine hooks or wire brushes. A moving belt, also covered with wire brushes, is on top of this cylinder. The cylinder pulls the fibers in one direction, disentangles them, and arranges them parallel in the form of a thin film. This film is drawn through a funnel-shaped device that molds it into a round ropelike mass called *card sliver,* about the thickness of a broomstick. Card sliver produces *carded yarns* or *carded cottons* serviceable for inexpensive cotton fabrics.

DOUBLING ■ After carding, several slivers are combined. This results in a relatively narrow lap of compactly placed staple fibers. The compactness of these fibers permits this cotton stock to be attenuated, or drawn out, to a sliver of smaller diameter without falling apart.

COMBING ■ When the fiber is intended for fine yarns, the sliver is put through an additional straightening called *combing*. In this operation, fine-toothed combs continue straightening the fibers until they are arranged with such a high degree of parallelism that the short fibers, called *noils,* are combed out and completely separated from the longer fibers. (This procedure is not done when processing man-made staple fibers because they are cut into predetermined uniform lengths. Since these fibers do not need the combing separation, they are processed for spinning into yarns by the Direct Spinner, the Perlok Process, or the Pacific Converter, depending upon the desired end uses of the yarns. These techniques are discussed more fully in the description of spun rayon staple yarn in Chapter 15.)

The combing process forms a *comb sliver* made of the longest fibers, which, in turn, produces a smoother and more even yarn. This operation eliminates as much as 25 percent of the original card sliver; thus almost one-fourth of the raw cotton becomes waste. The combing process, therefore, is identified with consumers' goods of better quality. Since long-staple yarns produce stronger, smoother, and more serviceable fabrics, quality cotton goods carry labels indicating that they are made from *combed yarns* or *combed cottons.*

DRAWING OUT ■ The combining of several slivers for the drawing-out process eliminates irregularities that would cause too much variation if the slivers were put through singly. The drawing frame has several pairs of rollers, each advanced set of which revolves at a progressively faster speed. This action pulls the staple lengthwise over each other, thereby producing longer and thinner slivers. After several stages of drawing out, the condensed sliver is taken to the slubber, where rollers similar to those in the drawing frame draw out the cotton further. Here the slubbing is passed to the spindles, where it is given its first twist and is then wound on bobbins.

Courtesy Pepperell Manufacturing Company

Cotton going through the opening machine where the fibers are loosened.

Cotton lap from the picker room where dust, leaf, twigs, and other foreign matter have been removed.

Courtesy Pepperell Manufacturing Company

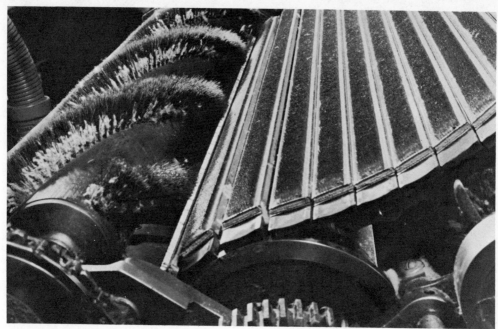

Courtesy Pepperell Manufacturing Company

Inside the carding machine, where the brushes clean and straighten the fiber.

Sliver leaving the carding machine, where the cotton has been further cleaned and disentangled.

Courtesy Pepperell Manufacturing Company

Courtesy Pepperell Manufacturing Company

Slivers are doubled to increase the density of the future cotton yarn.

Combed slivers are combined as they leave the combing machine to further increase the density and compactness of the future yarn.

Courtesy Pepperell Manufacturing Company

Courtesy Pepperell Manufacturing Company

On the spinning frame, the roving passes from the top through a series of rollers that draw out the cotton into a thread. The thread is twisted as it winds onto the bobbin.

ROVING ■ These bobbins are placed on the roving frame, where further drawing out and twisting take place until the cotton stock is about the diameter of a pencil lead. There are two stages of roving: intermediate and fine. The operations are identical, but each machine yields a finer product than the stock it received. *Roving* is the final product of the several drawing-out operations. It is a preparatory stage for the final insertion of twist. To this point, only enough twist has been given the stock to hold the fibers together. Roving has no tensile strength; it will break apart easily with any slight pull.

SPINNING ■ The roving, on bobbins, is placed in the spinning frame, where it passes through several sets of rollers running at successively higher rates of speed and is finally drawn out to *yarn* of the size desired. Spinning machines are of two kinds: ring frame and mule frame. The ring frame is a faster process, but produces a relatively coarse yarn. For very fine yarns, the mule frame is required because of its slow intermittent operation. The ring frame, which is in general use now, is more suitable for the manufacture of cotton yarns for mass production. Its hundreds of spindles, whirling thousands of revolutions a minute, and its constant spinning action provide a fast operation. The ring spinning frame completes the manufacture of yarn (1) by drawing out the roving, (2) by inserting twist, and (3) by winding the yarn on bobbins—all in one operation.

BLENDING FIBERS

When different types of fibers are combined or blended, the properties of the individual fibers are also combined, though modified, in the blended yarn. Blending has been done for many years to produce yarns for such fabrics as *union cloth,* which is made of cotton and wool. Fabrics made from some of the newer blends are sold under such trade names as *Cotron,* a blend of cotton and rayon; *Viyella,* a blend of cotton and wool; and *Cotdel,* a blend of cotton and Kodel. (The amount of fiber blended and the properties of the blend are discussed in the chapter dealing with the particular fiber.)

Blending may be done at any one of the fiber processing stages discussed. During the initial "opening" stage, appropriate amounts of each fiber can be weighed out and layers of them can be *sandwich blended* by spreading one on top of the other. Sections of the sandwich are then fed into a hopper or blending feeder for discharge into a mechanical mixer. When the fibers are *feeder blended,* each type of fiber is automatically weighed and fed directly from hoppers into a mechanical mixer.

When a lower percentage of one fiber is desired in a blend, it is *finisher picker blended.* Four of the breaker picker laps are blended together at the finisher picker stage and then fed to the carding machine.

Sandwich blending by this battery of machines automatically weighs out fibers in layers on top of each other as they are conveyed on a belt moving from left to right.

Courtesy Fiber Control Corporation

Card blended fibers can be produced by feeding one lap of the different fibers into the carding machine to produce a blended sliver. However, this procedure does not produce a precise, well-distributed blend.

When the fibers are to be combed, the blending would not be done until after the waste and shorter fibers are removed. Then, *drawing frame blended* fibers are produced by combined slivers of previously carded, combed, and parallelized fiber.

Sometimes fibers are *rove* or *spun blended.* This produces a rather random arrangement that is usually limited to the blending of colored fibers for such fabrics as tweed.

This beater blender controls removal of the blend from the sandwiching conveyor, maintaining the proportionate distribution of the fibers in the blend for discharge to the mechanical mixer.

Courtesy Fiber Control Corporation

The fuzzy yarn at left is spun rayon yarn. The smooth yarn at right is filament rayon yarn.

Courtesy American Viscose Corporation

FILAMENT YARNS

A reference was made earlier on page 30 regarding the production of yarns from the long strands or filaments of silk, as well as many man-made fibers. The spinning of such fibers is essentially a matter of producing individual filaments as *monofilament* yarn or of twisting several of these filaments together in a continuous ropelike fashion, producing *multifilament* yarn of the desired lengths of thousands of feet.

After spinning, yarn is sometimes reeled from bobbins into large skeins ready for bleaching, mercerizing, and dyeing.

Courtesy Spool Cotton Co.

There are various types of yarn, each having its own characteristics. These characteristics vary according to the construction and the treatment given in the manufacture of the yarn.

AMOUNT OF TWIST ■ The amount of twist to the inch is an important factor in finished consumers' goods. It determines the appearance as well as the durability and serviceability of a fabric. Fine yarns require more twist than coarse yarns. Warp yarns are given more twist than are filling yarns. To retain the twist in the yarns and prevent any tendency to untwist or kink, the yarns are given a twist-setting finish with heat or moisture, depending upon the kind of fiber used.

The amount of twist also depends upon the type of fabric to be woven:

1. Yarns intended for soft-surfaced fabrics are given only a slack twist. They are called *soft-twisted yarns*.

2. Yarns intended for smooth-surfaced fabrics are given many twists to the inch. Such *hard-twisted yarns* contribute strength, smoothness, elasticity, and some wrinkle resistance to fabrics.

3. Yarns intended for crepe fabrics (with rough, pebbly, or crinkled surfaces) are given a maximum amount of twist, which also adds wrinkle resistance.

From spools or cones, mounted on creel, separate yarns are wound on a warp beam.

Courtesy Bibb Manufacturing Co.

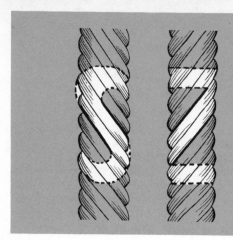

The S and Z twists are diagrammed here. The importance of the direction of the twist is illustrated in the diagrams of thrown silk threads shown in Chapter 14.

In this case, the direction of the twist also contributes to the wrinkle resistance. The direction of twist may be observed by holding the yarn in a vertical position. If the spirals conform to the direction of the slope of the central part of the letter S, the yarn has an S twist; if they conform to the slope of the letter Z, the yarn has a Z twist.

Permanent crepe effects, such as chiffon, georgette, crepe de chine, canton, and flat and French crepes, are produced by the use of hard-twisted yarns, some of which have left twist, others right twist. These yarns are placed alternately in the warp or in the filling, or in both. When the finished fabric is later washed or dyed, such yarns kink in different directions, producing the crepe surface.

Another satisfactory method of obtaining crepe effects during the construction of the fabric is by the use of slack warp yarns, which may or may not be wound on a separate warp beam. These yarns are held less taut than the other warp yarns and produce a permanent crinkled pattern. Seersucker and matelassé are produced in this way and prove very serviceable.

YARN COUNT ■ In the spinning process, there is always a fixed relation between the weight of the original quantity of fiber and the length of the yarn produced from that amount of raw material. This relation indicates the thickness of the yarn. It is determined by the extent of the drawing-out process and is designated by numbers, which are called the *yarn count*.

The standard for the yarn count in cotton is 1 pound of fiber drawn out to make 840 yards of yarn; the resultant thickness or size is known as count No. 1. If the yarn is drawn out farther, so that 1 pound makes twice 840 yards, it is identified as No. 2. Thus, a No. 2 yarn will be finer than a No. 1. No. 10 denotes a still finer yarn, as it indicates that 1 pound of cotton is drawn out to ten times 840 yards. The higher the number of the yarn count, the finer the yarn in size. Yarn counts up to 20 are called coarse yarns; 20 to 60 are medium yarns; above 60 are fine yarns. Up to 20, the count rises by single numbers. Only even numbers are used between 20 and 60. Above 60, the count rises by intervals of 5 until 100, after which an interval of 10 is used. The size of mercerized cotton sewing thread used for general purposes is No. 50 or No. 60. The very finest cotton yarns spun have been as high as No. 400, the product of one pound of cotton drawn out to a strand 336,000 yards long (almost 200 miles). Extemely fine yarns are difficult and costly to manufacture because of the greater care required in spinning and the greater amount of twist to the inch.

The size of yarn to be used in a fabric is determined by the purpose of the fabric. Yarns of varying sizes may be used to obtain the nubbed or novelty effects and rough textures characterized by ratiné, bouclé, or éponge.

There are presently different standards for yarn counts of different fibers. While the standard base of 1 pound is used for cotton, linen, and wool, the length of drawing for each of these fibers is different. Furthermore, yarn counts of such filament fibers as silk and nylon are designated according to denier, which is an entirely different system of measuring yarn diameter. This difference has created an increasingly difficult situation in view of the greater number of fibers, the blending of these fibers into yarns, and the growth of international textile trade. There is a growing awareness of the need for a single common standard system of measuring yarn diameter.

The International Organization for Standardization (IOS) has adopted the Tex System. This organization has established a fixed relationship between the weight and length of all yarns: one Tex equals one gram per thousand meters. The greater the weight, the thicker the yarn, and consequently the higher the Tex number.

This system was started in 1960 with the support of the American Society for Testing Materials (ASTM), which proposed a three-stage approach to the changeover. During the first stage, technologists and yarn manufacturers are urged to familiarize themselves with the new system and to include Tex numbers in parentheses following the customary yarn count numbers.

After a period of time deemed sufficient, Tex numbers will be used as the regular designation and the former yarn count numbers will be in parentheses. Eventually, only the Tex number will be used.

PLY YARNS ■ When two or more strands or yarns are twisted together, they are designated as *ply yarns*. They are termed two-ply, three-ply, and so on, according to the number used in their construction. A single yarn may be of relatively good quality; but where durability is all-important, ply yarns are preferable, assuming that the yarns have the same length of staple. Good-quality broadcloth for men's shirtings, for example, is made with ply yarns.

Yarn construction and yarn count are expressed in the following manner. The term 1/30s denotes the use of a single yarn having a yarn count of 30. In the same way, 3/30s denotes the use of a three-ply yarn—that is, three strands twisted together, each having a separate yarn count of 30. A three-ply yarn, indicated by 3/30s, would be equivalent to a single yarn having a yarn count of 10. In the same way, 2/10s (containing two single strands of 10s) is equivalent in size to 1/5s.

When the number of yards in a pound of cotton is to be calculated for any given size of yarn, the yarn count is multiplied by 840 yards. For example, if the required size of a yarn is 2/10s, the fraction should be reduced to 1/5s; then the 5 is multiplied by 840; and the result is 4,200 yards.

DOUBLED YARNS ■ Another type of yarn construction is the *doubled yarn*. This consists of two or more single strands treated as one in the weaving process, but the strands are not twisted together. The doubled yarn must not be confused with ply yarns, which are stronger because they are twisted. Doubled yarns are used for ornamental effect; they do, of course, contribute a certain amount of additional strength. Because doubled yarns have little twist, they produce luster and softness.

NOVELTY YARNS ■ The spinning process can produce decorative effects by varying the amount of twist or by twisting together yarns of different diameters, each of which may have different amounts of twist per inch. Such yarns can give fabrics almost limitless textural effects of various color combinations. Fabrics made of novelty yarns cannot generally be as durable as fabrics made of uniform yarns that have been evenly spun. A safe rule for the consumer is to remember that longer service may be expected from flat, smooth fabrics made from evenly spun yarns rather than from novelty yarns of complex character.

Slub Yarns. The consumer's desire for ornamental effects has popularized the production of yarns that are given only a small amount of drawing out. Such yarns, called slub yarns, have soft untwisted areas at frequent intervals throughout their length. They are coarse, with slight twist, having varying diameters that show irregularities typical of an incomplete spinning operation.

If simulation of linen is desired, the use of slub yarns is easily understood. Where durability is a main consideration, their practicability is justly questioned, because a heavy yarn protruding above the level of surrounding yarns is subjected to friction and the fabric soon shows signs of wear at those points after continued use. In the past, slub yarns were generally used in fabrics that possessed an especially compact construction and consequently were characterized by marked durability. Today, slub yarns do not always imply compact construction in the fabric of which they are a part. They do furnish ornamental effects, and are frequently used for that purpose in shantung and tweed.

Flake Yarns. Flake yarns are variations of the slub yarns. The flake or slub effect is made by inserting soft, thick tufts of roving between binder yarns at intervals. The result is a flake yarn of varying thickness and softness, caused by the soft-effect ply held in place by the uniform binder. This type of yarn is limited to fancy-effect uses.

Spiral Yarns. The general appearance of spiral yarns is that of a coarse yarn wound around a fine yarn, giving the effect of a spiral. The thicker yarn is given a slack twist and wound spirally around the fine yarn (sometimes referred to as the *core yarn*), which is given a hard twist. Other names for the spiral yarns are *corkscrew* and *eccentric*. Spiral yarns may be made for different purposes. They may be constructed in such a way as to give the decorative spiral effect of a candy-cane pattern. Sometimes the core yarn is completely hidden by the spiraling outer yarn, as in the case of lastex where the core yarn is rubber while the outer yarn may be of cotton, nylon, or other textile.

Ratiné Yarns. Ratiné yarns are a variation of the spiral yarn type, although the method of manufacture differs. The outer (effect) yarn and the core yarn are twisted in a spiral manner, but at intervals a longer loop is thrown out by the effect yarn, which kinks back on itself and is held in place by a third yarn called the binder. The binder is added in a second twisting operation going in the opposite direction of the effect yarn. The ratiné yarn's small loops on its surface give the yarn a taut, rough-surfaced effect. The technique may be applied to all major fibers and is popular for combinations of yarns made of such fibers as cotton and rayon.

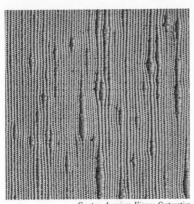

Courtesy American Viscose Corporation

Shantung, showing characteristic slub yarns in filling.

Courtesy American Viscose Corporation

Tweed, showing characteristic slub yarns in warp and filling.

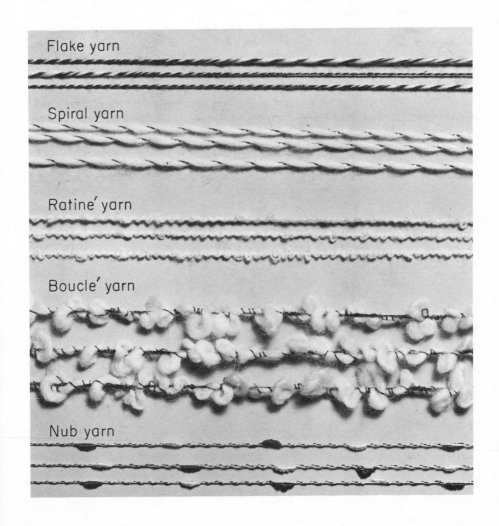

Flake yarn

Spiral yarn

Ratine' yarn

Boucle' yarn

Nub yarn

Homespun fabric showing the soft, thick tufts of roving of the flake yarns.

Bouclé, Loop, or Curl Yarns. Bouclé, loop, or curl yarns are comparable to the ratiné yarn type, but in bouclé yarns the surface is softer and has a more pronounced novelty effect. This effect is accomplished by allowing one of the plies to remain slack during the twisting operation, causing it to twist on itself and form a loop. The size of the loop will vary depending on the speed of the rollers. These yarns are popular for knitted fabrics. They are also used to create fabrics with a looped pile to resemble fur, such as karakul, for trimmings and coating fabrics.

Nub, Knop, Knot, or Spot Yarns. Nub yarns are made by twisting the effect ply around the other ply many times within a very short space, causing bumps or nubs that may be spaced at intervals along the yarn. Variations are possible where, for example, two effect plies, each of different color, may be used, and the nubs arranged so that the colors are alternated along the length of the yarn. In some instances, nub yarns are bound by a binder or third thread; in other cases, the effects can be created without the binder.

REVIEW QUESTIONS

1 How are fibers made into yarns?

2 Describe the carding process and what it does to the cotton fibers.

3 Explain why a fabric woven from slub yarns may not wear well.

4 Why would it be difficult to make fabric directly from roving?

5 (a) What is meant by yarn count? (b) Why is it important?

6 How do filament yarns differ in the manner in which they are made from yarns of staple fibers?

7 In what way do differences in the raw material affect the formation of yarn?

8 Describe the combing process and what it does to the fibers.

9 What are the qualities that determine the choice of a yarn?

10 Explain the meaning of 1/60s, 4/20s, 3/30s.

11 Explain the difference between ply yarns and doubled yarns.

12 How is variation in yarns obtained in the spinning process?

13 How does twist in a yarn affect the finished fabric?

14 What kind of fabrics use yarns spun with a very slack twist?

15 What are the purposes and characteristics of the different types of novelty yarns?

SUGGESTED ACTIVITY

Prepare a rough diagram to illustrate the processes involved in the manufacture of yarn.

TEXTURED YARNS

4

The yarns discussed in Chapter 3 are made of fibers in their normal forms. While they are produced in many varieties to provide various effects, each yarn's characteristics are limited by the normal condition of the fiber's shape, its thickness, its length and surface texture, as well as such inherent qualities as elasticity, resilience, and warmth.

Consumers often wish that certain characteristics could be combined into one yarn for a particular kind of fabric. They welcome new, interesting, and useful properties in fabrics made from yarns that normally cannot provide these characteristics. Consequently, techniques have been developed that change the surface or shape and texture of the fibers and, in turn, affect the characteristics of the yarns. These *textured* yarns provide consumers with the variations in fabric properties that they seek. For convenient identification, they may be grouped into three types: *stretch, high bulk,* and *loop bulk.*

STRETCH YARNS

There are four kinds of stretch yarns: (1) those made by giving a special mechanical *heat-setting* treatment to *thermoplastic* filament fibers, such as nylon or the polyesters; (2) those made of *elastomeric* fibers, such as spandex or rubber; (3) those made of *bicomponent* fibers, such as two different types of nylon produced as a single filament; and (4) those made of specially *chemically treated* natural fibers, such as cotton.

There are also several different techniques that are used in producing each kind of stretch yarn.

HEAT-SET THERMOPLASTIC YARNS ■
The long, smooth, endless strands of man-made filament fibers, such as nylon, have varying amounts of natural ability to stretch when pulled and to spring back to their original sizes when allowed to relax. However, when subjected to certain methods that use heat to set crimp in these thermoplastic filament yarns, the crimp greatly increases their stretchability.

A *thermoplastic yarn* is one that can be put into any shape or position desired and, after being subjected to a predetermined level of heat for a specific period of time, it will retain that shape despite washing, dry cleaning, stretching, or compressing. This heat-setting technique is employed in many ways, and depending on the method of manufacture and the fibers used, the properties of the yarn will also vary.

Thermoplastic stretch yarns have many advantages over untreated filament yarns. They have a soft touch and a dull appearance like that of wool rather than the sometimes undesirable sheen of some filament yarns. The resultant textural appearance of stretch yarns provides opportunity for desirable novelty effects. Fabrics or garments made of these yarns have a higher degree of absorbency and adsorbency than ordinary filament yarns, since stretch yarns provide loops and kinks to hold the moisture. This results in providing better perspiration conductivity and consequently increases comfort to the wearer. The pockets of air caused by the coils in the yarns also act as an insulative barrier, which makes the garment warmer.

Garments made of such stretch yarns wash easily and dry-clean readily. They are as strong and durable as garments made of yarns of similar fibers that have not been processed into stretch yarns. In fact, the stretch characteristic is more likely to result in less strain on the yarns, fabrics, and seams of garments during the ordinary stress of putting on, wearing, and taking off. The stretchability also provides greater comfort, shape retention, and wrinkle resistance and allows the garment to conform to the figure and to fit better. Solving the fitting problem is not only an advantage to the consumer but also to the manufacturer, who finds it more economical to produce fewer specific sizes, and to the retailer, who needs less space to store fewer sizes and finds it easier to fit the consumer.

There are four general types of heat-set thermoplastic yarns: *coil, curl, crimp,* and *wavy.* All are treated to provide a springlike or accordionlike characteristic to the yarn. The methods of accomplishing this vary, thereby giving different shapes to the yarns but producing somewhat similar results.

Coil Types: Conventional Method. This method utilizes conventional twisting equipment with heat-setting techniques. It consists basically of untwisting nylon or polyester yarns, inserting a measured high twist (from 47 to 114 turns per inch depending upon the denier or thickness), heat-setting the yarn in that condition in a high-pressure steam autoclave at approximately 260 degrees Fahrenheit for an hour or less, and then untwisting the yarns to a predetermined level. As a result, the torque or tendency to twist back to its heat-set condition causes the filaments to bulk up into a springlike condition. To give balance to the yarn, a set of filaments previously given an S twist is generally plied a few turns with a previously Z twisted set of ends.

Helanca, a well known stretch yarn introduced by the Heberlein Patent Corporation in 1947, is produced by this conventional method. It is now produced under license by many companies. This yarn can be stretched three times its relaxed length in heavier deniers and from four to five times in lighter yarns. Helanca has excellent recovery to its original size on release of the tension and will provide a snug fit and shape retention to garments made from it. It has a firm, crisp hand and a bulking power up to three times its uncoiled condition. The two basic types are *Helanca Hi-Test* and *Helanca SP.* Helanca Hi-Test has greater stretch than Helanca SP and is used in the manufacture of such garments as men's, women's and children's hosiery, women's blouses and lingerie, men's briefs, and children's underwear.

Helanca SP and SP300 (*SP* is the abbreviation for "sport") has less bulk, has a higher elastic pull, and is slightly less elastic. It is used in fabrics for sportswear, such as ski pants, and for upholstery. Helanca yarn can be combined with a rubber-core yarn to produce firm, elastic fabrics for foundation garments and swimsuits.

Burmilized and *Shape 2 U,* trade names owned by Burlington Mills Corporation, are made of any one of several thermoplastic monofilament fibers. The processing technique is similar to that of Helanca, but it varies in the method and the amount of twisting. *Chadalon,* a trademark of Chadbourn Gotham, Inc., is a similar yarn used for hosiery.

Coil Types: False-Twist Method. Most of the world's stretch yarn is made by this method because it is more economical and much faster to produce. It is basically a technique of temporarily putting a very high twist in a multifilament yarn, heat-setting the yarn in this twisted condition, cooling it quickly, and then untwisting the yarn. The operation is based on the principle that a stationary multifilament yarn that is held at both ends and twisted at the center by an eccentrically placed hook will develop equal amounts of twist in opposite directions on each side of the guide hook. The opposite direction of the twist in the yarn as it passes out of the false-twist spindle cancels out the twist in the yarn. However, since the yarn is made of a thermoplastic fiber that has been heat-set in a coiled condition, the yarn develops a coillike, bulky, springy character.

On emerging from the false-twist spindle, the yarn has a built-in torque (or twist) in either the S or the Z direction, depending upon the direction of the rotating spindle. Since fabrics made of yarns in this condition would be distorted, yarns of opposite torques are usually plied or sometimes doubled to provide balance.

The amount of stretchability and the texture of the yarn is dependent upon such factors as the denier, the amount of false twist used, the amount and method of heat applied, and the ply of the yarn. The principal varieties are as follows.

Helanca generally has less stretch than the other yarns made by the false-twist method. It is used for sweaters and crepe-textured fabrics that need a more relaxed fit.

Fluflon yarn, manufactured by the Universal Winding Company, is usually made of nylon but could be made of other thermoplastic fibers. The yarn may be made into singles or plied. Fluflon yarn has a high degree of elasticity. It stretches up to four times its original length and relaxes to its normal size. The yarn has a very soft hand and a variety of uses.

Superloft is another trademark of Universal Winding Company for stretch yarns made of any thermoplastic fiber. It has good bulk but less stretch than Fluflon.

Whitin ARCT, manufactured by the Whitin Machine Works, is a nylon stretch yarn. It can be stretched up to five times its relaxed length and, when relaxed, it can bulk up to three times its stretched diameter.

Cumuloft is a Chemstrand Division nylon stretch yarn. Its characteristics are the same as Whitin ARCT.

Saaba is a false-twist yarn that has been modified by a second heat-setting treatment at a lower temperature. The technique reduces the stretch but increases the bulk. The trademark is owned by Universal Winding Company.

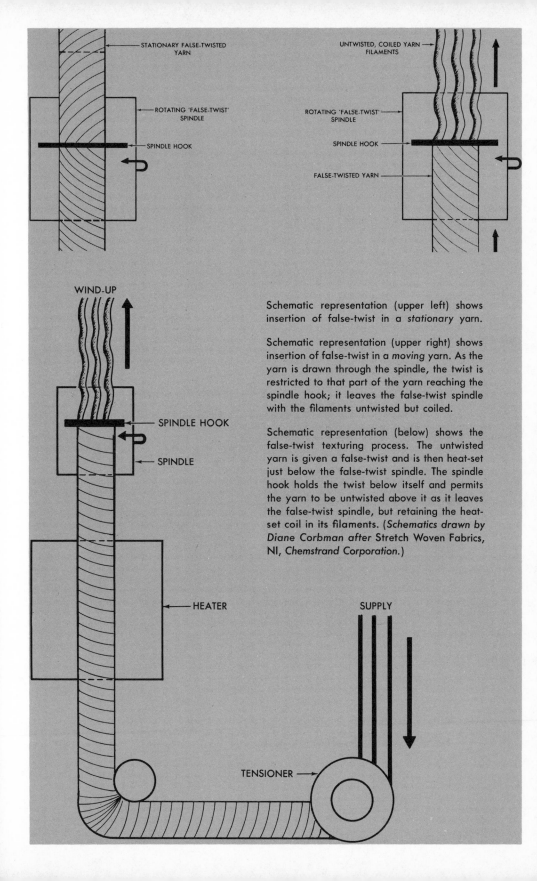

STATIONARY FALSE-TWISTED YARN

ROTATING 'FALSE-TWIST' SPINDLE

SPINDLE HOOK

UNTWISTED, COILED YARN FILAMENTS

ROTATING 'FALSE-TWIST' SPINDLE

SPINDLE HOOK

FALSE-TWISTED YARN

WIND-UP

SPINDLE HOOK

SPINDLE

HEATER

SUPPLY

TENSIONER

Schematic representation (upper left) shows insertion of false-twist in a *stationary* yarn.

Schematic representation (upper right) shows insertion of false-twist in a *moving* yarn. As the yarn is drawn through the spindle, the twist is restricted to that part of the yarn reaching the spindle hook; it leaves the false-twist spindle with the filaments untwisted but coiled.

Schematic representation (below) shows the false-twist texturing process. The untwisted yarn is given a false-twist and is then heat-set just below the false-twist spindle. The spindle hook holds the twist below itself and permits the yarn to be untwisted above it as it leaves the false-twist spindle, but retaining the heat-set coil in its filaments. (*Schematics drawn by Diane Corbman after Stretch Woven Fabrics, NI, Chemstrand Corporation.*)

Curl Types: Stress-Curled Method. This is essentially an adaptation of the method of obtaining a random curl in a paper ribbon by pulling it between one's thumb and the edge of a dull blade.

Agilon is the trade name of the stretch yarn first developed by this process and patented by the Deering Milliken Research Trust. This thermoplastic yarn is softened by heating and passed with a slight pressure over a dull knife edge, which deforms the filaments by flattening one part of their curved surfaces. The actual contracting and stretching characteristic of the yarn is added to the fabric made from this yarn in the washing or scouring process, which is part of the finishing operation. The yarn develops very short sections of marked curl and torque, but since they change position at random, the net result is a balanced no-torque effect in the fabric.

Agilon yarn is produced in monofilament and multifilament forms. It has an additional distinguishing feature in that a filament fiber, such as nylon, can have a staple fiber, such as cotton or wool, spun around it. Therefore, the textural characteristics can vary; Agilon yarn can simulate any kind of yarn made of any kind of fiber, whether smooth or rough, soft or harsh.

Depending on the denier and processing of the yarn, Agilon can stretch up to three times its length and return to its original length on release of the tension. Unlike some other stretch yarns, Agilon yarn does not immediately snap back with an almost rubber-band action after it has been released. It recovers its original shape more slowly. This "gentle elasticity" results in less strain on the fabric and no binding to the wearer, which insures increased comfort. Garments made of Agilon yarn include men's, women's, and children's hosiery, creped fabrics for women's blouses and lingerie, and pile fabrics, such as velvets, artificial furs, and fleeces.

Crimp Types: Stuffer Box Method. This process is essentially one of tightly cramming thermoplastic yarn into a container and heat-setting it in this cramped condition, thereby forming a random zigzag crimp. There are several widely used varieties.

Ban-Lon yarn is licensed by Joseph Bancroft & Sons Company. The yarn is made of thermoplastic fibers that are permanently crimped by forcing them into a heated stuffing box. Ban-Lon yarn is composed of multifilament or staple fibers and has a soft hand with a dull appearance. It may impart a crepelike surface to the fabric. Ban-Lon has a moderate stretch and clings to the form. The yarn has a bulking capacity of two to three times its stretched diameter. It may be utilized in woven or knitted fabrics and is popular for men's socks and women's blouses and sweaters.

Textralized yarn is also licensed by Joseph Bancroft & Sons Company. The method of production is similar but a finer denier yarn is used, producing a yarn that has greater stretch (up to two times its relaxed state) but the same bulking power. This yarn is used for both woven and knitted fabrics.

Spunized yarn is produced by the Hartford Spinners process from thermoplastic yarn in a laced-chain arrangement, passed through a stuffer box, and heat-set. The yarn is soft and quite bulky, but it has limited stretch.

Wavy Types: Knit-Deknit Method. This technique requires that a thermoplastic yarn be knitted into a fabric and then heat-set. The yarn is subsequently unraveled from the fabric. The loops, formed in knitting and then heat-set, remain permanently in the yarn and give it a wavy or crimpy character.

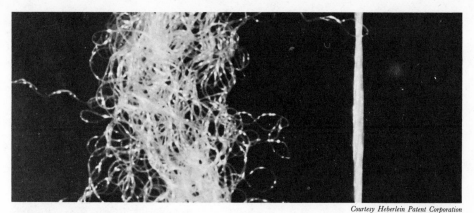

Courtesy Heberlein Patent Corporation

Helanca relaxed (left) and stretched (right).

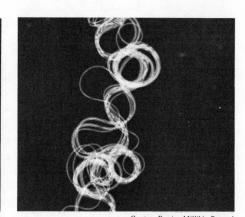

Courtesy Deering Millikin Research   *Courtesy Deering Millikin Research*

At left, 40-denier Agilon nylon yarn with undeveloped crimp. At right, 40 denier Agilon nylon yarn, fully developed, showing the curled effect that provides its stretch property.

ELASTOMERIC YARNS ■ All of these yarns are elastic because of the inherent nature of the basic fiber: rubber or spandex.

Lastex. Everyone is familiar with the elasticity of rubber. In fact, it is this characteristic that brought about the production of rubber yarn as the first stretch yarn. It has been produced for many years under the trademark *Lastex*. This yarn has a rubber core with a ply of cotton or some other yarn wound around it. The construction combines the elasticity of rubber with the texture and hand of the other fiber, which hides the rubber.

Lastex yarn can be produced in weights fine enough for sheer fabrics and laces and heavy enough for foundation garments. Stretched Lastex has a strong tendency to return to its relaxed condition, which makes it an excellent yarn for supportive or holding purposes. It is not affected by laundering or dry cleaning, but the use of chlorine bleach or excessive amounts of dry-cleaning fluid should be avoided. Over a period of time, Lastex loses its elasticity as the rubber tends to dry out and deteriorate. Fabrics of Lastex yarn are heavier than fabrics made of other types of stretch yarns.

Spandex. Spandex is a man-made fiber and has the distinctive property of stretching about five to seven times its relaxed state without breaking. This high degree of elasticity, along with its relatively light weight and its resistance to most solvents (including the common dry-cleaning and laundering agents), make it superior to rubber. Spandex fibers have a comfortable hand, wear very well, and retain their natural whiteness. They do not dye easily and may fade.

Spandex fibers, such as Lycra and Vyrene, are also produced as core-spun yarns. These yarns have a spandex core (which could be as little as 5 to 15 percent of the entire yarn) with a layer of any staple fiber spun around the core as it is held under a predetermined amount of tension. When it is relaxed after spinning, the spandex core returns to its normal length, which pulls the outer layer of spun fibers into a more compact formation. This technique can control the degree of stretchability of the core-spun yarn from a very low degree to twice its relaxed state. Since the core yarn is encased in the layer of staple fibers, the yarn takes on the hand and appearance of these fibers.

Spandex yarns differ from the heat-set thermoplastic stretch yarns in that they have a stronger pull or tendency to recover to original size. This provides more positive support to the body. They are therefore very useful for foundation garments, support hose, and swimsuits. They are also used for lingerie and outerwear, depending upon the type of yarn used, such as core spun.

A variation of the use of spandex fiber that is under development has been called *intimate blend spinning*. This stretch yarn is composed of a spandex staple blended with any other staple fiber that is desired in the yarn by the fabric producer. As with other blends, the characteristics of the yarns and fabrics produced would depend upon the kind and the amount of fiber blended, the kind of spun yarn, and the fabric construction.

BICOMPONENT YARNS ■ This yarn is made of a filament of two types of a man-made fiber extruded simultaneously through the spinneret opening. The fibers adhere in "siamese" fashion. As the yarn is processed, one type, which shrinks more than the other, pulls on the other type attached to it and causes the whole filament to become distorted and crimped. Such yarns are free of torque. *Cantrece,* which is used for hosiery, is a nylon bicomponent yarn produced by Du Pont.

CHEMICALLY TREATED NATURAL FIBER YARNS ■ Manufacturers of cotton fabrics have been interested for a long time in the development of yarns and fabrics that have stretch. The natural properties of cotton—cool hand, texture, absorbency, washability, and durability—could be enhanced by the addition of stretch capability. The competitive production of ingenious man-made stretch yarns has given great impetus to the experimentation and development of cotton stretch yarns. There presently are three techniques.

Heat-Set Thermoplastic Cotton Crimping Process. Cotton yarn can be treated with one of several polymeric chemicals, which gives it thermoplastic properties. The yarn is then processed by the same heat-setting and crimping methods that are applied to man-made thermoplastic yarns. Cotton yarns produced by this method have as high as 200 percent stretch, and fabrics woven of these yarns may have up to 100 percent stretch. The higher the thread count, the lower the stretch. Return to original size is not immediate and is generally about 75 percent, though it is completely restored by washing or dry cleaning.

Cotton Yarn Cross-Linking Process. Cotton yarn can be treated with a resin similar to the ones used for cotton wash and wear finishes. This resin is known as a cellulose cross-linking chemical. It gives cotton yarns and fabrics a "memory" and causes them to return to their original state (the same principle as wrinkle resistance). After the yarn has been treated, it is twisted and set with heat. It is subsequently *back-twisted* in the reverse direction. As the treated yarn tries to return to its original twist, it pulls itself up into tiny coils. This provides the springlike action of stretch.

A variation of this process is that of *false-twisting* the resin-treated cotton plied yarns, heat-setting them, and then untwisting the plies. The cotton singles retain their coiled characteristics and thus have the springlike stretch action.

At present, this process is relatively expensive and not too commercially feasible. Performance of the yarns and fabrics is similar to that of the heat-set thermoplastic crimping process.

Slack Mercerization Process. Another method used to provide stretch in cotton is to give the woven cotton fabric a special finish by the *slack mercerization* process. (This finish is discussed further in Chapter 8.) Essentially, it is a technique of passing the cotton fabric through caustic soda as the warp is held at constant tension while the width is allowed to relax. The resultant slack in the filling causes the yarns to contract. Under tension, the filling in the finished fabric may stretch from 15 to 20 percent. The fabric returns to about 80 percent of its original size, and it is completely restored by washing. The advantages of this method over the others are the increased strength and the low cost of production.

BULK YARNS

HIGH-BULK YARNS ■ The high-bulk yarns are relatively thick and soft, and they may also have the additional characteristic of stretch. They are always made of crimped-staple synthetic fibers that are usually an acrylic, such as Orlon, Acrilan, or Creslan. Blends of these fibers can also be made with other synthetic as well as natural fibers. Some high-bulk yarns are spun with a slack twist, sometimes with crimped staple, to produce a soft, thick, spongy yarn; such yarns generally do not have much natural stretch. Frequently, high-bulk yarns are made by blending stretched fibers with fibers that have been stretched and relaxed. During the dyeing operation, the stretched fibers relax; and their contraction causes the other already relaxed fibers to crimp and curl. This produces a soft, thick, but lightweight stretch yarn. Agilon and Fluflon yarns may be produced as stretch high-bulk yarns.

High-bulk yarns have the soft hand of wool or cashmere. Although they are lightweight, they are warm because the crimped fibers form air spaces within the thick yarn to provide insulation. High-bulk yarns have good water adsorbency; water droplets will accumulate on the surface of the fibers in the air spaces. The fabrics do not feel clammy when moist, and they tend to dry more quickly than wool fabrics. Garments made of high-bulk yarns wash and dry-clean readily. But they may pill—that is, form little balls of fiber on the surface of the fabric. To avoid this, garments should be turned inside out and washed gently. Light brushing with a very soft brush will help reduce the pilling. When

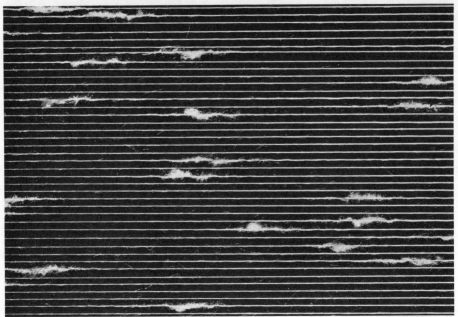

Courtesy Eastman Chemical Products, Inc.

Loftura acetate textured yarn.

knitted garments made of these yarns are washed, it is best to block them, since knitted garments of slack-twisted yarns tend to sag.

The durability of garments made of high-bulk yarns depends primarily on the durability of the synthetic fiber used and the amount of twist in the yarn. The more twist in the yarn, the greater the durability; however, the more twist, the less bulk in the yarn. Among the products made of high-bulk yarns are blouses and sweaters.

LOOP-BULK YARNS ■ These yarns are made of any of the continuous-filament fibers, such as rayon, acetate, nylon, or polyester. The textured appearance and hand of the yarns resemble that of cotton or fine wool. Yet the yarns have many of the desirable characteristics of the filament fibers used. There are variations in the technique of making textured yarns. They all involve the process of passing smooth filament yarn across high-pressure air jets that cause the individual filaments to loop up and become tangled so that a permanently textured surface of randomly situated tiny loops develops along the yarn. Different textures and effects are possible depending on the size of the loops, the closeness of the loops, the yarn size, the amount of twist in the yarn, the number of plies, and the nature of the plies. Bouclé type yarns can be produced; core and effect yarns can be made by twisting loop-bulk yarns around spun yarns.

Loop-bulk yarns are dull and have the fuzzy or rough appearance and texture of staple yarns. They have bulk without weight, which provides high-cover power of 50 to 150 percent of the untreated filament yarn as well as opacity. These yarns have little stretch, depending upon the fiber used. Garments made of loop-bulk yarns launder and dry-clean readily, dry quickly, and need little or no ironing. The air spaces caused by the loops provide for moisture adsorption and some insulation, which makes the fabrics comfortable to wear.

58　CHAPTER 4

These fabrics will not pill, as those made of some staple fibers, such as nylon or acrylic staple. Loop-bulk yarns are used for a wide variety of textile products, such as shirts, blouses, and rugs.

Among the trade names of loop-bulk yarns are the following:

Taslan, by E. I. du Pont de Nemours & Company, Inc.
Lofted Chromspun, by Eastman Chemical Products, Inc.
Loftura Estron, by Eastman Chemical Products, Inc.
Bulked Celaperm, by Celanese Corporation of America
Skyloft, by American Enka Corporation
Aerocor, by Owens Corning Fiberglas Corporation

REVIEW QUESTIONS

1 (a) What are the properties of heat-set stretch yarns? (b) Give some common trade names.

2 (a) Describe briefly each of the several techniques to produce heat-set stretch yarns. (b) Is one method better than another? Why?

3 (a) How are yarns of elastomeric fibers different from heat-set stretch yarns? (b) Name two elastomeric fibers.

4 What is meant by core-spun yarn?

5 What is bicomponent yarn?

6 How can cotton fiber be made into stretch yarn?

7 What is the difference between high-bulk yarns and loop-bulk yarns?

8 What are the main purposes of bulk yarns?

SUGGESTED ACTIVITIES

1 Obtain samples of heat-set stretch yarns and elastomeric yarns. (a) Compare them by examination for structure. (b) Compare their stretchability.

2 Obtain samples of high-bulk and loop-bulk yarns and identify their characteristics.

WEAVING

5 YARN TO FABRIC

The second stage of development of fiber into fabric is the weaving process. Although there are other methods of cloth construction, that of weaving, or interlacing, yarns is used most frequently. The interlacing, or weaving, process probably became known before spinning. Primitive man may have observed the interlaced grasses and twigs in the nests of birds, and thus discovered how he could make clothing for himself, baskets and nets, and thatchlike huts and fences. Or he may have seen rushes naturally interlacing as they grew. Spinning developed when man discovered that the raw materials could be improved before they were woven. In the course of time, rude looms were made, which were crudely simple and hand operated. The modern power loom used in the textile industry today still contains essentially the same parts and performs the same operations as the simple hand-operated loom.

PREPARATION FOR WEAVING

In the weaving operation, the lengthwise yarns that form the basic structure of the fabric are called the *warp*. The crosswise yarns are the *filling*, also referred to as the *weft* or the *woof*. The filling yarns undergo little strain in the weaving process. In preparing them for weaving, it is necessary only to spin them to the desired size and give them the amount of twist required for the type of fabric for which they will be used.

Yarns intended for the warp must pass through such operations as spooling, warping, and slashing to prepare them to withstand the strain of the weaving process. These operations do not improve the quality of the yarn. In *spooling*, the yarn is wound on larger spools, or cones, which are placed on a rack called a *creel*. From this rack, the yarns are wound on a *warp beam*, which is similar to a huge spool. An uninterrupted length of hundreds of warp yarns results, all lying parallel to one another. These yarns are unwound to be put through a starch bath called *slashing*, or *sizing*. The slasher machine covers every yarn with a starch coating to prevent chafing or breaking during the weaving process. The sized yarns are passed over large steam-heated copper cylinders that remove the moisture and set the size. They are then wound on a final warp beam and are ready for the loom.

On the conventional loom, the *warp* yarns that are to run lengthwise in the fabric are wound on a cylinder called the *warp beam,* which is at the back of the loom. The warp also extends to a cylinder called the *cloth beam,* which is at the front of the loom and on which the fabric is rolled as it is constructed. Supported on the loom frame between these two cylinders, the warp yarns are ready to be interlaced by the filling yarns that run in the width of the cloth, thus producing the woven fabric.

In any type of weaving, four operations are fundamental. They are performed in sequence and are constantly repeated. If these operations are carefully noted, the more varied and advanced constructions of fabric will be readily understood. The essential parts of the loom are: warp beam, cloth beam, harness or heddle frame, shuttle, and reed. These parts perform the following operations.

Shedding—raising warp yarns by means of the harness or heddle frame

Picking—inserting filling yarns by means of the shuttle

Battening—pushing filling yarns firmly in place by means of the reed

Taking up and letting off—winding the finished fabric on the cloth beam and releasing more of the warp from the warp beam

Right: Warp yarns pass through the eyes of the heddles (see enlargement) and are raised or lowered as one unit. Below: the warp yarns are evenly separated and held parallel as they pass between the teeth of the reed.

Courtesy Steel Heddle Mfg. Co.

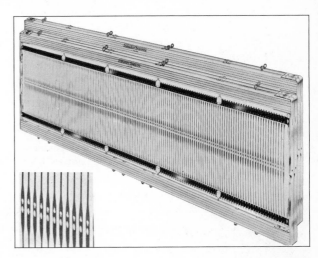

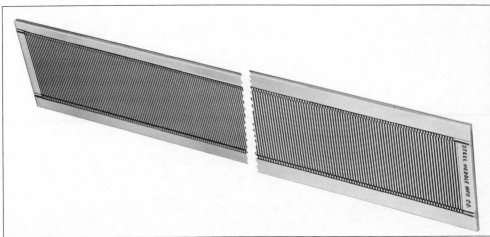

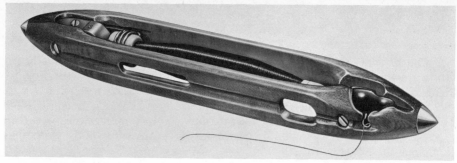

Courtesy Steel Heddle Mfg. Co.

The bobbin of filling yarn lies inside the shuttle, and the yarn is pulled through a small opening in the side as the shuttle moves swiftly across the loom.

SHEDDING ■ On a primitive loom, the weaver had to raise each alternate warp yarn with his finger or with a stick to insert the filling yarns into the warp. Weaving was therefore a very slow process. The raising of the warp yarns formed an opening, or shed, through which the filling yarn was inserted. This first weaving operation therefore became known as *shedding*.

On the modern loom, simple and intricate shedding operations are performed automatically by the heddle frame. This is a rectangular frame to which a series of wires, called heddles, are attached. As the warp yarns come from the warp beam, they must pass through openings in the heddles. Each opening may be compared to the eye of a needle. The operation of drawing each warp yarn through its appropriate heddle is known as *drawing in*.

In the simplest weave construction, the heddle frame raises or lowers certain groups of alternate warp yarns so that the filling yarns alternate in passing under one group of warp yarns and over another. The heddle frame is better known

This loom in operation shows how the harness and heddles lift and lower units of warp yarns to form the shed through which the shuttle passes. The reed automatically moves forward to batten each newly woven yarn.

Courtesy Crompton & Knowles Corporation

←HARNESS

←HEDDLES

←REED

←SHED

Courtesy Draper Corporation

This shuttleless loom has fingerlike arms that extend from the disclike compartments on its sides and feed the filling yarn through the shed. Woven cloth is wound on a roll at the bottom front of the loom.

as the *harness,* and that term is used hereafter in referring to the number of harnesses used for the different types of weaves.

PICKING ■ As the harnesses raise the heddles, which, in turn, raise the warp yarns, the filling yarn is inserted through the shed by a small carrier device called a *shuttle.* The shuttle contains a bobbin of filling yarn, which emerges through a hole in the side as the shuttle moves across the loom. A single crossing of the shuttle from one side of the loom to the other is known as a *pick.*

The shuttle itself has often created problems of splintering and catching yarns, thus causing the loom to stop. This has led to certain modifications of shuttle structure, such as molding it from a nonsplintering plastic substance. The Draper shuttleless loom employs a fingerlike arm on both sides. The arm on one side feeds the filling yarn halfway through the shed of warp yarns to the arm on the other side, which reaches in and takes it across the rest of the way. Another type of loom uses an air jet to carry the filling yarn from side to side.

BATTENING ■ All warp yarns pass through the heddle eyelets and through openings in another frame that resembles a comb and is called a *reed.* With each picking operation, the reed pushes automatically, or battens, each filling yarn against the portion of the fabric that has already been formed. This third essential weaving operation is therefore called *battening*. It gives the fabric a firm compact construction.

TAKING UP AND LETTING OFF ■ With each shedding, picking, and battening operation, the newly constructed fabric must be wound on the cloth beam. This process is known as *taking up*. At the same time, the warp yarns must be released from the warp beam; this is referred to as *letting off*.

SELVAGES

As the shuttle moves back and forth across the width of the shed, it weaves a self-edge called the *selvage* on each side of the fabric. The selvage prevents the fabric from raveling. It is usually made more compact and stronger than the rest of the fabric by using more or heavier warp yarns or by using a stronger weave. There are several kinds of selvages, depending upon economy of production and the expected use of the fabric.

PLAIN SELVAGES ■ These selvages are constructed of the simple plain weave with the same size yarn as the rest of the fabric, but with the threads packed more closely together. Such selvages are fairly durable and firm.

TAPE SELVAGES ■ The tape selvages are sometimes constructed with the plain weave but often are made of the basket weave, which makes a flatter edge. Tape selvages are made of heavier yarns or ply yarns, which provide greater strength.

SPLIT SELVAGES ■ Split selvages are made by weaving a narrow width fabric twice its ordinary width with two selvages in the center. The fabric is then cut between the selvages, and the cut edges are finished with a chain stitch or hem.

FUSED SELVAGES ■ These selvages are made on fabrics of thermoplastic fibers, such as nylon, by heating the edges of the fabric. The fibers melt and fuse together, sealing the edges. This technique is sometimes used to split wide fabrics into narrower widths or to prevent edges of jersey fabric from curling.

CONSTRUCTION OF CLOTH DESIGNS

In the textile industry, a pattern, or draft, of the weave to be used in the construction of a fabric is designed on cross-sectioned paper by the textile designer. A draft of the design is indispensable when setting up a loom for a particular weave or color effect, as it indicates the particular harness and heddle through which each warp yarn is to be drawn. The horizontal squares represent the filling yarns; the vertical squares represent the warp. The student may obtain a working knowledge of weaves by reproducing such designs on graph paper and then carrying out the actual weaving operations on a miniature loom made of stiff cardboard or a cigar box.

The durability of a fabric depends on: (1) the kind and quality of the fiber, (2) the tensile strength of the yarn, (3) the amount of twist in the yarn, (4) the use of ply yarns as compared with singles, and (5) compactness of construction. Compactness is one of the most significant factors when considering the durability of a fabric. It is determined by the closeness of the yarns after the fabric is woven. A closely woven fabric has a larger quantity of yarns than a loosely woven one and is therefore more serviceable. A garment made from such a fabric shrinks less in washing, slips less at the seams, and keeps its shape.

A fabric of compact construction has a high thread count. *Thread count,* also known as *cloth count,* is determined by counting the number of warp yarns and filling yarns in a square inch of fabric. These yarns are commonly referred to as *ends* and *picks,* terms that are synonymous with *warp* and *filling,* respectively. To ascertain the thread count, it is necessary to have a pick glass, sometimes called a thread counter, which is a magnifying glass mounted on a small stand with a square opening in its base. Through this opening, warp and filling yarns are magnified and counted. If the square opening is a ¼-inch size, the number of yarns counted in the quarter inch, when multiplied by 4, gives the number of yarns in 1 inch of the fabric. Some pick glasses have a ½-inch square opening; others have a full square inch. The largest size minimizes the possibility of error in computation.

Thread count should not be confused with yarn count. Yarn count measures the degree of fineness in yarns; thread count measures the number of warp and filling yarns in a square inch of fabric. While these counts are separate devices of measurement, there is a direct relationship between them. If coarse sheeting with a low thread count is to be constructed, thick or coarse yarns will be used. These give the fabric greater resistance to hard wear.

TYPICAL THREAD COUNTS ■ Thread counts range from as low as 20 threads to the inch, used in tobacco cloth, to as high as 350 threads to the inch, found in typewriter-ribbon fabrics. An example of thread count used as a standard is illustrated by the Summary of Types of Muslin and Percale Sheets in Chapter 11. With some finished goods, such as sheeting, thread count is sometimes given as a single number, which is the addition of warp and filling. A total thread count of 140 threads to the square inch, for example, means that each sheet must have 74 warp yarns and 66 filling yarns to the square inch. The first number indicates the warp; the second is the filling. Thus a 74 × 66 is described as a 140.

BALANCED CONSTRUCTION ■ A fabric is said to be well balanced if the number of warp yarns and filling yarns are almost equal. For example, a piece of muslin with a thread count of 64 × 60 is considered well balanced. A piece of gauze with a thread count of 28 × 24 is also well balanced. In contrast, a broadcloth with a count of 100 × 60 has poor balance. Although good balance of warp and filling produces a fabric with good wearing qualities, a balanced construction is not always obtainable with certain staple fabrics. Broadcloth shirting, for example, uses approximately twice as many warp yarns as filling yarns. The nature of its construction, therefore, makes it impossible for it to be well balanced according to thread count; yet it is a durable fabric if its thread count is high.

Sometimes, a fabric may have good balance in its thread count, but it may be altogether unsatisfactory because of weakness in either warp or filling yarns. The factor of tensile strength of both sets of yarns must, therefore, always be taken into consideration when a fabric is being judged. Both yarn count and thread count determine the suitability and value of finished goods. A safe rule to remember is that a high-count fabric even with poor balance will give better wear than a low-count fabric with good balance.

A fabric's strength can be tested by grasping the fabric with both hands and pressing down and apart with the thumbs close together and parallel. This should be tried in both directions of the cloth. If the yarns are weak, the fabric will split, indicating low durability. If the count is low, the yarns will slide or spread apart into an elliptical opening, indicating weakness under strain or tension at points of stress, such as the seams.

CLASSIFICATION OF WEAVES

The manner in which groups of warp yarns are raised by the harnesses to permit the insertion of the filling yarn determines the pattern of the weave, and in large measure the kind of fabric produced. Weave patterns can create varying degrees of durability in fabrics, adding to their usefulness and also to their appearance. In a simple weave construction, consisting of the filling going under one warp and over the next, two harnesses are needed: one to lift the odd-numbered warp yarns, and a second to lift the even-numbered warp yarns. More than two harnesses are required for advanced weaves, and as many as forty for figured weaves.

The three basic weaves in common use for the majority of fabrics are plain, twill, and satin, with respective variations. Important constructions are also obtained from the following weaves: pile, double cloth, gauze, swivel, lappet, dobby, and Jacquard.

PLAIN WEAVE ■ The plain weave is sometimes referred to as the tabby, home-spun, or taffeta weave. It is the simplest type of construction and is consequently inexpensive to produce. On the loom, the plain weave requires only two harnesses. Each filling yarn goes alternately under and over the warp yarns across the width of the fabric. On its return, the yarn alternates the pattern of interlacing. If the yarns are close together, the plain weave has a high thread count, and the fabric is therefore firm and will wear well.

As the manufacture of the plain weave is relatively inexpensive, it is used

The construction design for the plain weave resembles the familiar checkerboard. The way in which filling yarns (black squares and yarns) pass under and over alternate warp yarns (white squares and yarns) is shown at left. When fabric is closely constructed in the plain weave, there is no distinct pattern, as shown in muslin at right.

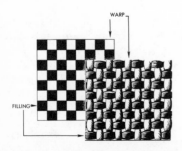

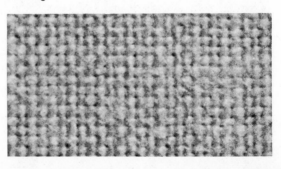

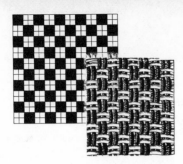

The basket weave (left) is a variation of the plain weave. Two (instead of one) filling yarns pass under and over two (instead of one) warp yarns. This weaving method results in a simple, attractive pattern, so named because baskets have long been woven in this manner. Monk's cloth (right) shows how the interweaving of two filling yarns with two warp yarns constructs a loosely woven fabric with an attractive basket weave pattern.

extensively for cotton fabrics and for fabrics that are to be decorated with printed designs, because the surface that it produces is receptive to a direct print. The appearance of the plain weave may be varied by differences in the closeness of the weave, by different thicknesses of yarn, or by the use of contrasting colors in the warp and filling. The last method gives the effect of a design. In addition, two variations of the plain weave afford simple decorative effects; namely, the basket weave and the ribbed, or corded, weave.

FABRICS IN PLAIN WEAVE. In cotton: batiste, broadcloth, bunting, calico, cambric, challis, chambray, cheesecloth, chintz, crash, crepe, crinoline, cretonne, duck or canvas, flannelette, gingham, Indianhead, lawn, longcloth, muslin, madras, nainsook, oilcloth, organdy, osnaburg, outing flannel, percale, percaline, ratiné, seersucker, scrim, sheeting, tarlatan, voile.

In linen: airplane cloth, art linen, cambric, crash, dress linen, handkerchief linen, sheeting, theatrical gauze.

In wool: albatross, blanket cloth, challis, flannel, homespun, nun's veiling, tweed.

In silk, rayon, or other filament yarns: canton crepe, chiffon, crepe de chine, flat crepe, georgette, mousseline de soie, radium, taffeta, voile.

Basket Weave. The variation of the plain weave known as the *basket weave* uses doubled yarns to produce the design that resembles the familiar pattern of a basket. Two or more filling yarns with little or no twist are interlaced with a corresponding number of warp yarns. They are woven in a pattern of 2×2, 3×3, or 4×4, instead of 1×1, which is the plain weave.

The weave used in the popular oxford shirting varies slightly from the regular basket weave in that it has a 2×1 construction; but the size of the single yarn—a coarser yarn used as the filling—is approximately equivalent in size to the two separate warp yarns. As the coarser yarn has no twist, the fabric is of soft texture and has a degree of luster.

Many variations of the yarn construction of the basket weave are possible. For example, there may be a 3×2 or a 5×3, and so on. The size or thickness of the combined warp yarns will, however, always equal the size or thickness of the corresponding filling yarns. This provides a certain degree of balance and pattern to the fabric.

The basket weave produces an attractive, loosely woven fabric that stretches easily and hangs well. It is therefore suitable for drapery and covering fabrics

The design for oxford cloth shows how a large filling yarn having no twist is woven under and over two single, twisted warp yarns.

such as monk's cloth. Due to the characteristic looseness of construction and the low tensile strength of yarns that have little or no twist, this weave is not considered desirable for clothing purposes where the factor of durability is a primary consideration.

FABRICS IN BASKET WEAVE. In cotton: monk's cloth, hardanger cloth, oxford shirting or suiting, panama cloth, Shirley cloth.

In wool, silk, rayon, or other filament yarns: shepherd's check or plaid.

Ribbed Effects. Ribbed, or corded, effects are further variations of the plain weave. The rib may be produced in the warp or in the filling by alternating fine yarns with coarse yarns, or single yarns with doubled yarns. Ribbed effects are popular, but the consumer should remember that sometimes inferior yarns are used in their manufacture, especially when the yarns that make the rib are hidden in the thickness of the cloth. As these yarns do not show on either side of the fabric, sometimes extremely short-staple yarns or yarns with insufficient twist are used. A ribbed fabric will not be durable if the ribs are too pronounced, because the coarse yarns that produce the rib tend to pull away from adjacent fine yarns. Also, in ribbed effects, an entire yarn is exposed to friction, thus lessening the durability of the fabric.

FABRICS IN RIBBED EFFECTS. Filling-ribbed fabrics include: poplin and broadcloth in cotton; bengaline, faille, taffeta; ottoman in silk, rayon, and other filament fibers. Warp-ribbed fabrics, usually referred to as *waled* or *corded,* include Bedford cord, piqué, and dimity.

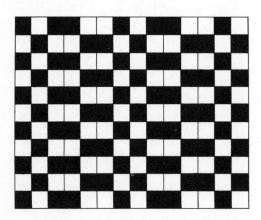

The drawing at left shows a ribbed or corded effect running in the direction of the warp. The drawing below shows the ribbed effect running in the direction of the filling.

 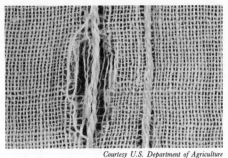

Courtesy U.S. Department of Agriculture

An example of a well-constructed ribbed fabric is shown at left. When too coarse a yarn is combined with fine yarns for a ribbed effect, the fine yarns adjacent to the rib soon break when subjected to strain or to heavy wear, as shown at right.

TWILL WEAVE ■ A distinct design in the form of diagonals is characteristic of the second basic weave, called the *twill*. Changes in the direction of the diagonal lines produce variations, such as the herringbone, corkscrew, entwining, and fancy twills. Increased ornamentation may be obtained by varying the diagonal and yarn colors. The values of the twill weave include its strength and drapability. The diagonally arranged interlacings of the warp and filling provide greater pliability and resilience than the plain weave. Also, twill fabrics are frequently more tightly woven and will not get dirty as quickly as the plain weave, though twills are more difficult to clean when they do get soiled. The yarns are usually closely battened, making an especially durable fabric. Twill weaves are therefore commonly used in men's suit and coat fabrics and for work clothes, where strong construction is essential.

In the twill weave, the filling yarn interlaces more than one warp yarn but never more than four, as strength would be sacrificed by so doing. On each successive line, or pick, the filling yarn moves the design one step to the right or to the left, thus forming the diagonal. Whichever the direction of the diagonal on the face of the fabric, the design runs in the opposite direction on the reverse side.

When the direction of the diagonal starts from the upper left-hand side of the fabric and moves down toward the lower right, it is called a *left-hand* twill. When the direction of the diagonal starts from the upper right-hand side of the

The common herringbone twill.

The characteristic diagonal of the twill weave.

Courtesy National Association of Wool Manufacturers

fabric and moves down toward the lower left, it is called a *right-hand* twill. Although there is no advantage of one over the other, the direction of the diagonal can aid in the recognition of the face of the fabric.

The *steepness* of the diagonal can indicate strength and durability in the fabric. In order to obtain a steep twill, more warp yarns must be used than filling yarns. And since warp yarns have a higher twist and are stronger than filling yarns, the steeper the twist the stronger the fabric is likely to be.

Twill weaves are named according to the number of harnesses required to make the design. A three- or four-harness twill is frequently used. The word "shaft" may be substituted for "harness," as in *three-shaft* or *four-shaft twill.*

Twill weaves are also classified as *even* or *uneven* according to the number of warp and filling yarns that are visible on the face of the fabric. The even twill, for example, shows an equal number of warp and filling yarns in the recurring design, such as two over and two under. This pattern makes what is called a four-shaft twill, and it requires four harnesses.

Most twill weaves are uneven. An uneven twill may show more warp than filling yarns in the recurring design; this is called a *warp-face twill.* If more filling yarns than warp yarns show on the face, the weave is called a *filling-face twill.* Warp-face twills are generally stronger than filling-face twills because the stronger warp yarns on the face of the fabric can take more abrasion and wear. Warp-face twills generally have much more warp than filling yarns; consequently, such fabrics hold their shape better and drape better due to the warp's greater twist and resilience.

Twills are described in terms of the interlacing of the warp yarns over and under the filling yarns. An uneven four-shaft twill, for example, that has three warp yarns riding over one filling yarn is referred to as a three up and one down, or $\frac{3}{1}$. On the other hand, a three-shaft twill that has one warp yarn riding over two filling yarns is referred to as a one up and two down, or $\frac{1}{2}$.

FABRICS IN TWILL WEAVE. Wool fabrics are usually right-hand twills, such as broadcloth, cashmere, cheviot, covert, flannel, gabardine, mackinaw, melton, pilot cloth, serge, tweed, whipcord, and worsted cheviot.

Silk fabrics are also right-hand twills. They include foulard, merveilleux, silk serge, and surah.

Cotton fabrics are usually left-hand twills. They include canton flannel, covert cloth, coutil, denim, drill, gabardine, hickory shirting or hickory stripe, jean, khaki, middle twill, outing flannel, silesia, ticking, venetian cloth, and whipcord.

The twill weave is not used much in the production of linen, as linen yarns make a naturally strong fabric. However, it may be found in linen ticking, twill toweling, and towel drills.

This drawing shows a three-shaft twill—two warp yarns are interlaced with one filling yarn in each repeat. This is a right-hand, filling-faced twill because the diagonal moves from the upper right down to the lower left, and more filling than warp appears on the face of the fabric. It is also referred to as a one up and two down twill ($\frac{1}{2}$) because the warp goes over one and under two filling yarns.

LEFT-HAND TWILLS   **RIGHT-HAND TWILLS**

Even $(\frac{2}{2})$ Even $(\frac{2}{2})$

Uneven, Filling-Faced $(\frac{1}{2})$ Uneven, Filling-Faced $(\frac{1}{2})$

Uneven, Warp-Faced $(\frac{3}{T})$ Uneven, Warp-Faced $(\frac{2}{T})$

The basic diagonal of the twill weave is shown in all of these drawings. The direction of the diagonal and the number of harnesses used produce different surface designs.

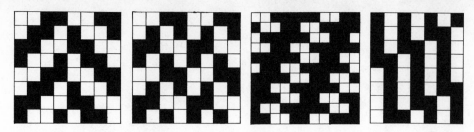

These variations of the twill weave show broken twills (herringbone) in the first two drawings; a gabardine in the third; and a corkscrew twill in the fourth.

SATIN WEAVE ■ In basic construction, the satin weave is similar to the twill weave but generally uses from five to as many as twelve harnesses, producing a five- to twelve-shaft construction. It differs in appearance from the twill weave because the diagonal of the satin weave is not visible; it is purposely interrupted in order to contribute to the flat, smooth, lustrous surface desired. There is no visible design on the face of the fabric because the yarns that are to be thrown to the surface are greater in number and finer in count than the yarns that form the reverse of the fabric. The satin weave may have a warp- or filling-face construction.

Warp-Face Satin Weave. Warp-face satin is woven so that the warp may be seen on the surface of the fabric. For example, in a five-shaft construction, the warp may pass over four filling yarns and under one; in a twelve-shaft construction, the warp may pass over eleven filling yarns and under one. Since the warp lies on the surface and interlaces only one filling at a time, the lengths of warp between the filling are called *floats*. These floats lie compactly on the surface with very little interruption from the yarns going at right angles to them. Reflection of light on the floats gives satin fabric its primary characteristic of luster, which appears in the direction of the warp.

The long floats found in the satin weave might be considered a disadvantage because they represent a minimum of interlacings, and therefore a potential weakness in the fabric. Furthermore, to increase the smoothness and luster of the fabric, the yarns are given a minimum of twist and are therefore relatively weak. The longer the float, the greater the chance that the surface of the fabric will snag, roughen, and show signs of wear. However, the luster makes the fabric suitable for dressy wear and the smoothness, for use as lining.

Satin-weave fabrics drape well because the weave is heavier than the twill weave, which, in turn, is heavier than the plain weave. More harnesses are used for satin weave, thus compressing a greater amount of fine yarn into a given space of cloth. This compactness gives the fabric more body as well as less porosity, which makes the fabric warmer. The quality of drapability also makes satin fabrics preferable for evening wear, and the warmth contributes to its value as lining material.

DESIGNING A SATIN CONSTRUCTION. When making a design for a satin construction, the interlacings on successive lines must be separated by a proper interval to avoid forming the contiguous diagonal. When the proper interval for any shaft construction is selected, the design will not repeat itself until the number of successive picks that make up the desired shaft have been interlaced. In a five-shaft construction, for example, the design begins to repeat on the sixth line; in an eight-shaft, on the ninth line; in a twelve-shaft, on the thirteenth line.

WARP-FACE SATIN WEAVE

Point Design*

Yarn Layout

Five-Shaft Construction

Warp floats are seen interlacing every fifth filling.

Eight-Shaft Construction

Warp floats are seen interlacing every eighth filling.

Twelve-Shaft Construction

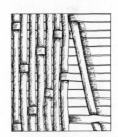

* White squares indicate where warp yarns pass under filling yarns.

Warp floats are seen interlacing every twelfth filling.

FABRICS IN WARP-FACE SATIN WEAVE. In silk or rayon: damask, double-faced satin, duchesse, merveilleux, satin-faced crepe, slipper satin.

In cotton: damask, sateen, ticking, venetian cloth.

In linen: single and double damask.

Point Design*

Yarn Layout

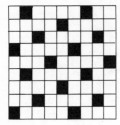

Five-Shaft Construction

Filling floats are seen interlacing every fifth warp.

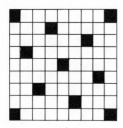

Eight-Shaft Construction

Filling floats are seen interlacing every eighth warp.

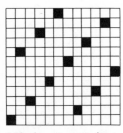

Twelve-Shaft Construction

* Black squares indicate where filling yarns pass under warp yarns.

Filling floats are seen interlacing every twelfth warp.

Filling-Face Satin Weave. The filling-face satin weave is also called the *sateen* weave; however, this sometimes causes confusion because some cotton and rayon fabrics are also identified as sateen. In this construction, the filling yarn lies on the surface of the fabric as it passes regularly over and under the warp yarns. For instance, a filling yarn may pass over four warp yarns and under one. The floats are consequently made up of the filling yarns, and the luster appears in the filling direction.

The diagram at left (labeled with letters T, R, U, S, V, M, P, N, Q, O, K, I, L, J, F, G, H, D, E, A, B, C and interval markers 1 2 3 4 5) shows an eight-shaft filling-face satin construction.

The diagram at left shows an eight-shaft filling-face satin construction. Each horizontal line of blocks represents a filling yarn or pick. The blocks covered by letters are the points at which the filling yarns interlace the warp yarns on each successive pick. In the eight-shaft warp-face satin construction, the filling is carried across the back, creating the float in the warp. The basic idea of warp-faced satin can be seen when this diagram is turned sideways. Satin cloth is shown at right.

DESIGNING A FILLING-FACE SATIN CONSTRUCTION. An eight-shaft construction illustrates here the rules that must be followed to select a suitable interval.

1. Arrange in pairs the numbers that will add up to the desired shaft number. For an eight-shaft filling-face satin, the shaft number is 8. The pairs are: 1 and 7, 2 and 6, 3 and 5, 4 and 4.

2. Eliminate the pair that contains the number 1 and the number below the shaft number, which is 7 in this case. A contiguous diagonal would result if these intervals were used, producing the conventional twill weave.

3. Next, eliminate the pairs that have a common divisor and those that are divisible into the shaft number. This step eliminates 2 and 6, 4 and 4. The pair 3 and 5 remains. These numbers are the only intervals that can be used in an eight-shaft construction. If any of the eliminated numbers were used as an interval, the fabric would show no interlacing whatever for one or more warp yarns; in fact, there would be no fabric because it would fall apart.

Now that the only possible interlacings have been worked out, the design can be constructed. (See the accompanying drawing.) For convenience, here the interlacing begins in the lower left square, at A. The horizontal rows of squares represent filling yarns—that is, the successive picks on the loom. The vertical rows represent the warp yarns.

The interval to be used for this particular design could be 3 or 5; in this case, 5 has been selected. As this is to be an eight-shaft construction, the interlacing on the first pick will be 7 squares (warp yarns) apart at B and C.

To find the warp yarn that will interlace on the second pick, count 5 to the right, beginning with the square above the interlacing that is already started at A; thus, the interlacing occurs at D. Adjacent interlacing on the same line will be 7 squares apart, at E.

To find the warp yarn that will interlace on the third pick, start with the square above D. Count 5 to the right, and interlacing G is plotted. Adjacent interlacings will be 7 squares apart.

On the fourth pick, interlacing I is found by counting 5 to the right of the square above F; J is found by counting 5 to the right of the square above G (or 7 squares from I).

This same procedure determines the interlacing points on successive picks, additional interlacings always being 7 squares apart.

On the ninth pick, the design starts to repeat, which proves the accuracy of the construction of an eight-shaft weave.

Where it is not possible to plot subsequent interlacing by continuing to count to the right, because of the small area of the design, interlacings on successive picks can be determined by counting 3 to the left instead of 5 to the right. If the interval 3 had been used to count to the right, 5 would have been used to count to the left.

FABRICS IN FILLING-FACE SATIN WEAVE. In cotton: damask, sateen, ticking. In linen: single and double damask.

PILE WEAVE ■ The pile weave is a fancy weave that also includes a plain or a twill construction. In contrast to the three basic weaves that produce a flat surface on a fabric, the pile weave introduces a decorative third dimension, creating an effect of depth. Its construction is especially desirable when softness, warmth, and absorbency are desired. Pile-weave fabrics are also durable if the proper yarns and adequate compact construction are used. In the manufacture of rugs, for example, a strong, tightly twisted staple with compact construction in the base cloth will withstand long wear.

The pile is produced by weaving an additional warp yarn or filling yarn into the basic structure. The additional yarn is drawn away from the surface of the fabric by thick wires, which form loops at regular intervals. These loops may be cut or closely sheared, or left uncut if a loop surface is desired.

When the pile is produced by an extra warp yarn, the result is a warp-pile fabric, of which terry, carpet, and plush are examples. Fabrics are classified as plush when the pile is more than ⅛-inch high. When the pile is produced by an extra filling yarn, the result is a filling-pile fabric, of which velveteen and corduroy are examples.

In certain cut-pile fabrics, the wires used to form the loops are equipped with razorlike ends, so that the loops are cut when the wires are withdrawn, thus producing the cut pile exemplified by velvet carpet. Cut pile fabrics are produced economically by constructing double-cloth fabrics, as explained in the following section, then cutting the two cloths apart.

Pile effects can also be created by using varying tension in the warp yarns. In the manufacture of rugs, such as chenille, Wilton, velvet, and tapestry, various processes are used for pile effects, including hand knotting.

Cut-pile fabrics have certain limitations. They catch lint and spot easily. The grain or direction of the pile can be disturbed, causing the appearance of

The drawing at left shows the pile weave as it looks after the wires that have raised the filling yarns have been withdrawn. Cut pile, shown in the drawing at right, can be produced by using wires equipped with razorlike ends that cut the loops as the wires are withdrawn.

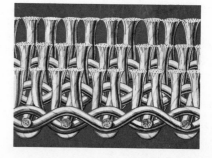

dark areas. In garment construction, the direction of the grain must be properly matched, otherwise there will be an impression of mismatched colors. Some cut-pile fabrics may be laundered, depending upon the fiber used, but they must be thoroughly rinsed so that they will not be stiffened by soaps or detergents. If they need be ironed, they should be pressed with a steam iron. To avoid crushing, ironing should be done on the wrong side. Uncut-pile fabrics may wear better but are not as soft or warm.

FABRICS IN PILE WEAVE. In cotton: chenille, corduroy, duvetyn, frieze, plush, terry (turkish toweling), velour, velveteen.

In wool: frieze, plush, velour, rugs of all kinds.

In silk, rayon, and other filament yarns: chenille, frieze, fur fabrics, plush, transparent velvet, velour, velvets of all kinds.

Linen is seldom made in the pile weave.

DOUBLE-CLOTH WEAVE ■ In the double-cloth weave, two fabrics are woven on the loom at the same time, one on top of the other. The fabric may have a plain weave on one side and a twill weave on the other. Each of the fabrics requires its separate sets of warp and filling yarns. They are combined by interlacing some of the warp or filling yarns or by means of a complete fifth set of stitching yarns. The surfaces of such fabrics may show different patterns or color on each side by varying the yarns as to color and size. A true double-cloth weave is never a pasted construction.

Because the double-cloth weave produces two pieces of fabric combined into one, fabrics so woven are commonly regarded as strong and warm. Warmth, however, is due primarily to the insulative properties inherent in a fiber; bulk and thickness alone do not give warmth. Also, strength cannot be judged by mere thickness or weight. It cannot be assumed that a double-cloth weave will have the qualities of warmth and strength; on the contrary, the fabric may be heavy, bulky, and needlessly expensive. Sometimes, this method of construction is chosen to use a cheaper material on the reverse side of the fabric, thus reducing the cost of a heavy fabric.

FABRICS IN DOUBLE-CLOTH WEAVE. In cotton: double-faced blankets, bathrobe blankets.
In wool: polo cloth, steamer rugs, overcoatings.
In silk and other filament yarns: upholstery fabrics of all kinds.

GAUZE WEAVE ■ The gauze weave must not be confused with the weave used in manufacturing gauze bandages or cheesecloth; these materials are made with the plain weave. The true gauze-weave construction produces a fabric very light in weight and with an open-mesh effect. Curtain materials and some cotton dress goods are woven with this weave. Such lightweight fabrics have a strength that could not be provided by the plain weave. In the gauze weave, strength is gained by the manner in which the yarns are intertwisted: each filling yarn is encircled by two warp yarns twisted about each other.

The double-cloth weave can be produced by either of two methods shown at right: the V method in the upper drawing or the W method in the lower. Cutting the yarn that holds the two cloths together makes two separate cut-pile fabrics.

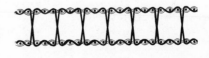

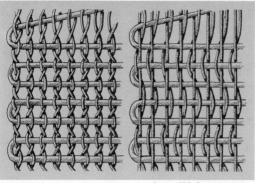

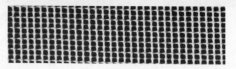

The drawing shows the gauze weave (left) and the leno weave (right). Note how the filling yarns in the gauze weave are encircled by two warp yarns twisting around each other, a construction that gives strength although the mesh is open. In the leno weave, the second of each of two warp yarns merely passes around the first yarn. Shown above is marquisette, which is constructed with a leno weave.

Courtesy U.S. Dept. of Agriculture

The gauze weave is sometimes referred to as the *leno weave* because it is made on a leno loom, but the true leno weave is a variation of the gauze weave.

On the leno loom, the action of one warp yarn is similar to the action of the warp in the plain weave. The *doup attachment,* a hairpin-like device at the heddle, alternately pulls the second warp yarn up or down to the right or left with each passage of the shuttle. This causes the pair of warps to be twisted, in effect, around each filling yarn. The leno is sometimes used in combination with the plain weave to produce a stripe or figure on a plain background. Generally, the term "leno" is used synonymously with "gauze."

FABRICS IN GAUZE WEAVE. In cotton: grenadine, marquisette, mosquito netting, rice net, mesh shirtings.

In silk, rayon, and other filament yarns: bolting cloth, curtain madras, grenadine, marquisette.

SWIVEL WEAVE ■ The swivel weave is the method by which decorative effects, such as dots, circles, or other figures, are interwoven on the surface of a fabric while it is being constructed on the loom. The weaving of the design requires an extra filling yarn and additional small shuttles. A separate shed is made for these shuttles. While the fabric is being constructed, the row of small shuttles drops across the width of the loom, and each shuttle interweaves its separate design with a circular motion on a small area of the warp. A long thread is carried on the undersurface of the fabric from one design to the next. Different colors may be used in each of the designs because each figure is woven by its own shuttle containing its own miniature bobbin.

The decoration produced by the swivel weave is not considered durable, because the swivel yarns are cut when the fabric is completed and cannot be securely fastened. The cut ends roughen the undersurface of the fabric and may pull out if it is handled carelessly in laundering.

FABRICS IN SWIVEL WEAVE: dotted swiss, grenadine, curtain madras.

Dotted swiss has a swivel weave construction into which an additional warp thread is interwoven and subsequently clipped on the reverse side of the fabric (left), producing intermittent dots on the face (right).

LAPPET WEAVE ■ The lappet weave is also used to superimpose a small design on the surface of a fabric while it is being woven. In the lappet weave, the design is stitched into the fabric by needles that operate at right angles to the construction. Thus, the lappet weave is very similar to embroidery.

The lappet design is made with one continuous additional warp yarn carried on the back of the fabric from one design to the next. Only one color is possible. The floating threads on the back are cut away when the fabric is completed, but the ends are fastened securely and will not pull out easily.

FABRIC IN THE LAPPET WEAVE. Dotted swiss produced by the lappet weave is superior to swivel-weave dotted swiss.

DOBBY WEAVE ■ The dobby weave is a patterned weave used to construct designs that cannot be produced by the plain, twill, or satin weaves. The designs are simple, limited in size, and usually geometric in form. They are found in shirtings and tie fabrics. The dobby weave is created on a plain loom by means of a mechanical attachment, called a *dobby* or *cam*, which raises or lowers as many as twenty-four to forty harnesses containing the series of warp yarns that form the pattern. Although a large number of harnesses is used in this construction, the design is always small and does not make use of long floats. The most familiar type of dobby weave is bird's-eye, the small diamond pattern that has an eye in its center.

FABRICS IN DOBBY WEAVE. In cotton: bird's-eye, huckaback.

In linen: cretonne, huckaback, mummy cloth.

In wool: granite cloth.

A twenty-harness dobby loom with a swivel for weaving fabric with small designs.

Courtesy Draper Corporation

JACQUARD WEAVE ■ In any of the weaves that have been described, the number of harnesses determines the construction. For example, two harnesses are required for the plain weave, three or more for the twill, and five to twelve for the satin weave. As many as forty can be manipulated by the special attachment of the dobby. The dobby designs are not intricate, however. They are limited to straight lines, edges, steps, or small circular lines.

For curves, swirls, and large-sized figures, it was necessary to devise a different mechanism that would allow an unlimited range of intricate designs. This need is met by the Jacquard attachment, named after its inventor, Joseph Marie Jacquard, a Frenchman. The Jacquard mechanism controls thousands of heddles, which lift one or more warp yarns independently of others without the use of harnesses. Its action is similar to that of the player piano, where each note is governed by a hole on the music roll and is sounded when the hole passes over a certain opening.

The card puncher has a paper design before him. Following a line of checks across the design paper, he inserts steel punches in the cardboards specified on the paper design. Each hole in the card controls the loom mechanism that raises the desired warp yarns in the fabric surface, thus producing the weaving design.

Courtesy Textile World

The Jacquard design is first worked out on squared paper. Cards are then perforated to correspond with the design; they are laced together and placed on the Jacquard attachment. The moving cards pass over a battery of needles mounted on top of the loom. Each needle controls a string, which, when released, picks up the heddle to which it is tied. The perforations on the cards allow the needles to drop through, and lift certain strings, which, in turn, lift single heddles independently of others. The preparation of a Jacquard weave is the most expensive part of its construction. Setting up the loom may take several weeks or months; but once set, the pattern to be produced can be used and reused for different materials. This is the most expensive form of weaving, and it is chiefly used for linen and for upholstery materials.

This Jacquard head loom in operation shows the laced cards at the top of the loom (see insert). The long slanting strings control the heddles immediately below the cards. The heddles raise and lower the warp yarns in accordance with the pattern punched on the cards above; the filling yarn makes the design as the shuttle passes across the loom.

Courtesy Crompton & Knowles Corporation

Courtesy American Viscose Corp.

Damask produced by the Jacquard.

Courtesy American Viscose Corp.

Brocade produced by the Jacquard.

Floats are inevitable in the Jacquard weave because of the elaborate designs. As in the satin weave, long floats may affect the wearing quality of the fabric; also, long cotton yarns exposed to friction cause lint. Compact construction of the fabric, however, offsets the tendency to friction and wear. The consumer should select the better-quality fabrics when purchasing those having the Jacquard weave, especially when purchasing linen damask because table linens receive hard wear and repeated washings.

FABRICS IN JACQUARD WEAVE. In cotton: damask, matelassé, tapestry.

In linen: single and double damask.

In wool: tapestry.

In silk, rayon, and other filament yarns: brocade, brocatelle, damask, and tapestry.

BASIC WEAVES

WEAVE	CHARACTERISTICS	ADVANTAGES	LIMITATIONS
PLAIN	No distinct design unless yarns have contrasting colors	Maximum yardage; easily produced; inexpensive; strong; adaptable for direct printing and other finishing processes	Sleazy fabric if thread count is low
Basket	Basket pattern	Attractive; inexpensive; drapable; absorbent	Not durable for apparel; soils easily
Ribbed	Corded effects	Ornamental	Not serviceable if of inferior construction
TWILL	Distinct diagonal design	Strong, firm texture; increased drapability; interesting designs	Requires care to keep clean; develops shine
SATIN	Luster; interrupted diagonal design discernible with magnifying glass	Beauty contributed by luster; smooth; maximum drapability	Excessively long floats may snag and roughen fabric

Persons who handle fabrics must be able to identify the warp and the filling yarns, because the direction of the warp determines the way in which the fabric should be cut when a garment is made from it. In a new piece of yard goods, the direction of the warp is easily distinguished. The length of the fabric indicates the warp yarns. Also, if a piece of the fabric shows part of the selvage, which is the firm edge of the cloth, then the yarns parallel to the selvage are warp yarns. The opposite yarns are the filling yarns. When a sample of fabric contains no selvage, the warp and filling may be identified by observation of the weave.

1. In plain weaves, a greater number of yarns running in one direction indicates the warp.

2. In twill weaves, the filling yarns run in the direction of the diagonal, which may be toward the right or toward the left.

3. In satin weaves, the floating yarns are more likely to be the warp yarns. When one runs a finger over the fabric in both directions, the finger will slide more easily in the direction of the floats. Usually the floats will be in the warp, unless the fabric is cotton. Cotton is more likely to have the floats in the filling.

When the name of the fabric is known, its characteristic features aid in distinguishing the warp and filling. For example, the ribs of dimity and of piqué run in the direction of the warp; the ribs of rep, faille, bengaline, and poplin in the direction of the filling. When colored stripes show in such fabrics as chambray, madras shirtings, and in some dress goods, the direction in which the stripe runs usually indicates the warp.

When the warp and the filling cannot be identified by the foregoing aids, the sets of yarns may be examined for the following characteristics.

1. Exerting tension on a sample by holding it in both hands and pulling, at the same time pressing with the thumbs and forefingers, will show which set of yarns is stronger. The stronger set will be the warp, because warp yarns have to withstand the tension of the heddles in the weaving process. The filling yarn, which emerges from the bobbin of the shuttle as it crosses the fabric, is under little tension.

2. When one set contains yarns of varying sizes, this set is usually the warp. Filling yarns are usually of the same size.

3. The set of yarns that can be more easily stretched is the filling.

4. Yarns of inferior quality are commonly used as filling in inexpensive fabrics. When both sets of yarns are carefully compared, the inferior yarn is usually the filling.

5. When a yarn has a hard twist, as in serges and overcoatings, it is generally the warp yarn.

6. Yarns with slack twist usually are the filling yarns. Yarns with little twist are used as filling when a soft, lustrous effect is desired.

7. If one set consists of thicker yarns, this indicates the filling, as the bulk produced by heavier yarns dispenses with the need for a great amount of twist.

8. If ply yarns are used, they probably indicate the warp.

9. In a napped fabric, the warp runs in the direction of the napping, because the fabric has been run through the machine in the direction of its length.

10. In light cotton or silk fabrics, a marked evenness between the yarns indicates the warp. This evenness is the result of the mechanical movement of the reed as it battens the filling yarns when the cloth is being constructed. In patterned weaves, such as a herringbone twill, the impact of the battening operation leaves small reed marks that distinguish filling from warp yarns.

IDENTIFYING THE RIGHT SIDE OF A FABRIC

For cutting and sewing purposes, it is necessary to identify the face of a fabric. When the cloth is on a bolt, identification is easy because the fabric is wound or folded with the right side inside to keep it clean. Off the bolt, other characteristics may be observed. If one side of the fabric is shinier than the other, the more lustrous side is the face. If a printed fabric has a more distinct design on one side, that is the right side. When the fabric has a nap, the face is, as a rule, the fuzzier side. When slub yarns are used, they tend to be more outstanding on the right side. Recognition of the weave characteristics also helps.

TWILL WEAVE ■ Since twills often have a diagonal with a distinct wale or ridge on the face, the right side may be identified in this manner. Even when there is no wale, the diagonal of the twill is likely to be more discernible on the face of the fabric. The cloth should be held so that the warp yarns (identified by methods described on page 83) run up and down.

SATIN WEAVE ■ If the fabric is very smooth and lustrous, the fabric should be examined closely for floats, which would be on the face. By partially separating out a thread along the edge of the material, one could observe whether the yarn forms the characteristic floats of the satin weave. A magnifying glass will help.

PILE WEAVE ■ The prime purpose of the pile weave is to provide textural interest. Therefore, the pile will be on the face of the fabric.

FANCY WEAVES ■ The smoother sides of swivel and clip-spot weaves are the right sides. The back of the cloth will show the ends of the clipped yarns used for the design. The lappet weave usually has a trail thread passing on the back of the fabric from one design to the next in the row. The dobby design, including piqués, are clearer and more outstanding on the face. In Jacquard patterns, the figure also stands out (sometimes figuratively) from the background.

REVIEW QUESTIONS

1 Explain why lappet ornamentation is permanent and swivel is not.

2 Why are harnesses not required in the Jacquard weave?

3 Describe the basic operations of the weaving process, naming specific parts of the loom.

4 Compare the pile weave and its uses with the double-cloth weave and its uses.

5 Differentiate between plain weave, ribbed weave, basket weave, and twill.

6 Compare the advantages and disadvantages of the twill and satin weaves.

7 Which of the three basic weaves is (a) the most durable, (b) the most beautiful, (c) the most inexpensive to produce? Give reasons for the answers.

8 What weave would you prefer in a shirt, suit, curtains? Why?

9 Why was the Jacquard weave revolutionary in the weaving industry?

10 Contrary to common belief, why does the gauze weave embody strength?

11 Differentiate between damask and a fabric made by the dobby weave.

12 How can one identify the face of a fabric?

13 How can the warp be differentiated from the filling in a fabric?

14 (a) What is a swivel design? (b) On what kinds of garments would it be used?

15 (a) What is the selvage? (b) What are the different types? (c) Which is best and why?

16 Is it of any advantage to the consumer to know the basic differences between the three foundation weaves? Why?

SUGGESTED ACTIVITIES

1 Construct designs for variations of the plain and the twill weaves.

2 Construct a design for producing a ribbed effect in the warp.

3 Obtain samples of fabrics woven in each of the basic weaves described. Mount each fabric on a card and identify the weave.

4 Wind a piece of yarn or string around a square piece of cardboard, about 4 by 4 inches, so that on each side of the cardboard there are parallel yarns in close rows. These are similar to the warp yarns on a loom. Thread another piece of yarn of a contrasting color in a large needle. Insert it through the parallel rows to produce the weave pattern of the three foundation weaves.

KNITTING

6 YARN TO FABRIC OR GARMENT

Second in importance in fabric construction is knitting. Its popularity has grown tremendously within recent years because of the increased versatility of techniques, the adaptability of the many new man-made fibers, and the growth in consumer demand for stretchable, snug-fitting fabrics, particularly in the greatly expanding areas of sportswear and other casual wearing apparel. Today, the usage of knitted fabrics ranges from hosiery, underwear, sweaters, slacks, suits, and coats, to rugs and other home furnishings.

Hand knitting was an early invention of man. The earliest known knitted fabric was a pair of thick, hand-knitted wool socks found in an Egyptian tomb, which probably dated back to the 4th century B.C. But the art seems to have been perfected in western Europe in the fifteenth century. The word "cnyttan" was first mentioned in English literature in 1492. Hand knitting spread rapidly throughout Europe within a few generations. Primitive needles of bone or wood were first used, producing a coarse mesh. The Spaniards began to use steel needles, which produced a closer mesh and a more evenly knit fabric. In 1589, the Reverend William Lee, an Englishman, invented the first knitting machine, which knit 8 loops to 1 inch of width. As this construction was too coarse a mesh, he improved the machine so that it was possible to knit 20 loops to 1 inch. Today, the average is 28 loops; and the modern knitting machine still operates on the same general principles established by William Lee.

KNITTED CONSTRUCTION

Knitted fabrics may be constructed with a single yarn that is formed into interlocking loops by the use of hooked needles. The loops may be either loosely or closely constructed according to the purpose of the fabric. Crocheting is knitting in its simplest form. A chain of loops is produced from a single thread by means of a hook. The interlocking loops of the knitted construction permit the fabric to stretch in any direction, even if low-grade yarn having little elasticity or yarn that lacks natural elasticity is used.

Woven fabrics are constructed by the interlacing of two or more yarns, which does not allow the fabric to stretch to any marked degree. If a certain amount of stretching is necessary, woven fabric must be cut on the bias; that is, in a diagonal direction. Even then the fabric can be stretched only in the direction of the diagonal cutting. The advantage of stretchability in knitted fabrics is an important consideration where fit and comfort are concerned—they fit the figure but do not bind it. Knitted fabrics also give warmth because of the insulative air pockets contained in this type of construction. Yet they are porous and provide "breathing" comfort as body movements cause the loops to expand and contract, thereby pushing air through close-fitting garments. Knitted fabrics are very absorbent, light in weight, and wrinkle resistant. It is usually unnecessary to iron them after laundering.

Certain kinds of knitted fabric have one serious disadvantage: if one of the loops breaks, a hole is made, which starts a run. This disadvantage can be eliminated by variation in the stitch, which protects the fabric from raveling if any single stitch is broken. Some knitted fabrics tend to lose their shape and sag. This tendency can be avoided by using a more closely constructed knit, giving the yarn a tighter twist, and using such special techniques as the double knit. Knitted fabrics may shrink considerably unless special techniques and shrink-proofing processes, such as Pak-nit or Perma-sized, are used. Also, unless the fabric is heavily napped or foam laminated, it is not windproof.

EVALUATING CONSTRUCTION OF KNITTED FABRIC ■ It will be recalled that thread count (the number of threads per square inch) is used to evaluate the construction of woven fabrics. The construction of knitted fabrics is evaluated by the number of stitches or loops that can be counted in any square inch. When the interlocking loops run lengthwise, each row is called a *wale*. A wale corresponds to the direction of the warp in woven fabrics. When the loops run across the fabric, each row is called a *course*. A course corresponds to the filling or weft. Thus, a knitted fabric having 40 loops or stitches in 1 inch of width, and 50 loops in 1 inch of length, is said to have 40 wales and 50 courses.

The construction of the knitted fabrics varies with the type, and each type has its own particular appearance and properties.

Some constructions, such as jersey and rib knitting, are made with a latch needle, which has a latch or swinging finger that closes onto the hook of the needle as it pulls the yarn through a loop to form a new loop. Other knits, such as the tricot, milanese, and simplex, are made with a spring-beard needle that has a fine springy hook, which slightly resembles a beard. This type of hook must be used with a sinker and a presser to close it as it forms the loop. However, because of its fineness, the spring-beard needle can be used in the knitting machine in much closer formation to produce more finely constructed fabrics with smaller loops.

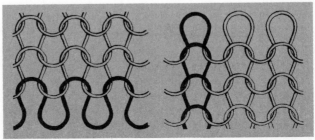

At left, a course in a plain circular-knit fabric; at right, a wale.

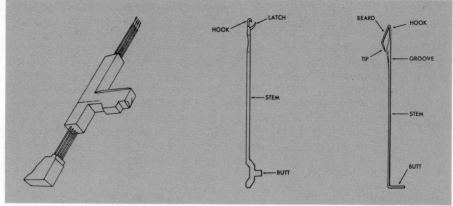

Courtesy CIBA Review

At left, a working arrangement of a group of needles in its lead. At center, a latch needle. At right, a spring-beard needle.

The quality of the needle will affect the quality of the knitted fabric. If the thickness of the hook varies from one needle to the next, the stitches will vary in width. Also, if the needles vary in length, so will the loops. Obviously, these variations will affect the appearance, texture, and performance of the knitted fabric.

CLASSIFICATION OF KNITTED FABRICS

Knitted fabrics are divided into two general types: (1) those produced by weft knitting, where one continuous yarn forms courses across the fabric; (2) those produced by warp knitting, where a series of yarns forms wales in the lengthwise direction of the fabric.

WEFT KNITTING ■ There are three fundamental stitches in weft knitting: (1) plain knit stitch, (2) purl stitch, (3) rib stitch. Novelty stitches are variations of these three. The hand method of knitting is weft knitting. On a machine, the individual yarn is fed to one or more needles at a time.

Plain-Knit Stitch. The *plain knit* is the basic form of knitting. It can be produced in *flat knit* or in *tubular* (or *circular*) form. The flat knit is also called *jersey stitch* because the construction is like that of the turtleneck sweaters originally worn by English sailors from the Isle of Jersey; it is sometimes called *balbriggan stitch* after the hosiery and underwear fabrics made in Balbriggan, Ireland.

The knitting is done with a row of latch or beard needles arranged in a linear position on a needle plate or in a circular position on a cylinder. All of the needles are evenly spaced side by side and are moved by cams, which act on the needle butts. The spacing of the needles is referred to as the *gauge, gage,* or *cut.* As applied to many flat knits and some circular ones, gauge refers to the number of needles in 1½ inches; for example, a 60-gauge machine would have 40 needles per inch. As applied to circular and flat machines that have needles adjustably or slidably mounted, *cut* refers to the number of needles per inch.

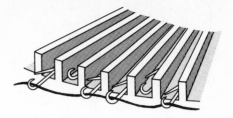

At left, a section of a circular needle plate showing the arrangement of latch needles. At right, a section of a cylinder showing the arrangement of latch needles.

The plain knit is made by needles intermeshing loops drawn to one side of the fabric. These loops form distinctive vertical herringbonelike ribs or wales on the right (or face) side of the fabric. On the reverse (or back) side, the courses can be readily seen as interlocking rows of opposed half circles. This construction gives the face of the fabric a sheen, while the back is dull.

The flat knit produces a relatively lightweight fabric compared to the thicker fabrics produced by other stitches. It has a high rate of production (up to five times faster than weaving), is inexpensive, and lends itself readily to variation in design by pattern devices. Single or double yarns may be employed.

As the fabric will stretch more in the width than in the length, the plain-knit stitch is widely used for underwear, gloves, hosiery, and sweaters. Most jersey sweaters are knitted with two-ply yarns, providing greater strength and shape retention.

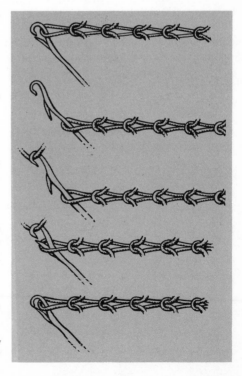

Stitch formation with a latch needle on a weft knitting machine, top to bottom:
The closed needle after drawing off a loop.

The needle latch opens as the finished loop slips over it onto the needle stem.

The thread caught and being drawn by the descending needle head.

The previously finished loop pushes the latch closing the needle head while the new loop is formed.

The first loop slips over the needle head onto the newly formed loop.

Courtesy CIBA Review

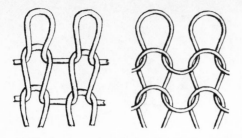

Plain knit, showing right (face) side at far left and reverse (back) side at near left.

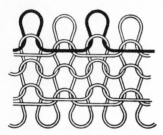

A "run-resistant" circular knit.

Courtesy CIBA Review

A section of a garment knitted in the jersey stitch.

Purl Stitch. This construction is also referred to as the *links-and-links stitch* (after the German word *links,* meaning *left*). It is made by needles using hooks on both ends to alternately draw loops to the front of the fabric in one course and to the back in the next course. The fabric looks the same on both sides and resembles the back of the plain knit. It is a slower and more costly technique.

The use of double-hook needles enables ready changeover during fabric construction to include flat and rib stitches, which makes it possible to duplicate virtually any hand-knitted structure. It lends itself to the heavy, jumbo stitch that produces the familiar bulky effect. Because the purl stitch has crosswise stretch and excellent lengthwise stretch, it is widely used in infants' and children's wear.

A links-links double-latch needle with complete head and latch at each end.

Courtesy CIBA Review

Fabric made on a links-links flat-knitting machine.

Courtesy CIBA Review

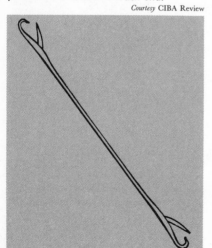

At near right, diagram of the rib stitch. At far right, fabric sample of 2 x 2 rib stitch.

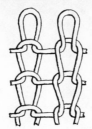

Rib Stitch. Rib-knit fabrics have alternating lengthwise rows of plain and purl stitches constructed so that the face and back of the fabric appear alike. This is produced by having two sets of needles, generally at right angles to each other. Each set of needles alternately draws loops in its own direction, depending upon the width of the rib desired. For example, rib stitches can be 1×1, 2×2, 2×1, 3×1, and so on. A combination of 1×1 and 2×2 is called an *accordion rib*. Rib construction is costlier because of the greater amount of yarn needed and the slower rate of production.

The rib stitch has excellent widthwise elasticity, particularly in the 2×2 rib structure. This characteristic has resulted in its extensive use in apparel where snugness of fit is essential, such as wristbands of sleeves and waistbands of garments. It is also widely used for underwear and socks for men and children.

Variations of the rib stitch include the full-cardigan stitch, the half-cardigan stitch, the interlock stitch, the cable stitch, and the double-knit stitch.

The *full-cardigan stitch* is a bulky rib knit and is produced by one set of needles knitting and the other set of needles tucking on the first course. They reverse on the next course, with the plain needles tucking and the rib needles knitting. The fabric has the same appearance on both sides, looking like slightly stretched jersey fabric.

The *half-cardigan stitch* is a variation of the full-cardigan stitch. It is produced by one set of needles alternately tucking and knitting on alternate courses. The construction on the back of the fabric is the reverse of the face. A variation of this stitch is the *rack stitch*, which has a herringbone pattern on the face.

At near right, diagram of the full-cardigan stitch. At far right, fabric sample of the full-cardigan stitch.

Half-cardigan stitch showing face side at left, reverse side at center, and fabric sample at right.

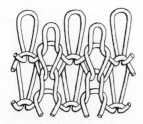

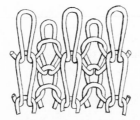

The drawing shows the needle set-out for interlock knitting. The left photo is sample of a cable stitch; the right photo is sample of a double-knit stitch.

The *interlock stitch* is also a variation of the rib stitch, resembling two separate 1 × 1 rib fabrics interknitted. To accomplish this, production is slow. The fabric is relatively heavy and is restricted to single yarns, which tend to pill more readily than ply yarns when spun from certain of the man-made fibers, such as nylon. The fabric has the same appearance on both sides, and the pattern scope is limited. The limited widthwise but excellent lengthwise extensibility of this stitch has been used to advantage for knit shirts and other sportswear. The fabrics made with the interlock stitch are extremely soft, firm, and absorbent.

The *cable stitch* is formed by small groups of plain wales plaited with one another in ropelike fashion. One familiar form is made of two groups of three wales each, thus utilizing six needles. At regular intervals during the construction, the groups interchange their knitting actions producing the twisted cable effect. The interesting appearance and textural effect has made this construction popular for outerwear, particularly sweaters.

The *double-knit stitch* has become very popular. It lends itself to such apparel as sportswear and women's suits and dresses, and it is being promoted for men's suits and slacks. The fabrics are knitted with two sets of needles producing firmness, body, and dimensional stability. This gives such fabrics hand and drape similar to that of woven cloth. Yet, the double knits are naturally shape retentive, wrinkle resistant, and quite durable.

There are several forms of double-knit construction. One type, called *double jersey,* looks like a fine-ribbed fabric on the face and a fine jersey on the reverse. The cloth is quite compact, yet a bit spongy.

Another type of double knit is *double piqué.* The surfaces of these fabrics can vary to look like diamond or honeycomb piqué, or the reverse side of wale piqué. These are produced on circular machines. The Swiss double piqué is made with a smaller, finer loop than the French double piqué.

 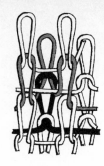 

The drawing at left shows a Swiss double piqué stitch. At right, a French double piqué stitch, with a fabric sample.

WARP KNITTING ■ Warp knitting differs from weft knitting, basically, in that each needle loops its own thread. The needles produce parallel rows of loops simultaneously that are interlocked in a zigzag pattern. Warp knitting may be flat or tubular and can be produced in many varieties of patterns. It can yield cloth with a dimensional stability almost equal to that of woven fabric. Yet, a modern 28 gauge machine can produce a cloth 168 inches wide at a rate of 1,000 courses per minute—that is, 4,700,000 stitches per minute, or more than 40 square feet of fabric per minute. This speed coupled with the use of yarns of man-made fibers has resulted in a great production of warp-knitted fabrics that enjoy popularity because of their smoothness, possible sheerness, wrinkle and shrink resistance, strength, and abrasion resistance.

Products ranging from hairnets to rugs may be produced by warp knitting, depending upon the machine and technique employed. The six types of warp knitting are tricot, milanese, simplex, raschel, ketten raschel, and crochet.

Tricot Knit. The word *tricot* comes from the French word *tricoter*, which means *to knit*. The tricot production began between 1775 and 1780 with the invention of the *warp loom* by an Englishman named Crane. Tricot knits are used in a wide variety of fabrics for such purposes as lingerie, blouses, dresses, and bed sheets.

The gauge in tricot knit is expressed in terms of the number of knitting elements per bar inch. They range from the coarsest of 14 to the finest of 44,

Stitch formation with a spring-beard needle on warp knitting machine, left to right: (a) The needle returns after drawing off a loop. (b) The thread guide lays the thread over the needle stop. (c) The needle draws the thread to hook it. (d) The thread is pulled through the first loop to form another one.

Courtesy CIBA Review

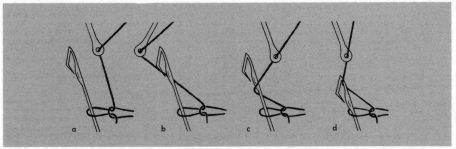

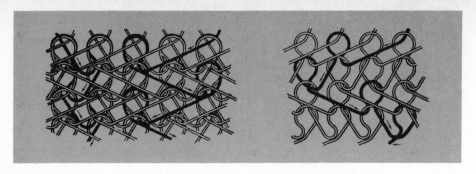

At left, a double-warp (two-bar) tricot; at right, a single-warp (one-bar) tricot.

with the most popular being 28 gauge. The lighter the gauge, the lighter the fabric and the greater its strength per ounce.

Tricot fabrics have many good attributes. They are porous and permit passage of water vapor and air for body comfort. They also offer bulk without undue weight. Tricot fabrics are soft, wrinkle resistant, and have good drapability. They have controllable elasticity, and they do not run or fray. Tricot construction contributes to good abrasion resistance and high bursting and tearing strength. Other factors that contribute to the fabric's strength are the fiber and yarn structure.

Milanese Knit. The milanese stitch, though accomplished by a different technique, produces a fabric almost identical to the tricot. (Tricot differs in that faint horizontal lines are discernible.) Milanese fabrics are superior to tricot in smoothness, elasticity, regularity of structure, and split and tear resistance.

Tricot fabric being woven on a high-speed warp knitting machine.

Courtesy Allied Chemical Corporation

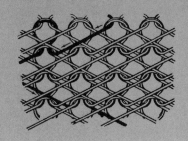

A diagram of the milanese stitch.

However, production has declined considerably in recent years due to the low production rates of milanese machines and their limitations in scope of patterns.

Simplex Knit. *Simplex* fabrics are produced with spring-beard needles on a machine that is essentially two tricot machines arranged back to back. The gauge ranges from 28 to 34 on fabrics of 84- to 112-inch widths.

Most simplex fabrics are made of cotton, are relatively heavy, and are double faced. They are used for such purposes as gloves, handbags, sportswear, and slipcovers. Eyelet and other openwork may also be produced on the simplex machine.

Raschel Knit. The raschel knit is made with latched needles rather than the bearded type used for tricot, milanese, and simplex. It ranks in importance of production with tricot, but it surpasses it in variety of products, which range from veilings and laces to pile fabrics. The gauges of these materials are measured in terms of the number of needles per 2 inches. The finest gauges, used for elastic cloths, are 48 and 56. The 18 gauge is used for such products as outerwear and bedspreads. The great majority of these materials are made on a *pillar and inlay principle* that uses one bar of needles knitting vertical rows of loops, or pillars, with each row connected by a horizontal inlay thread.

Raschel machines are extremely versatile. They can knit every type of yarn made of *any* kind of fiber, including metallic and glass, and in *any* form, whether staple or filament, standard or novelty. This versatility naturally extends the possible characteristics and properties of the fabrics produced.

Ketten Raschel Knit. This knit is also called the *chain raschel*. It is a variation of the tricot knit that produces a coarse gauge of 14 to 20 needles per inch on widths of 90 to 120 inches. The machine can be equipped to produce raised pattern effects in one or more colors by a *shell-stitch construction*. Since the ketten raschel knit is produced with bearded needles, the fabric is finer and has a better hand as well as superior elasticity and cover.

These magnifications of warp-knit "Nylsuisse" fabric show some variations from basic warp-knit stitches.

Courtesy CIBA Review

Courtesy Wildman Jacquard Co.

The circular Jacquard knitting machine employs spools of yarns of various colors (see enlargement) to obtain the design governed by the action of the punched tapes, shown connected around the middle of the machine.

Crochet. This basic stitch is used in hand-crochet work employing a pillar chain. Using either latch or beard needles, this construction is used in a wide variety of fabrics ranging from nets and laces to bedspreads and carpets.

JACQUARD KNITTING ■ Both weft and warp knitting can incorporate the Jacquard mechanism to produce multicolored designs. The Jacquard punched-card technique used in weaving can also be adapted to knitting. Cards control the selection or inhibition of the needles to produce the pattern.

PILE KNITTING ■ With the development of acrylic, modacrylic, and olefin fibers, the production of *pile knits* has grown since 1955. Weft and warp knitting machines produce imitation fur fabrics and rugs that are similar in appearance to woven fabrics but are more flexible, and have better drape. These fabrics are lightweight and easy to care for. They usually can be laundered and cold tumble-dried. The pile should then be combed or brushed.

Production of Pile Knits. The techniques for knitting pile fabrics are quite complicated. The slower and more common method uses a plain knit with heavy yarn for the background and a carded sliver for the pile. As the needles pull the ground yarn to form loops, they catch and draw the sliver through, causing the fibers to get locked into place as the stitch is tightened. Production runs from 5 to 11 yards per hour.

A newer, faster method uses circular-knitting units operating on a cut-loop and ground-yarn principle. Another technique is the cut-pile and ground-yarn method on a raschel machine.

The needles of this circular-pile knitting machine form loops from the ground yarns as they come off the spools and draw the carded slivers from the cans through these loops, causing the fibers to get locked into the stitches and forming the pile effect.

Courtesy Wildman Jacquard Co.

A Jacquard knitted sweater of Orlon Sayelle acrylic fiber.

Courtesy E. I. duPont de Nemours, and Co., Inc.

To simulate natural fur coats, the materials are processed through the following special finishes.

1. *Heat setting* to preshrink the fabric in length, giving it stability and expanding the diameter of the pile fibers. (If the fabric is made by the uncut-loop method, it must be napped to cut the loops prior to heat setting.)

2. *Tigering,* which uses a roll of wire brushes to remove loose fibers from the face of the fabric.

3. *Rough shearing* by helical knives (similar to those of a reel-type mower) to the desired height.

4. *Electrofying,* a polishing technique that gives a desired luster by combing the fabric in both directions with a heated, grooved cylinder.

5. *Wet application* of certain chemicals, such as silicones and various resins (depending upon the pile fiber), to further increase the smoothness and luster.

6. *Electrofying* a second time to bring out the luster.

7. *Finish shearing,* a light shearing to remove loose fibers raised by a previous treatment.

8. *Embossing,* sometimes done instead of shearing when the fabric is to simulate the curl of such furs as karakul, Persian lamb, or broadtail. The fabric may first be processed through an offset and swirling machine with rows of narrow rotary wire brushes, which permanently deform the lay of the fibers in adjoining strips and cause variations in light reflection. The fabrics are then passed under heated embossing steel rollers that are cut to resemble the natural curl of the fur they are intended to imitate. The curl is permanently heat-set into the fabric.

The imitation fur fabrics, which must be labeled as required by law, are much less expensive than genuine fur fabrics. They are soft, resilient, durable, and warm. When not made of wool, they cannot be damaged by moth larvae. They may be dry-cleaned or laundered, depending on the construction. Of course, on close examination, they do not have the same appearance or luxuriant hand of genuine fur.

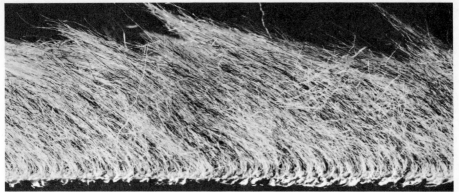

Courtesy CIBA Review

Close-up side view of knitted pile fabric.

This furlike coat is made of a knitted pile fabric of Acrilan acrylic fiber. It is warm, lightweight, and washable.

Courtesy Chemstrand Div.

HOSIERY

Before the sixteenth century, the Anglo-Saxon word *hosa* designated a woven cloth garment that covered the lower portion of the body as well as the legs. As knitting was popularized and practiced to a great extent throughout England and Scotland, it soon became customary to knit the leg coverings separately by hand. In the course of time, these garments became known as stockings. Wool was used for such hand knitting.

When William Lee invented the knitting machine, the English queen encouraged him to adapt it to the knitting of silk stockings rather than wool ones because she feared that such a machine would take away the livelihood of the wool hand-knitters. But credit for the later development of machine-knit silk stockings must be given to France, as Lee was invited to that country to set up his machines there when the queen of England failed to grant him a patent. Misfortune still followed Lee, and he died in France before the full value of his knitting machine became apparent.

Hosiery is a major product of knitting, and its cost is often a large item in the clothing budget of the consumer. The construction of hosiery should be of interest because it has a bearing on the serviceability of the article. In most cases, the better-constructed hosiery is well worth its extra cost, provided it is given proper care in wearing as well as in laundering.

YARNS USED FOR HOSIERY ■ The selection of hosiery yarn depends upon the purpose for which it is to be used. Different types of hosiery are available for sportswear and dresswear for women, children, and men. The yarns may be made of spun staple or filament, and they may be textured. The fiber used will also contribute particular characteristics to the hosiery.

Cotton. Cotton is suitable for hosiery because it is soft, absorbent, and dries quickly. It has less tendency to run when a thread is broken. The durability of cotton hosiery is enhanced when it is made of lisle and mercerized yarns.

Wool. Wool is desirable for some hosiery because of its warmth. The high absorbency of wool is another good feature. Of course, the grade of the wool yarns used has an important bearing on the quality and price of the hose.

Rayon. This was the first man-made fiber to be used for hosiery. But it does not possess the elasticity or strength necessary to produce good-looking, fine hosiery for women.

Nylon. Nylon has proved to be the outstanding fiber for hosiery. Before nylon was developed in 1940, silk had always been the most popular fiber for hosiery because of its strength, elasticity, and pleasing, soft, luxurious texture. Because nylon filament yarn is stronger and more elastic than silk, it has become the first yarn acceptable for fine hosiery in place of silk. Nylon has a greater resistance to abrasion and outlasts silk in the heels and toes of stockings. It lacks the absorbent quality of silk, however. Nylon filament hosiery snags easily and, once a thread is broken, a run develops quickly unless constructed with a run-resistant stitch.

Nylon yarn can be spun into fine deniers, so that a large variety of styles, types, and weights of women's nylon hosiery can be made. At first, the full-fashioned construction was used, but the use of the circular-knit construction on high-count needle machines has increased because nylon can be preset by heat. A preboarding operation stabilizes the nylon stocking fabric against distortion of stitch by subjecting it to conditions higher in temperature than those that will be subsequently encountered.

One kind of nylon developed by Du Pont especially for women's hosiery is *Cantrece*. Its characteristics, as described on page 335, are a little different from the conventional nylon. Cantrece has greater resilience and fit regardless of the size and shape of the leg, and the fit does not diminish even after continued wear. The superior resilience and fit reduces the straining and wearing effect of stress at the ankle, calf, and knee. Cantrece has a soft, matte finish. It retains a wrinkle-free appearance without letdown or looseness throughout its entire wear-life.

The nylon staple can also be spun into woollike yarns, which are usually knitted into men's hosiery. Spun nylon hosiery is soft and warm, and the yarn is even more abrasion-resistant than nylon filament yarn; therefore, spun nylon hosiery is very durable and will wear for a very long time—it will, in fact, outwear all other hosiery. Spun nylon hosiery launders easily and does not shrink. The one big disadvantage of this type of hosiery is its tendency to cause the feet to perspire.

Nylon is the most common fiber used to produce textured yarns that have stretch characteristics, as described in Chapter 4. Stretch nylon hosiery has fewer size ranges, fits well without binding, and is durable.

Spun Acrylic. These yarns are often made into men's hosiery, but they do not have the abrasion resistance and wearing qualities of spun nylon. They have low absorbency and a cashmerelike feel but will not produce durable hosiery.

Spandex. Spandex yarns, both covered and uncovered, are particularly well suited for support hosiery for men and women, including women's sheer dresswear.

TYPES OF HOSIERY CONSTRUCTION ■ There are two basic types of hosiery construction: *full-fashioned* and *circular* (*or seamless*). While a third type, *cut and tailored,* has been generally discontinued, features of it are retained in "hybrid" constructions utilizing the two basic methods.

Full-fashioned Hosiery. Full-fashioned hosiery receives its name from the narrowing process performed during the knitting operation to shape the hose to fit the leg. The fabric is knitted flat. Loops are dropped at appropriate points between the knee and the ankle, thus tapering the width of the stocking. Stitches are also dropped to shape the instep and the heel. When the selvages are joined together, the stocking is fully shaped. The joining produces a noticeable seam on the back of the hosiery. Small dots, called *fashion marks,* appear on both sides of the seam indicating where the stitches were decreased during the narrowing process. Lines or wales radiate from these fashion marks.

Because full-fashioned hosiery is shaped in the knitting operation, its fit is assured and its shape is retained after wearing and washing. All parts of full-fashioned stockings have the same number of loops to the inch.

A variation in the method of constructing full-fashioned hosiery employs the thermoplastic properties of nylon. The entire leg and foot are knitted to the same width, but progressively tighter stitches are utilized for the graduated body shape. After seaming, the stocking is placed on a *board shape* and heat-set to the desired leg shape. This technique eliminates the fashion marks and radiating wales.

Circular-knit Hosiery. Circular hose is knit from hem to toe on a circular machine and is often called *seamless* hosiery. There are the same number of stitches in the width of circular-knit hosiery from top to toe. The shaping is accomplished by gradually reducing the size of the loops from the top to the toe. The heel and toe are shaped by a circular *fashioning* mechanism that drops successive courses in the knitting process. In women's hosiery, two or three gores or segments will appear in the heel; children's and men's hosiery usually have two-segment gore heels.

Circular-knit hosiery for women was formerly considered less desirable and was less expensive than full-fashioned hosiery. To imitate the full-fashioned hosiery, circular-knit hosiery was given a mock seam and additional stitches were knitted at the back of the leg. Today, circular-knit hosiery of nylon are extremely popular. Since the hose is heat-set on a board shape, it provides excellent fit. Circular-knit hosiery eliminates the problem of unsightly twisted or crooked seams on the back of the leg, and it imparts the bare-leg appearance preferred by many women.

A variation of the circular knit is the *fashioned seamless* stocking. This is now in limited production, usually for certain kinds of hosiery specialities. Fashioned seamless hosiery is knit on a special flat machine. The hose is started at the toe, where only a small number of needles is used. As the stocking is widened from ankle to calf and finally to hem, one needle at a time is added to obtain the full-fashioned effect. The added stitches form a V at the back of the leg, which identifies fashioned seamless hose. The fashioned seamless construction makes a comfortable stocking because the seam in the foot is eliminated.

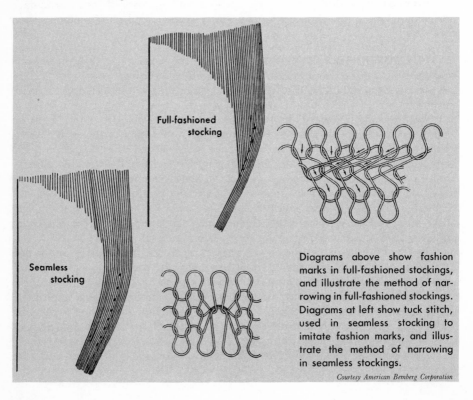

Full-fashioned stocking

Seamless stocking

Diagrams above show fashion marks in full-fashioned stockings, and illustrate the method of narrowing in full-fashioned stockings. Diagrams at left show tuck stitch, used in seamless stocking to imitate fashion marks, and illustrate the method of narrowing in seamless stockings.

Courtesy American Bemberg Corporation

At left, unfinished, seamless stocking just off a circular knitting machine. At right, the same stocking after being heat-set on a board shape.

Courtesy CIBA Review

Hybrid Construction of Hosiery. Stocking leg shapes are sometimes cut out of lace machine fabrics as well as from raschel or Jacquard knitted fabrics. These cut blanks are then joined to welts and feet made from other circular- or flat-knitted fabrics, which produces such hosiery as lace stockings and sweater-set hose.

Other varieties combine plain stockings or knee-high hose with sewed or topped-on lace, elastic, or plain welts. Further variations include the construction of seamless tights, which are long stockings with wide top sections knit on circular hosiery machines, then cut on opposite sides of each pair and seamed in the front, back, and through the crotch.

WOMEN'S NYLON HOSIERY ■ Nylon is the most popular textile for hosiery among women. Nevertheless, many women find fault with the durability of their nylon hosiery. For greater service, the following factors should be considered when purchasing nylon hosiery.

Types of Stocking Fabric. The manner in which hosiery is knit has a great deal to do with its durability, appearance, and fit. There are two main types of knit: plain and mesh. The *plain knit* of which most hosiery is made has several advantages. It stretches in both directions, has a smooth clear texture, and provides unequaled sheerness. The outstanding disadvantage of the plain knit is that a break in any loop can cause a run.

The *mesh knit* can be produced in a variety of patterns. Usually, the fabric is of a run-resistant construction. The yarn can snag but will develop only a hole in the fabric rather than a run because the loops are interlocked. Since most mesh-knit fabrics are less stretchable than plain-knit, special attention

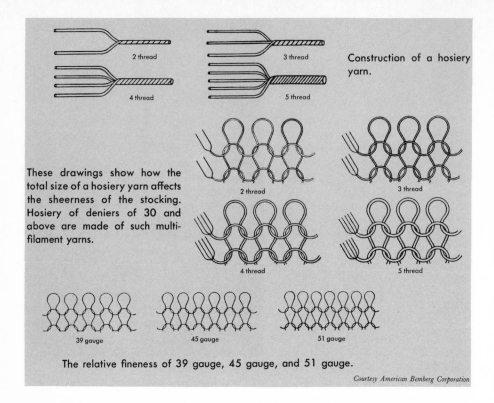

2 thread

3 thread

Construction of a hosiery yarn.

4 thread

5 thread

These drawings show how the total size of a hosiery yarn affects the sheerness of the stocking. Hosiery of deniers of 30 and above are made of such multifilament yarns.

2 thread

3 thread

4 thread

5 thread

39 gauge

45 gauge

51 gauge

The relative fineness of 39 gauge, 45 gauge, and 51 gauge.

Courtesy American Bemberg Corporation

should be given to proper fit to avoid unnecessary strain on any part of the stocking. A half-size larger stocking is recommended to make up for this lack of stretch. Mesh-knit hosiery is not as smooth or as sheer and flattering to the leg as plain-knit, but it tends to be more serviceable.

Another type of mesh hosiery is the *micro-mesh* knit. Because this hosiery is constructed with the loops knitted in one direction, the stocking will run in only one direction: from the foot toward the welt.

Sheerness of Hosiery. The sheerness of nylon hosiery depends on the fineness (denier) of the yarn used and the closeness (gauge, for full-fashioned, and needles, for seamless hosiery) of the stitches or loops. The term *denier* indicates the weight of the nylon yarn. The higher the denier, the heavier or thicker the yarn; the lower the denier, the finer the yarn. Nylon deniers most commonly range from 7 (the finest yarn) through 10, 12, 15, 20, 30, 40, 50, 60, and 70.

The term *gauge* refers to the closeness of fineness of the loops across the width of the full-fashioned stocking. The gauge, which indicates the number of stitches or loops per 1½ inches across a knitted row, may range from a low of 39 through 42, 45, 48, 51, 54, 57, 60, 66, 75, and 90. Since each needle makes a loop, the more needles used, the more loops there will be and the finer the gauge. Since a high gauge uses more and finer stitches, it uses more nylon yarn and gives greater strength to the stocking. The higher the gauge and the finer the stitch, the greater the wearing quality and snag resistance.

In seamless hosiery, the closeness of the loops is measured in terms of *needles* on the circular stocking knitting machine. Like gauge, the higher the number of needles, the closer and finer the knit. Sometimes, a seamless stocking is also referred to by its equivalent gauge count—that is, 400 needle count is similar to 51 gauge, a 432 needle count is as closely knit as 54 gauge, and a 474 needle count is similar to 60 gauge.

Gauge affects the appearance and durability of hosiery, but it is the combination of denier and gauge that determines the sheerness of the hose. For example, 45 gauge, 15 denier hosiery is sheerer than 51 gauge, 15 denier hosiery, but the 45 gauge stocking will probably not wear as well because it is not so closely knitted. Likewise, 54 gauge, 15 denier hosiery should wear even better because of the greater number of stitches to each 1½ inches of the stocking. When comparing hosiery deniers and gauges, similar components must be used. Each stocking is a combination of the quality of knitting, the quality of the yarn, the denier of the yarn, the gauge, and the construction features. The following facts are helpful when purchasing hosiery.

15 denier, 51 gauge—filmy and supersheer, for evening wear

20 denier, 51 gauge—sheer weight, desirable for evening wear

30 denier, 51 gauge—average weight, for afternoon or business

40 denier, 45 gauge—duty weight, often preferred for daytime wear at home

60 to 70 denier, 45 gauge—service weight, best for outdoors and for extra long wear

Construction of Hosiery. For hosiery to wear well, it must be properly constructed. The fact that strong nylon yarn is used, or that a high gauge is employed in knitting the stocking, does not automatically ensure long-wearing hosiery. The *seams* in full-fashioned hosiery should be straight, sturdy, narrow, and trim, with no raw fabric edges showing. Nylon thread should be used because it assures long-wearing and fast-drying fine seams. When correctly sewed, the heel reinforcing, welt, and fashion marks will match on both sides of the

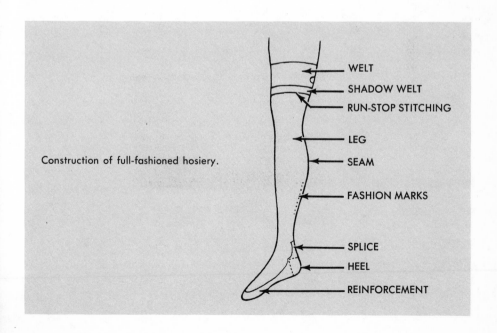

Construction of full-fashioned hosiery.

WELT
SHADOW WELT
RUN-STOP STITCHING
LEG
SEAM
FASHION MARKS
SPLICE
HEEL
REINFORCEMENT

seam. The *welt,* or hem, should be 3 to 4 inches long to permit firm anchoring of the garter. The welt should be sufficiently wide and elastic to fit the thigh without binding. It should measure 7 or 8 inches when flat and should stretch to about 12 or 13 inches to be comfortable on the average leg.

There should be a well-constructed *shadow welt,* or *afterwelt,* directly below the welt, which gives added strength to the upper part of the hosiery by taking up the garter strain. Just below the welt or the shadow welt, there should be a row of *"run-stop" stitching* around the stocking, which discourages runs, starting in the welt, from running into the body of the stocking. This stitching can be made in several ways, such as by interlocking the loops during the knitting process.

WOMEN'S HOSIERY SIZE—BASED ON SHOE SIZE AND SHOE WIDTH

SHOE SIZE	SHOE WIDTH				
	AAA	AA	A or B	C or D	E or EE
4	8½	8½	8½	9	9
4½	8½	8½	9	9	9½
5	9	9	9	9	9½
5½	9	9	9½	9½	9½
6	9½	9½	9½	9½	10
6½	9½	9½	9½	10	10
7	9½	9½	10	10	10½
7½	10	10	10	10½	10½
8	10	10	10½	10½	10½
8½	10½	10½	10½	10½	11
9	10½	10½	11	11	11
9½	11	11	11	11	11

WOMEN'S HOSIERY LENGTH—BASED ON STOCKING SIZE

STOCKING SIZE	STANDARD LENGTH		
	Short	Medium	Long
8½, 9	28"	30"	—
9½	28"	31"	34"
10	—	31"	34"
10½, 11	—	32"	34"

Reinforcement in the toe, heel, and sole is desirable for greater durability and should be in proportion to the weight and style of the hosiery. Some styles of sheer hosiery are made with little or no reinforcement. Fortunately, nylon is strong and can withstand unusual rubbing and abrading before it will wear through. The *volume* of the stocking is another important consideration. Since nylon hosiery has unusual two-way stretch, flat measurement alone is not sufficient to assure that the stocking is correctly sized. Good construction requires

HOSIERY RUNS AND BREAKS—CAUSE AND CORRECTION

CAUSE	POSSIBLE CORRECTION
Too much pull from garters. Lack of elasticity of garter or sharp edge on garter clasp.	Wear longer stockings. Have elastic and garters in good condition.
A skimpy welt or not enough elasticity in welt.	Buy stockings with plenty of stretch in the hem or those with a special stretch-top feature.
Stocking too tight or too long.	Buy stockings with more ample tops and of correct length. Garters should never be put into sheer leg fabric or shadow welt.
Too sheer a stocking for the occasion.	Wear stockings of heavier denier yarn or higher gauge knit.
Improper fastening of garter.	Always fasten garters into hem of stockings. Garters fastened into sheer leg fabric, shadow welt, or on the seams frequently result in tears and runs. Handle hose carefully.
Snags or pulled threads.	Avoid contact with sharp or rough objects, as broken or rough fingernails or toenails, zippers, crinoline skirts, and the like. Buy stockings that fit the leg more snugly. Loose, poorly fitting stockings are more readily snagged.
Strain at knee.	Buy longer stockings.
Excessive strain and wear above heel reinforcement.	Buy larger foot size.
Reinforcement too thin.	Buy hosiery with heavier reinforcements. Use lightly reinforced hosiery or sandal-foot types only for more dressy occasions.
Stocking snagging on rough shoe lining.	Have shoe lining repaired. Wear shoes with snug-fitting heels.
Stocking too short in foot causing runs in toe reinforcing.	Buy larger-sized stockings.
Runs above toe reinforcing when too long stocking is folded under.	Buy smaller-sized stockings.
Insufficient reinforcement.	Buy hose of heavier denier or more heavily reinforced in toe.
Reinforcement worn through.	Buy stockings more heavily reinforced or of heavier denier for the occasion. Check rough shoe linings.
Friction from bunions, calluses, or similar abrasion.	Take proper care of feet.
Friction from arch supports.	Buy hose with heavier foot reinforcements.

that stockings should conform to standard leg-form sizes. This volume should not be skimpy but rather should be adequate in both girth and length of the foot, leg, and thigh.

Regardless of the quality of construction, no hosiery will give proper service unless the wearer selects the correct foot size in accordance with the width and size of her shoe, and the correct leg length.

When stretch nylon yarns are used, the top of the welt should measure 12 to 13 inches across. A narrower width would tend to bind, while a wider width would not provide sufficient elasticity and snugness. The stocking should be able to stretch about 7 inches at the instep, otherwise strain in this area might result in holes at splicing and sole reinforcement points.

Grading of Hosiery. Hosiery is graded as *first quality, irregulars, seconds,* and *thirds.* Stockings are classified as irregulars if there is an irregularity in dimension, size, color, or knit, but without any breaks, runs, tears, or mends in the fabric or yarn. Seconds and thirds have a substantial number of imperfections, including runs, mends, and defects in the yarn, fabric, or finish.

MEN'S, CHILDREN'S, AND INFANTS' HOSIERY ■ Men's, children's, and infants' hosiery, with minor exceptions, is circular-knit and is made of any of the various kinds and combinations of yarns, in many styles and in color effects.

Stretch yarns have become very popular in men's and children's hosiery. Sizes of small, medium, and large provide the consumer with greater shopping ease and wardrobe flexibility for the family. Such hosiery is comfortable and tends to fit the leg better, reducing or eliminating the problem of sagging.

MEN'S AND CHILDREN'S HOSIERY SIZES[1]

SHOE SIZE	MEN	CHILDREN AND INFANTS	SHOE SIZE	MEN	CHILDREN AND INFANTS
1	..	4			
1½	..	4	7½	10½	6
2	..	4	8	10½	6½
2½	..	4	8½	11	6½
3	..	4½	9	11	7
3½	..	4½	9½	11	7
4	..	4½	10	11½	7
4½	..	4½	10½	11½	7½
5	9	5	11	12	7½
5½	9½	5	11½	12	7½
6	9½	5½	12	..	7½
6½	10	5½	12½	..	8
7	10	6	13	..	8

[1] Courtesy National Association of Hosiery Manufacturers.

DYEING OF HOSIERY ■ Most stockings are dip-dyed or piece-dyed. This method is satisfactory if proper care is taken to ensure evenness of color, for the flesh background quickly reveals inadequately dyed hosiery. By stretching the seamed part of the stocking, the consumer can tell whether the dyeing was well done. Unevenness of color indicates poor or incomplete penetration of the dye. Hosiery is sometimes yarn-dyed. Ingrain stockings are made from yarns that were dyed before knitting. The amount of ingrain hosiery produced today is very small. A richer color results, but the hosiery is not as durable as when piece-dyed.

CARE OF HOSIERY ■ Hosiery should be washed after each wearing, as perspiration weakens the fiber. Unusual care is necessary in washing, as rough skin or sharp fingernails cause snags that eventually result in runs. Rings should be removed when hosiery is being handled. Lukewarm water with suds made from mild soap or soap flakes should be used, and the suds squeezed through the hose. The hosiery should be thoroughly rinsed in clear, warm water. Cantrece nylon should be rolled quickly in a towel and then hung on a smooth rod in the same manner as other nylon hosiery. Stockings should never be wrung or twisted. When drying, they should not be exposed to the direct heat of the sun nor hung near a hot radiator or stove. These precautions apply to all types of hosiery. For wool stockings, the additional precautions for washing any wool fabric should be observed. In addition to careful washing, the following suggestions will also help lengthen the wear of hosiery.

1. Purchase at least two pairs of stockings of the same color, to match pairs when a single stocking has been damaged.
2. Keep stockings in a separate box, when not in use, to prevent contact with anything that may mar their texture.
3. Select the proper size of hose according to well-fitted shoes. The stocking should be at least a half-inch longer than the wearer's foot.

OUTERWEAR

Knitting has long been employed to produce sweaters and shirts. These garments may be constructed in several ways. Front, back, and sleeve sections may be *flat knit* and subsequently seamed together. The seamed, flat-knit sleeves may be stitched to a body that has been *circular knit*. Sweaters and blouses may also be *full-fashion* knitted, with the full-fashioned marks showing the contour shaping of the sleeves in the area of the shoulders.

The type and method of knitting used is dependent upon many factors, including cost of production; the kind of garment (such as a cardigan or pullover), the kind of fiber (such as wool or one of the acrylics), and the kind of yarn (such as bulk or stretch). The techniques vary, depending upon the particular combination of these factors.

While these factors are discussed in various sections of the text, several other considerations should be kept in mind when selecting a sweater or knitted shirt. The quality of the ribbing at the sleeves and waistband should be such that these areas are not binding but elastic, shape retentive, and well-finished. Seams should be straight and buttons should meet buttonholes properly to avoid puckering and unevenness. The grosgrain tape backing the buttons and buttonholes should be well placed and secure. The shoulders should fit comfortably.

Full-fashioned fabric made on a flat-knit machine.

Courtesy CIBA Review

Full-fashioned goods being flat knitted with the aid of a racking mechanism. Note the two needle bars and the thread feed.

Courtesy CIBA Review

There are several factors that cause knitted underwear to differ from other knitted goods. The fiber and yarn used in underwear should be soft and able to absorb perspiration so that the body will be comfortable in all seasons. The stitch must offer sufficient cover and yet provide enough porosity for body ventilation. In order to provide proper fit, construction must allow for changes in dimension due to the finishing processes.

Underwear is made principally on circular-knit machines in various gauges. Most T-shirts and lightweight summer fabrics are made with the plain stitch on weft machines. The range of lightweight summer to heavyweight winter fabrics generally results from combinations of yarn size and needle spacing and the use of one set of needles, as in the plain knit, or two sets of needles, as in the rib knit. So-called "fleece-lined" fabric used in some underwear, as well as sweatshirts, is constructed of a plain knit employing an extra soft-spun, thick yarn. The yarn is knitted into the back of the fabric in longer course-wise loops and then brushed to produce a soft fuzzy nap.

Rib fabrics used for underwear are usually of the 1 × 1 construction. Other ribs used are the 2 × 2 and, sometimes, the alternating front and back or *panel rib,* which are not as elastic as the regular rib knits. Some better quality underwear is made on the Interlock machine, which simultaneously interknits two 1 × 1 fabrics.

The quality of underwear depends not only upon the fiber, yarn, and knitted construction but also upon the cutting, trimming, finishing, and sizing operations. The consumer should observe the evenness and neatness of the seams. The size should be full and protected against shrinking by such processes as Permasized or Pak-nit (as described on pages 132–33).

REVIEW QUESTIONS

1 How does the construction of knitted fabrics differ from woven fabrics?

2 What is the chief advantage gained by the knitted construction?

3 Why is a knitted fabric always a warm fabric?

4 (a) What is a disadvantage of the knitted construction? (b) How can it be eliminated?

5 How would you evaluate the construction of knitted fabrics?

6 Compare the designations for construction and sheerness of full-fashioned and seamless hosiery.

7 What are the characteristics of the basic types of weft knits?

8 What are the advantages of the double-knit construction?

9 What are the characteristics of the basic type of warp knits?

10 How is pile knitting accomplished?

11 (a) What are the types of hosiery construction? (b) What is preferable, and why?

12 How would you judge a pair of women's stockings?

13 (a) What is meant by gauge of hosiery? (b) What is meant by denier?

14 How will the gauge and denier of nylon hosiery influence a consumer's choice?

15 What is the difference between mesh and micro-mesh hosiery?

16 How will the fit of shoes affect the wear of hosiery?

17 Why is it important to examine the reinforcements of hosiery?

18 What are the average lengths of hosiery for women?

19 What considerations should be given to the care of hosiery?

20 Compare cotton, wool, rayon, nylon, and acrylics for use in men's hosiery.

21 What factors should one consider when selecting a sweater?

22 (a) What is "fleece-lined" underwear? (b) How is it made?

23 How are fabrics simulated to look like fur?

7 MINOR FABRIC CONSTRUCTIONS

Some methods of fabric construction that have been in existence for a long time have been of relatively minor importance due to their limited practical application. Yet, they retain a place of significance in the textile industry. Felt, braid, net, and lace are examples of these.

More recently, relatively new techniques of fabric construction have been developed. These are nonwoven processes (other than felting), as well as tufting and mali processes. These methods of fabric production are in their infancy, so to speak, but they promise to become increasingly important.

NONWOVEN FABRICS

The art of producing fabrics directly from fibers matted together began before spinning and weaving were invented. Yet, nonwovens presently account for only about five percent of all the textile fabrics produced. Modern techniques have evolved and are still being developed to improve the quality and usefulness of nonwoven fabrics. These techniques differ, depending upon whether felt or some other form of nonwoven is being manufactured.

FELT ■ History records that the patron saint of the felt industry, Saint Feutre of Caen, France, put wool fibers in his sandals to make them more comfortable during his long walking trips. The pressure, moisture, and heat from his feet caused the fibers to interlock into a matted layer. Today, felt is made from wool with or without the admixture of another animal fiber, vegetable fiber, or man-made fiber.

The Felting Process. Felting was originally based upon the physical characteristics of the crimp and scaly surface of wool fibers that cause them to cling and intermesh and allow them to be pressed into a compact fabric. In the wool felting process, two carding operations make the fibers parallel and of even thickness in the form of a fine web. Several webs may be built up until a sufficient amount of weight or thickness has accumulated. Timing is important during these processes, so that the web will not be broken or have weak areas. The mass, or batt, may then be cut, and the edges trimmed to the desired width.

Finished felt may vary in thickness from a few thousandths of an inch to 3 inches. Any thickness can be obtained by superimposing batts on one another and felting them together. Batts are usually about 40 yards long and 60 to 90 inches wide; their weights vary from 18 to 50 pounds.

The batts are evenly sprinkled with warm water, passed over a steam box to warm the fibers thoroughly, and then pressed between two rollers. The top roller rests on the batt and, with an oscillating motion, exerts the pressure that, combined with moisture and heat, produces the final felting action.

After the batts have been processed, they are allowed to drain and cool off for about twenty-four hours. The timing for each raw material or blend used in the felt is very important. The felt is then dampened with a suitable lubricant, such as a soap and soda combination, for the fulling process, by which it is subjected to a pounding action with hammers. The fulling time varies from five minutes to half an hour. The longer the felt is fulled, the firmer it will be. But this operation cannot be continued too long, or the quality of the felt would be spoiled. Final operations include washing, stiffening, ironing, brushing to raise a nap, and shearing to produce a smooth even surface. Felt may be made water-repellent and may be flameproofed or mothproofed. It may be dyed against fading, perspiration, cleaning, and washing.

Before 1952, it was believed that felt could be made only from wool or fur. Then technicians at Du Pont created a process for making felt from man-made fibers by carding, cross-lapping or air dispersion, followed by passing the batt through a needle-punching machine containing numerous barbed needles. This machine forces fibers into a three-dimensional entanglement that gives the necessary adhesion, structure, and body to the fabric. Controls are provided for uniformity, density, and hardness. A shrinking treatment further contributes to these properties. Felts made by this process are resistant to mildew, rot, chemical degradation, and abrasion.

Wool Felt. In most satisfactory grades of wool felt, at least one-half of the fiber comprises wool, as the wool fiber surpasses all others in the physical quality of cohesiveness that makes this type of fabric construction possible. Short-staple wool fiber, or noil, is used for felt; but the finer the grade of staple used, the stronger the felt. Some lower-priced grades of felt are also made chiefly from wool. Other felts are made by combining cotton, kapok, or rayon with wool. These felts may be distinguished from fur felt by the dull appearance, harder feel, and comparatively rougher texture.

Acetate, nylon, and acrylic fibers are also blended with wool. They contribute cross-dyeing color effects and improve the fabric's drapability. These blends also reduce the finished felt's tendency to shrink.

Fur Felt. The short fibers of such fur-bearing animals as the rabbit, muskrat, nutria, and beaver are important in the manufacture of felt for hats. Fur felt is usually made from a mixture of fibers, and the better grade contains beaver. Fur contributes softness, smoothness, resilience, and water repellency.

Properties of Felt. Felt has no warp, filling, or selvage, which simplifies its use in garment construction. Because it does not have a system of threads, it will not fray or ravel. On the other hand, its structure makes sewing difficult; hidden mending of tears and holes is impossible. Because it is made without twisted yarns and without interlacing, felt has little tensile strength and, when it tears, it does so in a ragged, fuzzy manner. It has practically no elasticity or draping quality. However, felt can be cut or blocked into any shape. It has good resilience and will retain its shape unless subjected to undue tension.

Wool felt has high thermal insulating properties, and it provides warmth. It absorbs sound and shock, and is more impervious to water than untreated woven or knitted fabrics. Since wool felt shrinks, it should be dry-cleaned.

Uses of Felt. The properties of felt affect its application. Lack of tensile strength and drapability limit the use of felt as a general clothing fabric, but it is especially adaptable for blocking into hats. Felt is also suitable for such articles as slippers, shoe insoles, earmuffs, pennants, and table padding. Because of its insulative and noise absorptive properties, felt has various industrial uses.

OTHER NONWOVENS

To differentiate them from felt, other nonwovens are defined by the American Society for Testing Materials as fabrics constructed "of fibers held together with a bonding material." The history of nonwovens began in the 1930's when a few textile firms began experimenting with cotton waste fibers. Significant commercial production began during World War II. While the development of man-made fibers and chemical bonding agents have given added impetus, this industry is still in its infancy.

METHODS OF MANUFACTURE ■ The processing and manufacture of nonwovens vary with the fibers and bonding agents used. The fibers include cotton, wool, acetate, rayon, nylon, polyester, acrylic, and glass. Generally, a combination of fibers is employed. The staple, which is usually not waste, ranges from $\frac{1}{2}$ to 6 inches in length. The fibers are processed through a series of opening, conditioning, and blending operations, and through the addition of appropriate resin, rubber, acrylic, or other bonding agents. Webs or layers of fiber are then formed.

WEB FORMATION ■ Web formation is dependent upon the particular technique employed.

Parallel-Laid Web. Fibers are passed through carding machines that put them into parallel alignment. Thin webs of parallelized fiber, produced by successive machines and running in the same direction, are laid on each other to form a multi-layer web. This technique produces a fabric which has high lengthwise strength but low crosswise strength. The fabrics produced are used chiefly for disposable products.

Cross-Laid Web. After fibers are passed through a carding machine to form thin webs of parallelized fiber, the webs are crisscrossed successively on each other. This technique is more costly to produce, but the fabric has greater crosswise strength than the parallel-laid web type.

Random-Laid Web. Loose fiber is blown onto a rotating, perforated drum. Internal vacuum causes the fiber to adhere to the drum, forming a heavy matte that is then passed to a lickerin, or rotating drum with teeth, which breaks up the web. These particles are blown onto a second vacuum drum forming a highly uniform web of randomly placed fibers. The thickness of the web can be regulated as required. Fabrics from these random-laid webs have uniform weight.

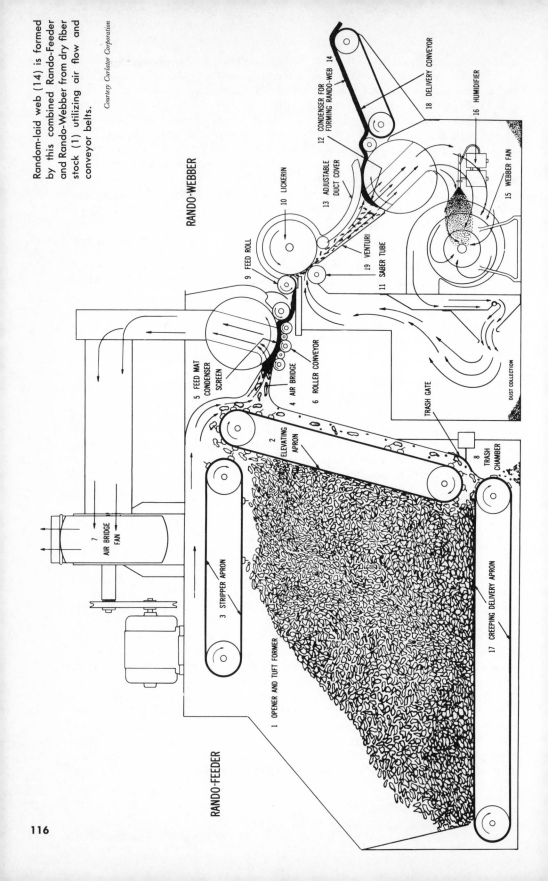

Random-laid web (14) is formed by this combined Rando-Feeder and Rando-Webber from dry fiber stock (1) utilizing air flow and conveyor belts.

Courtesy Curlator Corporation

RANDO-WEBBER

RANDO-FEEDER

1 OPENER AND TUFT FORMER
2 ELEVATING APRON
3 STRIPPER APRON
4 AIR BRIDGE
5 FEED MAT CONDENSER SCREEN
6 ROLLER CONVEYOR
7 AIR BRIDGE FAN
8 TRASH CHAMBER
9 FEED ROLL
10 LICKERIN
11 SABER TUBE
12 CONDENSER FOR FORMING RANDO-WEB 14
13 ADJUSTABLE DUCT COVER
15 WEBBER FAN
16 HUMIDIFIER
17 CREEPING DELIVERY APRON
18 DELIVERY CONVEYOR
19 VENTURI

TRASH GATE

DUST COLLECTION

116

Wet-Lay Random Web. This method is based upon paper-making technique. Fibers are mixed with certain chemicals, processed through beaters and pulpers, and then passed onto a wire screen. The excess moisture is drawn off, leaving a web that is then compressed in a manner similar to other nonwovens.

High-Velocity Sprayed Web. This technique is used with thermoplastic fibers. They are first sprayed onto a belt, which produces a random web. Subsequently, heat and pressure are applied to the web causing the fibers to fuse.

BONDING THE WEB ■ There are three principal methods of bonding the fibers in the web to form fabrics. Because the method used and the particular binder applied affect the characteristics of the finished fabric, the intended use of the fabric must be anticipated beforehand.

Resin Bonding. If the fibers are absorbent, the web may be saturated with a suitable bonding agent either by spraying, printing, padding, or immersing in a bath just before it is passed between two rollers that compress the web and squeeze out the excess liquid. The web is then dried and heat-cured at temperatures ranging from 200 to 400 degrees Fahrenheit, depending upon the material used.

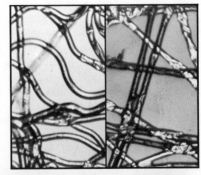

The flexibility of "Reemay" may be predetermined by the use of crimped polyester fibers as shown in the microscopic view (near right). Microscopic view of a sheet of "Reemay" (far right), shows a nonwoven fabric of thermoplastic polyester fiber bonded by heat. The triple exposure photo below shows the high strength and shape retention of "Reemay" nonwoven fabric despite tension in different directions.

Courtesy Du Pont Magazine

Thermoplastic Bonding. Thermoplastic fibers with a low melting point may be blended into either a nonthermoplastic fiber web or a web composed of thermoplastic fibers that have a high melting point. The web may then be either calendered or embossed by passing it between rollers heated to the low melting point of the added thermoplastic fibers that fuse and bond with the other fibers.

Stitch Through Bonding. Thermoplastic thread may be used to stitch laminated webs together. The application of heat causes the thread to soften, shrink, and bond to the web structure, making it more compact.

FINISHING NONWOVENS ■ Finishing techniques for nonwovens are limited. Dyeing is usually done after the fabric has been formed. They may be calendered for smoothness or embossed for textured effects. They may also be printed or flocked. Softness may be added to improve the hand.

CHARACTERISTICS OF NONWOVENS ■ The particular set of properties that a nonwoven fabric may have is dependent upon the combination of factors in its production. The range of characteristics is wide. The appearance of nonwovens may be paperlike, feltlike, or similar to that of woven fabrics. They may have a soft, resilient hand, or they may be hard, stiff, or boardy with little pliability. They may be as thin as tissue paper or many times thicker. Nonwovens may be translucent or opaque. Their porosity may range from high, free airflow to minute to impermeable. Their strength may range from low tear and burst strength to very high tensile strength. They may be fabricated by gluing, heat bonding, or sewing. The drapability of nonwovens varies from good to none at all. Some nonwovens have excellent launderability; others have none. Some may be dry-cleaned.

While these fabrics already have many desirable properties, research is being conducted to produce nonwovens that would meet or perhaps exceed the qualities of woven cloth.

USES OF NONWOVENS ■ The properties of nonwovens offer both unique and limited applications. Their newness, however, has met with understandable consumer hesitancy. Further developments and consumer education are likely to broaden their application. Today they are being used for apparel, such as aprons, skirts, and caps; for home furnishings, such as napkins, draperies, towels, and sheets; for medical applications, such as bandages and bed pads; and for industrial purposes, such as filters, insulation, and packaging.

TUFTING

The technique of tufting was developed by the early settlers of the southeastern United States. They worked wick ends (trimmed off their homemade candles) into fabrics to give them pile or tufted designs. These became popularly known as candlewick bedspreads. During the 1930's, machinery was developed to mass-produce such fabrics for cotton rugs, robes, and bedspreads. However, tufting was of little significance until 1950, when the first broadloom carpet was made by this technique. Today more than 85 percent of the carpets are produced by this method. Tufting has also been adapted to the manufacture of blankets, and there is much promise for its widespread use for that purpose.

METHOD OF MANUFACTURE ■ Tufting is done by punching extra yarns into a ground fabric of desired weight and yarn content. Rows of needles, each of which carries a yarn from a spool held in a creel, simultaneously punch through the horizontally held fabric to a predetermined distance. As the needles are withdrawn, hooks move forward to hold the loops, thus forming uncut pile. When cut pile is desired, knives that are attached to the hooks move in scissor-like fashion and cut the loops as the needles are drawn up. The fabric moves a predetermined distance forward each time the needles are retracted.

The tufts of yarn are held in place by their own blooming, or untwisting, and by the shrinkage of the ground fabric in the finishing process. In rugs, where there is much abrasion, the back is coated with latex to hold the tufts.

Tufting is extremely rapid and therefore economical. A fabric can be tufted as rapidly as 3 yards per minute; a length of blanket fabric can be made in two minutes; a rug can be tufted at about 645 square yards per minute. Both cut and uncut pile may be combined. Sculptured and textural effects can be obtained by controlling the depths of the individual needle punchings.

MALI FABRIC-FORMING TECHNIQUES

A new method of constructing fabrics has been invented recently. The principle was developed in East Germany by Heinrich Mauersberger, who had been trying to improve a knitting machine. One day he observed his wife mending a threadbare tablecloth with an ordinary sewing machine. She reinforced the cloth by passing it back and forth as the needle moved up and down stitching the fabric. This gave him the idea for his machine, Malimo. (The name was derived from "Ma," the first two letters of his last name, "li" from his home town of Limbach, and "mo" from the German word "molton," meaning the flat, napped woolen fabric known in English as "melton").

The machines have been successfully operated in several European plants and several major American fabric mills are also using them. There are three types of machines: the *Malimo,* which produces flat fabrics; the *Malipol,* which produces pile fabrics; and the *Maliwatt,* which fortifies nonwoven fabrics.

MALIMO TECHNIQUE ■ Essentially, the Malimo constructs a fabric by placing a layer of warp yarns over a layer of filling yarns and locking the criss-crossed layers together with a multiple needle and thread system, using an interlocking chain stitch. This procedure is done at the rate of 1200 to 1400 stitches per minute. As many as 144 filling yarns, or picks, at a time can be fed directly into the machine from creels. This contrasts sharply with the single bobbins used in the shuttle of the conventional loom. The Malimo machine is capable of producing fabrics up to 63 inches wide at speeds of 2 to 3 yards per minute—a rate of about twenty times that of the conventional loom.

In addition to the speed and economy of production, Malimo fabrics constructed in this manner do not ravel and have exceptional resistance to tearing. Since the warp and filling are under less tension than in a loom, it is possible to use yarns with less twist. Also, the need to strengthen the warp yarns by slashing is eliminated. Conventional finishing procedures are used.

Variations in fabric construction are possible. For instance, a two-yarn system or a backing fabric may be used in place of warp threads, and either an

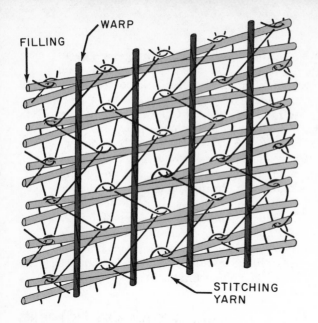

The following diagrams (courtesy Crompton & Knowles-Malimo, Inc.) illustrate the Malimo technique. In the diagram at left, the warp yarns are laid on the filling yarns and the unconnected yarns are joined with an interlocking chain (tricot) stitch to form a solid, ravel-free Malimo fabric.

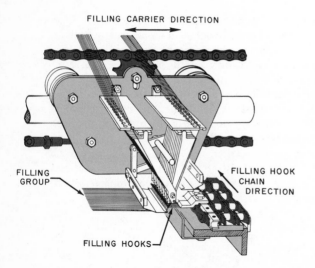

The filling carrier moves back and forth across the width of the fabric being formed and places the group of filling yarns on constantly moving filling-hook chains.

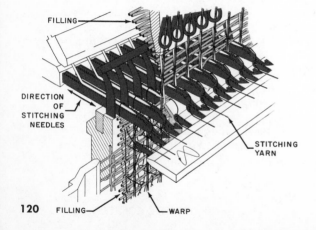

The needles knit the filling and warp yarns together by looping, or stitching, them together with a third yarn.

This side view cross-sectional diagram shows how the filling and warp yarns are stitching together by the Malimo fabric-forming technique.

FILLING

RETAINING PIN

WARP

WARP GUIDE

STITCHING YARN

NEEDLE CLOSING WIRE

STITCHING THREAD GUIDE

STITCHING NEEDLE

FORMED FABRIC

A side view cross-sectional diagram shows how a pile fabric is constructed from a flat backing fabric by stitching loops into it to form a Malipol pile construction.

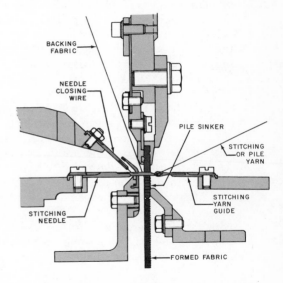

BACKING FABRIC

NEEDLE CLOSING WIRE

PILE SINKER

STITCHING OR PILE YARN

STITCHING NEEDLE

STITCHING YARN GUIDE

FORMED FABRIC

A side view cross-sectional diagram illustrates the Maliwatt technique of stitching a yarn through a batt of loose fibers to form a feltlike fabric.

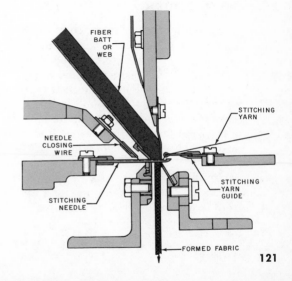

FIBER BATT OR WEB

STITCHING YARN

NEEDLE CLOSING WIRE

STITCHING NEEDLE

STITCHING YARN GUIDE

FORMED FABRIC

interlocking chain stitch or a plain chain stitch may be used, depending upon the desired fabric characteristics. They can be made to resemble closely woven or knitted goods. By varying the counts of filling and warp yarns and the gauge and length of the stitch, an infinite number of fabric weights, constructions, and design effects are possible. The wide range of fabrics produced by the Malimo machine have many uses, including coats and other wearing apparel, blankets, draperies, upholstery, and industrial purposes.

MALIPOL TECHNIQUE ■ Pile fabrics are constructed on the Malipol machine. A backing fabric, or scrim, of either woven, knitted, or Malimo structure is conveyed at full width and under proper tension to the stitching area. Stitching needles then pierce the fabric, and, with the aid of pile sinkers, the stitching yarn is converted into pile loops of predetermined height on one side of the fabric. The stitching or pile yarns can be fed into the machine from beams or creels. Pile heights may be varied from 3/64 inch to 1 inch. Depending upon yarn count and constructions, the Malipol machine is capable of constructing pile fabrics up to 67 inches wide at rates of more than 100 yards per hour.

Exceedingly dense pile can be obtained by this technique. The loops can be cut to form cut-pile fabrics and, since the pile yarns are firmly stitched into the backing fabric, the pile cannot be readily pulled out. Colored stitching yarns may be used to create stripe designs. Fabrics produced include pile linings, imitation furs, blanket materials, floor coverings, and upholstery.

MALIWATT TECHNIQUE ■ By overstitching fiber batting or card webs, the Maliwatt machine rapidly forms a firm fabric. A batt or web of loose fibers is conveyed by a lattice arrangement to the stitching area where it is compacted and interlaced with either an interlocking chain stitch or a plain chain stitch, depending upon the desired fabric characteristics. Additional variations can be achieved through the use of a wide range of yarn counts of any type of fiber.

Maliwatt fabrics, which can be produced as wide as 100 inches, can retain the natural fluffiness of the fibers by regulating the stitching. Feltlike fabrics with various degrees of stiffness can be obtained by impregnating various substances or by using finishing techniques. The fabrics produced are used for interlinings for garments and for industrial purposes.

BRAIDING OR PLAITING

Another form of fabric construction is the diagonal or lengthwise interlacing that is most familiar as the method of braiding or plaiting long hair. Braid is formed on a braiding machine by interlacing three or more strands of yarn so that each strand passes over and under one or more of the others.

Braids are divided into two types: (1) flat braids, in the form of strips or narrow flat tapes; (2) round braids, tubular in form, which may be hollow or have a center core of some material. Both types of braiding are produced from any of the textile fibers, as well as from metal threads, tinsel, straw, wire, or leather. This principle of fabric construction is used for making shaped articles, such as straw hats and small rugs; narrow fabrics, such as ribbons and braids for millinery and accessory dress materials; cords and tapes, such as fishlines, shoelaces, wicks, parachute and glider cords, and elastic of various types; and cord coverings for tires, tubing, hose, wires, and cables.

Netting is an open-mesh form of fabric construction that is held together by knots at each point where the yarns cross one another. The mesh varies in size and type, and ranges from the very open fish net to the finest and most delicate lace designs. The open-mesh construction is characteristic of both nets and laces. The true lace construction is always made with a design. *Bobbinet,* which is a machine-made net with an hexagonal mesh and no design, is not a true lace.

Laces were first made only by hand, and hand laces have always been highly prized as trimming for apparel and as decorative pieces for the home. Unusually beautiful and intricately designed laces are retained in families as heirlooms and are displayed in museums as works of art. Real laces, such as needlepoint, bobbin (pillow), darned, crocheted, and knotted are now duplicated so expertly by machine that the average consumer is not able to determine whether a lace is machine-made or handmade. Linen yarns are generally used for expensive laces, but cotton, silk, rayon, and other yarns are used for other qualities and types. Lace may be made by knotting or by looping, braiding, stitching, or twisting. Machine-made laces are made on the *Leavers, Nottingham, Bobbin,* and *Schiffli* machines.

LEAVERS LACE ■ The Leavers machine, which was invented in 1813, was developed to incorporate the Jacquard principle and other improvements. Today, it can produce the most intricate patterns from any type of yarn into fabrics up to 10 yards wide. Leavers machines produce laces that are used to a great extent in the dress industry.

NOTTINGHAM LACE ■ The Nottingham machine produces a coarser fabric than the Leavers. Its large overall patterns are used for such purposes as table-cloths.

BOBBIN LACE ■ The Bobbin machine employs the braiding principle. The lace produced has a fairly heavy texture, with an angular appearance and a uniform count. Bobbin lace lacks the fine texture and flowing lines of the laces produced by other machines.

SCHIFFLI LACE ■ Although the Schiffli design closely resembles lace, it is produced by an embroidery technique on the Schiffli machine developed in St. Gall, Switzerland. It is produced now by Swiss descendants living in the northeastern part of New Jersey, around Union City.

The machine was named *Schiffli,* which means "little boat," because of the shape of the shuttle. It employs 682 to 1020 needles to produce fine and intricate designs in appliques and embroideries on all kinds of fabrics, particularly sheer fabrics such as batiste, lawn, and organdy. The pattern is controlled by punched cards similar to those used in the Jacquard loom. The finished material has the appearance of expensive handwork but costs much less. The fabrics produced range from narrow trimmings to widths of up to 15 yards, including pile construction.

USES OF LACES ■ Laces may be classified according to their uses into the following categories.

Allover lace has the design spread over the width of the fabric and repeated in its length. Many kinds of design motifs and colors are used. The fabric can be produced in widths of more than one yard that are devoid of scallops. The fabric comes in bolt form and is used for blouses, dresses, and evening wear.

Flouncing comes in 12- to 36-inch widths and is used for ruffles. It has a straight top edge and is scalloped at the bottom.

Galloon has scalloped edges on top and bottom. It comes in widths of up to 18 inches and is used either as a banded applique on a fabric or as an insertion between two pieces of fabric.

Insertion may be sewn either between two pieces of fabric or to the top or bottom edge of a single piece of fabric.

Beading is a narrow galloon, insertion, or edging lace that has openings through which ribbon can be interlaced.

Edging comes in widths of 18 inches or less and has a straight top edge and a scalloped bottom. It is used to trim such garments as dresses, blouses, and lingerie.

Medallion is a single lace design that is used as an applique on a ground fabric for dresses, blouses, lingerie, or napkins.

REVIEW QUESTIONS

1 Describe the felting process.

2 For what purposes is the braided construction used?

3 Why are at least three strands required in braiding?

4 Why is braiding confined to the production of shaped articles?

5 Why is wool preferred in making felt fabric?

6 Why are fur fibers used in the production of expensive felt hats?

7 How is felt used for industrial purposes?

8 How does net differ from woven fabric?

9 What characteristics limit the use of felt for garments?

10 How do nonwovens differ from felt (a) in construction, (b) in fiber content?

11 What are the important properties of nonwovens (other than felt)?

12 What limitations do nonwovens have?

13 Indicate some uses for nonwovens.

14 Compare tufting to the pile weave (a) in construction, (b) in properties?

15 (a) Describe the Malimo construction. (b) What are its main advantages?

16 Distinguish net from lace.

17 Compare the kinds of laces made on the several types of lace machines.

18 Describe the uses for lace.

8 FINISHING PROCESSES

APPEARANCE AND SERVICEABILITY

Newly constructed fabric as it comes from the loom does not represent finished consumers' goods. It must pass through various finishing processes that make it suitable for many different purposes. Finishing enhances the appearance of the fabric and also may add to its serviceability and durability, thus increasing its value. Familiarity with finishing processes enables the consumer to recognize and judge quality in fabrics. The untrained purchaser is influenced too readily by quantity rather than by quality. He is likely to choose the large, the bulky, the heavy. As manufacturers and retailers conduct their businesses to meet existing demand, textile fabrics are finished to a large extent to satisfy this type of purchaser. This explains why many fabrics are "oversized" and others are weighted. If fabric is not properly constructed and if finishing processes are used to conceal inferior construction or to simulate superior quality, the durability of the finished product is questionable.

This does not mean that all finishing is intended to deceive the consumer, for no type of finish should be labeled as spurious until the purpose of the fabric has been considered. A sustained demand for a particular kind of finished fabric usually explains its continued production.

CONVERTING GRAY GOODS

Finishing processes have assumed such great importance in the textile industry that this phase of textile manufacturing is undertaken by a highly specialized group of middlemen called *converters*. Conversion of "gray goods," or goods "in the gray," includes the various types of finishing processes as well as subsequent dyeing and printing.

The converter contracts for a volume purchase of gray goods and converts this unfinished product into finished consumers' goods in accordance with either solicited demand, based on orders taken by his selling force, or with anticipated demand, which is an estimate of the immediate market.

The term *gray goods* does not imply that the fabric is gray in color. It is another form of the term *greige goods*, originally applied only to unfinished silk fabrics, but now used to denote any unfinished fabric as it comes from the loom.

KINDS OF FINISHING PROCESSES

Finishing may take many forms, for it must be adapted to the kind of fiber and yarn used in the fabric and, most important of all, to its intended purpose. One type of gray goods may emerge from a certain finishing process in a form suitable for curtains, while the identical gray goods put through other finishing processes can be used for dress material.

Even the factor of thread count, so important in the evaluation of a fabric, can be changed by the kind and amount of finishing. Cotton can be given the soft finish required for such fabrics as batiste, nainsook, and lawn, the napped finish required for flannelette and duvetyne, the hard stiffened finish typical of cambric and linene, or the lustrous effect of chintz.

The most common finishing processes are listed here. The list does not represent a sequence, nor are all the processes applicable to all kinds of gray goods. Some fabrics must be put through more than one process. Some of the first-named operations are essential preparatory processing for other final finishes, since each fabric is given its own characteristic finishes.

Singeing or gassing	Beetling
Bleaching	Napping
Mercerizing	Gigging
Slack Mercerizing	Shearing
Shrinking	Crepe and crinkled effects
Fulling and other wool-shrinking processes	Shape-retentive finishes
Tentering	Water repellency
Crabbing	Waterproofing
Decating (or decatizing)	Flameproofing
Stiffening	Mothproofing
Weighting	Mildewproofing
Calendering	Antibacterial finishes
Schreinering	Slip resistance
Embossing	Heat-reflectant finishes
Moiréing	Foam laminating
Ciréing	Fabric bonding

SINGEING OR GASSING ■ If a fabric is to have a smooth finish, singeing is one of the first essential preparatory processes. Practically all cotton fabrics, except those that are to be napped, are singed. Spun rayon fabrics are also frequently singed, but wool, silk, and man-made fibers are not because they would form unsightly rough melt balls on the surface of the fabric. Singeing burns off lint and threads as well as all fuzz and fiber ends, leaving an even surface before the fabric passes through other finishing processes or a printing operation.

Singeing is accomplished by passing gray goods rapidly over gas flames, usually two burners to a side, at a speed of 100 to 250 yards per minute. After the cotton cloth leaves the burners, it is pulled through a solution of an enzyme, squeezed out in a heavy mangle, and usually allowed to lay for several hours to allow the enzyme to digest the starch with which the warp yarns were sized. Rayons sized with gelatin do not need any enzyme treatment. In some plants, the singed goods pass directly into a steamer where the sizing is digested rapidly by the heat and moisture.

Singeing may also be done in the yarn stage, especially when the yarns are to be used for fine-quality cotton goods. Usually such yarns are fully mercerized,

Courtesy United Piece Dye Works

As the gray goods passes through the open gas flames of two infrared platens at over 100 yards per minute, hair, fuzz, and lint are singed simultaneously from both faces of the fabric. Singeing produces a smooth fabric surface—prerequisite to flawless dyeing—and eliminates the problem of "balling" in spun rayon fabrics.

and singeing in this case is referred to as *gassing.* Mercerized gassed yarns are sold in the trade as *lisle.* Lisle hosiery was formerly of major importance in both men's and women's styles, but it is being replaced by inexpensive, stronger nylon.

BLEACHING ■ If cloth is to be finished white or is to be given surface ornamentation, all natural color must be removed by bleaching. This is also necessary if discoloration or stains have occurred during the previous manufacturing process. Bleaching can be done in the yarn stage as well as in the constructed fabric. The kind of chemicals to be used depends upon the kind of textile fiber of which the fabric is composed. When cloth has been bleached for finishing, it is called *bleached goods.*

In the case of cotton goods, 85 percent of these fabrics are bleached by continuous peroxide methods. In this system, the singed goods are put through a rapid de-size steamer, washed, impregnated with a mild 3 percent solution of caustic soda, and pulled up into the top of a huge J-shaped container (called a *J-box*) that is equipped to maintain a temperature close to 212 degrees Fahrenheit. The J-box is big enough to hold the goods for at least an hour. After this time period, the fabric is hauled out of the J, given a hot wash, impregnated with a 2 percent solution of hydrogen peroxide, and put in a second J for another hour. Washing follows, and the fabric goes to the dryers fully bleached. Variations on this process include single-J methods, faster routines, and combinations of peroxide and chlorine bleaching.

Some fabrics are bleached by the older method of first boiling off the goods in *kiers,* which are large steel vessels that hold about 5 tons of cloth. The goods are boiled for 12 hours under pressure of a 3 percent solution of caustic soda plus soap and sodium silicate. Then they are washed with cold water, pulled out of the kier, washed again, and "soured" by passing them through a weak solution of sulfuric acid to neutralize the alkali. After another washing, they are passed into a 2 percent solution of sodium hypochlorite and piled into bins or pulled up into J-boxes. After laying there about an hour, they are thoroughly washed, given a "white sour" by running them through a weak solution of sulfur dioxide in water, washed again, and dried for finishing.

All bleaching processes reduce the strength of the fiber. If durability is more important than appearance, the consumer should select gray goods rather than bleached material. With continued laundering, gray goods will gradually become quite white as natural impurities are washed out and the sun bleaches them.

Sunlight is still the primary bleaching aid for fine linens, which are spread out on the grass for several weeks with intermediate washings between "grassings." This process is known as *grass bleaching.* The longer the linen remains in the sunlight, the whiter it gets; however, it correspondingly weakens. Commercially, wool is bleached by *stoving,* a process of exposing the scoured fabric to the fumes of burning sulfur. The material is further whitened by immersing it in a bath of hot hydrogen peroxide for several hours and then thoroughly rinsed. Silk also responds well to peroxide. Both silk and wool tend to yellow with age, and a touch up with peroxide will restore the whiteness.

Man-made fibers as a class require less preparation to whiten. However, not all are easy to bleach. There is little foreign matter in these fibers, but some are inherently off-white and are difficult to whiten. Rayon and acetate are both easy to bleach with either peroxide or chlorine-based bleaches.

Nylon and Zantrel do not respond well to ordinary bleaches. A stronger oxidizing agent, such as peracetic acid or sodium chlorite, is required. The latter is less harmful to the fiber and, in fact, it is beginning to be used extensively in cotton bleaching.

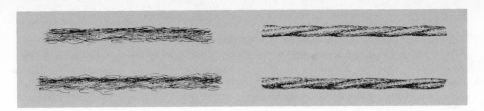

The highly magnified cotton yarn at left shows its appearance *before* gassing and mercerization. Note the dullness of the yarn and the fuzz on its surface. The highly magnified cotton yarn at right shows its appearance *after* gassing and mercerization. Note the smooth, lustrous appearance and absence of fuzz.

The other man-made fibers respond to chlorine or peroxide. The polyesters and most acrylics (Orlon, Acrilan, Creslan, and Zefran) may be bleached with chlorine. Zefran should not be bleached with peroxide; Verel should not be bleached at all. Glass fibers are inert to chemical attack for all practical purposes and do not need bleaching.

In addition to the usual bleaches, mills sometimes utilize *optical bleaches.* Actually, optical bleaches are not true bleaches but fluorescent white chemicals that are absorbed into the fabric and give off a bluish-white light, thereby hiding the yellowish hue.

MERCERIZING ■ Mercerizing is an important preparatory process for cotton fabric. It is also used in the finishing of linen. The fabric is usually singed before mercerizing, but mercerizing can either precede or follow bleaching. Mercerizing causes the flat, twisted, ribbonlike cotton fiber to swell into a round shape and to contract in length. The fiber becomes much more lustrous than the original fiber, and its strength is increased by as much as 20 percent. Its affinity for direct, vat, and reactive dyes is much greater. Sometimes mercerizing is done at low concentrations solely to improve the dye pickup. The improvement more than pays for the cost of processing.

Mercerization can give cotton broadcloth a silklike appearance and cause cotton damask to be mistaken for linen. When lisle yarn or high-quality mercerized yarn is used, a silklike luster results.

The process consists of passing the fabric through a cold 15 to 20 percent solution of caustic soda. It is then stretched out on a tenter frame where hot-water sprays remove most of the caustic. A special washer at the end of the tenter removes the balance of the alkali. The process is continuous. Good results require adequate saturation, sufficient tension (caustic soda induces a 20 percent shrinkage if the fabric is relaxed), and thorough washing.

DURENE FINISH. This is a standardized process of mercerizing that utilizes a fine quality of cotton yarn. Manufacturers who maintain standards established by the Durene Association of America are allowed to label their product "Durene Yarns." These yarns are made of fine long-staple combed cotton and are always of two-ply construction.

SLACK MERCERIZING ■ In order to maintain and expand the important position of cotton in our economy and have cotton keep up with the growth of man-made fibers, the United States Department of Agriculture, at its Southern Regional Research Laboratory in New Orleans, Louisiana, embarked upon an experimental program to impart the property of stretch to cotton. During the early 1960's, an extension or variation of the principle of mercerization was one of the techniques developed (as well as others described on pages 56–57). The technique has been applied to yarn as well as to woven and knitted fabrics and has shown most promise in producing woven fabrics with stretch in the filling direction.

To obtain stretch in the filling direction only, cotton fabric is held under tension in the length, relaxed in the width, and treated with a strong cold caustic soda solution for about one minute. It is then washed in clear water (at or near boiling temperature) and dried. This slack mercerization causes contraction of the yarns not held under tension (in this case, the filling yarns). Subsequently, the dried fabric will stretch from 15 to 20 percent in the filling direction with about 80 percent recovery, in inverse relation to the compactness of construction. Complete recovery occurs with laundering.

This amount of stretch allows comfort and easy movement to the wearer. It is considered adequate for such apparel as shirts, blouses, and dresses. It also provides better-fitting cotton fabrics, despite the lack of complete stretch recovery. Stretch fabrics made by slack mercerization can have four times as much abrasion resistance as untreated fabrics.

Improved stretch and recovery can be obtained by treating the slack mercerized fabric with a wash and wear or cross-linking resin. When a resin is

Cotton filling yarn and cotton fiber in this photo were removed from cotton twill fabric after slack mercerization. Note the crimp in the yarn and in the fiber.

Courtesy U.S. Dept. of Agriculture, Southern Utilization Research and Development Division

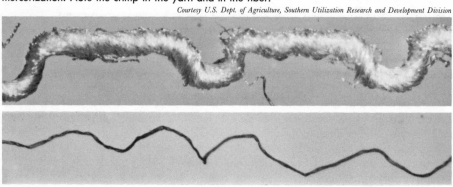

Cotton filling yarn and cotton fiber shown here were removed from plain weave fabric after slack mercerization.

Courtesy U.S. Dept. of Agriculture, Southern Utilization Research and Development Division

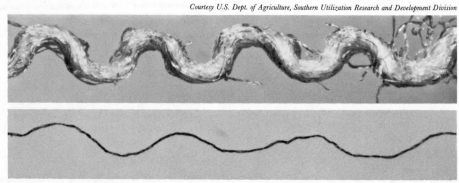

used, however, the fabric loses from 30 to 50 percent of its strength, but techniques are being developed to reduce this loss.

Slack mercerization of knitted goods has been primarily applied to all-cotton hosiery. The hose are loosely knit to about twice the normal length and from 25 to 30 percent less than the normal width. They are then slack mercerized, which causes about 50 percent reduction in the length only and provides a permanent lengthwise stretch quality. The hose are then bleached and dyed. These socks have the properties of good cotton. They have a good hand, are absorbent, and do not bind, but rather cling lightly to the leg. While the hose tend to "grow", or sag, somewhat during a day's wear, they recover their shape with laundering.

SHRINKING ■ When fibers are spun into yarn, they are under constant tension during the weaving process. Their physical condition is changed, but not permanently fixed: the fibers tend to revert to their natural state, causing shrinkage. The yarns are made to assume a final condition by shrinking the fabric in a preparatory finishing process that minimizes subsequent shrinkage, such as immersion in cold water, followed by hot water, steaming, or a chemical treatment. Any such method permits the manufacturer to label his product as preshrunk. But even when textile fabrics are preshrunk, they are liable to further shrinkage when washed. The amount of additional shrinkage that may occur after washing is sometimes stated on the label.

To realize maximum preshrinkage in finishing, the fabric must be given a preshrinking operation in which no tension is exerted while the fabric is damp. General adoption of such preshrinking methods for all fabrics is not feasible. Additional expense is incurred, and in some cases prized qualities inherent in certain fabrics are sacrificed.

In general, the factors that control shrinkage are the stability of the fiber and the construction of the fabric. Construction is based on the type of weave, the amount of twist in the yarn, the thread count, and the yarn count. For example, percales shrink from 3 to 8 percent, depending upon thread count, and flannelettes may shrink 10 percent or more. In terms of fitted garments, a 3 percent shrinkage of a man's shirt would reduce the collar from size 15 to 14½; a 5 percent shrinkage in a woman's dress would reduce size 16 to 14 in general fit and to size 12 in length. The final finishing process also affects shrinkage; for example, a water-repellent quality in a fabric offers resistance to subsequent shrinkage.

If the label on a fabric mentions shrinkage, the fabric must conform to rulings on shrinkage issued by the Federal Trade Commission. One important provision states that if a product is to be labeled preshrunk or shrunk, the label must specifically indicate how much additional shrinkage is to be expected. Formerly, a manufacturer's label reading "fully shrunk" or "will not shrink" or "shrink-proof" did not guarantee that substantially more shrinkage would not take place with continued laundering.

A machine known as a *launderometer* is used to make washing tests in testing laboratories. A similar, though larger, machine is used for determining shrinkage. Measured distances are marked in indelible ink or with fine threads on unwashed samples of the fabric, which are washed in boiling water in cylinder machines. After an interval, the samples are removed, dried, and pressed. Any change in the measurements marked on the samples determines the amount of shrinkage.

Compressive Shrinkage. Compressive shrinkage was originally developed for woven cotton fabrics. A standardized method was first patented by Cluett, Peabody & Co., Inc., under the trademark of *Sanforized Finish,* which reduced the residual shrinkage in cotton and linen to not more than 1 percent. Tests have been developed to ensure that proper application of this process conforms to this standard. The fabric is deliberately shortened in both width and length, resulting in a tighter and closer weave and, consequently, a higher thread count. The process is carried out on a machine about 65 feet long in the following manner.

1. Normal shrinkage is determined by subjecting a test sample of the fabric to ordinary washing conditions, using the United States Government wash test.
2. Careful measurements before and after the wash test indicate how much the fabric shrinks in length and width.
3. The compressive-shrinkage machine is set to shrink the fabric to the exact dimensions that the wash test indicated.
4. The fabric is dampened with pure water and live steam, which soften it in preparation for the adjustments to be made in length and width.
5. The width is adjusted by a stretching action, in which the fabric is gripped along its selvages.
6. The fabric is then held firmly against a heavy wool blanket, which is under controlled tension.
7. As the tension of the blanket is relaxed to the desired measurements, the fabric shrinks uniformly in length.
8. The fabric is then carried around a heated drum while drying, and the surface finish is restored.
9. A sample is tested again to make certain that additional shrinkage will not exceed 1 percent.

A process similar to this is identified by the Springs Mills, Inc., under the trademark of *Springshrunk.* It also has a maximum residual shrinkage of 1 percent.

Another method of mechanical shrinking, somewhat similar to compressive shrinkage, is *Rigmel,* which was developed and patented by the Bradford Dyeing Association. A cotton fabric is put through a standard wash test to determine the precise potential shrinkage in inches per yard, and it is subsequently shrunk to planned dimensions that anticipate a residual shrinkage of a 1 percent maximum.

Rayon fabrics may also be preshrunk by a process known as *Sanforsetting.* This term has a resemblance to the term Sanforized, which shrinks cotton up to 1 percent. Both processes are owned by the same company and are somewhat similar. Sanforsetting, however, has a residual shrinkage of not more than 2 percent.

Compressive shrinkage techniques have more recently been developed for cotton knitted goods. The Compax Corporation developed and patented the trademark process of *Pak-nit,* which guarantees less than 1 percent shrinkage in length. The process compacts the fabric in a specially designed machine by running it through rollers operating at progressively slower rates of speed, which causes overfeeding of the fabric and consequent lengthwise compression. In effect, this compression forces fabric shrinkage in advance, thus eliminating the usual shrinkage due to finishing and laundering.

A related shrinkage-control technique for cotton knitted goods is the *Redmamized* finish developed by F. R. Redman Company. The fabric is dampened and stretched widthwise to reorient the knitted loops, and then dried in a tension-less state by blasts of air, which causes a permanent shortening of the loops. A shrinkproofing process developed for, and applied to, knitted cotton goods that has proved to be effective is the *Perma-sized* finish.

Cylinder Method. This method for shrinking wool uses two perforated cylinders, which steam the fabric as it is rolled off one cylinder and rewound on the other. The steamed fabric is then wound loosely around a wood roller, where it dries and cools slowly and naturally.

London Shrinking. London shrinking is a cold-water process of preshrinking wool fabrics. Lengths of wool fabric are retained between wet blankets for about twenty hours while the moisture of the blankets penetrates into the fibers of the cloth. The cloth is then dried slowly and subsequently subjected to a hydraulic pressure of about 3,500 pounds. Cold-water shrinking originated in London. It is considered one of the best methods.

Chlorination Process. This is a chemical method of treating wool so that the fabric will be shrink proof. The wool fabric is treated with a dilute solution of calcium or sodium hypochlorite. Some of the scales of the fibers are removed, causing fusion of the outer and inner part of the fibers. As a result, shrinkage decreases. When this protective scaly covering is removed, however, the felting quality is lessened, and the durability of the fabric is affected. But luster and affinity for dyes are increased. Steaming or fulling does not have this result. Chlorinated wool is chiefly used in woolen underwear, socks, and sweaters. Among the trade names for this process are *Harriset, Hypol, Kelpie, Kroy, Sanforlan, Schollerizing,* and *Protonizing.*

A variation of this process is *Drisol,* which utilizes the action of chlorine gas from sulfuryl chloride to shrink-proof wool.

Chemical Treatment. A method that works on wool fiber in much the same way as the chlorination processes is based on treating the wool in a solution of potassium permanganate, which is also nearly saturated with common salt. The salt confines the reaction of the permanganate to the surface of the wool. Excellent shrinkage control is possible. The process is called the *McFee* method, for the inventor, who is connected with the Commonwealth Scientific Research and Development Institute in Australia.

Resin Treatment. By adding certain thermosetting resins (mostly based on melamine) to wool fabrics, shrinkage can be controlled to a considerable extent. The resin is cured in the fiber and tends to prevent slippage of the fibers past

The effect of chlorination on wool fiber serations, left to right: unmodified, slightly modified, modified, severely modified.

Courtesy CIBA Review

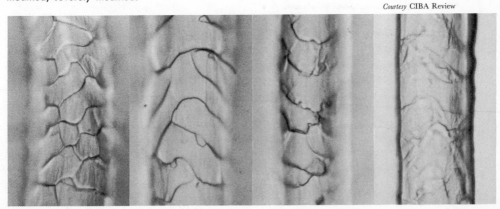

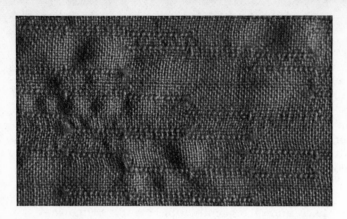

Uneven tension on the filling or warp ends in weaving can result in "bubbling" when relaxation shrinkage occurs unevenly in dry cleaning or steam pressing. The problem cannot always be corrected by pressing, especially when the finish, which had a stabilizing effect on the fabric, has been disturbed.

Courtesy CIBA Review

each other in any wet processing. The hand of the fabric may be affected, and shrinkage control cannot be predicted for all types of fabric. The goal is a residual shrinkage of 2 percent, but these resin systems are not much used at this time. Some trade names for the process include *Resloom, Lanaset,* and *Pacifixed.*

Another method recently developed for controlling the shrinkage of wool is the *Wurlan* process. This method was developed by the Western Regional Research Laboratory of the United States Department of Agriculture. Wool fabric is passed through a diamine, squeezed out, and then passed through a solution of an diacyl chloride. By a process of interfacial polymerization, a nylontype resin is formed on the surface of the wool fibers. The film is extremely thin and needs no further treatment. Other polymers can be applied in the same way. Among these are the polyurethanes, polyureas, polycarbonates, and polyesters. The process shows a good deal of promise, and has been commercially successful in a small way. Based upon this technique, J. P. Stevens & Co. has introduced its washable-wool process under the trademark *Stevens H₂O*. The maximum residual shrinkage in the first three washes are guaranteed not to exceed 3 percent, with negligible shrinkage thereafter. The garments are automatic machine washable. They should be washed in warm water in a normal wash cycle, spun dried, and dried further by hanging the garment on a line.

FULLING ■ The process of fulling, an important operation in the finishing of wool fabrics, actually operates as a preshrinking process for wool. The fibers are cleaned, scoured, and condensed by a combination of moisture, heat, soap, and pressure. Sometimes, chemicals are added to increase the adhesion of the fibers. The condensing is a natural result of the felting property of wool fiber—shrinkage takes place because the fibers are drawn together. As a result, the fabric has a fuller, more compact body.

TENTERING ■ This process is applied at various stages of finishing. Usually, the fabric is wet when it is run into a tenter; drying and evening of the fabric width are the primary purposes of *tentering*. The tenter frame consists of two endless chains carried in rugged rails with a distance between them that can be adjusted. The chains are equipped with clips or pins, which grip the selvage of the fabric and carry it into the heated housing where a blast of hot air removes any moisture. Pin frames are mostly used on woolens or knitted goods; clip frames are favored for cotton. The tiny holes or marks of the clips are sometimes noticeable in the selvages of yard goods. Tentering is a continuous operation in

Courtesy United Piece Dye Works

After being relaxed during dyeing and finishing, all fabrics are coaxed back to normal width on a tentering frame. The endless chain of ''mechanical fingers,'' or tenter-frame clips, grips the fabric selvages on entering the machine, which has been set for the narrowest width of the fabric. Gently but firmly, the fingers stretch the fabric to a predetermined width as it passes down the widening 60- to 120-foot length of the tenter, over live steam and subsequently heat, which dries and sets the fabric.

that the goods enter one end of the frame, usually 90 feet long, and emerge from the other. The frame is equipped in most modern plants with devices that straighten the filling and keep it at right angles to the warp, thus avoiding biased goods.

CRABBING ■ In finishing wool fabrics, a stretching process called *crabbing* passes the cloth over rollers into hot water or steam. The fabric is then put into cold water, after which it is pressed. This process is similar to tentering, as the fabric is stretched or loosened where necessary and finally set at the width at which the warp and filling yarns are in proper relation to each other. Consequently, there is no hidden strain on any portion of the fabric. Crabbing also prevents the formation of creases or other forms of uneven shrinkage in subsequent finishing operations.

DECATING ■ A finishing process that may be applied to wool fabrics to set the nap and develop the luster is called *decating*, or *decatizing*. In wet decating, the material is tightly wound on a perforated iron roller and immersed in a trough of hot water that is circulated through the fabric. In dry decating, steam is used instead of hot water. Decating may be applied to rayon and other manmade fabrics to improve the hand, color, and luster of the fabric, or to overcome uneven or blotchy dyeing.

TEMPORARY STIFFENING ■ Cotton and linen can be given stiffness, smoothness, weight, and strength by immersion in a solution of starch. This process is commonly known as *starching*. A small amount of starch in consumers' goods (especially cotton fabrics) helps to retain freshness while they are on the dealers' shelves. Cotton fabrics that are usually starched are organdy, lawn, voile, and buckram. Some starching is acceptable, but the consumer should avoid purchasing fabrics that have too much starch because it could conceal inferior construction. Starch fills in the openings in the constructed cloth, creating an appearance of greater compactness; thus, a low thread count is not immediately discernible at the time of purchase. If a fabric loses body after one or more washings, it has been overstarched.

Excessive starching can be detected by rubbing the fabric between the hands, which causes the starch to come off in the form of a fine powder. An absolute test for any starching can be made by touching the fabric with a drop of weak iodine; if starch is present, a blue color appears.

Other substances used for stiffening fabrics are flour, dextrine, glue, shellac, fats, wax, and paraffin. The starches give weight; glue gives stiffness; fats give softness; wax and paraffin produce luster. Starch that is baked brown before using is known as *dextrine,* or *British gum;* in this form, it gives a soft dressing to a fabric.

Cotton fabrics are sometimes stiffened with clay chalk, barium sulfate, calcium sulfate, or magnesium sulfate to make them especially heavy and close in texture. Some stiffenings, such as starch, make cotton fabrics susceptible to mildew, but this tendency can be offset by the addition of zinc chloride to the sizing bath.

In addition to starch, soluble oils and fats are often used to modify the stiffness of the starch and to develop a more pleasing feel to the fabric. In some cases, the starch is applied to the back of the goods only in an operation called *back starching*. This finish is used for low-count printed goods that require considerable loading but also must retain a bright print pattern. Cheap mattress ticking is often finished in this manner. Along with the starch, these finishes require a lot of talc, China clay, sulfonated oil, and a binder to hold the starch in the fabric.

Other terms used in referring to temporary stiffening are *sizing* and *dressing*. While both terms are generally used today in preparing the warp for weaving, the term "dressing" usually applies to the warp of wool.

PERMANENT STIFFENING ■ Permanent-stiffening effects can be achieved by chemical processes that change the cellular structure of the fiber. By this method, sheer and medium-weight cottons are given stiffness, which sometimes lasts throughout the life of the fabric. These processes are known by specific trade names. They vary in method, in the chemicals used, and in the degree of permanency of the final finish. All have the property of making the fabric smoother, and it soils less easily because dirt tends to slide off rather than to cling. As a result, fabrics with permanent sizing usually require less laundering and may therefore last longer. Some of these permanent finishes are as follows.

ANKORD. Ankord, a starchless finish given to cotton and rayon gray goods, increases tensile strength, improves luster, and reduces shrinkage.

CLEARIGHT. This is a starchless process that imparts lasting crispness. Clearight is generally used on sheer fabrics.

KANDARIZED. This process imparts a permanent crispness and abrasion resistance.

SAYLERIZING. Saylerizing is a starchless finish similar to Bellmanizing. It gives permanent crispness to medium-weight as well as to sheer cottons.

SHEERCROFT. Sheercroft is a starchless finish that imparts crispness and increases luster, giving cotton a linenlike appearance.

STABILIZED. The Stabilized process gives a finish similar to sizing. It also adds body to spun rayon and to cotton, but the finish is not permanent.

STAZE-RIGHT. This finish gives luster and crispness to organdies and marquisettes and is resistant to washing and dry cleaning.

BASCO. This starchless finish increases strength and gives permanent luster and a linenlike appearance to fabrics.

TRUBENIZING. Trubenizing is a patented process that prevents wilting in collars and cuffs. Fabric made of acetate yarns is used to interline the collars and cuffs, which are then immersed in acetone and pressed with a hot iron; the result is a permanent stiffness that does not require starching. This process also gives rise to the term *fused* collars and cuffs.

WEIGHTING ■ Silk may be treated with tin salts to increase the weight of the fabric and improve its hand and drape. The weight and body of the fabric are increased by immersing it in a solution containing metallic salts. The salts permeate the yarns and become a permanent part of the fabric but cannot be detected by handling. If excessive metallic salts are used in the weighting, they eventually weaken the fabric. The Federal Trade Commission has issued specific regulations with respect to kinds of weighting and their proper labeling.

Only low-grade wool fabrics are weighted. As much as 40 percent additional weight can be obtained by felting extremely short wool fibers into the fabric. These fibers, called *flocks,* are obtained when wool fabrics are washed, brushed, and sheared. An excessive amount of flocks can be detected by brushing and shaking the fabric vigorously. Careful examination of the selvage will also reveal flock particles. Treating wool fabric with magnesium chloride causes an excessive water content, referred to as "watered stock."

Napped cotton goods may also be adulterated by adding flocks. These flocks, forced into the fabric under air pressure, can be detected by brushing and shaking.

CALENDERING ■ Calendering is essentially an ironing process that adds sheen to the fabric. The method varies according to the type of finish desired. Calenders are heavy machines made up of at least two rolls. One is usually of chilled steel; the other, of a softer material like wool paper, cotton fiber, corn husks, or combinations of cotton and corn husk. The rolls are supported in vertical frames. Plain rolling calenders may have as many as seven rolls—four steel and three corn husk or cotton. The steel rolls may be equipped to be heated by gas or steam. In operation, the goods pass rapidly between the nips formed by the rolls. This is done at an average rate of 150 yards per minute, and under pressure of 40–60 tons and sometimes 100 tons; the goods are then wound up on the back of the machine.

Courtesy Pepperell Manufacturing Co.

Close-up of a rolling calender, showing cloth passing through the nip formed by the heavy rolls, which exert a smoothing and pressing action.

Another type of calender that is used to produce glazed finishes is the friction calender, which is geared so that the highly polished, hot steel roll goes faster than the goods passing through the nip.

Some rolling calenders are set up to pass the cloth through one nip several times so that the pressures built up in the calender nips are transferred to three or four layers of cloth at once. This operation is called *chasing,* and was once highly favored for broadcloth shirtings. Unfortunately, to get the best effect of this process, it has to be done after shrinking the fabric, and it invariably stretches the fabric so that it cannot be guaranteed to have only 1 percent residual shrinkage.

Near right: untreated wool fabric showing heavily crimped fibers that are not aligned longitudinally and are devoid of lustre. Far right: uncurled, parallelized, and highly lustrous wool fibers after treatment with Wool Lustring Agent CIBA. Below: schematic drawing of a lustring machine.

Courtesy CIBA Review

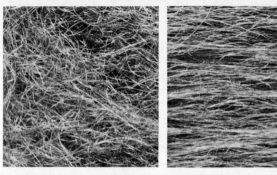

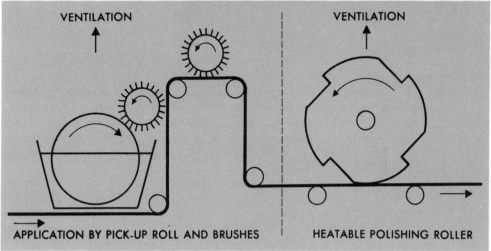

VENTILATION · VENTILATION

APPLICATION BY PICK-UP ROLL AND BRUSHES · HEATABLE POLISHING ROLLER

GLAZING ■ A stiff polished or glazed surface can be obtained by the application of starch, glue, mucilage, or shellac followed by friction calendering. The process makes a fabric resistant to dust and spots and minimizes shrinkage. This finish is found principally on chintz. *Vita-glaze* is a typical trademark.

Wool fabrics are sometimes calendered or polished. The process adds a soft luster. Typical of such fabrics are wool broadcloth and sheen gabardine.

SCHREINERING ■ *Schreinering* is an inexpensive method for imparting luster to low-priced cottons. Steel rollers, finely engraved with lines and exerting a pressure of 4,500 pounds, impress on the fabric diagonal ridges ranging from 125 to 600 to the inch. Reflection of light from these ridges gives the fabric a lustrous effect somewhat similar to that produced by mercerization. But the luster produced by schreinering is not permanent, because the imprinted ridges disappear with repeated launderings. This finish is suitable, however, for lingerie fabrics and for linings and sateens, as the slightly rough surface produced by the diagonal ridges reduces the tendency of fabrics to cling. If the fabric has been mercerized, the additional schreinering produces a luster simulating that of silk.

EMBOSSING ■ The process of producing raised figures or designs in relief on surfaces of fabrics by passing the cloth between heated engraved rollers is known as *embossing*. The process can be applied to fabrics made of all types of fibers with the exception of wool. This finish is permanent when applied to fabrics made of thermoplastic fibers. It is not permanent when applied to untreated fabrics made of natural fibers or man-made fibers that are not thermoplastic; however, if these fabrics are treated with certain chemical resins, the embossing is considered to be permanent. To preserve the embossed finish of such fabrics, they should be washed in lukewarm water with a mild soap, never be bleached, and be ironed on the wrong side while damp.

When plain-woven fabrics treated with these chemical resins are embossed, they can resemble fabrics that are generally more expensive. The decorative effects also enhance the beauty of the cloth. Various trade names, such as *Picolay* and *Clokay,* have been given to particular fabrics of this type. There have also been trade names, such as *Everglaze,* which apply to a group of fabrics similarly treated to produce a variety of effects.

MOIRÉING ■ Attractive, lustrous wavy designs known as *moiré* can be produced by a process that is essentially one of minute surface embossing or pressing of a fabric with crenellated, or ridged, rollers. The best moiré results are obtained on fabrics that have rib effects in the filling. The pattern is imprinted on the raised filling yarns by rollers, which exert over 100,000 pounds pressure to the square inch. The luster is produced by the divergent reflection of light on the impressed lines of the design.

The technique requires the fabric to be cut lengthwise in two. The matched halves are rolled up on separate wooden rolls, or shells, passed over a wavy ridged bar under considerable tension, and wound up together. They are then put through a heavy, heated steel calender, and the patterns that have been induced in the goods by shifting the filling locally over the crenellated bar are embossed on the goods. The reason for cutting the fabric in two is that no two looms weave exactly alike, and it is upon the exactness of the spacing of the filling threads in the original piece that good moiré depends. Patterned moiré is done by passing the goods over a rubber roll engraved in relief with the pattern, while at the same time a brush engages the outside surface of the fabric and shifts the filling at the outlines of the engraving. The width of the moiré stripes is determined by the width of the crenellations in the bar used.

A moiré pattern on a rayon fabric is not permanent. Silk holds the pattern longer but will gradually diminish. Dry cleaning is recommended.

On acetate, moiré is definitely permanent because acetate fabrics have a melting reaction when subjected to the heat of the moiréing process, thus conforming and hardening to the pattern as the cloth cools. A similar condition can be obtained with nylon because of its tendency to melt and to hold a shape.

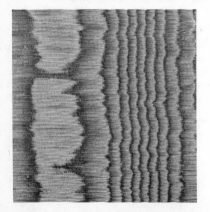

The best moiré results are obtained by imprinting the pattern on ribbed fabrics. Luster is produced by divergent reflections of light on the lines of the design.

Courtesy American Viscose Corporation

An entirely different method of moiréing cotton is obtained by treating the fabric with a chemical and then embossing the cloth. The moiré is permanent provided the fabric is cared for properly. It should be washed with a mild soap in lukewarm water and never should be bleached.

CIRÉING ■ The *ciré* process may be applied to silk and rayon, usually satins and taffetas. Wax or a similar compound is applied to the fabric, followed by hot calendering. The result is a supergloss almost metallic in appearance.

BEETLING ■ *Beetling* is a common finishing process for linen. The yarns are flattened by the impact of wooden mallets. This hammering actually closes the weave and gives the cloth a firm, flattened, lustrous appearance. All table linen is put through this process, but dress linens are never beetled.

Beetling differs from calendering. The smoothness and gloss obtained by the calendering process are the result of horizontal pressing and are not permanent; in beetling, the action performed is a vertical impact that permanently flattens the yarns.

Cotton fabrics can be made to simulate linen by beetling, as the process gives cotton the firm feel and lustrous appearance of linen.

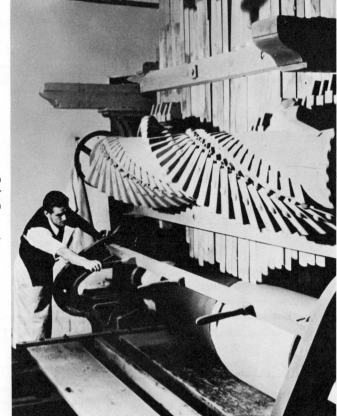

"Beetles" are great wooden blocks, used to beat the cloth for as long as 60 hours to give Irish linen its permanent sheen.

Courtesy Irish Linen Guild

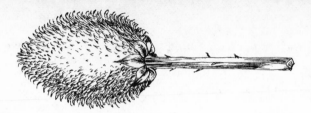

The teasel, a dried flower head with stiff, hooked bracts, is used to produce the fuzzy surface on napped fabrics.

NAPPING ■ A napped fabric should not be confused with a pile-weave fabric. In the pile weave, the thickness is a true third dimension produced by loops from an extra warp or filling yarn. In the napped fabrics, the thickness is only a surface fuzziness that is the result of a brushing process. When a fabric is to be napped, the yarns intended for the construction of the cloth are given only a slack twist in the spinning process.

The fuzzy finish produced by napping makes a soft fabric, which provides warmth because of the insulative air cells in the nap. The thicker the nap, the more air cells, and the warmer the fabric. In men's suitings, where long wear is desired, a napped surface acts as a protection against objectionable luster. The fact that stains can be removed easily from a napped surface is an additional advantage. On the other hand, napping may also serve to cover up a sleazy construction as well as weaving imperfections. It is generally considered that excessive napping tends to weaken the fabric, especially where a heavy nap has been produced.

Single napping signifies that both sides of a cloth have been napped in one direction; *double napping* signifies that both surfaces have been napped in opposite directions, which produces greater surface density, increased firmness, and greater warmth. Flannelette, wool flannel, suede cloth, and duvetyne exemplify napped fabrics. Cotton and spun rayon fabrics are napped when a soft, fuzzy surface is desired.

Vegetable burrs called *teasels* are used for napping finer grades of wool fabrics. Long cylindrical rollers containing closely set wires, which act like brushes, also perform the teaseling operation. As the brushes slide over the revolving fabric, they pull the top fibers and raise the protruding ends above the surface of the cloth in the form of a fleecelike nap. If a heavy nap is desired, teaseling is repeated several times.

Gigging. Wool fabrics may be napped, or they may be subjected to a raising process called *gigging*. The fabric is first saturated with water. When the fibers of a moist wool fabric are raised, they tend to curl and shrink. When brushed in one direction, a smooth and lustrous appearance results.

SHEARING ■ Pile-weave fabrics and fabrics that have been napped are usually sheared to give an attractive smooth surface to the cloth. Shearing levels all surface irregularities caused by the plucking action of the teasels in the napping process. Shearing is done by a cylindrical machine having rotating spiral blades whose action resembles that of a lawn mower. After shearing, the fabric is automatically brushed to remove the sheared ends of the yarns.

CREPE AND CRINKLED EFFECTS ■ Permanent-type crepe effects are obtained by using hard-twisted yarns in the weaving process, as described in Chapter 5. Crepe surfaces can also be produced by certain finishing processes, but the results are not so satisfactory. One finishing method imprints a crinkled effect by means of engraved rollers, similar to that produced when the thumbnail is drawn across tissue paper. The finish disappears with repeated washings, however.

In another finishing method, caustic soda is impressed on the fabric in the form of figures or stripes. The fabric is then washed. The part imprinted with the soda shrinks, and the other part puckers. A similar effect is obtained by using strips of wax in place of the caustic soda. *Plissé* crepes are produced by these methods. The degree of permanency of these crepe effects can be detected by pressing the thumb heavily on a portion of the fabric and stretching it sidewise at the same time. The ease with which the pressed portion will be smoothed, leaving no or little ripple on its surface, will indicate the relative permanency of the crepe.

A chemical method gives a crepe effect to silk by treating the fabric with concentrated sulfuric acid for a few minutes, followed by rinsing and neutralization with a weak alkali. There is a decrease in luster and a slight loss in strength. This method calls for careful manipulation, because too long an exposure in the acid injures the silk.

A permanent crinkle may be obtained on a fabric that will melt, such as nylon. The fabric is put through a hot roller on which there are raised figurations. The contact of the fabric against the raised hot surfaces causes it to melt and pucker at those points.

Crepe fabrics tend to stretch and shrink when subjected to any wetting operation.

A rotating spiral blade shears irregularities from napped and pile fabrics. A brush (shown in lower part of photo) removes the sheared ends.

Courtesy National Associated Wool Industries

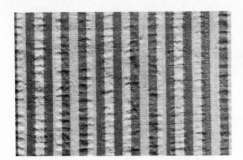

Courtesy American Viscose Corporation

Seersucker (left) shows crinkled effect obtained by the use of slack warp yarns. Matelassé (right) shows crinkled effect produced by the Jacquard.

SHAPE-RETENTIVE FINISHES ■ Unlike wool, silk, and man-made thermoplastic fibers, the cellulosic cotton, linen, and rayon fibers do not have good resilience. Fabrics of cellulosic fibers lack the ability to retain their shape—they wrinkle and crush easily. To make them competitive with other fibers in a market that demands easy care for apparel, a variety of shape-retentive finishes have been developed.

The initial process was for the purpose of making spun-rayon fabrics *wrinkle-resistant*. This was followed by similar treatment for cotton and linen. With further development, chemical finishes were added to cotton fabrics for what has become known as *wash and wear* cottons. A further extension of this is the recent development of *permanent press,* which is used on cotton and cotton-blend fabrics as well as wool and wool-nylon blends.

Wrinkle-Resistant Finishes. These finishes are also sometimes referred to as crease-resistant finishes. Actually, the term *crease-resistant* is a misnomer since the purpose of this finish is to prevent deformation of the fabric by undesirable and unintentionally introduced folds and rumples. The purpose is to keep the fabric flat and smooth as compared to creases or pleats that are deliberately placed in a fabric. Some finishes are more wrinkle-resistant than others, but fabrics treated with any of these finishes tend to smooth out when properly hung after wearing.

Durable wrinkle-resistant finishes have been developed for cotton and linen and to a lesser extent for rayon. These finishes are all based on resins or reactants that will combine chemically with the fiber through a process known as *cross-linking,* whereby adjacent molecular chains of cellulose in the fiber are linked or tied together to provide greater molecular rigidity and to prevent intermolecular slippage. The original chemical finish used was urea-formaldehyde; then came melamine formaldehyde and a host of variations on both basic chemicals including formaldehyde. These had a distinct disadvantage of giving off a fish odor, particularly when wet.

The latest reactants are based on vinyl sulfones and on epichlorohydrin. The latter confers only wet wrinkle-resistance, although experimental work has produced a technique that provides both wet and dry wrinkle-resistance. In the meantime, dry wrinkle-resistance is obtained by aftertreating the fabric with a resin like dimethylolethylene urea.

All of these finishes reduce by 30 to 50 percent the tensile and tear strength of the fabrics to which they are applied, as well as reduce the abrasion resistance.

This is due to the resultant "brittleness" of the fiber caused by the cross-linkage of the molecular chains. Also, the fiber becomes less absorptive and garments of such finished material are less comfortable in humid weather. The United States Department of Agriculture and other interested groups are now working on other techniques that will produce the desired wrinkle-resistant effect without cross-linkage and the concomittant disadvantages.

The durability of a finish depends upon its quality, the amount of fabric saturation, the care in applying and oven-curing it, as well as the care with which the consumer follows the instructions on the garment label. Of the many patented processes on the market, several of the better known are as follows.

ANTICREASE FINISH. In the anticrease process, a solution of formaldehyde resins is baked into the cloth, penetrating the fibers and resulting in a softened flexible fabric. Fabrics so treated are not absolutely wrinkle-resistant, but they resist crushing, recover easily, and tend to shrink less in laundering. Because of the added weight of the resin, drapability is increased. This finish may be used on cotton, linen, rayon, and acetate fabrics.

BOUNCE. This is a permanent wrinkle-resistant finish for cottons.

PRESTWICK. This is a permanent formaldehyde type of finish that imparts wrinkle resistance and dimensional stability to cottons, rayons, and blends.

PERMA-PRESSED. A wrinkle-resistant process applied to cotton fabrics.

UNIDURE. This finish is applied to spun rayons to avoid excessive wrinkles. Wrinkles that do occur will hang out. Unidure adds body to the fabric and improves the brightness and fastness of color. It also reduces shrinkage and stretch and is not affected by dampness and wilting weather.

WAT-A-SET. This is a wrinkle-resistant finish for cotton fabrics.

WRINKLE-SHED. This process gives cottons an excellent wrinkle-resistant property. It is difficult to wrinkle such cotton fabrics, and any wrinkles will hang out overnight.

VITALIZED FINISH. The Vitalized finish, also known by its English trade name *Tebelized,* is a patented wrinkle-resistant process similar to the Anticrease finish. It gives additional "vitality," or elasticity, by the use of synthetic resins. It is applicable to both cotton and linen cloth. Fabrics so treated are heavier and shrink less. Washing or dry cleaning does not affect the finish.

ZESET. This wrinkle-resistant finish also provides dimensional stability to cotton and rayon fabrics. The finish is not chlorine-retentive, and white fabrics will not yellow when bleached.

Wash and Wear Finishes. These are also referred to as drip-dry finishes. They are of the same types as the wrinkle-resistant finishes. Garments made of fabrics with wash and wear finishes will dry smooth and need little or no ironing after washing, depending upon the quality of the finish and the construction. The fabrics have a good, soft hand and a neat appearance. Wash and wear finishes have been used primarily on broadcloth and oxford shirting but are also applicable to other types of cotton fabrics.

Each company has its own trade name for its drip-dry finish, and its effectiveness depends on the particular process. Among the most widely advertised finishes are AMC—Bradford, Arrow Wash-and-Wear 100% Cotton, Belfast, Dri-Smooth, Manhattan Mansmooth, Minicare, Sanforized Plus, Van Heusen Vantage All Cotton, and Vanalux.

Garments made of fabrics treated with drip-dry finishes usually may be commercially laundered. The primary advantage, however, is that such garments launder easily at home and need no ironing. This tends to increase their wear since home laundering is less harsh. In some cases, it is advisable to use a mild soap. Since some wash and wear finishes cause yellowing when a chlorine bleach is used, labels should be carefully read before using a bleach. Do not wring the garments or spin-dry them in a washing machine or in a dryer. Rinse them well, hang them on wooden or plastic hangers, buttoned and straightened out, and allow them to drip-dry. Metal hangers may cause rust stains.

Not all drip-dry finishes produce the same results. Some garments tend to pucker at the seams when they dry; some require quick, light ironing with a cool iron. Since the care of drip-dry finished garments varies with the particular finish, read the instructions on the garment tag to determine which is best suited to your needs. In any event, follow the care instructions for most satisfactory results.

It should be noted that not all fabrics that have drip-dry characteristics have a wash and wear finish. Some fabrics (studied in later chapters) are constructed entirely of thermoplastic man-made fibers or of such fibers in blends with natural fibers. The extent to which garments made of such fabrics will drip-dry and have shape retention is dependent on the inherent properties of the fibers and on the proportion of thermoplastic fibers in the fabric—not on the finish.

Permanent-Press Finishes. The latest development in shape-retentive finishes is the *permanent press,* also referred to as *PP* and *delayed,* or *deferred, cure.* They are the outgrowth of the manufacturers' difficulty in shaping wrinkle-resistant goods —that is, pressing creases into trousers and putting pleats in skirts made of such material. To overcome this difficulty, processes have been developed so that, generally, the fabric is treated or sensitized with the finish but not cured or set for permanent shape-retention until after the garment has been constructed.

Presently, all the finishes contain some type of cross-linking chemical, which reduces by 30 to 50 percent the strength and durability of all-cotton fabrics. The permanent crease itself represents a particularly weak spot with further reduced abrasion resistance. In dyed goods, this weakness will first appear as a light-colored streak. One way to lessen abrasion is to launder the garment inside out, since this will reduce the wear on the crease.

Since the cross-linkage occurs only in cellulosic fibers, the loss of strength can be reduced by blending cotton or rayon with polyester fiber. A blend of at least 50 percent polyester fiber with 50 percent cotton or rayon is required for significant strength retention. A blend of 65 percent polyester fiber with 35 percent cotton will result in only about 10 percent strength reduction due to the finish. The polyester fiber also improves the abrasion resistance, hand, and appearance, as well as color and styling potential.

There are a number of permanent-press finishes on the market, and they may be readily identified by their trademarks. As indicated in the descriptions that follow, their methods of processing and their characteristics vary. These trademarks apply to both all-cotton and cotton-polyester blends, and the ultimate properties are affected accordingly.

KORATRON. The Koratron Company, Inc., was the pioneer in this field, introducing a permanent-press finish commercially in 1963. The patented process, utilizing the cross-linking chemical imidazolidone and produced under the trademark of Permafresh 183, impregnates the fabric at the mill or finishing plant. The cloth is dried at low temperature so as not to obtain a chemical reaction that would cure or set the finish. The sensitized goods are then shipped to the garment manufacturer.

Under strict quality control of Koratron, the manufacturer cuts and sews the garments, over-sizing them up to a half size. This is done to offset shrinkage during oven-curing. Koratron sensitized zippers, waistbanding, and pocketing material are used. The garments are pressed into shape with specially designed pressers. Pants, for example, are pressed with the proper roundness at the waist, shape at the hip, smoothness at the seams, and sharpness at the crease. At this point, the curing occurs and produces a "memory-shaping," or shape-retentive, quality. The garments, placed on special hangers, are then put on a conveyor and passed through an oven where heat of about 320 degrees Fahrenheit permanently sets the shape given on the pressing machine. Quality testing is maintained by washing and drying samples of garments five times and evaluating them for smoothness of surface, lack of puckering, smoothness of zipper area, sharpness of crease, overall appearance, and dimensional stability.

STA-PREST. This is the trademark of Levi Straus & Co., which employs the Koratron process under license.

SUPER-CREASE. This is the trademark of the patented process developed by J. P. Stevens & Co., Inc. It utilizes a sulfone cross-linking chemical that eliminates chlorine-retention and unpleasant odors. The hand of the fabric is not affected.

The process is similar to the deferred-cure method described previously. The fabric is padded with the sulfone chemical that cross-links with the cellulose when the fabric is passed through an alkaline solution. The cloth can also be Sanforized. After the garment is cut, sewed, and pressed, it is oven-cured for permanent shape-retention.

DAN-PRESS. This is the deferred-cure process of Dan River Mills, Inc. To overcome shrinkage during the process, trousers, for example, must be oversized ¼ inch at the inseam and at the waistband. Dan-Press fabrics are made of cotton and polyester blends, which have greater strength and abrasion resistance over all-cotton fabrics.

CONEPREST. This is a pre-cured process of Cone Mills, Inc. It differs from the deferred-cure technique in that the fabric is treated with a resin and completely cured at the mill. The usual shrinkage from oven-curing occurs at this time. Sometimes, fabrics are given an added Sanforized-Plus treatment for greater shrinkage control.

The completely treated and cured fabric is shipped to the manufacturer, who cuts and sews garments to size. Intended crease lines are then sprayed with the Coneprest solution. The solution causes the sprayed area of the fabric to temporarily lose its wrinkle-resistant quality. The garment is then pressed at an appropriate temperature above 325 degrees Fahrenheit at a predetermined pressure ranging from 25 seconds to 3 minutes. This technique re-cures the finish and produces a permanent crease and a shape-retentive garment.

SHARP/SHAPE. This is a pre-cured process of Everprest, Inc. The finished fabric is shipped to the manufacturer for cutting and sewing into garments. Permanent press is achieved with special press equipment, and no further curing is required. The process is considered to be especially effective for stretch fabrics of cotton and cotton-nylon blends.

NEVER-PRESS. This process, developed by Wamsutta, is a somewhat different approach to achieving permanent press. Fabrics are woven with a prescribed balance of warp and filling yarns of a predetermined blend. They are subsequently given a special resin finish and completely cured. The fabrics, which have a maximum residual shrinkage of 1 percent, are shipped to the manufacturer for cutting and sewing into garments. Durable creases are set on the pressing machine under the prescribed procedure of 250 degrees Fahrenheit for 15 seconds with steam.

Super-Crease provides permanent creasing of cotton and cotton-polyester blended fabrics. It is durable to both home and commercial laundering, with or without chlorine bleach. Both pairs of slacks shown were washed innumerable times, but never ironed. Pair at left was treated with Super-Crease; pair at right was not, although it was made of identical fabric.

Courtesy J. P. Stevens & Co., Inc.

It should be noted that all the permanent-press trademarks that have been discussed refer to all-cotton or cotton-blended fabrics that have been chemically treated to obtain the desired shape-retentive effect with easy care and no ironing requirements for the consumer. There are, however, fabrics constructed wholly or partly of thermoplastic fibers, such as triacetate, nylon, polyesters, and acrylics, which have their own inherent permanent heat-setting characteristics. They are frequently sold under specific trademarks, such as *Burmi-Crease.* The degree of shape retention depends upon the kind and amount of thermoplastic fiber used as well as the quality of the thermosetting technique. The labels on such garments may state that no ironing is necessary; others may advise little or no ironing.

Durable-Press Wool Finish. Wool has its own natural "memory." It is elastic, resilient, and tends to return to its original shape after tension or compression is exerted. The Wool Bureau sponsored a process that will add long-lasting creases or pleats to wool fabrics, as well as retain the natural quality of wool.

The process requires that the crease area of the garment be sprayed with a chemical-reducing agent, such as monoethanolamine sulfite, which temporarily inhibits the wool's resilience. When the garment is pressed, the heat resets the wool's "memory" with this crease so that the fabric always tends to return to the new creased condition. Moisture increases this reaction, and, when wet (worn in the rain, for instance), the crease tends to become sharper.

WATER REPELLENCY ■ A water-repellent fabric is one that will resist absorption and penetration of water for a given period of time, depending upon the length of exposure and the force of the water. Eventually, however, water will penetrate even a water-repellent fabric.

These fabrics have qualities not found in truly waterproof fabrics. They are porous, which permits the body to breathe, and are therefore comfortable. The hand and appearance of the fabric is good and very much like the untreated fabrics.

Penetration of water through a fabric is dependent upon the kind of fiber in the fabric, the tightness of the yarn twist, the compactness of the construction of the fabric, and the finish used to discourage water from soaking through the yarns and pores of the fabric. Some fibers, such as nylon and the polyesters, are hydrophobic—that is, they do not readily absorb water. Other fibers, such

In this water repellency test, after sufficient "rain" has fallen, the moisture in the cup set beneath each fabric swatch is withdrawn into a graduate and measured carefully to determine how much water—if any—has penetrated the fabric.

Courtesy Dow Corning

as cotton and rayon, absorb water readily. Consequently, the more hydrophobic fibers used, the more inherently water-repellent the fabric will be. For this reason, raincoats are often made of a 100 percent polyester fiber, such as Dacron, or of a polyester-cotton blend.

Some fabrics are specifically made with a cotton yarn that, when wet, will swell sufficiently to close the pores of the fabric so that the tightened construction will resist water penetration. One such fabric is *Shirley cloth,* which is made of low twist 3-ply cotton yarn with an oxford-weave construction.

Since the effectiveness and durability of water-repellent finishes vary, labels should be read carefully. A garment labelled as *shower resistant* will protect the wearer from a light rain but will be penetrated by a heavy rain after fifteen minutes. A garment labelled as *rain resistant* will provide protection for a few hours of exposure in a moderate rain. A garment labeled as *storm resistant* will resist water penetration for many hours. It should also be noted that greater water repellency will be obtained when a double thickness of water-repellent fabric is used—for instance, across the shoulders. Also, seams should be sewed with water repellent thread; untreated thread will carry water through the garment to the clothing worn underneath.

The quality and durability of the water-repellent finish are very important factors. These may be determined by recognition of the kind of finish used and the care instructions given to the wearer. There are two general types of water-repellent finishes: nondurable and durable. The least expensive are the least durable.

Nondurable Finishes. This type of water repellent is usually based on a paraffin wax-aluminum acetate emulsion that is applied to the goods in a simple padding and drying operation. A recent development in this type has been the substitution of zirconium salts for aluminum to give even better repellency. Although these finishes have excellent ratings of water repellency, they will withstand only very light laundering, will lose their repellency with repeated washings, and, generally, will not tolerate dry cleaning. Typical trademarks are *Aridex, Aquasec, Cravanette M-2, Impregnole,* and *Wata-tite.*

Durable Finishes. There are several types of durable water repellents, and the degree of effectiveness and durability varies for each. One of the first, based upon a pyridinium compound, is applied to cotton, linen, and viscose rayon fabrics. This type of finish permeates the fiber and becomes part of it. It also endures repeated washings as well as dry cleanings. Other advantages claimed are that stains and spots can be sponged off with a damp cloth, that the fabrics resist perspiration and wrinkling, and that the finish manifests a softness of texture that improves the fabric's appearance. Two well-known trademarks are *Zelan* and *Cravenette Long Life.*

Another type of durable water repellent is based on a combination of melamine resins and stearamides and is used on cotton, rayon, and blends containing these fibers. These are marketed under the trademarks of *Permel, Permel Plus,* and *Cravenette Plus.* These have excellent repellency and good tolerance to laundering and dry cleaning.

Silicone compounds are excellent water repellents. Application of this finish to the fabric results in coating the individual fibers of the yarn. Water and water-borne substances, such as beverages, "bead up" and roll off the fabric. The finish is usually more resistant to dry cleaning than to laundering, and instructions on hangtags should be closely observed. Depending upon additional

STAIN	UNTREATED		BEST PREVIOUS TREATMENT		"SCOTCHGARD" TEXTILE TREATMENT	
	Stain Resistance	Stain Removal	Stain Resistance	Stain Removal	Stain Resistance	Stain Removal
FRUIT JUICES (water base, low viscosity)	FAIR	EASY	EXCELLENT	EASY	EXCELLENT	EASY
CATCHUP (water base, high viscosity)	POOR	MEDIUM	GOOD	MEDIUM-EASY	EXCELLENT	EASY
WHISKEY (alcohol-water base)	POOR	MEDIUM	POOR	MEDIUM	EXCELLENT	EASY
GRAVIES (oil-water emulsion, low viscosity)	POOR	DIFFICULT	FAIR	DIFFICULT	EXCELLENT	MEDIUM
OLIVE OIL (oil base, low viscosity)	NO RESISTANCE	VERY DIFFICULT	NO RESISTANCE	VERY DIFFICULT	EXCELLENT	EASY
MAYONNAISE (oil base, high viscosity)	NO RESISTANCE	VERY DIFFICULT	NO RESISTANCE	VERY DIFFICULT	EXCELLENT	MEDIUM

Courtesy 3M Company

treatments, fabrics may also have a soft hand and be wrinkle resistant. Typical silicone finishes are *Cravenette 330, Hydropruf, Ranedare-S,* and *Syl-mer.*

A recently developed group of repellents, called *stain repellers,* are effective against both water- and oil-borne stains. They are very durable to laundering and dry cleaning. They are based on fluorocarbon compounds and are applied by pad-dry-cure processes similar to those used for wash and wear resins. These stain-repellent finishes have gained great favor, particularly for such home furnishings as upholstery, because of the relative ease with which food stains can be removed. Finishes of this type are marketed as *Scotchgard* and *Zepel.*

The best all-around water repellent from the standpoints of effectiveness and durability is not available to the general public, primarily because it is rather costly. This is the *Quarpel* finish, developed by the Quartermasters Corps of the United States Army. The finish effectively repels water, which keeps under-clothing dry even after several days of exposure to a steady downpour. It is a combination of the pyridinium and the fluorocarbon types, and it will withstand up to 15 launderings at the boiling point or repeated dry cleanings without seriously affecting its performance.

Spilled milk lies on the surface of a fabric treated with Scotchgard stain repeller.

Courtesy 3M Company

ZEPEL—PROTECTION AGAINST COMMON FABRIC STAINS

SOILS & STAINS	WET STAINS	DRIED STAINS
GREASE, FAT	Small residue may remain after blotting with dry tissue	Completely removed with solvent or dry cleaning
INK STAINS Fluid Ink	Rolls off; remainder blots off with water: no residue	Completely removed with laundering†
Ball Point Ink	Partly removed with solvent; some residue	Partially removed with solvent or by dry cleaning
GRASS STAINS	Partially removed with water and/or alcohol; small residue may remain	Almost completely removed with water, alcohol, or laundering
FRUIT, FRUIT JUICE	Rolls off or blots off with water; no residue	Completely removed with water and detergent or by laundering
PERSPIRATION	Wipes off with water; no residue†	Completely removed with water and detergent or by laundering†
COFFEE, TEA	Rolls off or blots off with water; no residue	Completely removed with water and detergent or by laundering
COSMETICS Liquid or Cream Deodorant	Rolls off or blots off with water; no residue	Completely removed with solvent or dry cleaning
Lipstick	Blots off with solvent; some small residue†	Almost completely removed by laundering or dry cleaning†
Hair Oil	Blots off or blots off with solvent; no residue	Completely removed with dry cleaning
MUD	Residue wipes off with water	Completely removed with water and detergent or by laundering

† *Results of preliminary tests*

Courtesy E. I. du Pont de Nemours & Co., Inc.

WATERPROOFING ■ For a fabric to be truly waterproof, it must be completely sealed with a substance that is insoluble in water. The familiar rubber-coated garb of policemen and firemen is a good example. Older methods include coating the fabric with linseed oil to produce the well-known fisherman's slicker; oiled silk is produced by a similar process.

Modern waterproofing materials include the vinyl resins, which do not oxidize and crack as readily as rubber. Synthetic rubbers are also more durable to outside influences than natural rubber. The fabrics used in most of today's waterproof materials are cotton and nylon. The latter, coated with vinyl resins, has largely superseded the heavy canvas tarpaulins used to protect merchandise in transit.

The *Koroseal* process can be applied to any finished fabric except acetate. It makes fabrics impervious to water, wind, moths, and mildew, and resistant to acid, grease, sunlight, perspiration, and stains. Koroseal fabrics do not contain any rubber or oil; consequently, they will not deteriorate by cracking, sticking, or peeling and therefore serve a multitude of uses. The coating applied to the surface of the fabric is a plasticized white powder, polyvinyl chloride, which is obtained by compressing two gases—acetylene from coal and limestone, and hydrogen chloride from salt. The result is a tough, stretchable plastic coating having unusual properties.

A waterproofing finish that claims superiority to vinyl and acrylic coatings is sold by Kenyon Piece Dyeworks, Inc. under the trademark of *K-Kote*. Treated fabrics will not crack, and they can be either machine washed or dry-cleaned. Water-borne spots can be removed with a damp cloth, and the fabric requires little or no ironing because of the wash and wear quality given by the finish. K-Kote is neither brittle in cold weather nor tacky in hot weather, and it is durable enough to last the life of the garment to which it is applied.

The slick, or satiny, effect is usually applied to the outer side of the fabric, with a more subdued finish on the inside. Both sides feel the same. One variation has a clear finish on the outside and a colored finish, which takes the place of a lining, on the inside. In any case, the fabric is soft, pliable, and has a natural hand—that is, there is no obtrusive tactile awareness of coating.

K-Kote has been applied to nylon and blended fabrics for the outerwear and raincoat markets, but it has also been found applicable to almost any kind of material. It has been used to coat silk, cotton, and blended fabrics in home furnishings.

ABSORBENT FINISHES ■ To increase the absorbency of cellulosic fibers, which improves their effectiveness and comfort for such use as towels and undergarments, ammonium compounds may be applied to cotton, linen, and rayon fabrics.

The absorbency of nylon 6 and nylon 6, 6 may be increased by treating them with a solution of nylon 8, which is more absorbent. This process is known as *Nylonizing*. Another finish used to increase nylon absorbency is known as *Nylonex*. *Hysorb* is a compound of surfactants and synthetic resins used to give absorbent properties to fabrics of other man-made fibers.

FLAMEPROOFING ■ Only mineral, asbestos, glass, or metal substances are completely fireproof. Textile fabrics cannot be made fireproof, but they can be chemically treated to retard inflammability. Fabrics so treated may be regarded as flameproof, which means that they will not flame or burn actively. *Flameproofing* is a practical form of fire protection where a fire-resistant quality is desirable, as in fabrics used for awnings, mattresses, work clothes, or draperies, as well as for sheer and napped fabrics of cotton and rayon.

The objection to most fire-retardant compounds is that the fabric so treated loses this quality in washing or in dry cleaning. Also, such compounds sometimes affect the feel of a fabric, causing it to lose softness and flexibility. Where the fire-retardant quality is lost in washing or in dry cleaning, it can be restored by reprocessing with a commercial fire-retardant compound. Some of the trademarked names that indicate a fire-retardant quality are *Du Pont, Fire-Retardant, Saniflame, Neva-Flame*. These are applicable to all fabrics except acetate. *Permaproof 300* has been described as the first finish that permits cloth to be laundered repeatedly without losing its fire-retardant properties.

Among the most effective flameproofing compounds is one that uses ammonium sulfamate. It makes a fabric fire-resistant without imparting a harsh quality. The fabric must be reprocessed after washing, but this is not necessary after dry cleaning, as the ammonium sulfamate finish is fast to dry-cleaning solvents.

The newer, more durable flame-resistant finishes are based on phosphorus-bearing resins developed by the Southern Regional Research Laboratory of the United States Department of Agriculture. Carrying the tongue-twisting name of tetrakis (hydroxymethyl) phosphonium chloride, it is better known by the trademark, *THPC,* of the Hooker Chemical Company. It is fairly expensive and has only recently been made available to chemical compounders and finishers.

The finish is applied by padding followed by drying and curing, which is easily done in plants equipped to handle wash and wear finishes. The goods treated with THPC lose some tensile strength and abrasion resistance, and they are somewhat stiffer in hand than the untreated fabrics. The finish will withstand commercial laundering. It is used on fabrics for work clothes for steel workers, welders, and the military.

Another fire-retardant is *Fyran.* It is a stable, neutral compound that does not stiffen the fabric even in fairly high-percentage applications, and there is usually no perceptible difference in appearance or hand between the treated and the untreated fabric. Fyran is especially valuable for treatment of cotton or rayon fabrics before napping. It may be used successfully for flameproofing such items as finished garments, paper or textile decorations, and draperies. It is usually applied by padding and drying, but it may also be applied by spraying or brushing.

Fyran is not removed from fabrics by dry cleaning, but since it consists of water soluble materials, it is removed by laundering or rinsing. Laundries and cleaning establishments can easily apply this treatment to draperies, blankets, and wearing apparel as a special customer service.

Fabrics may be given a fire-resistant quality by a simple home method of immersing them in a solution of 70 percent borax and 30 percent boric acid. If the fabric to be treated is already water-repellent, soap should be added to the solution so that an even wetness and absorbency will be obtained. This method does not alter the appearance of the fabric, but the treatment must be repeated after every washing.

MOTHPROOFING ■ Wool fabrics are sometimes mothproofed as one of the finishing operations to the cloth by impregnating the yarns with a chemical. Of all these preparations, tests seem to indicate that the most effective are *Mitin F F, Eulan C N,* and *Lanoc C N.* These are fast to other finishing processes as well as dry cleaning, but are only moderately fast to washing.

Simple home methods of moth-damage prevention comprise daily brushing of apparel after wearing, frequent exposure to sunlight, and dry cleaning before placing the garments in airtight storage and cold storage at a maximum temperature of 40 degrees Fahrenheit. For additional protection, various commercial compounds are available for use in the home. Among these are naphthalene and paradichlorobenzene (moth balls, flakes, and cakes). These do not act as a repellent, as is commonly thought. They will actually kill the moth, eggs, and larvae, provided the closet, chest, or package containing the wool fabrics is airtight. The atmosphere must be thoroughly saturated for these substances to be effective. The container should be hung above the clothes so that the vapor will flow down over them.

Many sprays are also available. Some of these—such as *Atomoth, Berlou, Boconize, Larvex,* and *Ya-De*—contain either a fluoride or silicofluoride. These are very stable to exposure to light and air and are not removed by dry cleaning. They are, however, water-soluble and also may give rise to white markings when the fabric is rubbed. They also may cause a harshening of the fabric's hand. Products containing carbon tetrachloride, such as *Moth Gas,* are also effective. Others containing arsenic, such as *Per Mo,* are poisonous to humans as well as to moth larvae.

Products containing DDT in concentrations of at least 5 percent kill moth grubs quickly. These sprays are sold under such proprietary names as *Black Flag, Erustomoth, Gulf Trak,* and *SLA.* However, DDT has the disadvantage of eradication by dry cleaning or washing.

One of the most effective mothproofing agents is based on a chemical called *dieldrin.* Applied to the wool during the end of the dyeing process or any other wet process, this material is absorbed by the wool and is there for the life of the fabric. It is still effective after laundering and dry cleaning. The active ingredient of *Moth Snub* is dieldrin.

A more recent development is the work of a United States Department of Agriculture scientist, Dr. Roy Pence, who has discovered what he calls *antimetabolites.* These substances, which can be applied easily to wool, make the fiber useless to the moth larva as food. Consequently, it starves to death before it has consumed enough fiber to damage the fabric.

MILDEWPROOFING ■ Cellulosic fibers are particularly susceptible to mildew; silk and wool are also suceptible, but to a lesser extent. Such untreated fabrics will become stained, malodorous, and eventually deteriorated by the fungus if allowed to remain in a moist condition for a period of time.

Shower curtains or other cotton fabrics may be mildewproofed at home by soaking the material in very soapy water, then, without rinsing, dipping it into a solution of copper sulfate. Antiseptics, such as boric acid and carbolic acid, also prevent rapid growth of the mildew fungus.

One compound that is not easily washed out is a .05 percent solution of phenyl mercuric acetate in water. This is one of the most effective mildewproofing agents.

Certain organo-metallic compounds, such as of tin and copper, are powerful mildew retardants. Copper imparts a greenish color to fabrics. Certain resins based on melamine formaldehyde, such as *Mel-Tron 80* of Crown Chemical Corporation, are also valuable for mildewproofing. The *Arigal* process, developed by CIBA, is another example. An extension of mildewproofing is rotproofing, which is very important in military applications.

ANTIBACTERIAL FINISHES ■ Chemical antiseptic finishes impart a self-sterilizing quality to a fabric. The appearance and feel of the fabric are unchanged, and no chemical odor remains. Dry cleaning does not impair the finish. *Cyana-finish, Hygienized, Permafab, Sani-Age, Sanitized,* and *Vita-Fresh* are trademarked names exemplifying these finishes.

SLIP RESISTANCE ■ In fabrics that have a low thread count, the warp yarns sometimes slip along the filling yarns. Unusual wear or strain on some part of a fabric may cause the same action, known as *slipping.* It is not frequent with rough-surfaced fabrics made of hard-twisted yarns. Permanent firmness can be given to fabrics by immersing them in synthetic resins, then stretching and drying them under tension. The deposit of resin at the points of interlacing in the weave prevents the yarns from slipping. This treatment is advantageous for smooth-surfaced rayons, as the smoothness of the synthetic yarn causes it to slip and fray. Fabrics labeled "slip-resistant" should be examined closely for thread count, as the resinous coating may be used to create an effect of compact construction. One such finish is *Estralok A* of Crown Chemical Corporation.

HEAT-REFLECTANT FINISHES ■ It may be desirable to conserve the heat of the body if conditions are cold or to protect it from the heat if conditions are hot. For cold conditions, a properly treated fabric with a metallic substance faced toward the body will reflect its radiated heat back to the body rather than permit it to escape. For hot conditions, the same treated material with the face outward will reflect the outside heat away from the body. Similar considerations apply to insulating a window, a room, or a tent.

One such excellent finish, developed by Deering Milliken Research Corporation, is sold under the trademark of *Milium*. A fabric to be used as a lining can be coated with this resinated metal (usually aluminum) spray, which adds less than an ounce to the weight of the lining and does not interfere with the porosity or pliability of the fabric. Tests using a wind velocity of 15 miles an hour have shown that a wool outer fabric with a Milium satin lining is approximately equal in warmth to an untreated satin lining plus an 8½-ounce wool interlining with the same outer fabric. Another similar finish is *Temp-resisto*. The quality and durability of the finish depend upon the quality of the resin and its ability to withstand darkening and removal by laundering or dry cleaning. The degree of reflectiveness is also affected by the closeness of the weave. A sleazy, open construction will result in much loss of reflective ability since the heat will pass through the open pores.

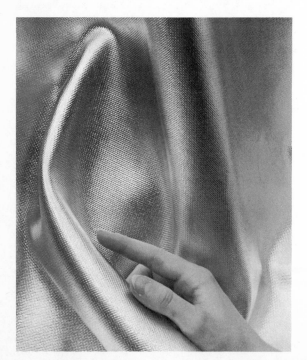

Scotch-Shield brand aluminized film type 103, a 5-millionths-thick film of aluminum, assumes the texture of the material to which it is bonded.

Courtesy 3M Company

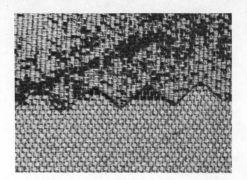

Aluminum particles used as a heat-reflective finish on lining fabrics are easily removed by rubbing action during dry cleaning if not held securely enough to the cloth by the binder. The dark color of the fabric (top) shows through the partially removed finish.

Courtesy CIBA Review

A variation of the metallic heat-reflectant technique involves the application of an extremely thin metal foil to a woven fabric so that the foil conforms to the surface contours of the fabric and is ruptured at its interstices. The degree of air permeability may vary, depending upon the closeness of the weave. Developed in England as *Flectavent,* it is produced in this country under the trademark of *Foylon.* Another process that applies aluminum foil to fabric is *Scotch-Shield.*

FOAM LAMINATING ■ The heat-insulative properties of dead or trapped air spaces have been formerly limited to the nature of the fiber, yarn, and fabric construction. The principle has been extended to the application of a solid foam to woven and knitted fabrics. One type is the ether urethane foam commonly found in furniture upholstery; similar types are ester urethane foam and LF 70 heat laminatable ethers. The foam thicknesses range from ⅟₁₆ to ⅛ inch and have an accepted range standard of 40 to 60 air cells per linear inch.

Since the bulk of foam laminates is air, separated by extremely thin walls of urethane, its outstanding features are the insulative properties combined with light weight. Foam sheets are warmer than the equivalent thickness of unlaminated fabrics or any of the fiber-filled quilted materials. The degree of insulation depends upon the small cell size of the foam and its thickness. Skimping on the thickness could neutralize the insulative effect. Since fabric porosity is an important factor for body comfort, the foam can be produced in a manner that provides for some of the air spaces to be continuous so that the moisture can gradually pass through the material. This permits natural regulation of body temperature and tends to prevent overheating or chilling from moisture collection.

The draping quality of foam-laminated fabrics varies depending upon the thickness of the foam, its density, and its fabrication. Techniques imparting

A cross-section of washable knitted nylon velour (top) laminated to a foam backing.

Courtesy CIBA Review

Courtesy Nopco Chemical Company

A solid bun of urethane foam is peeled into a sheet of foam for lamination to a fabric.

special designs, such as the waffle pattern, and patterned application of bonding adhesives have shown much promise for improved pliability and drapability with reduced bulky or "ballooning" appearance. Foam laminates move readily with the fabric to which they adhere as well as to body movements. They possess sufficient stretchability to reduce binding and increase action comfort— both distinct advantages when applied to stretch fabrics. Foam laminates have good dimensional stability, shape retentiveness, and resiliency.

Generally, foam-laminated fabrics may be laundered if the base fabric is launderable. They may also be dry-cleaned. Temporary swelling, possible peeling, or deterioration that might result from the application of dry cleaning solutions depends upon the quality of the foam and the care taken in applying it to the fabric. While urethane foams do tend to discolor, this problem is being met by new dyeing methods as well as such "hiding" techniques as flocking and printing, by other surface treatments on smooth-faced or polished foam, and by sandwiching the foam sheet between two fabrics. However, the sandwiching technique gives the fabric a heavier hand.

Urethane foams can be odorless. They are nontoxic, nonallergenic, and can be safely worn without fear of skin irritation.

The two basic methods of adhering the foam to the fabric are *heat* bonding and *adhesive* bonding. The method used is dependent upon the manufacturer's objectives. Heat bonding requires the use of either an ester urethane or an LF 70 ether foam sheet that is sufficiently heated (about 250 to 300 degrees Fahrenheit) to melt its surface immediately before it comes in contact with the

The waffle pattern of Nopco-foam on the back of this fabric facilitates better draping quality. The foam is heat-bonded to the fabric.

Courtesy Nopco Company

cloth and is pressed between two rollers. The tacky foam surface unites with the fabric and produces a material with a cloth face and a foam back. This method is very fast (40 to 70 yards can be processed per minute), but an additional cost allowance must be made for some foam burn-off. Heat-laminating must be done after such processes as preshrinking, otherwise there will be puckering and possible delamination. Other processes, such as repellency finishes, must be applied after heat-laminating to ensure proper adherence.

A modification of the heat-bonding process applies the same basic technique to a thin ether-urethane foam sheet ($\frac{1}{32}$-inch thick) sandwiched between two layers of cloth. The method competes with fabric-to-fabric bonding techniques.

Adhesive bonding of ether urethane foam to fabric may be accomplished by applying with a spray or roller a resin, a synthetic rubber cement, or another mastic before pressing the cloth and foam between rollers. For increased "body breathing" comfort and better drape and hand, the adhesive may be applied as dots, lines, or scattered patterns. Special finishes, such as repellencies, may be applied to the fabric before laminating. Adhesive-lamination is slower—about 20 to 25 yards per minute. Additional time is required for curing, but there is no burn-off loss. There is a greater chance that adhesive-bonded cloth and foam will separate when washed or dry-cleaned, depending upon the care exercised in processing.

Urethane foams are sold under a variety of trade names that are owned by either the foam producers or the laminating processors. The end product will be affected by both the nature of the foam and the method of bonding.

Curon. This foam is heat-laminated. Reeves Bros., Inc., produces the foam, laminates knitted and woven fabrics with it, and also licenses other mills and convertors to process fabrics under this trade name. A waffle design Curon is produced for greater drapability.

Nopco-Foam. This foam is sold by the Nopco Chemical Company. They produce it in flat, waffle design, and smooth or polished form. Mills and converters heat-bond it to their fabrics and merchandise the laminated fabrics under their own trademarks.

Vomar. This is a trade name owned by the Allied Polymer Corporation for a foam made by Nopco. It is merchandised by various fabric firms.

Scott Apparel Foam. Manufactured by the Scott Paper Company, this foam is sold to mills and converters for laminating to knitted and woven fabrics. It may be laminated by heat or adhesive. Some fabricators feature this foam under their own trade names. However, the quality control standards have been set up by Scott.

Astrotex. This trade name is owned by Princeton Knitting Mills for its fabrics laminated with Scott Apparel Foam.

Bondaknit. Abasco Fabrics, Inc., merchandises its knitted fabrics that are bonded to Scott Apparel Foam under this trade name.

Feathalite. Guilford Woolen Fabrics, Inc., uses this trademark for its woven fabrics laminated to Scott Apparel Foam.

Chem-Stitch. This is the trade name owned by Hicks and Otis for a process that applies a pattern of specially formulated adhesive-bonding, low-density, high-loft ether urethane foam. It produces a permanent quiltlike effect on the face of the fabric that is wash and dry-clean resistant. The process is licensed to converters.

Top left: knitted woolen bonded to nylon tricot.

Top right: woven worsted bonded to rayon jersey.

Bottom left: ribbon fabric bonded to acetate jersey.

Bottom right: raschel-knitted rayon bonded to acetate jersey.

Courtesy Coin Sales Corporation, Inc.

FABRIC-TO-FABRIC BONDING ■ This technique uses specially developed adhesives that effect a permanent bond between two fabrics. It can be applied to a wide variety of fabrics of different fibers, constructions, and textures. The original soft hand and drapability of the fabric combination is retained after washing or dry cleaning. The process gives dimensional stability to knitted goods and produces a self-lined fabric. The latter factor contributes to fabric shape retention, opacity, and lower garment construction costs, as well as to unusual styling possibilities. Sheer, lacy fabrics may also be given opacity and drape by bonding a lining to them.

The process is gaining wide recognition and is being adopted by leading mills under such trademarks as *Coin*, which is advertised as a "two-faced" fabric. Other trademarks include *Everline, Lockline,* and *Perma-Line.*

REVIEW QUESTIONS

1 Describe one important preparatory finishing process for smooth-surfaced fabrics.

2 Name six finishing processes for producing luster.

3 In each pair of the following finishes, which type is preferable and why? (a) waterproof or water-repellent (b) fireproof or flame resistant.

4 (a) What is the purpose of weighting? (b) Why would it be unwise to buy a heavily weighted silk garment?

5 Explain two finishing methods by which a crinkled effect is achieved.

6 (a) What is the result of beetling? (b) How does it compare with schreinering?

7 How is starch used in finishing fabrics?

8 (a) Explain the calendering process. (b) What is chasing?

9 How may a finishing process deceive the consumer?

10 Discuss shrinkage, telling (a) why it occurs, (b) whether it can be prevented entirely, (c) methods preferable for cotton, (d) methods preferable for wool.

11 (a) Discuss the advantages of napping. (b) Name the disadvantages, if any.

12 (a)What fabrics are naturally wrinkle-resistant? (b) How can this quality be produced in other fabrics?

13 (a) What method of bleaching is preferable? (b) Is there any advantage in buying unbleached fabrics?

14 Why are finishing processes necessary?

15 Explain tentering and crabbing.

16 What is meant by a drip-dry or wash and wear garment?

17 How effective is the drip-dry finish?

18 How are fabrics embossed?

19 Under what circumstances will embossing on fabrics be permanent?

20 Differentiate between mercerizing and slack mercerizing in terms of their effect on cotton.

21 Differentiate between wrinkle-resistant and permanent-press finishes in terms of properties and limitations.

22 What is the principle of each of the two types of heat reflectants?

23 (a) What is foam lamination? (b) Describe its effectiveness.

24 What are the characteristics of bonded fabrics?

SUGGESTED ACTIVITY

Visit the yard-goods department of a large retail store. Obtain the name of the finishes of ten different fabrics by noting the labels. Describe the fabrics' appearance and finish characteristics.

DYEING

FINISHING WITH COLOR

As the textile fibers have been examined and tested for their differential qualities and as the spinning and weaving processes have been explained, the qualities of durability and serviceability have been constantly stressed. When the yarn is woven into fabric, the interesting and intricate designs of weaves begin to add beauty of appearance as well as serviceability. The various finishing processes suggest additional means of enhancing the appearance of the newly formed fabric. It remains for the dyeing and printing processes to provide lasting beauty and delight to the eye. Both these processes add color to fabrics, and color delights by stimulating or soothing. Dyeing and printing differ in the method by which color is applied to fabric. In the dyeing process, fiber, yarn, or fabric is immersed in a solution of dyestuff and is thus saturated with the dye. In printing (described in the following chapter), a pattern or a design is imprinted on the fabric in one or more colors by using dyes in paste form.

SELECTION OF DYE

To select the proper dye for a fiber, it is necessary to know which dyes have an affinity for the vegetable, animal, or man-made fibers. In general, the dyes used for cotton and linen may be used for rayons, but acetate requires a special class of dyes. When a dye colors fabric directly with one simple operation of immersion, without the aid of an affixing agent, the dye is said to be a *direct dye* for that fiber. Direct dyes are the easiest to produce, the simplest to apply, and the cheapest in their initial cost as well as in application. They are not, however, as colorfast to light and washing as some other dyes. The term *bleeding* describes dyes that run in washing. When dye rubs off a fabric exposed to the friction of wear, it is termed *crocking*.

Requirements for colorfastness differ. Fastness to *light* is important in draperies, for example, as they must stand strong light daily but do not need to be washed frequently. Fastness to *washing* is important in dress fabrics and household linens because they must undergo frequent washings. Therefore, both the kind of fiber to be dyed and the intended use for the fabric enter into the selection of the dye.

Primitive man obtained dyes from flowers, nuts, berries, and other forms of vegetable and plant life, as well as from mineral and animal sources. These sources have provided such "natural dyes" throughout civilization. They are no longer used in quantity by the dyeing industry, but they are still used in Oriental countries to a certain extent for rug dyeing and in many parts of the world for native handicraft.

The principal vegetable dyes are: fustic, sumac, catechu or cutch, madder, henna, saffron, logwood, indigo, and alizarin. Animal dyes, such as cochineal, squid sepia, lac, and Tyrian purple, are obtained from species of fish and small insects. Minerals provide such dyes as Prussian blue, chrome yellow, and iron buff.

SYNTHETIC DYES

Although synthetic dyes were first derived from coal tar in 1856, they were not developed in the United States to any great extent until World War I, when the supply of imported synthetic dyes was cut off. Since then, the United States has built up a dye industry that is unsurpassed. Innumerable dye compounds made from coal tar have now supplanted natural dyes. These synthetic dyes are constantly being improved as to beauty of color and colorfastness. Lasting beauty of color is an important factor in consumers' finished goods. Durability of color depends on: (1) selection of the proper dye for the fiber to be dyed; (2) selection of the method of dyeing the fiber, yarn, or fabric.

The synthetic dyes may be categorized into about 14 classes. The classification is based upon the particular type of chemical composition of the dye and/or the method of its application.

A view of an automated dye center where such factors as color formulation and dye temperature are controlled.

Courtesy Burlington Industries, Inc.

BASIC DYES ■ The first coal-tar dye was a so-called *basic* dye. It was developed to give many bright shades for silk and wool. The chemical agent that binds the dye to a fiber, which otherwise has little or no affinity for the dye, is known as a *mordant*. Basic dyes are used with a mordant for cotton, linen, acetate, nylon, polyesters, acrylics, and modacrylics.

When used on natural fibers, basic dyes are not fast to light, washing, perspiration, or atmospheric gases; they tend either to bleed or crock. They give good fastness and bright shades to acrylics for which they are principally used. Basic dyes are frequently used as an aftertreatment for fabrics that have been previously dyed with acid colors.

OXIDATION BASES ■ This is one of the oldest of synthetic dyes. Aniline black, one of the most intense and fastest blacks available, is an example of this group. Excellent browns are also available for printing. They are used primarily for cotton and can be applied with oxidizing agents and careful processing to wool, silk, and acetate.

ACID DYES ■ Acidification of basic dyes led to the creation of acid dyes that are used mostly on wool and silk. They are also being more widely used for dyeing acetate, nylon, acrylics, modacrylics, and spandex. These dyes have also been found useful in printing chlorinated wool and silk.

Acid dyes are inexpensive and fairly fast to light, but they are not fast to washing and have only fair fastness to dry cleaning. They have low resistance to perspiration.

Wool may be given increased fastness to both light and washing by boiling the fabric in a chromate solution after the first dye bath. This is called *after-chroming.*

ACID-MILLING DYES ■ A further development of the acid colors was the acid-milling dyes, which have superior wetfastness, good lightfastness, and less tendency to bleed onto surrounding white areas.

ACID-PREMETALIZED DYES ■ These are another outgrowth of the acid dyes. Carrying one or two molecules of chromium bound to the dye in their structure, they require a strong acid bath to get the color into the fabric. The metal improves the colorfastness, which is greater than for acid or acid-milling dyes. Acid-premetalized dyes are used a great deal on wool, nylon, and acrylics. The colors are good, though no brilliant blues or greens are obtainable.

NEUTRAL-PREMETALIZED DYES ■ These dyes have one molecule of metal, usually chromium, bound to two molecules of dye to improve fastness properties. The shades are not so bright as acid colors. These dyes are used on wool, silk, nylon, acrylics, modacrylics, and vinylidene-derived fibers. Since the generally good fastness properties are similar for all of these fibers, the neutral-premetalized dyes are used for their blends.

MORDANT OR CHROME DYES ■ These dyes are related to acid dyes but are more complex. They require the addition of sodium or potassium bichromate in the dye bath or after the dyeing is completed to obtain the mordant or binding action of the chrome. They are the fastest dyes to wet processing available for wool and are therefore principally used for wool requiring maximum fastness. They are also used with less effective fastness for cotton, linen, silk, rayon, and nylon. They provide a wide range of colors that are duller than the acid dyes.

SUBSTANTIVE DIRECT DYES ■ This group is one of three types of direct dyes, all of which dye cellulosic fibers directly and without a mordant in bright, full shades. Some direct dyes may be used on wool, silk, and nylon. They are applied to cotton or rayon from a water solution, and when salt is added, the color is forced out of solution onto the fiber. The dye colors often have only fair fastness to light, poor fastness to washing, and are not very bright. They are often referred to as *commercial colors,* a term that indicates that the dyes are not the best available for the purpose.

DEVELOPED DYES ■ This is another group of direct dyes. In addition to their primary use for cellulosic fibers, they are also used to color wool, silk, and nylon. The process requires a base to be dyed on the goods. This is followed by a *diazotizing* process, whereby the dye is chemically changed and treated with a fresh set of chemicals, called *developers,* that form the completed dye. Developed dyes are fairly fast to washing because they have been literally built into the fiber.

AZOIC DYES ■ This is the third group of direct dyes that is further identified as naphthol and rapidogen types. They are quite fast to washing and vary from poor to excellent lightfastness. Azoic dyes are used to a very great extent on cotton and for special purposes on nylon and acetate.

The method of applying these dyes is somewhat similar to that of developed dyes, as it involves diazotizing. The fabric is first immersed in naphthol, which impregnates the fibers; it is then dipped into the diazotized color bath. The dyeing is followed by thorough soaping and rinsing. Naphthol or azoic dyes are sometimes referred to as *ice dyes* because ice is frequently used to bring the dyes to a low temperature and assure efficient dye formation. A complete color range is available, but these dyes are used primarily for bright reds, yellows, and blacks.

DISPERSE DYES ■ These dyes were developed originally for dyeing acetate fibers and have since found wide use in dyeing triacetate, nylon, polyester, acrylic, modacrylic, and olefin, as well as cellulosic fibers. While they are not soluble in water, they are supplied in a finely ground form that will disperse in water. The particles will dissolve in the fibers and, by this action, the fabric is dyed. Disperse blacks are usually made by a process similar to the one described for developed direct dyes.

Other shades are dyed just as are direct dyes except that salt is never added to the dyebaths. The disperse dyes have one weakness, particularly in the blue shades: they are susceptible to nitrous oxide gas in the atmosphere and will gradually fade to a pink color. Inhibitors applied at the dyehouse can slow down the fading process. Peculiarly enough, disperse blues applied to nylon do not gas-fade. The disperse dyes as a class are fairly fast, except that the ones least sensitive to gas-fading on acetate are the least lightfast.

SULFUR DYES ■ Sulfur dyes, first made in 1879, are used for cotton and linen. These dyes are fast to washing, light, and perspiration, but they have one weakness: excessive chlorine bleaching will strip the color.

Sulfur dyes are insoluble in water and must be made soluble with the aid of caustic soda and sodium sulfide. (One or two manufacturers produce sulfur dyes that have already been made water soluble.)

Sulfur dyeing is done at high temperature and with a large quantity of salt, which helps to drive the color into the fabric. After immersion in the dye bath, followed by rinsing, the fabric is oxidized to the desired shade by exposure to the air or, chemically, by the use of potassium bichromate and acetic acid. The oxidizing process must be carefully controlled because penetration of the dye is retarded by premature oxidation. Also, oxidation changes sulfur to sulfuric acid, which may be harmful to the fabric. Excess chemicals and excess dye must be completely removed by thorough washing. Sulfur dyes penetrate more thoroughly than any other dye because of the high temperature and the alkalinity of the dye bath. They are excellent for khaki and for the heavy piece goods used in work clothes. Sulfur dyes produce dull colors, such as navy, brown, and black. They are used for blacks more than any other dye. If stored for a great length of time, fabrics become tender.

VAT DYES ■ The first synthetic vat dye was an indigo created in 1879. Vat dyes are the fastest dyes for cotton, linen, and rayon. They also may be applied to wool, nylon, polyesters, acrylics, and modacrylics with the use of a mordant. Vat dyes are not only resistant to light and to acids and alkalies, but they are equally resistant to the strong oxidizing bleaches used in commercial laundries. In this respect, vat dyes excel sulfur dyes, which are not fast to chlorine washing.

A label stating that a garment is vat-dyed is not a guarantee that the fabric is absolutely fast to washing if it is of brilliant color. The name *Indanthrene* on labels indicates that a special type of dye has been used that is particularly fast to light and to washing. This type was among the first of the synthetic vat dyes.

The old-fashioned method of fermenting and steeping indigo in a vat gave vat dyes their name. They are prepared today on the same principle, but they are chemically purer and the process is shorter. Vat dyes are expensive because of the initial cost as well as the method of application. They are insoluble pigments; but they are made soluble in water by the use of a strong reducing agent, such as hydrosulfite dissolved in the alkali, sodium hydroxide. The fabric is immersed in this solution. Subsequent exposure to air or immersion in an oxidizing bath (bichromate) restores the dye to its insoluble form as a part of the fiber.

REACTIVE DYES ■ This interesting class of colors was the first really new development (1957) since the vat dyes. There are now several varieties of reactive dyes, which actually react with fiber molecules to form a chemical compound. While these dyes were first designed for cellulosic fibers, types are now available for wool, silk, nylon, acrylics, and blends of these fibers. Some advantages of reactive dyes are their excellent fastness to light and washing and their brilliant shades, which are rivaled only by acid dyes on silk.

There are several chemical ways of combining the dye with cellulosic fibers, and all have about the same potential. The dyes can be applied from alkaline solutions in a one-step process of pad and dry, or they can be applied from neutral solutions and then alkalized in a separate run. Heat is also used to develop the shade. In all cases, the fabric is well soaped after dyeing to remove any unfixed dye (color that has combined with the water in the dye bath and is of no value in the dyeing of the goods).

PIGMENT DYES ■ These dyes, developed in recent years, utilize a technique of coloring that has become increasingly important. The colors, confined to light shades, bright colors, and such metallic colors as gold, are applied usually to cotton cloth but are also used on fabrics of man-made fibers. Actually, they are not true dyes because they have no affinity for the fiber and are applied and held to the fabric with resins, which are then cured at high temperatures.

Pigment dyeing gives excellent lightfast colors and generally good all-around fastness. However, if the shade is too deep, the color will crock. Great improvements in the pigments and resins have made it possible to dye in much darker shades than was possible at first.

COLORLESS DYES ■ These so-called "dyes" are also called *fluorescent whiteners* or *optical brighteners.* The whiteness is really caused by absorption of ultraviolet light and reflection of visible blue light. Optical brighteners are available for cotton, wool, acetate, nylon, and acrylics. They may be applied during bleaching, before resin finishing, or with the resin.

Though lightfastness varies, it is generally fair depending upon the compound and the fiber to which it is applied. Washfastness also varies but is generally good; further brightness buildup occurs from washing in household detergents.

SELECTION OF DYEING METHOD

Textiles may be dyed at any stage of their development from fiber into fabric by the following methods.

Stock dyeing, in the fiber stage

Top dyeing, in the combed wool sliver stage

Yarn dyeing, after the fiber has been spun into yarn

Piece dyeing, after the yarn has been constructed into fabric

Cross-dyeing, a combination of either stock dyeing or yarn dyeing, with subsequent piece dyeing

Solution pigmenting or dope dyeing, before the man-made fiber is extruded through the spinneret

STOCK DYEING ■ This term is used when a textile fiber is dyed in a loose condition before it is spun. This is done by putting it in large vats and circulating dye liquor through the mass of fiber at elevated temperatures. Although the dye liquor is pumped through the fiber in large quantities, there are areas where the dye does not penetrate completely. However, in subsequent blending and spinning operations, these areas are so mixed with the thoroughly dyed fiber that an overall even color is obtained. In stock dyeing, which is the least expensive method of coloring, the color is well penetrated into the fibers and does not crock readily. Stock-dyed fiber does not spin as readily as undyed fiber because it loses some of its flexibility, but lubricants added in the final rinsing overcome most of this difficulty.

PRINCIPAL CLASSES OF SYNTHETIC DYES AND THEIR CHARACTERISTICS

DYE CLASS	GENERAL DESCRIPTION	USES	FASTNESS								
			Light	Washing	Staining (Bleeding)	Dry Cleaning	Hot Pressing	Crocking	Gas Fading	Seawater	Perspiration
Basic	First synthetic dye (1856); organic base dissolved in inorganic acid. Limited use today, except some used for acrylics. Complete color range; colors bright	Cotton (with mordant), wool, silk, nylon, polyesters, acrylics, modacrylics. Direct printing on acetate; discharge printing on cotton	Poor; selected types excellent on acrylics	Poor on natural fibers; good on others in wide range of shades	Bleeds easily on wool, silk; good resistance on man-made fibers	Mostly poor; good on acrylics	Not affected	Good resistance on acrylics	Not susceptible	Very poor; good on acrylics	Generally poor; some blues good; good on acrylics
Oxidation Bases	One of earliest synthetics; aniline black, still one of the most intense and fastest blacks available. Excellent browns for printing	Primarily for dyeing cotton; also wool, silk, acetate. Direct, resist, and discharge printing	Excellent	Very good	Very good	Very good	Not affected	Very good	Not susceptible	Not affected	Good
Acid	Originated from basic dye acidification; complete color range	Primarily for wool and silk; also acetate, nylons, acrylics, modacrylics, spandex. Printing on chlorinated wool, silk, acetate	Generally very good; range poor to excellent	Poor	Bleed easily; stain adjacent fibers	Good	Not affected	Excellent	Not susceptible	Fair	Fair
Acid-Milling	Similar origin to acid dyes. Complete color range; duller than acid dyes	Same as acid; also stock and top dyeing	Generally very good; range poor to excellent	Good	Good resistance; generally will not stain adjacent fibers	Good	Not affected	Excellent	Not susceptible	Good	Fair to good

Acid-Premetalized	Require strong acid bath; based on structure of one or two molecules of chromium to one molecule of dye; metal assists dye fastness; blues and greens duller than acid dyes; tendency to dye unevenly on nylons	Suitable for carpeting, decorative fabrics, women's wear, swimwear of wool, nylon, acrylic fabrics	Good to excellent	Fair to good	Generally good resistance to staining other fibers	Good	Not affected	Good to excellent	Not susceptible	Fair to good	Good
Neutral-Premetalized	Derived from acid dyes based on structure of one molecule of metal (usually chromium) bound to two molecules of dye; shades fairly bright but less so than acid colors; fastness similar for various fibers	Wool, silk, nylons, acrylics, modacrylics, vinylidene-derived fibers; blends of these fibers due to similar fastness properties for various fibers	Very good to excellent	Fair to good	Generally good resistance	Good	Not affected	Good to excellent	Not affected	Good to excellent	Good
Mordant (Chrome)	Related to acid dyes; require addition of chrome derived from potassium or sodium bichromate; fairly complete color range but duller than acid dyes	Primarily for wool requiring maximum fastness: carpeting, decorative fabrics, men's wear; also silk, nylons, cellulosic fibers. Printing on wool and silk	Good to excellent, depending on depth of shade, dyeing method	Good	Considerable staining of adjacent fibers, particularly silk, nylons; more resistant to cellulosics	Fair to good	Not affected	Fair to good	Not affected	Good	Generally good; some greens fair
Substantive Direct	Dye cellulosics directly; some dye wool, silk, nylons; union dyes for cotton-wool blends. Complete shade range; colors duller than basic or acid dyes	Primarily for cellulosic fabrics. Some good for cotton-wool blends; some good for better quality fabrics. Much used for printing on dischargeable dyed backgrounds	Good to excellent	Poor	Good resistance	Good	Good	Very good in most shades on cotton, rayons	Not affected	Poor to good, depending on color	Good

PRINCIPAL CLASSES OF SYNTHETIC DYES AND THEIR CHARACTERISTICS (Continued)

DYE CLASS	GENERAL DESCRIPTION	USES	FASTNESS								
			Light	Washing	Staining (Bleeding)	Dry Cleaning	Hot Pressing	Crocking	Gas Fading	Seawater	Perspiration
Developed	Dyes processed using copper salts, copper-resin compounds develop new dye in fiber. Used for cellulosics, wool, silk, nylons. Complete shade range; colors duller than basic or acid dyes	Same as substantive dyes.	Good to excellent	Fair	Good resistance	Good	Good	Very good in most shades on cotton, rayons	Not affected	Poor to good, depending on color	Good
Azoic (Naphthol and Rapidogens)	Also known as insoluble azos and ice colors; ice helps to reduce temperature of bath to facilitate dyeing. Complete shade range; yellows, reds, blacks most used. Bright shades at moderate cost	Primarily for cotton goods; limited use on acetate, nylons. Extensive printing use since colors are dischargeable and work with other groups	Good to excellent, depending on type, shade, depth	Good; some sensitive to chlorine bleach	Fair, sometimes stain adjacent whites; some bleed in peroxide bleach	Good	Good	Depends on dyeing technique and after treatment	Not affected	Good	Generally good
Disperse	Developed for acetate (1922). Insoluble in water; supplied in paste or finely powdered form; particles disperse in water and dissolve in fibers. Good shade range	Primarily for acetate; also triacetate, nylons, polyesters, acrylics, modacrylics, olefins, as well as cellulosic fibers. Wide use in apparel, decorative fabrics. Used for dyeing and printing	Fair to excellent, depending on fiber	Fair to good; better on polyesters than on acetate or nylons	Stains wool badly	Good	Some color change possible	Good	Poor to good resistance, depending on fiber. Blues and violets on acetate very sensitive, less sensitive on nylons and polyesters	Good	Good
Sulfur	First created in 1879. Generally insoluble in water. Complete shade range except for true red; colors not bright	Applicable to stock, yarn, piece goods; used for heavy woven and knitted cotton goods as well as linen and jute. Some printing	Poor to fair for yellows and browns; good to excellent in heavy	Poor to good; most sensitive to chlorine bleach	Fair to good, depending on shade, depth, aftertreatment	Good	Good	Poor to good, depending on shade, depth	Not affected	Good	Good

Class	Characteristics									
Vat	Synthetic indigo original (1879). Insoluble in water; require reduction to apply. Incomplete but adequate shade range	Generally excellent	Good	Good resistance	Good	Generally good; some color change with certain dyes	Fair to good, depending on dye, depth of shade	Generally not affected; a few are susceptible	Good	Good
Reactive	First available in 1957; several chemical varieties. Form chemical combination with fiber, distinguishing class from others. Produce brightest shades on cotton	Good to very good on most fibers; poor to moderate on nylon	Good; generally sensitive to chlorine bleach	Good resistance	Good	Not affected	Good	Not susceptible	Good; some fair, particularly in chlorinated pool	Good
Pigment	Generally organic coloring materials; all insoluble in water with no affinity for fiber. Fixed on fiber with resinous binders and cured at high temperatures. Complete shade range in bright colors	Very good to excellent	Good	Good	Good, if properly bound	Good	Good for light to medium shades; very poor for dark shades	Majority not susceptible; a few sensitive	Good	Good
Optical Brighteners (Colorless Dyes)	Also called fluorescent whiteners. Brightness caused by absorption of ultraviolet light and reflection of visible blue light. Applied during bleaching or in the final finish (before resin finish or with the resin)	Fair	Varies but generally improves with build-up of whiteners in household detergents	Not affected	Not known to be affected	Not known to be affected	Not known to be affected	Not known to be affected	Not known to be affected	Not known to be affected

Data based upon Dye Chart—1963, Textile World

Courtesy Pepperell Manufacturing Co.

Cotton staple being stock-dyed in a kettle containing 1,000 pounds of fiber.

Woolens are often stock-dyed. The completeness of this method is reflected in the expression "dyed in the wool," which is used to attribute the quality of thoroughness. Stock dyeing produces mixture effects and color blends, of which oxford suitings and tweed homespuns are examples.

TOP DYEING ■ One step nearer to the finished yarn than stock dyeing is what is called *top dyeing* in the worsted industry. Top is wool that has been combed to take out the short fibers, then delivered from the combs in a ropelike form about 1¼ inches thick. The top is wound on perforated spools and the dye liquor is circulated through it. Very even dyeing is possible with this method.

YARN DYEING ■ When dyeing is done after the fiber has been spun into yarn, the fabric is described as *yarn-dyed*. This method is also sometimes referred to as *skein dyeing;* the yarn is on packages, or spools, or is in the form of skeins when immersed in the dye bath. The dyestuff has a chance to penetrate to the core of the yarn, similar to the penetration of the fiber in stock dyeing. Yarn-dyed fabrics are usually deeper and richer in color. Yarn-dyed fabrics intended for laundering must be quite colorfast, or bleeding will occur. The primary reason for dyeing in the yarn form is to create interesting checks, stripes, and plaids with different colored yarns in the weaving process. Chambrays, for example, are usually woven with a colored warp and white filling. Other combinations of different-colored yarns are checked gingham, shepherd's check, plaid, seersucker, and heather mixtures.

Warpbeam dyeing, a form of yarn dyeing, is done by steeping the yarns on a warp-beam in a dye vat.

Courtesy Textile World

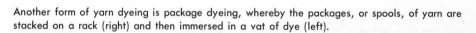

Another form of yarn dyeing is package dyeing, whereby the packages, or spools, of yarn are stacked on a rack (right) and then immersed in a vat of dye (left).

Courtesy Burlington Industries, Inc.

Close-up of fabric in rope form being fed into dye bath in rear.

Courtesy Burlington Industries, Inc.

PIECE DYEING ■ The great bulk of dyed fabric on the market is dyed in the piece, or after it is woven. This method gives the manufacturer maximum flexibility for his inventory to meet large or small demands for a given color as fashion requires. The goods are dyed by three general methods. Where yardage warrants it, cellulosic fabrics are dyed in continuous ranges. It is possible to do the same with nylon and wool fabrics, but the latter is seldom handled in this way.

Small lots of fabrics of all fibers are dyed in batches, either in the open width on jigs, on perforated beams, or on becks that rotate the fabric in rope form in the dye bath. Polyesters are often dyed under pressure in either rope or open width. The choice of method depends, in most cases, on the character of the goods.

Piece dyeing is thoroughly satisfactory as regards levelness, penetration, and overall fastness, assuming that the proper dyes have been used for the job. The method has been extended to fabrics of all fibers. The higher temperatures that are possible with pressure speed up the dyeing process.

CROSS DYEING ■ Cross dyeing is a combination of stock dyeing or of yarn dyeing with subsequent piece dyeing. Cross dyeing produces varied effects. For instance, either the warp or the filling yarns may be stock-dyed or yarn-dyed, one set of yarns being left undyed. The fabric is piece-dyed after weaving; thus,

Courtesy Burlington Industries, Inc.

Fabric may be piece-dyed on a jig, whereby the cloth is immersed into troughs of dye and subsequently rewound into rolls.

color is given to the undyed yarn in a second dye bath, and the yarns that were originally stock-dyed or yarn-dyed acquire some additional coloring, which blends with the piece-dyed portion of the fabric.

If yarns of vegetable fibers have been combined with yarns of animal fibers in a fabric that is to be piece-dyed, two separate dye baths must be used. The fabric is dipped into both solutions, each of which affects the fiber for which it has an affinity. This provides colorful effects.

A mordant can be included in a single dye bath to cause the dye to adhere to the fiber for which it does not have an affinity. Thus, the more expensive method of cross dyeing, requiring two dye baths, need not be used.

Still another method of cross dyeing is to immerse a fabric composed of two different types of fibers into one dye bath containing two different dyes, one specific for each of the fibers. For example, a fabric composed of viscose rayon and acetate yarns may be cross-dyed in this manner. When the fabric is removed from the dye bath, the viscose rayon yarns will be one color, and the acetate yarns will be another color.

SOLUTION PIGMENTING OR DOPE DYEING ■ In producing man-made or synthetic fibers, a great deal of time and money can be saved if the dye is added to the solution before it is extruded through the spinnerets into filaments. This method also gives a greater degree of colorfastness. A process called *solution* *pigmenting* or *dope dyeing* has been used with varying degrees of success for man-made fibers ranging from rayon through saran and glass fiber. Effective results have been obtained.

Two outstanding examples of the solution pigmenting process for acetate fiber are Chromspun and Celaperm. The former is the trade name for the process developed by the Tennessee Eastman Company; the latter is the trade name for a similar process developed by the Celanese Corporation of America. These solution pigmenting processes were developed to overcome problems in dyeing acetate yarns and fabrics where grays and blues would gas-fade. The pigment colors are the fastest known—much faster than any of the customary dyeing techniques. Therefore, where warranted, they are to be preferred when fastness to almost any known factor is important.

TESTS TO DETERMINE COLORFASTNESS

Beauty of color in any fabric is of no value to the consumer unless the dye may be considered fast under the conditions in which the fabric will be used.

Swatches of colored fabric are put into containers of water and soap or detergent and rotated in this Launder-Ometer to test colorfastness to washing.

Courtesy Atlas Electric Devices Co.

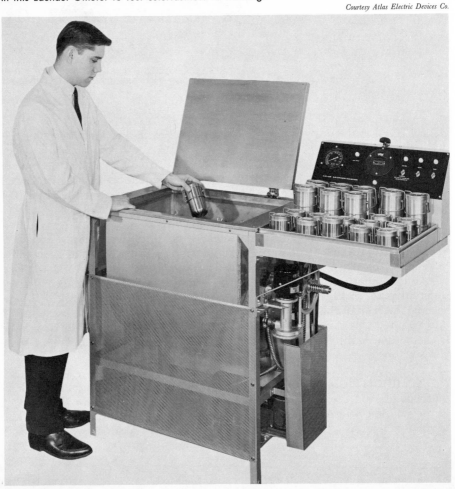

Color must meet such tests as washing, ironing, steaming, perspiration, strong light, and dry cleaning. The United States Government tests fabrics for colorfastness to maintain and enforce trade standards. Retail stores often have laboratories for testing consumers' goods to maintain merchandise standards for their own protection as well as to give their customers proper value for the price paid. The consumer may also test fabrics for colorfastness at home. Garments will give additional wear and retain a fresh, new appearance if they are properly cleaned at home or at a commercial cleaner in accordance with the results of the tests to which samples of the garment's fabrics have been previously subjected.

FASTNESS TO WASHING ■ The usual method for determining fastness to washing is to wash and then iron under a white cloth a sample of the fabric while it is still wet. If the dye bleeds on the cloth, the color cannot be considered fast. Home washing is not a rigorous enough test for fabrics that will be washed in commercial laundries. A more adequate test is to immerse the sample in water containing a bleach, such as Clorox, because similar strong compounds are used in the laundries.

FASTNESS TO IRONING ■ To test for fastness to ironing, iron the sample with a very hot iron. After the sample has cooled, compare it with the original fabric. If the color is unchanged, the fabric is fast to ironing.

FASTNESS TO STEAMING ■ To test for fastness to steaming, place a sample between the folds of a white cloth, and steam it over a teakettle. If the color is fast, it should be unchanged, and no dye will show on the white cloth.

FASTNESS TO LIGHT ■ To test for fastness to light, cover half a sample of fabric with opaque paper and expose it to outdoor light for perhaps 20 days. Then compare both halves. If the exposed portion shows perceptible fading, the fabric is not fast to light. A more specific time for exposure cannot be given, because the intensity of sunlight varies in different localities. Usually, resistance to exposure of 20 days is considered good.

This test is performed in a much shorter time in textile testing laboratories by the use of the Fade-Ometer, an apparatus having very strong electric lamps or a special carbon arc light. If a fabric can withstand an exposure of 40 hours in this machine with no perceptible loss of color, it is said to have superlative fastness to light. A fabric has good fastness to light if it withstands an exposure of 30 hours.

FASTNESS TO PERSPIRATION ■ To test for fastness to perspiration, soak a sample of the dyed fabric for 10 minutes in a weak acid, such as a dilute acetic acid solution. Do not rinse. Roll the sample in a piece of undyed cloth. Permit gradual drying, and leave the material rolled for a few days. If comparison with the original color shows that the shade of the dyed fabric has changed, or if the dye appears on the cloth in which the sample was rolled, the color is not fast to perspiration.

The effects of both acid and alkaline perspiration can be determined by the standard Government test, which recommends the use of two solutions. *For acid perspiration:* 10 grams sodium chloride; 1 gram lactic acid, U.S.P. 85 percent; 1 gram disodium orthophosphate, anhydrous. Make up to 1 liter with water. *For alkaline perspiration:* 10 grams sodium chloride; 4 grams ammonium carbonate, U.S.P.; 1 gram disodium orthophosphate, anhydrous. Make up to 1 liter with water. Samples of the dyed fabric are placed against pieces of undyed cloth and left for a few days in each solution. The pieces of dyed fabric and undyed cloth are then squeezed and allowed to dry. Any indication of staining denotes poor fastness to perspiration.

The Fade-Ometer is used for testing colorfastness to sunlight. Samples of fabric are exposed to the rays of the machine for a period of hours or days. After removal, the samples are compared with an unexposed piece of fabric to determine the extent of loss of color.

Courtesy Atlas Electric Devices Co.

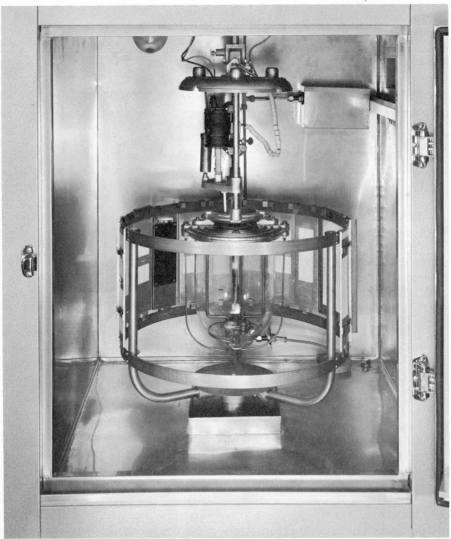

FASTNESS TO CROCKING ■ To test for fastness to crocking, rub a dry sample against a white cloth; make the same test with a wet sample. If the color does not rub off on the white cloth, the color is fast to rubbing or crocking.

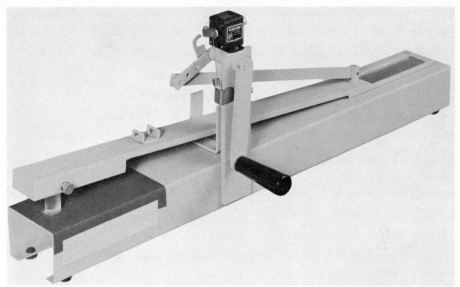

Courtesy Atlas Electric Devices Co.

This Crockmeter drags one colored fabric across another to determine whether the dye will rub off.

FASTNESS TO GAS FADING ■ Flames from heating appliances cause nitrogen in the atmosphere to unite with oxygen, forming nitrogenous compounds that cause some acetate dyes to lose color if the fumes come in contact with the fabric. This is known as gas fading or acid fading in acetate; blue is especially susceptible. An antifume finish of an alkaline nature can be applied to a fabric to minimize gas fading by the use of an inhibiter in the dye. Fabrics can be tested to determine the permanency of their antifume finish by exposure for about 20 hours in a chamber containing the combustible fumes of a gas burner.

REVIEW QUESTIONS

1 Explain the difference between dyeing and printing.

2 Explain the importance of dyeing from the consumer's point of view.

3 What two factors enter into the selection of a dye?

4 What types of fabrics need to be colorfast (a) to washing, (b) to light, (c) to perspiration?

5 What are the essential differences between stock, yarn, and piece dyeing?

6 Explain the following terms: (a) crocking, (b) bleeding, (c) gas fading.

7 Discuss both the limitations and advantages of direct dyes.

8 (a) What is a mordant? (b) Explain how it is used in dyeing.

9 Discuss the advantages and the limitations of acid dyes.

10 Why is salt often put into a dye bath?

11 What happens to sulfur-dyed fabrics if stored for a long time?

12 (a) What is vat dyeing? (b) When would it be used?

13 What is meant by an optical brightener, or colorless dye?

14 What characteristic is common to yarn dyeing and skein dyeing?

15 (a) What is solution dyeing? (b) What are its advantages?

16 When is cross dyeing used?

17 Why may warp yarns be dyed in the fiber stage or in the yarn stage instead of using the piece-dyeing method entirely?

18 What factors determine the durability of a dye?

19 Describe briefly the stages of the dyeing process.

20 What kinds of dyes are used primarily (a) for the animal fibers, (b) for the vegetable fibers, (c) for man-made fibers?

21 Explain how to test colorfastness (a) to light, (b) to washing, (c) to crocking.

SUGGESTED ACTIVITIES

1 Obtain small samples of colored fabrics, and test them for colorfastness. Report your testing procedure and your findings.

2 Examine the labels on three pieces of apparel or household furnishings. Copy each label on a sheet of paper, and write your interpretation of each label in terms of the textile information that you have acquired.

10 COLOR AND DESIGN DECORATION

The yarns produced in the spinning process create some form of decoration in the fabric. Later, in the weaving process, decoration is also obtained by the pattern of the weave. The checkerboard pattern of the plain weave, the variations of the basket construction, the diagonal of the twill weave, and the luster of the satin weave produce simple designs. This type of decoration becomes more elaborate as fabric construction advances to the use of the third dimension in the pile weave, to the open-mesh lacelike effect of the lappet weave, and to the intricate effects of the Jacquard weave.

When fabric passes through finishing operations, it is given lustrous effects that contribute further to its final appearance. Other finishing processes create the additional effects of soft napped surfaces and the crinkled designs seen in seersucker, matelassé, and similar crepes. Dyeing makes an important contribution to fabric decoration by the many beautiful colors it produces and the color harmonies obtained by combinations of the various dyeing methods. Fabric can be still further enhanced by printing color designs on the finished cloth.

DISTINGUISHING PRINTING FROM DYEING

To know whether a fabric has been dyed by immersion or whether the color has merely been printed on the cloth, examine the outline of the design. On the printed fabric, the outline or edges of the design are sharply defined on the right side. The entire design seldom penetrates to the wrong side.

On sheer fabrics, the design may show up favorably on the wrong side because dyestuffs will penetrate sheer construction. Such fabrics may intentionally simulate woven designs, which use yarn-dyed warp and filling. Examine some of the raveled yarns. If the design has been imprinted, the yarns will show areas on which the color is not equally distributed.

DYES USED FOR PRINTING

Most classes of dyes are adaptable to one or more of the various types of printing. The choice depends on the purpose for which the goods will be used, the fiber or fibers involved, and what the potential customer would be willing to pay. Good fastness properties in prints are available today at a modest cost, and there is no reason why the consumer should settle for less than satisfactory fastness.

Of the various dye classes, the *vat, reactive,* and *naphthol* colors will generally produce the needed fastness properties for most purposes. Another class, called *pigment* colors, are not truly dyes but are of utmost importance in printing. These colors are fixed to the fiber by means of resins that are very resistant to laundering or dry cleaning. The pigments themselves are among the fastest known colors to all normal influences. For light to medium shades they are unbeatable; but for full or dark shades they are impractical because the colors are not really absorbed by the fiber and will crock, or rub off. This problem may be solved by improved resins, better pigments, or more effective anticrock agents.

For cotton printing, vat and reactive dyes are used. Pigments and some naphthols are also used. Very cheap prints can be made with basic colors mixed with tartar emetic and tannic acid, but today's domestic market has scarcely any room for such prints. Silk is usually printed with acid colors; wool, treated with chlorine to make it more receptive to color (and to prevent shrinking), is printed with acid or chrome dyes.

METHODS OF DECORATION WITH COLOR

One form of applying color decoration to a fabric after it has otherwise been finished is called *printing*. Fabric that is to be printed must be singed, bleached, and cleaned. The methods producing color designs are as follows.

Block printing	Thermacrome transfer printing
Roller printing	Warp printing
Duplex printing	Photo printing
Discharge or extract printing	Batik dyeing
Resist printing	Tie dyeing
Stencil printing	Composition or paste designs
Screen printing	Flocking
Rotary screen printing	Spray painting

In most of these methods, the dye is imprinted on the fabric in paste form, and any desired pattern may be produced. The dyes are usually dissolved in a limited amount of water to which a thickening agent has been added to give the necessary viscosity to the print paste. Originally, corn starch was much favored for this purpose in cotton printing; today, gums or alginates derived from seaweed are preferred because they are easier to wash out and do not, themselves, absorb any color (which would be subsequently washed out in the final soaping and printing). Furthermore, the gums allow better penetration of color, which is important to good printing. Most pigment printing is done without thickeners, as such; the thickening is obtained by mixing together resins, solvents, and water to produce the necessary viscosity for printing.

BLOCK PRINTING ■ Block printing is the hand method and the oldest method of printing designs on fabric. It is not commercially important because it is too slow—printed fabric cannot be produced inexpensively in large enough quantities by the hand-blocked method. Block printing has usually been done in countries where labor is less costly than in the United States. Today, fabric is block-printed only in comparatively short lengths of material. Block printing is found chiefly in decorative pieces for the home or in expensive linens for upholstery purposes.

To make hand-blocked prints, the design must first be carved on a wooden or metal block. The dyestuff is applied in paste form to the design on the face of the block. The block is pressed down firmly by hand on selected portions of the surface of the fabric, imprinting the carved design as many times as desired on a specific length of cloth. To obtain variation of color in the same design, as many additional blocks must be carved as there will be additional colors. The portions of the design that will appear in different colors must be separately imprinted by hand before each design is complete. The more colors used, the

The high fidelity of a print pattern depends on the accuracy of the engraving and registration of the copper rollers. Separate rollers for each color in the fabric design are outlined by pantograph, then hand-etched, polished, and chrome-plated.

Courtesy United Piece Dye Works

more valuable and expensive the hand-blocked print will be, because of the enhanced beauty of design as well as the labor involved in the hand printing.

You can recognize hand-blocked prints by noting slight irregularities in the detail and in the repetition of the design and by comparing areas for slight variations in color. These irregularities are imitated by machine printing, however, to give machine prints the characteristic appearance of expensive hand-blocked prints.

ROLLER PRINTING ■ Roller printing is the machine method of printing designs on cloth by engraved rollers. It turns out color-designed fabrics in vast quantities at the rate of thousands of yards an hour. This method of producing attractive designs is relatively inexpensive when compared with any hand method. It is a machine counterpart of block printing. In roller printing, engraved copper cylinders or rollers take the place of the hand-carved blocks. Just as there must be a separate block for each color in block printing, so must there be as many engraved rollers in machine printing as there are colors in the

In roller printing, engraved copper rollers transfer print design to fabric. Note color pans and furnisher-rolls supplying color to the rollers. In the foreground are counterweights controlling "doctor-blades" (hidden from view by copper rollers), which continuously remove excess color from the engraving.

Courtesy United Piece Dye Works

design to be imprinted. With each revolution of the roller, a "repeat" of the design is printed.

Originally, the design for each of the rollers was engraved by hand with an awl; then a skilled craftsman duplicated the artist's design onto copper rollers. Today, the engraving is frequently done by *pantograph* transference. Separate photographs on individually sensitized copper plates are taken for each color of the design. An artist then paints the appropriate color of the pattern on each plate. The engraver traces the outline of the design on the plate with one arm of a pantograph, which simultaneously cuts the design (with a diamond needle on its other arm) into the curved surface of a copper roller. Next, a chemical resistant is coated over the areas of the roller that will print the color, and the roller is treated with acid. The acid etches the unprotected areas; the protected raised areas are the design pattern to be used for color printing.

Another method of reproducing a design on a roller is by photo engraving. A film of a photograph pattern is placed over a sensitized roller. After exposure, the roller is etched. This technique reproduces the photograph's detail and shading.

Each roller is polished for uniform smoothness so that the dye will spread evenly on the raised areas. They are then locked into precise positions on the machine. The number of rollers used depends upon the number of colors in the design, and as many as sixteen rollers can be employed.

Each of the engraved rollers first comes in contact with a companion roller that has been submerged in the dye paste to be used for its part of the design. A sharp blade, called the *doctor blade,* scrapes the excess dye from the roller. As the fabric passes under the engraved rollers, the design is imprinted on it. A mordant is generally used in the dye paste to fix the color.

DUPLEX PRINTING ■ Duplex printing simulates a woven pattern by printing the fabric on both sides. The fabric may be passed through the roller-printing machine in two separate operations or through a duplex printing machine in a single operation. Duplex printing produces an equally clear outline on both sides of the fabric. The design is applied so skillfully by careful registration of the printing cylinders that the result may be mistaken for a woven design. But the difference can be detected by raveling a yarn.

BLOTCH PRINTING ■ Blotch prints may have a colored background as well as a colored design, and both may be printed at the same time. This method is used chiefly for cottons and linens.

DISCHARGE PRINTING ■ In the discharge method of printing, fabric is often dyed in the piece and then printed with a chemical that will destroy the color in designed areas. Sometimes the base color is removed and another color printed in its place, but usually a white area is desirable to brighten the overall design. When properly done, discharge printing is thoroughly satisfactory; however, the discharged areas may literally fall out of the fabric if the goods are not thoroughly washed after printing (a rare situation today). The usual method of producing discharge prints is to print the design, such as polka dots, with a paste containing caustic soda and sodium hydrosulfite. A steaming follows and then there is a good washing to remove the by-products of the reaction.

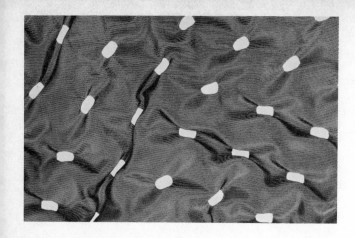

The lacquer used in this stencil print curled and became brittle after the inferior plasticizer was leached out during dry cleaning.

Courtesy CIBA Review

RESIST PRINTING ◼ In resist printing, bleached goods are run through cylinders that print a pattern on the fabric in the form of a resist paste, a resinous substance that cannot be penetrated when the fabric is subsequently immersed in a dye. The dye will affect only the parts that are not covered by the resist paste. After the fabric has passed through a subsequent dyeing process, the resist paste is removed, leaving a pattern on a dark ground. In the discharge method, the fabric is first dyed, and the color is then extracted by an imprinted chemical; in the resist method, a resist paste is first imprinted, and the fabric is then dyed. The durability of the fabric is not affected by the resist method.

STENCIL PRINTING ◼ Stencil printing originated in Japan. Its high cost limits its use and importance in the United States. In stencil printing, the design must first be cut in cardboard, wood, or metal. The stencil may have a fine, delicate design, or there may be large spaces through which a great amount of color can be applied. A stencil design is usually limited to the application of only one color and is generally used for narrow widths of fabric.

SCREEN PRINTING ◼ Originally, this technique was referred to as *silk-screen printing* because the screens were made of fine, strong silk threads. Today, they are also made of nylon, Dacron, Vinyon, and metal.

For screen printing, the artist's design is copied onto a series of very fine screens, one for each color to be printed. Each screen's design may be drawn by hand and a coating of lacquer or other impermeable substance applied to all parts of the screen that are not part of its design. More usually, today, the design is photographed and a negative is used for each sensitized screen to opaque, or block out, those areas not part of the screen's color design. Each screen is then fitted onto a wooden or metal frame.

The fabric to be printed is attached to a backing spread on a long table. A screen representing one color of the design is set by hand over the fabric in the first position by metal brackets on the sides of the table to hold it in place. The printing paste, or dye, is poured on the screen and forced through its unblocked areas onto the fabric with a rubber-edged squeegee. The frame is then raised and placed on the next section of the fabric, and the operation is repeated until the entire length of the cloth is printed with that one color. This process must be repeated for each color to be used in the design.

Whereas the hand screen printing is time-consuming and limited to relatively

*Photos Courtesy Geigy Chemical Corporation
and Printex Corporation*

In hand screen printing, the fabric to be printed is laid out on a table and a screen for each color of the design is precisely placed.

Two men work together passing the squeegee to each other as they force the dye through the screen.

Each screen of the series is progressively moved to succeeding sections of the fabric to repeat the same color of the design.

The hand screen printed fabric shown below is hung on a rack above the printing table to air-dry.

short lengths of sixty yards of fabric, electronically controlled automatic machines screen print hundreds of yards of cloth at rates of up to 450 yards per hour. The back of the fabric to be printed is coated with an adhesive, which causes it to adhere to a backing on a rubber conveyor belt that serves as the table top for the printing operation. A series of screens, one for each color set in frames with automatically operated squeegees, are printed above the belt. As the fabric advances, the screens are automatically lowered to the cloth and the appropriate color is properly applied with the automatically regulated squeegees. The cloth is continuously fed into an oven to be dried. The modern screen-printing machine is very expensive, but it will print up to 20 colors in one run. The method's versatility and production rate, however, compensate for its initial high cost.

The chief advantages of screen printing are that the colors can be produced in brighter, cleaner shades than are possible with roller printing and the designs to be repeated can be much larger. The technique also lends itself to experimental and creative designs. Short runs of unique designs provide an exclusive pattern often sought by couturiers and interior decorators. The process is slower than machine roller-printing; therefore, it is not quite as economical for large-sized yardages. However, the automatic screen-printing machines now available have cut down the cost differences considerably. Screen printers so equipped are no longer looked upon as small-yardage operators. Most roller printing plants today have auxiliary screen-printing machines to get out samples and intermediate-sized yardages that are not profitable on the roller machines.

In screen printing, it is possible to have designs consisting of squares, circles, and ovals because the areas not to receive the dye are painted out by the lacquer. If clearly defined geometric designs were attempted in cardboard or metal stencils, obviously, the cut area would fall away.

On a knitted fabric, such as jersey, screen printing is the only printing method that can be used. Other methods smear the dye, as a knitted fabric stretches when it receives the impact of the rollers.

Rotary screen printing combines the basic principles of the roller and the screen printing techniques.

Courtesy Textile World

In automatic screen printing, electronic controls set each screen on the fabric, release a measured amount of the appropriate color, and run the squeegee on a rail passing over the screen.

The fabric is automatically moved along on a conveyor belt successively from one screen to the next to receive different parts of the colored design.

The fabric passes under the last of a series of screens before being moved into the dryer. As many as 20 screens may be employed to obtain as many colors.

The automatic machine screen printed design is inspected as it leaves the dryer.

Photos Courtesy Geigy Chemical Corp. and Printex Corp.

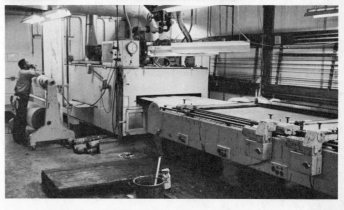

ROTARY SCREEN PRINTING ■ More recently, a machine that utilizes seamless cylindrical screens made of metal foil has been introduced from Holland. Prints of various types and intricate designs and with shadings of up to 12 colors can be obtained with a high degree of accuracy and sharpness.

As the fabric to be printed is fed under constant tension into the printer portion of the machine, its back is coated with an adhesive, which causes it to adhere to a horizontal conveyor printing blanket. The fabric passes under the rotating screens through which the printing paste is automatically fed from pressure tanks. A squeegee in each screen forces the paste through the screen onto the fabric as it moves along at rates of up to 85 yards per minute. The cloth then passes into a drying oven.

THERMACROME TRANSFER PRINTING ■ This process for printing cotton, woolen, and man-made woven and circular-knitted fabrics was recently developed in England. The technique is to transfer thermoplastic ink designs from paper to the fabric (a technique similar to that of transferring decals). One of the unique features of this process is that circular-knitted fabrics can be printed around the circumference without slitting the goods.

Identified as the *Thermacrome* process, thermoplastic ink designs on paper are transferred to the fabric by applying heat under pressure. Several narrow reels of transfer paper are set up on the machine to accommodate fabric widths of up to 36 inches. No aftertreatments are necessary. Clarity of design and fastness of color is said to be as good as other printing techniques. The process can print fabrics at rates up to 180 yards per hour at costs claimed to be about one-half that of screen printing.

WARP PRINTING ■ Warp printing is roller printing applied to warp yarns before they are woven into fabric. Fine white or neutral-colored filling yarns are generally used for weaving, so that the design on the warp will not be obscured. This method produces designs with soft, nebulous, but striking effects. Great care must be taken to keep the warp yarns in their proper position so the outline of the design will be preserved. Warp printing is used for expensive cretonnes and upholstery fabrics.

A variation of warp printing is *Vigoureux printing* or *melange*. Utilizing a variation of roller printing, horizontal or cross-striped designs are printed on the ropelike wool tops or slubbings. Subsequently, when the tops are spun into yarn, the stripes are attenuated and pulled apart so that they appear as scattered flecks of color in the woven cloth.

PHOTO PRINTING ■ In photo printing, the fabric is coated with a chemical that is sensitive to light. Any photograph may be printed on the fabric. The results are the same as when printing photographs on paper. All details can be reproduced if the photographer and technician are careful.

BATIK DYEING ■ The hand method of producing designs, known as *batik*, originated in Java. It enjoys frequent renewal of popularity in the United States. Batik is somewhat similar to the machine method of resist printing. The design is drawn on the fabric, and beeswax containing paraffin is deposited through a small cup-shaped instrument on the areas that are not to be colored. The fabric is then immersed in a tepid dye bath and absorbs the dye in those areas not

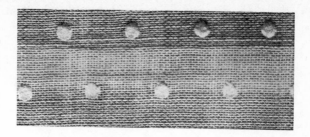

Pasted designs, like the dots in this fabric, may disappear in laundering if an inferior adhesive is used.

Courtesy U.S. Department of Agriculture

covered by the wax. After the fabric is dried, the wax is removed by applying heat or benzine. The result is a silhouette design or a dyed background. The process is repeated if additional colors are to be added.

Sometimes, in the last application of color, the wax is permitted to crack, and the last dyestuff partially penetrates the other dyed portions, producing the multicolored design characteristic of batik. The American method differs from the Oriental in that light colors are applied first, followed by the wax; the deeper shades are then built in. In the Oriental method, the dark shades are applied first, and the portions to be kept light are waxed.

TIE DYEING ■ The results of tie dyeing are similar to batik, but the designs can be only circular in form, as the dye is resisted by knots that are tied in the cloth before it is immersed in the dye bath. The outside of the knotted portion is dyed, but the inside is not penetrated if the knot is firmly tied. Partial penetration occurs when the knot is not tight, causing gradations and irregularities of color that produce indistinct but attractive designs. The process is repeated as many times as desired by making new knots in other parts of the cloth and immersing the fabric in additional dye baths. This gives a characteristic blurred or mottled effect, the result of the dyes running into each other. Like other hand methods, tie dyeing is expensive. Because the method creates interesting designs, the patterns are imitated in roller printing.

COMPOSITION OR PASTED DESIGNS ■ The rollers used to imprint color by means of dyes, chemicals, or resist pastes can also apply lacquer or colored paste to fabric as small designs. Modern adhesives make such designs very resistant to normal laundering. Substances that can be baked into the fabric are also used for this decorative effect. When this is done, the designs become so much a part of the cloth that they may be considered permanent, seldom being destroyed by washing or dry cleaning.

FLOCKING ■ The technique of adhering minute pieces of fiber, called *flock*, to form designs on fabric has been used to a limited extent for about 600 years. It has become more widely used in recent years because of modern methods. Using a suitable adhesive (instead of a dye), a design is roller printed onto a fabric. Then, flock of cotton, wool, viscose rayon, or nylon are applied to the fabric in a manner that causes them to adhere in an upright position and produce a pilelike, velvet-textured design. The flock are usually of colored fiber, thereby adding to the decorative appeal.

Cotton and wool waste fiber are often ground or random-cut into flock. However, since such production results in uneven and angular ends that do not

SCHEMATIC DIAGRAM OF MECHANICAL FLOCKING

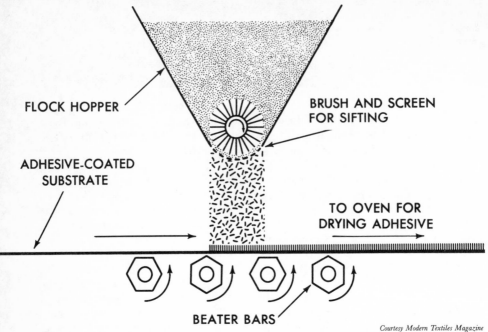

FLOCK HOPPER

BRUSH AND SCREEN
FOR SIFTING

ADHESIVE-COATED
SUBSTRATE

TO OVEN FOR
DRYING ADHESIVE

BEATER BARS

Courtesy Modern Textiles Magazine

The beater bars' vibration of the fabric causes the flock to flow over the surface of the cloth, stand erect, and penetrate into the adhesive coated fabric, producing an inexpensive pile design.

Durability of flocking is influenced by the adhesive used. Natural rubber adhesive used to hold the flock on this fabric swelled, loosened, and curled when it was dry-cleaned.

Courtesy CIBA Review

SCHEMATIC DIAGRAM OF ELECTROSTATIC FLOCKING

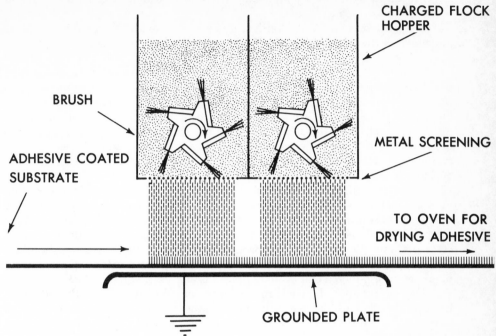

CHARGED FLOCK HOPPER

BRUSH

METAL SCREENING

ADHESIVE COATED SUBSTRATE

TO OVEN FOR DRYING ADHESIVE

GROUNDED PLATE

Courtesy Modern Textiles Magazine

The electrically charged air directs and propels the flock into the adhesive-coated fabric producing a dense, uniform pile in the design.

Close-up view of an electrostatic flocking unit showing nylon flock being propelled onto a woven jute substrate.

Courtesy Modern Textiles Magazine

affix as well as straight ends, precision-cut flock of rayon and other man-made fibers (such as nylon and acrylics) are preferred. The flock generally range in length from ⅖₅ inch to ¼ inch.

Flocking may be accomplished by a *mechanical* method of beating the underside of the adhesive-coated fabric with rotating multisided beater bars as the flock is sifted onto the surface of the fabric. The fabric's vibrations, produced by the beater bars, cause the flock to flow over the surface of the fabric and stand erect those fibers that do not land flat on the adhesive. Continued vibration causes the erect fibers to penetrate deeper into the adhesive, and, as more fibers fall on the already erect fibers, they become similarly oriented and build up a pile effect. With this method (which has the advantage of being relatively inexpensive), the fibers become more deeply imbedded and, therefore, more permanently attached. However, since many fibers adhere at various angles, the flocking may not be as dense as desired.

Another technique utilizes an *electrostatic* principle. As the flock are sifted onto the fabric, they pass through an electrostatic field, or electrically charged air space. This directs and propels the fibers in the longitudinal direction of the current toward the fabric, which causes them to stick to the adhesive in an erect position. This method can produce a denser flocking because the fibers uniformly adhere upright to the fabric. However, it is a more expensive technique, requiring more complicated apparatus and better-quality flock.

Depending upon the background fabric, or substrate, the depth of the pile, the flock used, and the pattern, flocked fabrics may be created for various purposes. Flocking is used for curtains, draperies, carpeting, and wearing apparel.

SPRAY PAINTING ■ Designs may be hand-painted on fabric, or the dye may be applied with a mechanized airbrush, which blows or sprays color on the fabric. Spray painting is used when surface coloring is to be done quickly and economically; for example, designs on tablecloths. Direct, acid, or vat dyes dissolved in water, alcohol, or other organic solvent may be used.

Pattern flocking, using different colored flock and controlling the deposition of each to certain areas, can be done on a substrate that is coated with one overall coat of adhesive.

Courtesy Modern Textiles Magazine

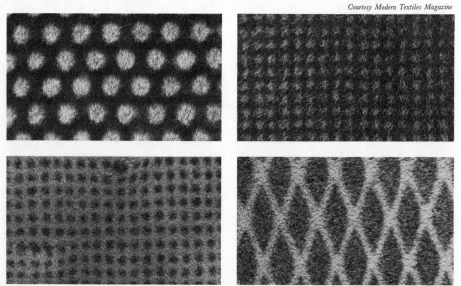

DECORATION OF FABRICS BY PRINTING AND DYEING

TYPE OF DECORATION	HAND METHOD	MACHINE METHOD
Block printing	Design carved on blocks; dye applied to block; block pressed on fabric	Similar blocks pressed on fabric by machine; design tends to be more regular.
Roller printing		Design etched on roller; companion roller transmits dye to etched roller, which transmits it to fabric
Discharge printing		Bleached goods first dyed; chemical bleach printed on fabric; color discharged
Resist printing		Resist paste put on fabric; fabric dyed; paste removed
Stencil printing	Design cut in stencil; color applied over stencil	
Screen printing	Design sketched or photographed on sheer silk, nylon, Dacron, Vinyon, or metal screen; background of design opaqued; color applied to screen as stencil and forced through screen	Similar screens; up to twenty set in electronically controlled machine that regulates speed of operation, amount of dye forced through each screen, fabric movement
Rotary screen printing		Cylindrical seamless metal screen; dye paste forced through screen as it rotates on moving fabric
Thermacrome transfer printing		Thermoplastic ink designs transferred by heat and pressure from paper to fabric
Warp printing		Engraved rollers print design only on warp yarns; fabric then woven, using white or neutral filling yarn
Duplex printing		Design printed back to back on both sides of fabric; gives effect of woven pattern
Photo printing	Photographs printed on sensitized fabric	
Batik dyeing	Design put on fabric; wax deposited on background of design; fabric dyed; wax removed	
Tie dyeing	Fabric knotted or tied in parts with string; dipped into dye; fabric untied	
Composition or paste designs		Lacquer figures or colored paste glued or baked on surface of fabric
Flocking		Very short, usually colored fibers adhered to fabric in design effect, conforming to pattern of adhesive applied with roller
Spray painting	Mechanized airbrush applies surface coating	

1 How can spinning and weaving processes produce decoration (a) in fabrics, (b) in finishing processes?

2 What is meant by block printing?

3 Explain roller printing and duplex printing.

4 Differentiate between discharge and resist printing.

5 Why is the discharge-printed fabric the least desirable?

6 What is the difference between a blotch and a duplex print?

7 How could one determine whether a color design is printed or woven?

8 How do screen printing and stenciling differ?

9 Compare the methods of rotary screen printing and automatic screen printing.

10 What are the values of Thermacrome transfer printing?

11 Describe warp printing and its result.

12 How does Vigoureux printing differ from warp printing?

13 Compare and contrast the batik method and the resist method of decoration.

14 (a) How are composition or paste designs made? (b) Are they durable?

15 Describe tie dyeing, and explain why it is expensive.

16 (a) Describe the flocking techniques. (b) How effective and durable are they?

17 Can batik and tie dying be imitated on a machine?

18 What are the several methods of hand decoration with color?

19 Why are most fabrics machine-printed?

20 What are the characteristics of a well-printed fabric?

Cotton is a fiber that grows from the surface of seeds in the pods, or bolls, of a bushy mallow plant. It is composed basically of a woody substance called *cellulose*.

HISTORY OF COTTON

Ancient historical records show that cotton was first cultivated in Oriental countries at least three thousand years ago. India is believed to be the oldest cotton-growing country. Cotton was known and used in all the Mediterranean countries, being introduced into Italy by the Arabs and into other parts of Europe by the Crusaders. The use of cotton in England is mentioned in writings of the thirteenth century, although its use did not become general until the first half of the sixteenth century. In the United States, cotton was cultivated in the early seventeenth century. The impetus of the Industrial Revolution, represented in the cotton industry by the invention of the spinning frame and the spinning mule in England, and by the invention of the cotton gin in the United States, resulted in vastly increased cotton production and manufacturing. Today, cotton fields extend across southern United States from Virginia to California.

Cotton fabrics have been so well known and so extensively used throughout the world for hundreds of years that the spinning of the cotton fiber into yarn, the weaving of cotton yarn into fabric, and many of the finishing processes used for cotton goods come first to mind and naturally serve as foremost examples in a study of fiber and fabric. Cotton has been of service to mankind for so long that its versatility is almost unlimited. New uses are constantly being discovered. Cotton is considered nature's most economical fiber; it is low-priced as a raw material and as a finished product. It can be depended on to serve many purposes. Not only is cotton a textile in its own right, but its by-products form the base for some of the man-made textile fibers.

VARIETIES OF COTTON

Different varieties of cotton are grown in various parts of the world. Some of their basic characteristics differ. Variations among cotton fibers also occur because of such factors as soil, moisture, climate, weather conditions, fertilizer, and insect damage. The quality of cotton fiber is based on its whiteness, fineness, length, and strength. The relative fineness and strength is generally in direct relationship with the length of the staple, the shortest staple being the coarsest and weakest.

The particular variety of cotton is often identified by the name of the country or geographic area where it is produced, and although it may have been successfully transplanted, its name may still be based on the place of origin. The kind and quality of the cotton has come to be associated with its name. The following are the better-known varieties of cotton in the United States.

SEA ISLAND COTTON ■ Sea Island cotton received its name from Sea Island off the coast of Georgia. This cotton is now successfully grown on other islands, such as those in the British West Indies and off the southeastern coast of the United States, as well as along the seacoast of the mainland. As nearness to the ocean provides the moisture so necessary to the proper development of good-quality cotton, Sea Island cotton has an extremely fine long staple, ranging from 1½ to 2½ inches in length. Wherever this variety has been successfully transplanted, it has produced the finest and the longest staple of all cotton fibers. Sea Island cotton is used for the highest-quality cotton fabrics, including laces, fine sewing thread, and imitations of silk.

EGYPTIAN COTTON ■ Consumers have long associated Egyptian cotton with high quality. However, the label "Egyptian Cotton" does not necessarily indicate superiority, since there are many varieties of Egyptian cottons. Some of these are excellent to very good. Others are only average quality. The more important of these are presented here.

Sakel, or *Sakellaridis,* is the best variety of Egyptian cotton. It is a lustrous, light-cream-colored, fine fiber with a length of 1⅜ to 1¹¹⁄₃₂ inches. Its fineness and strength permit the spinning of Sakel into yarns of 200s, which can be used for the manufacture of the very best sheerest cotton fabrics. It is also used for fine quality white-on-white and broadcloth. Through crossbreeding, Sakel has given rise to the best American Egyptian cottons, which are used in making the finest cotton goods today.

Due to its low yield per acre, its low resistance to wilt disease and boll damage, the production of Sakel is, however, only about 1.5 percent of the entire cotton crop of Egypt. There are two other very good varieties of Egyptian cotton.

Malaki owes its origin to crossbreeding between Sakel and Sea Island. Its fineness and strength are in close competition to that of Sakel. However, it is dark brown in color, a serious disadvantage since strong bleaching is required. The fiber length is 1⁷⁄₁₆ to 1²¹⁄₃₂ inches. Malaki represents about 8 percent of the total Egyptian cotton acreage. It is used for a wide variety of cotton fabrics.

Karnak, a long-staple cotton, is given the largest acreage in Egypt. It is about as fine as Sakel and is 1⅜ to 1⅝ inches in length. It is light brown in color and must be thoroughly bleached to obtain the desired whiteness which results in some weakening of the fiber.

Ashmouni is a good-to-fair variety of Egyptian cotton. It is not as strong as

Karnak nor quite as fine. It is also shorter in length, averaging about 1$\frac{5}{32}$ inches.

Giza 30 is another widely used variety of Egyptian cotton. It is of fair strength but not as strong as Ashmouni; it is finer in diameter and consequently produces a thinner, though weaker, yarn. The staple length of Giza 30 cotton fiber averages about 1$\frac{7}{16}$ inches.

PIMA COTTON ■ Crossbreeding of superior strains of American Pima and Egyptian Sakel cottons have produced several types of cotton that are all identified as strains of Pima. They are grown in the Upper Rio Grande Valley of Texas, in New Mexico, Arizona, and southern California. The most recently developed strain is Pima S-2, which is given the largest acreage. It has almost uniform staple length averaging about 1$\frac{3}{8}$ inches. This uniformity of length contributes considerably to the production of more uniform and stronger yarns that can be obtained from cotton of varied lengths. In addition, Pima is a fine, strong, lustrous, silky, almost white fiber. These outstanding characteristics make Pima highly desirable, and since there is more Pima available than Sea Island or Sakel cotton, it is more commonly known and more popular. Pima is used for high quality white-on-white broadcloth as well as other cotton fabrics where strength and a silky smoothness, softness, and luster are desired.

Several years ago, some Pima cotton farmers formed the SuPima Association of America to promote their product. They advertise their cotton under the trade name of SuPima. They consider their Pima cotton to be a superior variety and confidently authorize their SuPima labels for fabrics made of Pima cotton provided by farmer members of their association.

UPLAND COTTON ■ American Upland cotton supplies the bulk of the United States' cotton crop and is used for most popular-priced fabrics. The particular type of Upland cotton from which these fabrics are made is important because the quality and characteristics vary among the types. Generally speaking, Upland cotton fibers are fairly white and strong, dull, and range in staple length from $\frac{3}{4}$ to 1$\frac{1}{4}$ inches. As a group, their characteristics are not as good as those of Sea Island, Sakel, or Pima cotton. Of the several types of Upland cotton, there are four varieties that are best and account for the major acreage planted.

Deltapine is the leading variety of Upland cotton produced in the United States. It is grown in Arizona, Kentucky, Louisiana, Mississippi, and Tennessee. It has a staple length of about 1$\frac{1}{32}$ to 1$\frac{3}{32}$ inches. It is whiter than Pima S-2 but is duller, weaker, and much coarser.

Acala is the next leading variety of Upland cotton, which is grown in California, Nevada, New Mexico, and Texas. It is a longer staple than Deltapine, ranging from about 1$\frac{1}{16}$ to 1$\frac{1}{4}$ inches. It is also finer, stronger, and whiter.

Stoneville cotton is planted in approximately equal acreage with Acala but is grown in Arkansas, Louisiana, Mississippi, and Missouri. It has a relatively uniform fiber length, about 1$\frac{1}{16}$ inches. This uniformity contributes to its good spinning ability. However, the fiber is the coarsest of the Upland cottons. It is not as strong or as white as Acala, but it is stronger than Deltapine.

Lankart cotton is the fourth leading variety and is grown in Oklahoma and Texas. Its staple length is about $\frac{15}{16}$ inch, and it is weaker, coarser and yellower than the previously mentioned Upland cottons.

PERUVIAN AND BRAZILIAN COTTONS ■ These varieties of cotton are related to the group of Egyptian, Sea Island, and Pima cottons. Peruvian and Brazilian varieties have a very wide range of qualities. They vary from fine to coarse and crimpy, resembling somewhat the texture of wool (a characteristic that has been utilized in the past for blending it with wool) with a staple length generally ranging from 1 to 1¼ inches.

ASIATIC COTTON ■ Asiatic cotton is grown in India, China, Asia Minor, Iran, and Japan. Of relatively short staple, nearly all being less than 1 inch in length, its use is limited to low-grade cotton goods.

FROM FIELD TO MILL

CULTIVATING COTTON ■ Cotton can be cultivated only in warm places, which is the reason for its cultivation in the southern part of the United States. Cotton requires about two hundred days of continuous warm weather with adequate moisture and sunlight; frost is harmful to the plant. The ground must be thoroughly plowed, and the soil pulverized. In the United States, usually in March or April, carefully selected cotton seeds are planted in rows. Approximately thirty-five days pass before the seeds develop. The plants require careful fertilization.

The cotton plants must be protected from being crowded out by weeds. A variety of techniques are employed depending upon such factors as topography, soil texture, frequency of cultivation, and necessity of irrigation. The plants are generally thinned out and weeded when they are from 5 to 7 inches tall. This may be done by hand or by mechanical rotary hoes. Flame cultivators, which throw out small flames from jets set low to the ground between the rows of young cotton plants, are sometimes used to burn the thin-stemmed weeds and grass and leave the stronger, woody cotton plants unharmed. Some farmers use geese as cultivators since the geese voraciously eat the young weeds and grass but do not bother the cotton plants. Chemicals, specifically developed to kill certain weed and grass seeds, are often spread or sprayed on the ground at the time the cotton is planted. Other chemicals are sprayed on weeds after they emerge, but care must be taken to avoid contact with the cotton plants as they could be damaged.

Buds appear a few weeks after the plant emerges. They begin to bloom as creamy white blossoms about three weeks later in June or July. These blossoms change to pink and then to reddish purple. Within three days their petals fall off, leaving the ripening seed pod. The fibers that grow from the surface of the seeds cause the pod to expand to about an inch in diameter and to an inch and a half in length to form the cotton boll. During this period, the plant is subject to attack by many insects (particularly the boll weevil that lays its eggs inside the buds), which, when they are hatched, feed inside the maturing boll. To protect the plants, insecticides are sprayed by hand, tractors, or airplanes.

The cotton bolls grow to full size by August or September, a month and a half to two months after the blossoms first appeared. When fully grown, the cotton plant may be from 3 to 6 feet in height. Its wide green leaves conceal some of the bolls, which begin to burst with fleecy white cotton fiber. This indicates that the cotton is ready for harvesting.

Courtesy Deere & Company

This mechanical picker can pick cotton bolls from two rows at one time.

HARVESTING ■ Not all cotton bolls open at the same time. Only those that burst, thus exposing the fiber, are ready for picking. Consequently, a hand-picked cotton field must be gone over several times. When mechanical pickers are used, the bolls are left on the plant until they are all mature. Although some leaves will have fallen off by then, the plants are defoliated by spraying them with a chemical, causing the remaining leaves to wither and fall. The full, ripe bolls are then picked by machine, one or two rows at a time.

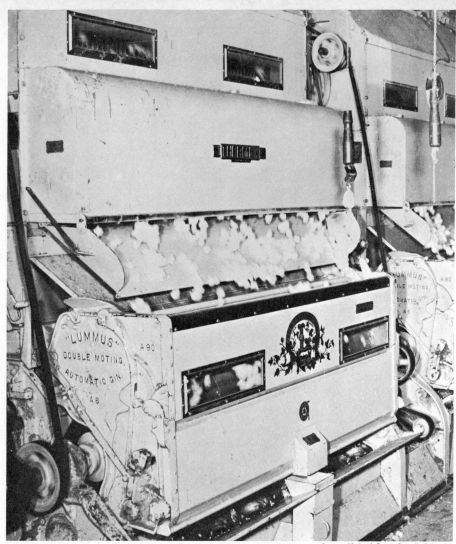

Courtesy National Cotton Council of America

Cotton fiber, which has entered the cotton gin from a pneumatic conveyor, is here seen falling on covered gin saws after sand and coarse soil have been removed. The saws separate the seeds from the fiber; the fiber is removed from the sawtooth by a blast of air and is whisked toward the back. The seeds then fall into a conveyor at the bottom of the machine.

GINNING AND BALING ■ When the raw cotton is harvested, it contains seeds, leaf fragments, dirt, and other material that must be removed before the fiber can be baled. Cotton seeds alone constitute approximately two-thirds of the weight of the raw cotton when first picked. The seeds are removed by the cotton gin. (The cotton gin was invented by Eli Whitney in 1794. Whitney's invention was not immediately accepted, and he suffered serious financial loss. It was subsequently promoted by others and became a major impetus in the growth of the cotton industry and the dominance of southern United States as a cotton producer.)

Essentially, the cotton gin has rows of revolving saw-toothed bands that pull the fiber away from the seeds as well as remove other extraneous material. The cotton seeds are one of the valued by-products. The cotton fiber is compressed into rectangular bales, which are covered with jute or polypropylene bagging and bound with iron bands. These bales weigh about 500 pounds each.

BY-PRODUCTS OF COTTON

The raw cotton passes through several cleaning processes before it is baled as well as after it is unbaled at the cotton mill. As a result, the grower obtains valuable by-products that amount approximately to one-sixth of the entire income derived from the cotton plant. Cotton is therefore important because of its contributions to other industries as well as to the textile industry.

COTTON LINTERS ■ Linters are the short, fuzzy hairlike fibers that remain on the seeds after they have been separated from the fiber in the cotton gin. The cotton linters are removed by a second ginning process. They are used in the manufacture of rayons and acetates, plastics, shatterproof glass, guncotton, photographic film, fast-drying lacquers, and for other purposes.

HULLS ■ The hulls, which are the outside portion of the cotton seeds, are obtained after the linters have been removed. The hulls are rich in nitrogen, an important plant food, and are used as fertilizer and also in the manufacture of paper, plastics, cattle feed, and as a base for explosives.

INNER SEEDS ■ The meat of the seed inside the hull yields *cottonseed oil,* which is used in cooking oils and compounds and in the manufacture of soap. The residue of the inner seed becomes cattle feed.

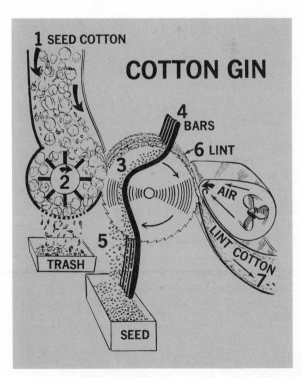

Shown in the drawing are the following basic principles of the cotton gin: (1) Seed cotton enters gin. (2) Roll throws seed cotton against fast-turning saws. (3) Saw teeth take cotton up and against bars. (4) Bars near saws on both sides let lint pass through but hold back seed. (5) Seed falls into conveyor. (6) Lint on sawtooth is struck by blast of air and, (7) blown into lint cotton conveyor pipe.

Courtesy Bibb Manufacturing Company

1 SEED COTTON

COTTON GIN

4 BARS

6 LINT

2

3

AIR

5

TRASH

SEED

LINT COTTON 7

PROCESSING, BLENDING, AND MIXING COTTON

As observed in Chapter 3, cotton fiber may be spun alone or blended with other fibers in making yarns. Cotton yarns are also combined or mixed with other yarns in making fabrics. These techniques contribute to fabrics such desirable cotton properties as softness, strength, absorbency, and affinity for color.

FINISHING COTTON FABRICS

The finishing processes given to cotton were reviewed in Chapter 8. They may be summarized as follows.

Full bleaching—for clear whiteness

Mercerizing—for strength, luster, and affinity for dyes

Singeing—for smoothness

Stiffening—for smoothness and body

Weighting—for bulk

Preshrinking—for serviceability

Compressive shrinkage—for maximum preshrinking

Insulating—for warmth

Calendering—for luster

Schreinering—for luster

Beetling—for flattened effects

Napping—for softness, warmth, and absorbency

Crepe effects—for wrinkle resistance

Water repellency—for resistance to water and rain

Drip-dry—for no ironing

Embossing—for decoration

Slack mercerizing—for stretch

The types of dyes used for cotton and their degree of fastness to light and to washing were explained in Chapter 9.

SIMULATING LINEN ■ Cotton yarn can be spun to simulate the irregularities characteristic of linen fiber. The fabric is woven in the damask and other patterns usually associated with linen fabrics and is then sized, beetled, and calendered similarly to linen.

SIMULATING WOOL ■ Cotton fibers can be treated with chemicals to give them the roughness characteristic of wool fibers. The fibers are spun into thick yarns to increase the similarity. The finished fabric is napped or roughened to produce a woollike surface. Because Peruvian cotton fiber has crimp, an inherent similarity to wool fiber, it is sometimes mixed with American Upland cotton to simulate wool.

SIMULATING SILK ■ The highest quality of cotton fiber, when spun to a high yarn count and then mercerized, simulates silk. The use of the satin construction in weaving produces a silklike luster. The cotton fabric may be singed and calendered to smooth its surface and to increase the luster. Cotton fabrics are frequently schreinered to obtain an added lustrous effect.

EVALUATING COTTON FABRICS

Manufacturers now place labels on finished consumers' goods to give such information as the thread count, fiber content, expected shrinkage, permanency of crispness (if any), and fastness of dye to strong light, washing, and dry cleaning, with general instructions on the maintenance and care of the fabric. Such labels are designed to protect the consumer. If he understands them, he can estimate how long the fabric or garment that he is purchasing may be expected to give good wear. These labels also protect the manufacturer from the consumer's possible misunderstanding of the quality and durability of a fabric and from complaint if it is improperly handled when washed or dry-cleaned.

The information gained in previous chapters of this book concerning the essential qualities of the fibers and their spinning into yarn and construction into fabric can now be applied to the actual purchase of consumers' goods.

Strength. Cotton fiber is relatively strong due to the intrinsic structure of layers of criss-crossed, minute, spiralled fibrils that compose the fiber cell. Strength is also determined by the character of the cotton yarns, which should be of long staple and tightly twisted. Compact construction, represented by high thread count, helps a fabric keep its shape and give longer wear. A sample of the fabric may be tested for strength by holding it in both hands and pressing down firmly with the thumbs while pulling. If the cloth gives easily, it will not stand the strain of wear. Strength can be substantially improved by mercerizing.

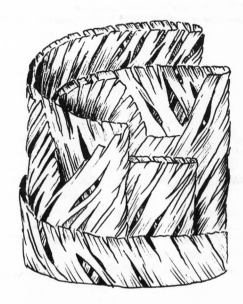

Diagram of inner layer of an enlarged cotton fiber shows how fibrils criss-cross and double back. This structure contributes greatly to the strength of cotton.

Courtesy CIBA Review

Amount of Sizing. If a cotton fabric is oversized, rubbing or tearing a sample swatch will cause shedding of excess starch. Holding the fabric to the light will reveal defects in construction that may have been concealed by sizing. Washing a sample will remove excess sizing, showing sleazy construction. An absolute test for starch is made by dipping a sample in a very dilute iodine solution; a dark-blue color indicates starch.

Elasticity. Cotton fiber has very little natural elasticity. This characteristic can be altered to varying extents by hard-twisting the fibers into creped yarns, and by using such fabric construction techniques as knitting. Recently, the slack mercerization technique has been used to give cotton fabrics some stretch in the warp and/or filling, thereby reducing the binding characteristic of the cotton fabrics.

Resilience. The tendency of cotton fabrics to wrinkle easily may be offset by finishing processes that give a wrinkle-resistant quality.

Heat Conductivity. Cotton fabrics make excellent summer clothing because cotton is a good conductor of heat. Crisp, clean, fine cotton fabrics look cool as well as feel cool. Napped or pile-weave cotton fabric has a warmth-giving quality.

Absorbency. Once the outer protective cuticle of the fiber is broken down by finishing processes, such as kiering and mercerizing, the fiber becomes very absorbent. Cotton fiber is composed primarily of cellulose, which is very absorbent. Its hollow center, or lumen, aids in conveying moisture. Such factors as the amount of twist in the yarn will also affect the absorbency, since a low-twisted yarn will be more absorbent than a high-twisted one. Fabric structure, such as a pile weave, will affect absorbency. Also, the compactness of the weave influences the absorbency because the looser the structure the more absorbent the fabric will be.

Cleanliness and Washability. Although cotton attracts dirt particles because of its roughness, this disadvantage is offset by the washability of the fiber. Cotton fabrics are not injured even in strong, hot solutions of alkalies; therefore, they can stand laundering with strong soap. They withstand rough handling and considerable heat in ironing.

Reactions to Bleaches. Cotton may be safely bleached with ordinary household bleaches. However, the bleach should be put into the water before the clothing so that it is thoroughly mixed and diluted to avoid the oxidizing or yellowing that may be caused by over-concentration from sodium hypochlorite bleaches, such as *Clorox* and *Rose-X*. Labels on wash and wear fabrics should be observed since some of these finishes are chlorine retentive—they turn yellow when subjected to sodium hypochlorite bleaches. Bleaches containing sodium perborate, such as *Snowy,* are safe.

Shrinkage. A great amount of shrinkage will occur if cotton fabric is loosely woven and stiffened with starch, which is usually lost in washing. Preshrinking finishing processes minimize shrinkage in cotton fabrics.

Effect of Light. Cotton fiber oxidizes, turning yellow and losing strength from exposure to sunlight over a protracted period of time. Cotton fabrics should therefore be shaded from direct sunlight.

Resistance to Mildew. Cotton fabrics, especially sized fabrics, mildew readily when permitted to remain in a damp condition. New processes, in many cases, offset this tendency to mildew.

Resistance to Moths. Cotton is not digestible to moth larvae, so that the fabric will not be attacked by moths. But in fabrics containing cotton and wool, the larvae may damage the cotton to get at the wool.

Reaction to Alkalies. Cotton is not harmed by alkalies. In fact, a solution of sodium hydroxide is used to mercerize cotton, making it stronger, smoother, and more lustrous.

Reaction to Acids. Cotton is not damaged by such volatile organic acids as acetic acid (vinegar). However, it is tendered if such nonvolatile organic acids as oxalic and citric (found in orange, lemon, and grapefruit juices) are allowed to remain on them, and particularly if heat is also applied. They should, therefore, be rinsed with cool water as soon as possible. Concentrated cold or hot dilute mineral acids, such as sulfuric acid, will destroy cotton.

Affinity for Dyes. Cotton has a good affinity for dyes. It is dyed best with vat dyes, which provide good color fastness. Fastness of dye to washing can be tested by washing a sample in hot water. Fastness to light can be tested by exposing a sample to light for a week or more. Penetration or thoroughness of dye can be tested by raveling a yarn and examining its unexposed surfaces.

Resistance to Perspiration. Acid perspiration has a slightly deteriorating effect on cotton.

CONSTRUCTION OF SHEETS

As sheets are an important item in the budget of the American family, the labeling of sheets is explained here.

THREAD COUNT ■ Sheets are labeled as belonging to one of seven types: backfilled, 112, 128, 140, 180 carded, 180 combed, and 200. The figures are obtained by adding the number of warp and filling yarns to the square inch, which represent the thread count. The higher the count, the closer and more uniform the weave; the more compact the weave, the greater the resistance to wear.

Types including backfilled, 112, 128, and 140 are known as *muslin,* which is made from cotton yarns that have been carded but not combed. Of these types, 140 represents the best quality, giving greater durability, because such sheets are made from good-quality carded cotton yarns that are coarser and heavier and more compactly constructed than the first three types. Heavy muslin sheets are practical and economical because they are moderately priced and withstand wear longest, particularly when subjected to hard laundering.

Types including 180 carded, 180 combed, and 200 are known as *percale.* Percale is woven from fine-quality long-staple cotton yarns. In the case of 180 carded percale, the sheet is woven with 180 carded threads to the square inch. The 180 combed percale is woven with 180 combed threads to the square inch. Combed yarns are smoother, more lustrous, and stronger than yarns that are merely carded. The 180 combed percale is therefore superior and a little more expensive than the 180 carded percale. The 200 percale, woven with 200 combed threads to the square inch, is constructed of the finest cotton yarn and is considered the most luxurious of cotton sheets. The thread count is high in all percale sheets because of the fineness of the yarns and their compact construction. Such yarns make lightweight sheets of fine texture, desirable for summer use. There is

TYPES OF MUSLIN AND PERCALE SHEETS

GRADE	WEAVE OR THREAD COUNT	POINTS TO CONSIDER IN BUYING	PRICE
Back-filled muslin	Woven with less than 112 threads to each square inch	Loosely woven; excess starch washes out, leaves sheets sleazy	Lowest
Light-weight muslin	Woven with not less than 112 threads to each square inch	Wears well considering low price. For limited household service	Low
Medium-weight muslin	Woven with not less than 128 threads to each square inch	Strong; gives satisfactory wear. Widely used for everday household service	Medium
Heavy-weight muslin	Woven with not less than 140 threads to each square inch	Sturdy; longest wearing muslin. Used where durability is prime consideration, as in hospitals, many hotels, etc.	Highest price muslin
Percale (carded)	Woven with carded yarns, not less than 180 threads to each square inch	Lightweight; durable. Smooth, pleasant to sleep on, easy and economical to launder	Medium
Percale (combed)	Woven with all combed yarns, not less than 180 threads to each square inch	Lightweight; extremely strong and durable. Soft and unusually smooth; easy and economical to launder	Medium
Finest quality percale	Not less than 200 threads to each square inch	The finest, most luxurious sheets available. Light, fine, soft texture, beautiful appearance. Made of finest all-combed yarns	Highest price percale

Courtesy Cannon Mills, Inc.

a gain in luxury but a slight sacrifice in durability because, all other conditions being equal, the heavier fabric gives the longer wear.

Sheets are generally labeled. But you can always examine the sheet itself for quality. By holding it up to the light, you can determine whether it is firmly, closely, and uniformly woven. It should look smooth. Lengthwise and crosswise threads should be of the same even thickness, rather than thick or thin in spots. There should be no weak places, knots, or slubs, and the yarns should run straight and unbroken.

SELVAGE ■ Sheets should be made with a tape selvage in which extra threads are woven. The selvage should be firm and strong, clean, neat, and with no loose threads.

WEIGHT ■ Many weights of sheets are available, varying from 3¼ to 5¼ ounces per yard. But good weight should be the result of compact construction, not of excessive sizing. Government regulations on sheets permit a certain amount of sizing depending on the grade of the sheet. In the lowest grade of sheet, an excessive amount of sizing may be used to give the material greater body. Since this washes out, leaving the sheet thin and sleazy, it is advisable for the consumer to test sheets for sizing by rubbing parts of the sheet together over a dark surface. If much of a white powdery substance comes out, the sheet is "loaded" or sized. Sheets labeled "no weighting" indicates no overdose of sizing.

LENGTH AND WIDTH ■ Sheets should always be long enough and wide enough to tuck underneath a mattress at least 6 inches on all sides. The better grades of sheets are torn to size to make certain that the length is absolutely even; therefore, the size is given as a torn size, which means before hemming. After hemming, sheets are shorter; top hems are usually 3 inches wide on muslin, 4 inches wide on percale sheets; bottom hems are 1 inch wide on both. After washing, there is another decrease in length of approximately 5 inches, or 5 percent, due to shrinkage. Sheets for standard length beds should be 108 inches long. As about 10 inches must be deducted from the stated torn size for hems and shrinkage allowance, 98 inches remain for use. The average mattress is 74 inches long and 6 inches thick. Thus, 6 inches will be left for tucking under when a sheet is used to cover the mattress directly, and when used as an upper sheet, there will be a sufficiently wide turnover to protect blankets. Larger queen-size beds require sheets from 113 to 120 inches long; sheets for king-size beds should be at least 122 inches long.

Careful consideration should also be given to the width of sheets. For a double bed, a sheet should be 81 to 90 inches wide. Extra-wide double and queen-size beds require sheets 90 inches wide; a king-size bed requires a sheet 108 inches wide. A three-quarter bed requires a sheet 72 inches wide, and a single bed, a width of 63 to 72 inches.

There are also fitted, or contour, sheets, the corners of which conform to the shape and size of the mattress. These sheets, as a rule, are preshrunk. Contour sheets are sized according to the mattress or the type of bed as listed.

Cot	XL Twin	Queen
Youth	XL Full	King
Three-quarter Bed		Super
Day Bed		XL Super

CONSTRUCTION OF TERRY TOWELS

The primary function of a terry towel is to absorb moisture from wet skin. It must, however, be strong enough to withstand the strain of the rubbing and pulling, twisting and tugging of the user and of constant laundering. A terry towel, therefore, should be constructed of an uncut pile with a sound underweave. One cannot purchase towels merely by a brand name because the name identifies only the manufacturer, not a particular quality. A company may manufacture many different grades and qualities of towels under the same brand name.

WEAVE ■ The underweave, which supplies the strength of the towel, should be firm, close, tight, and preferably of a twill weave. It is difficult to examine the weave because the loops hide it. It can be more readily seen in the plain portion or near the hem or selvage of the towel. To examine the weave better, the towel should be held up to the light. If light shows through in tiny and regular pin points, the weave is uniform and good; if the light shows loose and open spots, then the weave is poor.

The loops of the pile, which absorb the moisture, should be closely packed. In a well-constructed towel, the moisture absorbed remains in the surface loops and does not reach the underweave. A better-quality towel, therefore, will absorb more moisture and dry faster after use. Another consideration is that the longer the loops, the greater the absorbency of the towel. Also, loosely twisted loops are more absorbent than tightly twisted ones. On this point, however, personal choice must be a factor, since some people prefer soft towels with loosely twisted loops, some prefer medium-soft towels, and others prefer a rough, hard towel with tightly twisted loops. In a well-constructed towel, good absorbency may be expected, since the close weave will result in a close, thick pile.

The magnified views below show single-crop (upper left) and double-crop (upper right) construction in terry cloth. The enlarged view (lower left) shows how the loops, or uncut pile, in terry cloth are formed. The enlarged cross section (lower right) shows how terry loops are formed on both sides at the same time.

Courtesy Dundee Mills, Inc.

Courtesy Dundee Mills, Inc.

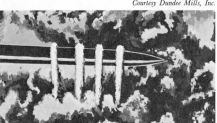

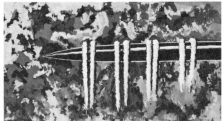

Courtesy Cannon Mills, Inc.

Courtesy Cannon Mills, Inc.

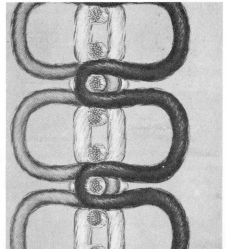

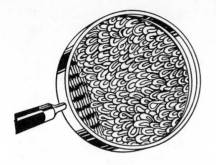

Courtesy Cannon Mills, Inc.

The loops (left) do the drying, and the ground weave (right) does the wearing.

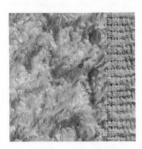

Courtesy Cannon Mills, Inc.

Three types of selvages, left to right: fast, overedged, hemmed.

HEM AND SELVAGE ■ The hems of the towel should be sewn with small close stitches and finished with the edges either backstitched at the corners or turned and continued across the width of the hem. There are three types of satisfactory selvages, if properly made. One is the fast selvage, which is the ordinary type of selvage found on any fabric. It should be closely woven. The second is an overedged selvage, and the third the hemmed selvage.

LENGTH AND WIDTH ■ Terry towels are divided by size into five groups: guest, small, bath, extra large, and beach. The guest towels are 11 × 18 inches. The small size, used for hands and face, are from 16 × 26 to 18 × 36 inches. The bath size are from 20 × 40 to 22 × 44 inches. The extra-large bath towel is 24 × 46 to 25 × 48 inches. The beach size is 35 × 70 to 36 × 72 inches.

GLOSSARY OF COTTON FABRICS

airplane fabric. Plain weave. Closely woven, desized, durable medium-weight and lightweight fabric originally used in the manufacture of airplane wings and parts. Made of combed and mercerized yarns; usually in square weave. Many fabrics go under this name. Most important is fancy, irregular broken weave.

armure. Drapery fabric with a small woven design, usually on a rep foundation. Can be either Jacquard or dobby weave. Pattern is made by floating warp threads over the surface, giving a raised effect.

backing or back cloth. Gray goods, usually print cloth, used to take up surplus dye and to reinforce fabric on the printing machine.

balloon cloth.   Plain weave. Of finest Pima yarns. High thread count. The extremely fine yarns give the fabric luster. Usually mercerized. When used for balloons, given a special coating. Also used for frocks, shirts, typewriter ribbons.

batiste.   Plain weave. A sheer, soft-finished fabric of the lawn family. Comes in various grades from coarse to very fine. Generally woven of combed yarns, but occasionally of carded. Often given high mercerization; bleached, dyed, or printed. Sometimes embroidered.

beach cloth.   A strong, coarse fabric of plain weave, heavy yarns, and low thread count. Has the appearance of crash. There are a number of versions of this fabric.

Bedford cord.   A carded yarn, wale, or cord material. Two-ply warp yarns and heavier single or ply yarns used as a backing. These heavy yarns are caught at intervals in the weaving of the fabric. Single yarns sometimes used in cheaper versions; the effect of the cord is obtained in the weaving. Wale runs in warp. Can be napped in back, bleached, dyed, or printed. Often the face of the fabric is given a suede finish.

bengaline.   Rib effect in filling with a high luster. Has somewhat the appearance of grosgrain. For draperies and frocks.

bird's-eye (diaper cloth).   Fabric woven on a dobby loom of carded yarns in tiny geometric designs that look like the eye of a bird, or in diamond effect. Heavier filling yarns are loosely twisted, making the fabric absorbent.

blanket cloth.   Plain or twill weave, 60 × 80 inches and over. Thick, soft filling yarns, heavily napped both sides. Often yarn-dyed in plaids or stripes.

book cloth.   Coarse, plain-weave print cloth or sheeting. Dyed, heavily sized, often pyroxylin coated, or embossed.

box loom.   Fabrics made with right-hand and left-hand twist in filling, notably box-loom crepe. Such fabrics as ginghams and plaids are also made on box looms.

broadcloth.   Plain, closely woven fabrics of either carded or combed yarns with a fillingwise rib effect. Originally a poplin or adapted from poplin construction, broadcloths are of lighter weight with a finer rib. Ribs are made by using finer warp yarn and medium filling. Many more warp threads than filling. Better broadcloths are combed ply yarns and have high thread counts of 144 × 76. Coarser fabrics often have both ply and single carded yarns.

brocade.   Basic weave is satin. Elaborate lustrous design woven on a Jacquard loom. Has a raised appearance, usually on a filling-faced satin ground but often on twill or rep. The design is on the surface only. Multicolored yarns used.

brocatelle.   A heavier version of brocade. Woven on a Jacquard loom with two, three, four, or more shuttles. Ordinary warp yarns but fewer twists in filling yarns. Has extra backing threads. The floating warp yarns over the backing yarns make the design stand out in relief.

bunting.   Plain weave, in low or medium thread count. Open weave similar to cheesecloth or scrim. Dyed or printed.

calico.   A low-count or medium-count cotton print cloth with special designs called calico designs. Many Early American designs are in use.

cambric.   Originally linen, now cotton print cloth or lightweight sheeting construction. Given special sizing and calendered finish.

canton flannel.   Warp-faced twill flannel with a heavy, soft filling yarn and lighter warp than filling yarn. Has a long nap on one side only. Comes unbleached or bleached. For men's work gloves, infants' wear, linings.

challis.   Plain or twill weave, printed or dyed. Given a soft finish and very slight nap.

chambray.   Pattern is formed by the use of colored yarn warp and natural or white filling. This gives a tiny check or mottled effect. There are endless variations of this fabric, such as stripes, satin stripes, and so on. The end-to-end chambrays are woven with alternate colored and natural or white yarns in warp and all natural or white yarns in filling, or vice versa. Many novelties on the market.

cheesecloth (and tobacco cloths).   Loose, open, plain light weave with low thread count. Print cloth yarns. Cheesecloths range from 25 to 55 inches in width. Tobacco cloths are 36 inches and over in width with a somewhat lower thread count than cheesecloth. When bleached, starched, or permanently finished, known also as scrim. Other names, depending on finish, are gauze, bunting.

chenille.   Fluffy or fuzzy faced fabric made with a cotton warp yarn and a cotton chenille filling yarn that has a fuzzy pile protruding from all sides. Some imitations made by tufting, using no chenille yarn.

cheviot.   A strong twilled fabric woven with a colored stripe or check.

chiffon.   A sheer voile with a dull finish; of fine, hard-twisted yarns. Often dyed or printed.

chintz.   A print cloth or high-count fine sheeting with bright attractive floral or geometric designs, both large and small. Often given a permanent or semi-permanent glaze; then known as glazed chintz. For draperies, slip covers, frocks.

clokay.   A plain woven fabric with an embossed surface of some geometric pattern. Rather compact weave. Embossed design is permanent if the fabric is laundered only in lukewarm water with a mild soap.

corduroy.   A ribbed pile fabric with a high, soft luster. Made with extra filling threads or extra warp threads. In weaving, the extra filling yarns form loops or floats over the ground threads. After weaving, the loop threads are cut on a special machine. Threads are then brushed, forming a pile.

cottonade.   Generally three-harness, left-hand, warp-faced twill of coarse yarns. Comes mostly in dark stripes on a solid or medium-dark ground. Durable finish.

coutil.   A strong three-harness herringbone or reverse-twist twill weave of high count. For suits, corsets, and other purposes requiring a durable fabric.

covert.   A medium-weight or medium-lightweight fabric with warp-faced left-hand twill. Usually of two-ply warp yarns and single or two-ply filling. Mixed yarns, such as natural and color in warp and matching color alone in filling. Has a mottled appearance. Often made with slack-twisted single yarns consisting of two rovings, one white and one color in warp and all color in filling.

crash.   Name given to fabrics having coarse, uneven yarns in both plain and twill weaves. Usually sheeting, osnaburg, or twill-weave construction with a special finish. Used for toweling and drapery purposes. In lighter weights used for suits and dresses.

crepe. Has a pebbly or crinkled surface produced by use of special crepe yarns. Can be either crepe, granite, or plain weave. Generally, mixed-twist crepe yarns used in both warp and filling, occasionally crepe yarns used only in the warp or the filling. Mostly woven on a box loom.

cretonne. Generally a medium or heavy sheeting or osnaburg printed in bold, bright designs. Used for draperies and other household articles.

crinoline. Cheesecloth, tobacco cloth, or loosely woven sheetings given a stiff starched or plastic finish. Gives a firm appearance and feel.

damask. Design, woven on Jacquard loom, on both sides of the fabric. Usually given a lustrous, smooth finish when used for tablecloths and a soft or lustrous finish for draperies or upholstery.

denim. A durable fabric of the twill family. Usually of single hard-twisted yarns with colored warp and natural or white filling.

dimity. A sheer white, dyed, or printed fabric of plain weave with a spaced rib made with warp cords. This rib may be single, double, or in groups. Comes also in checks and other novelty versions. Coarser small-check dimities are known as pajama checks.

dobby. Woven on a dobby loom. All material with small figures, such as dots and geometric designs; floral patterns woven in the fabric, such as certain shirtings, huck towels, diaper cloth, certain dress goods, drapery and upholstery fabrics. Can be dyed, bleached, or yarn-dyed in many colors.

domett flannel. See also "outing flannel." Plain or twill weave. Generally white with a longer nap than outing flannel, although the names are interchangeable. Soft filled yarns of medium or light weight.

dotted swiss. Generally a voile or lawn construction woven with either clip spots or swivel dots. The clip spot is the more popular version. The fabric is given a crisp, clear finish, which may be permanent or semipermanent. Often yarn-dyed dots are woven on a white ground, or a dark ground has white dots. Many imitations on the market, pigment dots, flock dots, and others.

drill. A durable fabric of medium weight. Usually, three-harness warp-faced twills made of carded sheeting yarns. Comes in various weights and thread counts ranging from 60 × 36 to 80 × 48. When dyed, known as khaki, tickings, silesia, herringbones. One thread goes over two filling yarns, then under one.

druid's cloth. See "monk's cloth."

duck. The name "duck" covers a wide range of fabrics. It is one of the most durable fabrics made. A closely woven, heavy material. The most important fabrics in this group are known as *number duck, army duck,* and *flat* or *ounce duck.* Number and army ducks are always of plain weave with medium or heavy ply yarns; army ducks are the lighter. Ounce ducks always have single warp yarns woven in pairs and single or ply filling yarns. Other names for variations of these fabrics are sail duck, belt duck, hose duck, tire duck (such as breaker, cord, chafer), wide and narrow duck, biscuit duck, harvester duck, oil press duck, wagon duck, enameling duck, boot duck, canvas, and so on. Generally of ply yarns in warp and yarns of various sizes and weights in filling. Thread counts range from 54 × 40 to 72 × 40.

duvetyne. See "suede cloth."

éponge. See "ratiné."

express stripe. Warp-faced twill with a woven stripe. A durable fabric. An even number of unbleached and blue yarns are used in the pattern, forming a stripe.

friezette. An uncut loop or pile ribbed fabric similar to a heavy rib or rep. Of heavy yarns, usually mixed in color.

gabardine. A distinctive steep-diagonal warp-faced twill of carded or combed yarns. Twill is to the left if made with all single yarns, and to the right when ply warp and single filling are used. Thread counts range from 110 × 76 to 130 × 80.

gauze. See "cheesecloth." Usually bleached; often specially treated, as when used for bandages. Better cheesecloths are also used for less expensive infants' items under trade names.

gingham. Plain-weave, medium-weight, or lightweight fabrics. Can be either combed or carded yarns. Usually woven on a box loom. Colored and white yarns or multicolored yarns form the pattern. Same number and variation of yarns in the warp as in the filling, forming squares, plaids, and similar patterns. Strange to say, a solid-color gingham is called a novelty gingham. Endless variations in color and design. Tissue ginghams are sheer ginghams made with lighter-weight yarns.

glazed chintz. Generally a print cloth or percale or a lightweight sheeting having bright, attractive floral or geometric designs. The fabric has a semi-permanent or permanent glaze finish. Sometimes calendered or given a plastic finish. Fine twills are also used for this purpose.

granite. See "mummy cloth."

grosgrain. Plain-weave fabric similar to poplin but with a heavier rib effect and coarser, lower thread count. Made with single or with ply filling.

hickory cloth. Resembles ticking somewhat, but of lighter weight and not so firm a weave.

holland. Usually a low-count print cloth or high-count cheesecloth, heavily sized and glazed. Occasionally, sheeting constructions are used.

hopsacking. Made of yarns about the same weight as osnaburg in a loose and low thread count. Sometimes made with spiral yarns. It has a soft texture and is of the homespun family of cottons. Sometimes made with fine warp and heavier filling. Many versions of this fabric.

huck. Small-figured dobby weave used for towels. Has a rough surface. Comes bleached or with yarn-dyed striped border.

Indianhead. A porous fabric of a plain weave. The yarn is somewhat thick. The fabric feels wiry, resembling butcher linen but not as stiff or as lustrous.

jaspé. A durable, narrow woven stripe made on a dobby loom with multicolored threads or with different shades of the same color. Has a shadow effect. Sometimes printed versions are shown in the market. Often small dots are woven into the fabric. Used for draperies and slip covers.

jeans. Three-harness warp-faced twills of lightweight sheeting yarns. One warp thread goes over two or more filling threads, then under, moving one pick higher for each return filling thread. Sometimes made in chevron or herringbone versions.

kasha cloth. Flannel with napped face and mottled color. Usually tan or brown. An unbleached soft filled sheeting. Mixed yarns are used with sized warp yarns that take dye and filling yarns with natural wax that do not take dye. When bale-dyed, has a mottled appearance.

khaki. See "twill."

lawn. Sheer and medium-sheer plain-weave fabrics made with lightweight yarns and medium to high count. Can be bleached, dyed, or printed. When finished, it is also known by the name of such special finishes as batiste, organdy.

linene. See "osnaburg."

longcloth. Also known as *fineplain.* A plain-weave, closely woven, high-count fabric. The weight is between a print cloth and lawn. Generally combed finer yarns, and with more threads to the square inch than percales. A few are made of print cloth yarns.

madras. Usually woven in stripes, cords, dobby, and Jacquard. Mostly all white, but in a number of cases done with a patterned warp and white filling, such as white and color warp, or color-and-color warp and white filling, or vice versa. Often a stripe is woven in solid colors. A number of variations of the above.

marquisette. Lightweight open-mesh fabric of low thread count. Can be either a gauze or leno weave. Made with ply or single yarns. Dots and figures can be woven in. Either combed or carded. Generally the ply yarns are combed. Can be bleached, dyed, or printed.

matelassé. Woven on a box loom. A real matelassé is a double warp-faced fabric, stitched together in warp and filling. Face of cloth has a fine warp and filling, the back a fine warp and heavy filling. Other matelassé crepes are made by interlacing crepe yarns with ordinary yarns in warp and filling, or in filling only. Comes in dobby or Jacquard designs. Has a slightly quilted appearance.

moiré. A fabric with a compact plain weave with a shimmering effect on the surface. The finish is permanent provided the fabric is washed with luke-warm water and a mild soap. Bleach should not be used.

moleskin. Mostly a right-hand filling-faced twill with a soft, smooth, shiny face. High thread count, usually many more fine filling threads and fewer heavier warp threads. Generally a napped back.

monk's cloth. Basket weave, a variation of the plain weave. Made with heavy rough yarns. Can be a 1 × 1, 2 × 2, 4 × 4, or 8 × 8 thread; the best known is the 4 × 4. These four threads in warp and filling are placed flat together and woven over and under in a plain weave; the resulting appearance is that of a basket.

mummy cloth. Sometimes called *granite cloth;* also *momie cloth.* Although this fabric has the appearance of crepe with a crinkled surface, it is not made with crepe yarns but with ordinary yarns and is woven on a dobby loom. Can be bleached, dyed, or printed.

muslin. Coarse type of cotton fabric made of carded yarns; of various thread counts up to 140. Gray print cloths and lightweight sheetings known as unbleached muslins.

nainsook. Plain weave. Mostly fine combed-yarn lawns, given a soft finish and light luster. Comes bleached and sometimes dyed.

netting. A lightweight or heavy open-construction, knotted fabric. The knots come at each corner of the square. Ranges in weight from very sheer to very heavy fabrics, from fine nets to fishing or laundry nets.

oilcloth. Sheetings or print cloths that are printed, bleached, or dyed, and given a special linseed oil and pigment preparation.

organdy. Plain weave. A sheer transparent lawn of lightweight yarns. Slightly lower construction than ordinary lawns. The filling is slightly finer than the warp yarns. Fewer filling than warp threads. Comes in many variations, such as permanent crinkles, leno effects, embroidery, plain or crinkled mixtures, clip spots. Bleached, dyed, or printed. Stiff finish, either starched or permanent stiff starchless finish.

osnaburg. A plain weave made of low-grade cotton, medium and heavy coarse yarns. Low thread count. When made of waste mixed with low-grade cotton, it is known as part-waste osnaburg; when of short-staple, low-grade white cotton, known as clean osnaburg. Woven with colored stripe and check effects, known as crash toweling. Comes in both wide and narrow widths and in innumerable variations in weight and thread count. Known also under the names of drapery crash, linene, hopsacking, suiting. Has a number of uses.

outing flannel. Can be either plain or twill weave. Lightweight or medium-weight soft filled single yarn with nap on both sides. Mostly yarn-dyed. Woven in stripes, plaids, or checks. Sometimes bleached or piece-dyed, and occasionally printed.

oxford. A plain weave of medium and heavy weights. Made with a variety of yarns. The majority of oxfords are of combed yarns, with heavier filling than warp yarns. Cheaper grades are mixed carded and combed yarns, and some-times all carded yarns. Two warp yarns, placed flat next to each other, are woven over and under one heavier filling thread. Usually mercerized. A number of variations of this weave are on the market. For shirtings, frocks, and similar purposes.

pajama check. A lightweight or medium-weight plain-weave fabric with small-sized or medium-sized cord checks. Usually carded yarns. Of the dimity family.

percale. Plain-weave medium-weight-yarn fabric in the print cloth group. Thread count, 80 × 80 and over. Usually given a firm finish. Can be bleached, dyed, or printed. Has innumerable uses.

percaline. In the lightweight, low-count print cloth or lawn group with a bright, soft finish. Usually mercerized. Made in both fine and cheap versions. Used for the lining of furs.

picolay. A compact fabric with a plain weave. The cloth is embossed with a diamond pattern to resemble diamond piqué. With careful laundering, the design is permanent.

piqué. Has a warp or filling wale or cord, usually warp. Can be of carded or combed yarns. It is woven on a dobby loom or with a dobby motion. A heavy stuffer yarn is used in back of the cloth; this heavy yarn is caught at intervals by a filling thread. Groups of fine warp yarns are woven on the surface over the back stuffer yarn, forming a rib. Many of the cheaper versions are woven with-out this stuffer yarn. Other versions of piqué are irregular or novelty wales, woven dots, bird's-eye, diamond squares, ladder effects.

plissé. A plain-weave crepe or crinkled fabric that has been specially treated. The plain fabric, which can be print cloth, lawn, or lightweight sheeting, is bleached, dyed, or printed, then covered with a gum in the desired pattern—stripe, check, floral, or geometric. The fabric is then passed through a caustic soda bath. The soda crinkles or crepes the fabric, leaving the gummed sections plain. When the gum is washed off, the crinkled pattern is revealed.

plush. Plain-weave fabric with occasional twill or novelty versions. A deep velvetlike pile woven on a cam loom in what is known as a velvet weave. Many plushes are made on a Jacquard loom in patterns with many colored yarns. The ground yarns are generally two-ply carded. The double fabric is woven face to face and the warp yarns severed on the loom. Generally piece-dyed, and occasionally printed.

pongee. Plain-weave fabric adapted from the early silk fabric of that name. Generally combed yarns. More and heavier filling yarns than warp. Schreinered to have a silklike finish.

poplin. Has a heavier rib effect than broadcloth. Heavier filling than warp yarns, and more threads in the warp than filling. Print cloth yarns mostly. Combed yarns in the better cloths. Many mixtures made. Poplin comes in many variations, such as slubs, nubs, and yarn-dyed checks and stripes. Mainly dyed solid colors or printed. Often given special finishes, such as water-repellent, fire-retardant, mildewproof.

print cloth. Carded cloth made with same yarns as cheesecloth, but with more warp and filling threads to the inch. Most print cloths are made in narrow widths up to 40 inches. Given a range of finishes, thus producing cambric, muslin, lawn, longcloth, and printed percales.

ratiné. A loosely woven fabric of plain weave, with a rough, nubby appearance. This is obtained by the use of ratiné yarns; that is, one heavy and two fine, twisted together at different tensions, thus forming a knotty ply yarn. In less expensive versions, ordinary yarn is used in the warp with ratiné yarn in the filling. Can be bleached, dyed, or printed, and given a high luster or other finishes.

rep. Plain weave. Has a rib running across the fabric. The rib stands out more than in broadcloth or poplin. Usually given a high luster, although not always. Rib produced by heavy warp ends or extra floating filling. Also formed by using two warp beams with slack and tension warp ends. Two slacks are woven as one, and the tension is woven plain.

sateen. A satin weave. Usually woven so that the surface is smooth and the finish lustrous, resembling satin. Can be either a strong warp-faced sateen or a softer filling-faced sateen. Often, though not always, filling sateens have a softer finish than warp sateens. Either carded or combed yarns.

scrim. A durable plain weave. Generally ply yarns and low thread count. Somewhat similar to voile but a much lower thread count. Cheesecloth with a special finish is often referred to as scrim. Comes in many variations. Usually has a selvage. Generally carded, but a few combed varieties on the market.

seersucker. A plain weave. Usually a medium-weight or medium heavy-weight fabric with a woven crinkled stripe, check, or plaid. Yarn-dyed or bleached, occasionally overprinted. The woven crinkle is made by alternating slack tension in warp yarns. Not to be confused with plissé.

shantung. Plain weave. Has a rib effect formed by slub yarns. Certain parts of the yarn are not given the usual number of twists. These places form the slub in the rib.

sheetings. Plain weave. Mostly carded but occasionally combed yarns in all weights, light, medium, and heavy. Generally about the same number of yarns in warp as in filling, but often warp yarns are heavier than filling. Sheetings come in both wide and narrow widths. Yarn sizes range from 10s to 29s.

silesia. Generally a lightweight twill lining with a calendered glaze.

suede cloth. Sheeting napped on one side to resemble leather suede. Duvetyne, which is similar to suede, has a longer nap.

tapestry. A closely woven yarn-dyed figured material with two or more sets of warp and filling, often plied. Woven on a Jacquard loom. Comes in both fine and coarse versions. The reverse side is smooth.

terry cloth. A fabric having uncut loops on both sides. Woven on a dobby loom with terry arrangement. Various sizes and numbers of yarns used in picks and ends, forming different versions of terry cloth. Can be woven on Jacquard loom to form designs. Can be yarn-dyed in different colors to form patterns. Bleached, piece-dyed, even printed.

tickings. A variety of fabrics are known by this name. The main weave is a closely woven, strong yarn twill. Spaced colored and natural or white yarns repeated in the warp, and all natural or white in the filling, forming a stripe. Several color combinations used, such as blue and white, brown and white, red and white. Heavy warp sateens as well as heavy sheetings are printed and sold as tickings. Jacquard damask tickings woven in lovely damask effects also sold for this purpose, as well as other fabrics, such as drills.

tobacco cloth. See "cheesecloth."

twill. Cotton fabric in twill weave. Right-hand or left-hand twills. Known as drills, jeans, gabardines, denims, serge, canton flannel, cottonade, tickings, and others, depending on finish and thread count.

typewriter ribbon cloth. Fine fabric of plain weave. Often balloon cloth. Made with finest regular yarns, then cut into strips, and specially finished.

velveteen. Twill or plain weave with a short, lustrous pile. Ply or single yarns are used, either combed or carded. Many more filling yarns than warp. The extra soft-twisted filling threads that float over surface of cloth are cut, forming the pile. Thickness of pile depends on number of threads used. Can be dyed or printed.

venetian. Durable warp-faced eight-harness sateen of fine reverse-twist yarns.

voile. A soft yet firm sheer fabric of plain weave. Generally made of combed hard-twisted single yarns, although ply yarns are also used. About the same number of yarns in warp as in filling. Occasionally dots are woven in, and a crisp finish given the fabric; then it is sold as swiss.

whipcord. Serviceable fabric with prominent steep twill effect. Often mercerized and preshrunk. Generally a left-hand warp twill. Many finished with slight nap on back of cloth. Some woven in solid colors, others have mixed warp and solid matching color filling.

wigan. Usually made of print cloth or lightweight sheetings. Dyed in dark colors and starched and calendered. Used mostly for interlinings.

The preceding glossary is based upon material prepared by The Cotton Textile Institute, Inc.

1 (a) What are the by-products of the cotton plant? (b) For what are they used?

2 How would you judge cotton fabrics?

3 Name the more important varieties of cotton grown in the United States, according to their quality.

4 What climate is necessary for the growth of cotton?

5 Discuss the advantages of cotton fabrics.

6 How can cotton be made to simulate (a) linen, (b) wool, (c) silk?

7 What is the difference between muslin and percale?

8 (a) How are sheets labeled? (b) What is the basis for labeling?

9 (a) How may the strength of a fabric be determined? (b) How may the amount of sizing be determined?

10 (a) Why are long fibers separated from short fibers? (b) How may the consumer identify finished goods made from long staple?

11 Name some of the finishing processes used for cotton fabrics.

12 (a) What is ginning? (b) What are linters? (c) What are hulls?

13 Why is the more expensive method of vat dyeing used for such an inexpensive fiber as cotton?

14 (a) What determines the strength of a terry towel? (b) How can the consumer determine whether a towel is strong?

15 (a) What determines the absorbency of a terry towel? (b) How can the consumer determine whether a towel will be absorbent?

16 What care should be taken when laundering cotton fabrics?

17 What characteristics does cotton contribute to blends or mixtures in yarns and fabrics?

SUGGESTED ACTIVITY

Obtain three samples of fabrics used in cotton clothing. Attach to each a record showing the name of the fabric, kinds of yarns, weave, thread count, and finish. State the uses and relative durability of each sample.

12

A NATURAL CELLULOSIC FIBER

LINEN

Linen fiber is obtained from the stem of the slender flax plant. These fibers, held together under the stem's bark principally by a gummy substance (*pectin*), form the body of the flax plant. The linen fiber is composed basically of the woody substance, *cellulose*.

HISTORY OF LINEN

The fiber obtained from the stem of the flax plant was probably the first textile fiber to be used by mankind. Historical records show that linen cloth was produced and used far back in antiquity, the earliest record being the use of flax for fish nets by the neolithic lake dwellers of the Stone Age some ten thousand years ago. The Bible contains references to the use of linen. The bodies of early Egyptian kings and nobles were swathed in yards of delicate linen, indicating that the art of spinning and weaving had reached a high state of perfection in that country six thousand years ago. Such linen burial wrappings have been found to be in good condition, proving the amazing durability of the flax fiber.

Linen has always been considered the fabric of luxury. In some ancient countries, linen was used only for ceremonial purposes, as the symbol of purity. The descriptive phrase "pure linen" is customarily used to describe all-linen fabrics. Linen always looks cool, crisp, and clean, and gives an attractive and immaculate appearance to the persons and objects it adorns.

In some countries, certain grades of linen are more readily available and are less expensive than cotton, which is generally considered the most economical fabric. But in the United States, fine-quality linens still retain the reputation of luxuriousness and expensiveness because the finest linens are imported into this country. The flax plant must be grown in countries where there is plenty of cheap labor as well as natural facilities for extracting the fiber. Even the manufacture of the fiber into fabric requires unusual care throughout each process to retain the strength and beauty of the fiber.

The seed of the flax plant is valuable as the source of *linseed oil,* which is used in the manufacture of paints, varnishes, linoleum, oilcloth, patent leather, and oiled silk. To obtain the seed, flax must be allowed to overripen. As over-ripening destroys the value of flax as a textile fiber, the method of raising the plant is influenced by the purpose for which it is required.

FLAX-PRODUCING COUNTRIES

The countries that produce flax of various grades are Australia, Austria, Belgium, Czechoslovakia, France, Germany, Ireland, The Netherlands, New Zealand, Poland, Scotland, and the U.S.S.R. Flax is grown in Canada and in the United States (Michigan, Minnesota, and Oregon), but chiefly for its seed.

QUALITIES AND GRADES OF FLAX

Courtrai flax, which comes from the Lys district in Belgium, produces the finest and strongest yarns. The water of the Lys River in Belgium and of the Scheldt River in The Netherlands is free from minerals and has proved especially desirable for decomposing the woody tissues of the plant, a necessary step in treating the linen fiber.

Belgium has a reputation for producing the best quality of linen, but Ireland is noted for the best workmanship. Irish linen is also prized for its fine white color and strength. The flax is spun while it is wet, and the cloth is grass-bleached, two processes reserved for good-quality linen.

Scotch linen is lighter in color than Irish linen. It is used extensively in making heavy-grade fabrics, such as twine and canvases for tarpaulins.

French linen ranks high. It is characterized by fine designs and the use of round yarns, as the cloth is not put through the beetling process.

Russian flax is used for medium and coarse yarns, which are dark gray in color. Russian linen sometimes cracks because the fiber is not so carefully processed as in the countries that have a reputation for fine-linen production.

German linen is generally of medium grade. Austria, Czechoslovakia, and Poland also produce medium-quality flax.

FROM FIELD TO MILL

CULTIVATING ■ The flax plant requires deep, rich, well-plowed soil and a cool, damp climate. Premature warm weather affects the growth and the quality of the fiber. Level land with a plentiful supply of soft fresh water is essential. As the soil in which flax is grown must be enriched for six years before it will yield a good harvest, only one crop in seven years can be raised on a specified portion of land. The crops, therefore, must be carefully rotated. Shorter periods of rotation have been tried with success.

The flaxseeds are sown by hand in April or May. When the plants are a few inches high, the weeds must be pulled by hand with extreme care to avoid injury to the delicate sprouts. In three months, the plants become straight, slender stalks from 2 to 4 feet in height, with tapering leaves and small blue or white flowers. The plant with the blue flower yields the finer fiber. The white-flowered plant produces a coarse but strong fiber.

Flax is pulled from the ground at harvest time but not cut. Most of this pulling is done by hand.

Courtesy Irish Linen Guild

HARVESTING ■ By the end of August, the flax turns a brownish color, which indicates that the plant is about to mature; it is ready for harvesting. There must be no delay at this stage; otherwise, the fiber will lose its prized luster and soft texture. The plants are often pulled out of the ground by hand; however, there is a machine which can efficiently pull the flax. If the stalk is cut, the sap is lost; this loss affects the quality of the fiber. The stalk must be kept intact, and the tapered ends of the fiber must be preserved so that a smooth yarn may be spun. The stalks are tied in bundles, called *beets,* in preparation for extraction of the fiber.

PREPARATION OF THE FIBER ■ The seeds and the leaves are removed from the stems of the flax plant by passing the stalks through coarse combs. This process is called *rippling.* The bundles of plants are then steeped in water. The plants are weighted down with heavy stones to insure complete immersion. This allows the tissue or woody bark surrounding the hairlike flax fiber to decompose, thus loosening the gum that binds the fiber to the stem. This decomposing or fermentation is called *retting.*

Dew Retting. Dew retting is the method used in the U.S.S.R. The flax straw is spread on the grass and is exposed to the atmosphere for 3 or 4 weeks. This method produces strong flax, dark gray in color.

Pool, or Dam, Retting. This method is used in Ireland. It requires less time than dew retting, from 10 to 15 days. As stagnant pools of water are used, this method sometimes causes overretting, which is responsible for brittle and weak flax fibers. Pool retting darkens the flax, giving it a bluish-gray color.

Stream Retting. This method produces the best quality of flax fiber, as the process of fermentation can be retarded and easily controlled. Bundles of flax straw are weighted down in streams of cool, soft running water for 5 to 15 days.

Courtesy Irish Linen Guild

Bundles of flax being stacked in a retting dam.

This method, which produces strong, superior linen of a pale yellow color, is used extensively in the River Lys in Belgium.

Chemical Retting. Chemical retting can shorten the retting process, but chemicals will affect the strength and color of the flax fiber. Soda ash, oxalic soda, and caustic soda in warm water, or boiling in a dilute sulfuric acid solution are the chemical methods used.

Vat, or Mechanical, Retting. This method shortens the retting process and is used primarily in France, Northern Ireland, and United States. The flax is immersed in wooden vats of warm water at temperatures ranging from 75 to 90 degrees Fahrenheit, which hastens the decomposition of the woody bark. The flax is removed from the vats and passed between rollers to crush the decomposed bark as clean water flushes away the pectin, or gum, and other impurities. Linen produced by this method is more susceptible to mildew.

Retting only loosens the woody bark. If flax is not retted enough, the removal of the stalk without injury to the delicate fiber is difficult. If flax is overretted, the fiber is weakened. The retting operation, as well as all other processes for producing linen fabric, therefore, requires great care.

MANUFACTURING PROCESSES

BREAKING ■ The stalk becomes partially separated from the fiber when the wet plants are laid in the fields to dry. When the decomposed woody tissue is dry, it is crushed by being passed through fluted iron rollers. This *breaking* operation reduces the stalk to small pieces of bark called *shives*.

SCUTCHING ■ The scutching machine removes the broken shives by means of rotating wooden paddles, thus finally releasing the flax fiber from the stalk. This operation can be done by hand as well as by machinery.

HACKLING ■ The simple combing process known as hackling straightens the flax fibers, separates the short from the long staple, and leaves the longer fibers in parallel formation. For very fine linen, hackling is usually done by hand and is repeated, a finer comb being used with each hackling treatment. Coarse linen is hackled by machine.

SPINNING ■ The short-staple flax fibers, called *tow,* are used for the spinning of irregular linen yarns. Tow is put through a carding operation, similar to the carding of cotton staple, which straightens the fibers and forms them into a sliver ready for spinning into yarn. The long-staple fibers are used for fine linens. These are called *line,* sometimes *dressed flax.* Line fibers are from 12 to 20 inches in length. They are put through machines, called *spreaders,* which combine fibers of the same length, laying them parallel so that the ends overlap. The sliver thus formed passes through sets of rollers, making a rove for the final spinning process, which inserts the necessary twist.

Although flax is one of the strongest fibers, it is inelastic and requires carefully controlled warm, moist atmosphere for both methods of spinning.

Dry Spinning. Dry spinning does not use moisture. It produces rough, uneven yarns, which are not especially strong. These yarns are used for making coarse, heavy, and inexpensive linen fabrics.

Wet Spinning. This method requires a temperature of 120 degrees Fahrenheit, which is conducive to the production of soft, fine, even yarns. By passing

After retting, flax is shaken out by hand and spread in the fields to dry.

Courtesy Irish Linen Guild

the roving through hot water, the gummy substance on the fiber is dissolved, permitting drawing out the roving into a fine yarn of high yarn count.

LINEN YARN COUNT ■ The standard measure of flax yarn is the *cut*. If 1 pound of flax fiber is drawn out to make 300 yards, the yarn is known as No. 1s. When drawn out to make twice 300 yards, it is labeled No. 2s. The higher the yarn count, the finer the yarn. Exceptionally fine linen yarns for fine laces have been spun as high as 600s.

CONSTRUCTION OF LINEN FABRICS

The inelasticity of the flax fiber presents a problem in the weaving process because the fiber breaks easily under strain. A dressing, applied to the warp yarns by passing them over rotating brushes, helps linen yarns to withstand the strain of being lifted by the heddles during weaving. A very moist atmosphere is also required.

GENERAL USES ■ Linen fabrics usually have a balanced or squared construction, with the exception of double damask and certain sheer linens. The thread count, therefore, is always expressed as one number.

With the exception of some toweling, linen is seldom made in the pile weave. The pile weave increases absorbency, and this quality is already possessed to a large degree by any linen fabric. The twill weave is seldom used, as the fiber possesses natural strength; for the same reason, ply yarns are not necessary. The plain, satin, and Jacquard weaves are predominant. The twill weave, however, is used for linen drills in the South American market.

DAMASK TABLE LINENS ■ Fine table linens are always woven with the Jacquard construction; there are two kinds of construction, depending on the

After scutching, the fibers are hackled by hand by drawing them over successively finer sets of steel combs to remove pieces of straw and disentangle the fibers.

Courtesy Irish Linen Guild

The hackling machine is used to produce coarser linens. The hanks of flax suspended at the top of this machine are being hackled by the horizontal rows of combs that pass down behind them.

Courtesy Irish Linen Guild

weave. The designs in damask result from the manner in which the warp yarns pass over the filling yarns. The background is always the same on both sides.

A five-shaft satin construction on the Jacquard loom is used for *single-damask linen*. Most single damasks have the same number of warp and filling yarns, and the thread count ranges from 100 to 200 to the square inch. Some better single damasks have more filling than warp yarns, being overwefted by about 10 to 15 percent more filling than warp. But the cheaper qualities are usually underwefted—that is, some skimping is done with respect to the equalization of filling and warp.

The weave used for *double-damask linen* is an eight-shaft satin construction on the Jacquard loom. There are twice as many filling yarns as warp yarns, which gives greater distinctness to the pattern. The thread count ranges from 165 to 400 to the inch.

Originally, double-damask linen was considered superior to single damask. Today, the weave alone does not produce a superior product, because inferior yarns as well as high-quality yarns are used in all weaves. Double damask may range in quality from mediocre to excellent, and is superior to single damask only if good yarns and quality construction with higher thread count are used.

If single and double damasks having thread counts approximately the same are compared, the single damask is preferable because shorter floats give greater serviceability. The threads hold more firmly. A double damask with a thread count less than 180 threads is not advisable for home use.

FINISHING PROCESSES

Linen is generally scoured before it is given a finish, and the finish used depends upon the intended purpose and use of the fabric. The most common treatment given to linen is bleaching.

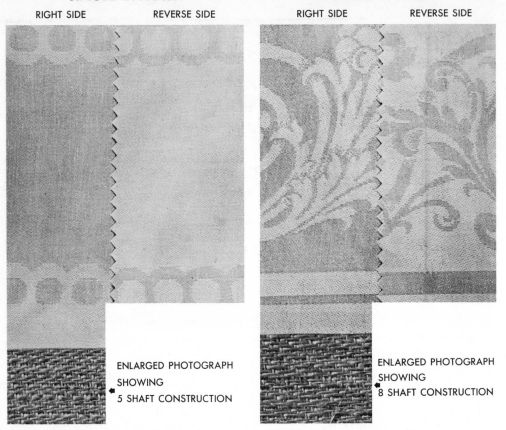

ENLARGED PHOTOGRAPH SHOWING 5 SHAFT CONSTRUCTION

ENLARGED PHOTOGRAPH SHOWING 8 SHAFT CONSTRUCTION

The construction and appearance of single damask (left) may be compared with double damask (right). Double damask is superior only if good yarns and quality construction are used.

BLEACHING ■ Linen is usually bleached in the piece except when it is to be used for such purposes as yarn-dyed fabrics and dress linen. The two methods used are *grass bleaching* and *chemical bleaching.*

Grass bleaching produces the finest results. It is accomplished by spreading the linen out in the fields so that it is gradually bleached in the sun. This process is time consuming but less injurious to the linen; it is therefore considered more desirable.

Although chemical bleaching is the method chiefly used, it may adversely affect the durability of the finished fabric due to the weakening effects of the chemicals. The process requires boiling the linen in a lime solution for 8 to 10 hours to remove such impurities as wax, then rinsing it in water, bleaching it with hydrochloric acid, washing the fabric again, and then treating it with caustic soda to neutralize any acid that remains.

OTHER PROCESSES ■ Bleaching produces four grades in the finished product: fully bleached, three-quarters bleached, half or silver bleached, and quarter bleached. Unbleached linen makes a fifth grade. A fully bleached linen fabric is less enduring than any other grade. Unbleached linen is the strongest because

Courtesy Irish Linen Guild and British Information Service

Fine Irish linens are laid "on the green" for sun bleaching, which produces the best results.

Modern chemical bleaching is chiefly used, though not for the finest linens.

Courtesy Irish Linen Guild and British Information Service

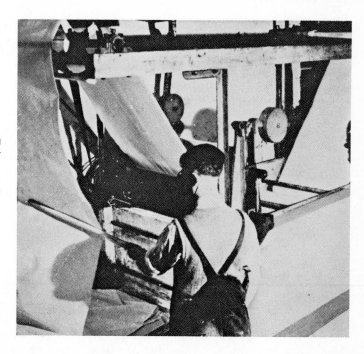

the natural strength of the fiber has not been weakened by the bleach. It is sometimes called gray linen or brown linen. The natural characteristics of linen are enhanced by the following finishing processes, which are discussed in detail in Chapter 8.

Beetling—for flexibility and uniform thickness

Calendering—for luster and smoothness

Mercerizing—for luster

Sizing—for added body

Wrinkle resisting—for resilience and easier care

Linen is never napped. The fiber does not lend itself to this process, nor would napping be desirable for long-staple yarns of hard surface. Where some crease resistance is obtained by reducing the yarn to short staple, the strength of the linen, which is its chief attribute, is sacrificed. Thus, any fuzziness in a linen fabric indicates the use of short staple or the presence of cotton.

DYEING LINEN

Linen is seldom yarn-dyed. The surface of the natural flax fiber is hard and nonporous and is, therefore, impenetrable to dyes. The cells of the fiber are held together with tissue that can be broken down only in a severe bleaching process. Highly colored linens, therefore, will not give lasting service because they must have been fully bleached to absorb the dye. The colors are therefore usually pastel or dark but dull shades.

EVALUATING LINEN FABRICS

The term "linen" has long been used to refer to such household necessities as tablecloths, napkins, towels, pillowcases, sheets, and decorative coverings. Every consumer knows that these articles are not necessarily made of pure linen. They may be made of cotton or spun rayon, even of linen mixed with such fibers. It is, however, always a woman's ideal to possess pure linens, because they satisfy a desire for the beautiful and the luxurious and may remain in families as heirlooms. When linens are chosen wisely, their additional cost is well worthwhile. There is no doubt that linen is still the best fabric for table covering because of its durability as well as its exceptional beauty when thus displayed.

There are several well-known trade names that are recognized as representing fine quality linen. *Moygashel,* produced by Stevenson & Sons, Ltd., enjoys a reputation for excellent quality. *Meadow Bleach* and *Yorkflax,* produced by York Street Flax Spinning Company, Inc., and *McBratney* linens, of Robert McBratney & Co., Inc., are also fine quality linens. The Irish Linen Guild has promoted its quality products under the *Irish Linen* label.

Even when a fabric is labeled "pure linen," it is necessary to know whether the yarns are line or tow. Fine linen fabrics, such as high-grade table damask and dress linens, are usually made of line, the long uniform staple. Line may be distinguished from tow by untwisting and examining the length of the fibers. The popular peasant linen is made of tow, but it is constructed with a very fine weave.

Pure linen is free from lint; therefore, the presence of lint indicates adulteration with cotton, or possibly oversizing. Cotton yarns are frequently mixed with linen to produce inexpensive fabrics. The name *Union Linen* is given to a fabric of which half or more is cotton. *Linene* is a trade name for an all-cotton fabric that simulates linen.

Strength. Linen is especially durable, being two or three times as strong as cotton. Among the natural fibers, it is second in strength to silk.

Sizing. As excessive sizing indicates the probability of poor construction or imperfections in weave, a sample may be tested for oversizing by holding it to the light, by rubbing, or by washing.

Weight. In linen, weight may be considered a criterion of durability. Damask weighs from 4 to 7 ounces to the square yard.

Elasticity. Linen has no significant elasticity. It is, in fact, the least elastic of natural fibers. In order to fit comfortably, linen garments should neither bind nor pull at the seams.

Resilience. Linen fiber is relatively stiff and has little resilience. Therefore, it wrinkles easily, which somewhat offsets its otherwise excellent qualities as a fabric for summer apparel. But it is possible to buy dress linens that have been given one of the patented wrinkle-resistant processes described in Chapter 8.

Due to its stiffness, linen fabrics should not have creases pressed firmly into them. Deep repeated folds, as in tablecloths, should be avoided because these creases eventually cause the otherwise strong yarns to crack and break long before they ordinarily would.

Heat Conductivity. Linen is most suitable for summer apparel, as it allows the heat of the body to escape.

Absorbency. When absorbency is the main consideration, linen is preferable to cotton. It absorbs moisture and dries more quickly. It is therefore excellent for handkerchiefs and towels.

Cleanliness and Washability. Linen launders well and gives up stains readily; its softness is enhanced with repeated washings. Since linen can be boiled and made sterile, it is desirable for surgical dressings and bandages. Bacteria do not thrive on linen because of its hard, smooth surface. Because of its stiffness, linen must be thoroughly damp when it is ironed or a steam iron may be used.

Reaction to Bleaches. Linen does not stain as readily as cotton, but it is also more difficult to bleach. Like cotton, it is weakened by sodium hypochlorite bleaches.

Drapability. Linen has more body than cotton and drapes somewhat better.

Shrinkage. Linen does not shrink a great deal; in fact, it shrinks less than cotton.

Effect of Heat. Linen scorches and flames in a manner similar to cotton.

Effect of Light. Linen is more resistant to light than cotton, but it will gradually deteriorate from protracted exposure.

Fastness of Color. When buying colored linens, look for the words "Guaranteed Fast Color" on the label, or get a guarantee of colorfastness from the store. If a label states that the fabric is "vat-dyed," it has been given the fastest color possible to withstand washing.

Resistance to Mildew. Like cotton, linen is vulnerable to mildew.

Resistance to Moths. Also like cotton, linen is not damaged by moths.

Reaction to Alkalies. Linen, like cotton, is highly resistant to alkalies. Linen may also be mercerized.

Reaction to Acids. Linen is damaged by hot dilute acids and cold concentrated acids. Cold dilute acids will not harm linen.

Resistance to Perspiration. Acid perspiration will deteriorate linen.

GLOSSARY OF LINEN FABRICS

art linen. Closely woven round thread linen, used chiefly for embroidery, generally in the plain weave. Bleached, unbleached, and colors. Also used for dresses and table linens.

bisso linen. Fine, sheer linen; sometimes called altar linen. Made of wiry yarns. Has a crisp feel. Used for altar cloths.

cambric. Fine, closely woven fabric with a high thread count. Plain weave; white and colors. Used chiefly for handkerchiefs.

canvas. Many fabrics come under this heading. Two principal types: (1) Open-mesh canvas; used for embroidery; made of hard-twisted yarns; very durable. Most popularly known in this group is Java canvas. (2) Close-woven canvas; made from coarse hard-twisted yarns in the plain weave; in various weights. Finishes range from heavily sized to soft.

crash. A relatively coarse fabric made of uneven slack-twisted yarns. Made in various qualities; plain weave. Used for towels, suitings, dresses, depending on the weight.

damasks. In satin weave as well as the Jacquard pattern. Two types: single damask and double damask. Single damask has a five-shaft satin construction; thread count ranges from 100 to 200 to the square inch; if given a high thread count is more durable than double damask. Double damask is more lustrous because of the longer float of the eight-shaft construction; reversible because the design is made on both sides; thread count ranges from 165 to 400 to the square inch.

handkerchief linen. Same as linen cambric. Sometimes called *linen lawn* or *linen batiste.* Plain weave, often corded.

huckaback. Coarse fabric, having rough surface. Variations in weave; may have small figures. Color range from semibleached to white.

sheeting. Firmly constructed plain-weave cloth. Used industrially. The closer constructions used for bed linens. May be unbleached or white.

toweling. General name that covers all types of linen woven in special widths for towels. Some are terry, huckaback, crash, bird's-eye, glass.

The preceding glossary is based upon material prepared by the Linen Trade Association.

REVIEW QUESTIONS

1 Why is linen a desirable fiber?

2 Why is linen not used as frequently as cotton?

3 What disadvantages may there be in the use of linen fabrics?

4 Why are linens expensive?

5 What kind of climate is necessary for the growth of flax?

6 (a) What are the methods of retting? (b) Which method is used in Russia? in Ireland? in Belgium?

7 Which method of retting produces the finest linen?

8 From what part of the flax plant is the fiber taken?

9 What are line and tow?

10 Would you prefer a cotton blouse to a linen blouse? If so, why?

11 (a) What country grows the flax plant for its seed? (b) For what is the seed used?

12 Why should the short fibers be separated from the long fibers?

13 (a) What characteristic of the linen fiber makes it difficult to spin? (b) Why would a wet fiber be more easily twisted?

14 (a) In what weaves are linen yarns woven? (b) Name some fabrics in each weave.

15 What finishing processes are given to linen fabrics?

WOOL
HAIR

TWO NATURAL PROTEIN FIBERS

Wool fiber and hair fiber are the natural hair growth of certain animals and are alike in that they are composed of *protein*.

HISTORY OF WOOL, HAIR

Originally, wool was borne on wild species of sheep as a short, fluffy undercoat concealed by hair. When wild sheep were killed by primitive man for food, he used the pelts as covering for his body. The fluffy undercoat probably became matted by usage, thus giving early man the idea of felting it into a crude cloth. It is believed that ancient shepherds in the first century A.D. discovered that Merino sheep could be bred to improve the fleece.

At first, wool was a very coarse fiber. Its development into the soft, fleecy coat so familiar on domesticated sheep is the result of long-continued selective breeding. The breeding of the animals and the production of the wool fiber into fabric are more costly processes than the cultivation of plant fiber and its manufacture. Consequently, wool fabrics are more expensive than cotton and linen. But wool provides warmth and physical comfort that cotton and linen fabrics cannot give. These qualities, combined with its soft resiliency, make wool desirable for apparel as well as for such household uses as rugs and blankets.

Hair fibers have all the qualities of wool and, in general, are even more expensive than wool. Vicuna is the world's costliest textile product and surpasses all other textiles in fineness and beauty. These hairs are often mixed with wool, adding rather than detracting from the quality of any wool fabric in which they appear.

WOOL

The quality of the wool fiber is determined by the breeding, climate, food, general care, and health of the sheep. Cold weather produces a hardier and heavier fiber. Excessive moisture dries out natural grease. Insufficient or poor food retards growth. Certain countries are suitable for large-scale sheep raising and consequently produce the greatest quantities of wool. The chief wool-producing countries are Argentina, Australia, British Isles, India, South Africa, and the United States.

CLASSIFICATIONS FOR WOOL

CLASSIFICATION BY SHEEP ■ There are about forty breeds of sheep. Counting the crossbreeds, there are over two hundred distinct grades of sheep. Those that produce wool may be classified into four groupings according to the quality of the wool produced.

Merino. Merino sheep produce the best wool. The variety originated in Spain and was so prized for its outstanding quality that during the Middle Ages it was a capital offense to export a Merino sheep from Spain. The staple is relatively short, ranging from 1 to 5 inches, but the fiber is strong, fine, and elastic and has good working properties. Merino fiber has the greatest amount of crimp of all wool fibers and has a maximum number of scales, totaling as many as 3,000 to the inch—two factors which contribute to its superior warmth and spinning qualities. Merino is used in the best types of wool clothing. The Ohio Merino, Austrian Silesian, and French Rambouillet are all varieties of Merino sheep. Other types are now found in Australia, New Zealand, South America, South Africa, and Spain.

Class-Two Wools. These sheep originated in England, Scotland, Ireland, and Wales. They have helped make the British Isles famous for their fine wool fabrics. They are, however, no longer limited to that area and are now raised in many parts of the world. While not quite as good as the merino wool, this variety is nevertheless a very good quality wool. It is 2 to 8 inches in length, has a large number of scales per inch, and has good crimp. The fibers are comparatively strong, fine, and elastic and have good working properties. Some of the better-known sheep of this variety include Bampton, Berkshire, Blackface, Cornwall, Devonshire, Dorset, Hampshire, Hereford, Exmoor, Kent, Norfolk, Shropshire, Southdown, Sussex, Oxford, Welsh Mountain, Wiltshire, Westmoreland, Irish, and Ryeland.

Class-Three Wools. These sheep originated in the United Kingdom. The fibers are about 4 to 18 inches long, are coarser, and have fewer scales, and less crimp than merino and the class-two wools. As a result, they are smoother, and therefore have more luster. These wools are less elastic and resilient. They are nevertheless of good enough quality to be used for clothing. In fact, some of these sheep, such as Leicester, Cotswold, Cheviot, Harris, Lewis, and Shetland, have given their names to wool fabrics.

Class-Four Wools. This class is actually a group of mongrel sheep sometimes referred to as half-breeds. The fibers are from 1 to 16 inches long, are coarse and hairlike, have relatively few scales and little crimp, and are therefore smoother and more lustrous. This wool is less desirable, having the least elasticity and strength. It is used primarily for carpets, rugs, and inexpensive low-grade clothing.

CLASSIFICATION BY FLEECE ■ Sheep are generally shorn of their fleeces in the spring, but the time of shearing varies in different parts of the world. In the

Top: Merino Ram
Center left: Cheviot Ram
Center right: Southdown Ewe
Bottom left: Blackface Ewe
Bottom right: Dorset Ram

Courtesy Australian News and Information Bureau

Courtesy American Cheviot Sheep Society, Inc.

Courtesy American Southdown Breeders Assn.

Courtesy American Suffolk Sheep Society

Courtesy Continental Dorset Club

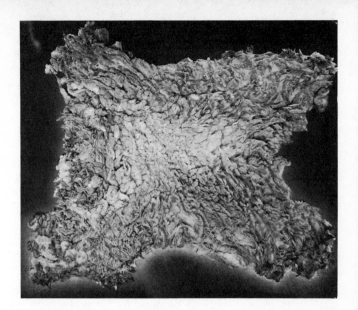

A fleece just after shearing.

Courtesy U.S. Department of Agriculture

United States, shearing takes place in April or May; in Australia, in September; in Great Britain, in June or July. Texas and California sheep are shorn twice a year because of the warm climate.

Sheep are not washed before shearing. Sometimes, they are dipped into an antiseptic bath, but this is done only when prescribed by law. Formerly, sheep were shorn with hand clippers; today the fleeces are removed in one piece by machine clippers, which shear closer as well as faster.

A skilled worker can shear up to 200 sheep a day. Traveling by truck from southwestern United States in the early spring, shearers work their way to the northern ranches and then south again.

Wool shorn from young lambs differs in quality from that of older sheep. Also, fleeces differ according to whether they come from live or dead sheep, which necessitates standards for the classification of fleeces.

Lamb's Wool. The first fleece sheared from a lamb about six to eight months old is known as *lamb's wool* and sometimes referred to as *fleece wool,* or *first clip.* This wool is of very fine quality; the fibers are tapered because the ends have never been clipped. Such fibers produce a softness of texture in fabrics that is characteristic only of lamb's wool. Because of its immaturity, however, lamb's wool is not as strong as fully developed wool of the same sheep.

Hogget Wool. Hogget (hogg or teg) wool comes from sheep, 12 to 14 months old, that have not been previously shorn. The fiber is fine, soft, resilient, and mature, and has tapered ends. Hogget wool is a very desirable grade of wool and, because of its strength, is used primarily for the warp yarns of fabrics.

Wether Wool. Any fleece clipped after the first shearing is called *wether wool.* This wool is usually taken from sheep older than 14 months, and these fleeces contain much soil and dirt.

Pulled Wool. When sheep are slaughtered for meat, their wool is pulled from the pelt by the use of lime, by sweating, or by a chemical depilatory. Such wool fiber, called *pulled wool,* is of inferior quality for two reasons: (1) because sheep that are raised for meat generally do not have a good quality of wool,

(2) because the roots of the fibers are generally damaged by the chemicals and the tension exerted in pulling.

Dead Wool. The wool fiber known as *dead wool* is sometimes mistaken for pulled wool. The term is correctly used for wool that has been recovered from sheep that have died on the range or been accidentally killed. Dead wool fiber is decidedly inferior in grade; it is used in low-grade cloth.

Cotty Wool. Sheep that are exposed to severe weather conditions or lack of nourishment yield a wool that is matted or felted together and is hard and brittle. This very poor grade is known as *cotty wool*.

Taglocks. The torn, ragged, or discolored parts of a fleece are known as *taglocks*. These are usually sold separately as an inferior grade of wool.

WOOL PRODUCTS LABELING ACT

There has never been a sufficient supply of new wool stocks to take care of a steadily increasing demand for wool. To meet this situation, wool fibers have had to be recovered from old clothing, rags of all kinds, and waste from wool manufacturing; all are important sources. This wool is variously called "salvaged," "reclaimed," "reworked," or "remanufactured," but it is best known in the textile industry as *shoddy*. This term is misunderstood by the average consumer, who is inclined to believe that wool fabric containing remanufactured fibers is necessarily of inferior quality. This is not so.

The hardier, though less resilient, remanufactured fibers when obtained from good original stock and combined with new wool from lamb, hogget, or wether fleeces, add durability to the soft new wool. Thus, remanufactured fibers contribute ability to withstand hard wear, although there is some sacrifice in warmth, softness of texture, and resiliency. They also make wool clothing available to consumers who cannot afford expensive wool fabrics.

To correct wrong impressions concerning the use of remanufactured wool, and also to protect consumers against unscrupulous practices, the United States government passed the Wool Products Labeling Act, which became effective in July, 1941. This act provides that every article of wool clothing must be labeled according to the type of wool used in its manufacture. The label must state: (1) the amount of wool fiber in the fabric, (2) the percentage by weight of "new or virgin wool" fibers, (3) the percentages of "reprocessed" fibers or "reused" fibers, (4) the percentage of each fiber other than wool, if such fibers constitute 5 percent or more of the total, (5) the aggregate of other fibers, and (6) the nonfibrous loading, filling, or adulterating substance.

New definitions of the type of wool fibers used in labeled garments were established by this act. Note that the law does not require labeling as to the type of sheep or the type of fleece from which the wool has come. It is therefore of only partial and limited value to the consumer.

WOOL ■ The simple term "wool," according to government standards, must always mean "new wool" that has not been made up in any form of wool product. New wool comes directly from a fleece. It has never been previously spun, woven, felted, or worn.

One fleece produces various qualities of wool fiber (numbered 1 to 14 on the diagram), with number 1 yielding the softest, finest, and longest fibers.

The term *virgin wool* is now used by the textile industry to designate new wool from a sheep's fleece, but the term is too all-inclusive to serve as a criterion of quality. Although the term testifies to the fact that virgin wool does not contain remanufactured wool fibers, it can be used to identify the less desirable fibers of a fleece as well as a specially fine quality of wool. Virgin wool may also include pulled or dead wool, which may be of definitely inferior stock. You should not feel that a fabric labeled "100 percent new wool" is necessarily more serviceable than one containing any of the remanufactured wool fibers, for there are many different grades of new wool. It is important to remember that a high grade of reprocessed wool makes a more serviceable fabric than one having a low grade of new wool.

REPROCESSED WOOL ■ According to the government classification, "reprocessed wool" is fiber that has been reclaimed and remanufactured from "unused" wool materials. Such materials may be combings and scraps of wool obtained during the manufacturing processes, sample swatches, or pieces of all-wool cloth from apparel manufacturing.

REUSED WOOL ■ The government gives the special classification of "reused wool" to fiber salvaged from all kinds of "used" consumers' goods.

MANUFACTURING PROCESSES

PREPARATION ■ Fleeces vary from 6 to 18 pounds in weight, average about 8 pounds each, and ultimately provide about 3 pounds of scoured wool. Since wool is sold according to the lowest grades in the fleece, it is often trimmed of the poorer quality edges, rolled up, tied, and packed in sacks weighing about 225 to 350 pounds. The trimmed skirtings are baled separately. In Australia, the fleece is separated at the time of shearing according to its quality. Superior wool comes from the sides and shoulders, where it grows longer, finer, and softer, and is treated as one fleece; wool from the head, chest, belly, and shanks is treated as a second fleece.

Domestic wool reaches the mill in loosely packed bags; imported wool comes in tightly compressed bales. Each fleece contains different grades or *sorts* of wool, and the raw stock must be carefully graded and segregated according to length, diameter, and quality of the fiber. The raw wool or newly sheared fleece is called *grease wool* because it contains the natural oil of the sheep. When grease wool is washed, it loses from 20 to 80 percent of its original weight. The grease, known as *yolk,* is widely used in the pharmaceutical and cosmetic industries for lanolin compounds because is can be absorbed by the human skin.

Sorting and Grading. Wool sorting is done by skilled workers who are expert in distinguishing qualities by touch and sight. As many as twenty separate grades of wool may be obtained from one fleece if the sorting is especially rigid. Each grade is determined by type, length, fineness, elasticity, and strength.

The standard for wool grading in the United States is based upon the quality of wool produced by Merino sheep because it yields the finest quality wool in terms of diameter, scales, and crimp. For example, first-quality wool is identified as "fine" and is equivalent to the quality of wool that could be obtained from a full- to three-quarter-blood Merino sheep; second quality is equivalent to the kind of wool that could be obtained from a half-blood Merino. The poorest qualities are identified as common and braid; they are coarse, have little crimp, relatively few scales, and are somewhat hairlike in appearance.

The grading system on the world market is based upon the British numbering system, which relates the fineness, or diameter, of the wool fiber to the kind of combed, or worsted, yarn that could be spun from 1 pound of scoured wool. For example, the first in quality would be that wool which is fine enough for and capable of being spun from 1 pound of fiber into the highest wool yarn counts of 80s, 70s, and 64s (see page 245 for explanation of wool yarn count). The second in quality is fine enough to be capable of being spun into yarn counts of 62s, 60s, and 58s. The poorest grade is that wool which is capable of being spun into yarn counts of only 40s and 30s. An equivalent grading scale of the British and United States systems follows.

COMPARATIVE WOOL GRADING TABLE

UNITED STATES SYSTEM	BRITISH SYSTEM
Fine (full- to three-quarter-blood)	80s, 70s, 64s
Half-blood	62s, 60s, 58s
Three-eighths-blood	56s
Quarter-blood	50s, 48s
Low-quarter-blood	46s
Common	44s
Braid	40s, 36s

Garnetting. Reprocessed and reused wool fibers are obtained by separately reducing the unused and used materials to a fibrous mass by a picking and shredding process called *garnetting*. The fibers are then put through a dilute solution of sulfuric or hydrochloric acid, which destroys any vegetable fibers that may be contained in the raw stock. This process is known as *carbonizing,* and the resultant wool fibers are called *extracts.* The new staple ranges from ¼ to 1½-inch lengths.

The quality and cost of reprocessed and reused wool fibers depend on the original stock from which they were obtained. A good grade of reprocessed wool may cost five times as much as a poor grade of virgin wool.

Scouring. The next step in preparing raw wool for manufacturing is a thorough washing in an alkaline solution; this process is known as *scouring.* The scouring machines contain warm water, soap, and a mild solution of soda ash or other alkali; they are equipped with automatic rakes, which stir the wool. Rollers between the vats squeeze out the water. If the raw wool is not sufficiently clear of vegetable substance after scouring, it is put through the carbonizing bath of dilute sulfuric acid or hydrochloric acid to burn out the foreign matter.

For some consumers' goods, the term "naphthalated wool" is used, which means that the grease and dirt found in the fleece when originally sheared from the sheep's back have been removed by a series of naphtha baths followed by clear water to remove the naphtha. When wool has been thus treated by a cleansing agent, dyestuff penetrates better. For some purposes, wool is degreased by extracting the grease with a solvent, such as perchloroethylene. Excess solvent is evaporated off and recovered, and the wool is ready for further processing. This method is used both on stock and piece goods.

Drying. Wool is not allowed to become absolutely dry. Usually, about 12 to 16 percent of the moisture is left in the wool to condition it for subsequent handling.

Oiling. As wool is unmanageable after scouring, the fiber is usually treated with various oils, including animal, vegetable, and mineral, or a blend of these to keep it from becoming brittle and to lubricate it for the spinning operation.

DYEING ■ If the wool is to be dyed in the raw stock, it is dyed at this stage. The advantage of stock dyeing has been described in Chapter 9. Some wool fabrics are piece-dyed, some are yarn- or skein-dyed, and some are top-dyed.

BLENDING ■ Wool of different grades may be blended or mixed together at this point. It is not uncommon for taglocks and inferior grades of wool to be mixed with the better grades. The use of a mixture with a coarser grade of fiber is a legitimate practice if the purpose is to make a hardier product and a less expensive one, provided the label on the finished goods indicates a true description of the raw materials used. In the manufacture of *Union* fabrics, a small amount of cotton is blended with raw wool. A greater amount of twist can be given to such yarns, with a resultant increase of strength in the fabric. Because of its crimp, Peruvian cotton is frequently mixed with raw wool stock. Such mixtures have a place in certain finished goods, but the amount of cotton used must be indicated on the label.

Depending upon the kind of ultimate fabric desired, such man-made fibers as nylon, polyesters, or acrylics may be blended with the wool. The wool con-

Courtesy Wool Bureau, Inc.

Various types of scoured wool are blended on a combination scale, which indicates the amount of each type of wool to be used in the blend.

tributes warmth, absorbency, body, drape, and hand. Discussions of the contributions of man-made fibers in such blends are presented in the appropriate later chapters.

CARDING ■ The carding process introduces the classifications of *woolen yarns* and *worsted yarns*. Manufacturing processes from this point differ, depending on whether the wool fiber is to be made into a woolen or a worsted product.

In the manufacture of woolen yarns, the essential purpose of carding is to disentangle the fibers by passing the wool fibers between rollers covered with thousands of fine wire teeth. Incidentally, this action also removes some dirt and foreign matter from the fibers. As the wool fibers are brushed and disentangled by these wires, they tend to lie parallel, which would make woolen yarns too smooth. Since woolen yarns should be somewhat rough or fuzzy, it is not desirable to have the fibers too parallel. By use of an oscillating device, one thin film or sliver of wool is placed diagonally and overlapping another sliver to give a crisscross effect to the fibers. This permits the fibers to be disentangled and somewhat parallel and at the same time provides a fuzzy surface to the yarn. After this carding process, the woolen slivers go directly to the spinning operation.

In the manufacture of worsted yarns, the essential purpose of carding is also to disentangle the fibers by passing the wool fibers between rollers covered with fine wire teeth. Since worsted yarns, however, should be smooth, the fibers are made to lie as parallel as this process will permit. Following this operation, the wool goes to the gilling and combing processes.

GILLING AND COMBING ■ The carded wool, which is to be made into worsted yarn, is put through gilling and combing operations. The *gilling* process removes the shorter staple and straightens the fibers. This process is continued in the combing operation, which removes the shorter fibers of 1- to 4-inch lengths (called *combing noils*), places the longer fibers (called *tops*) as parallel as possible, and further cleans the fibers by removing any remaining loose impurities.

The short-staple noils are not necessarily of poor quality. Combing noils may well be of good quality, depending on the original source of the wool. They may be used as filler for other types of wool fabrics; however, such fibers must be classified as reprocessed wool.

The long-staple tops, which are over 4 inches in length, excel in color, feel, and strength. They are used in the production of such worsted fabrics as serge, whipcord, gabardine, and covert.

DRAWING ■ Drawing is an advanced operation which doubles and redoubles slivers of wool fibers. The process draws, drafts, twists, and winds the stock, making the slivers more compact and thinning them into slubbers. Drawing is done only to worsted yarns.

Carded wool in fine spider-web form is being drawn from the cylinder (left) into wool sliver (right).

Courtesy Nat'l Association of Woolen Manufacturers

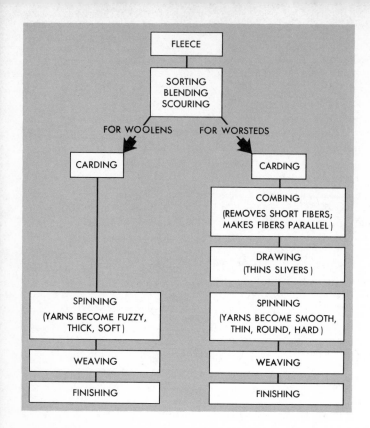

Diagram shows difference in the manufacture of woolen and worsted yarns.

ROVING ■ This is the final stage before spinning. Roving is actually a light twisting operation to hold the thin slubbers intact.

SPINNING ■ In the spinning operation, the wool roving is drawn out and twisted into yarn. Woolen yarns are chiefly spun on the mule spinning machine. Worsted yarns are spun on any kind of spinning machine—mule, ring, cap, or flyer. The two different systems of spinning worsted yarns are the English system and the French system.

In the English system (Bradford), the yarn is oiled before combing, and a tight twist is inserted. This produces smoother and finer yarns. The more tightly twisted yarn makes a stronger, more enduring fabric. In the French system, no oil is used. The yarn is given no twist; it is fuzzier, and therefore suitable for soft worsted yarns.

The differences between woolen and worsted yarns are as follows.

WOOLEN YARN	WORSTED YARN
Short staple	Long staple
Carded only	Carded and combed
Slack twisted	Tightly twisted
Weaker	Stronger
Bulkier	Finer, smoother, even fibers
Softer	Harder
Uneven twisting	Even twisting

YARN COUNT ■ The fineness or thickness of wool yarns is based on different systems for woolen and worsted. One pound of worsted yarn yielding 560 yards is identified as No. 1s. Ply yarns are numbered according to the number of the single yarn from which they are spun. Thus, 2/60s worsted means two-ply yarns of No. 60 singles, twisted together.

In woolens, the size of the yarn is based on two separate systems: the cut and the American run. The latter is more generally used.

The *cut system,* sometimes called the *Philadelphia* because of its use in that area, uses a base of 300 yards to the cut. Thus, 1 pound of woolen fiber drawn out to 300 yards sets a standard for No. 1s.

In the *American run system,* sometimes called the *New England,* 1 pound of woolen yarn yielding 1,600 yards is identified as No. 1s.

WARPING ■ The yarn that leaves the spinning frame is not of sufficient length to serve as warp yarn on the loom. It is first wound on bobbins or spools and placed on a large rack or frame called a *creel.* As in the warping operation explained in Chapter 5, the warp yarns on the bobbins or spools are evenly wound on the warp beam. They may be immersed in a solution of starch, gum, or similar compound to make them smooth and strong for weaving. In the production of better-quality wool fabrics, a hard-twisted two-ply yarn is frequently used for the warp yarn, as the plied construction gives greater strength.

WEAVING WOOLEN FABRICS ■ Basically, the weaving process for wool resembles the process described in Chapter 5. The short, curly woolen yarns obtained in the carding process are made into woolen fabrics by using the plain weave, sometimes the twill. The weave pattern is not always discernible because woolen fabrics often have a napped surface. The thread count of woolens is usually less than that of worsteds because the construction is not so compact.

Woolen fabrics are soft, fuzzy, and thick; they are warmer than worsted, but not so durable. Napping gives woolens a soft surface, which acts as a protection against objectionable luster. But napping can conceal poor construction and the quality of the yarns used; therefore, woolens can be more easily adulterated than worsteds. The napped surface tends to catch and hold dirt, but stains can be easily removed. If poorer yarns have been used in woolens, the fabric is less expensive than worsted. Woolens are desirable for sportswear, jackets, sweaters, skirts, blankets, and similar general use.

WEAVING WORSTED FABRICS ■ The worsted yarns, which have been specially carded and combed, are woven into fine worsted fabrics with distinctive patterns, chiefly by means of the twill weave. The plain weave is infrequently used. The thread count of worsteds is higher than that of woolens because the finer yarn permits closer construction.

Worsted fabrics are flat, rough, and harsh when worn next to the skin. They are more durable than woolens and more resistant to dirt. They wrinkle less and hold creases and shape, but they become shiny with use.

Worsted fabrics are costlier than woolens. They are appropriate for tailored and dressy purposes, for spring and summer coats and suits, and for tropical suits. They are suitable for business wear.

Top drawing shows smooth worsted yarn produced from long-staple fibers; bottom drawing shows uneven woolen yarn, with protruding short ends, produced from short-staple fibers.

INSPECTING AND CORRECTING FLAWS ■ Prior to various wet- and dry-finishing processes, wool fabrics are *perched*, or examined, for defects that are marked with chalk. Some flaws are corrected by *burling* with a kind of tweezers (called *burling irons*) to remove loose threads and push knots to the back of the cloth and by *specking* to remove specks, burrs, and other foreign matter. *Mending* and *sewing* may be required to correct minor catches and similar defects.

FINISHING WOOL FABRICS

FULLING ■ After the weaving process, woolen and worsted gray goods are placed in warm soapy water and are pounded and twisted to make the wool fibers interlock. This application of heat, moisture, and pressure, followed by a cold rinse, is called *fulling* (also *felting* or *milling*). Sometimes, chemicals are used to help moisten, soften, and lubricate the fibers so that matting will occur.

Fulling produces a desired shrinkage and gives the fabric additional thickness and a firmer, fuller texture. The longer the fulling operation, the greater the shrinkage, with consequent increase in the strength of the fabric.

The fulling process and other finishing operations for woolens and worsteds yield *flocks*, extremely short staple ranging from ⅛- to ¾-inch lengths. Flocks are felted into the poorer grades of woolens to add weight. They are also blended with other raw wool stocks. Other waste material reclaimed from fulling is termed *mungo*. This is the lowest grade of waste. It is used for blending and is combined with yarn for low-grade wool fabrics.

CRABBING ■ To set the cloth and the yarn twist permanently, wool fabric is passed over several cylinders that rotate in hot water and is then immersed quickly in cold water. The cloth is held firmly and tightly to avoid wrinkling. Repetition of the treatment with increased pressure results in setting the cloth and the finish.

DECATING ■ Decating, or decatizing, is a shrinking treatment that is sometimes used instead of London shrinking (discussed on pages 133, 247). Decating, however, is faster and gives reasonable protection against further shrinking. There are two decating techniques, and the one that is used depends upon the luster desired in the finished fabric.

Dry Decating. If the luster is to be set, the fabric is wound under tension on a perforated roller that is then placed in a preheated boiler equipped with a vacuum system. Steam is first forced from the inside of the roller through the layers of fabric for two or three minutes; then the process is reversed. The fabric is then removed and cooled by air.

Wet Decating. If the luster is to be increased, the fabric, wound under tension on a perforated roller, is placed in hot water (140 to 212 degrees Fahrenheit) that is first forced through the roller and fabric and then reversed. The hotter the water or steam used, the more effective the process will be. The cloth is then removed, cooled with cold water or cold air, and dried.

LONDON SHRINKING ■ This is a superior preshrinking treatment given to better-quality wool fabrics. It is a cold-water process by which the cloth is interleaved with wet blankets, dried slowly for twenty-four hours, and then set under 3500 pounds of pressure per inch.

ADDITIONAL FINISHING PROCESSES ■ Wool fabrics are also given the following finishing processes.

Shearing—cutting and shaving for a uniform surface
Singeing and steaming—for hard finish of worsted fabrics
Pressing—improving appearance and giving final shape to the cloth
Steaming, sponging—removing excess glaze
Napping or gigging—to raise a fuzzy surface
Piece dyeing—to impart color in the fabric
Tentering—for desired uniform width
Water repellency—for all-weather wear
Shrinkproofing—for stability
Mothproofing—for durability

These finishes are fully discussed in Chapter 8.

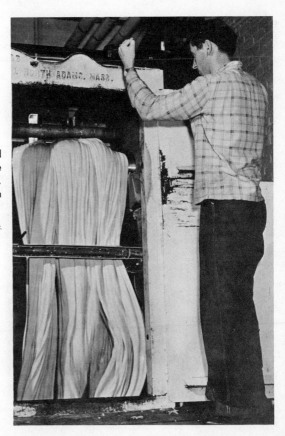

Woven pieces are sewed end to end and fed into the fulling machine where, in moisture and heat, the cloth is tumbled and pounded. This shrinks the fabric in length and width to give it body and evenness.

Courtesy Wool Bureau, Inc.

UNFINISHED WORSTEDS

Unfinished worsteds have the durability and tailored appearance characteristic of worsted fabrics and the comfort, greater warmth, and freedom from luster characteristic of woolens.

The soft texture of unfinished worsteds is due to additional manufacturing processes, such as fulling, brushing, or napping. Since they require more processing, the term *unfinished* gives a wrong impression.

The napped surface in the unfinished worsted gives softness of texture, serves the functional purposes of napped fabrics, and gives the beauty found in woolens. In addition, the fabric possesses the durability of worsteds. With continued wear, however, the nap rubs off, and these areas show an objectionable luster or shine. Such consumers' goods can be renapped by a cleaning establishment, but this is generally avoided since the renapping can weaken the cloth. You can enjoy longer serviceability by selecting an unfinished worsted in a light color. Light colors, such as gray, do not show luster as readily as the darker shades.

DIFFERENCES BETWEEN WOOLEN AND WORSTED FABRICS

	WOOLEN FABRICS	WORSTED FABRICS
Fiber	Short, curly fibers	Long, straight fibers
Yarn	Carded only; slack twist; weaker yarns	Carded and combed; tight twist; greater tensile strength than woolens; generally yarn-dyed
Weave	Indistinct pattern; usually plain weave, sometimes twill; thread count generally less than worsteds	Distinct pattern; chiefly twill weave, infrequently plain weave; more closely woven than woolens
Finish	Soft finish; fulling, flocking, napping, steaming; since napping can conceal quality of construction, woolens are easily adulterated	Hard finish; singed, steamed; unfinished worsteds are napped; adulteration more difficult as fillers would be easily discernible
Appearance and touch	Soft, fuzzy, thick	Flat, rough, harsh
Characteristics	Warmer than worsteds, not so durable; nap acts as a protective agent against shine; soft surface catches and holds dirt; stains easily removed	Wrinkle less than woolens, more durable; hold creases and shape; become shiny with use; feel harsh when next to skin; more resistant to dust
Uses	Generally less expensive than worsteds if poorer yarns are used; desirable for sportswear, jackets, sweaters, skirts, blankets, winter use	Costlier yarns; appropriate for tailored and dressy wear; spring and summer coats and suits, tropical suits; good for business wear
Typical fabrics	Tweed, homespun, flannel, broadcloth, shetland, cassimere	Gabardine, whipcord, serge, worsted cheviot, tropical worsted, Bedford cord

Genuine Harris Tweed is always identified by a label such as this containing the registered number and the association symbol.

The label reads:

HAND WOVEN
Harris Tweed
REG. U.S. PAT. OFF.
NO 353,757
COPYRIGHT 1937
GRANTED BY THE BRITISH GOVERNMENT BOARD OF TRADE TO THE HARRIS TWEED ASSOCIATION LTD.
HARRIS TWEED
FACSIMILE OF THE TRADE MARK APPEARS ON THE CLOTH
MADE FROM 100% PURE SCOTTISH WOOL

EVALUATING WOOL FABRICS

It is apparent that the quality and characteristics of wool fabrics are dependent upon the kind of sheep, its physical condition, the part of the sheep from which the wool is taken, and the manufacturing and finishing processes applied to the fabrics. While it might appear that these factors present a complicated problem in discerning preferred wool fabrics, there is much information and evidence available to the consumer to help him make satisfactory selections.

While it is not required that the labels on wool fabrics mention the type of sheep wool, fabrics made of Merino wool are frequently identified by label and in advertisements because they are preferred for their softness, warmth, resilience, and fineness. It should be noted, however, there are trade names that are similar but not identical in spelling to Merino; such fabrics do not necessarily contain Merino wool.

Another wool fabric that may be readily identified is the Harris Tweed. Harris sheep produce a quality of wool particularly well suited for durable tweeds. Harris sheep, which are raised on the Outer Hebrides Islands, have a coarse but strong fiber, which is spun into yarn and woven on looms in the cottages of the members of the Harris Tweed Association. These tweeds are preferred for their quality of construction, durability, and exclusive designs. These fabrics are identified by the Association's symbol and the registered number of the particular bolt of cloth.

The indication of the amounts of new, reprocessed, and reused wools is also helpful. The presence of reprocessed or reused wool in a fabric does not condemn it so long as the product is properly labeled and the consumer understands the limitations as well as the advantages of such wool fabrics. A fabric made of new or virgin wool may be of inferior quality if it is made of inferior grades or of extremely short staple. The yarns should be examined for fineness and crimp of fiber, as these factors have a direct relationship to the quality of wool used.

The identification of the fiber (or fibers) blended with the wool is also important. To consider the characteristics and contributions of these fibers to the blend, refer to the chapter that discusses each of them.

Strength. As wool is the weakest of the natural textile fibers, the fabric may be made more durable by the use of selected grades of reprocessed or reused wool, although the durability is gained at the expense of texture and resiliency. To determine whether temporary body (without strength) has been given by the use of flocks, brush and whip the fabric vigorously. Then examine the surface and selvages for powdery particles, which are the sign of short staple. Also examine the structure of the fabric to determine whether it has been weakened by excessive napping.

Wool fabric is strengthened by the use of ply yarns. A hard-twisted two-ply yarn may be regarded as an assurance of durability. Tightly twisted single yarns also make a strong fabric.

Elasticity. One might look upon wool's elasticity as a compensation for its relative weakness. Depending upon the quality of wool, the fiber may be stretched from 25 to 30 percent of its natural length before breaking. This characteristic reduces the danger of tearing under tension and contributes to free body movements. To preserve this natural elasticity, wool garments should be hung properly after wearing and allowed to relax sufficiently to regain their shape.

Resilience. Because wool fiber has a high degree of resilience, wool fabric wrinkles less than some others; wrinkles disappear when the garment or fabric is steamed. Good wool is very soft and resilient; poor wool is harsh. When buying a wool fabric, grasp a handful to determine its quality. If the fabric retains the wrinkles and feels stiff, this may indicate a mixture with cotton or an inferior grade of reused wool.

Heat Conductivity. As wool fibers are nonconductors of heat, they permit the body to retain a temperature close to the 98.6 degrees required for health. Wool garments are excellent for winter clothing and are protective on damp days throughout the year. The scales on the surface of a fiber and the crimp in the fiber create little pockets of air that serve as insulative barriers and give the garment greater warmth. Low-twisted yarns will also contribute to the warmth of the garment. Lightweight wool of sheer construction is comfortable for summer wear because of its thermostatic quality.

Drapability. Wool's excellent draping quality is aided by its pliability, elasticity, and resiliency. One of the outstanding competitive features that wool has over many man-made fibers is its superior drapability.

Absorbency. Initially, wool tends to be water repellent. One can observe that droplets of water on the surface of wool fabrics are readily brushed off. However, once the moisture seeps between the scales of the fiber, the fiber's high degree of capillarity will result in ready absorption. Wool can absorb about 20 percent of its weight in water without feeling damp; consequently, wool fabrics tend to feel comfortable rather than clammy or chilly. Wool also dries slowly.

Cleanliness and Washability. Dirt tends to adhere to wool fabric. Unless thoroughly cleaned, wool retains odors. Consequently, wool requires frequent dry cleaning, or laundering if the fabric is washable. Extreme care is required in laundering. Wool is softened by moisture and heat, and shrinking and felting occur when the fabric is washed. Since wool temporarily looses about 25 percent of its strength when wet, wool fabrics should never be pulled or wrung while wet. They should be lifted and squeezed.

To control the possibility of shrinking or stretching when laundering a wool sweater or a similar garment, wash it in cold water with an appropriate detergent, such as *Woolite*. To dry the garment, roll it in a towel, squeeze gently to remove as much moisture as possible, then spread it out to its original shape on a towel or heavy cardboard.

Reaction to Bleaches. Household bleaches that contain sodium hypochlorite or other chlorine compounds are harmful to wool. However, a bleach containing hydrogen peroxide or sodium perborate, such as *Snowy,* may be safely used.

Shrinkage. Shrinkage is greater in woolens than in worsteds, but all fabrics made of wool are subject to shrinkage, depending upon the preshrinking treatment. If the fabrics are dry-cleaned, the shrinkage will be less. "Chlorinated wools" are wools that have been subjected to shrinkproofing, but this treatment reduces the strength of the fabric.

The recently developed ultra-thin polymer resin films, made by the basic Wurlan process, is an excellent wool-shrinkage-control technique. This process was developed by the United States Department of Agriculture and is now used on fabrics by various wool manufacturers and processors under their own trade names.

If fabrics have been preshrunk or treated for shrinkproofing, this fact should be stated on the identifying labels. These tags should also indicate whether residual shrinkage may be expected, how much shrinkage may be expected, and how the garments should be cared for.

Effect of Heat. Wool becomes harsh at 212 degrees Fahrenheit and begins to decompose at slightly higher temperatures. It will scorch at 400 degrees Fahrenheit and will eventually char. However, it is not easily combustible—it will smolder but not flame when fire is removed. Wool has a plastic quality in that it can be pressed and shaped at steam temperatures, whether in fabric, as for slacks and jackets, or in felt, for hats.

Effect of Light. Wool is weakened by prolonged exposure to sunlight.

Fastness of Color. Because of their high affinity for dyes, wool fabrics dye well and evenly. The use of chrome dyes assures fastness of color.

Resistance of Mildew. Wool is not ordinarily susceptible to mildew; but if left in a damp condition, mildew develops.

Resistance to Moths. Wool fabrics are especially vulnerable to moths. They should be protected in some manner as discussed in Chapter 8.

Reaction to Alkalies. Wool is quickly damaged by strong alkalies. It is imperative to use a mild soap or detergent when laundering wool fabrics.

Reaction to Acids. Although wool is damaged by hot sulfuric acid, it is not affected by other acids, even when heated. This property permits wool to be carbonized without damage.

HAIR

Hair fibers that have the qualities of wool are obtained from certain kinds of animals throughout the world. The hair of these animals has been so adapted by nature for the climate in which they live that the cloth produced from the fiber gives warmth without weight. Some of these animals are used primarily as burden carriers; others are bred for their fleeces, which produce the most expensive fibers in the textile industry.

These hair fibers are used alone or are combined with sheep's wool for construction into fabrics whose cost varies according to the amount and quality of the blend. The consumer must be careful to analyze descriptions of certain of these blends. Parts of the names of rare animals are sometimes used to convey false or nonexistent values to mixtures of cotton and wool that contain such insignificant quantities of the lowest grade of hair fibers that they could not possibly add quality to the fabrics.

CAMEL'S HAIR

Camel's hair is a fine hair that is known to the American consumer chiefly in the form of high-quality coat fabrics. This textile fiber is obtained from the two-humped Bactrian camel, which is native to all parts of Asia. The climate of the desert countries, where the camel is used as a burden carrier and as a means of transportation, is exceedingly hot during the day and extremely cold at night. This constant change has produced a protective hair covering that is a nonconductor of both heat and cold; it is also naturally water-repellent. In the spring, the year's growth of hair, which hangs from the camel in matted strands and tufts, falls off in clumps to make room for the new growth. Masses of hair that are shed throughout the year are also accumulated. The camel is sometimes plucked to obtain the down or underhair.

Camel's-hair fabrics are ideal for comfort, particularly when used for over-coating, as they are especially warm but light in weight. Camel's hair is characterized by strength, luster, and smoothness. The best quality is expensive when used alone. It is often mixed with wool, thus raising the quality of the wool fabric by adding the fine qualities of camel's hair. The price of a mixed cloth is naturally much less than that of a fabric that is 100 percent camel's hair.

In the textile industry, camel's hair is divided into three grades. Grade 1 is the soft and silky light-tan underhair found close to the skin of the camel. This is short staple or noil of from 1¼ to 3½ inches, but it is also the choicest quality. Until recent years, it was the only true camel's hair used in the manufacture of apparel. In wool, noils represent the less valuable short staple; in the hair fibers, the short fibers are the prized product and are the only ones used in high-grade hair fabrics.

Grade 2 is the intermediate growth, consisting of short hairs and partly of coarse outer hairs, ranging from 1½ to 5 inches in length. Grade 3 consists entirely of coarse outer hairs measuring up to 15 inches in length and varying in color from brownish black to reddish brown. This grade has no value for apparel manufacture; it is suitable only for cordage and for low-quality rugs.

MOHAIR

Mohair is the hair of the Angora goat, native to the province of Angora, Turkey. This species of goat is now raised in the United States, principally in Oregon, California, and Texas. Some of the domestic mohair, particularly that obtained from Texas, is of excellent quality. Imported mohair is of long staple, 9 to 12 inches long, and represents a full year's growth. The domestic goat is shorn twice a year, yielding a shorter staple, from 8 to 10 inches. Imported mohair can be spun to a fineness of 60s in yarn count. The highest count possible for domestic fiber is 40s. The domestic fiber has a great amount of coarse, stiff hair, known as *kemp,* which does not process readily or allow thorough penetration of dye.

Mohair is a smooth, strong, and resilient fiber. It does not attract or hold dirt particles. It absorbs dye evenly and permanently, and its fine silklike luster permits interesting decorative effects. Mohair fiber is more uniform in diameter than wool fiber. Under the microscope, it shows almost no scales; its indistinct scales do not project from the shaft, as is characteristic of wool fiber. Mohair, therefore, does not shrink or felt as readily as wool.

When mohair is used in pile fabrics, the naturally strong fiber combined with the strength of the pile weave makes an especially durable and serviceable fabric. Mohair fabrics are wrinkle-resistant and do not mat readily because of the natural resiliency of the fiber. The fabric can also be made mothproof. Because mohair is very resilient and is stronger than wool or the other hair fibers, it is used to great advantage in quality floor coverings, better grades of upholstery and drapery materials, and summer suitings.

CASHMERE

The Cashmere goat is native to the Himalaya Mountain region of Kashmir, India, and China. The fleece of this goat has long, straight, coarse outer hair of little value; but the small quantity of underhair, or down, is made into luxuriously soft woollike yarns with a characteristic highly napped finish. This fine cashmere fiber is not sheared from the goat but is obtained by frequent combings during the shedding season. The microscope reveals that cashmere is a much finer fiber than mohair or any wool fiber obtained from sheep. The scales are less distinct and are farther apart; the fiber appears to be made of sections placed within each other.

Cashmere first became familiar in the beautiful soft, light cashmere shawls for which India has been famous. Today, it is used for such garments as sweaters, sports jackets, and overcoats. Cashmere is desirable because it is soft, lighter in weight than wool, and quite warm; however, because it is a soft, delicate fiber, fabrics produced from cashmere are not as durable as wool.

LLAMA

The llama is allied to the camel in species, having many of the characteristics of that animal, but being about one-third in size. The llama is the traditional burden carrier in the higher parts of the Andes Mountains in South America, primarily Bolivia and Peru, and has not been bred for its fleece. Its hair fiber is generally coarse and brownish in color and is valued because it may be mixed with the hair of the alpaca, an animal of the same species that is raised for its fleece alone. Some noils are obtained from the undercoat of the llama.

When llama is part of a blend of fibers, it gives exquisite natural colors that can be found in few fabrics. Llama mixtures have a characteristic high insulative property with little weight and are used for high-quality coat fabrics, as they embody the essential qualities of wrinkle resistance, fastness of color, and extreme durability.

Top: Angora Goat
Center left: Camel
Center right: Llama
Bottom left: Alpaca
Bottom right: Vicuna

Courtesy Arthur Ambler

Courtesy American Museum of Natural History

Courtesy S. Straack & Co., Inc.

Courtesy New York Zoological Society

Courtesy S. Straack & Co., Inc.

In the higher regions of the Andes, 14,000 feet above sea level, is found another fleece bearer, the alpaca, a domesticated animal that resembles the llama and is related to the camel. The fiber is valued for its silky beauty as well as for its strength. The hair of the alpaca is stronger than ordinary sheep's wool. It is also water-repellent and has a high insulative quality. The staple is relatively long, ranging from 6 to 11 inches; yet it is as delicate, soft, and lustrous as the finest silk.

Alpaca consists of two varieties of fiber: soft, woollike hair, and stiff beard, or outer hair. Of the many colors obtainable, ranging from white to brown and black, the reddish-brown variety is considered the most valuable.

A more highly selected type of alpaca is the *suri*—a superbreed just as the Merino is the highest type of sheep. The fiber of the suri is sought by manufacturers of outer apparel because the staple is longer, silkier, and finer and has curl throughout its length. A crossbreed, with the alpaca as sire and the llama as dam, produces the *misti*. Another crossbreed, the *huarizo,* is the result of breeding a llama sire and an alpaca dam.

VICUNA

The rare animal whose fiber makes the world's most costly and most exquisite cloth, surpassing all others in fineness and beauty, is found in an almost inaccessible area of the Andes Mountains, at altitudes between 16,000 and 19,000 feet. The vicuna, one of the wildest of animals, is less than 3 feet high and weighs 75 to 100 pounds. A single animal yields only ¼ pound of hair; thus forty animals are required to provide enough hair for the average coat. To preserve the species, the vicuna is now under the protection of the Peruvian and Bolivian governments. Attempts to domesticate this animal have not been very successful but are still being made in Peru. The fiber of the vicuna is the softest and most delicate of the known animal fibers; yet it is strong for its weight, is resilient, and has a marked degree of elasticity and surface cohesion. It is the most expensive fiber used in suitings and overcoat fabrics of tan to orange-brown.

GUANACO

The guanaco, native to southern Argentina where it is both wild and domesticated, is related to the llama and alpaca. The fiber is extremely soft and silky. It is also light, resilient, and warm, and the color is a honey biege. Because of these characteristics and its limited availability, it is expensive. It is generally blended with wool, frequently lamb's wool, so as not to mask the fiber's soft texture.

ANGORA

The angora rabbit produces long, fine, silky white hair that is clipped or combed every 3 or 4 months. The finest angora comes from France, Italy, and Japan. The angora rabbit is also raised in many other parts of the world, including the United States. The fiber's smooth, silky texture makes it difficult to spin, and the fibers tend to slip out of the yarn and shed from the fabric;

nevertheless, the fiber is desired for its texture, warmth, light weight, and pure white color. It is sometimes dyed in pastel shades. Angora rabbit hair is used primarily for sweaters, mittens, baby clothes, and millinery.

GLOSSARY OF WOOL AND HAIR FABRICS

alpaca. The lower grades of alpaca were originally used as linings, and the better grades for fine dress goods. The fabrics sometimes being sold as alpaca merely resemble an alpaca fabric in finish; the use of the term for such fabrics is incorrect.

astrakhan. Rough fabric with closely curled face resembling Astrakhan lamb's pelt. Often made with cotton warp or cotton back.

batiste (wool). Lightweight wool fabric in plain weave similar to plain cambric. Should be all wool unless otherwise described.

Bedford cord. Vertically ribbed fabric of substantial construction used for severe wear. Rib is pronounced and runs in same direction as warp. Originally an all-wool fabric, now also made of other fibers. Term describes weave rather than material.

bengaline. A thin fabric made generally of silk and wool, usually with a relatively inconspicuous rib running at right angles to the warp. The name does not denote any particular fiber blend.

bolivia. A soft plushlike fabric of wool, usually containing some special wool fiber, such as alpaca or mohair. The term is properly applied only to an all-wool product, closely woven and of fine stock.

bouclé. A fabric woven from curled or specially twisted yarn in such a way as to produce small loops on the surface, giving a kinky appearance. The curled nap does not cover the entire surface but occurs at intervals, distinguishing it from astrakhan. Usually made in coating weights but also in lighter weights for dress goods.

broadcloth. A fine wool fabric openly woven and then fulled to achieve uniform texture. The surface is then napped, closely sheared, and polished. The term originally was applied only to wool fabrics, but it is also applied to a cotton fabric used principally for men's shirtings. Not only is the fiber content of these fabrics wholly dissimilar but also the construction, finish, and use, so that they cannot be confused.

camel's hair. In undyed form, camel's hair is light tan. Fabrics that merely have this distinctive color cannot be correctly called camel's hair. The best grade is very expensive, and even then camel's hair is sometimes mixed with sheep's wool or other fibers.

candlewick. A soft woolen dress fabric made in imitation of the candlewick bedspread, with tufted patterns similarly constructed.

cashmere. A real cashmere fabric is woven only from the hair of the Cashmere goat. It is of fine close twill weave and extremely soft. The total amount of cashmere wool available is strictly limited.

cassimere (not to be confused with cashmere). Cassimere is a woolen fabric closely woven with a plain twill weave, and fulled. Most unclassified woolen fabrics are referred to as cassimeres.

challis. A lightweight sheer fabric of all wool or of silk and wool. Sometimes made with a woven pattern but more often printed with designs after weaving. The designs are commonly of the type found in silk goods. Challis is made of fine yarn; it is very thin, light in weight, and soft and pliable.

cheviot. Rough, somewhat harsh woolen fabric, woven from finer yarns than used in typical tweeds. Usually in plain colors or herringbones but may be in other fancy patterns. Woven from woolen yarns except for more expensive cheviots made from worsted yarns, generally in high colors, and referred to as worsted cheviots.

chinchilla. A thick, heavily napped fabric with a close curled surface in imitation of chinchilla fur. The tufts are close together, covering the entire surface. Generally dyed in the piece in solid colors. Used for women's and children's coats and hats.

covert. Twilled fabric made from highly twisted woolen or worsted yarns, usually of two colors, which give it a speckled appearance. Closely woven with a fine, smooth face. Used largely for men's topcoats and women's coats or mannish tailored suits.

crepe (wool). Wool crepe is a lightweight worsted fabric with a more or less crinkly appearance, obtained by using warp yarns that are tightly twisted in alternate directions. The term is often applied to lightweight worsted fabrics for women's wear that have little or no crepe surface.

doeskin. A very close and compact wool fabric with exceptionally smooth face. The weave is similar to a satin, but the smooth finish generally obliterates any trace of the weave on the face.

flannel. A fulled and napped woven fabric, made generally of woolen yarn but sometimes with worsted yarn used in the warp or filling. Usually woven with a twill weave, which may be obscured by the nap. Counts range from 56×30 to 86×52; distinguished for its softness. Used for bathrobes, skirts, men's suits and trousers. Cotton flannel or flannelette is not dissimilar in appearance.

fleece. Wool fabric with deep, soft nap. Term properly applied to flat woven or knit woolen fabrics as well as to those woven on the pile principle. The long nap or pile provides many air spaces, resulting in a fabric with high insulative properties.

gabardine. A firm, hard-finished worsted fabric in the twill weave with a fine diagonal wale.

homespun. A coarse and loosely woven woolen material made to simulate homemade cloth—in effect, a coarse, rough tweed. Yarn is usually heavy and contains coarse wool fiber unevenly spun.

hopsacking. A rough open-weave woolen fabric made of coarse yarn, usually in a basket weave. Used for novelty effects.

jersey. Elastic knitted fabric made from either woolen or worsted yarn. The rib is clearly discernible on one side of the fabric.

kersey. A medium-weight woolen fabric, well fulled in the finishing, with a napped and closely sheared surface that obscures the weave. Used extensively for military and civil uniforms.

mackinaw. A heavy woolen fabric, heavily fulled or felted, sometimes napped, with the result that no weave is apparent on the surface. In general construction, the same as melton except that the latter is usually made in plain colors, whereas mackinaw cloth is commonly woven with large distinctive plaids or color effects. Usually made of the coarser wools.

melton. Well-fulled or felted overcoating fabric with smooth finish and close-cropped nap. Generally in plain colors. Coarser meltons similar to mackinaw cloth, but sometimes made of fine, soft wools to produce smooth coating fabric with finish similar to broadcloth.

mohair. Yarns and fabrics of mohair are bright and lustrous. Warp yarns of cotton or worsted generally used in flat mohair fabrics. Mohair pile fabrics used in automobiles and for upholstery usually have pile introduced as warp, but in such fashion that the special system of threads is not subjected to severe tension.

nun's veiling. A fine, lightweight plain-weave woolen fabric, very soft and thin, originally for veils but now used for women's and children's dresses. Plain colors.

plaid back. A type of construction used in overcoatings. The face may be finished like melton, fleece, or similar fabrics. The back is a fancy or tartan plaid.

poplin (wool). Originally a fabric having a silk warp and a filling that consisted of a wool yarn heavier than the silk, thus producing a ribbed surface something like a rep. Now made of different fibers or combinations.

rabbit's hair. Rabbit's hair is used in combination with other fibers. It is soft and lustrous. In the better fabrics, enough hair may be present to justify the use of the term.

ratiné. A rough, pebbly woolen fabric the surface interest of which is obtained by the use of novelty yarns with a fancy twist.

Saxony. A term applied to certain flannels and to smooth woolen fabrics made from fine wools similar in nature to Saxony wools.

serge. A fabric with a diagonal twill and a smooth finish. The twill is visible both on the face and on the back; counts range from 48 × 34 to 62 × 58. Dark blue is the color most commonly used, but other plain colors are made for certain purposes.

sharkskin (wool). A term descriptively applied to wool fabrics woven in a 2 and 2 right-hand twill, with a 1 and 1 color arrangement of yarns in the warp and filling. This combination of weave and color results in color lines running diagonally to the left, opposed to the direction of the twill lines, and a distinctly sleek appearance and feel that suggests the texture of the skin of the shark. Modifications of this design are often loosely designated as sharkskin.

sheers (wool). General classification for thin lightweight women's-wear fabrics. Usually woven from worsted yarns, although some woolen fabrics are sufficiently thin to be classified as sheers.

Shetland. The term is now applied to fabrics made of wool with the characteristics of Shetland Islands wool. Shetlands are extremely soft. The herringbone weave is common.

snow cloth. Fabrics designed for outdoor winter use. May be meltons, kerseys, heavy flannels, and similar fabrics. Often indicates these fabrics have been given water-repellent finish.

suede (wool). A fine soft fabric with closely clipped nap made to imitate suede leather.

tropical weights. Lightweight suitings of woolen or worsted, usually the latter, used for men's and less frequently for women's summer suits. The weave should be firm but open, as the fabric is especially designed for hot-weather wear.

tweed. A term broadly applied to the sturdier types of fabrics made of the coarser grades of wool. Tweed fabrics originally derived their interest from the color effects obtained by mixing stock-dyed wools. More recently the term includes monotones, which derive their interest from weave effects. The most popular weaves for tweeds are the plain, the twill, and variations of the latter.

velour (wool). A smooth, sleek fabric with a closely cut pile face. The upright pile, which yields in any direction, gives the fabric an exceedingly smooth feel.

vicuna. Short, soft, exceedingly fine hair fiber, very valuable because of the limited supply. It is rarely used by itself, although a few vicuna coats are manufactured each year. Sometimes mixed with wool to produce special soft coating fabrics. The term and certain derived and coined names have been much misused.

whipcord. Sturdy wool fabric with pronounced diagonal wale, closely woven and smooth-finished. Used for riding habits and other garments subjected to hard wear; in heavier weights for upholstery.

The preceding glossary is based upon material furnished by the Associated Wool Industries.

REVIEW QUESTIONS

1 What are the advantages of wool fabrics?

2 Name the classification of fleeces according to quality.

3 What countries supply the world with wool?

4 Explain the United States government classifications of wool.

5 What qualities are found in fleece wool?

6 (a) How are grease and dirt removed from the fleece? (b) What by-product is obtained from the grease?

7 Name six differences between woolens and worsteds.

8 Name three woolen fabrics and three worsted fabrics.

9 What are unfinished worsteds?

10 How would you judge quality in wool fabrics?

11 What finishing processes are used for woolens?

12 Which finishing processes are used for worsteds? Why?

13 How do worsteds compare with woolens as to appearance and touch?

14 (a) Which type of wool fabric is warmer: woolen or worsted? Why? (b) Which is stronger? Why? (c) Which is higher in price? Why?

15 Discuss the properties of wool in terms of (a) strength or durability, (b) warmth, (c) absorbency.

16 Discuss the care of wool fabrics in terms of (a) cleaning and washing, (b) shape retention, (c) moth protection.

17 What information should you look for in determining the quality of wool fabrics?

18 Differentiate among mohair, cashmere, and angora hair.

19 Why might some camel's hair coats be inexpensive?

20 Compare llama, alpaca, vicuna, and guanaco fiber.

ANOTHER NATURAL PROTEIN FIBER

14

SILK

Silk is the very fine strand of fiber that is a solidified *protein* secretion produced by certain caterpillars to encase themselves in the form of cocoons.

HISTORY OF SILK

The possibility of making cloth from the filament that the silkworm spins into a cocoon was first discovered in China about 2600 B.C. Legend tells us that a cocoon accidentally dropped into a cup of tea that a Chinese princess was having in her garden. The hot liquid softened and loosened the fiber, which the princess pulled and drew away from the cocoon as a continuous strand. Another story cites Empress Si-Ling-Chi as the first producer of silk fiber from which she made a silk robe for her husband. From antiquity until the more recent establishment of the Chinese Republic, she was venerated as the "Goddess of the Silkworm."

The Chinese who first cultivated the silkworm and developed a silk industry endeavored to keep the source of the raw material secret. Their silk fabrics were highly prized. Caravans carried silks into the Near East where they were traded for hundreds of years. It is believed that silk was introduced into Europe by Alexander the Great in the fourth century B.C. As the desire for silk fabrics expanded, the interest in its production also increased. About 3000 years after its original discovery, the secret was stolen out of China.

A large silk industry eventually developed in southeastern Europe and subsequently spread westward because of the Moslem conquests. Spain began to produce silk in the eighth century. Italy began silk production in the twelfth century and was the leader for 500 years. In the sixteenth century, France became the rival of Italy in the production of silk fabrics of excellence and beauty.

Attempts have been made to cultivate the silkworm in the United States, but they have not succeeded commercially because of the higher labor and production costs in this country. The silk industry is an important one, however, because the United States has become the greatest importer and consumer of silk. That part of the industry that manufactures raw silk into fabrics closely touches the lives of American consumers. The possession of silk fabrics has always represented an ideal of luxury to Americans, perhaps more than to the inhabitants of other countries. Silk will probably always be prized by the consumer even though some man-made fibers now have qualities that were formerly possessed only by silk.

SILK-PRODUCING COUNTRIES

When farmers in the Asiatic countries first raised silkworms, the many diseased worms and defective cocoons resulted in poor grades of finished goods. The farmers were raising silkworms only as an additional means of support. Japan was the first country producing silk in large quantities to use scientific methods in cultivating the silkworm on farms as well as in factories. Japan has therefore always ranked highest in the production of fine silk, although satisfactory types are made in other silk-producing countries—China, Italy, Spain, France, Austria, Iran, Turkey, Greece, Syria, Bulgaria, and Brazil. The cultivation of the silkworm requires extreme care and close supervision, and the reeling of the filament from the cocoons can be undertaken only by skilled operators whose training is the result of many generations of experience.

CULTIVATION OF COCOONS

Since the discovery, so many years ago, that the fiber, or filament, composing the cocoon of the silkworm can be unwound and constructed into a beautiful and durable fabric, silkworms have been bred for the sole purpose of producing raw silk. The production of cocoons for their filament is called *sericulture*. Experiments have proved that the cocoon of the *Bombyx mori*, a species of moth, produces the finest quality of raw silk. In sericulture, all four stages of the life cycle of this moth are important, because some of the better cocoons must be set aside to permit full development, thus supplying eggs for another hatching. Under scientific breeding, silkworms may be hatched three times a year; under natural conditions, breeding occurs only once a year. The life cycle is as follows.

1. The egg, which develops into the larva or caterpillar—the silkworm
2. The silkworm, which spins its cocoon for protection, to permit development into the pupa or chrysalis
3. The chrysalis, which emerges from the cocoon as the moth
4. The moth, of which the female lays eggs, so continuing the life cycle

Within three days after emerging from the cocoons, the moths mate, the female lays 350 to 400 eggs on numbered cards, and the moths die. Based upon Louis Pasteur's discovery that the insect is subject to a hereditary infection, the moths are then examined microscopically. The cards of eggs from moths that have been infected are burned. By this careful, scientific regulation, Japan has not only protected and fostered sericulture but has developed into the leading producer of silk fiber.

Each healthy egg hatches into what is called an *ant*. It is a larva about ⅛ inch in length. The larva requires careful nurturing in a controlled atmosphere for approximately twenty to thirty-two days. During this period, the tiny worm has a voracious appetite. It is fed five times a day on chopped mulberry leaves. After four changes of skin, or moltings, the worm reaches full growth in the form of a smooth grayish-white caterpillar about 3½ inches long. Its interest in

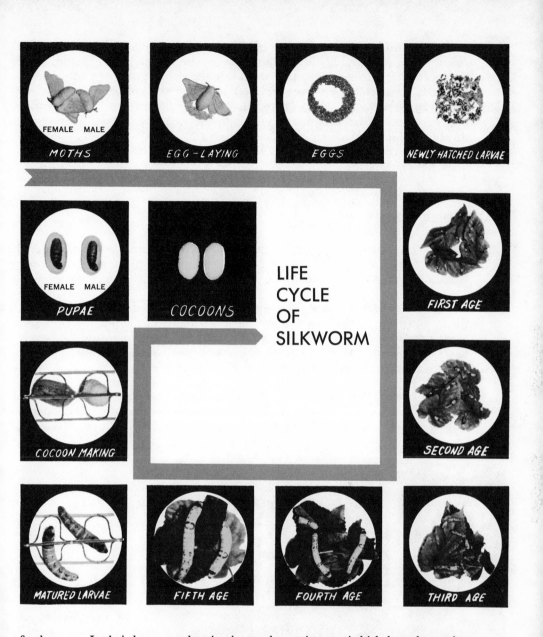

LIFE
CYCLE
OF
SILKWORM

MOTHS — FEMALE MALE

EGG-LAYING

EGGS

NEWLY HATCHED LARVAE

PUPAE — FEMALE MALE

COCOONS

FIRST AGE

COCOON MAKING

SECOND AGE

MATURED LARVAE

FIFTH AGE

FOURTH AGE

THIRD AGE

food ceases. It shrinks somewhat in size and acquires a pinkish hue, becoming nearly transparent. A constant restless rearing movement of the head indicates that the worm is ready to spin its cocoon. Clusters of twigs or straw are provided for this purpose.

Of importance to the silk industry is the small opening under the caterpillar's jaws, called the *spinneret*. The silkworm begins to secrete a proteinlike substance through its spinneret, and with a bending motion, the filament is spun around the worm in the form of the figure eight. The silkworm is hidden from view within twenty-four hours; in three days, the cocoon is completed. It is about the size and shape of a peanut shell. The filament is in the form of a double strand or *fibroin,* which is held together by a gummy substance called *sericin,* or *silk gum.* The liquid substance hardens immediately on exposure to the air. If left undisturbed, the chrysalis inside the cocoon develops into a moth within two weeks. To emerge, the moth must break through the top of the cocoon by secreting an alkaline liquid that dissolves the filament. As this cutting through damages the cocoon so that the filament cannot be unwound in one long thread, the life cycle is terminated at this point by a process known as *stoving* or *stifling.* The cocoons are heated to suffocate the chrysalis, but the delicate silk filament is not harmed.

FILATURE OPERATIONS

The cocoons that are raised by silk farmers are delivered to a factory, called a *filature,* where the silk is unwound from the cocoons and the strands are collected into skeins. Some cocoons are scientifically bred in such factories.

SORTING COCOONS ■ The cocoons are sorted according to color, size, shape, and texture, as all these affect the final quality of the silk. Cocoons may range from white or yellow to grayish, depending on the source and the type of food consumed during the worm stage. Cocoons from China are white; Japanese cocoons are creamy white and yellow; Italian cocoons are yellow.

SOFTENING THE SERICIN ■ After the cocoons have been sorted, they are put through a series of hot and cold immersions, as the sericin must be softened to permit the unwinding of the filament as one continuous thread. Raw silk

Cocoons being picked from nests of twigs originally provided to aid the silkworms in their spinning.

Courtesy International Silk Guild

Sorting cocoons.

Courtesy International Silk Association Inc.

consists of about 80 percent fibroin and 20 percent sericin. At this time, only about 1 percent of the sericin is removed because this silk gum is a needed protection during the further handling of the delicate filament.

REELING THE FILAMENT ■ The process of unwinding the filament from the cocoon is called *reeling*. The care and skill used in the reeling operation prevent defects in the raw silk. As the filament of a single cocoon is too fine for commercial use, three to ten strands are usually reeled at a time to produce the desired diameter of raw silk thread. The cocoons float in water, bobbing up and down, as the filaments are drawn upward through porcelain eyelets and are rapidly wound on wheels or drums while the operator watches to detect flaws. As the reeling of the filament from each cocoon nears completion, the operator attaches a new filament to the moving thread. Skilled operators have an uncanny ability to blend the filaments, always retaining the same diameter of the rapidly moving silk strand. The sericin acts as an adhesive. It aids in holding the several filaments together while they are combined to form the single thread. On old-style reeling machines at high speed, an operator could handle five to seven threads, and on the newest models he can handle twenty-five threads.

The usable length of the reeled filament is from 1,000 to 2,000 feet, approximately a quarter of a mile long. The remaining part of the filament is used as valuable raw material for the manufacture of spun silk.

The term *reeled silk* is applied to the raw silk strand that is formed by combining several filaments from separate cocoons. The diameter of the silk fiber is so fine that an estimated 3000 cocoons are required to produce a yard of silk

Reeling silk cocoons.

Skeins of reeled silk.

Books of reeled silk.

Photos Courtesy The Central Raw Silk Assn. of Japan

fabric. The silk filaments are reeled into skeins, which are packed in small bundles called *books,* weighing 5 to 10 pounds. These books are put into bales, weighing about 133.33 pounds. In this form, the raw silk is shipped to all parts of the world.

MANUFACTURE OF SILK YARNS

From the filature, the books of reeled silk are put through the following manufacturing processes.

SILK THROWING ■ Reeled silk is transformed into silk yarn—also called silk thread—by a process known as *throwing.* The term is derived from the Anglo-Saxon word "thrawn," meaning "to twist." Persons engaged in this work are called *throwsters.* Silk throwing is analogous to the spinning process that manufactures cotton, linen, or wool fibers into yarn. Unlike those fibers, the manufacture of silk yarn does not include the processes for producing a continuous yarn by carding, combing, and drawing out. The raw silk skeins are sorted according to size, color, and length or quantity, then soaked in warm water with soap or oil. This softening of the sericin aids in handling the thread. After mechanical drying, the skeins are placed on light reels from which the silk is wound on bobbins.

During this winding operation, single strands may be given any desired amount of twist. If two or more yarns are to be doubled, they are twisted again in the same direction or in a reverse direction, depending on the kind of thread to be made. To equalize the diameter, the thread is run through rollers. The thread is then inspected and packaged and is ready for shipment to manufacturers for construction into fabric.

KINDS OF THROWN SILK THREADS ■ Several kinds of silk yarns or threads are used in the manufacture of silk goods. The type of yarn and the amount of twist depend on what the weaver desires.

Singles. Usually, three to eight strands of silk filaments are twisted together in one direction to form a yarn called a *single.* Loose-twist singles, having two or three twists per inch, are used primarily for the filling yarns in many silk fabrics. Hard-twist singles, having a much greater number of twists per inch, are used in the sheer fabrics.

Tram. Tram is used only as a filling yarn. Usually, two to four untwisted singles are combined with only a slight twist of about three to five turns per inch. The number of turns may be increased for especially heavy silk fabrics. Tram is rarely twisted more than five turns to the inch, except in such fabrics as radium and taffeta, which use a special hard-twisted tram of about thirty turns per inch.

Voile. This yarn is used for such sheer crepes as voile. It is composed of three untwisted singles combined with thirty-five to forty S turns per inch.

Georgette or Crepe de Chine. This yarn is composed of two untwisted singles combined with a very hard S or Z twist of seventy to seventy-five turns per inch. The result is a very fine, strong, elastic yarn used for warp yarns and for such sheer fabrics as georgette or crepe de chine.

Organzine. Organzine is used primarily for warp yarns. It is composed of two or more singles, each of which has sixteen Z turns per inch. These singles

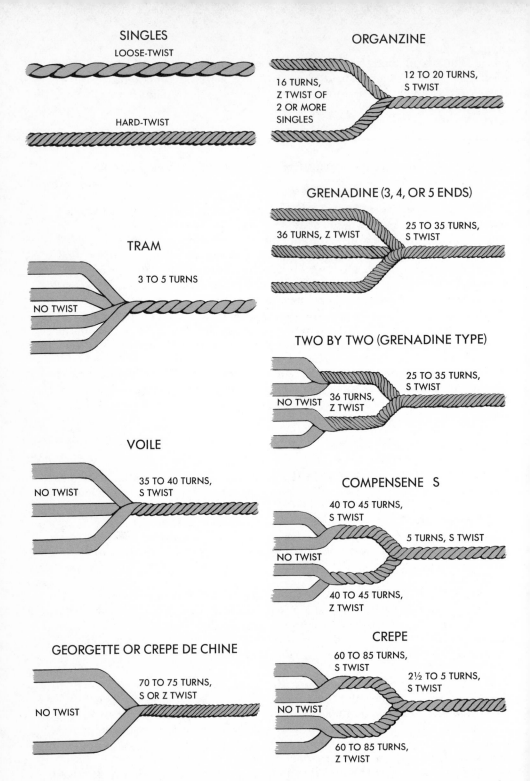

SINGLES

LOOSE-TWIST

HARD-TWIST

ORGANZINE

16 TURNS, Z TWIST OF 2 OR MORE SINGLES

12 TO 20 TURNS, S TWIST

TRAM

NO TWIST

3 TO 5 TURNS

GRENADINE (3, 4, OR 5 ENDS)

36 TURNS, Z TWIST

25 TO 35 TURNS, S TWIST

TWO BY TWO (GRENADINE TYPE)

NO TWIST

36 TURNS, Z TWIST

25 TO 35 TURNS, S TWIST

VOILE

NO TWIST

35 TO 40 TURNS, S TWIST

COMPENSENE S

40 TO 45 TURNS, S TWIST

NO TWIST

5 TURNS, S TWIST

40 TO 45 TURNS, Z TWIST

CREPE

60 TO 85 TURNS, S TWIST

2½ TO 5 TURNS, S TWIST

GEORGETTE OR CREPE DE CHINE

NO TWIST

70 TO 75 TURNS, S OR Z TWIST

NO TWIST

60 TO 85 TURNS, Z TWIST

The types of thrown silk yarns are illustrated above. The term *turns* means "turns per inch."

are then combined by twisting them around each other in the opposite S twist twelve to twenty turns per inch, which causes them to interlock more tightly, resulting in a firmer, stronger yarn.

Grenadine. This yarn is composed of three to five singles, each given a twist of about thirty-six Z turns per inch, then combined by being twisted around each other in the opposite S direction twenty-five to thirty-five turns per inch. Although these yarns have a high twist, they are nevertheless fine and are used for such sheer fabrics as organdy and grenadine.

Two by Two (Grenadine Type). Each of two pairs of untwisted singles is twisted about thirty-six Z turns per inch, then twisted around each other twenty-five or thirty-five turns in the S direction. These yarns are consequently much like the grenadine yarns but are heavier. Their weight, body, and high twist make them desirable for crepe fabrics.

Compensene S. This yarn is made of each of two pairs of untwisted singles. One pair is twisted together forty to forty-five S turns per inch; the other is twisted the same number of Z turns per inch. These twisted pairs are then twisted around each other five S turns per inch. The opposing directions of these twists prevent kinking but give elasticity. These yarns are often used for knitted fabrics.

Crepe. Some crepe fabrics are made of crepe yarns. These yarns are composed of each of two pairs of untwisted singles. One pair is twisted sixty to eighty-five turns per inch in the S direction; the other is twisted the same number of turns per inch in the Z direction. They are then twisted around each other two and one-half to five S turns per inch.

YARN COUNT OF THROWN SILK ■ The size or the yarn count of silk threads is based on a system of weight known as *denier*. A denier represents a weight of 5 centigrams—that is .05 or ½₀ gram. The standard length of a raw silk skein is 450 meters. A 450-meter skein weighing ½₀ gram contains a 1 denier thread, which is an extremely fine thread. To find the denier of 450 meters of silk thread weighing 70 centigrams (the usual weight of skeins from Japan), divide 70 by .05, or ½₀. The result is 14. The denier is expressed as 13/15 to allow for variation in the diameter of the thread.

In the laboratory, the denier size of a silk thread is obtained by a different method of figuring. The weight of a 450-meter skein is multiplied by 20 because 20 denier equals 1 gram (since 1 denier equals ½₀ gram). For example, if the 450-meter skein weighs 2.16 grams, multiplying this weight by 20 gives 43.2 denier, which is expressed as a 42/44 denier to allow for variation.

The most common size of raw silk from Japan is 13/15 denier, which is as fine as a 350s cotton yarn. In the spring crop, a 13/15 denier requires four to five cocoons to a thread, whereas the summer and autumn crops require five to six cocoons to the thread. As each cocoon comprises two filaments, a 13/15 denier may contain eight to ten or ten to twelve filaments, depending on the season. The greater the number of cocoons used, the coarser the thread and the higher the denier.

DEGUMMING ■ Thrown silk threads still contain some sericin that must be removed in another soap bath to bring out the natural luster and the soft feel of the silk. As much as 25 percent of the weight is lost by the degumming process. When the gum has been removed, the silk fiber or fabric is a creamy-white color, beautifully lustrous, and luxuriantly soft.

Degumming may take place after the silk thread is thrown in order to prepare it for yarn dyeing, or it may be done in any finishing process after the fabric is woven. For example, the tightly twisted yarns used for crepe effects still contain sericin. A small amount of sericin is sometimes left in the yarn or in the fabric to give the finished product added strength or a dull finish. Ecru and souple are examples of silk fabrics from which sericin has been partially removed.

WEIGHTING ■ The amount of weight that silk loses in the degumming process is an appreciable factor in manufacturing costs because the manufacturer buys silk by weight. As is customary in any business, the price of the finished product must offset this loss; therefore, silk has always been an expensive fabric. The weighting of silk fabric with metallic substances to make up for the weight lost by degumming is an accepted practice in the silk industry. This procedure lowers the cost of silk to the consumer.

Weighted silk is less compactly woven than unweighted silk and less silk is used in the construction of the cloth. In other words, weighting rather than compact construction can give firmness and body to a silk fabric. Weighting is done during the dyeing process. To weight colored silks, stannic chloride is used, followed by treatment with sodium phosphate. Black silks are weighted with metallic mordants, such as iron salt and logwood.

A small amount of metallic weighting, correctly applied to a fabric that is well woven to hold the weighting, is not considered injurious. In addition to lowering the cost, it is claimed that weighting gives silk crispness, luster, and firmer body and feel. When weighted silk is pleated, the crease is retained. Weighted silk, however, loses the natural elasticity of the silk fiber and is subject to deterioration when exposed to sunlight, perspiration, and dry cleaning. When the fabric is not properly constructed, threads shift. If the fabric is not woven sufficiently wide to allow for natural shrinkage, there is an unsatisfactory amount of shrinkage.

Taffeta is a commonly used fabric that is usually heavily weighted, because today there is little demand for pure-dye taffeta. Weighted taffeta is apt to crack and split at the places subjected to the strain of wear and when folded for a length of time. (Rayon and acetate taffeta do not contain any metallic weighting.) Because the consumer cannot determine the percentage of weighting in a silk fabric, the Federal Trade Commission ruled in 1938 that weighted silk must be marked as such, and the percentage of weighting must be indicated on the label.

SPUN SILK ■ Short lengths of inferior silk filaments obtained from waste material are not used in producing reeled silk. After the short lengths have been carded and combed, they are spun together much as cotton, linen, or wool yarns are spun. Spun silk threads are soft, but they are less lustrous than reeled silk and are not as strong or elastic. Spun silk fabric tends to become fuzzy after wearing because the yarn is made of short staple.

There are several sources of staple silk: (1) pierced cocoons, the result of breeding moths that have emerged from their cocoons; (2) double cocoons, the result of two cocoons having been spun by two silkworms too close together and is sometimes called *douppioni* silk; (3) floss, brushed from cocoons before reeling; (4) frison, the coarse and uneven silk fiber at the beginning and end of each cocoon; (5) scrap, the machine waste left from reeling, throwing, and the like.

Spun silk is less expensive than reeled silk. Although spun silk has less strength and elasticity than reeled silk because of the shorter staple used, it possesses all the general characteristics of reeled silk. Tub silk fabric, for example, is made of spun silk, yet it gives good service when the quality of the fiber is good. Spun silk is used for shantung and pile fabrics; for dress trimmings, linings, elastic webbing, and sewing silk; for summer wash silks, for velvets, for umbrella fabrics, and for insulative materials.

The waste derived from the processing of spun silk yarn is also used. The Trade Practice Rules of the Federal Trade Commission require that such fiber be labeled as *waste silk, silk waste, noil silk,* or *silk noil.* For obvious reasons, the last two designations are most frequently used. Silk noil may be reprocessed into spun yarn and woven into textured fabrics for draperies, upholstery, and sportswear. These fabrics are dull and rough and have a cottonlike appearance but are generally more resilient.

Yarn Count of Spun Silk. The method of determining the size of spun silk thread is similar to that used for cotton yarn. In cotton, the term 2/60s signifies a two-ply yarn consisting of two single strands twisted together, each having a yarn count of 60.

In spun silk, a two-ply yarn is indicated by the figures 60s/2. Although this term appears to be only the reverse of the cotton term, it does not mean the same. In spun silk, 60s/2 means that two yarns with a separate yarn count of 120 have been doubled, producing a ply yarn with a new count of 60.

FINISHING PROCESSES

Finishing processes that enhance the appearance of fabrics and add to their serviceability are given to silk fabrics. The most essential finishes are as follows.

Singeing—for smoothness
Bleaching—very little is required for silk that is completely degummed
Stiffening—for body
Embossing—if such patterns as moiré are desired
Calendering—for enhancing luster
Ciréing—for body and luster
Water repellency—for use as rainwear
Steaming—for raising pile weaves
Wringing and stretching—for softening the fiber and increasing the luster
Pressing—for removing wrinkles from finished fabric by passing it through heated rollers, then soaking in dilute acid to develop luster

For more detailed information the reader is referred to Chapter 8.

PURE-DYE SILK

As silk is weighted during the dyeing process, the term *pure-dye silk* indicates that weighting was not added at that time. According to the Federal Trade Commission rulings, pure-dye silk is defined as a fabric made exclusively of silk fibers containing "no metallic weighting whatsoever." But the use of such water-soluble substances as starch, glue, sugar, or gelatin in the dyeing and finishing processes is allowed. Such foreign substances are limited to 10 percent for white or colored silks and 15 percent for black silks. Well-constructed pure-dye silk requires a greater amount of silk thread than weighted silk because pure-dye silk is usually more compact. Thus it is generally superior, having the qualities of elasticity and durability, because the natural elasticity of the silk fiber has not been lessened and its great natural strength has been retained.

WILD SILK

The silkworms that hatch from a wild species of moth, the *Antheraea mylitta,* live on oak leaves instead of the mulberry leaves that form the food of the cultivated species. This coarser food produces an irregular and coarse filament that is hard to bleach and hard to dye. The tannin in the oak leaves gives wild silk its tan color, and the silk is commonly woven with the naturally colored thread; it is rarely dyed except in solid shades. Wild silk is less lustrous than cultivated silk as only a low percentage (about 11 percent) of sericin is removed in the degumming process. Wild silk fabrics are durable and have a coarse irregular surface. They are washable and are generally less expensive than pure-dye silk. Typical fabrics are rajah, shantung, tussah, and pongee.

The standard wild silk thread differs from the standard reeled silk thread in size, as it is made from eighteen cocoons. It averages 32/34 denier.

EVALUATING SILK FABRICS

In spite of its high cost, silk has been one of the most popular fabrics because of its unique properties. Soft, supple, strong, and lighter in weight than any other natural fiber, silk is prized for its lightness with warmth, sheerness with strength, and delicacy with resiliency.

Strength. Silk is the strongest natural fiber. The continuous length of the filaments in thrown yarns provides a factor of strength above what is possible with short natural fibers. The smoothness of the silk filament yarns reduces the problem of wear from abrasion. The inherent strength of silk along with its fine diameter and lightness has made it a highly desirable fiber for sheer, yet durable, fabrics. The strength of silk fabric is also affected, of course, by its construction as well as its finish.

Spun silk yarn, though strong, is weaker than thrown silk filament yarns. The quality of spun silk depends upon the source of the staple. Douppioni and pierced cocoon silk are generally stronger than the other silk staple, which tend to be less uniform.

Elasticity. While silk is an elastic fiber, its elasticity varies, as may be expected of a natural fiber. Silk fiber may be stretched from $\frac{1}{7}$ to $\frac{1}{5}$ its original length before breaking. It returns to its original size gradually and loses little of its elasticity. This characteristic means less binding and sagging, thus contributing to the wearer's comfort. It should be kept in mind that the elasticity of the yarn and the fabric is affected by the kind of yarn used (thrown or spun), the construction of the fabric, and the finish that it is given.

Resilience. Silk fabrics retain their shape and resist wrinkling rather well. This is particularly true of the fabrics made from pure-dye silk and from wild silk. Fabrics that contain a large percentage of weighting or those made from the short-staple spun silk have less resilience.

Heat Conductivity. Like wool, silk is a protein fiber; therefore, it is also a nonconductor of heat. Because silk prevents body heat from radiating outward, it is desirable for winter apparel, including scarves. Thin silk fabrics are also comfortably warm when used for lingerie, pajamas, robes, and linings. The warmth-giving quality is lessened by weighting because the metallic content causes the fabric to become a conductor of heat.

A question often raised is why silk is used for summer fabrics when it is a nonconductor of heat. The answer is that silk, being fine and strong, may be made into very fine yarns and woven into very sheer fabrics. This permits the body heat and the air to pass freely through the open construction of such cloth.

Drapability. Silk has a pliability and suppleness that, aided by its elasticity and resilience, give it excellent drapability.

Absorption. The good absorbtive property of silk also contributes to its comfort in a warmer atmosphere. Silk fiber can generally absorb about 11 percent of its weight in moisture, but the range varies from 10 percent to as much as 30 percent. This property is also a major factor in silk's ability to be printed and dyed easily.

Cleanliness and Washability. Silk is a hygienic material because its smooth surface does not attract dirt, and when dirt does gather, it is given up readily by washing or dry cleaning. Care should be exercised in laundering silk—always use a mild soap. Wringing or strong agitation in the washing machine should be avoided as silk weakens slightly when wet.

All silks water-spot easily, but subsequent washing or dry cleaning will restore the appearance of the fabric unless it has a special finish. Taffeta, for example, may be given a finish that could be permanently stained by water. Dry cleaning is preferable for weighted silks, but wild-silk and spun-silk fabrics may be washed.

Reaction to Bleaches. Strong bleaches containing sodium hypochlorite will deteriorate silk. A mild bleach of hydrogen peroxide or sodium perborate may be used with normal caution.

Shrinkage. Because of the straightness of the filament, smooth-surfaced silk fabrics have only a normal shrinkage, which is easily restored by ironing. Crepe effects shrink considerably in washing, but careful ironing with a moderately hot iron will restore the fabric to its original size.

Effect of Heat. Silk is somewhat sensitive to heat. It will begin to decompose at 330 degrees Fahrenheit; therefore, it should be ironed while damp with a warm iron.

Effect of Light. Continuous exposure to light weakens silk faster than either cotton or wool. Raw silk is more resistant to light than degummed silk, and weighted silk has the least light resistance. Silk drapery and upholstery fabrics should be protected from direct exposure to the light.

Resistance to Mildew. Silk will not mildew unless left for some time in a damp state or under the extreme conditions of tropical dampness.

Resistance to Moths. Silk is not attacked by moths.

Reaction to Alkalies. Silk is not as sensitive as wool is to alkalies but can be damaged if the concentration and temperature are high enough. Use mild soap in lukewarm water when laundering.

Reaction to Acids. Concentrated mineral acids will dissolve silk faster than wool. Organic acids do not harm silk.

Reaction to Perspiration. Silk fabrics are damaged by perspiration. The silk itself deteriorates, and the color is affected, causing staining. Garments worn next to the skin should be washed or otherwise cleaned after each wearing.

Affinity to Dyes. Silk has a very good affinity for dyes. It readily absorbs basic, acid, and direct dyes. Prints on silk are taken so well that the color on the back of the fabric often differs only slightly from the face.

Dyed silk is colorfast under most conditions, but its resistance to light is unsatisfactory. The resistance of weighted silk is particularly poor; therefore, silk is not recommended for window curtains. Pure-dye silks may be redyed by the consumer, provided a suitable commercial dye is used and the directions on the container are carefully followed.

GLOSSARY OF SILK FABRICS

bengaline. A ribbed fabric having cotton or wool yarns for the filling and silk for the warp. Similar to poplin but having a heavier ribbed effect. Used for coats, suits, dresses.

broadcloth. A fine, smooth, closely woven fabric in plain colors or in woven stripes; also known as silk shirting. It has a plain weave. Used for shirts and dresses.

brocade. Most figured silk fabrics in a Jacquard weave are known as brocades. The pattern is raised above the general surface of the fabric. Used mainly for elaborate evening wear.

brocatelle. Similar to brocade but usually heavier with a pronounced raised design. Used primarily for upholstery and draperies.

canton crepe. Characterized by a heavy filling and a finer warp. Heavier than crepe de chine, having pronounced crinkle and greater durability. Used chiefly for dresses.

chiffon. A transparent sheer fabric in a plain weave. Extremely light in weight but very strong. It usually has a soft finish. Used for evening dresses, lingerie, blouses, and handkerchiefs.

China silk. A very soft, extremely lightweight silk made in a plain weave, used chiefly for linings. Irregularities of threads, caused by the extreme lightness and softness of China silk, are characteristic of the fabric.

crepe. Fabrics with a crinkled effect, produced either by the use of tightly twisted yarns or by the method of weaving.

crepe-back satin or satin crepe. Satin weave with a crepe-twist filling. As the fabric is reversible, interesting effects can be obtained by contrasting the surfaces. Used for dresses, blouses, linings.

crepe de chine. Soft but strong; lighter in weight than canton crepe. Has a fine crinkled effect produced by alternately twisted filling yarns. Popular for dresses, lingerie, blouses, and scarves.

crepe meteor. Similar to georgette in construction on the reverse side. Satin construction on its face, thus showing more luster than any of the flat crepes. Light in weight, drapes well, has a soft feel and finish.

damask. Reversible figured silk fabrics woven on the Jacquard loom. Pattern flatter than in brocade. Used for upholstery and draperies; the lighter weights, for dresses and lingerie.

ecru silk. Thrown silk with small amount of sericin removed.

faille. A silk fabric of the grosgrain type. In plain weave with flat ribs in the filling. Has good body and wears well if not too loosely constructed. Usually slightly lustrous finish. Used for dresses, coats, and handbags.

faille crepe.   Lighter weight than faille with creped filling. Used for dresses.

faille taffeta.   Stiff and crisp with a fine cross-ribbed appearance. Used for dresses and coats.

flat crepe.   Similar to crepe de chine but with a flatter surface.

foulard.   A lightweight silk fabric with a soft finish. Made with a twill weave. Usually printed with small figures on dark and light backgrounds. Suitable for dresses, robes, and scarves.

georgette.   Highly creped sheer silk fabric, chiefly for dresses and blouses.

gloria silk.   A very closely woven, lightweight cloth generally constructed of plain weave, but sometimes of twill or satin. Made with silk warp and a cotton, worsted, or nylon filling. Much used as an umbrella cloth.

grosgrain.   A fine cross-ribbed fabric of close texture having a heavy filling, which is sometimes made of cotton yarns. Ribs are rounder than in faille; heavier than in poplin. Used chiefly for ribbons and trimmings.

habutai.   Similar to China silk but heavier. A closely woven, pure-dye fabric. Used for lamp shades, dresses, blouses, lingerie, curtains.

lamé.   Silk in which metal threads form the pattern or the background. Used for evening wear.

marquisette.   Very sheer silk fabric in the gauze weave. Sometimes called silk gauze. Used for evening dresses and trimmings.

matelassé.   A fabric having a raised figured pattern in a blistered quilted effect. Woven on a Jacquard loom. Used for dresses and blouses.

merveilleux.   An all-silk or silk-and-cotton mixture in twill weave. Used as lining in men's outer apparel.

moiré.   Watermark designs embossed on plain-weave fabrics that have crosswise ribs.

mousseline de soie.   Sheer transparent silk in a plain weave. Similar to chiffon but with a more open texture and a stiffer finish produced by the use of sizing. Used chiefly for evening dresses.

ottoman.   Heavy plain-weave fabric with wide, flat crosswise ribs that are larger and rounder than in faille. Filling may be cotton, silk, or wool. Used for dress coats, suits, trimmings.

pongee.   Also called *tussah silk*. Made from wild silk. Has a rough, uneven texture. Generally in its natural colors of cream to light brown, but may be dyed. Used for dress goods and household decoration.

radium.   A lustrous, supple fabric having the drapability of crepe and the crispness of taffeta. Plain weave. Used for women's dresses, slips, negligees, blouses, linings, draperies.

satin.   Silk fabric with a highly lustrous surface and usually a dull back. Made in different weights according to its uses, which vary from lingerie and dress goods to drapery and upholstery fabrics. May be made with a cotton back. Sometimes double-faced for use as ribbon.

shantung.   Low in luster, heavier and rougher than pongee. A plain weave in which irregular (slub) filling yarns are used. Sometimes used to describe a heavy grade of pongee made in China.

souple silk. Silk dyed in the skein, only part of the sericin being removed.

surah. A soft, strong silk with a twill weave. Used for dresses and scarves.

taffeta. A smooth, closely woven fabric in a plain weave. Often weighted to produce its characteristic crispness. Sometimes has a moiré pattern. Used for dresses, suits, coats, and lingerie.

velvet. Silk velvet has a silk pile and a silk back. Some velvets are made with a silk pile and a rayon or cotton back. *Transparent velvet* is a sheer velvet having a rayon pile and a silk back. *Panne velvet* has a special luster that is produced by pressing the pile in one direction.

REVIEW QUESTIONS

1 (a) Name the silk-producing countries. (b) What is the cultivation of silk called?

2 Describe the life cycle of the silkworm.

3 What process in the production of silk is analogous to the spinning process for other fibers?

4 Describe the degumming process and its effects on various types of silk fabrics.

5 What is the difference between weighted silk and pure-dye silk?

6 (a) Why is silk weighted? (b) What are the advantages of weighting? (c) What are the disadvantages?

7 What is spun silk?

8 (a) How does wild silk differ from cultivated silk? (b) How does the difference affect the consumer?

9 Why are most wild silk fabrics tan in color?

10 Name some fabrics usually made from wild silk.

11 For what purposes is pongee most desirable?

12 What finishing processes are given to silk fabrics?

13 Why is silk not recommended for window curtains?

14 For what purpose would you select silk rather than other fabrics? Why?

15 List the essential qualities of silk, and show the effects of each quality on finished goods.

SUGGESTED ACTIVITY

Make a chart comparing the properties of the natural fibers: cotton, linen, wool, silk.

15

RAYONS: FOUR BASIC VARIETIES

A rayon fiber is composed of pure cellulose, the substance of which the cell walls of such woody plants as trees and cotton are largely comprised. We are already familiar with cellulose in the form of such products as paper.

Rayon fibers are made from cellulose that has been reformed, or *regenerated;* consequently, these fibers are identified as *regenerated cellulosic fibers.*

HISTORY OF RAYONS

The production of a fiber such as rayon, the first of the man-made fibers, had been prophesied as long ago as 1664 by Robert Hooke, the English naturalist. He believed that it was possible to make an "artificial glutinous composition, much resembling, if not full as good, nay better, than that excrement, or whatever other substance it be out of which the silkworm wire-draws his clew." In 1710, René A. de Réaumur, the French scientist, suggested the possibility of making silk filaments out of gums and resins; for example, threads of varnish. One hundred and thirty years later, in 1840, an apparatus was invented that drew synthetic filaments through small holes. In 1855, Georges Audemars, a Swiss chemist, discovered how to make cellulose nitrate. This was the first step toward the nitrocellulose process of making rayon. Almost thirty years later, in 1884, Count Hilaire de Chardonnet produced the first synthetic textile fibers from nitrocellulose. He became known as the "father of rayon." Chardonnet obtained the original French patent and won the financial support that built the world's first rayon factory. These and other chemists of their day, as well as those who are constantly experimenting today on new fibers, have been guided by a desire to produce beautiful, smooth, light, supple fabrics with just the right amount of luster—the characteristics for which silk has long been noted—at a price within the income of every consumer.

Man-made textile filaments were officially recognized in 1925 when the Federal Trade Commission permitted the use of the name *rayon* for yarns obtained from cellulose or its derivatives. As the production and types of man-made fibers had increased and been given various trade names, the Federal Trade Commission ruled again in 1937 that any fiber or yarn produced chemically from cellulose must be designated as "rayon."

Wood pulp and cotton are the sources of pure cellulose used to produce rayon fiber.

Courtesy American Viscose Corporation

Over the period of the next fifteen years, however, confusion developed among garment manufacturers, and particularly among consumers, because there were as many as four different types of rayon with some similar and some different properties. Some rayons would fade faster than others; some would dry more quickly than others; some would stick to the iron and melt, others would iron nicely. The cause of this lay in the fact that there were basically two groups of rayons: one consisting of regenerated pure cellulose, the other of a cellulose compound. These different compositions gave different properties. The Federal Trade Commission therefore ruled that as of February 9, 1952, there would be two categories of cellulosic fibers: rayon and acetate. All fabrics and garments containing rayon and/or acetate must now be labeled as such and the percent of content of each fiber indicated. The rules also incorporated the first official designation of rayon and acetate products as "man-made" rather than "synthetic." In the chemist's terminology, rayon and acetate are not synthetic because natural materials—cotton linters and wood pulp—are used in their manufacture, rather than chemical elements.

BASIC METHOD OF PRODUCING RAYON FILAMENT

The natural process by which the silkworm transforms the cellulose of mulberry trees into two fine filaments is simulated in the process of making rayon.

A liquid substance of cellulose is forced through a metal cap or nozzle about the size of a thimble. This nozzle is called a *spinneret* because it performs the same function as the silkworm's spinneret. The cap is usually made of a platinum-rhodium alloy because that metal is not affected by acids or alkalies; it is perforated with small holes that are almost invisible to the naked eye. Through each of the tiny holes, a filament is extruded, which is solidified by a liquid bath as it comes from the spinneret. This is similar to the hardening by air of the raw-silk substance spun by the silkworm. The number of holes in the spinneret ranges from 1 to 20,000, and filaments of equal size are simultaneously produced. In a subsequent operation, these filaments are combined by twisting to make any required diameter of rayon yarn.

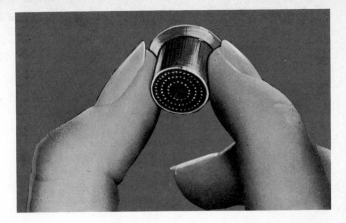

The spinneret that forms the spinning solution into filaments.

Courtesy American Viscose Corporation

TYPES OF RAYON

Although Chardonnet produced the first man-made textile fibers from nitrocellulose over eighty years ago, the nitrocellulose process is no longer a significant factor in the world production of rayon. Today there are four principal methods of making rayon. The fibers differ in important characteristics because the methods differ in specific features of manufacture. These rayons—*viscose, cuprammonium, high wet-modulus,* and *saponified*—are classified as *regenerated rayons* because the original raw material (cellulose) is changed chemically into another form, which is then changed (regenerated) into cellulose again. These changes produce the final product—purified cellulose in fiber form.

VISCOSE RAYON ✔

THE VISCOSE PROCESS

Viscose rayon is made from cotton fiber or wood pulp usually obtained from spruce, hemlock, and pine trees. The chemical process of dissolving wood pulp was first discovered in 1840 by F. G. Keller, a noted German weaver. The viscose method of using wood pulp to manufacture rayon was developed in 1892, more than fifty years later, by C. F. Cross and E. J. Bevan, both English scientists. The first viscose manufacturing plant in the United States was established in 1910.

In the viscose process, wood chips or cotton fibers are treated to produce sheets of purified cellulose that resemble white blotters. The cellulose sheets are then soaked in caustic soda, producing sheets of alkali cellulose. This substance is broken up into fluffy white flakes or grains called *cellulose crumbs,* which are aged for two or three days under controlled temperature and humidity. Liquid carbon disulfide is then added. This turns the cellulose into cellulose xanthate, a light-orange substance that is still in crumb form. The cellulose xanthate crumbs are dissolved in a weak solution of caustic soda and transformed into a thick viscous solution, called *viscose,* resembling honey in color and consistency. If the rayon is to be delustered, titanium dioxide is added at this point. The viscose is aged, filtered, and vacuum-treated to remove air bubbles, as they would cause the filament to break. It is then forced through the holes of the spinneret into sulfuric acid, which coagulates the cellulose of the soluble cellulose xanthate to form pure regenerated cellulose filaments.

Courtesy American Enka Corporation

To regenerate the cellulose for the viscose rayon process, cellulose sheets are soaked in caustic soda to produce alkali cellulose.

Alkali cellulose crumbs are poured into a vat to be soaked in carbon disulfide, thus forming cellulose xanthate.

Courtesy American Enka Corporation

Courtesy American Enka Corporation

The cellulose xanthate crumbs are removed from the vat to be dissolved in weak caustic soda.

Controlled variations in certain characteristics of viscose rayon are possible. It has been noted that the luster can be regulated from *bright* to *semidull* or *dull*, depending upon the amount of delustering agent that is added to the viscose solution before extrusion through the spinneret. Dyes may be added to the solution to produce *solution-dyed* filaments which have a high degree of color permanency. Variations in the chemical composition of the coagulating bath cause different rates of coagulation on the inside and the outside of the fiber that result in variations in the thickness of the "skin" of the fiber; this in turn provides a *latent crimp* that will emerge when the fiber is immersed in water. The diameter of the fiber may be varied to give a thick and thin effect by changing the pump pressure and drawing off the filaments as they are extruded. The shape of the spinneret holes may be varied to change the appearance of the fiber; *Krispglo,* for example, is a flat filament that is highly reflective and therefore lustrous. The strength, or *tenacity,* of the fiber may be increased by aligning the molecules through stretching, which produces a high-tenacity rayon for such purposes as tire cord. These variations in production techniques have increased the versatility of rayon and have made viscose the major type of rayon used.

YARN PRODUCTION

Upon extrusion from the spinneret, the viscose rayon fibers are processed by one of several methods into filament or spun staple yarns.

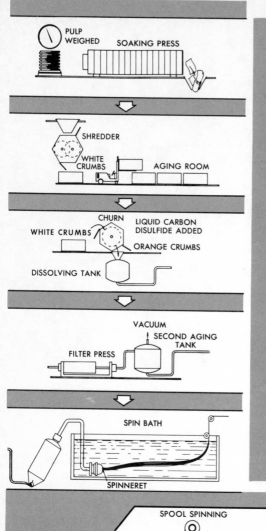

PULP
WEIGHED
SOAKING PRESS

SHREDDER
WHITE CRUMBS
AGING ROOM

CHURN
WHITE CRUMBS
LIQUID CARBON DISULFIDE ADDED
ORANGE CRUMBS
DISSOLVING TANK

VACUUM
SECOND AGING TANK
FILTER PRESS

SPIN BATH
SPINNERET

PRODUCTION

OF

VISCOSE

RAYON

YARN

Courtesy American Enka Corporation

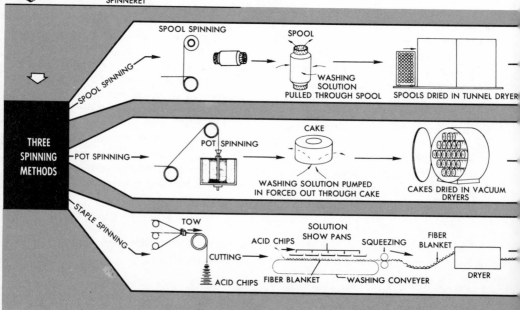

THREE SPINNING METHODS

SPOOL SPINNING

SPOOL SPINNING
SPOOL
WASHING SOLUTION PULLED THROUGH SPOOL
SPOOLS DRIED IN TUNNEL DRYER

POT SPINNING

POT SPINNING
CAKE
WASHING SOLUTION PUMPED IN FORCED OUT THROUGH CAKE
CAKES DRIED IN VACUUM DRYERS

STAPLE SPINNING

TOW
CUTTING
ACID CHIPS
ACID CHIPS
FIBER BLANKET
SOLUTION SHOW PANS
WASHING CONVEYER
SQUEEZING
FIBER BLANKET
DRYER

PROCESSING ■ There are three methods of processing the viscose rayon as the fiber is extruded.

Pot, or box, spinning. The filaments are removed from the coagulating bath by being passed over a series of godet wheels. The resultant slight tension on the fibers causes a certain amount of molecular alignment and consequent strengthening of the filaments. The fibers are led through a funnel moving up and down in a covered cylinder, called a *Topham box,* which whirls around and builds by centrifugal force a hollow "cake" of filament against the cylinder's wall. This action also gives the filaments a slight uniform twist. After the cake is removed, it is thoroughly washed, treated to remove any trace of residual chemical substances, bleached, rinsed, dried, and wound on spools.

Spool spinning. The filaments may be drawn from the coagulating bath over guides and rollers and wound on perforated spools. A washing solution is forced through the spools' holes to cleanse the filaments that are then bleached, rinsed, dried, and wound on cones or spools or put up in skeins.

Continuous process. Upon extrusion from the spinneret, the filaments may be carried in one continuous process over the godet wheels through a series of reels as they are washed, purified, bleached, dried, twisted, finished, and wound onto the desired package for the particular desired use. (This process is not included on the schematic shown on these pages.)

FILAMENT YARNS ■ The rayon filament yarns are processed in a manner similar to thrown silk yarns. The filaments can be thrown, or twisted, as indicated in the pot and continuous spinning processes, or they may be thrown after being received in spool form.

The count of rayon yarn is expressed in denier, the unit of weight explained in Chapter 14. The denier of rayon yarn is controlled by the size and the number of holes in the spinneret. The number of denier required to weigh one skein of yarn, 450 meters long (the standard length), is the denier that indicates the size of the yarn in that skein. Because the sizes of yarns differ according to the purposes for which the yarns are intended, the weights of the skeins differ

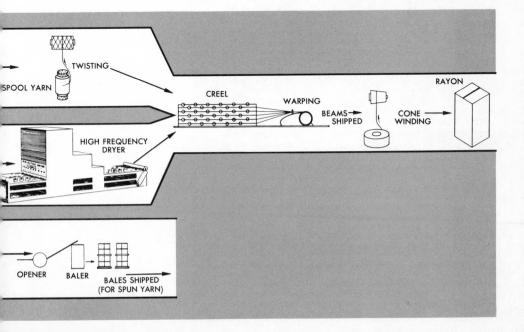

The filaments of spool-spun viscose rayon are twisted and wound on cones.

In spool spinning, the coagulated viscose is drawn over guides and rollers and wound on a revolving spool.

Spools of viscose pass through the tunnel drier after being bleached and rinsed.

The pot-spun yarn is washed by pumping the washing solution through the hollow cake from the center to the outside.

Photos Courtesy American Enka Corporation

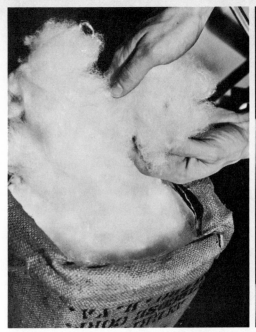

Photos Courtesy American Viscose Corporation

Staple fibers from which spun yarn is made.　　　A cake of long-filament rayon yarn.

even though the skeins are of the standard length. The finer the yarn, the less the skein weighs, and the lower the figure that expresses its weight in denier.

Monofilament Yarns. Monofilament yarns are composed of a single filament. The viscous solution is extruded through a spinneret with only one hole. Spinnerets, each with a different-sized hole, are used, depending on the denier of yarn desired. Monofilament yarn is used for a variety of products including hosiery. The term *monofil* is applied to a type of monofilament yarn used in the millinery industry as a substitute for horsehair, which has limited use because of its short length.

Multifilament Yarns. Multifilament yarns are composed of more than one filament, usually a great many twisted together. These filaments are extremely fine, supple, pliable, and stronger than monofilament yarns of the same denier. They are used for a wide variety of fabrics including sheers. The continuous filament yarns may be used to produce smooth fabrics or creped-surface fabrics, depending upon the amount of twist given to the yarns.

Viscose rayon multifilament yarns to be used for apparel and upholstery fabrics are composed of 10 to 980 filaments, which may vary from 1 to 6 denier each. Thus, when 40 or more filaments are combined, the yarns will vary from 40 to 240 denier. A yarn designated as 100/40 would be 100 denier and be composed of 40 filaments.

SPUN YARNS ■ The filament yarns can be adapted for other effects by reducing them to short lengths, usually 1 to 6 inches, and spinning the staple similarly to the spinning of cotton or wool. The counts of spun rayon yarns conform to the base of the system used; for example, count No. 1 would be 1 pound drawn 840 yards on the cotton system, 1600 yards on the woolen system, and

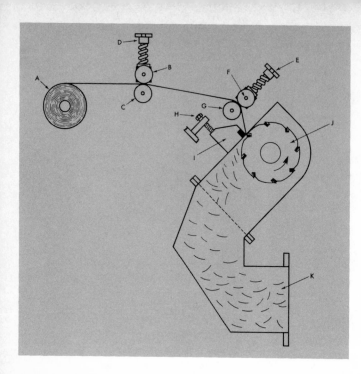

The operating sequence of a staple cutter is as follows:

A Reel of tow

B Top pull roll, under spring pressure

C Bottom pull roll

D Adjusting screw for top pull roll

E Adjusting screw for top tension roll

F Top tension roll

G Bottom tension roll

H Bed knife adjusting screw

I Bed knife with hardened insert

J Rotating cutterhead, with eight fly knives making a shearing cut across the fiber

K Discharge chute with flanged outlet for air suction

Courtesy Taylor, Stiles & Company

560 yards on the worsted system. In each of these systems, of course, the higher the count, the finer the spun yarn.

Both conventional and direct spinning methods are used.

Conventional Spinning. Filaments ranging from 1.5 to 50 denier each may be gathered from the spool spinning process into a group, or *tow,* of 600 to 250,000 filaments. The tow may then be precision cut while wet into predetermined lengths, washed, purified, bleached, rinsed, and dried. As the staple dries, it shrinks somewhat and develops a degree of crimp that facilitates later processing into yarn.

Some rayon fiber manufacturers process the tow through washing, purifying, bleaching, rinsing, drying, and then dry-cutting into predetermined staple lengths. This method has the disadvantage of producing uncrimped staple, but it permits production of staple as needed from stored tow. It also permits fiber processors, such as yarn manufacturers, to cut as much staple as they may need.

Depending upon the kind of yarn desired, the staple must be spun on a cotton, woolen, or worsted system. The process conforms to the description of these methods of opening, breaking, carding, combing, and so forth, as described in Chapters 3 and 13.

Such spun rayon yarns have a different character from the filament rayon yarns. According to the amount of twist inserted in the spinning process, spun rayon yarn can be made stronger, less lustrous, and adaptable to napping and other finishes, producing fabrics that resemble wool, linen, or cotton. Such short-staple rayon can also be combined with any of the other fibers to make effective and useful fabrics. This blending would not be possible with the long rayon filament. Thus, spun rayon provides new finishes and a variety of low-priced fabrics that formerly were made only from natural fibers.

Direct Spinning. A more economical method of producing spun yarn is to reduce the filaments in the tow to staple without disturbing the parallelism of the fibers. This eliminates the need for opening and breaking, and since the fibers are of desired length and have no foreign matter or neps, the carding and combing operations are also unnecessary. There are three basic methods of accomplishing this.

1. The tow may be processed through the Pacific Converter (other machines are the Greenfield and the Campbell), which cuts the filament into either uniform or varied lengths of up to six inches. This method permits blending with other fibers and produces a crimped sliver as described in the schematic below. The sliver is then passed along for further processing into cotton, woolen,

The photograph of the Pacific Converter shows tows (left) being combined and passed under cutter roll (center), then through draft and shuffling sections (center) to diagonal roll (right), then crimped (right) and into coiler can (right). The bottom illustration is a schematic of the Pacific Converter.

Courtesy The Warner & Swazey Co.

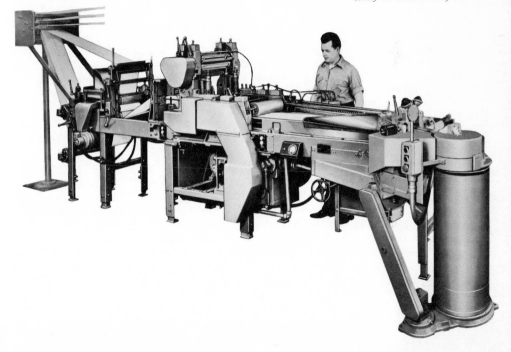

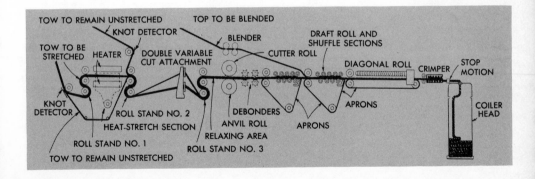

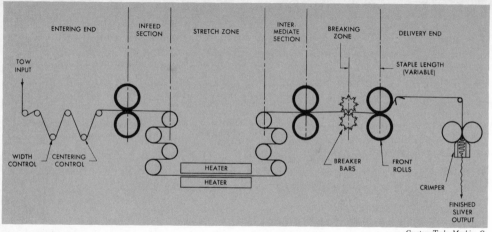

Courtesy Turbo Machine Co.

The schematic above shows how the Turbo Stapler reduces tow to sliver in one machine by the "Perlok" principle. This action takes place in the "breaking zone" and may be described as a modified, controlled stretch breaking process. To understand the process, visualize a single fiber end as it leaves the intermediate nip rolls. It passes between the breaker bars and approaches the front roll nip, being carried under practically no tension by adjacent fibers. As it enters the front rolls, tension is suddenly applied and a break occurs in the area of stress concentration created by the abrasive breaker strips. This fiber, now reduced to staple length, is rapidly carried through the front rolls. The original end, from which it came, is again carried toward the front rolls, and the process repeats. Each end in the tow is exposed to the same process, but the breaks occur at different, perfectly random times. There are, therefore, no coterminal fibers, and evenness and parallelism are excellent.

or worsted type yarn of high quality with excellent uniformity of evenness and count.

2. The tow filaments may be broken into staple by the Perlok process. The technique is the same as that described on page 57 for the production of high-bulk yarn. The schematic above indicates the movement of the tow through the breaking zone where tension is applied suddenly between the break bars and the front rolls, which causes the individual filaments to break at their weakest points. This results in random breakage of the fiber into staple without disturbing their parallelism. The process is repeated as the staple is moved along to a crimper, where it emerges as crimped sliver. The sliver is then spun into yarn using any one of the desired spinning systems.

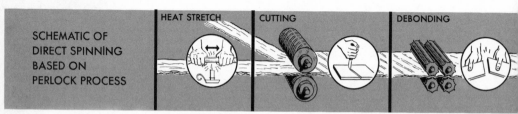

SCHEMATIC OF DIRECT SPINNING BASED ON PERLOCK PROCESS	HEAT STRETCH	CUTTING	DEBONDING

Courtesy The Warner & Swazey Co.

Heat stretched tow and relaxed tow enter simultaneously to form a proportionate blend. Speed of the infeed rolls may be varied to provide controlled stretch.

A driven helix blade cutter, acting against a revolving anvil, cuts continuous tow into uniform or variable lengths as desired.

The cut sheet passes between two sets of deeply fluted rolls that flex the fibers separating all of the individual ends after cutting.

3. Another technique of reducing tow to staple is based upon the Perlok process but uses the Direct Spinner. This method is in much less use because the staple and yarn produced have certain limitations, as will be noted in the following description.

Tow is fed from one set of rolls onto a conveyor belt, then to a second set of rolls moving at a higher rate of speed. The tension created by this difference in speed and the grip exerted by the faster rolls cause the random breakage of the fibers at their weakest points. The fibers are then drafted into sliver form and directly spun in the conventional manner. However, with this procedure, it is not possible to blend the staple with other fibers. It may also be noted that the staple does not have any crimp.

Since the filaments are stretched to the breaking point and the fibers are then twisted into yarn without having sufficient opportunity to relax, direct-spun yarns will have a high rate of shrinkage in the wet-finishing processes. This disadvantage may be turned into an advantage when such yarns are used to produce novelty nubby effects in fabrics, creped surfaces, or compact constructions.

TRADE NAMES OF VISCOSE RAYON

Many companies manufacture viscose rayon. All utilize the same basic principle of producing regenerated cellulose fiber by the viscose process and any of the several methods of spinning the fiber. To identify and promote their products, these manufacturers have copyrighted trade names for their respective viscose rayon fibers and yarns. These trade names also identify variations in production that affect certain characteristics of the fibers and yarns, such as dull, staple, crimp, solution-dyed, or high tenacity. While the retailer and the consumer will find fabrics and garments advertised, labelled, or tagged with these trade names, all viscose rayon of the same type has relatively similar quality and properties. Acquaintance with these names helps not only in recognizing the textile as viscose rayon but also in being alert to special characteristics. In this regard, the chart on pages 290–291 should be of assistance.

FINISHING PROCESSES

The many types of yarn that can be made from viscose rayon permit the production of a wide variety of fabrics. Spun rayon yarns can be made into fabrics resembling cotton, linen, or wool; rayon filament yarns can be made into fabrics

POSITIVE NIP	SHUFFLING	FORMING SLIVER	CRIMPING AND COILING
Three sets of nip rolls, separated by two shuffling sections, draft the fibers extending them lengthwise without strain to form a thinner sheet.	A serpentine action takes place when the fibers are passed between fluted rolls and a leather apron, producing further fiber separation.	After passing through the third draft roll section, the cut sheet is lifted from the apron and rolled diagonally upon itself, forming a continuous sliver of staple fiber.	Crimping rolls at the delivery end of the apron crimp the sliver imparting added strength. A ball bearing coiler head lays the sliver into the can ready for further processing.

VISCOSE RAYON TRADE NAMES

TRADE NAME	MANUFACTURER	TYPE	SPECIAL CHARACTERISTICS
Avicolor	American Viscose Div. FMC Corporation	Multifilament, staple	Solution-dyed
Avicron	American Viscose Div. FMC Corporation	Multifilament	
Aviloc	American Viscose Div. FMC Corporation	Multifilament	High tenacity
Avisco	American Viscose Div. FMC Corporation	Multifilament, staple	
Avron (Avisco XL)	American Viscose Div. FMC Corporation	Staple	
Beaunel	Beaunit Fibers Div. of Beaunit Corp.	Staple	
Beautrel	Beaunit Fibers Div. of Beaunit Corp.	Staple	
Briglo	American Enka Corp.	Multifilament	Bright luster
Celanese Rayon	Celanese Corp. of America, Fiber Div.	Multifilament, staple, tow	
Coloray	Courtaulds North America Inc.	Staple	Solution-dyed
Comiso	Beaunit Fibers Div. of Beaunit Corp.	Staple, tow	Super-high strength
Drapespun	I. R. C. Fibers Midland-Ross Corp.	Multifilament	
Dul-Tone	I. R. C. Fibers Midland-Ross Corp.	Multifilament	Dull
Dy-lok	I. R. C. Fibers Midland-Ross Corp.	Multifilament	Colored
Englo	American Enka Corp.	Multifilament	Dull
Enka Rayon	American Enka Corp.	Staple	
Enkrome	American Enka Corp.	Multifilament, staple	
Fibro	Courtaulds North America Inc.	Staple	
Hi-Narco	Beaunit Fibers Div. of Beaunit Corp.	Multifilament	Semihigh tenacity
I. T.	American Enka Corp.	Staple	Improved tenacity
Jetspun	American Enka Corp.	Multifilament	Solution-dyed
Kolorbon	American Enka Corp.	Staple	Solution-dyed
Krispglo	American Enka Corp.	Multifilament	Flat filament, solution-dyed
Lekroset	I. R. C. Fibers Midland-Ross Corp.	Multifilament	Twist reduction, process

VISCOSE RAYON TRADE NAMES (Continued)

TRADE NAME	MANUFACTURER	TYPE	SPECIAL CHARACTERISTICS
Lintella	Beaunit Fibers Div. of Beaunit Corp.	Multifilament	Thick and thin
Narco	Beaunit Fibers Div. of Beaunit Corp.	Multifilament	
Narcon	Beaunit Fibers Div. of Beaunit Corp.	Staple, tow	Super-high strength
Newbray	New Bedford Rayon Div. Mohasco Industries, Inc.	Multifilament	Bright
Newdull	New Bedford Rayon Div. Mohasco Industries, Inc.	Multifilament	Dull
Rayflex	American Viscose Div. FMC Corporation	Multifilament	
Skybloom	American Enka Corp.	Staple	
Skyloft	American Enka Corp.	Multifilament	Bulked
Softglo	American Enka Corp.	Multifilament	Semidull luster
Strawn	I. R. C. Fibers Midland-Ross Corp.	Multifilament, staple	Flat
Super L	American Viscose Div. FMC Corporation	Staple	
Super Narco	Beaunit Fibers Div. of Beaunit Corp.	Multifilament	Super-high tenacity
Super Rayflex	American Viscose Div. FMC Corporation	Multifilament	High tenacity
Suprenka M	American Enka Corp.	Multifilament	Super-high tenacity, high elongation
Suprenka MS	American Enka Corp.	Multifilament	Super-high tenacity, low elongation
Suprenka 6000	American Enka Corp.	Multifilament	Super-high tenacity
Suprenka 2000	American Enka Corp.	Multifilament	High tenacity
Tyrex	American Enka Corp. Beaunit Fibers Div. of Beaunit Corp. I. R. C. Fibers Midland-Ross Corp.	Multifilament	Super-high tenacity
Tyrop	I. R. C. Fibers Midland-Ross Corp.	Multifilament	
Tyweld	I. R. C. Fibers Midland-Ross Corp.	Multifilament	Treated
Villwyte	I. R. C. Fibers Midland-Ross Corp.	Multifilament	

resembling silk. To enhance the appearance of these fabrics and to improve their serviceability, they can be given various finishes. The most common finishes are as follows.

Calendering—for smoothness

Embossing—for decorative effects

Napping (spun rayons only)—for softness and warmth and to improve resemblance to wool

Stiffening—for body

Preshrinking—for greater dimensional stability

Water repellency—for resistance to water and rain

Wrinkle resistance—for better shape retention

These finishes are discussed in greater detail in Chapter 8. Printing and dyeing procedures are discussed in Chapters 10 and 9 respectively.

EVALUATING VISCOSE RAYON FABRICS

In studying each of the natural fibers, cotton was rated highly for its economy and versatility. It was shown that linen excelled cotton in certain qualities, such as strength, luster, absorbency, cleanliness, and crispness. With respect to warmth and resiliency, wool and silk rank first.

The development of a man-made fiber possessing many of the above-mentioned prized qualities of the natural fibers is a tribute to the ingenuity of man. If the supply of natural fibers were insufficient or even nonexistent, man-made fibers could fully meet the situation.

Variations in the properties of viscose rayons are directly dependent upon the kind of fiber desired. Similar viscose rayon fibers have similar properties. Of course, the type of yarn that is used, as well as how the material is constructed, will contribute to the ultimate properties of the fabrics. The following discussion represents, in general, the properties of viscose rayon.

Strength. Viscose rayon is about half as strong as silk. It is also weaker than cotton and linen, but stronger than wool. Yet, although viscose rayon is weaker than most natural fibers, it produces fairly durable, economical, and serviceable fabrics whose smoothness of surface favorably withstands the friction of wear.

Strength combined with sheerness of construction is possible in rayon fabrics by means of multifilament yarns. High-tenacity yarns afford a lightness with strength that surpasses silk.

Smooth-surfaced rayon fabrics are unusually slippery; therefore, the seams of rayon garments will slip unless the French seam or the flat felled seam is used. Also, when cut on the bias, loosely constructed rayon fabrics may slip.

Elasticity. Viscose rayon has greater elasticity than cotton or linen but less than wool or silk. Therefore, while viscose rayon fabrics have some inherent extensibility, undue strain might cause them to sag and even burst. High-tenacity rayon is generally less elastic than regular rayon.

Resilience. Viscose rayon lacks the resilience natural to wool and silk and creases readily; but it should be remembered that the resistance of a fabric to creasing depends on the kind of yarn, weave, and finishing process. For example, the extremely fine filaments used in multifilament rayons have a greater resistance to creasing, and any of the crepe surfaces produced by tightly twisted yarns also resist creasing. Fabrics treated with one of the better patented crease-resistant finishing processes are highly resistant to creasing. Also, a soft surface produced by napping, typical of spun rayon, has some degree of crease resistance because of the softness and flexibility of the short staple, which recovers easily from wrinkles. Crimped staple offers increased resilience to spun yarn.

Drapability. Viscose rayon possesses a marked quality of drapability because it is a relatively heavy-weight fabric. The filament can be made as coarse as desired, depending on the holes in the spinneret; and the yarn can be made heavy without the use of metallic filling, thus producing body substance in the fabric. Higher tenacity rayons are stiffer and do not have the good draping quality of regular viscose rayons.

Heat Conductivity. Viscose rayon is a good conductor of heat and is therefore appropriate for summer clothing. Spun rayon fabrics, however, are adaptable to winter apparel because they can be napped. The fuzzy surface provides some insulation, although the warmth will certainly not be as great as can be provided by wool or silk.

Absorbency. Viscose rayon is one of the most absorbent of all textiles. It is more absorbent than cotton or linen and is exceeded only by wool and silk in absorbency. The combination of high heat conductivity and high absorbency of rayon makes it very suitable for summer wear. One limitation in this regard, however, is that rayon loses up to 70 percent of its strength while it is wet and therefore cannot take too much strain when it is wet. Also, as viscose rayon absorbs moisture from the air there is a tendency to sag, but as the humidity reduces the fabric shortens. This presents a disadvantage for its utilization in curtains.

Cleanliness and Washability. The smoothness of viscose rayon fibers helps to produce hygienic fabrics that shed dirt. Some viscose rayon fabrics wash easily, and depending on the finish that may be given to them, they will not become yellow when washed or dry-cleaned. White viscose rayon remains white and therefore needs no bleaching. Since viscose rayons temporarily loses strength when wet, they must be handled with care when washed. When laundered, a mild soap and warm water should be used. The garments should be squeezed, not wrung, to remove the water. When in doubt about whether a garment should be washed, it is safer to dry-clean it because viscose rayon dry-cleans very well.

Effect of Bleaches. It has been mentioned that white viscose rayon does not normally discolor. However, with prolonged exposure to sunlight, certain finishes or blends with such fibers as cotton may cause some discoloration. Household bleaches containing sodium hypochlorite (such as Clorox), sodium perborate (such as Snowy), or hydrogen peroxide may be safely used. However, it is always advisable to be careful of the amount of bleach used as well as the temperature of the water.

Shrinkage. Viscose rayon fabrics tend to shrink more than cotton fabrics of similar construction. Crepe weaves and knitted fabrics always shrink more than flat-woven fabrics because of the nature of the construction. Spun viscose rayon fabrics shrink more with repeated laundering than fabrics made of the filament yarns. Spun viscose rayon fabrics can be given a shrink-resistant finish, such as Sanforset, which makes them suitable for apparel that must be frequently washed. Spun viscose rayon blended with wool tends to reduce the great amount of shrinkage characteristic of wool.

Demonstration of the washability of Avicron viscose rayon.

Courtesy American Viscose Corporation

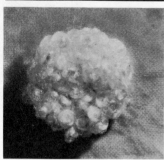

Effect of Heat. Since viscose rayon is a pure cellulosic fiber, it will burn in much the same manner as cotton. Napped or pile viscose rayon fabrics are susceptible to flash burning and must therefore be flameproofed. Application of heat at 300 degrees Fahrenheit causes viscose rayon to lose strength; above 350 degrees Fahrenheit it begins to decompose. When ironing, it is wise either to use a moderately hot iron on a dampened fabric or a steam iron.

Effect of Light. Viscose rayon has generally good resistance to sunlight, though prolonged exposure of intermediate-tenacity rayon results in faster deterioration and yellowing.

Fastness of Color. Viscose rayon fabrics absorb dyes evenly. Colored viscose rayons have a high resistance to sunlight; they withstand strong light better than silk. This property makes them especially adaptable for window curtains. Of course, over a period of time, viscose rayon fabrics will fade. To overcome this, pigmented rayon, in which the dyestuff is put into the spinning solution thus becoming an integral part of the fiber, has been developed. Pigmented, or solution-dyed viscose rayon, is absolutely fast to light, washing, atmospheric gases, perspiration, crocking, and dry cleaning. Trade names for pigmented viscose rayon yarns include *Jetspun* and *Coloray*. Solution-dyed rayons, however, are not produced in large quantities and are not widely used because there is not a large sustained demand for specific shades.

Decorative Effects. Viscose rayon is often combined with other textile fibers to produce novel and decorative effects. This can be accomplished by combining different types of yarns as well as using such techniques as cross dyeing. Viscose rayon can also be given a moiré finish, but it is not permanent and will come out with washing or dry cleaning.

Resistance to Mildew. Like cotton, viscose rayon has a tendency to mildew. Such fabrics, therefore, should not be allowed to remain damp for any length of time.

Resistance to Moths. Moths are not attracted to cellulose. Consequently, mothproofing treatments are not necessary for viscose rayon.

Reaction to Alkalies. Concentrated solutions of alkalies disintegrate viscose rayon. A mild soap and lukewarm water is therefore recommended when laundering such garments.

Reaction to Acids. Viscose rayon reacts to acids in a manner similar to cotton. Being pure cellulose, the fabric is disintegrated by hot dilute and cold concentrated acids.

Resistance to Perspiration. Viscose rayon is fairly resistant to deterioration from perspiration. The color, however, is not usually as resistant as the fabric and will fade if not solution-dyed.

CUPRAMMONIUM RAYON

THE CUPRAMMONIUM PROCESS

The cuprammonium process of making rayon was first developed by L. H. Despaisses in France in 1890. However, the process was abandoned a few years later because it could not compete commercially with the more economical viscose process. It was subsequently successfully revived in Germany in 1919 by the J. P. Bemberg, A. G., company as a result of the invention and application by Dr. E. Thiele and Dr. E. Elsaesser of a *stretch-spinning* technique, which produced very fine denier fibers with a soft hand and high flexibility. In 1926 the American Bemberg Corporation began production of cuprammonium rayon in Elizabethton, Tennessee.

The cuprammonium process uses purified cellulose obtained from cotton linters or, more usually, wood pulp. The pulp is mixed with copper sulfate and ammonia at low temperatures. The name *cuprammonium* is derived from these two substances. Caustic soda and stabilizing agents are added to maintain the solution's equilibrium and control its cellulose content. The solution is filtered for impurities and deaerated, prior to extrusion through the spinneret for further treatment, to form pure regenerated cellulose filaments and yarn.

Flow chart of the manufacturing process of cuprammonium rayon yarn.

Courtesy American Viscose Corporation

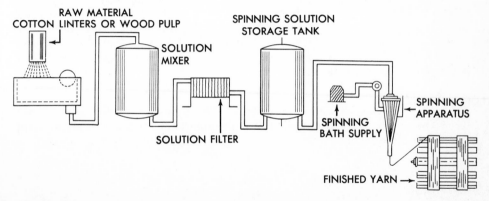

RAW MATERIAL
COTTON LINTERS OR WOOD PULP

SOLUTION MIXER

SPINNING SOLUTION STORAGE TANK

SPINNING APPARATUS

SPINNING BATH SUPPLY

SOLUTION FILTER

FINISHED YARN →

YARN PRODUCTION

Upon extrusion from the spinneret, the cuprammonium solution is processed into multifilament yarns.

PROCESSING ■ The two methods of spinning cuprammonium rayon are by conventional reel spinning and continuous spinning.

Conventional Reel Spinning. As the solution is pumped through large-sized holes of the spinneret, it passes into a glass funnel where most of the ammonia and about one-third of the copper sulfate is removed, causing the solution to coagulate into filaments. On its way through the funnel, the filaments are uniformly stretched to finer diameters. As the filaments leave the funnel, they enter a bath of mild sulfuric acid that hardens them as its reaction removes the remaining ammonia and copper salt, leaving filaments of pure cellulose. The yarn is then wound on reels and subsequently washed, rinsed, lubricated, and dried.

The stretch-spinning feature of the cuprammonium process produces fine yarn that can be given a great amount of twist. For its weight, it has greater elasticity than viscose rayon filaments. The fine threads can be woven into the sheerest of fabrics. The high twist contributes to drapability.

Continuous Spinning. In 1944 a technique for continuous spinning was introduced with the development of a continuous machine by Dr. Hugo Hofmann. The cuprammonium solution is pumped through 120 spinning funnels forming two banks of 60 parallel filaments. These filaments are passed through a solution of hot sulfuric acid in a pretreatment pan where they contract to approximately one-third their original diameter and are ultimately converted into cellulosic fiber. The banks of filaments are passed from the pretreatment pan through an acid trough for further purification and then into water to wash off the acid. The filaments are then lubricated or sized, dried, oiled, wound on spools or skeins, and conditioned in controlled humidity for a few days. This method is more economical because it requires no handling of the filaments from the spinneret through the winding machine.

As has been indicated, cuprammonium rayon is produced in multifilament form only. These yarns may be twisted or untwisted because, unlike viscose rayon, cuprammonium filaments are not separated; they adhere to each other unless subjected to relatively high friction. Cuprammonium yarn generally ranges from 40 to 900 denier having from 30 to over 700 filaments each. The most popular deniers for fabrics are 50 to 100.

Variations in certain characteristics of cuprammonium rayon are possible. Dyes may be added to the solution to produce *solution-dyed* yarns. A cuprammonium rayon yarn that is solution-dyed at varied intervals along its length has been produced under the trade name of *Parfé*. Techniques have been developed to produce novelty filament yarns having smooth, slub, and nubby effects. The finer deniers are suitable for a wide range of apparel, such as dresses, blouses, and sportswear. The heavier deniers are used for interesting textural effects for upholstery and related fabrics.

FINISHING PROCESSES

The finishes that are applied to cuprammonium rayon fabrics are fewer than for viscose rayon. For example, since cuprammonium rayon comes only in multifilament form, it is never napped. The fine filaments make the fabrics extremely pliable and the amount of sizing is therefore limited. The most common finishes are as follows.

Calendering—for smoothness
Dyeing—for fibers that are not solution-dyed
Printing—for decorative effects
Stain resistance—for ease of care

TRADE NAMES OF CUPRAMMONIUM RAYON

Cuprammonium rayon is sold under any one of several trade names as shown below. The fibers are all chemically the same—that is, they are all made from cellulose and have the same chemical properties. Variations in certain physical properties, such as solution-dyed effects and slub effects, can give the fabrics a unique appearance. These variations may be identified by the respective trademarks.

CUPRAMMONIUM RAYON TRADE NAMES

TRADE NAME	MANUFACTURER	TYPE	SPECIAL CHARACTERISTICS
Bemberg, Regular	Beaunit Fibers Div. of Beaunit Corp.	Multifilament	Reel spun
Bemberg, 44 HH	Beaunit Fibers Div. of Beaunit Corp.	Multifilament	Spool spun
Cupioni	Beaunit Fibers Div. of Beaunit Corp.	Multifilament	Entangled slub
Cuprel	Beaunit Fibers Div. of Beaunit Corp.	Multifilament	Texturized
Cupracolor	Beaunit Fibers Div. of Beaunit Corp.	Multifilament	Solution-dyed
Dream Slub	Beaunit Fibers Div. of Beaunit Corp.	Multifilament	Large slub
Flaikona	Beaunit Fibers Div. of Beaunit Corp.	Multifilament	Flake slub
Multi-Cupioni	Beaunit Fibers Div. of Beaunit Corp.	Multifilament	Short-entangled slub
Nublite	Beaunit Fibers Div. of Beaunit Corp.	Multifilament	Short-entangled slub
Ondelette	Beaunit Fibers Div. of Beaunit Corp.	Multifilament	Flake slub
Parfé	Beaunit Fibers Div. of Beaunit Corp.	Multifilament	Space-dyed
Strata	Beaunit Fibers Div. of Beaunit Corp.	Multifilament	Thick and thin
Stratella	Beaunit Fibers Div. of Beaunit Corp.	Multifilament	Thick and thin

EVALUATING CUPRAMMONIUM RAYON FABRICS

Cuprammonium yarn has a subdued luster and a soft hand, giving it a silklike appearance and feel. But because it is a cellulosic fiber, many of its other properties are quite similar to those of viscose rayon. Since it can be produced in extremely fine deniers, it is very suitable for triple sheer, fancy sheer, and chiffon fabrics as well as heavier-weight cloth.

Strength. Cuprammonium rayon is about as strong as regular viscose filament yarn but weaker than intermediate- and high-tenacity viscose rayons. The production of thick and thin, slub and nubby effect multifilament yarns make it possible to produce textured fabrics, usually made of spun yarns. Such cuprammonium yarns have relatively good wearing qualities because they are made of filament rather than staple yarns; they have a smoother surface that results in less friction and provides greater abrasion resistance. However, like viscose, cuprammonium rayon loses up to 70 percent of its strength when it is thoroughly wet.

Elasticity. Cuprammonium rayon yarns are generally slightly less elastic than viscose yarns. They therefore tend to sag less but, on the other hand, cannot take undue strain.

Resilience. A desirable characteristic of cuprammonium rayon is its fair degree of resilience. It does not wrinkle too easily; rumpled fabrics tend to smooth out and wrinkles will iron out nicely.

Drapability. Cuprammonium rayon is especially suitable for drapery fabrics because the numerous fine filaments make the material extremely pliable.

Heat Conductivity. Cuprammonium rayon is a good conductor of heat and is therefore appropriate for summer clothing. Its ability to be produced in very fine denier and woven into lightweight, sheer fabrics makes it highly desirable for warm-weather apparel.

Absorbency. Cuprammonium rayon is slightly less absorbent than viscose rayon under normal conditions, but it is equally absorbent under more humid conditions. Therefore, cuprammonium fabrics, particularly lightweight ones, tend to be relatively comfortable in warm, humid weather.

Cleanliness and Washability. Depending upon the construction of the garment, apparel made of cuprammonium rayon may be laundered, though some shrinkage may occur. The smooth surface of cuprammonium yarn tends to shed dirt. However, the relatively high absorbency may result in easy staining unless such fabrics are given a spot-resistant finish. A mild soap and warm water should be used. Since cuprammonium rayon temporarily loses strength when wet, the garments should be handled with care to avoid wringing, pulling, or other great stress. Of course, cuprammonium fabrics may be dry-cleaned.

Effect of Bleaches. White cuprammonium rayon normally remains white. Bleaches are therefore unnecessary unless it has discolored because of the fibers blended with it or yellowed because of excessive heat. Under such circumstances, the ordinary household bleaches may be used with usual care.

Shrinkage. Cuprammonium rayon will shrink when laundered, but shrink-resistant finishes reduce this effect. Less shrinkage will occur if cool water is used.

Effect of Heat. Heat of 300 degrees Fahrenheit causes cuprammonium to weaken, scorch, and begin to decompose. Exposure to flame will cause it to burn like paper. When ironing, it is wise either to use a moderately hot iron on a dampened fabric or a steam iron.

Effect of Light. Much like cotton, cuprammonium rayon has generally good resistance to deterioration from sunlight.

Fastness of Color. Cuprammonium rayon has a good affinity for dyes; it takes dyes evenly and prints very well. It holds color well but, over a period of time, it will fade. However, solution-dyed cuprammonium has excellent color fastness.

Resistance to Mildew. Like cotton and viscose rayon, cuprammonium rayon will mildew when allowed to remain damp for any length of time. It should therefore be treated the same as cotton for removing mildew odor and stain.

Resistance to Moths. Being a cellulosic fiber, cuprammonium rayon is not attacked by moth larvae.

Reaction to Alkalies. Cuprammonium rayon is unaffected by mild alkalies. Mild soaps and detergents are therefore safe to use. However, strong alkali solutions cause swelling, loss of strength, and ultimate deterioration.

Reaction to Acids. Hot dilute and cold concentrated mineral acids, such as sulfuric and nitric acids, destroy cuprammonium rayon. Milder organic acids, such as citric acid, will cause tendering, and the fabric should be rinsed after exposure to them.

Resistance to Perspiration. Cuprammonium rayon has good resistance to perspiration. This contributes to its usefulness for garments worn next to the skin, particularly in warm weather. Since color may fade, however, solution-dyed cuprammonium is preferable.

HIGH WET-MODULUS RAYON

Several properties of viscose and cuprammonium rayon represent limitations, particularly for their use as substitutes for cotton. The most significant limitation is their wet strength: both of these rayons lose up to 70 percent of their strength while wet. The tensile strength of a fiber is identified as its *tensile modulus*—the relative amount of pulling force that it can endure before breaking.

In 1960, commercial production was initiated for a rayon that approximated the natural strength of cotton and retained most of that strength, even when wet. It was consequently identified as a *high wet-modulus rayon.* Subsequently, it also became known as a *modified rayon.*

There are three general varieties of this type of rayon in commercial production. They are *Zantrel, Lirelle,* and *Avril.* While all are cellulosic and have basic characteristics similar to high-grade cotton, they do differ from each other in certain respects. Commercial production of a fourth variety, *Nupron,* was recently begun; while initial tests indicate good performance and strong competition, more definitive information must be awaited in order to be evaluated properly. Two newer varieties, *Nupron* and *Xena* were introduced in 1966 but adequate information about their properties and performance are not yet available.

··· Zantrel

The development of Zantrel originated with the research of a brilliant Japanese scientist, Dr. Shozo Tachikawa. In 1938 he began experimentation in his own laboratory to produce man-made cotton, and by 1951 he had made considerable progress. However, because his laboratory techniques were impractical for commercial production, a European textile firm, CTA, subsequently acquired an option to the patents and adapted Tachikawa's laboratory techniques to commercial production. By 1958, CTA had developed a process for the manufacture of the fiber, identified as *Z-54*.

A license to produce the fiber in the United States was obtained in 1959 by the Hartford Fibers Co. Commercial production, begun in 1960 under the trademark of *Zantrel,* was subsequently acquired by the American Enka Corporation.

METHOD OF MANUFACTURE OF ZANTREL FIBER

The production of Zantrel fiber requires the use of much highly specialized, costly equipment. Treatment of the purified cellulose requires different chemical compositions, concentrations, and temperatures, as well as much greater critical control of the process than is required for the viscose or cuprammonium rayons.

The objective of the process is to control the cellulose molecular length and arrangement in the fiber, for the longer the chain of molecules and the more longitudinally parallel they can be made to each other the stronger the fiber will be. The individual molecules, or monomers (*mono,* meaning "one"), of cellulose are formed into long-chain polymers (*poly,* meaning "many"). Upon extrusion from the spinneret, controlled stretching orients these polymers so that they tend to straighten out and lie parallel to each other. Where these cellulose polymers become parallel, they tend to group into bundles forming chemical bonds along the length of the fiber. The object is to achieve a desired amount of such orientation and bonding. This organization of fairly long-chain molecules into connecting groups, or bundles, forms a microfibrillar structure resembling that of cotton.

The fibril structure of Zantrel has led its manufacturer to further identify the fiber by the trademark, *Polynosic,* for its many (*poly*) fibrils (*nosi*). The similar structure of Zantrel Polynosic fiber and cotton fiber accounts for the difference between this type of rayon and the viscose and cuprammonium rayons. The long-chain molecular structure has a stronger and greater number of chemical bonds between the molecules, which are arranged into fibrils that are compactly spaced and rather uniform in size and distribution. This structure inhibits such swelling agents as water and alkalies from readily penetrating between the cellulose molecules and thereby weakening the chemical bonds that hold the structure together. There is, then, much less loss of strength in Zantrel when it is wet than occurs in viscose and cuprammonium rayons, which are composed of small bundles of shorter cellulose molecules, irregularly distributed and with consequently fewer and weaker chemical bonds.

YARN PRODUCTION

Zantrel fiber, which is produced in 1.0, 1.5, and 3.0 denier, is cut into staple ranging from 1¼- to 2-inch lengths. It may be processed into yarn on any of the conventional spinning systems. It may also be spun in blends with cotton or other man-made fibers.

The finishing processes given to Zantrel and Zantrel blend fabrics vary with the composition of the fabric and its desired end use. Listed below are some typical finishes.

Singeing—for clear, smooth surface
Bleaching—for whiteness
Resin impregnation—for wrinkle resistance and wash and wear care
Compressive shrinkage—for greater dimensional stability
Calendering—for smoothness
Plissé—for crinkle-textured effects

These finishes are more fully discussed in Chapter 8. Wrinkle-resistant resin treatments need only a light application to Zantrel fabrics to obtain the desired results, and the fabrics are not weakened by the finish as much as is cotton. Fabrics of 100 percent Zantrel are not mercerized. However, blends of Zantrel and cotton may be mercerized to give improved luster and strength to the cotton.

EVALUATING ZANTREL FABRICS

Zantrel fabrics fall into the price range of combed cotton. Their natural soft luster and luxurious hand are similar to that of Sea Island cotton. The quality of the fabric will, of course, be affected by such factors of yarn and fabric construction, as previously considered. The following characteristics and performances may be expected of Zantrel fabrics.

Strength. Zantrel is approximately as strong as such cotton as Upland, and it is considerably stronger than either regular viscose or cuprammonium rayons. A major feature is its relatively high wet strength. Zantrel loses some strength when wet but not as significantly as do viscose and cuprammonium rayon. (Another form, under the trademark of Zantrel 700, is somewhat stronger but is better suited for certain industrial uses than for apparel.)

The abrasion resistance of Zantrel fabrics is somewhat lower than that of similar cotton fabrics. Fabrics of 100 percent Zantrel are therefore not well suited for apparel that is expected to be hard-wearing, such as children's clothes or work clothes.

Elasticity. Zantrel is less elastic than viscose or cuprammonium rayon but slightly more elastic than cotton. In this regard, Zantrel fabrics tend not to sag but rather to hold their dimension.

Resilience. Fabrics of Zantrel have some natural wrinkle resistance that is slightly better than viscose or cuprammonium rayon. This may be enhanced without great loss of strength by the application of a wrinkle-resistant resin finish.

Drapability. Fabrics of Zantrel fiber are highly drapable. They have a markedly better drape than either viscose or cuprammonium rayon as well as having a supple, firm hand.

Heat Conductivity. Being a cellulosic fiber, Zantrel is a good conductor of heat. It has a cool, comfortable feel and is suitable for warm weather.

Absorbency. Due to its molecular structure, Zantrel is a little less absorbent than viscose or cuprammonium rayons or cotton. Nevertheless, it is sufficiently absorbent to feel comfortable in warm, humid weather. Also, since Zantrel does not swell as much as those rayons when wet, there is less tendency to distort or sag.

Cleanliness and Washability. Because Zantrel fiber is round and has a smooth surface, it tends to shed dirt and stay cleaner than the rougher cellulosic fibers. Zantrel fabrics are completely washable. However, since Zantrel loses some strength when wet and does not have abrasion resistance that is as good as cotton, reasonable care should be taken in laundering it to avoid heavy rubbing action, pulling, or twisting. Soaps and detergents used for cotton may also be used for Zantrel fabrics. Wash and wear characteristics may be imparted by using an appropriate resin finish, which has a less weakening effect on Zantrel than occurs on cotton or on viscose or cuprammonium rayon.

Effect of Bleaches. Household bleaches, such as those containing sodium hypochlorite, are not too effective on Zantrel fabrics, though they may be used. The most desirable bleaches are sodium chlorite and paracetic acid, which are generally used commercially.

Shrinkage. Like other cellulosic fibers, Zantrel will shrink. However, Zantrel fabrics can be given a compressive-shrinkage finish, such as Sanforized, so that the residual shrinkage may be as little as 1 percent.

Effect of Heat. Zantrel fabrics begin to scorch at 400 degrees Fahrenheit and burn at 465 degrees Fahrenheit. This indicates a greater resistance to damage by heat than cotton or the other rayons. Pressing may therefore be readily done with a hot iron and a damp cloth. When Zantrel does ignite, it burns in the same manner as other cellulosic fibers.

Effect of Light. Zantrel has good resistance to light, similar to that of other cellulosic fibers. For most apparel and decorative purposes, this is quite adequate. However, since prolonged exposure will weaken the fiber, it is not suitable for such outdoor purposes as awnings.

Fastness of Color. Zantrel can be readily colored with a wide range of dyes. Fabrics that have been vat-dyed have generally good all-around colorfastness.

Resistance to Mildew. Like other cellulosic fibers, Zantrel will be damaged by mildew. Damp conditions should be avoided.

Resistance to Moths. Being a cellulosic fiber, Zantrel is not attacked by moths.

Reaction to Alkalies. One of the desirable features of Zantrel is its good resistance to alkalies. This characteristic makes it possible to mercerize fabrics blended of cotton and Zantrel to obtain increased luster and strength in the cotton as well as an increased dye level in the blend.

Reaction to Acids. Zantrel reacts to acids in a manner similar to that of the other cellulosic fibers. Hot dilute acids or cold concentrated weak acids will disintegrate the fiber.

Resistance to Perspiration. Zantrel is fairly resistant; however, it is deteriorated by acid perspiration.

ZANTREL FIBER BLENDS

Zantrel fiber is readily blended with a wide variety of other fibers because it can be easily spun on any conventional system and reacts favorably to the usual finishing and dyeing techniques. It can be blended with cotton, triacetate, nylon, polyester, and acrylic fibers. Depending upon the blend percentage,

Zantrel may impart a crisp or lofty hand and a luster ranging from that of high-grade cotton to silk. A blend of 40 percent Zantrel and 60 percent carded cotton, for example, will produce a fabric that has a hand as good as or superior to that of 100 percent combed cotton and has the sheen of Pima cotton.

· · · Lirelle

Development of the high wet-modulus rayon fiber *Lirelle* (pronounced lĭ rĕl') was begun by Courtaulds North America, Inc. in 1955. Research was undertaken to determine what specific fiber properties of viscose rayon cause fabric shrinkage. It was observed that fibers having high resistance to stretch when wet produce relatively high dimensionally stable fabrics; that is, they tend to maintain their size and shape better. However, fibers with low resistance to stretch when wet—that is, stretch easily when wet—yield fabrics that have high shrinkage. This led to the development of a cellulose fiber of a molecular structure that would have a high stretch resistance when wet and that, importantly, would essentially retain its strength when wet—in other words, a high wet-modulus fiber. Commercial production of such a fiber, identified as *W-63,* was begun in 1963 and was subsequently marketed under the trade name of *Lirelle.*

METHOD OF MANUFACTURE OF LIRELLE FIBER

Production of Lirelle from purified cellulose is achieved under highly controlled conditions. The cellulose is processed so as to obtain long-chain cellulose molecules arranged relatively parallel to each other and running in the lengthwise direction of the fiber, the principle underlying all high wet-modulus fiber structure. As a result, there develops a strong attraction of the molecules for each other with a relatively low number of areas between these molecules for water to penetrate. This molecular arrangement gives the fiber tensile strength and chemical-reactive properties more like those of cotton than of viscose or cuprammonium rayon.

The extruded and oriented cellulose fiber is cut into staple and sold as W-63. When the yarns and fabrics produced from this fiber are processed and finished according to methods approved by Courtaulds under its quality control system, the product is marketed under the Lirelle trademark.

YARN PRODUCTION

The fiber is produced in 1.5 denier. It is cut into 1⁹⁄₁₆-inch staple, a length that is desirable for spinning into 100 percent Lirelle yarn and man-made fiber blends. When the fiber is to be blended with cotton, it is cut into 1¼-inch staple to conform more closely with the cotton-staple length. Conventional spinning systems, such as for cotton, are used with a minimum of modification to produce the desired yarn.

FINISHING LIRELLE FABRICS

The finishing processes given to these fabrics depend upon the desired end use.

Singeing—for smooth surface
Bleaching—for whiteness
Resin impregnation—for wrinkle resistance and wash and wear care
Compressive shrinkage—for greater dimensional stability
Water repellency—for weather protection
Calendering—for smoothness
Napping—for soft, textured surface
Schreinering—for increased luster

Fabrics blended of Lirelle and cotton yarns may be mercerized to improve the uniformity of dyeing, while increasing the luster and strength of the cotton fiber with little effect on the strength of the Lirelle fiber.

EVALUATING LIRELLE FABRICS

Lirelle fabrics have a rich luster almost equal to that of bright viscose rayon. The fabrics have a soft, pleasing hand. While the characteristics of Lirelle fiber may vary with the type of yarn, fabric construction, and finish, consideration of the basic properties will indicate the performance that may be expected of Lirelle fabrics.

Strength. Lirelle is stronger than Upland cotton and compares quite favorably with Pima cotton. Its molecular structure has even stronger bondage than Zantrel and is therefore a stronger fiber. It is, of course, much stronger than viscose or cuprammonium rayon. Lirelle does lose strength when wet, but its wet strength is approximately equal to that of dry Upland cotton. Lirelle fabrics may be expected to have a reasonably satisfactory abrasion resistance. Lirelle is therefore suitable for a wide variety of apparel, such as dresses, shirts, sportswear, lingerie, and sleepwear.

Elasticity. Lirelle, like Zantrel, has less elasticity than viscose or cuprammonium rayon but slightly more than cotton. Lirelle fabrics tend not to sag but to hold their shape.

Resilience. Lirelle has some resilience, which can be improved with a resin finish.

Drapability. Fabrics of Lirelle fiber have very good draping quality, making them suitable for such purposes as dresses and draperies.

Heat Conductivity. Being a cellulosic fiber, Lirelle is a good conductor of heat. Its cool, comfortable feel makes it suitable for warm-weather apparel.

Absorbency. Lirelle is a little less absorbent than viscose or cuprammonium rayon or cotton, but it is more absorbent than Zantrel. Its absorbency makes it suitable for comfortable apparel in warm, humid weather.

Cleanliness and Washability. Lirelle fiber has a slightly irregular but somewhat round shape and tends to shed dirt. Lirelle fabrics are completely washable. Wash and wear finishes given to Lirelle fabrics do not weaken them as much as they do cotton or viscose and cuprammonium rayon.

Effect of Bleaches. With reasonable care, bleaches of hydrogen peroxide, sodium hypochlorite, and sodium chlorite may all be used safely and effectively on Lirelle fabrics.

Shrinkage. As do other cellulosic fibers, Lirelle will shrink. However, it can be given a compressive-shrinkage finish, such as Sanforized, so that it will have a residual shrinkage of less than 1 percent.

Effect of Heat. Lirelle fabrics begin to scorch at about 300 degrees Fahrenheit and will ultimately burn like cotton. When ironing fabrics of Lirelle, the temperature should be set at "rayon" and the fabrics should be damp.

Effect of Light. Lirelle has good resistance to degradation by light, similar to that of other cellulosic fibers. This resistance is quite adequate for general apparel purposes.

Fastness of Color. The dyes normally used for cellulosic fibers can also be used for Lirelle fabrics. Prior mercerization increases their dyeability. Vat dyes provide generally good all-around colorfastness.

Resistance to Mildew. Since Lirelle is a cellulosic fiber, it will be damaged by mildew. Damp conditions should therefore be avoided.

Resistance to Moths. Lirelle is totally resistant to moth damage.

Reaction to Alkalies. Lirelle has good resistance to alkalies. Fabrics of Lirelle and cotton can therefore be mercerized to enhance their general appearance and quality.

Reaction to Acids. Hot dilute acids or cold concentrated weak acids will disintegrate Lirelle fiber.

Resistance to Perspiration. Lirelle is fairly resistant; it is affected by acid perspiration.

LIRELLE FIBER BLENDS

Lirelle blends extremely well with cotton. A blend of 50 percent Lirelle and 50 percent cotton has been found most suitable for woven fabrics; a blend of 65 percent Lirelle and 35 percent cotton is needed for the yarn evenness necessary for knitted fabrics. Such blends produce fabrics with a good hand and appearance similar to that of combed cotton; they also provide a desirable luster. Such fabrics have been found to have superior strength over 100 percent cotton. When treated with a wash and wear resin, the shape retention, the wash and wear properties, and the strength retention are superior to comparable 100 percent cotton fabrics.

Blends of Lirelle and other man-made fibers have been produced on a limited scale. These also appear to have promise in terms of appearance, comfort, strength, and shape retention.

· · · Avril

After several years of research and development, in 1961 the American Viscose Corporation (which subsequently became a division of the FMC Corporation) began commercial production of its high wet-modulus rayon fiber identified as *Fiber 40* and subsequently marketed under the trademark of *Avril*. While it is competitive with the other modified rayon fibers, it is similar only in general respects; certain of its characteristics are quite different.

METHOD OF MANUFACTURE OF AVRIL FIBER

Like other high wet-modulus rayon fibers, Avril is produced from purified cellulose by means of techniques modified from the basic viscose process, which provides greater control of the molecular structure of the fiber. The long-chain cellulose molecules are arranged lengthwise, relatively parallel to each other, thereby forming bonds in a microfibrillar structure that has a relatively low number of spaces between the molecules for water to penetrate.

The fiber is produced in 1.0, 1.25, 1.5, and 3.0 deniers. It is almost round and more closely resembles cuprammonium rayon in shape and smoothness than any of the other rayons. The fiber is sold as Fiber 40 to processors and, when the yarns and fabrics produced from this fiber are processed and finished according to FMC's quality control standards, the product is marketed as Avril.

YARN PRODUCTION

The fiber is cut into staple lengths of 1¼, 1⁹⁄₁₆, and 2 inches, depending upon the kind of yarn and the other staple with which it is to be blended. Conventional spinning systems, such as for rayon, are used to produce the desired yarn.

FINISHING AVRIL FABRICS

These fabrics are finished in the same manner as viscose rayon or cotton. Since Avril is whiter than cotton, bleaching is generally not required unless a higher level of whiteness is desired. Other finishes include the following.

Resin impregnation—for wrinkle resistance and wash and wear care

Compressive shrinkage—for greater dimensional stability

Calendering—for smoothness

Schreinering—for increased luster

Plissé—for crinkle-textured effect

Fabrics blended of Avril and cotton yarns may also be mercerized to enhance their appearance.

EVALUATING AVRIL FABRICS

Avril fabrics have a silky, lustrous appearance and a soft hand. They have been used in a variety of lightweight as well as heavier weight fabrics. Judgment of performance may be based upon the following characteristics.

Strength. The strength of Avril is about equal to Pima cotton and greater than Zantrel though, on the average, slightly weaker than Lirelle. When wet, Avril loses some strength and becomes a little weaker than wet Lirelle. It remains, of course, much stronger than viscose or cuprammonium rayon. Avril fabrics also have satisfactory abrasion resistance. They may therefore be expected to give good service in a variety of apparel from dresswear and sportswear to underwear and sleepwear.

Elasticity. Avril has very little elasticity, approximating that of cotton. Fabrics of Avril will not sag, which is an advantage in dress goods and draperies.

Resilience. Avril has better resilience than viscose or cuprammonium rayon, approximating that of Zantrel. When treated with a wrinkle-resistant finish, its resilience is also considerably improved with little loss of strength.

Drapability. Avril fabrics have a good hand with good draping quality. It has been found suitable for draperies as well as women's apparel.

Heat Conductivity. Like similar cellulosic fibers, Avril is a good conductor of heat and is therefore quite well suited for warm-weather apparel.

Absorbency. Avril is as absorbent as viscose rayon. It is also a little more absorbent than Lirelle. It is interesting to note, though, that despite the higher wet-modulus (strength) of Avril over Zantrel, Avril is more absorbent. This relatively high absorbency makes Avril well suited for a wide variety of apparel that may be comfortably worn in warm humid weather. Avril can also be used for towels and sheets.

Cleanliness and Washability. Avril fiber has a smooth surface with a round to oval shape; therefore, it sheds dirt easily. On the other hand, its absorbency of water-borne substances may cause spotting. It launders readily, however, and is resistant to damage by soaps as well as to the machine washing action. Avril fabrics do not become harsh from repeated washings. Wash and wear finishes contribute to their easy care with much less loss of strength than occurs with cotton or viscose and cuprammonium rayons.

Effect of Bleaches. With reasonable care, bleaches of sodium hypochlorite or sodium chlorite may be safely used. Hydrogen peroxide should not be used at home since special care must be given.

Shrinkage. Like other cellulosic fibers, Avril will shrink when wet. However, it can similarly be given a compressive-shrinkage finish so that it will have a residual shrinkage of less than 1 percent.

Effect of Heat. Avril fabrics scorch and flame at about the same temperature as viscose rayon. When pressing fabrics of Avril, the iron should be set at "rayon" and the fabrics should be damp.

Effect of Light. Avril has good resistance to light, similar to that of other cellulosic fibers.

Fastness of Color. Avril fabrics can be dyed in a full range of shades with a wide variety of dyes used for other cellulosic fibers. However, the fastness varies with the dye. Vat dyes, for example, provide good colorfastness.

Resistance to Mildew. Being a cellulosic fiber, Avril will be attacked by mildew unless kept in a dry condition.

Resistance to Moths. Avril is not attacked by moth larvae.

Reaction to Alkalies. Avril has very good resistance to damage by alkalies. Consequently, fabrics blended of Avril and cotton may be treated with caustic soda for mercerized and plissé finishes.

Reaction to Acids. Hot dilute acids or cold concentrated cold acids will destroy Avril fiber.

Resistance to Perspiration. While Avril is fairly resistant, it is affected by acid perspiration.

AVRIL FIBER BLENDS

Avril may be effectively blended with cotton to produce dimensionally stable fabrics. Avril contributes strength, improved luster, a soft hand, and an appearance of combed cotton to the blend. Resin-treated blends for wrinkle-resistance and wash and wear care are stronger than similarly treated 100 percent cotton fabrics.

Blends of Avril and other man-made fibers have produced favorable results. For example, when blended with viscose rayon, Avril generally adds comfort (due to its absorbency and draping quality), good appearance, pleasant hand, and strength.

COMPARISON OF HIGH WET-MODULUS RAYONS

The chart below is for the reader's general guidance. It is a summary composite based upon information supplied by the producers and evaluations of performance of the fibers as described in the literature included in the bibliography. The reader is reminded that variations do exist within each trade name as well as blend combination, type of yarn, fabric weight, construction, and finishing operation and that these factors will affect the performance of all the fibers. It is also possible that future changes in the chemical and physical compositions of these fibers may alter their performance.

COMPARISON OF PROPERTIES—THE HIGH WET-MODULUS RAYON FIBERS

	ZANTREL	LIRELLE	AVRIL
Strength	Fair; similar to Upland cotton	Very good; similar to Pima cotton	Good; approximates Pima cotton
Abrasion resistance	Fair	Good	Fair
Elasticity	Little	Little	Little
Resilience	Fair (improved with resin treatment, little strength loss)	Fair (improved with resin treatment, little strength loss)	Fair (improved with resin treatment, little strength loss)
Absorbency	Good	Very good	Superior
Laundering care	Avoid heavy rubbing, twisting; household bleaches not too effective	Same as for cotton; bleaches may be used with care	Avoid heavy rubbing or twisting; bleaches may be used with care
Ironing temperature	At cotton setting	At rayon setting	At rayon setting
Shrinkage	Shrinks unless preshrunk	Shrinks unless preshrunk	Shrinks unless preshrunk
Household bleaches	Not very effective	Sodium hypochlorite or peroxide effective	Only sodium hypochlorite safely effective
Resistance to light	Good	Good	Good
Resistance to mildew	Damaged	Damaged	Damaged
Reaction to alkalies	Good resistance	Good resistance	Good resistance
Reaction to acids	Poor resistance	Poor resistance	Poor resistance
Resistance to perspiration	Fair	Fair	Fair
Colorfastness	Good	Good	Good

THE FORTISAN PROCESS

As a result of many years of research, the Celanese Corporation of America developed during World War II an extremely strong fiber (stronger than nylon) that was immediately used for parachutes, cordage, and other military purposes. The process was patented by the company and given the trademark of *Fortisan*.

Fortisan is a type of regenerated cellulose fiber that, because of its unique method of manufacture, has properties that viscose and cuprammonium rayons do not have. This difference is due to the molecular structure of the fiber. Whereas the molecules of viscose and cuprammonium rayons are in a random pattern, the molecules in Fortisan rayon are aligned to run parallel in the yarn's direction.

Fortisan rayon is derived from cellulose acetate. After cellulose acetate yarn is produced (see pages 318–319), the dry filament yarn is passed through a chamber of highly compressed air and then into a steam chamber where it is softened. It is then passed with tension over a series of high-speed rollers that stretch the fiber, thereby aligning the molecules and reducing the diameter of the filaments. They are then saponified, whereby the acetyl groups from the cellulose acetate are removed by pumping a solution of caustic soda and sodium acetate through the spools of filaments. The resultant product is a fine, highly oriented, regenerated cellulose fiber, about one-tenth the diameter of the original yarn. The filaments are then washed to remove residual chemicals, dried, sized, and wound on skeins, cones, or spools.

YARN PRODUCTION

Fortisan rayon yarn is produced by the usual method of throwing or twisting a desired number of filaments into *multifilament* yarn of a particular denier, depending upon the fineness and strength desired.

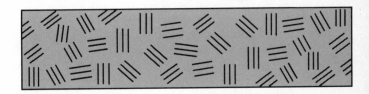

Schematic comparison of the molecular arrangement of viscose rayon (top) and the molecular arrangement of Fortisan (bottom).

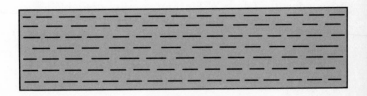

FINISHING PROCESSES

The limited use to which Fortisan has been put for consumer purposes, due to both its relatively high cost of production and the demand for its use in military and industrial purposes, has in turn limited the variety of finishes developed. It most frequently comes in smooth, soft-lustered fabrics that are white or have been piece-dyed. If other yarns are used, interesting cross-dyed effects are obtained. It may also be printed.

EVALUATING FORTISAN FABRICS

The great strength and fineness of Fortisan yarns make it highly useful for sheer fabrics, particularly for curtains. However, it is expensive. Therefore, it is frequently combined in fabrics with other fibers, being used in the warp only for its strength, supple hand, and shimmering effect caused by its luster. The labels of fabrics containing Fortisan should be carefully read for fiber content and considered in the light of the following characteristics of the fiber.

Strength. As has been stated, Fortisan is extremely strong. It is three times as strong as silk and is stronger than high-tenacity viscose rayon used for tire cord. In fact, it is stronger than all other textile fibers except a special type of Fortrel polyester fiber and glass fiber. Therefore, fabrics made of Fortisan are extremely durable.

Elasticity. Fortisan has low elasticity and is the least elastic of the rayons. Consequently, fabrics of Fortisan tend to hold their shape and sag very little.

Resilience. Fortisan is generally more resilient than either viscose or cuprammonium rayon. This quality, coupled with its low elasticity, gives it good stability and shape retention.

Drapability. The light, superfine nature of Fortisan fibers give it excellent draping quality.

Heat Conductivity. As a pure cellulosic fiber, Fortisan is a good conductor of heat. This quality, in conjunction with its fine denier, makes possible very cool fabrics.

Absorbency. Fortisan is less absorbent than any of the other regenerated cellulose fibers. For added comfort, it can be combined in fabrics with more absorbent fibers.

Cleanliness and Washability. Fortisan is a relatively smooth fiber and therefore tends to shed dirt. However, fabrics containing Fortisan should never be washed because Fortisan shrinks considerably when wet. Fabrics of 100 percent Fortisan dry-clean nicely.

Effect of Bleaches. Fortisan is chemically resistant to the usual household bleaches, but because it shrinks when wet, it is advisable to have stains removed by dry cleaning.

Effect of Heat. Fortisan reacts to heat in much the same manner as viscose rayon. When it is pressed, a moderately hot iron should be used to avoid scorching.

Effect of Light. Fortisan has excellent resistance to degradation by light. Consequently, fabrics of Fortisan are very desirable for curtains and draperies.

Fastness of Color. The dyes used for Fortisan are similar to those used for cotton, though it does not take the dyes as readily. Fastness therefore depends on the particular dye used. Fortisan is also produced in solution-dyed black, which has a high degree of fastness. Fabrics that are made in combination with other fibers can be cross-dyed to give interesting effects.

Resistance to Mildew. Like other cellulosic fibers, Fortisan is damaged by mildew unless proper care is taken to avoid exposure to damp conditions.

Resistance to Moths. Being a cellulosic fiber, Fortisan is not attacked by moth larvae.

Reaction to Alkalies. Strong alkaline solutions cause Fortisan yarn to swell and loose strength.

Reaction to Acids. Fortisan reacts to acids in a manner similar to cotton and viscose rayon. Hot dilute and cold concentrated mineral acids disintegrate Fortisan. Organic acids, such as citric acid, will tender the fiber, especially if heat is applied.

Resistance to Perspiration. Fortisan may be expected to have the same resistance to perspiration as viscose rayon.

GLOSSARY OF STANDARD FABRICS OF MAN-MADE FIBERS

The fabrics in this glossary were formerly made only of natural fibers— cotton, silk, linen, wool—or of blends of these fibers. When the man-made fibers rayon and acetate were developed, they were used alone, in combination, or in blends with the natural fibers. The newer man-made fibers described in the following chapters are also being used, and the labels attached to garments required by the United States government identify the fibers.

alpaca. A fabric originally containing hair of the alpaca. Now made in rayon-and-wool blends. Plain weave. Used for women's spring coats, suits, sportswear.

alpaca crepe. Two-ply. Gives somewhat the appearance of wool. Term used for a soft, dull combination crepe.

bark crepe. A fabric that produces the effect of rough bark on trees. A crepe with extreme surface interest.

batiste. Soft, thin lightweight fabric. Made of various fibers, including spun rayon. White, colors, or printed. Plain weave. Lingerie, dresses, blouses.

Bedford cord. A corded material that can be made with various fibers, particularly adaptable to rayon. Has tailored appearance. Cords run lengthwise. Novelty weave, a type of raised plain weave. Used for riding habits, coats, sportswear, suits.

bengaline. A ribbed fabric. Ribs run crosswise. A substantial, somewhat dressy fabric resembling poplin, but with a heavier rib. Plain weave of a 92×40 count. Used for women's formal coats, suits.

bird's-eye. A distinctive weave; small diamond twill pattern featuring a small dot in the center that resembles a bird's eye. Seen in bird's-eye piqué and diapers.

broadcloth. A fine, closely woven fabric originally made in cotton for shirtings and dress goods, and in wool for dress goods, suitings, and coatings. Now, also made in rayon in shirting and dress weights. Also in wool blends in suitings, coatings, and woollike dress weights. Plain weave. In all-rayon, used for sportswear, shirts, pajamas.

brocade. Originally, heavy silk with elaborate pattern. Now made with various fibers. Brocade has slightly raised designs or an embossed appearance as contrasted with damask, which has a very flat pattern. A contrast of surfaces in the weave may produce design, or different colors may be used. Novelty weave,

Jacquard. Example: satin or twill figures on plain, twill, or satin grounds. Used for draperies and upholstery; in lighter weights, for formal evening wear.

brocatelle. A fabric similar to brocade but having designs in high relief. Weave is usually a filling satin or a twill figure on plain or satin ground. Used for draperies, upholstery.

canton crepe. A crepe with modified rippled texture. Heavier than crepe de chine.

casement cloth. A term covering many curtain fabrics of various fibers. Variety of weaves are used.

cavalry twill. A sturdy, substantial fabric with a pronounced diagonal raised cord. Twill weave. Sportswear, uniforms, riding habits, ski wear.

challis. Originally a silk-and-worsted fabric. A light, soft, pliable fabric. Usually printed in small floral designs, but may also be plain color. Plain weave. Used for dresses, negligees, ties, shirts, pajamas.

chambray. A plain-weave fabric generally characterized by a colored warp and a white filling, giving a mixture effect. Used for sportswear, women's and children's summer wear, men's shirts, pajamas.

chenille. A tufted fluffy yarn that looks like a caterpillar. Also a fabric made from such a yarn. Used for rugs, mats, spreads, knitting yarn, robes.

chiffon. (1) Descriptive term indicating light weight, as chiffon velvet, chiffon taffeta. (2) Thin gauzelike fabric with soft or sometimes stiff finish. Plain weave. Evening dresses, formal blouses, trimmings.

corduroy. A fabric having ridges or cords in the pile. Formerly made in cotton only, now in combinations. Variation of plain weave. For men's and women's sportswear, children's wear, infants' wraps, slip covers, draperies.

covert. Originally a medium-weight suiting of woolen or worsted yarns. Now developed in spun rayon or blends with wool. In dress as well as suiting weights. It has a speckled effect in color. Twill, sometimes satin, weave. Used for sportswear, riding habits, suits, coats, raincoats.

crash. Term applied to fabrics having coarse uneven yarns and rough texture. Plain or twill weave, or twill variations. Used for sportswear, men's, women's, and children's summer suits and coats, draperies.

crepe. A fabric made of highly twisted yarn extremely versatile in texture, ranging from a fine, flat crepe to pebbly and mossy effects and, in extreme cases, to barklike, roughish textures. Rayon and acetate are used extensively in crepes. Fabrics of this family have a wide range of suitability in women's wear. Usually plain weave.

crepe de chine. Crepy fabric that in texture falls between canton and flat crepe. Mainly for lingerie; formerly for dresses.

crepe georgette. A lightweight semisheer crepe.

crepe marocain. Heavier dress-weight crepe. An exaggerated canton crepe in texture.

crepon. Originally wool crepe. Has a wavy texture with waves running lengthwise. Mostly used for prints.

damask. Flatter than brocade and reversible. Jacquard weave. Satin or twill filling figures woven on plain, twill, or satin ground formed by warp. For upholstery and hangings. Lighter weights for formal evening wear and wraps; also table linens, bedspreads, face towels.

doeskin.   Twilled fabric napped on one side. Twill or satin weave. Used for sportswear, coats, suits.

duvetyne.   Originally a soft woolen fabric with fine downy back. Twill or satin weave. Used for coats, suits, dresses.

éponge.   Soft, loose, spongy fabric similar to terry cloth. Novelty weave. Used for sportswear, summer suits, coats.

etched-out fabrics.   Also called *burnt-out*. A fabric containing two different yarns in which pattern effects have been produced by acid. The acid is used to treat one of the yarns so as to remove certain portions of it, creating a patterned effect. Any of the three basic weaves or their variations. Used for dresses, curtains.

faille.   A flat-ribbed fabric having body and drape. Ribs are wider and flatter than in grosgrain. Tailors well and wears well if not too loose in weave. Variation of plan weave. Good count is 200 × 64. Used for women's spring coats, suits, dresses.

felt.   An unwoven fabric that can now be made by using wool and a percentage of rayon or other fibers.

flannel.   Soft lightweight fabric with slightly napped surface. Originally made in wool; now made extensively in spun rayon or in wool blends. Plain or twill weave. Used in medium weight for dressses and sportswear; in light weight for shirts and sports blouses, children's wear; in heavier weight for suitings and coatings.

flat crepe.   Smoothest of crepe family. Inaccurately called French crepe.

foulard.   Soft, light fabric, originally silk or wool, now in rayon or acetate. Usually printed. Twill weave. For dresses, neckties.

frieze.   Originally a heavy woolen overcoating with nap on the face. Can be made in spun rayon and wool in similar texture. Double-cloth weave with twill construction. Used for overcoats.

frise.   Pile fabric of uncut loops. Variation of plain weave. For upholstery.

fur fabrics.   Large class of pile fabrics of various fibers, imitating furs by dyeing and special finishing. Fabric can be either woven or knitted. Any variation of basic weaves. Used for popular-priced winter coats and trimmings.

gabardine.   A firm, durable fabric with a steep diagonal. Modern gabardines are made in spun rayon, wool, cotton, or blends in both dress and suiting weights. Twill weave. Used for men's, women's, and children's wear, sportswear, suits, uniforms, riding habits, fabric shoes, raincoats.

gauze.   A light, sheer fabric having an open, lacy effect. Leno weave.

gros de Londres.   Cross-ribbed dress fabric with heavy and fine ribs alternating, or ribs of different colors. Plain weave or plain variations. Used for dresses, evening wear.

grosgrain.   Firm, stiff, closely woven ribbed fabric. Much grosgrain ribbon is made of rayon. Ribs heavier and closer than in poplin, rounder than in faille. Plain weave or plain variation. Used for neckties, ribbons, trimmings, millinery.

hopsacking.   A rough-textured fabric with open weave. Resembles sacking, as name implies. Plain weave. Used for men's slacks and shirts, women's sportswear, draperies.

jersey.   Plain knitted or ribbed. Originally wool, now featured extensively in rayon and acetate in plain and novelty effects. May also be had in wool blends. Used for women's dress fabrics, sportswear, underwear.

lamé.   Any fabric using metal threads in warp or filling or for decoration. Any weave. Used for formal evening wear.

linen-textured rayon.   A large and important category of rayon fabrics having the distinctive textures of linens. These range from sheer handkerchief-linen texture to heavier, rougher butcher-linen texture. Usually plain weave. Used in lighter weight for handkerchiefs, women's and children's dresses, table-cloths, towels, sheets, pillowcases; heavier weights for summer coats, suits, sportswear.

madras.   Soft fabric for shirts. May be white or yarn-dyed. Variation of plain or twill weave. Fancy effects in weaving with corded stripes or small figures. True madras has woven figures. For shirts, sportswear.

marquisette.   Loose, open, sheer fabric of leno construction in which warp yarns are in pairs, whipping around one another between picks of filling yarns. Each thread is locked. Novelty leno weave. Used for curtains, evening wear.

matelassé.   Cloth having a raised pattern as if quilted or wadded. Rayon matelassé crepe looks somewhat blistered. A novelty double weave showing a quilted effect: plain, twill, or satin. Used for women's dresses, evening wear.

milanese.   A type of warp-knit fabric, originally silk, used in gloves and women's underwear. Milanese has a distinctive diagonal cross effect.

mock romaine crepe.   Similar to romaine crepe in texture and appearance. Different filling construction.

mogador.   Originally a tie silk. Resembles fine faille. Plain weave. Used for ties, sportswear.

moiré.   A watered or waved effect, usually on taffeta or faille, produced by a special finish. Steaming or wetting will destroy the pattern on rayon fabrics. Plain weave. Used for women's dressy coats, suits, dresses, evening wear, bathrobes, dressing gowns, draperies, bedspreads.

mossy crepe.   Also called *sand crepe.* Texture gives fine moss effect.

mousseline.   Taken from "mousseline de soie," meaning "silk muslin." Firmer than chiffon, stiffer than voile. A sheer, crisp, formal fabric. Plain weave. Used for evening wear, collars, cuffs, trimmings.

net.   Originally all nets and laces were made with a needle or with bobbins. In modern nets, the same effect is produced by machinery. There are a variety of meshes. Used for curtains, trimmings, evening gowns, veiling; heavier nets for tablecloths, bedspreads, curtains.

ninon.   A sheer, crisp fabric, heavier than chiffon. Plain weave. Used for evening wear and curtains.

organza.   Thin, transparent, stiff, wiry fabric. Crushes but is easily pressed. Plain weave. For evening dresses, trimmings, neckwear.

ottoman.   Heavy cross-corded fabric having larger and rounder ribs than faille and bengaline. The heavy ribs may alternate with thinner ribs. Variation of plain weave. Used for evening wraps, formal coats, suits.

oxford shirting or suiting.   Basket-weave fabrics, which may be made in plaid or two-color effects. Heavy qualities suitable for summer suits, skirts, jackets; lighter weight for sportswear, shirts.

pin check.   Fine check made with different-colored yarns. Usually woven. Smaller than shepherd's check.

piqué. Originally a cotton fabric with raised stripes or welts running lengthwise or on diagonal. Knit construction may give similar effect, not so crisp. Variation of plain weave. Used for sportswear, children's wear, summer evening wear.

plush. Cut-pile fabric with a pile of greater depth than velvet. Variation of plain weave. Used for coats, trimmings, upholstery.

poplin. Originally made in silk. A cross-ribbed fabric between taffeta and bengaline in weight and appearance. The effect is created by a coarser yarn in the filling than in the warp. Plain weave. Used for women's wear, shirts, pajamas.

ratiné. A fabric made of nubby or knotty yarns. Frequently rough and spongy in texture. Plain weave or variation of basic weaves. Used for sportswear, dresses, draperies.

rep. A fabric with narrow ribs running lengthwise. Variation of plain weave. Used for women's wear, neckties, draperies, upholstery.

romaine crepe. A heavy sheer combination crepe similar to alpaca crepe but slightly flatter.

satin. A fabric with a lustrous surface in satin weave; compact structure of low twist yarns may have count of 200×64. *Crepe satin* is soft and lustrous, made of creped yarns in the filling with counts of about 128×68; used for women's dresses, formal wear, negligees, draperies, and bedspreads. *Panne satin* is a stiff slipper satin; used for formal evening or bridal wear. Panne or crepe satin is used for *lining satin,* usually lighter in weight than dress satin. Panne or crepe satin can be finished as *wash satin* for blouses and lingerie. *Upholstery satin* is heavy, usually with cotton back.

seersucker. A lightweight fabric with crinkled stripes. Does not require ironing after laundering. Originally made in cotton. May be plain, printed, or cross-dyed. Plain weave. Used for women's wear, children's wear, sportswear, and, in heavier weights, for men's summer suits.

serge. A twill fabric with a smooth finish. The twill is very fine and close. Made of spun rayon, wool, cotton, or blends. Twill weave. Used for women's dresses, suits, coats, children's wear, men's suits.

shantung. Originally a silk fabric typified by uneven yarns in the filling, resulting in an interesting slubbed or nubbed texture. Now made in rayon extensively. Plain weave of a 140×44 count. Used for sportswear, women's summer suits, pajamas, robes.

sharkskin. Originally a two-color worsted suiting in various weaves, with basket-weave effects most common. Plain, twill, and basic weave variations. (1) Sharkskin suiting is now also made in spun rayon and wool blends, for men's and women's suits. (2) Term also used to describe a well-known acetate sports fabric typified by heavy, semicrisp texture. Used for men's and women's sportswear, summer suits.

shepherd's check. Fabrics having small, even checks. Usually twill weave. Used for sportswear, women's suits, dresses.

surah. Soft, flexible, lightweight, lustrous twill-weave fabric. Used for sports dresses, tailored dresses, blouses, mufflers, ties.

taffeta. A plain, closely woven fabric with crosswise rib. Smooth, crisp, lustrous. Warp and filling are of the same or nearly the same yarn size. Plain weave. Used for dresses, children's wear, trimmings, linings, millinery, hangings, draperies, bedspreads, comforters, lamp shades. *Faille taffeta* has alternating thick and thin crosswise ribs. *Pigment taffeta* is made of dull or pigmented yarns. *Tissue taffeta* is of very light weight. Counts range from 60 × 15 to 140 × 64.

tartan. Originally, Scotch plaids in woolens or worsteds in the distinctive designs and colors of Highland clans. Used for children's wear in particular; also women's sportswear.

tricot. Correct name for jersey cloth. Most important of warp-knit fabrics. On the right side, it appears like rib knitting; on the wrong side, the ribs run crosswise. Used for underwear, dress fabrics, sportswear, bathing suits, gloves.

tricotine. Originally, worsted dress goods resembling gabardine but woven with a double twill. Twill weave. Used for women's suits, coats.

triple sheer. Term in common usage describing a tightly woven sheer fabric with a fine, flat surface. Almost opaque.

tweed. Originally, all-wool homespun made in Scotland. Now in blends. Roughish fabric with wiry, somewhat hairy texture, casual or sportslike in appearance. In mixtures, nubbed, and slubbed effects. Plain, twill, herringbone twill, or novelty weaves. Coats, suits, dresses.

velour. A woven fabric napped on one side. Originally made in wool. Now also made in blends. Plain or satin weave. Used for women's coats, draperies, upholstery.

velvet. Broad and inclusive term covering almost all warp-pile fabrics except plush, chenille, terry, velveteen, and corduroy. Velvets are woven double, face to face, and cut apart while still on the loom. *Chiffon velvet* is of light weight. *Lyons velvet* is the name given stiff velvets. *Panne velvet* refers to the finish on lightweight velvet; the pile is laid flat in one direction. *Transparent velvet* is a very lightweight velvet. Variation of plain weave. Used for evening wear, formal daytime fashions, negligees, draperies.

velveteen. A fabric with short pile resembling velvet but woven single. Variation of plain weave. Used for women's wear, children's wear, draperies, bedspreads.

voile. A light, transparent fabric similar to mousseline but softer and more clinging. Plain weave. Used for dresses, curtains.

whipcord. A twill fabric with pronounced diagonals. Twill weave. Used for riding habits, uniforms, sportswear.

The preceding glossary was adapted from Rayon Fabrics, *courtesy of American Viscose Corporation.*

REVIEW QUESTIONS

1 (a) What is the source of rayon? (b) What natural fiber does rayon resemble chemically?

2 (a) What are the different types of rayon? (b) Distinguish between types of rayon and rayon trademarks.

3 Compare the basic differences in manufacture of each of the major types of rayon.

4 Compare the characteristics of the several types of rayon in terms of (a) durability, (b) serviceability, (c) care.

5 (a) How are multifilament yarns made? (b) What are their main characteristics?

6 (a) What are spun yarns? (b) What are their main characteristics?

7 Describe how spun yarns are made by the conventional spinning methods.

8 Describe how spun yarns are made utilizing the Perlok "breakage" techniques and each of the two direct-spinning methods.

9 What is meant by the description of a rayon yarn (a) of 150/30; (b) of 30s, cotton system; (c) of 40s, woolen system; (d) of 40s, worsted system?

10 (a) What is the advantage of solution-dyed rayon? (b) Identify three such rayons by trademark.

11 What major finishes are applied to rayon fabrics?

12 What characteristics would fabrics made of blends of regular rayon and each of the natural fibers have?

13 Name and describe (a) five fabrics made of filament rayon and (b) five fabrics made of spun rayon.

14 (a) Name the high wet-modulus rayon fibers. (b) How is their structure different from the viscose and cuprammonium rayons?

15 What properties do the high wet-modulus rayon fibers have in common?

16 What properties do the high wet-modulus fibers have that are similar to the other cellulosic fibers?

17 In what respects do the high wet-modulus rayons differ from each other?

18 How does Fortisan differ from other rayons (a) in structure, (b) in properties?

SUGGESTED ACTIVITY

Obtain advertisements and/or labels with rayon trademarks for fabrics or garments and identify the type of rayon used.

The cellulose acetate fibers differ from rayon in that they are not pure cellulose products; they are chemical compounds of cellulose and have their own unique properties. In fact, the types of cellulose acetate fibers also differ from one another.

HISTORY OF CELLULOSE ACETATES

Cellulose acetate was developed in England during World War I by Henri and Camille Dreyfus as a nonflammable lacquer for the fabric used on the wings and fuselage of aircraft. In 1918 they perfected a technique for spinning the substance into lustrous filaments of "artificial silk." Subsequently, the fiber was produced by British Celanese, Ltd. Commercial production was begun in the United States in 1924 by the Celanese Corporation of America under the trademark of *Celanese*. Much later, other manufacturers in this country produced this type of fiber under their respective trademarks. All of these became generally referred to as *acetate* fiber according to the Federal Trade Commission ruling of 1952.

More recently, the Celanese Corporation of America undertook the production of a variation of this chemical synthesis. This product, a cellulose triacetate, is marketed by the Celanese Fibers Marketing Company under the trademark of *Arnel*.

ACETATE

THE ACETATE PROCESS

Cotton linters or wood chips are converted into sheets of pure cellulose. The cellulose is steeped in glacial acetic acid and aged for a period of time under a controlled temperature. After aging, it is thoroughly mixed with acetic anhydride. A small amount of sulfuric acid is then added as a catalyst to facilitate a reaction producing a thick, clear liquid solution of cellulose acetate. After further aging, this *dope,* as it is called, is mixed with an excess of water, causing the cellulose acetate to precipitate as white flakes. The flakes are dried, dissolved in acetone, and filtered several times to remove impurities. The result is a clear, white spinning solution of the consistency of syrup.

If delustered yarn is required, titanium dioxide is added at this stage to produce the desired degree of brightness: bright, semidull, or dull. This delusterant has no effect on the characteristics or properties of acetate other than on the luster. The variation in the amount of luster given to acetate increases its versatility. Acetate fibers not only have various degrees of sheen; they can also simulate as well as blend with other fibers, thereby providing a wider use of acetate.

Dyestuff may also be added to the spinning solution. Solution-dyed acetate, which has excellent colorfastness, is identified by such trademarks as *Celaperm, Chromspun, Color-sealed,* and *Colorspun.*

After the delusterant has been added, the spinning solution is forced through a spinneret and into a cabinet of heated air that evaporates the acetone and solidifies the filament. It is now ready for winding on spools, cones, or bobbins. No washing or bleaching is required as the solution was cleaned and filtered before it passed through the spinneret.

Further variations in the acetate filaments may be obtained by varying the shape of the spinneret holes. Normally, as the solution is pumped through round holes, the cellulose acetate coagulates into filaments with irregular cross-sectional shapes. However, when the solution is extruded through oblong holes, it produces flat, ribbonlike filaments that are highly reflective and impart a sparkle when woven into cloth. One such yarn is identified as *Estron Crystal.* Another variation, *Estron 50,* is extruded to produce doughnut-shaped filaments that give bulk, resilience, and added luster to the fabric. If greater bulk and covering

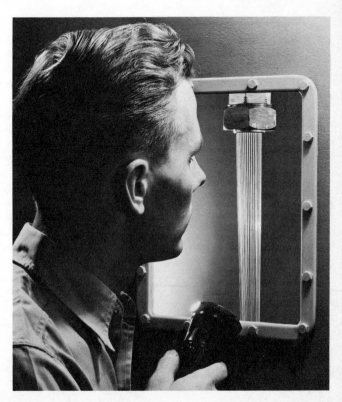

Acetate solution is forced under pressure through a spinneret and then falls in fine streams down a tall spinning shaft. The streams solidify into filaments in the warm air of the shaft. These filaments are drawn out of the shaft at the bottom and twisted together to form a single strand of yarn.

Courtesy Eastman Chemical Products, Inc.

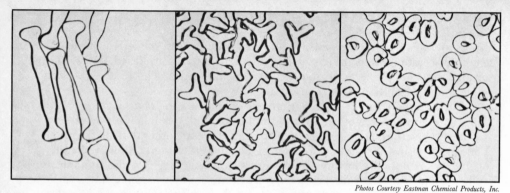

Photos Courtesy Eastman Chemical Products, Inc.

The flat surface of Estron "Crystal" acetate (left) reflects more light than regular acetate, thus creating a sparkle in woven fabric. The "Y" shape of Estron 10 acetate (center) gives maximum bulk and covering power and contributes stiff, crisp hand to fabrics. The round surface of Estron 50 acetate (right) adds luster to fabrics. The hollowness of the fiber increases bulk and gives more resilient hand.

power is desired, as well as a stiffer, crisper hand, Y-shaped filaments, such as *Celacloud* and *Estron 10,* may be produced.

YARN PRODUCTION

After the acetate filaments have been formed, they are processed into *filament, textured,* or *spun* yarns, and there are variations within each of these types.

FILAMENT YARNS ■ A wide variety of acetate yarns can be made in many different deniers depending on the number, size, and shape of the holes in the spinneret.

Monofilament Yarns. The acetate solution may be extruded through a spinneret with one hole. This will produce a single, or monofilament, yarn. The denier of such a yarn can be regulated by the size of the hole in the spinneret. These yarns are not very strong but provide good body and smoothness.

Multifilament Yarns. The majority of acetate yarns are composed of two or more filaments extruded simultaneously from the same spinneret and then eventually twisted (thrown) around each other in a manner similar to silk yarns. The denier of the multifilament yarns is dependent on the denier of the individual filaments as well as on the number of filaments in the yarn. Multifilament yarns are stronger than monofilament yarns because of the greater number of filaments and the amount of twist given to the yarns. They also have good drape.

TEXTURED YARNS ■ These yarns are really variations of filament yarns wherein the filaments have been processed to develop permanent kinks or loops. Such yarns offer bulk or loft, have the appearance of spun staple yarns, possess a warm, dry hand, but retain the advantages of continuous-filament construction. Examples are *Loftura, Sculptured,* and *Chavacette.*

SPUN YARNS ■ The relatively smooth, round acetate filaments can be reduced to staple, usually from 1 to 6 inches in length, and spun into yarns. The filaments in tow form may be cut by a staple cutter (the same as for rayon staple, page 286) and then spun on either the conventional cotton, woolen, or worsted system into yarns resembling one of these textiles; or they may be broken by the Perlok technique and spun into yarn by direct spinning on the Saco-Lowell or Pacific Converter system (as for rayon spun yarn, pages 288–289). Sometimes acetate staple is blended with other staples to obtain yarns and fabrics that will have characteristics of all the fibers used. These yarns are dull, fuzzy, and generally have the appearance and texture of natural fiber yarns.

TRADE NAMES OF ACETATE YARNS

Acetate yarns are produced by many companies and each company has its own trademark. The better-known acetate yarns appear in the chart on page 322.

FINISHING ACETATE FABRICS

Acetate fabrics can be given various finishes depending on the kind of yarn used and the effect desired. The more common finishes are listed.

Embossing—for pattern or design

Moiréing—for permanent watermarking effect

Napping—on spun acetate for softness and warmth

Sizing—for stiffness and body

Heat setting—for crease and shape retention

Water repellency—for resistance to water and rain

Wrinkle resistance—for better shape retention

The characteristics of acetate are quite different from those of all the other fibers considered in the text thus far. One of the most unique of its characteristics is its thermoplasticity; that is, it can be softened by the application of heat and placed or pressed into a particular shape. This permits the permanent embossing and moiréing of acetate fabrics. Also, creases and pleats heat-set into acetate fabrics are relatively durable and are retained better than in cotton, linen, wool, silk, or rayon, although some amount of re-pressing is usually desirable.

Although acetate is not very absorbent, it does absorb some moisture. A water-repellent finish, such as Zelan, given to acetate fabrics makes them satisfactorily water-repellent.

Flow chart of the manufacturing process of acetate.

Courtesy American Viscose Corporation

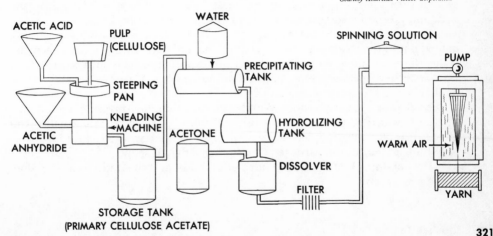

ACETATE TRADE NAMES

TRADE NAME	MANUFACTURER	TYPE	SPECIAL CHARACTERISTICS
Acele	E. I. du Pont de Nemours & Company	Multifilament	
Avicolor	American Viscose Div. FMC Corporation	Multifilament	Solution-dyed
Avisco	American Viscose Div. FMC Corporation	Multifilament	
Celacloud	Celanese Fibers Marketing Company	Staple	
Celafil	Celanese Fibers Marketing Company	Staple	
Celaloft	Celanese Fibers Marketing Company	Multifilament	Bulked filament
Celanese Acetate	Celanese Fibers Marketing Company	Multifilament, staple, tow	
Celaperm	Celanese Fibers Marketing Company	Multifilament	Solution-dyed
Chromspun	Eastman Chemical Products, Inc.	Multifilament	Solution-dyed
Estron	Eastman Chemical Products, Inc.	Multifilament	
Estron SLR	Eastman Chemical Products, Inc.	Multifilament	Dull yarn; resistant to weathering and sunlight
Loftura	Eastman Chemical Products, Inc.	Multifilament	Slub

EVALUATING ACETATE FABRICS

The properties of acetate fabrics will vary to some extent depending on the type of yarn used (filament, textured, or spun), on the type of fabric construction, and on the finish. Acetate has the following general properties.

Strength. Acetate is not a strong fiber. It is weaker than any rayon and is, in fact, one of the weakest textile fibers. Acetate has poor abrasion resistance and is therefore not suited for garments that are expected to take hard wear.

Elasticity. Acetate is more elastic than any rayon. However, its elasticity is limited, being much less than that of silk.

Resilience. Acetate is more wrinkle resistant than any rayon; consequently, the fabric will tend to return to its original shape much better than will rayon after it is pulled or crumpled. After wearing, acetate garments should be carefully hung to permit the yarns to relax to their original shape.

Drapability. Acetate fabrics have good body and flexibility and therefore drape very nicely.

Heat Conductivity. Acetate does not have as high a rate of heat conductivity as rayon and therefore is warmer. Acetate is consequently more useful for linings and warmer clothing, particularly if it is spun acetate. Of course, filament yarns woven or knitted into sheer fabrics will result in cooler fabrics because of their greater porosity.

Absorbency. Acetate is not very absorbent. It absorbs only half as much moisture as the rayons. This represents both advantages and disadvantages. Acetate fabrics get wet mostly on the surface and will not become saturated; therefore, they dry quickly. This makes acetate very suitable for shower curtains, umbrellas, and raincoats. It is also suited for bathing suits, particularly at the seashore because salt air does not have any deteriorating effect on acetate. On the other hand, acetate is uncomfortable in warm, humid weather because of its low absorbency. Acetate garments, such as blouses and lingerie, worn next to the skin feel clammy and uncomfortable because they do not absorb perspiration or atmospheric humidity.

Cleanliness and Washability. The smoothness of acetate fibers helps to produce hygienic fabrics that shed dirt and wash easily. They will not become yellow when washed or dry-cleaned.

Since acetate temporarily loses some strength when wet, such fabrics must be handled with care when washed. When laundered, a mild soap and warm water should be used. The garments should not be rubbed vigorously or wrung but should be handled gently and squeezed to remove the water. They will dry readily and should be hung so that the water will drip off.

When in doubt about the launderability of an acetate garment because of its tailoring or finish, it is always best to dry-clean it. Acetate garments dry-clean very well.

Effect of Bleaches. White acetate remains white, and acetate fabrics need not be bleached. If bleaching is desired, it should be done with a very mild solution of hydrogen peroxide or a very dilute solution of sodium hypochlorite, such as a dilution of Clorox, Rose-X, or the like.

Shrinkage. Acetate fabrics will shrink less than any rayon. Sometimes they are given a shrink-resistant finish.

Effect of Heat. Acetate is a thermoplastic fiber, but it gets tacky at about 350 degrees Fahrenheit. Acetate fabrics need less ironing than rayon fabrics. A warm iron will easily smooth out an acetate fabric, particularly if the fabric is a little damp. If the iron is too hot, it will melt the acetate causing it to stick to the iron and make the fabric stiff.

Effect of Light. Acetate is more resistant to the effect of light than cotton or any rayon except Fortisan. Over a period of time, acetate will be weakened from exposure to light.

Resistance to Mildew. Acetate is highly resistant to mildew. It is ideal for fabrics exposed to moisture, such as shower curtains.

Resistance to Moths. Moths, carpet beetles, and similar insects will not attack acetate. Mothproofing of all-acetate fabrics is not necessary.

Reaction to Alkalies. Concentrated solutions of alkalies disintegrate acetate.

Reaction to Acids. Acetate is more resistant to acids than rayon, but it will be decomposed by concentrated solutions of strong acids.

Affinity for Dyes. Since acetate fiber is not very absorbent, special acetate dyes were developed, but they are not so fast as one may wish. A full range of shades with moderate fastness to light and washing is available. The color is also affected by perspiration, but acetate's greatest weakness is poor fastness to atmospheric gases. Grays and blues particularly will gas-fade badly and change color to pink, red, and purple. Inhibitors can be added during the finishing process to minimize this effect.

Solution-dyed acetate fibers do not have these disadvantages. They are colorfast to light, atmospheric fumes, perspiration, crocking, washing, and dry cleaning.

Resistance to Perspiration. Acetate fabrics are fairly resistant to deterioration by perspiration, but the color will be affected if it has not been solution-dyed.

ACETATE FIBER BLENDS

Acetate fibers are sometimes blended with other fibers to reduce the price of a fabric or to obtain a desired combination of acetate properties with the properties of other fibers. Acetate yarns may be combined with other textile yarns in weaving fabrics for economy, cross-dyeing, or textural effects.

ACETATE AND WOOL ■ Acetate will reduce the tendency of a fabric to shrink, felt, or pill when blended with wool. The combination provides good shape retention and holds creases well. Although such a fabric may be relatively inexpensive, it will not be as durable as an all-wool cloth.

ACETATE AND RAYON ■ Of all the fibers discussed thus far, acetate fibers are most frequently blended with rayon. Acetate adds shape retention to fabrics. Garments made of such fabrics tend to wrinkle less because of the resilience of acetate. Such fabrics when pleated or creased tend to hold their shape well because of the thermoplastic characteristic of acetate. The easy care of rayon and acetate blended fabrics usually means little ironing for garments that have been laundered. Such fabrics, however, have reduced absorbency because of the acetate. They also may tend to shine when pressed if not given sufficient care.

ARNEL

METHOD OF MANUFACTURE

As early as 1914 and prior to the commercial production of cellulose acetate, fibers known chemically as *triacetate cellulose* were produced. They were, however, never fully exploited. Problems involving production, dyes, and finishes were not sufficiently pursued and solved.

With the advancement of chemistry and the development of advanced textile engineering techniques, the Celanese Corporation of America began commercial production of its triacetate cellulose fiber, Arnel, in 1954. The process of manufacturing Arnel is initially similar to the method of producing acetate except that triacetate cellulose is not reduced to diacetate cellulose (that is, acetate or cellulose acetate). After the cellulose triacetate solution is mixed with water, precipitated as white flakes, and then washed and dried, it is dissolved in a solution of methyl chloride with a small proportion of alcohol.

In its normal condition, Arnel is highly lustrous. To increase its versatility, it may be delustered by adding a delusterant to the spinning solution in a manner similar to the way acetate is delustered, so that either bright or dull fiber may be produced. The addition of the delusterant has no effect on the properties of the fiber other than to dull it.

The solution will accept a black dyestuff. Therefore, if desired, a fast, black solution-dyed Arnel fiber may be obtained.

The solution is pumped through a spinneret into a cabinet of air that evaporates the solvent and solidifies the filaments. It is then ready for processing into yarn.

YARN PRODUCTION

The triacetate Arnel filaments are made into either *multifilament* or *spun* yarns.

MULTIFILAMENT YARNS ■ Arnel multifilament yarns are produced in a wide variety of deniers. The denier of each fiber in the yarns is dependent on the size of the holes in the spinneret. The ultimate denier of each yarn is dependent on the number of fibers in the yarn.

Arnel multifilament yarns are made by twisting 15 to 160 filaments around each other. The subsequent denier of the thrown yarns ranges from 50 to 600 denier. The strength, texture, and draping quality of the yarns are dependent on the number of filaments, the denier of these filaments, and the amount of the twist in the yarns. The greater the twist, the stronger the yarn, but the higher the twist, the rougher or harder the yarn will feel. The lower the denier and the greater the number of filaments, the better the fabric will drape. Innumerable variations are possible to obtain the desired effects.

A special type of multifilament thick-and-thin yarn has been developed. This yarn varies in thickness throughout its length to give the impression of a spun slub yarn, but it has the general properties of multifilament yarns.

SPUN YARNS ■ Filaments of Arnel (generally in the range of 2.5, 3, and 5 denier per fiber) may be gathered as tow and crimped and cut into any of the standard lengths desired. The staple can then be spun on the conventional system used for cotton, woolen, or worsted yarns to produce yarns resembling these textiles. Arnel tow may also be broken into staple on a Perlok system and processed by direct spinning into spun yarn as described for rayon staple processing on pages 285–289. Arnel staple may also be blended with other staples to obtain yarns and fabrics that will have characteristics of all the fibers used.

FINISHING ARNEL FABRICS

Arnel fabrics can be given a variety of finishes depending on the effects desired. The most common finishes are as follows.

Embossing—for pattern or design
Water repellency—for resistance to water and rain
Spot resistance—for resistance to water and oil stains
Sizing—for stiffness and body
Antistatic—for protection against static and as a dust repellent
Heat setting—for crease and shape retention

Fabrics of Arnel can be given shallow and surface embossing patterns with heated engraved rollers. This technique can be used to obtain moiré and glazed effects. Such embossed patterns are durable to repeated home washings and to tumble dryers. Where pressing is required to remove mussiness, a light steam pressing will remove the wrinkles without reducing the shallow embossed texture.

Silicone resins, properly applied to Arnel fabrics, provide a durable water repellency. Such a finish also provides spot resistance against water-borne substances as well as a reduction in the spreading of oil stains when a cationic softener is used.

Sizing may be given to Arnel fabrics to provide stiffness, firmness, and body. The effectiveness of the sizing varies, depending on the technique used. For example, a silicone resin provides a durable finish that imparts the scroop and rustle desirable in taffeta. Some sizings help fabrics retain a very firm hand after repeated washings, but the cloth wrinkles easily and tears more easily than without such finishes.

Arnel fabrics have a tendency to develop static electricity when they are rubbed, as when worn. This may cause the fabric to crackle and cling undesirably. Also, the static electricity attracts and holds dust particles. Limited durable antistatic finishes have been developed. They are limited in that they greatly reduce the static behavior of the fabric, but are not absolutely antistatic, and the effectiveness of the finish is reduced with washing and dry cleaning.

Arnel is thermoplastic. Consequently, when properly heat-treated, Arnel fabrics may be heat-set so that they will retain their shape, creases, and pleats after repeated washings. Although the type of yarn used and the construction of the fabric have some influence on the effectiveness of the heat-setting finish, Arnel fabrics of either multifilament or spun yarns, whether woven or knitted, generally retain their shape well when properly heat-set.

EVALUATING ARNEL FABRICS

A wide variety of fabrics are being made of Arnel. Since these fabrics can be made of multifilament yarns and spun yarns and can be constructed in any of the standard manners, Arnel fabrics tend to look and feel like similar fabrics made of other textiles, such as cotton, wool, silk, rayon, and acetate. Arnel, however, lends its own distinctive properties to the finished fabric. As is true with other fibers, there are similarities between certain properties of Arnel and various other individual fibers. But Arnel has its own combination of distinctive characteristics with its own advantages and disadvantages. The general properties of fabrics made of Arnel are given here.

Strength. Arnel is not a strong fiber. Its strength approximates that of acetate. Arnel has poor abrasion resistance, like acetate, and a much lower abrasion resistance than wool. Arnel is therefore not suited for garments that are expected to take hard wear.

Elasticity. Arnel can be stretched about the same as acetate and has a slightly better recovery to original dimension. However, its elasticity is limited and is much less elastic than silk.

Resilience. Arnel is the most resilient of the cellulosic fibers. It also has very good shape-retentive qualities. Arnel fabrics will not wrinkle easily even at high humidity, and any wrinkles that may develop from packing or wearing will fall out readily when allowed to hang properly for a reasonable period of time.

Drapability. Arnel fabrics have good body and flexibility and drape very nicely.

Heat Conductivity. Like acetate, Arnel does not have a high rate of heat conductivity and is therefore warmer than cotton, linen, or rayon. This may be compensated by using finer yarns and sheerer construction, thus providing Arnel fabrics with year-round versatility.

Absorbency. Arnel is less absorbent than acetate. Since it does not absorb much water, Arnel is well suited for fabrics where some amount of water repellency is desirable. Also, because Arnel gets wet primarily on the surface rather than saturated within the fiber, fabrics made of Arnel dry rapidly when they are wet. On the other hand, the relatively low moisture absorbency of Arnel makes it uncomfortable when worn next to the skin in warm, humid weather. Sheerness of the fabric may counteract this characteristic to some extent.

Cleanliness and Washability. Under the microscope the appearance of Arnel fiber is similar to that of regular acetate. Being relatively smooth, the fibers tend to shed dirt. The fabric washes easily and has a high degree of shrink resistance. Arnel fabrics when wet are not weakened to the same extent as acetate and therefore can be safely home-washed and tumble-dried. All that is required for washing is reasonable care and the use of ordinary soaps or detergents. Ordinary hot-water temperatures of not more than 160 degrees Fahrenheit may be safely used.

Since Arnel fabric lends itself so readily to home laundering and can be heat-set, garments made of Arnel may be sold as "wash and wear." If proper heat-setting treatment has been given to the fabric, the garments will return to their original shape after laundering. They are likely to need little or no ironing if not wrung or crushed but allowed to dry while properly buttoned and carefully hung on a wooden hanger.

Fabrics made of Arnel have superior resistance to damage, such as glazing, even when ironed at high temperatures. No great precaution, therefore, need be taken when ironing is desired. If the construction of the garment does not permit laundering due to padding or interlining, clothing made of Arnel may be safely dry-cleaned.

Effect of Bleaches. Arnel has good resistance to household bleaches containing sodium hypochlorite or hydrogen peroxide.

Effect of Light. Fabrics of Arnel lose some strength when exposed to sunlight but are generally more resistant to light than silk, rayon, acetate, and semidull nylon. This indicates that Arnel fabrics are suited for curtains and can be used for normal outdoor wear.

Resistance to Mildew. Arnel has extremely high resistance to deterioration by mildew. Arnel fabrics do not lose strength or become stained from mildew and are well suited for a variety of purposes where they might be exposed to damp conditions.

Resistance to Moths. Fabrics made of Arnel are resistant to attack from moths and carpet beetles. Mothproofing is not necessary.

Reaction to Alkalies. Arnel has a very high resistance to alkalies. Fabrics of Arnel will be weakened only by very strong solutions at very high temperature. Ordinary household alkalies, such as strong soaps and ammonia, will have no harmful effect.

Reaction to Acids. In general, the effect of acids on Arnel is similar to their effect on acetate. Fabrics of Arnel are more resistant to acids than cotton, linen, silk, or rayon but would be decomposed by concentrated solutions of strong acids.

Affinity for Dyes. Dyes similar to those used for acetate may be used on fabrics of Arnel. But Arnel has a lower absorptive ability than acetate and does not take dyes as readily. Techniques have been developed, however, that result in more uniform color.

If properly treated, dyed fabrics made of Arnel are more resistant to fume or gas fading and crocking than acetate fabrics. In general, dyes that have good washfastness on acetate have an even higher fastness on Arnel. Lightfastness, perspiration fastness, and resistance to wet bleeding are similar to acetate. To obtain good fastness in black, Arnel is also produced in solution-dyed black filament and staple form. Such fibers have a very high degree of fastness to all conditions.

Resistance to Perspiration. Fabrics of Arnel have good resistance to perspiration. Such fabrics are not easily deteriorated or discolored by perspiration if properly finished.

ARNEL FIBER BLENDS

To obtain special styling and performance characteristics, blending of Arnel staple fiber with other fibers is sometimes advantageous. Processing and finishing characteristics, as well as the contribution to fabric performance, have a bearing on the selection of fibers and the percentages used in blends with Arnel.

Of all the fibers discussed so far, Arnel is most often blended with cotton, wool, or rayon.

ARNEL AND COTTON ■ Arnel provides easy care and shape retention when these fabrics are laundered. Arnel and cotton blended fabrics resist wrinkling and need little or no ironing. Cotton provides strength, abrasion resistance, and durability. Such fabrics are given greater absorbency by the cotton and are therefore less clammy and more comfortable in warm, humid weather.

This type of blend increases the styling properties and permits interesting cross-dyeing possibilities. Arnel and cotton blends have a cottonlike hand and appearance. To retain the intrinsic desirable properties of Arnel, such blends should not contain more than 30 percent cotton. Some blends contain 50 percent or more of cotton, permitting higher yarn counts; that is, finer yarns, which may be desirable where styling is the prime consideration. This greater amount of cotton will, however, decrease the desirable contribution of Arnel to the blend.

ARNEL AND WOOL ■ A wide variation of blend proportions is possible and feasible with Arnel and wool blends. The Arnel provides wrinkle resistance and shape retention. The wool provides a fair amount of abrasion resistance, drape, resilience, and absorbency. Such blends will not be as warm as all-wool fabrics, which may be of advantage for use in mild weather.

ARNEL AND RAYON ■ Blends of up to 30 percent rayon and the remainder Arnel are satisfactory. Rayon provides absorbency and contributes to such styling features as textural effects and cross dyeing. Arnel provides wrinkle resistance, shape retention, and easy care in handling and washing. However, such blends cannot take hard wear.

1 (a) What types of yarn are made of acetate fiber? (b) How are they made?

2 (a) What types of yarn are made of Arnel? (b) How are they made?

3 (a) What variations are made in producing acetate filaments? (b) What characteristics do they give to the yarn?

4 Give three trademarks each of (a) regular acetate (b) solution-dyed acetate (c) special varieties of filament acetate (d) textured acetate yarns.

5 Distinguish between triacetate and Arnel.

6 (a) What major finishes are applied to acetate fabrics? (b) How effective and durable are they?

7 (a) What major finishes are applied to Arnel fabrics? (b) How effective and durable are they?

8 Fabrics of Arnel are considered to be easy-care material. Why?

9 Name some fabrics (a) that could be made of acetate and (b) that could be made of Arnel. Name uses of each.

10 What would be the characteristics of fabrics that were made of blends of (a) acetate and wool, (b) acetate and rayon, (c) Arnel and cotton, (d) Arnel and wool, (e) Arnel and rayon?

Obtain one advertisement or label identifying an acetate fabric, an Arnel fabric, a blend of acetate and another fiber, and a blend of Arnel and another fiber. Make a chart comparing the properties described on the labels. Evaluate this information.

NYLON

THE POLYAMIDE FIBER

17

The word "nylon" is a generic term that designates a group of related chemical compounds classified as *polyamides.* Nylon is not a trademark—it is a textile just as cotton, linen, wool, silk, rayon, and acetate are textiles.

HISTORY OF NYLON

Responsibility for the discovery or invention of nylon belongs to E. I. du Pont de Nemours & Company. More specifically, the credit belongs to Dr. Wallace H. Carothers and his staff of organic chemists of that company's chemical department. Realizing that there was a need for a more active program of research to provide new developments that would insure the future growth of the company, the Du Pont Company began a long-range program of chemical exploration in 1928. Deviating from the applied research previously conducted, this fundamental research aimed primarily to develop basic knowledge of chemical materials and processes. Dr. Carothers was interested in obtaining a better understanding of polymerization. He wanted to know how and why certain molecules join to form "giant" molecules, such as those that occur in cotton, silk, and rubber. After many months of research, one of Dr. Carothers' assistants discovered that one polymer, which looked like clear, heavy molasses when molten, could be drawn out into a long fiber. When it cooled, the fiber could be drawn out farther to several times its original length. This strand was strong, lustrous, and silky. The question naturally arose as to whether this would make a good textile fiber.

At this point, the experiments became practical. The Carothers group was working with a type of compound called *polyesters.* A great many were synthesized. Each was deficient in one or more vital textile properties. Attempting to find a better fiber, they mixed polyesters and polyamides, which are related to polyesters. They were not successful and therefore decided to discontinue the mixtures and concentrate on the polyamides. One of the chemists filled a container, fitted with the tip of a hypodermic needle, with a hot viscous polyamide solution. He squirted a stream of it into the air, and the stream cooled into a fine filament. After the lustrous fiber was drawn and tested, it was found to be strong and pliable and had such promise that a large group of chemists and engineers were employed to make it a commercial success. During the next several years, research with a series of polyamides continued. In February, 1935, one of these was made from hexamethylene diamine and adipic acid. This polymer was called "6,6" because each of these component chemical compounds contains six carbon atoms per molecule. This "6,6" polymer proved to be best at that time.

The name *nylon* was given to this material. (The name has no meaning. It was chosen because it was short, catchy, and hard to mispronounce.) The discovery was made public in 1938. Since nylon is proteinlike in composition, the fiber was said to be similar in certain of its properties to silk, wool, and hair. Furthermore, this new fiber had many wonderful properties of its own. On May 15, 1940, nylon hosiery went on sale throughout the country. After that, nylon began to be used for a wide variety of garments. The Du Pont company subsequently licensed other companies to use its patents to produce nylon 6,6, and later variations in techniques were independently patented by others to produce this nylon.

Other experimentations with polyamides eventually led to the creation of other forms of nylon. In 1939 Schlak and Kleine of the I. G. Farben combine produced a German counterpart, nylon 6, from a polyamide called *caprolactum*, which contains 6 carbon atoms. Since then, other forms have been developed: examples are nylon 7 produced in the U.S.S.R., nylon 11 produced in Italy, and nylon 4 and nylon 6,10 produced in the United States. These nylons are all polyamides created from various raw materials in different ways, as found most economical by the producer. Chemically, they are similar but differ in molecular structure, which sometimes results in subtle differences in properties. Today, the major production in the United States is nylon 6,6 with less production of nylon 6, used primarily for carpeting and industrial fabrics. The major type produced in foreign countries is nylon 6.

METHODS OF MANUFACTURE

Nylon is actually a group of related chemical compounds. It is composed of hydrogen, nitrogen, oxygen, and carbon in controlled proportions and struc-

Flow chart of the manufacturing process of nylon 6, 6.

Courtesy E. I. du Pont de Nemours & Co.

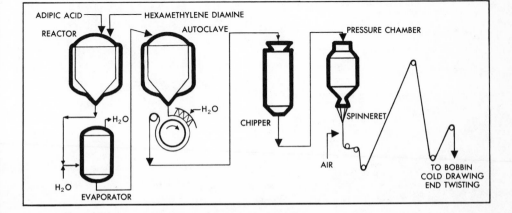

tural arrangements. Variations can result in types of nylon plastics, such as combs, brushes, and gears. We are here concerned with the production of nylon yarn. Since the two types of nylon that predominate the market are nylon 6,6 and nylon 6, we shall consider their basic methods of production, although variations in technique do exist among manufacturers.

NYLON 6,6 ■ By a series of chemical steps beginning with such raw materials as coal, petroleum, or such cereal by-products as oat hulls or corncobs, two chemicals called *hexamethylene diamine* and *adipic acid* are made. These are combined to form nylon salt. Then, since the nylon salt is to be shipped to the spinning mill, it is dissolved in water for easy handling. At the spinning mill, it is heated in large evaporators until a concentrated solution is obtained. The concentrated nylon salt solution is then transferred to an autoclave, which is like a huge pressure cooker. The heat combines the molecules of the two chemicals into giant chainlike ones, called *linear superpolymers*. This process gives nylon a molecular structure somewhat like wool and silk and is also the source of nylon's strength and elasticity. The linear superpolymer is then allowed to flow out of a slot in the autoclave onto a slowly revolving casting wheel. As the ribbons of molten nylon resin are deposited on the wheel, they are sprayed with cold water, which hardens them to milky-white opaque ribbons. The ribbons are removed from the casting wheel to a chipper, which transforms them into flakes.

NYLON 6 ■ Beginning with coal, a series of chemical steps produces another complicated chemical called *cyclohexanone-oxime*, which converts to a substance called *caprolactum* when it is treated with sulfuric acid. Polymerization of the molten caprolactum is begun by gently heating it in a steam-jacketed stainless steel vessel as it is constantly mixed. It is then filtered and pumped to a polymerization kettle where, under carefully controlled steam heat and pressure, the caprolactum is stabilized as a superpolymer. The molten nylon 6 polymer is then converted into chips in a manner similar to that of nylon 6,6.

SPINNING THE YARN ■ Nylon yarn can be made in several ways. The most important of these methods is the *melt process* that, depending upon the denier of

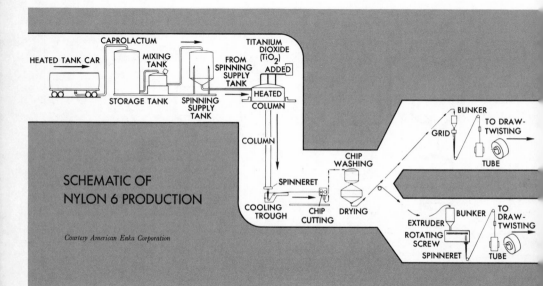

SCHEMATIC OF
NYLON 6 PRODUCTION

Courtesy American Enka Corporation

the yarn desired, generally uses either the grid or extruder spinning technique. In grid spinning, nylon flakes from several autoclaves are blended and poured into the hopper of the spinning machine to insure uniformity in the final nylon yarn. Through a valve in the bottom of the hopper, the nylon flakes fall onto a hot grid, which melts them. The molten nylon is pumped through a sand filter to the spinneret, a disk about the size of a silver dollar. The spinneret has one or more holes, depending on the purpose for which the yarn is to be made. As the filaments come out of the spinneret and hit the air, they solidify. After they cool, the filaments converge, pass through a conditioner where they are moistened sufficiently to make them adhere together, and are given a few turns per inch to form a single thread and facilitate further handling.

Extruder spinning is primarily used for heavier denier yarns. The chips flow by gravity into a device that forces them by screw action through heated zones. The combined action of the heat and screw pressure melts the chips. The molten liquid is subsequently processed in the same manner as described for grid-spun yarn.

Variations in the ultimate appearance of the nylon filaments may be accomplished. It is possible to obtain a bright, lustrous nylon that can be used for satin or a semidull or dull nylon for curtains. Nylon may be delustered by a process similar to delustering rayon and acetate. The delusterants are titanium oxide, barium sulfate, zinc oxide, or zinc sulfate. When any of these chemical compounds are mixed with the polyamide solution, they will cause the nylon to be delustered.

Although nylon is naturally white, the whiteness can be increased by adding an optical whitener to the molten polymer. An example of this is *Blanc de Blanc,* a very white nylon 6 fiber.

The nylon filaments are usually spun from round holes and have a round cross section; such fibers are smooth and slippery. The appearance and texture of the nylon filament can be altered by adjusting the shape of the holes of the spinneret. Nylon filaments may be spun to have a trilobal cross section. *Antron,* a nylon 6,6 fiber, and *Enkatron* and *Enkaloft,* which are nylon 6 fibers, are of this form. They have a unique luster, a dry, pleasing hand, greater opacity, and can be printed with a sharper definition and clarity.

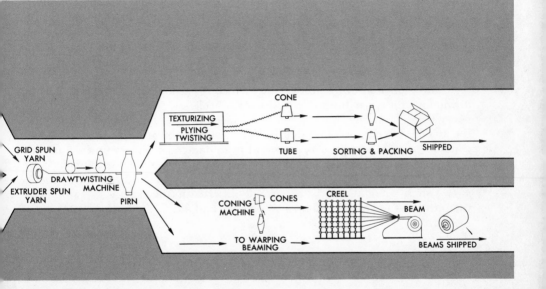

Courtesy American Enka Corporation

Polymerization of the molten caprolactum under controlled steam heat and pressure produces the stabilized superpolymer, nylon 6.

Nylon filaments can also be produced so that they develop a permanent crimp. *Crepeset* is a 20-denier monofilament nylon 6 fiber that is permanently crimped. As the trade name implies, the fiber is extremely well suited for producing crepe fabrics that do not require a high twist. Such fabrics have a crepe appearance but a soft, luxurious texture not usually associated with crepes.

DRAWING THE FIBER ■ Up to this point, the chemical structure of the filaments is about the same as the flakes from which they were made. The filaments are opaque, have poor pliability, and are not very strong because of the random arrangement of the linear superpolymer molecules. This can be changed, however, by stretching, or cold-drawing, the filaments from two to seven times their original length. The amount of stretching is dependent on the denier, elasticity, and strength desired. As the filaments are stretched, they become more and more transparent. The polyamide molecules straighten out, become parallelized, and are brought very close together. Up to a point, the nylon becomes stronger, more elastic, more flexible and pliable.

This elongation by cold-drawing, which is permanent, is accomplished by unwinding the yarn from one godet, or wheel, and winding it onto another godet that is rotating much faster. The speed of the second wheel determines the amount of cold-drawing; that is, if the nylon filament is to be stretched four times its original length, it is unwound from one godet and wound on another at a speed that will subject it to a four-fold stretch during the operation.

The yarn from the second godet is wrapped on a cylindrical tube called a *pirn*. A small amount of twist is normally inserted in the yarn as it is wound on the pirn so as to keep the filaments together and aid in the future processing of the yarn.

The diameter of the individual nylon filaments is determined by the rate of delivery from the pump to the spinneret, by the number of holes in the spinneret, and by the rate at which the yarn is drawn away from the spinneret. The size or denier of the yarn before drawing is determined by the diameter and number of filaments in the yarn. The denier of the yarn after drawing is determined by its original denier and the amount of cold-drawing. If it is drawn three times its original length, the stretched yarn will be one-third of its original denier. The individual filaments produced range from 0.1 to 15 denier.

MONOFILAMENT YARNS ■ Though single-filament, or monofilament, yarns of 7 denier are produced, 12 denier, 15 denier, or heavier yarns are more often manufactured. The monofilament yarns are used for hosiery and for industrial filters. These yarns are very fine and have little or no twist. Consequently, they are relatively weak nylon yarns. Heavier denier, strong monofilament yarns are also produced for various purposes.

In 1963 Du Pont introduced a new type of nylon monofilament yarn for hosiery under the trademark of *Cantrece*. It is a bicomponent fiber created by extruding nylon 6,6 and 6,10 solutions from a single spinneret to form the filaments adhering as one. It is a self-crimping yarn. Upon exposure to steam heat, Cantrece nylon develops a helical, or corkscrew, shape as a result of the different effects of the heat on the components of the fiber. The amount of crimp is dependent upon the temperature and rate of heating. The crimp provides

Nylon polymer, pressed out on this huge casting wheel, is sprayed with water and solidified into a strip resembling ivory.

Courtesy E. I. du Pont de Nemours & Co.

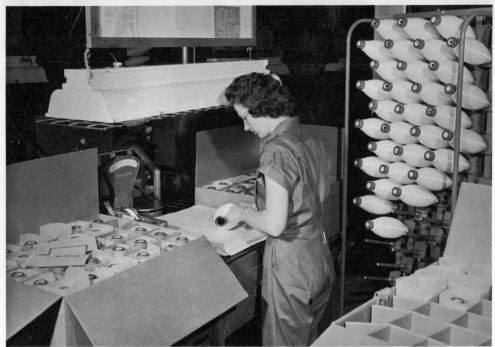

Courtesy American Enka Corporation

Inspecting and wrapping pirns of nylon 6 filament for shipment.

greater resilience and superior fit as well as fit retention and comfort. The improved fit characteristic is said to increase the life of the hose since there is less strain on the yarn.

MULTIFILAMENT YARNS ■ Multifilament yarns are made in both standard and high-tenacity forms. The number of filaments in each yarn varies according to the purpose of the yarn. The yarns generally range in denier from 20 to 210. Multifilament yarns are stronger than monofilament yarns because of the numerous filaments. The strength can be further increased by the amount of twist per inch given to the yarns.

STRETCH YARNS ■ Nylon filaments can be processed to have a crimp or coiled characteristic. This gives yarns made of such nylon filaments the ability to be greatly stretched, like a spring, and come back to shape when the tension is released. These yarns are produced under several trade names, of which one of the better-known is Helanca. (See pages 50–54.)

TEXTURED YARNS ■ Nylon filaments can also be processed to have a looped characteristic. Thrown yarns of these filaments have a texture and hand similar to yarns made of a staple fiber, such as cotton, but retain all the other characteristics of filament yarns. One of the best-known of these textured yarns is Taslan, discussed on page 58, which is used for sportshirts and similar apparel. Some textured filament yarns have a curly appearance that imparts a resilient, springy effect called *loft*. Examples of these are *Cumuloft, Enkaloft,* and *Nyloft,* which are used for rugs.

Another type of textured nylon is Antron 24, which has the latent ability to increase in bulk when subjected to a hot-wet finishing process developed by Du Pont (see photo below). This yarn has very high covering power, unique luster, rapid deep-dye rates, luxurious hand, and attractive texture, as well as resilience and durability. It is used for upholstery.

SPUN YARNS ■ Nylon filaments may be cut about 1 to 5 inches in staple length. The individual filaments range in denier from 1.5 to 15. The staple is usually crimped and spun on a cotton system. These yarns are fuzzy and soft. They have lower tensile strength but greater abrasion resistance. They are not as elastic as the filament yarns and take longer to dry.

TRADE NAMES OF NYLON YARNS

To identify and promote their respective products, manufacturers give trademarks to their nylon yarns that are found in advertisements and on labels or tags attached to garments and fabrics. Although the basic properties of these nylon yarns are similar, it is apparent that the characteristics of these yarns differ insofar as the type of nylon, the cross section of the fiber, and the yarn construction are concerned. See the chart on page 338.

FINISHING NYLON FABRICS

Nylon fabrics can be given various finishes.

Heat setting—for permanent shape
Embossing—for pattern or design
Moiréing—for effect
Molding—for shaping fabrics
Nylonizing—for increased absorbency
Water repellency—for protection against water

At left, close-up of untextured nylon filament yarn (bottom) and Cumuloft textured nylon filament yarn (top), showing the latter's curly, bulky appearance. At right, comparison of the bulk of Antron 24 nylon yarn before and after hot-wet finishing in a relaxed condition.

Courtesy Chemstrand Company   *Courtesy E. I. du Pont de Nemours & Co.*

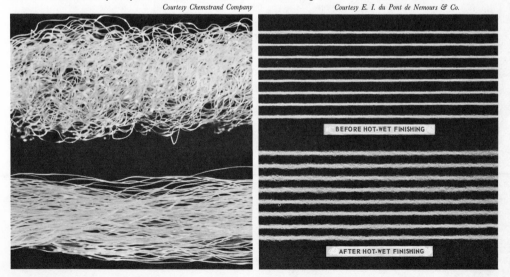

BEFORE HOT-WET FINISHING

AFTER HOT-WET FINISHING

NYLON TRADE NAMES

TRADE NAME	MANUFACTURER	TYPE	SPECIAL CHARACTERISTICS
Antron	E. I. du Pont de Nemours & Company	Multifilament, staple	Multilobal
Barbara	Sauquoit Corp.	Multifilament	Non-torque stretch
Blanc de Blanc	American Enka Corp.	Multifilament	Spun-dyed white
Cadon	Chemstrand Company	Multifilament	Multilobal
Cantrece	E. I. du Pont de Nemours & Company	Monofilament, multifilament	Bicomponent
Caprolan	Allied Chemical Corp.	Multifilament	
Celanese Nylon	Celanese Fibers Marketing Company	Multifilament	
Chemstrand	Chemstrand Company	Multifilament	
Crepeset	American Enka Corp.	Monofilament, multifilament	Crepe effect built in during manufacture
Cumuloft	Chemstrand Company	Multifilament	Textured
Diane	Sauquoit Corp.	Multifilament	Stretch
Enkaloft	American Enka Corp.	Multifilament	Textured multilobal
Enkalure	American Enka Corp.	Multifilament	Multilobal
Enka Nylon	American Enka Corp.	Monofilament, multifilament, staple	Type 6
Enkatron	American Enka Corp.	Multifilament	Multilobal
Firestone Nylon	Firestone Synthetic Fibers Company	Monofilament, multifilament	
Hazel	Sauquoit Corp.	Monofilament	Stretch
Heplon Nylon	Heplon Company	Staple	
Monosheer	American Enka Corp.	Monofilament	
Nomex	E. I. du Pont de Nemours & Company	Multifilament, staple	High temperature resistant
Nyloft	Firestone Synthetic Fibers Company	Multifilament	Textured
Nypel Nylon	Nypel Company	Monofilament	
Poliafil	Sauquoit Corp.	Fine denier	Type 6
Poliafil	Sauquoit Corp.	Fine denier	Type 6, 6
Qulon	Beaunit Fibers Div. of Beaunit Corp.	Multifilament	
Vectra Nylon	The Vectra Company	Monofilament, tapered, fine denier	
Wellon	Nickols Company	Staple	Type 6, 6

Courtesy American Enka Corporation

Nylon filament yarn being wound from a creel onto a warp beam.

An outstanding feature of nylon is that it is thermoplastic; consequently, a nylon fabric or garment can be heat-set by subjecting it to a high degree of heat while being held in a particular shape. After being heat-set, the fabric or garment will always retain its shape, creases, or pleats, and require little or no ironing. Washing, dry cleaning, or wear will not cause loss of shape. Properly done, heat-setting prevents nylon fabrics from shrinking.

Since nylon is thermoplastic, the application of a hot embossing roller will cause the nylon to melt in conformity with the embossing pattern. This results in a permanent finish that cannot be removed by wearing, washing, or dry cleaning. The same principle applies to nylon moiré. As with thermoplastic acetate, nylon moiré is permanent.

Because nylon is thermoplastic, fabrics made of nylon may also be *thermoformable,* which means that they can be molded into shapes by the application of pressure and heat. The fabrics may have a woven, knitted, or lace construction that has been only partially drawn in the manufacturing process. When such a fabric is preheated and then pressed in a heated mold, the drawing operation is, in effect, completed and the fabric is heat-set to the desired permanent shape. Examples of such products are hats, brassieres, and swimsuits.

Raised designs may also be created on nylon fabrics by printing the background area with phenol, which causes the treated nylon to shrink and the untreated areas to pucker.

Nylon is not very absorbent, which is a disadvantage for shirts and lingerie. To overcome this, nylon fabrics may be treated by a process known as *Nylonizing.* The technique utilizes nylon 8, which is more absorbent than other forms of nylon, to coat other nylon fabrics for improved absorbency.

Nylon fabrics may also be treated with a water-repellent finish, which makes them ideal for rainwear and for shower curtains.

EVALUATING NYLON FABRICS

Because nylon fabrics are produced in such a wide variety, they can be made to appear similar to cotton batiste and plissé, to the texture of linen, to jersey for sweaters, and to silk, rayon, or acetate shantung, and velvet. The properties of these fabrics depend on the type of nylon, the cross section of fiber, whether the fabric is made of multifilament or spun yarn, and how the fabric is constructed.

Although there are basic properties that all nylons share, the consumer should maintain an awareness of its variations when selecting or caring for nylon fabrics.

Strength. Nylon is produced in strengths of regular and high tenacity. Although one of the lightest textile fibers, it is also one of the strongest. It is surpassed in strength only by Fortisan rayon and glass. Its strength competes with the more recently developed forms of high-tenacity viscose rayon and the high wet-modulus Avril and Zantrel Polynosic rayons, as well as with Dacron and Fortrel polyester fibers.

The strength of nylon will not deteriorate with age. These advantages make nylon desirable for sheer hosiery, curtains, blouses, and dress fabrics. Nylon not only has great tensile strength with light weight, it is also tough and pliable. Nylon has the highest resistance to abrasion of any fiber. It can take a tremendous amount of rubbing, scraping, bending, and twisting without breaking down. Spun nylon yarn has even a higher abrasion resistance than filament nylon, which makes it desirable for socks and upholstery.

Elasticity. Nylon is one of the most elastic fibers that exists today, though it does not have the exceptional elastic quality of spandex fibers. After being stretched, nylon has a strong natural tendency to return to its original shape. Like any other textile, nylon has its own limit of elasticity. If stretched too much, it will not completely recover its shape. In addition, the type of yarn and the construction of the fabric may contribute to the behavior of the garment. For example, spun nylon is not as elastic as filament nylon. Knitted spun nylon fabrics, such as those used in sweaters, will sag more easily than knitted filament nylon fabrics, such as those used in tricot.

Of course, such stretch nylon yarns as Helanca and Agilon (discussed on pages 50–54) have exceptional elasticity. These yarns have given rise to a wide variety of stretch garments that retain their shape and comfortably conform to the contours of the body.

Resilience. Nylon has excellent resilience. Nylon fabrics retain their smooth appearance and wrinkles from the usual daily activities fall out readily. Pile fabrics, such as velvets and rugs, keep a neat uncrushed appearance.

Heat Conductivity. Nylon fabrics may or may not conduct heat well. The warmth or coolness of a nylon garment depends on the weave of the fabric and on the type of yarn used. The smoothness, roundness, and fineness of nylon filaments permit the manufacture of very smooth low-denier yarns, which can be packed very closely when weaving the fabric. If nylon fabric is woven compactly, it will not be porous. The tight construction will not permit air to circulate through the fabric, and the heat and moisture of the body will not readily pass through it, but will build up between the fabric and the body, and the wearer will feel very warm. Such fabrics are good for winter apparel, such as windbreakers, but are not suitable for summer garments.

On the other hand, these fine nylon filament yarns may be woven into extremely thin, lightweight, sheer fabrics. These materials are very porous and permit the circulation of air. Consequently, they are cool and can be used for summer blouses and curtains.

Spun nylon yarn will produce warm fabrics. These yarns are composed of thousands of short crimped fibers twisted together, which provide millions of tiny dead-air spaces that act as insulators. This insulation makes spun nylon fabrics warm and therefore useful for such apparel as sweaters and winter socks.

Drapability. Fabrics of nylon filament yarn have excellent draping qualities. Lightweight shears may have a flowing quality, medium-weight dress fabrics can drape very nicely, and heavier-weight Jacquards also drape well.

Absorbency. Nylon does not absorb much moisture. Fabrics made of nylon filament yarns will not readily wet through the material—most of the water remains on the surface and runs off the smooth fabric, which therefore dries quickly. Such fabrics are useful for raincoats and shower curtains. Spun nylon fabrics, however, will not dry quickly. Droplets of water tend to cling to the sides of the thousands of staple fibers, clogging the air spaces and relatively increasing the drying time for spun nylon fabrics. Nylon's low absorbency has a disadvantage in that the fabric feels clammy and uncomfortable in warm, humid weather.

Cleanliness and Washability. Dirt particles do not cling to nylon filament yarns because of its smooth surface. Consequently, spots often come clean merely

Time and money are saved by hosing dirt off these ruffled nylon costumes used daily in a musical show.

Courtesy Du Pont Magazine

by using a damp cloth. To wash nylon garments by hand or washing machine, use warm water (about 100 degrees Fahrenheit) and a detergent or soap with a water softener.

White nylon fabrics should always be separated from colored fabrics before washing because the nylon will pick up color (even from the palest pastels) and develop a dingy grey appearance that is extremely difficult to remove. Garments should be thoroughly rinsed to obtain thorough removal of soil particles and drip-dried to obtain maximum freedom from wrinkling.

Nylon filament fabrics dry very quickly. They need little or no ironing because the garments are usually heat-set to retain their shape, pleats, or creases.

Spun nylon has a tendency to pill, or form balls, on the surface of the fabric. To minimize this, such fabrics should not be rubbed. They should be washed gently, preferably by hand. Brushing with a soft brush will reduce the pilling.

Effect of Bleaches. With proper care, nylon fabrics retain their whiteness and should not need bleaching. However, if the nylon does become yellow or grey due to either the finish on the fabric or the absorption of color from other fabrics in the same water, a good common household bleach may be used with reasonable care.

Shrinkage. Nylon has good dimensional stability and retains its shape after being wet.

Effect of Heat. Like acetate, nylon will melt if the iron is too hot; therefore, the iron should be set at the proper heat level. Special care must be taken with fabrics made of nylon 6 because it has a lower melting point (420 degrees Fahrenheit) than nylon 6,6 (480 degrees Fahrenheit). One can identify the type of nylon by its trademark, as shown on the chart on page 338.

Effect of Light. Bright nylon is more resistant to the effects of sunlight than most other fibers. Dull nylon will deteriorate a little more quickly than bright nylon; however, even dull nylon has good resistance to light.

Resistance to Mildew. Mildew has absolutely no effect on nylon. Mildew may form on nylon, but it will not weaken the fabric.

Resistance to Moths. Moths and other insects will not attack nylon because it has no attraction for them.

Reaction to Alkalies. Nylon is substantially inert to alkalies.

Reaction to Acids. Nylon is decomposed by cold concentrated solutions of such mineral acids as hydrochloric, sulfuric, and nitric acids. A boiling dilute 5 percent solution of hydrochloric acid will destroy nylon.

Affinity for Dyes. Nylon 6 has greater affinity for dyes than nylon 6,6 and can be more easily dyed with a wider range of dyes. Both types of nylon retain their color and have good resistance to fading.

Resistance to Perspiration. Nylon fabrics are resistant to perspiration. The color, however, may be affected.

NYLON FIBER BLENDS

The consumer uses many textile products that do not possess all the properties he would like them to have. He would, for example, prefer overcoats with sufficient warmth but less weight; cool, light summer clothes that would not lose their fresh, clean appearance on hot sticky days; fabrics that would wash readily, dry quickly, and not lose their shape. Textile designers and engineers are producing new fabrics to meet such needs. These combine or blend two or more fibers to give the desired properties to the fabrics.

NYLON AND COTTON ■ When properly combined with cotton, nylon adds strength, which allows the development of unusually fine textures not possible to obtain from cotton alone. Nylon provides smoothness, silkiness, and dirt rejection. It also reduces the weight of the fabric and increases its wrinkle resistance. The cotton gives softness and moisture absorption. This combination permits the weaving of fabrics that are soft, supple, and extremely serviceable. If the combination is not properly balanced, the cotton may shrink, causing the fabric to pucker. Also, the nylon fibers may cut the cotton fibers. A blend of at least 17 percent high-tenacity Du Pont 420 nylon staple with cotton will produce an extremely durable fabric.

NYLON AND WOOL ■ The proper combination of nylon and wool will produce a lighter weight fabric with greater durability. Such a fabric will retain the hand, drape, and warmth of wool as well as the elasticity, resilience, and shape retention of nylon. The properties of the fabric will be in direct proportion to the amount used of each of the two fibers. A blend of 10 to 15 percent nylon and the remainder wool is considered satisfactory.

NYLON AND SILK ■ In this combination, the silk improves the hand and provides moisture absorption. The nylon improves the stability or shape retention, as well as the elasticity and strength.

NYLON AND RAYON ■ In this blend, the nylon gives wrinkle resistance and strength. The rayon gives suppleness, drape, and moisture absorption. Such a combination makes possible a fine-quality fabric of extremely light weight. As with cotton, if the combination is not properly balanced, the rayon may shrink, causing the fabric to pucker. Also, an improper blend of nylon and rayon may result in the nylon fibers cutting the rayon fibers. Like cotton, rayon staple blended with high-tenacity Du Pont 420 nylon staple can produce fabrics with 70 percent longer wear than all-rayon fabrics if the nylon is blended in a proportion of at least 17 percent. This blend is desirable for such garments as classed as wash and wear type.

NYLON AND ACETATE ■ The acetate in such a blend provides a luxurious hand and the nylon gives light weight and strength. As with cotton or rayon, improper blending may result in the nylon cutting the acetate fiber, and in some fabrics puckering may occur. Also, neither nylon nor acetate absorbs much moisture. Such fabrics may feel clammy and uncomfortable in warm and humid atmospheres.

NYLON AND ARNEL ■ A blend of 15 percent nylon and 85 percent Arnel in gabardines for shirts, slacks, and fabrics for outerwear is a satisfactory combination. The nylon provides strength to give good durability. Fabrics of this blend hold their creases and pleats and shape well. They can be laundered easily and need little or no ironing. Garments made of such a blend are among those classed as wash and wear type.

1 Who was responsible for discovering nylon?

2 (a) What is nylon? (b) May any company manufacture it?

3 (a) What are the major differences between nylon 6,6 and nylon 6? (b) For what is each used primarily?

4 How does Antron nylon differ from regular nylon 6,6?

5 (a) What is Cantrece nylon? (b) What is its outstanding feature?

6 What is *Nylonizing?*

7 What is meant by thermoformable nylon fabrics?

8 What types of yarns can be made of nylon? Describe them.

9 Why are some nylon fabrics warm while others are cold?

10 Why do some nylon fabrics dry faster than others?

11 What advantage does heat setting give to nylon garments?

12 Is nylon damaged (a) by mildew, (b) by moths?

13 What is the reaction of nylon (a) to alkalies, (b) to acids, (c) to perspiration?

14 (a) What are the properties of a nylon/cotton fabric? (b) What are its disadvantages?

15 What are the outstanding properties of a nylon/wool fabric?

18

THE POLYESTER FIBERS

DACRON
KODEL
FORTREL
VYCRON

Polyester fibers are long-chain polymers produced from elements derived from coal, air, water, and petroleum. As defined by the FTC, these fibers are chemically composed of "at least 85 percent by weight of an ester of a dihydric alcohol and terephthalic acid." While it is difficult for the average layman or consumer to comprehend this technical definition, it is apparent that there are variations in the composition and therefore in the properties of polyester fibers. In fact, as described in this chapter, manufacturers have purposely varied their products to better serve particular needs.

HISTORY OF POLYESTERS

The groundwork for the development of polyester fibers was laid by Dr. W. H. Carothers in his experiments with giant molecular structures. Seeing more immediate promise in the polyamides, he ultimately concentrated his research on them and, as a result, developed nylon. However, Dr. Carothers had published much research information on polyesters, and after studying his works, British research chemists decided to examine the possibilities of polyesters. During the period of 1939–1941, investigations were conducted in the laboratories of the Calico Printers Association, Ltd., by J. R. Whinfield, J. T. Dickson, W. K. Birtwhistle, and C. G. Ritchie. The work resulted in the development of a polyester fiber known in England as *Terylene*.

In 1946 E. I. du Pont de Nemours & Co., Inc., the company under whose auspices Carothers had engaged in the initial research, purchased the exclusive rights to produce this polyester fiber in the United States. Under the temporary name of Fiber V and in essentially the same chemical form, Du Pont conducted intensive development work. By 1951, the company was producing commercially this fiber, which is called *Dacron* (pronounced day'kron).

Subsequently, other companies became interested in polyester fiber. In 1958, Eastman Chemical Products, Inc., announced its own version of polyester, which it called *Kodel;* it is produced by its affiliate, Tennessee Eastman Company. The following year, the Celanese Corporation of America obtained licenses to use certain patents owned by Du Pont and entered the market with a polyester called *Fortrel,* which is now manufactured by the Celanese affiliate Fiber Industries, Inc.

The Beaunit Mills, Inc., also obtained certain licenses from Du Pont and in 1959 developed its version, which it introduced as *Vycron.*

In 1965 Chemstrand Company annuonced its *Blue C* polyester fiber to be available in the Spring of 1966. Specific information on this fiber's production and properties are not available at present. Because the Blue C trademark is used for other kinds of Chemstrand fibers, a fuller identification of this fiber must be noted to avoid confusion.

In 1966 American Enka Corporation introduced its *Enka* polyester fiber and Phoenix Works, Inc. announced its *Phoenix* polyester fiber. Adequate information about these fibers' production and properties are yet not available. Other companies are about to go into commercial production. Hercules, Inc. and Farberwerke Hoechst A G have formed Hystron Fibers, Inc. and expect to introduce *Trevira* polyester fiber late in 1967. American Viscose Division of F M C Corporation introduced its polyester Fiber 200, with the trade name of Avelen, early in 1967.

METHOD OF MANUFACTURE

The process of manufacture of Dacron polyester fiber is similar to that of nylon, but the chemicals used are different. The principal raw material is ethylene obtained from petroleum. The ethylene is oxidized to produce a glycol monomer dihydric alcohol that is then combined with another monomer, terephthalic acid in an autoclave at a high temperature in a vacuum. Polymerization takes place with the aid of catalysts. The molten polyester then flows from the vessel onto a casting wheel and forms into a ribbon as it cools to a porcelain-like hardness. The polymer is then cut into chips, blended for uniformity, and reheated to a molten condition. This viscous melt is extruded through a spinneret, and the filaments are subsequently drawn into the desired Dacron polyester fiber.

Variations in the manufacturing process depend upon the desired end results. Dacron is normally a bright fiber, but it may be made semidull or dull by the addition of a delusterant. The shape of the spinneret holes may be varied, which will affect the appearance and hand of the fiber. The extent to which the fiber is drawn will depend upon certain desired properties. The fiber is usually drawn to five times its original length, which consequently results in a fiber of one-fifth its original denier. Other characteristics affected are the strength, elasticity, and dyeability of the fiber. Crimp may also be added to give texture.

(It should be noted that the same polyester used to produce Dacron is also made in thin, transparent film form. It is marketed under the trade name of *Mylar* and used as a protective coating over metallic yarns, such as Lurex. Mylar is also used for magnetic tape for recording purposes.)

FORMS AND TYPES OF DACRON YARNS

Dacron polyester fibers are produced in two forms: filament and staple. As has been indicated, several types of Dacron are produced in each form, depending upon the desired end results.

FILAMENT YARNS ▪ There are six types of Dacron filament yarns. Each is produced in several deniers of multifilaments, which are thrown according to the desired number of twists per inch.

Dacron 51 is a bright, high-tenacity fiber. Yarns of this type are used where superior strength, stretch resistance (inelasticity), and resistance to chemicals are desired. They are used for such industrial purposes as filter cloths, conveyor belts, and laundry bags. Such yarns are also used for sails, ropes, and netting, as the fiber is resistant to seawater and various microorganisms.

Dacron 55 is a bright, regular-tenacity fiber. This type is used for sheer, crisp, lightweight fabrics, such as tulle, voile, and organdy. Its good light resistance as well as its stretch or sag resistance makes it very suitable for curtains.

Dacron 56, which may be characterized as the basic fiber, is semidull. It is used for a wide variety of apparel, such as dresses and lingerie. Dacron 57 is a duller version of Dacron 56 and is used for such apparel as shirts and blouses.

Dacron 62 is a basic-dyed, semidull fiber with a trilobal cross section rather than the usual roundness. As in the case of the trilobal Antron nylon discussed on page 333, this shape gives the fiber a silklike appearance and hand. Dacron 62 is more susceptible to such chemicals as acids and alkalies. It also takes dyes more easily than the other types of Dacron.

Dacron 69 is a specialty-type fiber that produces slub yarns. It is used for texture and novelty effects.

SPUN YARNS ▪ Dacron filaments of 3 and 6 denier are produced in tow form from large spinnerets with numerous holes, cut into staple, and subsequently spun into yarn. There are several types of Dacron staple for different end purposes.

Dacron 54 is the basic staple fiber. It is semidull and is cut into 1½- and 2½-inch lengths. This staple is spun into yarn on either the cotton or wool system, depending on the ultimate yarn desired. The spun yarns are used for summer suitings that require unusual resiliency and dimensional stability to prevent puckering and change in shape in humid weather. Spun yarns are also used for heavier weight fabrics for outerwear and for knitted fabrics because of their excellent shape retention and stretch resistance.

Dacron 64 is produced in 3-denier staple and may be spun into yarn on either the worsted or rayon system. These yarns are used for winter-weight and spring-weight fabrics. Such fabrics include finished worsteds like sharkskin, gabardine, and Bedford cord, as well as such napped unfinished worsteds as flannel and serge. Fabrics of Dacron 64 have greater resistance to pilling than fabrics of Dacron 54. Although Dacron 64 is the weakest of all the Dacrons, it is still twice as strong as wool and also has greater abrasion resistance. It also has greater dyeing versatility than the other Dacron staples.

Dacron 35 has pilling resistance similar to that of Dacron 64, but it is used where greater tensile strength is required.

Dacron 52, 67, and 68 are industrial types of high-tenacity Dacron staple. They are designed for resistance to chemicals and abrasion. They are used for such purposes as belts, ropes, and fire hoses. Type 68 has also been used experimentally for tire cord.

Dacron 88 is also referred to as Dacron Fiberfill. It is lightweight and has excellent resilience and loft, which provide comfort and insulation. It is also nonallergenic. Dacron Fiberfill is used in staple form for pillows, quilting, and sleeping bags.

The Turbo Stapler is designed especially to process acrylic and polyester fibers in tow form. It heat-stretches, breaks, and crimps the tow into even slivers, as shown in the photographs that follow.

A

A Tow is fed through an overhead creel and delivered to the stapler as a band up to 9-inches wide. It is controlled for proper width and centering as it passes around two bars, each with single quick-knob adjustment as shown.

B

B Tow passes through the first set of nip rolls at left, and around four snub rolls that are moving at the same speed. Tow then passes through two 10 by 14 inch heater plates. Next, the tow moves through the four intermediate snub rolls and around the intermediate nip rolls. The intermediate section operates at a higher speed than the in-feed rolls in order to develop tension on the tow passing through the draw zone. This stretch zone is the heart of the high-bulk yarn.

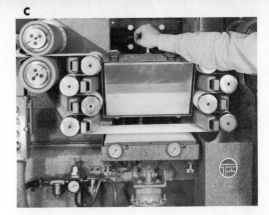

C The heater plates are individually thermo-statted in two zones for each plate. Temperature is continuously indicated at each of these four points. Plates automatically close when machine starts and open when machine stops. Top plate hinges back as shown for ease of cleaning. Pressure between plates is adjustable.

D As tow leaves the intermediate nip rolls, it passes between the breaker bars. The intermediate rolls at left are moving at a slower speed than the front rolls at right. The breaker bars, which are rotating at an intermediate speed, have an abrasive strip in each groove. The fibers in the tow are broken as they pass through this zone and the tow becomes sliver.

E Close-up of breaker bars.

F Close-up of crimper. Degree of crimp is controlled by two calibrated knobs.

FINISHING DACRON FABRICS

Several finishes can be given to Dacron fabrics to increase their usefulness. Among the most important are the following.

Heat setting—for permanent shape
Singeing—for improved hand and reduced pilling
Antistatic finish—for reduction of static electricity
Water and stain repellency—for comfort and ease of care

Fabrics made of Dacron filament yarn can be heat-set in about the same manner as nylon. Setting at temperatures ranging from 350 to 425 degrees Fahrenheit on a hot roller produces fabrics that are dimensionally stable to repeated washing and ironing. Fabrics made of Dacron spun yarn are effectively stabilized in normal dyeing and finishing operations.

Stabilized fabrics made of either Dacron filament yarn or spun yarn have excellent wrinkle resistance and recovery from wrinkling. Essentially permanent creases can be pressed into them at the ordinary ironing temperature for rayon (about 275 degrees Fahrenheit) and remain sharp even after the fabric is washed. Such creases, however, can be ironed out if desired. This means that such garments as suits made of Dacron staple will hold their shape and press in abnormally damp weather and even when wet.

Singeing has been found to be an effective method for reducing the pilling of spun-yarn fabrics made with Dacron 54 staple. While the Dacron 64 and 35 types are inherently pill resistant, singeing does yield a firmer hand. Careful control of the speed of the fabric movement and the height of the flame is maintained merely to remove fuzz and yet prevent melting of the fibers in the fabric, which will cause loss in fabric strength.

Dacron and Dacron blend fabrics may be given a water- and stain-repellent finish such as Zepel or Scotchgard, which are both very effective.

Dacron filament yarn is capable of 15 to 20 percent shrinkage in finishing. This means that such fabrics will not shrink to any significant extent thereafter. It is also possible to produce fabrics with very little porosity by this preshrinking procedure.

Dacron fabrics are subject to the accumulation of static electricity. Where this would prove objectionable, Dacron fabrics can be treated with antistatic agents. The electrostatic property of Dacron fabrics attracts lint, dust particles, hair, and similar substances. It therefore becomes difficult to keep dark fabrics looking neat and to prevent light fabrics from looking dingy. Such fabrics also cling to the body as the static electricity builds up. Consequently, several antistatic finishes have been developed. Some provide temporary protection, others are durable finishes. The consumer should carefully read the labels identifying such finishes to determine the maximum benefits that the finish has given the fabric.

EVALUATING DACRON FABRICS

It has been noted that Dacron fiber is produced in both filament and staple form and that each form has certain properties that affect the appearance and performance of the finished fabric. Furthermore, some Dacron filament and staple have properties designed for general consumer use while others are designed for industrial use. Within these two categories, there are further variations in properties. Therefore, while the ultimate user may be able to distinguish between fabrics of filament and spun yarn, he is not likely to be able to determine the particular type of Dacron used so that he can anticipate the precise properties and performance of the fabric. He must rely upon the manufacturer's ability to make the proper Dacron fiber selection. Within this framework, the consumer may expect a certain range of characteristics and certain standards of performance of the Dacron fabrics he purchases. Some of these are general, others are specific.

Strength. As a group, polyester fibers may be characterized as relatively strong fibers and, within this group, Dacron filament is one of the strongest. The range of strength for regular-filament Dacron is superior to all other similar polyester fibers except Vycron Type II. Fabrics of regular-filament Dacron yarns will therefore be very strong and durable. The high-tenacity filament Dacron used for industrial purposes is the strongest of all the polyesters, and some types are the strongest of all textiles except glass fiber. The staple fibers also have good strength but are weaker than the other polyester staple fibers.

The relative strength of regular Dacron combined with good abrasion resistance will provide relatively good service.

Elasticity. Polyester fibers do not have a high degree of elasticity, and Dacron is the least elastic of the group. Dacron is often characterized as having a high degree of stretch resistance, which means that Dacron fabrics are not likely to stretch out of shape too easily. This property makes Dacron particularly suited for knitted garments; the sagging and stretching that would ordinarily occur are reduced.

Resilience. Dacron has a very high degree of resilience. Not only does a Dacron fabric resist wrinkling when dry, it also resists wrinkling when wet. For example, a suit of Dacron will keep its pressed appearance after many wearings even in rain or moist, humid weather.

Heat Conductivity. Fabrics of Dacron polyester fiber are better conductors of heat than fabrics made of acrylic fibers (discussed in Chapter 19). Dacron fiber is round and, in the staple form, will not bulk up in a yarn as much as the acrylic fibers do. This results in a smoother yarn with less air spaces and less insulation. While a fabric of Dacron would not be as warm as a fabric made of the acrylics, silk, or wool, it would be warmer than if made of cotton, linen, or rayon. One of the reasons for the apparent greater warmth of Dacron is its low absorbency. However, Dacron Fiberfill is designed with crimp to provide bulk and insulative properties.

Drapability. Fabrics of Dacron have satisfactory drapability. The trilobal Dacron 62 is supple and has particularly good draping qualities, resembling those of silk.

Absorbency. Dacron is one of the least absorbent fibers. This low absorbency has two important advantages. Dacron fabrics will dry very rapidly since almost all the moisture will lie on the surface rather than penetrate the yarns. Furthermore, this low absorbency means that Dacron fabrics will not stain easily. Most substances that would stain other fabrics lie on the surface and can be wiped or washed off easily.

Fabrics of low absorbency generally have the disadvantage of being clammy and uncomfortable in humid weather because they will not absorb perspiration or atmospheric moisture. As a result, an absorbent fiber such as cotton is often blended with the Dacron.

Cleanliness and Washability. Since Dacron fabrics have a very low absorbency, stains lie on the surface and can easily be washed or dry-cleaned away. Strong soaps are not needed. Fabrics of Dacron filament yarn dry very quickly. Those of spun yarn dry comparatively rapidly if wrung out well. There is essentially no water shrinkage of Dacron fabrics; therefore, shirts, blouses, and even slacks made entirely of Dacron (including the sewing thread) may be safely laundered.

When ironing Dacron fabrics, it is best to use a moderately hot iron as for rayon. Excessive heat will cause Dacron to melt. (Burning tobacco will quickly melt holes in such fabrics. Certain resins are being used to coat the material, thus minimizing this danger.) Actually, little ironing is needed even after long wear or after being completely wet, because garments made of Dacron hold their shape and creases after being heat-set. Furthermore, the wrinkle resistance of Dacron is extremely good.

Effect of Bleaches. Fabrics of Dacron may be safely bleached because Dacron has excellent resistance to degradation from bleaches.

Shrinkage. As has been indicated, Dacron fabrics shrink as much as 20 percent during wet-finishing operations and they are generally heat-set in later treatments. Consequently, finished woven and knitted fabrics will not shrink. They have excellent dimensional stability.

Effect of Heat. Since Dacron gets tacky at 445 degrees Fahrenheit, fabrics should therefore be ironed at lower temperatures (usually the same as for rayon). At temperatures above 482 degrees Fahrenheit, Dacron will melt and flame but will extinguish when heat or flame is removed. Since sparks, burning cigarette ashes, and the like will easily melt holes in Dacron fabrics, appropriate care should be exercised.

Effect of Light. Dacron has good resistance to degradation by light. Over a prolonged period of time, however, Dacron definitely does deteriorate.

Resistance to Mildew. Dacron fabrics are absolutely resistant to mildew. They will not be stained or weakened.

Resistance to Moths. Dacron is unaffected by moths or by carpet beetles.

Reaction to Alkalies. At room temperature, Dacron has good resistance to weak alkalies and fair resistance to strong alkalies. This resistance is reduced with increased temperature. At boiling temperatures, it has poor resistance to weak alkalies and dissolves in strong alkalies.

Reaction to Acids. Dacron has excellent-to-good resistance to most acids. Such strong acids as sulfuric acid will cause decomposition if the temperature is high enough.

Affinity for Dyes. Dacron can be dyed with specialized techniques to a complete range of shades. The results have good-to-excellent washfastness and fair-to-good lightfastness. Pigment colors have a tendency to rub off and crock.

Resistance to Perspiration. Dacron is not easily affected by perspiration.

DACRON FIBER BLENDS

Dacron polyester fiber has been successfully blended with many other fibers. Various effects and combinations of properties are derived from these blends depending on the fibers used and on the percentages in the blends. One of the most important characteristics that Dacron provides is its high degree of shape retention for garments that require little or no ironing after they are washed.

DACRON AND COTTON ■ For satisfactory wash and wear purposes, fabrics for rainwear, tailored clothing, dress shirts, and sports shirts should have a blend of at least 65 percent Dacron with the cotton. Dacron will provide wrinkle resistance and shape retention. Cotton will provide absorbency and consequent comfort. However, unless properly constructed and properly cared for, a fabric of a Dacron and cotton blend may pucker and lose its shape if the cotton should shrink or if cotton thread is used in sewing. Dacron and cotton blends are well suited for fabrics to be given a permanent-press finish. The Dacron not only contributes its own inherent shape-retentive qualities but also retains its strength, thereby reducing the total potential strength loss from finishing that an all-cotton fabric would have.

DACRON AND WOOL ■ In combination with wool, Dacron provides outstanding wrinkle resistance and crease retention, so that wet or dry, the shape retention is improved according to the proportions used. The greater abrasion

Left: The proper blending of Dacron polyester and wool produces a fabric that has the good draping quality and resilience appropriate for men's suiting. Right: Permanent-pleated fabrics of a 65 percent Dacron and 35 percent cotton blend will keep their smooth, crisp look after washing and wearing.

Photos Courtesy E. I. du Pont de Nemours & Co.

resistance of Dacron also provides longer wear. The wool contributes good draping quality and elasticity. The wool also reduces the hazard of melted holes due to burning tobacco. A blend of 60 percent Dacron and 40 percent wool provides a cloth warm enough for year-round suits.

DACRON AND RAYON ■ In a blend with viscose rayon, Dacron gives greater resiliency, shape retention, and durability. The viscose rayon provides absorbency and variety of color and texture. For satisfactory wash and wear service, a blend of at least 55 percent Dacron with the rayon is desirable.

A blend of 65 percent Dacron and 35 percent high wet-modulus rayon provides a strong, durable, and serviceable fabric. The fabric has a good hand and drapes well. The rayon again provides the absorbency that Dacron lacks.

DACRON AND NYLON ■ Nylon contributes strength and abrasion resistance. Dacron contributes outstanding wrinkle resistance. Such a combination offers stability, easy laundering, quick drying, and resistance to damage from mildew and insects. The fabric will be clammy to the skin, however, in warm, humid weather. Since both fibers are thermoplastic and neither is very absorbent, any combination in the blend will provide good wash and wear characteristics. Care should be taken to avoid pilling of fabrics with this type of blend.

DACRON AND ARNEL ■ The most important contribution that Dacron makes to such a blend is its strength. Again, since both fibers are thermoplastic, fabrics made of such a blend will have excellent shape retention and provide good wash and wear service. The fabric, however, will pill, unless made of a fine-count yarn of this blend.

KODEL

METHOD OF MANUFACTURE

Tennessee Eastman Company states that the manufacture of its Kodel begins with dimethyl terephthlate and a "special suitable dihydric alcohol." This identifies the fiber as a polyester, but the base does differ from that used in the production of other polyester fibers. It is chemically identified by the tongue-twister 1,4-cyclohexylene dimethylene terephthlate. Variations in the manufacture of Kodel polyester fibers result in different forms with certain different properties.

The molten liquid polyester resulting from the chemical synthesis is forced through a spinneret with a large number of fine holes, cooled, and then gathered into bundles of continuous fibers forming a tow that looks like untwisted rope. The tow is drawn to a predetermined extent to make it shrink or stretch resistant. When desired, the tow may be permanently crimped to add bulk and texture. The tow may be cut into staple length or shipped uncut, according to the requirements of the recipient mill.

FORMS AND TYPES OF KODEL YARNS

All Kodel polyester fibers are eventually reduced to staple form, and they are always blended with other fibers into spun yarn. Each type of Kodel fiber has been engineered to satisfy different fiber-blend requirements and to attain certain desired characteristics. They may be bright or semidull.

Kodel II is designed primarily for woolen and worsted blends. It can also be blended with cotton, viscose rayon, or high wet-modulus rayon provided the blended spun yarn is heavy enough to furnish sufficient strength.

Kodel S is fundamentally the same as Kodel II but is solution-dyed in black. Its color is indestructible in any of the common textile processes or uses. It is employed in wool blends.

Kodel III is designed for strength and firm hand and is similar to Kodel IV except that it does not have the permanent whiteness. It is used to a limited extent by some mills.

Kodel IV features outstanding whiteness that results from its built-in ability to transform the invisible ultraviolet component of light into visible blue light. This additional blue light in combination with other reflected light rays gives the fabric a permanent white appearance that is superior to other fibers, including most polyesters. Kodel IV is particularly adaptable for blends with cotton or rayon.

Kodel Fiberfill is a staple similar to Kodel II that has been crimped to provide loft, added resilience, and insulation. It is used in pillows and quilting.

FINISHING KODEL FABRICS

The finish given to a fabric depends upon the properties of the particular Kodel fiber and the fiber with which it is blended. Some of the usual finishes are as follows.

Singeing—for smoothness and reduced pilling

Resin finishes—for ease of care

Water and oil repellency—for rainwear comfort and ease of cleaning

Antistatic finish—for reduction of static electricity

Kodel II is more resistant to pilling than other polyester fibers. Singeing is employed as desired to improve the general smoothness and, by removing fiber ends, further reduce pilling potential.

Blends of Kodel and wool may be fulled, crabbed, and decated to improve compactness and dimensional stability.

Kodel has built-in shape retention and, unlike other polyester fibers, does not have to be heat-set. The effectiveness of shape, crease, or pleat retention is directly related to the amount of Kodel in the fabric.

EVALUATING KODEL FABRICS

The performance of fabrics containing Kodel polyester fiber depends upon several factors. Since Kodel is always blended with another fiber, the properties of both fibers must be considered. In addition to the usual consideration of the construction and finish of the fabric, attention must be given to the kind of yarn and the particular type of Kodel fiber blended. The particular properties of the Kodel fibers should also be taken into consideration in making an evaluation.

Strength. Kodel II, which is usually blended with wool, is the weakest of all the polyester fibers. Kodel IV, used for blending with cotton or rayon, is about twice as strong; it compares favorably to Fortrel staple and is slightly stronger than Dacron staple. The differences in strength have a critical bearing on the blend proportions needed for a satisfactory fabric. The abrasion resistance of Kodel is fair.

Elasticity. Like other polyester fibers, Kodel has limited elasticity, but its elasticity is still greater than that of Dacron. Kodel II is a little more elastic than Kodel IV. This is one of the factors that makes Kodel II more compatible in blends with wool, which is elastic. Kodel IV is preferable for blending with the much less elastic cotton and rayons.

Resilience. The excellent resilience of Kodel II is even superior to that of Kodel IV. A sufficient blend of Kodel fibers with other fibers contributes to a fabric's shape retention and neat, fresh appearance that lasts with continued use and laundering.

Heat Conductivity. Kodel fibers have heat-conducting properties similar to those of Dacron. While not as good a conductor as the cellulosic fibers, it is better than wool, silk, or the acrylics. The conduction of heat can be reduced in a yarn, fabric, or filling by using crimped staple, which provides loft and bulk for greater insulation.

Drapability. Kodel fibers have a flexibility and soft hand similar to that of Fortrel staple, which is greater than that of the other polyester staples. The quality of drapability will depend upon the type of blend in the ultimate yarn as well as the fabric construction.

Absorbency. Like other polyester fibers, Kodel fibers have very little absorbency. Among the various polyester fibers, its types are consistently the least absorbent. Kodel therefore contributes water repellency, stain repellency, quick-drying properties to fabrics containing a sufficient amount of it.

Cleanliness and Washability. The round, smooth surface of Kodel and its very low absorbency are factors that help to keep the fabric looking clean and fresh. This is further enhanced by the permanent and superior whiteness of Kodel IV. Depending upon the fiber with which Kodel is blended, fabrics may be laundered with any household soap or detergent or dry-cleaned. The inherent wrinkle resistance and shape retention of Kodel is not materially changed by normal laundering procedures.

Effect of Bleaches. Kodel has good resistance to the usual household bleaches. The fluorescent effect of Kodel IV is permanent and therefore the need for bleaching is frequently unnecessary, depending upon the amount and type of the other fiber in the blend.

Shrinkage. Kodel has excellent dimensional stability. It has practically no dimensional change even in hot water. Thus, it has a controlling influence on the shrinkage of fabrics in which it is used.

Effect of Heat. Kodel fibers have good resistance to heat. They can be ironed safely at relatively high temperatures of about 400 degrees Fahrenheit. Pressing of fabrics blended of Kodel and other fiber is therefore no problem. Kodel will melt at temperatures above 482 degrees Fahrenheit. When it ignites, it burns slowly as it melts.

Effect of Light. Kodel has good resistance to sunlight degradation. Deterioration occurs over a prolonged period of exposure.

Resistance to Mildew. Kodel has excellent resistance to mildew.

Resistance to Moths. Kodel is not affected by moths or other household insects.

Reaction to Alkalies. Kodel has good resistance to most alkalies but disintegrates in strong alkalies at boiling temperatures.

Reaction to Acids. Kodel has good resistance to most mineral acids. It has fair resistance to concentrated sulfuric acid.

Affinity for Dyes. A full range of bright colors with good general fastness can be obtained with disperse and developed dyes.

Resistance to Perspiration. Kodel has very high resistance to degradation by perspiration.

KODEL FIBER BLENDS

Kodel polyester fiber is generally blended with cotton, viscose rayon, high wet-modulus rayon, or wool. The effectiveness of the blend depends upon the type of Kodel and the percentage of Kodel employed for different yarn counts.

KODEL AND COTTON ■ For blends with cotton, Kodel IV is preferred because of its additional strength and superior whiteness. A minimum of 50 percent Kodel IV blended with carded or combed cotton is satisfactory for fabrics of coarser yarns (that is, below yarn counts of 37s). Finer yarns of higher counts for lighter-weight fabrics require a minimum of 65 percent Kodel IV to obtain adequate strength and the desired ease-of-care characteristics. However, loosely woven or knitted fabrics containing Kodel IV tend to pill readily. For fabrics of such construction, the more pill-resistant Kodel II is preferred in a 50/50 proportion with combed cotton that is spun into the coarser yarn counts.

KODEL AND RAYONS ■ Kodel IV is also preferred in a blend with any rayon. The blends should be in the same proportions as for cotton to give sufficient strength and shape retention. Where greater pill resistance is desired, Kodel II should be used in a 50/50 blend for ease of care and optimum strength (though not as strong as a Kodel IV blend).

Generally, the same proportions are desirable for Kodel blends with high wet-modulus rayon. However, when Kodel II is used, the blend should not contain more than 50 percent of that fiber because a higher proportion lowers the overall yarn strength.

Although blends of Kodel and cotton or rayon may sometimes be given resin treatments to control dimensional stability, this finish is not necessary when Kodel is blended with high wet-modulus rayon. Such blends results in fabrics being permanently preshrunk in the usual wet-finishing operations.

KODEL AND WOOL ■ Kodel II should be used for blending with wool. It provides excellent pill resistance and fabric cover. For worsteds, a minimum of 55 percent Kodel should be blended with the wool for woven fabrics to provide the necessary strength, wrinkle resistance, crease retention, hand, and tailorability. In knitted worsteds, a minimum of 60 percent Kodel should be blended with the wool to obtain satisfactory machine washability and maintain dimensional stability, shape retention, and stitch clarity. The greater the amount of Kodel, the stronger the yarn and fabric.

The desired bulkiness of woolen yarns requires less Kodel and more wool. A minimum of 35 percent Kodel is needed to obtain the ease-of-care effect of the polyester fiber.

METHOD OF MANUFACTURE

The method of production of Fortrel is based upon the process established in the manufacture of Dacron. The polyester is the product of ethylene glycol and dimethyl terephthalate. While differences may exist in the catalysts used, in the condensation reaction, and in the drawing operations, the general method of melting the polymer chips in a vacuum chamber followed by spinning and drawing fibers from the molten polyester is similar to Dacron.

Depending upon the desired end results, there are variations in such aspects of the manufacturing process as the extent to which the fiber is drawn. Characteristics affected include the strength, elasticity, and dyeability of the fiber. Brightness may be altered by adding a delusterant; crimp may also be added.

FORMS AND TYPES OF FORTREL YARN

Fortrel polyester fibers are produced in two forms: filament and staple. Several types of Fortrel are produced in each form.

FILAMENT YARNS ■ There are four types of Fortrel filament yarns. Each is produced in several deniers of multifilaments that are thrown into yarn with the desired number of twists per inch.

Fortrel 700 filament is a bright, regular-tenacity fiber. The yarns are woven or knitted into fabrics with a smooth, crisp finish and used for a wide variety of apparel, such as dresses, blouses, lingerie, shirts, and sportswear, as well as for such home furnishing as curtains.

Fortrel 720 is a regular-tenacity filament with an optical whitener added. It is used for apparel and home furnishings fabrics where long-lasting superior whiteness in polyester filament yarns is desired.

Fortrel 730 is a textured yarn used primarily as a filling yarn in woven goods to add beauty to fabrics. It also is finding a widespread acceptance in double knits of 100 percent Type 730 or in blends with other fibers.

Fortrel 770 is a high-tenacity fiber used for industrial purposes. Because of its strength, high stretch resistance, and resistance to deterioration by heat, moisture, mildew, microorganisms, and most chemicals, Fortrel 770 is excellent for such items as belts, fire hoses, ropes, sewing threads, and tire cords.

SPUN YARNS ■ Fortrel filaments of 1.5 to 8.0 denier are produced in tow form and cut into staple lengths of 1¼ to 3 inches and spun into yarn on a conventional cotton, woolen, or worsted system. Fortrel "tops" can also be processed on the Pacific Converter or Turbo Stapler (as described for rayon yarn processing on pages 287–288) and spun into worsted yarn.

Fortrel 400 is the normal-tenacity staple designed for apparel. It has good shape retention as well as good abrasion resistance and stretch resistance. The spun yarns can be woven or knitted into fabrics for infants' wear, men's and women's suiting, and sportswear.

Fortrel 410 is like Type 400 but has an optical brightener that is claimed by the manufacturer to have superior whiteness.

Fortrel filament yarn may be woven into sheer, durable, easy-care fabrics.

Courtesy Celanese Fibers Marketing Company

Fortrel Fiberfill gives warmth and light weight to the quilt.

Courtesy Celanese Fibers Marketing Company

Fortrel 430 is a more pill-resistant staple for wool blends.

Fortrel 440 is a high-shrinkage staple designed for blends with natural or man-made fibers. The blended fabrics have considerable bulk, luxury of hand, and excellent resistance to pilling.

Fortrel 450 is a special binder-type fiber used for bonding purposes in industrial applications.

Fortrel 460 is a more pill-resistant staple for blending with cotton and high wet-modulus rayons. It contains an optical brightener for maximum whiteness.

Fortrel Fiberfill is a semidull crimped staple that has excellent resilience and loft. It is lightweight, has low heat conductivity, and is non-allergenic. It is used in staple form for pillows, quilting, and sleeping bags.

FINISHING FORTREL FABRICS

A variety of finishes may be applied to Fortrel and Fortrel blended fabrics, but the most important are as follows.

Singeing—for smoothness and reduced pilling

Heat setting—for permanent shape

Calendering—for smoothness and pilling resistance

Water and stain repellency—for rainwear, comfort, and easy cleaning

Embossing—for design and luster

Brushing, shearing, and singeing have been found very effective in improving the hand and pilling resistance of fabrics containing Fortrel fiber. The removal of the loose-end fibers by this means reduces the possibility that fiber ends will mat together into undesirable balls.

Calendering also improves the pilling resistance by flattening the fiber ends and smoothing the surface. It also provides increased luster and better covering power by reducing the size of the fabric pores.

Heat setting is a major finish given to fabrics of Fortrel. The thermosetting properties of the fiber permit shape formation and retention. Permanent creases and pleats may be pressed into such fabrics to provide easy wash and wear care with little or no ironing.

Durable water repellents, such as Syl-mer and Zelan, are very effective. Such water and oil repellents as Scotchgard are also effective and durable.

Shallow embossing, including schreinering, may also be applied to Fortrel and cotton blends to increase luster.

EVALUATING FORTREL FABRICS

Some characteristics are common to the various forms and types of Fortrel polyester fiber. However, special properties have been engineered for special purposes. Both the general and specific properties should be considered in anticipating fabric performance.

Strength. The strength of Fortrel fibers competes with that of Dacron. Regular-filament Fortrel is stronger than some types of regular-filament Dacron fibers. This is also true of the high-tenacity fibers. Fortrel staple is stronger than any type of Dacron staple, and it is competitive with Kodel IV polyester staple. All forms of Fortrel fiber have excellent abrasion resistance.

Because Fortrel fibers add strength and durability to the fabrics in which they are used, these fabrics may be expected to give good service and long wear.

Elasticity. Fortrel fibers are generally slightly more elastic than other polyester fibers, but they also have relatively good resistance to stretch. This is one reason for the good dimensional stability and shape retention of Fortrel fabrics.

Resilience. Fortrel has excellent resilience, particularly in staple form. It resists wrinkling in both wet and dry conditions, and the pressed appearance of garments is retained after repeated wearings. Suits, slacks, or dresses of Fortrel do not rumple easily; any wrinkles caused by sitting, packing, or wearing hang out readily.

Heat Conductivity. Fabrics of Fortrel fibers are not as good heat conductors as those of the cellulosic fibers, but they are better conductors than fabrics of wool, silk, or the acrylic fibers. At times, Fortrel fabrics can be uncomfortable if the yarns have a low twist, are a little bulky, and the weather is warm or humid. Fortrel Fiberfill is specially crimped to provide bulk and air spaces that contribute considerable insulative power.

Drapability. Fabrics of Fortrel have fairly good draping qualities. Fortrel staple has more flexibility than the filament. When Fortrel filaments are treated with a solution of hot caustic soda under carefully controlled conditions, the resultant fabrics have an improved drape and hand. However, this treatment weakens the fibers somewhat.

Absorbency. Fortrel, like other polyester fibers, has very little absorbtive ability. It has as little absorbency as some forms of Dacron and is less absorbent than others. It is, then, one of the least absorbent of textile fibers. Consequently, Fortrel fabrics tend to be water and stain repellent. Fortrel is well suited for rainwear, and it is quick-drying. On the other hand, the low absorbency of Fortrel makes it uncomfortable to wear next to the skin unless blended with a more absorbent fiber.

Cleanliness and Washability. Fabrics of Fortrel are easy-care materials. They do not stain easily and dirt can be readily laundered or dry-cleaned out. They may be laundered by hand or machine with the usual mild household soaps or detergents.

Fabrics of Fortrel have good dimensional stability. They retain their shape and creases after cleaning. They often need little or no ironing. For freshening up or for sharpening creases, the iron should be set at "rayon."

Effect of Bleaches. Any of the usual household bleaches may be safely used on Fortrel.

Shrinkage. As has been stated, fabrics of Fortrel have good dimensional stability. Heat-set fabrics will not shrink and will retain their shape.

Effect of Heat. Fortrel has a higher resistance to heat than some of the other polyester fibers. For example, exposure to temperatures of 300 degrees Fahrenheit for 1,000 hours reduces Fortrel's strength by only 50 percent. It melts at 485–510 degrees Fahrenheit. Above these temperatures, it will flame as it melts but will extinguish when the heat or flame is removed.

Effect of Light. Fortrel has good resistance to sunlight degradation. However, exposure over a prolonged period of time will deteriorate the fiber.

Resistance to Mildew. Fabrics of Fortrel are unaffected by mildew.

Resistance to Moths. Fortrel is not attacked by moths or other insects.

Reaction to Alkalies. Strong alkalies should be avoided. Fortrel has good resistance to weak alkalies and fair resistance to strong alkalies at room temperatures. As the temperature increases, its resistance decreases.

Reaction to Acids. Fortrel is exceedingly resistant to mineral and organic acids. Highly concentrated solutions of a mineral acid, such as sulfuric acid, at a relatively high temperature will partially decompose the fiber.

Affinity for Dyes. Fortrel can be dyed with appropriate disperse, azoic, and developed dyes at high temperatures, producing a good range of shades that have good-to-excellent washfastness and fair-to-good lightfastness. However, there has been some difficulty with pigment colors, which rub away with wear.

Resistance to Perspiration. Fortrel has no significant loss of strength from continued contact with either acid or alkaline perspiration.

FORTREL FIBER BLENDS

Fortrel polyester fiber is generally blended to contribute such qualities as shape retention, ease of care, and strength. The fibers with which Fortrel fibers are usually blended are cotton, wool, rayon, or triacetate. The proportion of fibers used varies, but a minimum of 50 percent Fortrel is required for its properties to be effective in the blend.

FORTREL AND COTTON ■ A blend of 65 percent Fortrel and 35 percent cotton is the most satisfactory combination for maximum strength, general durability, shape retention, and wash and wear care. Where greater absorbency and softer hand are desired, a 50/50 blend is preferable, but there will be a corresponding strength loss of as much as 20 percent as well as a slight loss in resilience. A 50/50 blend of Fortrel and cotton is also satisfactory for effective permanent-press finishes.

FORTREL AND WOOL ■ Blends of Fortrel and wool may range from 65 percent Fortrel and 35 percent wool to 60/40, 55/45, and 50/50, respectively. For optimum benefits of both fibers, the 60 percent Fortrel and 40 percent wool appears to be best for summer worsteds, while the 55 percent Fortrel and 45 percent wool are better for year-round garments. Where greater warmth is desired, the 50/50 blend for woolens would be preferable.

The greater the amount of wool, the less chance for pilling. Wool also contributes excellent draping qualities. A proper blend of the Fortrel provides wrinkle resistance, crease and shape retention, abrasion resistance, and strength.

FORTREL AND RAYON ■ Blends of Fortrel and viscose rayon are generally spun in a proportion of 65 percent Fortrel and 35 percent viscose or of 50 percent of each fiber. For maximum shape retention, ease of care, and durability, the first proportion is preferred, although absorbency will be a little less.

Similar blends are also spun of Fortrel and high wet-modulus rayons. The strength and durability of such blends is comparable to Fortrel and pima cotton blends and have the advantage of greater resilience and shape retention.

FORTREL AND ARNEL ■ Fortrel is usually blended on a 50/50 basis with Arnel. Both fibers have shape-retentive and wash and wear qualities but low absorbency. The prime advantage here is the strength and abrasion resistance contributed by Fortrel, since Arnel is a very weak fiber. However, this blend produces a yarn weaker than a similar blend of Fortrel and any cellulosic fiber.

METHOD OF MANUFACTURE

The production of Vycron polyester fiber is based upon the process for the manufacture of Dacron. However, variations have been developed for the production of Vycron types. For the manufacture of filament yarns, the filaments extruded from the spinneret are placed on a machine that heats the fibers, draws them out to impart the desired elongation and strength, and then twists them according to end-use requirements.

To produce staple, the filaments are treated as tow, drawn under varying controlled ratios and temperatures, sometimes crimped, then cut into 1- to 3-inch lengths. The staple is then prepared for shipment in bales to spinning mills.

FORMS AND TYPES OF VYCRON YARNS

Vycron polyester fibers are produced in both filament and staple form and in three principle types.

FILAMENT YARN ■ Vycron filament is generally used for apparel purposes, such as dresses and blouses.

SPUN YARNS ■ Vycron 2 is a staple used in blends with cotton or rayon to contribute superior strength and good shrinkage-control. Vycron 5 is a crimped type of staple used primarily in blends with wool and knitted fabrics where loft and bulk is desired.

VYCRON FIBERFILL ■ Vycron Fiberfill is a crimped staple used for pillows and quilting.

FINISHING VYCRON FABRICS

The finishes usually given to fabrics containing Vycron are similar to those generally given other fabrics containing polyester fibers.

EVALUATING VYCRON FABRICS

Properties such as shape retention and chemical resistance may be expected of Vycron because it is a polyester fiber. However, there are certain differences in properties between Vycron and the other polyesters as well as between the major types of Vycron.

Strength. Generally speaking, Vycron staple is the strongest of all polyester staple fibers. The strength of Vycron is excelled only by the special high-tenacity

Vycron Fiberfill polyester staple is used for quilting that contributes warmth with light weight to ski jackets.

Courtesy Beaunit Fibers

Dacron and Fortrel used for industrial purposes. This strength coupled with high abrasion resistance makes Vycron extremely well suited for durable apparel ranging from sportswear to dress and children's wear.

Elasticity. Among the polyester fibers, Vycron 2 is second only to Dacron in stretch resistance. Vycron 5 is, in general, the most elastic of the polyesters. This range makes its types readily useable with other fibers to provide dimensional stability to blends.

Resilience. Vycron has good wrinkle resistance, comparing satisfactorily to that of the other polyester fibers in a dry state. However, wet Vycron tends to retain wrinkles more readily.

Heat Conductivity. The heat conductivity of Vycron polyester fiber is quite good. The addition of crimp, however, will provide the yarn with loft and bulk and give increased insulative properties.

Drapability. Vycron has good pliability, a pleasing hand, and very good draping qualities, making it quite suitable for dresses, suits, and sportswear.

Absorbency. Vycron is not very absorbent. However, by comparison to the other polyester fibers, it is generally slightly more absorbent and therefore more comfortable.

Cleanliness and Washability. Fabrics that are knitted or woven of Vycron polyester fiber only or of Vycron blended with other fibers may be machine-washed in either warm soap or detergent suds as long as the Vycron accounts for the maximum fiber content. A three or five minute wash-rinse cycle is recommended.

To avoid setting wrinkles in the fabric and to obtain the maximum wash and wear quality from Vycron and Vycron blend materials, garments should be removed from the washing machine before the final spin-drying action. If the garment is being hand washed, it should not be twisted or wrung because this, too, tends to set wrinkles.

The garment should be drip-dried by hanging it on a wooden or plastic hanger. By finger-pressing the seams, hem, and collar, a wrinkle-free look can be achieved. No ironing is required, but a touch up with a warm iron will restore the fresh-as-new appearance.

Effect of Bleaches. Fabrics of Vycron may be safely bleached with any household bleach.

Shrinkage. Fabrics of Vycron have excellent shrink resistance that is built into the fiber.

Effect of Heat. Vycron softens at a lower temperature than the other polyester fibers; it is therefore advisable to press Vycron fabrics with a warm iron, as for acetate. Exposure to temperatures above 455 degrees Fahrenheit causes Vycron to melt and flame.

Effect of Light. Like other polyesters, Vycron has good resistance to sunlight degradation. Deterioration will occur with a prolonged period of exposure.

Resistance to Mildew. Vycron is unaffected by mildew.

Resistance to Moths. Vycron is not attacked by moths or other household insects.

Reaction to Alkalies. Vycron has good resistance to weak alkalies and to moderately concentrated alkalies at room temperature. Its rate of deterioration increases as the heat and strength of the solution increases.

Reaction to Acids. Vycron has good resistance to mineral acids. It will gradually dissolve in concentrated sulfuric and formic acids.

Affinity for Dyes. Vycron has good affinity for disperse dyes that provide good fastness in a wide range of colors.

Resistance to Perspiration. Considering its resistance to acids and alkalies, Vycron may be expected to have relatively satisfactory resistance to perspiration.

VYCRON FIBER BLENDS

Vycron is generally blended with cotton, rayon, or wool. The effectiveness of the blend is dependent upon the type and the proportion of Vycron to the other fiber. To be satisfactory, a minimum of 50 percent Vycron polyester fiber is necessary. The percentage of Vycron for optimum performance is 65 percent.

VYCRON AND COTTON ■ Vycron 2, being the strongest of the polyester staples, will provide maximum strength for a polyester and cotton blended fabric. This combination is also very desirable when a resin finish (for obtaining permanent-press features) is used to counteract the loss of strength in the cotton. Vycron and cotton blends provide excellent dimensional stability.

VYCRON AND RAYONS ■ Vycron blended with viscose rayon provides strength and shape retention; the rayon provides absorbency and softness of hand. For maximum effectiveness, the blend should be 65 percent Vycron and 35 percent cotton.

COMPARISON OF PROPERTIES—THE POLYESTER FIBERS

	DACRON	KODEL	FORTREL	VYCRON
Strength	Excellent for filament; good for staple	Very good to fair for staple	Excellent to good for filament; good for staple	Very good for filament; excellent to very good for staple
Abrasion resistance	Good	Fair	Excellent	Very good
Elasticity	Very low	Low	Slightly higher than others	Low
Resilience	Excellent	Excellent	Excellent	Excellent when dry; fair when wet; may develop wrinkles
Pressed-crease retention	Very good	Excellent (does not need heat-setting)	Very good	Very good
Dimensional stability	Excellent (when heat-set)	Excellent (does not need heat-setting)	Excellent (when heat-set)	Excellent (when heat-set)
Absorbency	Very little	Very little	Very little	Very little
Laundering care	Machine washable with usual soaps, detergents, bleaches	Same as for Dacron	Same as for Dacron	Should not be spun dry, twisted, wrung out; should be drip-dried
Household bleaches	Safe	Safe (unnecessary for Kodel IV)	Safe (unnecessary for Types 410, 460, 720)	Safe
Ironing temperature	Moderately hot iron	Moderately hot iron	Hot as for heavy rayon or cotton	Warm iron as for acetate
Resistance to pilling	Poor to good	Excellent	Poor to excellent	Fair
Resistance to light	Good	Good	Good	Good
Resistance to mildew	Wholly resistant	Wholly resistant	Wholly resistant	Wholly resistant
Resistance to chemicals	Very good	Very good	Very good	Good
Colorfastness	Good (pigment colors may crock)	Good (pigment colors may crock)	Good (pigment colors may crock)	Good (pigment colors may crock)
Resistance to perspiration	Very good	Very good	Very good	Good

Vycron and a high wet-modulus rayon make a well-balanced fabric with a 50/50 blend. Good strength is provided by both fibers; the modified rayon furnishes the absorbency and the Vycron polyester contributes increased dimensional stability and shape retention.

VYCRON AND WOOL ■ A 50/50 blend of Vycron and wool will provide a fabric of year-round weight. Such fabrics will have good drape and satisfactory shape retention. Blends of up to 65 percent Vycron provide lighter-weight fabrics that have relatively better shape retention but are more susceptible to pilling.

COMPARISON OF POLYESTER FIBERS

The chart on page 366 is for the reader's general guidance. It is a summary composite based on information supplied by the producers of these fibers and on evaluations of the performance of the fibers as described in the literature included in the bibliography. The reader is reminded that variations do exist within each trade name as well as blend combination, type of yarn, fabric weight, construction, and finish and that these factors will affect the performance. It is also possible that future changes in the chemical and physical compositions of these fibers may alter their performance.

REVIEW QUESTIONS

1 (a) What is Dacron? (b) May any company produce or imitate it? Why?

2 What types of yarns are made of Dacron? Explain their differences.

3 Discuss the washability and general care of fabrics made of Dacron.

4 How does the strength of Dacron compare to that of other fibers?

5 How is Dacron affected (a) by mildew, (b) by moths?

6 What reaction has Dacron (a) to alkalies, (b) to acids, (c) to perspiration?

7 Discuss the possible value of Dacron fabrics and blends for summer wear.

8 What are the outstanding properties of a Dacron/wool fabric?

9 Compare Kodel II and Kodel IV for blending purposes.

10 What blend proportions are preferrable for Kodel with other fibers? Why?

11 What differences are there in the properties of Kodel II, Kodel III, and Kodel IV?

12 (a) Describe the origin and general manufacturing process of Fortrel. (b) How does it compare to the manufacture of Vycron?

13 Identify the types of Fortrel and their major differences.

14 What blends of Fortrel and cotton are satisfactory? Discuss the merits of these blends.

15 What blends of Fortrel and rayon are satisfactory? Discuss their merits.

16 Evaluate the different proportions of Fortrel and wool blends.

17 Compare the properties of Vycron 2 and Vycron 5.

18 What blend proportions are preferable for Vycron with other fibers? Why?

19 Compare the strengths of the several polyester fibers.

20 Compare the elasticity of the polyester fibers.

21 What other differences exist among the polyester fibers?

22 In what respects are these fibers similar?

SUGGESTED ACTIVITY

Prepare a chart listing each polyester fiber and indicating the blend proportions that are desirable with cotton, rayon, and wool.

19

THE ACRYLIC FIBERS

ORLON
ACRILAN
CRESLAN
ZEFRAN
ZEFKROME

Basically, acrylic is a type of plastic. According to the definition set forth by the FTC, an acrylic fiber is "any long-chain synthetic polymer composed of at least 85 percent by weight of acrylonitrile units." This definition classifies a group of chemically related fibers and accounts for similarities in some of their properties. However, there are many differences in their specific chemical compositions, molecular structures, physical appearances, and methods of production.

HISTORY OF ACRYLICS

Dr. Carothers' discovery of the fiber-forming properties of linear super-polymers spurred researchers everywhere to investigate the fiber-forming possibilities of a host of polymers. The first acrylic fiber, *Orlon*, became a reality when in 1944 a "semiworks" was built under the auspices of the Research Section of Du Pont's Acetate Division. Until August, 1945, the development of Orlon acrylic fiber was concerned primarily with its possible aid in the war effort, but was not brought to fruition before World War II ended. By early 1946, Orlon looked promising enough for commercialization. Process development continued, and in October, 1948, the Du Pont Company built a plant near Camden, South Carolina, capable of producing 6½ million pounds of yarn a year. Production of Orlon started in May, 1950.

Following the lead of the Du Pont Company, The Chemstrand Corporation developed another acrylic fiber, which they named *Acrilan*. A plant was built in Decatur, Alabama; and operations, with a capacity of 30 million pounds annually, were started late in 1952.

For many years, the American Cyanamid Company manufactured a chemical known as *acrylonitrile* for use by other companies in the manufacture of such products as acrylic fibers. The company eventually decided to experiment in the production of its own acrylic fiber. After much experimentation, it produced in 1953 a fiber tentatively designated as X-51 at its pilot plant in Stamford, Connecticut. After spending fifteen years on research, the American Cyanamid Company began commercial production in 1958 of its own acrylic fiber, *Creslan,* in a new plant near Pensacola, Florida.

The development of *Zefran* was begun in 1949. Research in the laboratories of The Dow Chemical Company was concerned with polymers and particularly with polyacrylonitriles. One of the problems associated with polyacrylonitriles had been their low affinity for dyes and the limited fastness of the colors. After several years of intensive research, a chemical alloy with acrylonitrile was produced having properties similar to those of acrylic fibers plus superior dyeing properties. This fiber could be dyed with a wide variety of dyes including those used for natural fibers as well as those used for man-made fibers. This not only meant greater affinity for dyes but also greater possibilities for blending this new fiber with a wide array of other fibers without being hampered by dyeing problems frequently encountered with blending. Satisfied that they had a desirable product which was commercially feasible, The Dow Chemical Company established the trademark of that fiber as *Zefran*. Dow introduced its new fiber as a nitrile alloy in 1958, thereby differentiating its composition, as well as its properties, from the other acrylonitrile fibers. Upon establishment of the Federal Trade Commission's ruling in 1960, Zefran was classified as an acrylic fiber. It is now manufactured by the renamed Dow Badische Co. in Williamsburg, Virginia.

Subsequent to its development of Zefran, Dow introduced another acrylic fiber under the trademark of *Zefkrome*. Although it shares characteristics with its sister fiber, it has certain modifications based on a new concept in production. Zefkrome was developed as a precolored acrylic fiber.

ORLON

METHOD OF MANUFACTURE

The manufacture of Orlon resin is the result of a complicated chemical synthesis. Acrylonitrile may be made from acetylene or from ethylene, which are petroleum derivatives. When the ethylene is treated with hypochlorous acid, a chlorohydrin is formed. The chlorohydrin is reacted with sodium hydroxide to form ethylene oxide. Hydrocyanic acid is added to the ethylene oxide, producing cyanoalcohol, which is dehydrated to yield acrylonitrile. The acrylonitrile is then polymerized into polyacrylonitrile resin, a long-chain linear polymer. The polyacrylonitrile is dissolved in a suitable solvent, such as dimethylformamide, and extruded through a spinneret. By the addition of a delusterant, such as the one used for nylon, Orlon is made semidull. After coagulation, the filaments are oriented and stabilized by stretching.

Variations in the basic process that have been developed to meet specific needs change the fiber both in appearance and in certain properties.

FORMS AND TYPES OF ORLON YARNS

After orientation and stabilization, the Orlon filaments are shipped as tow or cut into staple lengths for spinning into yarn. The Orlon fibers are identified according to type and have particular characteristics suitable for particular purposes. These varieties provide Orlon acrylic fibers with considerable flexibility in application to serve numerous consumer uses.

Type 21 is produced as tow or staple and is identified as *Orlon Sayelle,* the

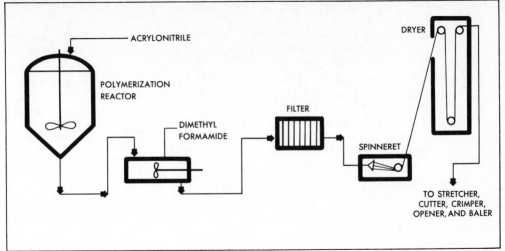

Flow chart of the manufacturing process of Orlon acrylic fiber.

Courtesy of E. I. du Pont de Nemours & Co.

trade name for Du Pont's bicomponent acrylic fiber. Two separate acrylic fiber components, each having different shrinkage potential, are extruded together and adhere as one fiber. When treated with heat and moisture in later finishing processes, one component shrinks more than the other and causes a permanent random-spiral crimp. (This crimp is in addition to the mechanical crimp put into the fiber in the early stages of production.) The random-spiral crimp enhances the loft, bulk, and covering power of the yarn, giving it a warm, soft, pleasing hand. The elasticity and resilience of the yarn are also considerably increased while still retaining the inherent crease-retentive property of the fiber. The crimp may be described as reversible—that is, the fiber has the ability of decreasing its crimp, thus elongating the fiber when wet and recovering its spiral crimp when dry. This unique characteristic provides excellent retention of its built-in elasticity in knitted fabrics after repeated laundering. This type of Orlon Sayelle, which is semidull, is extremely well suited for bulky, woolenlike yarns for such uses as knitted sweaters and socks.

Type 24 is an Orlon-Sayelle variant. It has been produced for use in knitted goods of finer yarns and gauge. This type is used in plied-yarn form to attain the maximum elasticity and bulk.

Type 28 is a bright staple developed for worsted-system properties. The fiber has an antistatic lubricant applied during its manufacture and does not require a supplemental antistatic finish. This type imparts a smooth hand and lustrous appearance to fabrics, and it is particularly well suited for knitted wear. Since this fiber is acid-dyeable, it can be blended with basic-dyeable fibers to obtain interesting cross-dyed effects.

Type 36 and 37 are staples specifically designed for rugs and carpets. Type 36 is for use in carpets of 100 percent Orlon pile yarn. Type 37 is designed for blending with wool or modacrylics in the pile. The fibers are engineered to reduce fuzzing and pilling. Carpets containing these fiber types have a thick, luxurious, resilient texture, maintain a neat appearance, and provide good durability. As is generally true of Orlon, they are stain resistant but are also subject to melting from cigarette sparks and the like.

Type 38 is a high-shrinkage tow suitable for furlike fabrics. When blended with fibers of low shrinkage in the pile and subjected to heat, this type of Orlon shrinks from 40 to 50 percent, thus forming the downlike noil hair of the fabric while the other component fiber serves as the guard hair. A typical combination of this sort is Orlon and Dynel.

Type 39 is produced in semidull and bright staple varieties with a built-in antistatic finish designed for blending on the woolen spinning system.

Type 42 is a general purpose variety, having properties suitable for many uses. It is produced in semidull, bright, and color-sealed black forms as tow or staple. It is available in regular-shrinkage and high-shrinkage varieties. The latter are used to produce high-bulk yarns.

Type 44 is similar to Type 42 except that it is acid-dyeable rather than basic-dyeable. Interesting cross-dyed effects are thus obtained in blended yarns and fabrics.

Type 72 is produced in semidull, bright, and specially whitened varieties. It is designed for the cotton spinning system for yarns used in lightweight fabrics. It has good adsorbency and wicking capacity. This, plus its softness, makes it more comfortable next to the skin than the other types of Orlon.

Type 75 is produced in semidull and bright varieties. It is designed for cotton and rayon system spinning.

SPUN YARN ■ The Orlon filaments range from 1.5 to 10 denier. The tow is usually processed through the Pacific converter or the Turbo stapler. The cut staple ranges from 1.5 to 5 inches, depending on the type of yarn to be made. The staple is crimped and spun on a cotton or wool system into fuzzy yarns. The more twist in the yarns, the finer, smoother, and harder the yarns will be. The less twist in the yarns, the thicker and softer the yarns will be. Spun yarns of Orlon with a low twist have the hand of cashmere. Soft spun Orlon yarns, however, are fuzzy and have a tendency to pill or form little balls on the surface of the fabric.

HIGH-BULK YARN ■ Orlon crimped staple may be spun into relatively thick, soft, spongy yarns called high-bulk yarns. Such yarns produce warm, lightweight fabrics with a luxurious hand. Sometimes Orlon crimped staple may be blended with other fibers, resulting in greater stretch as well as high bulk in the yarn. For further discussion, see pages 375–378.

FINISHING ORLON FABRICS

Several finishes can be given to Orlon fabrics to increase their usefulness. Among the most important are the following.

Heat setting—for permanent shape
Water repellency—for protection against water
Antistatic finish—for control of static electricity

An outstanding feature of Orlon is that a fabric or garment made of it can be given a permanent shape by being subjected to a high degree of heat. If properly heat-set, the fabric will retain its shape as well as its creases or pleats. Nor will washing, dry cleaning or wearing cause the garment to lose its shape.

Orlon is not a particularly absorbent textile. To make it even less absorbent, it may be treated with a water repellent, such as Aridex or Zelan. This process makes the fabric desirable for rainwear and children's playclothes.

EVALUATING ORLON FABRICS

The properties of Orlon fabrics depend on the type of Orlon acrylic fiber used as well as how the material is woven, knitted, or finished. The several types of Orlon provide for flexibility in application due to the differences in certain of their properties. Therefore, fabric and garment performance should be evaluated in terms of these particular characteristics as well as the general properties common to all Orlon acrylic fibers.

Strength. Orlon fiber is of moderate strength. It is, however, the weakest of the acrylic fibers. Compared to the natural fibers it is weaker than all with the exception of wool. Since Orlon fiber is used primarily as a replacement for wool, its greater strength is an advantage. The abrasion resistance of Orlon is good and compares favorably with that of wool.

Elasticity. Like the other acrylics, Orlon has little stretch. The low stretchability makes Orlon useful for knitted wear, since it is not likely to stretch unduly. Most of the stretch that does exist is due to the mechanical crimp put into the fiber. The additional random-spiral crimp of Orlon Sayelle provides good extensibility without straining the fiber. Thus, Orlon Sayelle provides freedom of movement without developing sag.

Resilience. Orlon acrylic fiber has very good resilience and therefore will not wrinkle easily. Orlon staple fabrics are not as lively in springing out from a creased position as Dacron and wool, but they are nevertheless good in this respect. The high resilience makes Orlon desirable for men's slacks and suits as well as for women's dresses.

Heat Conductivity. Like all acrylics, Orlon does not conduct heat rapidly; therefore, Orlon fabrics can be warm. Orlon fiber is dog-bone in shape, which provides overlapping and bulk (with little weight). As a result, staple Orlon fabrics have approximately 20 percent greater insulating power per ounce of fiber than wool fabrics. Since an ounce of Orlon fabric is thicker than an ounce of wool fabric, it is possible to obtain an Orlon fabric that, while being as thick and as warm as wool, is about 20 percent lighter in weight. The warmth of the yarns can be increased by bulking through the use of such special types as Orlon Sayelle and by blending with high-shrinkage Orlon.

Drapability. The drapability of Orlon varies with the type of fiber. Generally speaking, it provides satisfactory draping qualities.

Absorbency. Orlon, like the other acrylics, has low absorbency. Nevertheless, fabrics made of Orlon staple will take on quite a bit of water due to the staple's adsorbency, that is, the tendency for water droplets to cling to the surface of the individual fibers. Since these water droplets get into the air spaces between the fibers and evaporate slowly, Orlon spun-yarn fabrics dry slowly although not as slowly as wool fabrics.

This low absorbency gives Orlon the advantage of resisting stains. Many substances that are ordinarily absorbed by other fibers merely remain on the surface of fabrics made of Orlon yarns and can be easily removed by wiping, washing, or dry cleaning.

Cleanliness and Washability. Orlon fabrics do not soil or stain easily, and washing or dry cleaning quickly renews their freshness. A mild soap should, however, be used in laundering since strong soaps will damage Orlon. If desired, any ordinary cleaning fluid and household bleach may be safely used.

Soft, bulky Orlon yarns will pill. To reduce this tendency, such garments as sweaters should be laundered, while turned inside out, with as little rubbing as possible. After rinsing through mild suds and then lukewarm water, squeeze out the water, turn the garment right side out, spread it on a towel, and gently brush it with a very soft brush while drying. The tendency of Orlon to pill is reduced when it is blended with most other fibers. Tightly spun yarns of Orlon will not pill readily because they are harder, smoother, and not too fuzzy.

Sweaters of Orlon Sayelle require special attention. They can be washed either in a machine or by hand with equally satisfactory results. White sweaters should be washed with only white articles to avoid developing a dingy appearance caused by pick-up of dye particles; colored sweaters can be laundered with other colored garments. Neither white nor colored sweaters should be washed in the same load with lint-shedding fabrics. Sweaters trimmed with sequins or other delicate materials should be washed by hand and air-dried. Of course, sweaters of Orlon Sayelle can also be dry-cleaned.

When laundering sweaters of Orlon Sayelle by hand, use warm water (100 degrees Fahrenheit) with a detergent or soap and a water conditioner, such as *Calgon* or a similar product. Wringing or twisting the garment while washing or rinsing should be avoided. The sweater should be rinsed thoroughly in clear warm water until all the soap or detergent has been removed. A final rinse in fresh water containing a fabric softener, such as *Sta-Puf* or *Nu-Soft,* will maintain the soft texture of the sweater. The sweater should be rolled in a clean white towel and the excess water squeezed out—never wrung or twisted. The garment should then be bunched and spread out loosely on a flat surface (but not a towel) to dry. The sweater will appear larger in this condition, but as it dries, the reverse crimp in the fiber will cause the yarns to shorten and the garment will return to its original size. Bulky sweaters will take longer to dry than thinner sweaters.

When machine laundering sweaters of Orlon Sayelle, the washer should be set for a 5- to 8-minute agitation cycle or at the delicate-fabric setting at a high water level using warm water (100 degrees Fahrenheit). Any household detergent or soap and a water conditioner may be used. The sweater should be spun-dried and then must be tumble-dried at a low or medium temperature setting for about 30 minutes. Before the garment is removed from the dryer, it should be tumbled for about 5 minutes using the cold-temperature setting (although some dryers have special wash and wear cycles that are suitable). Remove the garments immediately after cooling. Garments that have been machine washed should not be drip-dried or flat-dried.

Effect of Bleaches. Fabrics of Orlon may be safely bleached with any of the household bleaches.

Shrinkage. The discussion regarding the various types of Orlon indicates that some Orlons will shrink in processing and that this characteristic is utilized in obtaining desired effects, such as high-bulk yarns and pile fabrics. However, once the finished product reaches the consumer, it may be expected to have excellent dimensional stability since the Orlon fiber will have practically no further shrinkage.

Effect of Heat. Orlon gets tacky at a temperature of 455 degrees Fahrenheit, which is slightly above that of nylon. At higher temperatures, it will melt.

Orlon fabrics should be ironed with a moderately warm iron; in fact, they may be ironed while dry. Old creases may be removed, and new ones added. Since fabrics of Orlon may be heat-set, it is often unnecessary to press them, but some ironing may be desired to smooth the cloth.

Effect of Light. Orlon has outstanding resistance to the effect of light. Its extreme resistance to such degradation makes it especially useful for fabrics that will be exposed to sunlight for an extended period of time.

Resistance to Mildew. Mildew may form on the surface, but it will have no effect on Orlon fabric. It may be easily wiped off.

Resistance to Moths. Orlon is unaffected by moths or their larvae or by carpet beetles.

Reaction to Alkalies. Orlon has fair-to-good resistance to weak alkalies.

Reaction to Acids. Orlon is exceedingly resistant to strong mineral acids as well as organic acids.

Affinity for Dyes. Formerly, it was difficult to dye Orlon; however, the Orlon now produced has greatly improved dyeability in a variety of dye types. Some types of Orlon are specific to acid dyes and some to basic dyes, which can provide interesting cross-dyed effects. Orlon can be dyed in a wide range of colors and hues. The colors have satisfactory fastness to washing and light.

Resistance to Perspiration. All indications are that Orlon fabrics are not readily deteriorated by perspiration, but the color may be affected.

ORLON FIBER BLENDS

Orlon has many desirable properties that may be imparted to fabrics containing fibers other than Orlon, depending on the relative amount of each fiber used.

ORLON AND COTTON ■ In combination with cotton, Orlon adds light weight and body. The cotton contributes strength and absorbency. The fabric is wrinkle-resistant, retains its shape well, and provides easy care. A blend of 80 percent or more of Orlon with cotton will provide the general characteristics of a wash and wear fabric, such as is used for sports shirts.

ORLON AND WOOL ■ One of the outstanding characteristics of Orlon is its bulk, so that when the staple is blended with wool, the resulting fabric is lightweight and yet warm. It also has a soft hand but there may be some pilling. Fabrics of this combination have very good crease retention and wrinkle recovery. These blends are washable. Where there is a good proportion of Orlon, the fabrics seldom need pressing. A good blend for a wash and wear tailored garment should have 60 percent or more Orlon with the wool, though too much Orlon makes the fabric too bulky. Such a blend will also be stronger than an all-wool fabric.

ORLON AND SILK ■ Orlon and silk provide interesting cross-dyed and textured effects. Such blends have outstanding hand and excellent stability. In addition to the good appearance, the combination gives long wear. The Orlon contributes easy-care qualities and shape retention; the silk contributes absorbency and strength. The fabric is very resilient and may be warm, depending on its weight.

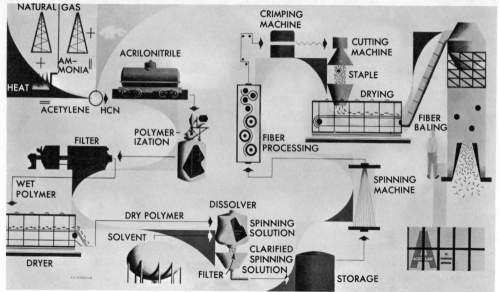

NATURAL GAS AMMONIA HEAT ACETYLENE HCN ACRILONITRILE CRIMPING MACHINE CUTTING MACHINE STAPLE DRYING FIBER BALING POLYMER-IZATION FILTER FIBER PROCESSING SPINNING MACHINE WET POLYMER DISSOLVER DRY POLYMER SOLVENT SPINNING SOLUTION CLARIFIED SPINNING SOLUTION DRYER FILTER STORAGE

A.F. ARNOLD

ACRILAN

Courtesy Chemstrand Company

Production of Acrilan acrylic fiber.

ORLON AND RAYON ■ To the versatility of rayon, Orlon adds wrinkle resistance and stability. New and unusual surface and dye effects, including cross dyes, are possible. Orlon provides a dry, warm, and soft hand. A wash and wear blend should have at least 70 percent Orlon with the rayon.

Orlon blended with a high wet-modulus rayon will provide a stronger fabric with the same general properties as that of a blend with regular rayon. An Orlon and modified-rayon blend could therefore have a lower proportion of Orlon.

ORLON AND ACETATE ■ A combination of Orlon and acetate in a fabric provides a soft, luxurious feel and excellent drapability. It also has excellent shape retention and good resilience. The fabric launders easily with mild soap and warm water, dries rapidly, and is easy to iron. The Orlon also provides greater resistance to sunlight. Neither Orlon nor acetate, however, is particularly absorbent, which presents a disadvantage in warm, humid weather. Such blends will be warm and clammy.

ORLON AND NYLON ■ The strength and abrasion resistance of nylon combined with the luxurious hand and covering power of Orlon produce attractive, warm, strong fabrics. Similar qualities of Orlon and nylon, such as wrinkle resistance, crease retention, and easy care, are increased when these fibers are combined. But such fabrics will not be very absorbent.

ORLON AND POLYESTER ■ Orlon improves the hand of a fabric when combined with a polyester fiber, giving better body comfort and warmth. The polyester fiber contributes even greater wrinkle resistance, especially under humid conditions. A 50/50 blend will provide good wash and wear characteristics. Such a fabric will generally wear well because of the strength of the polyester fibers and the good abrasion resistance of Orlon; however, it is likely to pill if care is not exercised.

METHOD OF MANUFACTURE

The processing of Acrilan is similar to that of Orlon. Natural gas and air are combined to form ammonia. Ammonia and natural gas are combined to produce hydrocyanic acid. Natural gas at elevated temperatures produces acetylene that, when combined with hydrocyanic acid, produces acrylonitrile. Then the acrylonitrile is polymerized. This polyacrylonitrile in powder form is dissolved by a suitable solvent and passed through spinnerets, and unlike Orlon acrylic fiber (which is extruded into air where it hardens), Acrilan fiber is formed in a coagulating bath to produce continuous filaments. The fibers, produced in semidull, bright, or solution-dyed varieties, are then washed, stretched, and crimped.

FORMS AND TYPES OF ACRILAN YARNS

The fibers, ranging from 1 to 15 denier, are produced in various types and processed into different forms of yarn depending upon the desired end uses.

FILAMENT YARNS ■ Acrilan is one of the two acrylic fibers produced in filament yarn form. There are two types—Type 13 and Type 40.

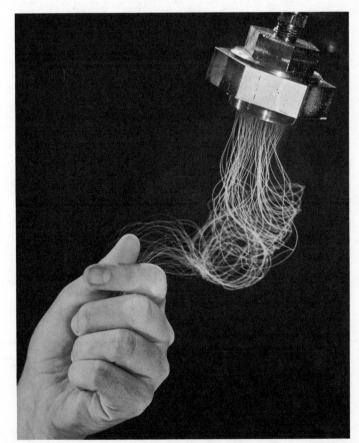

Acrilan acrylic fiber emerging from the spinneret.

Courtesy Chemstrand Company

Type 13 is particularly unique among acrylic fibers. It is semidull and solution-dyed in a wide range of colors, and it is produced in continuous filament form for processing into textured yarn. It is used for sweaters and other purposes where bulk yarns and textured effects are desirable. The solution-dyed feature provides excellent colorfastness; the filament form eliminates the problem of pilling.

Type 40 is also a continuous filament solution-dyed variety but is untextured to provide flat, smooth surface effects.

SPUN YARNS ■ Acrilan is also produced in several types of tow and staple. The tow is usually processed through the Pacific Converter or the Turbo stapler. The staple is cut in various lengths for processing on a cotton or wool system.

Type 16 is the basic variety of Acrilan acrylic fiber. It is produced in bright and semidull staple and tow forms. It is processed into various kinds of spun yarn. The yarn has a soft, pleasing hand, but there is a tendency to pill. It is used for a wide variety of fabrics for apparel.

Type 18 is a bright, solution-dyed staple. In other respects it is similar to Type 16.

Type 26 is produced in bright and semidull staple; Type 41, which is similar, is a semidull staple. Different potential-shrinkage properties allow for wet-processing development of different yarn textures and surface effects. The finished yarn has dimensional stability. Both types are used for pile yarn in carpets. They have gained considerable popularity due to their demonstrated ability to withstand heavy wear and their good durability on stairs, particularly on the edges where hard wear occurs. These types of Acrilan acrylic fiber have excellent resilience and retain their texture with little loss of thickness, which results in a lasting, good appearance. Acrilan carpet fiber is essentially static free. It is economical to maintain because, being an acrylic fiber, it has excellent stain resistance and ordinary soil is removed easily with water and a soap or detergent. It is resistant to mildew, moths, and other household insects, and is nonallergenic. It does, however, have the disadvantage of shriveling and melting when exposed to the heat of a flame or other burning objects, such as burning tobacco.

Type 36 is another basic variety of Acrilan acrylic fiber used for apparel fabrics. It is similar to Type 16 except that it is always semidull and comes in both regular and high-bulk varieties. It is also produced in tow and staple form.

Types 60 and 80 are semidull, staple varieties used for blankets. These blankets are lightweight and quite warm; they are also easy to care for, but there is some tendency to pill.

Type 70 is a white fiber for carpets. The whiteness facilitates dyeing to brighter and more vibrant colors.

Type 77 may be semidull or bright staple, and it is designed for sliver knitting used for pile knits (see pages 96–99). It is also used for fleece fabrics and coarse-count yarns for circular knitting and tufting.

Fiberfill is a crimped staple that is used in pillows because of its high resilience.

HIGH-BULK YARNS ■ Several of the yarn types discussed (both filament and staple) are used to produce various kinds of bulk yarns, and the properties and textural effects will vary with the type of fiber.

Acrilan may be finished similarly to Orlon. The principle finish is heat setting, which will permit semipermanent creases. Care must be taken in the process because dry heat in excess of 300 degrees Fahrenheit for more than a few minutes will yellow the fiber. With proper precautions, Acrilan fabrics will be bulky and silky.

EVALUATING ACRILAN FABRICS

Acrilan fabrics are made of various types of filament, spun, and high-bulk yarns. The characteristics of the fabrics depend on the type of fiber used and the kind of yarn produced, as well as the fabric construction and finish. The following properties of Acrilan acrylic fiber should be considered when judging Acrilan fabrics.

Strength. Acrilan is of moderate strength. It is slightly stronger than Orlon but weaker than the other acrylic fibers. Compared to those natural fibers with which it is sometimes blended, Acrilan is weaker than cotton but stronger than wool. It is also stronger than rayon and acetate. Its durability lies largely in the fact that it has good abrasion resistance as well as very good resilience.

Elasticity. Acrilan has little stretchability. This low elastic characteristic makes it particularly suitable for knitted wear and for garments where retention of shape is desired.

Resilience. As has been stated, Acrilan has very good resilience. It will not wrinkle easily and therefore is good for dresses, suits, and slacks. Some types are also used for rugs.

Heat Conductivity. Acrilan is similar in insulating value to the other acrylic fibers. In some forms, it is almost as warm as wool but lighter in weight. Thus, Acrilan can provide warmth with light weight. This combination makes Acrilan particularly suitable for blankets as well as for winter wear. It is cooler in filament form, since there is less bulking and insulative quality.

Drapability. The drapability of Acrilan varies with the type and form of the yarn as well as the fabric construction. However, it is generally quite satisfactory.

Absorbency. Like the other acrylic fibers, Acrilan has little absorbency. Nevertheless, Acrilan yarns, like Orlon yarns, have quite a bit of adsorbency and dry slowly because the water that gets trapped between the fibers evaporates slowly. This low absorbency gives Acrilan the advantage of resisting stains. Watery or oily substances, which stain other textiles, are not readily absorbed into Acrilan fabrics. They lie on the surface and can be easily removed by wiping, washing, or dry cleaning.

Cleanliness and Washability. It is relatively easy to keep Acrilan fabrics clean, and they may be readily dry-cleaned. Laundering is also no problem, although it is preferable to use a mild soap or detergent. Since Acrilan fabrics may be heat-set, it is often unnecessary to iron them, although some pressing with a moderately warm iron to smooth the cloth may be desired. Too hot an iron or heat for too long a period will cause yellowing.

Effect of Bleaches. Acrilan has good resistance to bleaches and, therefore, household bleaches may be used.

Shrinkage. Fabrics of Acrilan, when properly finished, have excellent dimensional stability. The consumer can therefore expect virtually no further shrinkage.

Effect of Heat. Acrilan shrinks when exposed to a temperature of 455 degrees Fahrenheit. At higher temperatures, it shrivels and decomposes.

Effect of Light. Acrilan has good resistance to the effect of sunlight although it is not so resistant as Orlon. Compared to other fibers, it is one of the most light-resistant textiles, and this indicates its value for outdoor uses.

Resistance to Mildew. Like the other acrylic fibers, Acrilan is wholly resistant to mildew. Any mildew that forms on the surface can be easily removed, and there will be no damage to the fabric.

Resistance to Moths. Acrilan is unaffected by moths. Together with its warmth and loft, Acrilan is, in this respect, well suited for both garments and rugs. This provides a particularly good advantage over wool.

Reaction to Alkalies. Acrilan has good resistance to weak alkalies. Its resistance decreases as the strength of the alkali, the temperature, and the length of immersion increase.

Reaction to Acids. Acrilan has good resistance to strong mineral acids as well as to organic acids.

Affinity for Dyes. Since some types of Acrilan are solution-dyed, they need not be dyed again and do have excellent colorfastness. Other types are dyed by a variety of dyes as appropriate to each type in a wide range of colors, which generally have good fastness to light and water.

Resistance to Perspiration. Acrilan is also resistant to perspiration.

ACRILAN FIBER BLENDS

Acrilan is readily adaptable to blending with other fibers. The chief blends are with cotton, wool, rayon, and acetate.

ACRILAN AND COTTON ■ In combination with cotton, Acrilan adds warmth, light weight, and wrinkle resistance. The cotton provides strength. The fabric can be laundered and pressed easily.

ACRILAN AND WOOL ■ The primary value of blending Acrilan and wool is to provide the same warmth as an all-wool fabric but with less weight. The

Acrilan acrylic fiber being measured for blending with other fibers, such as cotton, wool, rayon, or acetate.

Courtesy Chemstrand Div.

combination also provides a resilient, wrinkle-resistant fabric that nevertheless tends to retain creases and pleats. Acrilan will also add strength but too much of this fiber in the blend will make the fabric too bulky.

ACRILAN AND RAYONS ■ Various surface and color effects are possible by blending Acrilan and viscose rayon. The Acrilan provides greater resilience and shape retention. Such a fabric will also be warmer than an all-rayon fabric. Acrilan blended with a high wet-modulus rayon will provide similar results, but it will be stronger due to the greater strength (both wet and dry) of the modified rayon.

ACRILAN AND ACETATE ■ A combination of Acrilan and acetate produces a soft, warm fabric with good draping qualities, good shape retention, and resilience. The fabric can be easily laundered or dry-cleaned.

ACRILAN AND NYLON ■ The strength of nylon and the warmth of Acrilan together can produce a blend that would also be resilient and stable.

CRESLAN

METHOD OF MANUFACTURE

Creslan acrylic fiber is produced from a copolymer containing a high percentage of acrylonitrile. After polymerization, acrylonitrile copolymer is dissolved in a solvent, filtered, and deaerated to form a spinning solution. A delustering agent may be added. The spinning solution is extruded through a spinneret into an aqueous bath from which it emerges as filaments of 1.5 to 15 denier. The tow is washed to remove the solvent and stretched to impart fiber properties. It is also crimped and treated with an antistatic to aid textile processing. Creslan acrylic fiber is produced in bright and semidull varieties as filament, tow, or staple cut into lengths of 1½ to 4½ inches, depending on the processing needs.

FORMS AND TYPES OF CRESLAN YARNS

Several types of Creslan acrylic fibers are produced for different purposes as filament or staple. Modification of the method of manufacture of Creslan fiber permits the production of low-, medium-, and high-shrinkage varieties for staple use.

FILAMENT YARN ■ Creslan filament fiber is produced for apparel and for industrial purposes.

Type 63 is for apparel purposes. It is an extra-white filament that has a silk-like, luxurious hand. It takes dyes very well and provides processing and styling versatility.

SPUN YARNS ■ Creslan staple is spun into yarn for apparel, blankets, and rugs. Versatility in the production and application of these spun yarns is due to the variations in subtypes of the basic Types 58 and 61 Creslan acrylic fibers. Low-shrinkage Type 58, produced as staple, may be spun on a cotton, rayon, or woolen system. Low-shrinkage Type 61, used for similar purposes, is produced as staple for conventional spinning and as tow for processing on the Pacific converter or Turbo stapler into spun yarn.

BULK YARN ■ Low-, medium-, and high-shrinkage varieties of Types 58 and 61 Creslan staple may be blended and then spun into yarn. Subsequent immersion of such a yarn in boiling water results in hardly any shrinkage in the low-shrinkage fibers but a great deal in the high-shrinkage fibers. This results in a lightweight, spongy, bulky yarn.

FINISHING CRESLAN FABRICS

Fabrics of Creslan may generally be given the same kinds of finishes given to fabrics of other acrylic fibers. Like the other acrylic fibers, Creslan is thermoplastic. Fabrics and garments of Creslan fiber can be permanently heat-set. This is a major finishing treatment given to such products. They can be given pleats, creases, or any shape, heated under carefully controlled conditions, and thereafter retain the desired shape through repeated wearing, washing, and dry cleaning. Proper finishing establishes dimensional stability and enhances the aesthetic qualities inherent in Creslan.

EVALUATING CRESLAN FABRICS

The properties of fabrics of Creslan will depend on the properties of the fiber itself, the type of spun yarn used, and the construction of the fabric. The use of the Creslan trademark is controlled by the American Cyanamid Company through its quality testing program, which requires that fabrics meet certain standards in order to carry the name of its acrylic fiber. The performance of such fabrics is based upon the following general characteristics.

Strength. As compared to Orlon and Acrilan, Creslan staple fiber has from equal to above equal strength. It is, however, weaker than Zefran or Zefkrome acrylic fibers. On the other hand, Creslan filament is stronger than any of these staple, and the serviceability of Creslan fiber will vary with the type. Compared to all fibers, generally, Creslan is of moderate strength. Its resilience adds good abrasion resistance to its strength. Fabrics of Creslan, therefore, give good wear.

Elasticity. Creslan has very little stretchability whether in staple or filament form. Fabrics of Creslan will resist stretching and sagging.

Resilience. Creslan fiber has excellent resilience, and fabrics of Creslan will not wrinkle easily. Wrinkles that may form due to crushing will tend to fall out readily, thereby contributing to a neat appearance.

Heat Conductivity. Like other acrylic fibers, Creslan does not conduct heat rapidly. In filament form, the fibers can be made into yarns for fabrics that can feel comfortable but not warm next to the skin. On the other hand, the crimp plus potential shrinkage of the staple can produce spun yarns of various bulk and loft to provide warmth. Creslan is about 25 percent lighter than cotton and about 10 percent lighter than wool. Consequently, yarns of Creslan are relatively lightweight. Summer fabrics can be light and cool. Winter fabrics of Creslan can provide adequate warmth for such outerwear as sweaters, jackets, and coats.

Drapability. Creslan fiber has a good, pleasant hand, and the fabrics have good draping quality.

Absorbency. Generally speaking, Creslan is about the least absorbent of the acrylic fibers. Its wicking action, or adsorbency, accounts for its comfort when worn next to the skin. The low absorbency gives fabrics of Creslan the property of resisting stains. Such fabrics dry fairly rapidly when wet.

Cleanliness and Washability. Fabrics made of Creslan can be easily laundered with any mild soap in warm water. They may be safely put into automatic washers and dryers, and the fabrics tend to resist pilling. Strong soaps containing much alkali will cause yellowing, particularly if the water is very hot.

Creslan fabrics may be safely dry-cleaned. They have good dimensional stability. If properly constructed and finished, they will retain pleats and shape after washing or dry cleaning. If ironing is desired, Creslan fabrics may be pressed while damp with a warm iron as used for nylon.

Effect of Bleaches. Fabrics made of Creslan that are of Types 61 or 63 have a built-in extra whiteness and should not require bleaching. When bleaching is desired for any kind of fabric containing Creslan, sodium chlorite is recommended for the best results.

Shrinkage. When properly finished, fabrics of Creslan have excellent dimensional stability and do not shrink or pull out of shape.

Effect of Heat. Creslan staple gets tacky and sticks at temperatures of 400 to 440 degrees Fahrenheit, while Creslan filament sticks at temperatures of 430 to 460 degrees Fahrenheit. These temperatures indicate that fabrics of Creslan may be safely ironed, if need be, at temperatures about those used for nylon fabrics. Higher temperatures will cause Creslan to react as do other thermoplastic fibers: they will shrivel and melt.

Effect of Light. Creslan has excellent resistance to degradation by sunlight. It is therefore very well suited for fabrics for apparel and home furnishings that are likely to have lots of exposure to the sun (though colors may still fade, depending upon the dye used).

Resistance to Mildew. Creslan is absolutely resistant to deterioration by mildew.

Resistance to Moths. Creslan is unaffected by moths and their larvae or by carpet beetles.

Reaction to Alkalies. Creslan has fair resistance to alkalies. Exposure to alkalies at high temperatures will cause yellowing. Higher concentrations and higher temperatures will cause more severe damage.

Reaction to Acids. In general, Creslan has excellent resistance to acids. There is a tendency to bleach when the acid concentration is high.

Affinity for Dyes. Staple Creslan fiber can be dyed with a variety of dyes, depending upon the type. Filament Creslan fiber is readily dyeable with disperse and basic dyes. This provides versatility in dyeing, including cross-dyeing applications, with a wide range of colors of generally good fastness to light, washing, and crocking.

Resistance to Perspiration. All indications are that fabrics of Creslan are not readily deteriorated by perspiration.

CRESLAN FIBER BLENDS

Fabrics are presently available in blends of Creslan with cotton, wool, mohair, and rayons, all of which have a wide range of differences in hand, texture, appearance, and application.

CRESLAN AND COTTON ■ This blend may be expected to provide a relatively durable, serviceable fabric. A properly blended fabric that meets the established quality standards will retain the desirable wrinkle-resistant, shape-retentive, and wash and wear characteristics of Creslan. The cotton will contribute strength and absorbency. The blended fabric will be lightweight and comfortable.

CRESLAN AND WOOL ■ Depending upon the kind of yarn and the kind of finish used, fabrics of Creslan and wool may have textures ranging from soft to crisp. They provide good drape and are shape retentive and wrinkle resistant. Depending upon the fabric and garment, they may be washed and should need only light pressing.

CRESLAN AND MOHAIR ■ This blend provides a silky, luxurious hand and good draping qualities. Both fibers contribute resilience. Creslan adds the qualities of shape retention and easy care; mohair contributes strength.

CRESLAN AND RAYONS ■ Blends of Creslan and viscose rayon provide a comfortable fabric. The rayon provides absorbency; Creslan contributes resilience, shape retention, and easy care. For greater durability and service, a blend of Creslan and a modified rayon should prove a good combination.

ZEFRAN ZEFKROME

METHOD OF MANUFACTURE

Precise information concerning the production of Zefran cannot be given since the manufacturer is reluctant to divulge information concerning the manufacturing processes or the raw materials used. All that can be stated is that Zefran is a nitrile-acrylic alloy produced with somewhat the same general procedure used in the manufacture of acrylic fibers with modifications whereby a dye-receptive polymer is grafted to the acrylonitrile molecule. The copolymer alloy is extruded from the spinneret as white, bright, or semidull tow. It is stretched, crimped, and cut into staple lengths of 1½ to 4½ inches.

The process for producing Zefkrome acrylic fiber is a variant of the Zefran process. The production of Zefkrome introduces a new concept in that it is precolored by the manufacturer during an appropriate stage of processing prior to its finished form. (This method is not to be confused with solution dyeing, in which the color is incorporated into the solution prior to extrusion. The precolor technique permits greater flexibility in the manufacture of the product than does solution dyeing, and it still provides good color quality and excellent fastness.) As will be noted later in the discussion, the variation in the method of manufacture of Zefkrome results in certain modifications in properties from those of Zefran. The precolored fiber is produced as tow and then stretched, crimped, and cut into staple lengths of 2, 3, and 4 inches.

FORMS AND TYPES OF ZEFRAN AND ZEFKROME YARNS

Zefran staple is produced in two types: Zefran 100 and the newer basic dyeable Zefran 200. Zefkrome staple is produced only in one type. All can be processed into spun and high-bulk yarns on conventional textile equipment. These yarns contribute good wrinkle recovery, press retention, and dimensional stability to fabrics. They impart a pleasing hand and are nonirritating and nonallergenic.

SPUN YARNS ■ Zefran 100, produced in 2, 3, and 6 denier staple, is suitable for processing into yarn on the cotton, woolen or worsted system. Zefran 200 is produced in 3 denier staple and tow as well as 15 denier staple. All types can also be blended with cotton, rayon, or wool and spun into yarn. The yarns can be fuzzy or smooth.

Zefkrome is produced in 3, 6, and 15 denier and, depending upon the staple length, may be spun on a cotton or wool system. The yarns will accordingly vary in texture.

HIGH-BULK YARNS ■ The crimp imparted to Zefran and Zefkrome fibers is sharp and durable and provides loft and resilience. These fibers may be spun into yarns that are high in bulk and low in weight. Fabrics of Zefran and Zefkrome can be thick and resilient, having more warmth or insulating value than comparable fabrics of cotton, rayon, or wool.

FINISHING ZEFRAN AND ZEFKROME FABRICS

Various finishes have been and are being developed for fabrics of Zefran and Zefkrome. Such fabrics may be either dyed or printed in a wide variety of colors. They may be napped to give a soft, warm hand and heat-set to retain pleats, creases, and shape in fabric or garments.

EVALUATING ZEFRAN AND ZEFKROME FABRICS

The principle properties of the three types of Zefran and Zefkrome are generally similar. However, the variations that do exist are significant in the ultimate performance of the fabrics.

Strength. Zefran and Zefkrome are stronger than any of the other acrylic staple fibers, and Zefkrome is slightly stronger than Zefran. When compared to the natural fibers, they are weaker than cotton, linen, or silk but stronger than wool. Zefran and Zefkrome have very good abrasion resistance and can be used to produce relatively durable fabrics.

Elasticity. The elasticity of Zefran and Zefkrome is similar and approximates the low elasticity of Acrilan. This characteristic makes Zefran and Zefkrome suitable for garments that are required to hold their shape, such as knitted wear.

Resilience. Zefran and Zefkrome have excellent resilience. Fabrics of these fibers have an extremely high rate of wrinkle recovery. This characteristic makes these acrylic fibers highly desirable for blends.

Heat Conductivity. Neither Zefran nor Zefkrome has a high rate of heat conductivity. The cross-sectional shape is somewhat round and therefore the fibers lack the natural bulking characteristic of an acrylic fiber like Orlon. But both Zefran and Zefkrome can be permanently crimped to provide sufficient bulk in yarn form, producing the desirable insulative effect. In fact, fabrics of Zefran and Zefkrome can be produced that will be warmer than comparable fabrics of wool. These fabrics will also be lighter in weight than wool, though not quite so lightweight as fabrics of some of the other acrylic fibers.

Drapability. Both Zefran and Zefkrome have a pleasant, soft hand and provide satisfactory draping qualities.

Absorbency. Zefran is slightly more absorbent than Zefkrome, and both are a little more absorbent than any of the other acrylic fibers. They are, however, much less absorbent than any of the natural fibers or some of the man-made fibers. This means that, while fabrics of Zefran and Zefkrome will dry more slowly than fabrics of most acrylic fibers, they will dry faster than cotton, wool, or rayon.

The greater absorbency of Zefran and Zefkrome compared with the other acrylic fibers is due to their alloy composition. The grafted copolymer in the fibers' molecular structure provides some additional absorbency. This greater absorbency not only provides greater comfort in humid weather but also reduces the fabric's tendency to develop static electricity.

Cleanliness and Washability. Although fabrics of Zefran and Zefkrome are made of spun yarns and have varying degrees of fuzz that catch and hold dirt, Zefran and Zefkrome have the advantages of cleanliness and washability. They develop less static electricity than most other acrylic fibers and consequently do not easily attract or hold dust particles on their surfaces. Also, fabrics of Zefran and Zefkrome have excellent wrinkle recovery and excellent shape retention. Creases placed in fabrics of Zefran and Zefkrome stay in extremely well after repeated washing and require no ironing. This makes Zefran and Zefkrome highly suitable for wash and wear garments. For best results, the garment should be made entirely of Zefran or Zefkrome. When washing these fabrics, it is best to use a mild soap though hot water may be safely used. Such fabrics may also be safely dry-cleaned.

Effect of Bleaches. Ordinary household bleaches may be safely used on fabrics of Zefran and Zefkrome.

Shrinkage. Properly finished fabrics of Zefran and Zefkrome have very little residual shrinkage. Such fabrics also have good dimensional stability.

Effect of Heat. Zefran and Zefkrome have a sticking temperature of 490 degrees Fahrenheit. Consequently, if ironing is desired, fabrics of Zefran and Zefkrome may be safely ironed at temperatures of up to 350 degrees Fahrenheit, which is higher than for fabrics of other acrylic fibers. When subjected to flame or excessive heat, Zefran and Zefkrome will fuse and shrink away.

Effect of Light. Zefran and Zefkrome are highly resistant to degradation from exposure to sunlight. Along with other desirable properties, this indicates that Zefran and Zefkrome are very suitable for drapery and upholstery fabrics.

Resistance to Mildew. Zefran and Zefkrome are wholly resistant to mildew and are therefore undamaged even when hung or stored under damp conditions.

Resistance to Moths. Fabrics of Zefran and Zefkrome are unaffected by moths or other insects. Like the acrylic fibers, this offers a decided advantage over wool.

Reaction to Alkalies. Zefran and Zefkrome are resistant to weak alkalies. Although they will turn yellow when subjected to strong hot alkalies, they may be safely subjected to mercerizing conditions when blended with cotton.

Reaction to Acids. Zefran has excellent resistance to acids of up to 40 percent concentration.

Affinity for Dyes. Due to its composition, Zefran takes dyes better than most of the other acrylic fibers. Satisfactory dyes are available for essentially all colors and end uses. Vat dyes generally provide good-to-excellent lightfastness and excellent washfastness. Acid, basic, sulfur, direct, and acetate dyes may be used, but their colorfastness is not generally as good. Such dyes, however, may be necessary when Zefran is blended with fibers that require specific dyes to obtain certain colors.

Zefkrome is the only fiber that is precolored in the manufacturing process in a wide range of good shades. The process produces excellent colorfastness.

Resistance to Perspiration. There is no indication that perspiration will deteriorate Zefran, but the color may be affected.

ZEFRAN FIBER BLENDS

Zefran has been blended to a limited extent with cotton, rayon, and wool. Development of blends continues. The following results have been achieved.

ZEFRAN AND COTTON ■ A blend of Zefran and cotton provides a comfortable, durable fabric that will wash easily, dry fairly rapidly, and need little or no ironing. The Zefran provides shrink resistance, resilience, and shape retention. Cotton increases the absorbency and lowers the cost of the fabric.

ZEFRAN AND WOOL ■ A blend of 50 percent Zefran and 50 percent wool has twice the wrinkle recovery of an all-wool fabric and almost as much wrinkle recovery as an all-Zefran fabric. Due to the Zefran, garments of such a blend show excellent dimensional stability after repeated home washings. They show no appreciable shrinkage and need little ironing. They are warm, comfortable to wear, and do not pill. Zefran also provides greater strength, and the combination provides good abrasion resistance, making a durable fabric.

ZEFRAN AND RAYON ■ A major contribution of Zefran in a blend of Zefran and rayon is wrinkle recovery and dimensional stability. A blend of 50 percent Zefran with 50 percent rayon will have three times the wrinkle recovery of an all-rayon fabric and actually be more resilient than an all-wool fabric. Zefran will also provide greater strength. Rayon will provide greater absorbency and contribute to the comfort of such a fabric. Such a blend may be classified among the wash and wear fabrics.

COMPARISON OF ACRYLIC FIBERS

The chart on page 388 is a summary composite based on information supplied by the producers of these fibers and on evaluations of the performance of the fibers as described in the literature included in the bibliography. The reader is reminded that variations do exist within each trade name as well as blend combination, type of yarn, fabric weight, construction, and finish and that these factors will affect the performance. It is also possible that future changes in the chemical and physical compositions of these fibers may alter their performance.

COMPARISON OF PROPERTIES—THE ACRYLIC FIBERS

	ORLON	ACRILAN	CRESLAN	ZEFRAN	ZEFKROME
Strength	Fair	Fair	Fair to good	Good	Good
Abrasion resistance	Fair	Fair to good	Fair	Good	Good
Elasticity	Low; good extensibility for Sayelle	Low	Low	Low	Low
Resilience	Very good	Very good	Excellent	Excellent	Excellent
Absorbency	Little	Little	Little	Little	Little
Laundering care	Varies; requires care, use mild soap or detergent; may pill	Launders readily; some pilling may occur	Easy care with mild soap; relatively pill resistant	Easy care with mild soap; fair resistance to pilling	Easy care with mild soap; good resistance to pilling
Ironing temperature	Moderately warm	Moderately warm	Moderately warm	At rayon setting or slightly higher	At rayon setting or slightly higher
Shrinkage	Virtually none	Virtually none	Virtually none	Virtually none	Virtually none
Household bleaches	All safe	All safe	Requires sodium chlorite; some types have built-in whiteness	All safe	All safe
Resistance to light	Excellent	Very good	Excellent	Very good	Excellent
Resistance to mildew	Wholly resistant	Wholly resistant	Wholly resistant	Wholly resistant	Wholly resistant
Reaction to alkalies	Fair to good to weak alkalies	Good to weak alkalies	Fair to weak alkalies	Fair to weak alkalies	Fair to weak alkalies
Reaction to acids	Very resistant	Very resistant	Excellent resistance; tendency to bleach	Excellent resistance	Excellent resistance
Resistance to perspiration	Good	Good	Good	Good	Good
Colorfastness	Good	Good; excellent for solution-dyed types	Good	Good	Excellent

1 What is an acrylic fiber?

2 Give the trade names for the five acrylic fibers. Which companies produce each one?

3 How does Orlon Sayelle differ from regular Orlon acrylic fiber?

4 Compare the strength of the various acrylic fibers with each other and with other fibers.

5 Compare the elasticity of the various acrylic fibers with each other and with other fibers.

6 Discuss the washability and general care of fabrics made of acrylic fibers.

7 What general types of yarns can be made from each of the acrylic fibers?

8 Discuss the reactions of each of the acrylic fibers (a) to acids, (b) to alkalies, (c) to perspiration.

9 Discuss the affinity for dyes and the colorfastness of each of the acrylic fibers.

10 What are the general properties of acrylic fibers that tend to improve blends?

11 How are each of the acrylic fibers affected (a) by mildew, (b) by moths, (c) by other insects?

12 What are the main differences between Zefran and Zefkrome?

13 (a) Which acrylic fiber is solution-dyed? (b) Which is precolored? (c) What is the difference in processing?

As the identification implies, modacrylic fibers are modified acrylic fibers consisting of less acrylonitrile in combination with other polymers. Consequently, there are differences in production and in certain properties between acrylics and modacrylics.

HISTORY OF MODACRYLICS

The Carbide and Carbon Chemicals Company started experimenting with superpolymers in 1934. The company contributed much to the present knowledge of these substances, but it was not until 1949 that *Dynel,* a partly acrylic staple fiber, was developed. The first commercial plant started production of 5 million pounds annually in July, 1950. Since then, the company's name has been changed to the Union Carbide Chemicals Company, a division of Union Carbide Corporation; and the production and the use of Dynel have expanded.

In an effort to diversify its position in textile fibers, Eastman Chemical Products, Inc., a subsidiary of Eastman Kodak Company, also entered the acrylic fiber field. After due experimentation, the company announced the production of its own modified acrylic fiber, *Verel,* in March, 1956. Commercial production of Verel was begun in 1958 at newly developed facilities of the company's corporate associate, Tennessee Eastman Company, which also manufactures acetate fibers at Kingsport, Tennessee.

Until 1960 both Dynel and Verel were identified by their manufacturers as acrylics. Under the ruling of the Federal Trade Commission, they were reclassified as *modacrylics* and are now sold under that identification.

DYNEL

METHOD OF MANUFACTURE

The production of Dynel is derived from such basic substances as natural gas, salt, ammonia, and water. These are chemically combined to form two basic ingredients: acrylonitrile, which is the clear liquid used to produce acrylic and modacrylic fibers, and vinyl chloride, which is a gas used to produce vinyl plastics. When acrylonitrile and vinyl chloride are combined under heat and pressure, they copolymerize and form a white powdery resin. This resin is dissolved in acetone (the basic ingredient of nail polish removers) producing a viscous solution similar in appearance to that of acetate. It is then passed through spinnerets into a water bath from which it emerges as a tow or group of continuous filaments. The tow is dried, stretched, and annealed.

FORMS AND TYPES OF DYNEL YARNS

Dynel modacrylic fiber may be sold in tow form or cut into staple and crimped. It is generally produced as a semidull fiber, but it is also produced in several solution-dyed colors in the 3 denier weight. There are four types of Dynel fiber that can be processed into sliver for pile fabrics, into spun yarn for flat fabrics, or molded into such apparel as hats.

Type 150 is produced as uncrimped tow in a limited range of deniers. It is used for such specialty applications as wigs and hair pieces.

Type 180 is made in staple form in a variety of deniers. It has a wide array of uses from air filters to luxury furlike coats.

Type 183 is a controlled-high-shrinkage fiber produced in 3 denier tow or staple. It is used to produce high-bulk yarn and pile for furlike fabrics.

Type 197 is produced as bright or semidull staple. It is pill resistant and flame resistant as well as having a high level of abrasion resistance and soil resistance. It is suitable for carpets and other pile fabrics.

FINISHING DYNEL FABRICS

Dynel may be finished somewhat like the acrylic fibers. The outstanding feature is heat setting, which molds a fabric or garment into permanent shape and also permits permanent creases and pleats. These shapes are resistant to change due to wetting and are relatively permanent until the shaping temperature is again equaled or excelled.

The highly thermoplastic characteristic of Dynel gives it a thermoformable quality. Dynel fabrics, for example, may be permanently molded into hats. Wigs of Dynel may be given permanent settings.

Flow chart of the manufacturing process of Dynel.

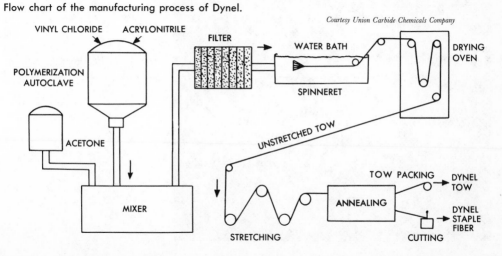

Courtesy Union Carbide Chemicals Company

The thermoplastic quality of Dynel is utilized in its dyeing. At temperatures above 205 degrees Fahrenheit, the fiber softens and the dyestuff penetrates to become an integral part of the fiber. The color thus becomes fixed in the fiber when it is cooled. During this process, however, the fiber becomes dull. Since the color of dull fiber is not as fast to light as lustrous fiber, Dynel must be semi-decated with steam to restore its luster and this must be followed by slow cooling to avoid setting creases.

EVALUATING DYNEL FABRICS

The manner in which the yarn is spun, the construction of the cloth, as well as the intrinsic properties of the Dynel fiber are all important factors in evaluating the fabric.

Strength. Dynel high-shrinkage fiber is the strongest of the three types, and all the Dynels are stronger than the other modacrylic fiber, Verel. Although Dynel is weaker than cotton, linen, or silk, it is two to three times as strong as wool. It is also stronger than regular rayon, acetate, Arnel, and the acrylics, but it is weaker than nylon. Dynel also has good abrasion resistance that assures long wear. This property makes Dynel very desirable for blending with other fibers that are not as strong.

Elasticity. Like the acrylic fibers, Dynel has very little stretchability, and the high-shrinkage type is even less elastic. This contributes to the dimensional stability and shape retention of Dynel fabrics.

Resilience. Dynel, particularly the type used for carpets, is highly resilient, thus assuring lasting loft (springiness) and softness. This resilience and loft make possible fabrics with an extremely pleasant and permanent nap that will not pill. Dynel is therefore a desirable fiber for blankets and such fabrics as flannel. Due to the high degree of resilience of Dynel, fabrics made of this fiber "bounce back" into shape. They do not wrinkle easily, and any wrinkles that may form fall out readily. Dynel fabrics hold their shape well even in damp weather.

Dynel emerges from the spinning bath as groups of endless fibers called tow.

Courtesy Union Carbide Chemicals Company

Dynel tow is cut to length, then crimped and sent by conveyor to the balers.

Courtesy Union Carbide Chemicals Company

Heat Conductivity. Dynel is a soft, bulky, warm fiber similar in insulating value to the acrylic fibers. It is about as warm and heavy as wool. The insulative property of Dynel produced in different deniers of various textures makes it very suitable for pile, furlike fabrics.

Drapability. The drapability of Dynel fabrics varies with the type and denier of the fibers. They may produce soft, flexible fabrics of good draping quality for skirts and drapes. On the other hand, they may produce slightly pliable or stiff materials for hats and for radio speaker grilles.

Absorbency. Dynel is the least absorbent of the modacrylic fibers. In fact, it is one of the least absorbent textile fibers, comparable to Kodel and Fortrel polyester fibers. This has certain disadvantages, such as making a garment uncomfortable in warm, humid weather. But it has the advantage of resistance to staining. Such stains as catsup, coffee, mustard, or ink come out in washing, leaving no trace.

Cleanliness and Washability. Dynel can be washed or dry-cleaned easily. It loses very little strength while wet and is not damaged by strong soaps or detergents. Dynel fabrics resist shrinking and retain their shape in washing and dry cleaning. The water temperature should, however, be below 160 degrees Fahrenheit; otherwise the fabric will become harsh. Dynel is one of the fastest drying fibers. Even heavily napped and knitted fabrics are relatively quick drying. Although Dynel can be washed in automatic washing machines, extreme agitation should be avoided as napped fabrics may pill.

Effect of Bleaches. Household bleaches may be safely used on Dynel fabrics.

Shrinkage. Properly finished Dynel fabrics have very good dimensional stability and normally will not shrink. However, when subjected to high temperatures, such as boiling water, Dynel fabrics could shrink unless held under tension. For this reason, fabrics of Dynel should be washed with water that is not too hot.

Effect of Heat. Dynel softens on application of heat and shrinks at about 260 degrees Fahrenheit. Dynel fabrics need little ironing. When ironing is desired, the iron should be warm or set at "rayon."

Although Dynel will melt and burn, it will not support combustion; it will stop burning when the flame is removed (unless the dyestuff is flammable).

Effect of Light. Although Dynel is not as resistant as Verel to the effect of sunlight, it has good resistance to deterioration from light. Dynel has about the same resistance as cotton to the effect of light. Over an extended period of time it darkens and weakens. It is satisfactory for use as curtains and draperies.

Resistance to Mildew. Like the acrylic fibers, Dynel is wholly resistant to mildew.

Resistance to Moths. Dynel is not damaged by moths or carpet beetles. Together with its warmth, this provides a particularly good advantage over wool. Dynel may therefore be safely used for rugs as well as clothing.

Reaction to Alkalies. Dynel has high resistance to strong alkalies. Common household cleaning alkalies, such as soap, ammonia, lye, and detergents, have no effect on Dynel. This resistance to such corrosive chemicals makes Dynel useful in industrial plants for clothes, gloves, filters, and the like.

Reaction to Acids. Dynel is extremely resistant to acids. In some industrial operations, Dynel work clothing is regularly washed in sulfuric and other strong acids to remove chemical contaminants.

Affinity for Dyes. Dynel can be dyed in a full range of light to dark colors with excellent fastness to fumes, crocking, washing, and good fastness to light. Almost the entire range of acetate dyestuffs, many of the direct dyes, and certain vat dyes can be used. As a result, dyestuffs can be selected to match nearly any color and withstand nearly every type of service required of the finished fabric.

As has been mentioned, solution dyeing is sometimes used in the production of Dynel. This technique is employed to produce such colors as black, brown, and gray for Dynel fibers that are to be used to make furlike fabrics. These dyes have excellent fastness to all conditions.

Resistance to Perspiration. Dynel is absolutely resistant to deterioration from perspiration.

DYNEL FIBER BLENDS

Dynel has been found to be an excellent blending fiber. It works well with other staple fibers and contributes worthwhile properties to fabrics.

DYNEL AND COTTON ■ In a blend of Dynel and cotton, Dynel contributes softness, warmth, and resistance to shrinkage. Cotton contributes strength. Together, the blend provides a durable, comfortable, launderable fabric. A satisfactory blend should contain 25 to 50 percent Dynel.

DYNEL AND WOOL ■ A combination of Dynel and wool provides a warm, resilient, wrinkle-resistant fabric. The Dynel contributes shape retention and greater strength. The bulking power of Dynel also means that more warmth is possible with less weight. The wool also reduces the tendency of Dynel to glaze and harden from a hot pressing iron or other application of heat. A satisfactory blend should have about 35 percent Dynel, with the rest wool.

DYNEL AND RAYON ■ To a rayon blend, Dynel contributes warmth, light weight, resilience, and shape retention. Rayon provides the needed absorbency for greater comfort. There should be a proportion of 25 to 30 percent Dynel with the rest rayon for satisfactory results.

DYNEL AND ACETATE ■ In combination, Dynel and acetate produce fabrics that are richly textured, warm, and resilient. They retain their shape and creases, and they drape well. Such a fabric, however, will have low absorbency. For satisfactory results, a combination of 25 to 30 percent Dynel with the rest acetate is desirable.

DYNEL AND NYLON ■ In a combination of Dynel and nylon, Dynel provides warmth, and nylon provides strength, abrasion resistance, and elasticity. Such a blend produces a resilient, wrinkle-resistant, shape-retentive fabric that launders easily and dries relatively fast.

DYNEL AND ORLON ■ One of the most outstanding of the successful Dynel blends is the furlike fabric of Dynel and Orlon made for women's coats. The original version of this blend was Borgana, a blend of Dynel and Orlon in the pile on a knit backing of 100 percent Dynel. Both fibers provided resistance to stretching and shrinking. Orlon contributed the softness, and Dynel was responsible for the luster and body.

As a result of Borgana's success, other similar fabrics were produced. Some used the same fiber combination. One used pile of Dynel and Orlon on a cotton back, and there were other combinations. The better known of these fabrics are O'llegro, Andante, Mutation, Glanara, Bakella, Dynasty, and Cloud No. 9. Their popularity has sprung from their ability to fill a long-felt need in the moderate- to better-priced coat field; that is, to provide warm, durable garments resembling expensive fur coats but at prices more people can afford.

VEREL

METHOD OF MANUFACTURE

The Tennessee Eastman Company, manufacturer of Verel, is reluctant to disclose its method of manufacture beyond the fact that it is composed of acrylonitrile and certain modifiers that are polymerized. The viscous solution is forced through a spinneret, and it coagulates as the solvent is removed. The filaments, which may be either bright or dull, are gathered into tow and then treated to make the fiber resistant to shrinking or stretching. The tow, composed of filaments of 3, 5, 8, 12, 16, or 24 denier, is then crimped and cut into staple.

FORMS AND TYPES OF VEREL YARNS

There are two basic types of Verel modacrylic fiber: Regular and Type III. Regular Verel is produced in six subtypes, and each type has a different degree and permanence of crimp to serve particular spinning processing and textural needs. These subtypes are as follows.

Type A is a general purpose fiber having a high crimp with good crimp retention.

Type B also has a high crimp but with less crimp retention.

Type C has a medium, nonpermanent crimp.

Type D has a low crimp, which is easily removed in the finishing process for pile fabrics.

Type F has a high crimp, which is also easily removed in the finishing process for pile fabrics.

Type HB has a very high, very permanent crimp.

Type III Verel is a high-shrinkage fiber. When subjected to boiling water, it will shrink from 43 to 48 percent. It is interesting to note that this characteristic diminishes over a period of time.

Since Verel is produced only in staple form, it can be made only into spun yarns on the cotton or wool system.

FINISHING VEREL FABRICS

Fabrics of Verel may be given finishes similar to those of other acrylic fibers. They may be dyed and may be napped to be given a very soft, luxurious, warm hand. Interesting textural effects can be obtained with the proper use of the appropriate type of Verel fiber. Verel fabrics may be heat-set to retain pleats, creases, and overall shape in garments.

EVALUATING VEREL FABRICS

All fabrics made of Verel are constructed from spun yarns. The spun yarn used to produce the fabric has a contributory effect on the characteristics of the fabric as well as on its construction. Even the type of Verel will have an effect on the characteristics of the fabric. The following properties, however, can be generally expected from fabrics of Verel.

Strength. Verel is of moderate strength. It is weaker than Dynel but compares favorably with the acrylics. Comparing Verel to the natural fibers, it is about twice as strong as wool but weaker than cotton, linen, or silk. Verel is stronger than regular rayon, acetate, and Arnel but is weaker than nylon. Fabrics of Verel have fairly good abrasion resistance.

Elasticity. The elasticity of Verel is comparable to Dynel and the acrylic fibers. It has very little stretchability, and there tends to be a moderate amount of recovery when it has been stretched. Verel fabrics therefore have good dimensional stability and shape retention.

Resilience. Verel has good resilience. Wrinkles tend to fall out easily, and wrinkles that persist will iron out readily at the "low" or "rayon" setting.

Heat Conductivity. Like the acrylic fibers, Verel does not conduct heat readily. In addition to its low heat conduction due to its chemical composition, Verel fibers have the added characteristic of having a cross-section dog-bone shape similar to that of Orlon fiber. As with Orlon fibers, this gives Verel fibers an overlapping quality that produces high bulk with relatively few fibers, which consequently makes fabrics lightweight. Also, the spun characteristic of Verel yarns provides air pockets among the staple that contribute insulation to the fabric. Like Dynel, it is suitable for warm, pile fabrics.

Drapability. The drapability of fabrics of Verel depends upon the type used and the denier and crimp of the yarn. The draping quality may be good.

Absorbency. Although Verel is less absorbent than either the natural fibers or rayon, acetate, Arnel, and nylon, it has some absorbency. In fact, it is much more absorbent than the acrylics and considerably more absorbent than Dynel. This means that Verel will not only absorb more moisture than the other acrylic fibers but will have a slightly more comfortable feeling in humid weather. Fabrics of Verel will dry more slowly than fabrics of the acrylic fibers.

Cleanliness and Washability. Fabrics of Verel may be washed or dry-cleaned by the conventional methods without difficulty. Verel has a tendency to pill, and the fabric should not be unduly rubbed. Soft brushing will reduce any pilling.

Verel is a thermoplastic fiber, and fabrics of Verel tend to retain their shape. Pleats and creases tend to stay in the fabrics after washing, and little ironing is needed.

Effect of Bleaches. Verel has an excellent white color and should not be bleached because such treatment causes the fiber to discolor.

Shrinkage. Properly finished fabrics of Verel will not shrink—they have good dimensional stability. Regular Verel fiber has very little shrinkage even at high water temperatures, and garments tend to retain their size and shape.

Effect of Heat. Like Dynel modacrylic fiber, Verel will not support combustion. It will, however, stick at temperatures above 390 degrees Fahrenheit. If ironing is done at a low setting, fabrics of Verel will iron easily. If the iron is too hot, such fabrics will stiffen and glaze.

Effect of Light. Verel is highly resistant to degradation from sunlight. This makes Verel well suited for drapery and similar home furnishing uses.

Resistance to Mildew. Verel is wholly resistant to mildew and can be safely used in damp climates.

Resistance to Moths. Verel is unaffected by moths or carpet beetles. This characteristic, along with its warmth and resilience, makes it suitable not only for clothing but also for rugs.

Reaction to Alkalies. Verel has good resistance to alkalies; however, excessive exposure to alkalies will cause discoloration. It is therefore best not to use strong soaps or other household cleaning agents.

Reaction to Acids. Verel has excellent resistance to acids.

Affinity for Dyes. Three classes of dyes—basic, acetate, and neutral-dyeing premetalized dyes—are considered the most effective for dyeing Verel in a wide range of colors from bright pastels to blacks and navies. Basic dyes are generally used when brighter shades are required, as for specialty fabrics. Acetate dyes may be used for brighter shades, in some cases, than can be obtained with premetalized dyes; but colorfastness is generally somewhat less. Neutral-dyeing premetalized dyes provide the best all-round lightfastness and washfastness.

The affinity of Verel to this variety of dyestuffs permits a multitude of dyeing effects including cross-dyeing when Verel is blended or combined with other fibers.

Resistance to Perspiration. All indications are that fabrics of Verel are not readily deteriorated by perspiration. The color may, however, be affected.

VEREL FIBER BLENDS

Verel has properties that make it very suitable for blending with other fibers. Some very desirable results can be accomplished.

VEREL AND COTTON ■ One of the important factors in determining the percentages of fibers in a blend of Verel and cotton is the cost. Cotton is relatively inexpensive and, therefore, the greater the amount of Verel in the blend, the more expensive the fabric. Fabrics containing up to 25 percent Verel are within reasonable price range.

To this type of blend, Verel contributes a soft, pliable hand with good drapability. Verel also provides dimensional stability, so that the fabric will not wrinkle easily, will resist shrinkage, and will retain its shape. Cotton contributes greater absorbency and additional strength. Fabrics of a Verel and cotton blend are used for underwear, children's sleepers, sports shirts, and outer garments.

VEREL AND WOOL ■ A blend of Verel and wool produces a warm fabric but light in weight due to the lightness and bulkiness of Verel fiber. Verel also provides greater strength, good shape retention, and wrinkle resistance. The thermoplastic characteristic of Verel also tends to hold creases and pleats in fabrics of such blends. Wool provides body and elasticity. Verel and wool blends are particularly well-suited for flannels.

VEREL AND RAYON ■ Verel has been satisfactorily blended with viscose rayon. Verel provides wrinkle resistance and shape retention. Rayon provides absorbency, coolness, and comfort.

VEREL AND ACETATE ■ Since both acetate and Verel are thermoplastic, such a blend can produce fabrics and garments with good wash and wear characteristics. In addition to the wrinkle-resistant and shape-retentive characteristics of both fibers, acetate can reduce the bulk of the fabric while Verel can add strength. One disadvantage of such a blend is the relatively low absorbency of both fibers, which would cause the fabric to be somewhat uncomfortable next to the skin in humid weather.

REVIEW QUESTIONS

1 How do modacrylics differ in composition from acrylics?

2 What are the trade names for the modacrylic fibers?

3 How do they differ from each other?

4 In what respects are they similar?

5 How do the several types of each of the basic modacrylics differ?

6 For what are these modacrylics best used?

7 What are the outstanding features of modacrylics?

8 What limitations do you see in modacrylics?

9 What blends are considered best for these modacrylics?

10 What features do these blends have?

21

THE SPANDEX FIBERS

LYCRA
VYRENE
GLOSPAN
BLUE C
NUMA

Spandex is an elastomeric fiber—that is, it has superior elasticity. Spandex fibers are capable of being stretched from about five to over seven times their length and returning immediately to their relaxed state upon release of tension. Yet, the elastic characteristic of spandex should not be confused with the elasticity of stretch nylon or rubber yarns. Spandex is different in both composition and properties from either of these. It may be described as being molecularly composed of a chainlike arrangement of soft, stretchable segments of polyurethane (the substance described on pages 157–159, which is used for foam laminating fabrics) linked together for reinforcement by hard segments. There is some degree of variation among the several spandex fibers.

HISTORY OF SPANDEX

For many years the only elastic substance that was available for use in apparel was rubber, and prior to 1930, yarn was cut from sheets of rubber. This method was replaced when a technique was developed for extruding liquid latex into a finer, round rubber yarn. To make the yarn suitable for garments, the rubber thread was covered by winding around it two layers of such yarns as cotton or rayon. These yarns became familiarly known by such names as *Lastex,* a trademark of the U.S. Rubber Company.

This type of yarn has several limitations: it is relatively coarse and heavy, and while the textile wrapping of such yarn may be dyed, the rubber thread does not take dyes readily and therefore shows or "grins through" when the yarn is stretched. The properties of these yarns are also affected by the particular properties of the textile plied around the rubber. In terms of serviceability, rubber has a relatively limited "flex life" and inadequate abrasion resistance. In addition, rubber is not too desirable for use next to the skin because it is deteriorated by oils, such as natural body oils, and various cosmetic and suntan lotions.

In 1947 the Heberlein Patent Corporation introduced *Helenca* stretch yarn, which is made from nylon filament. This was the first elastic yarn made entirely of a textile. Other similar stretch yarns soon followed. (See Chapter 4.) However, none of these are truly elastomeric yarns because the fibers themselves do not stretch materially—their stretchability is dependent upon the straightening out of the coil, curl, or crimp of the filaments. Furthermore, the amount of stretch is about one-quarter to one-half that of rubber. These stretch yarns do not have the ability to resist pulling, nor do they have the restraining power of rubber. While they have excellent stretch and form-fitting characteristics for such purposes as socks, tights, lingerie, and blouses, they lack the holding power needed for such garments as support hose and foundation garments.

This interest in elastic fibers was also pursued in another direction. Pioneer work done in the Du Pont laboratories led to the creation in 1947 of an experimental elastomeric textile identified as *Fiber K*. After much developmental effort, the fiber was introduced to the trade for evaluation in April, 1958. It was tested for the next year and a half by foundation garment manufacturers. This led to its commercialization as the first spandex fiber and the adoption by Du Pont of the *Lycra* trademark in October, 1959. The fiber met with some initial resistance from buyers who were skeptical about its alleged stretch and holding power. However, effective sales promotion overcame the resistance and the claims were proved. Having achieved good consumer acceptance, Du Pont began full scale production of Lycra in Waynesboro, Virginia, in 1962.

During this period, the U.S. Rubber Company was also much interested in elastomeric yarn, and they too engaged in research, development, and testing. After more than 10 years of preliminary work, in 1960 the company initiated production of its spandex fiber under the *Vyrene* trademark and began substituting it as the core for its Lastex yarn.

For many years the Firestone Tire and Rubber Company was also engaged in polyurethane research. *Spandelle* was it's first successful spandex fiber, which was made in 1958 at the Firestone Rubber & Latex Division in Fall River, Massachusetts. After much developmental work, a production plant was set up in 1961 by their subsidiary, the Firestone Synthetic Fibers Company in Hopewell, Virginia. The first commercial shipment of Spandelle was made in the fall of 1961 to Bauer & Black, a Division of the Kendall Co., for their now well-known *Fling* support hosiery. In the fall of 1962, Firestone formed a joint company with Courtaulds, Ltd. (of England) under the name of Elastomeric Fibers Co., Ltd. (EFCO). However, in 1966 Firestone discontinued its manufacture of Spandelle in the United States.

Other rubber companies also became very much interested in spandex. In 1963, for instance, Globe Manufacturing Company of Fall River, Massachusetts, introduced its *Glospan* spandex fiber.

The popularity of spandex fiber and the market demand for it has caused other textile companies to join into the competition. After considerable research at its Organic Chemicals Division in Bound Brook, New Jersey, the American Cyanamid Company introduced its spandex fiber, *Numa,* in 1964. The Chemstrand Division of Monsanto Company followed late in 1965 with the announcement of its *Blue C* spandex fiber.

The Celanese Fibers Company is currently engaged in developing a spandex fiber tentatively identified as *Fiber 32*. Union Carbide Corporation put its *Unel* spandex fiber into pilot-plant production in 1966, and Carr-Fulflex, Inc. also began manufacture of its *Duraspun* spandex fiber in that year. Thiokol Chemical Corporation also entered the field with pilot-plant manufacture of its spandex fiber in 1966. Other companies are also engaged in research programs.

In this highly competitive field, the specifics of the manufacture for each of the several spandex fibers are closely guarded by the respective producers. The chemistry and processing is generally described as being very complicated. Lycra, for example, is described as the result of the interaction of a diisocyanate with hydroxyl groups. All spandex fibers are segmented polyurethane and formed through spinnerets by either melt extrusion or solvent spinning. Variations among the methods of manufacture include the use of delustering agents, optical whiteners, and dye receptors.

TYPES OF SPANDEX FIBERS

The spandex fibers are generally produced as multifilaments that are coalesced, or fused together, at points of contact giving the appearance of mono-filaments. Monofilament spandex, such as Vyrene, is also available. Manu-facturers of multifilament spandex claim that this type provides greater flex life, suppleness, and draping quality. They also state that the multifilament type is less subject to damage from stitching because the needle passes between the filaments. The monofilament manufacturer counters with the advice that, if a blunt needle is used, it will push the fiber to the side and no puncture or damage will occur.

The deniers of the fibers range widely: from 40 to 3360. As a reference point, 70 denier is similar to the denier of nylon used for many fabrics. When 70 denier yarn is stretched 300 to 400 percent, the yarn reduces in diameter to almost 15 denier, which is the typical size for most women's nylon hosiery yarn.

LYCRA ■ This spandex fiber is produced as delustered, very white multifila-ment, each with a somewhat dog-bone cross section. These multifilaments are fused together at points of contacts in an irregular pattern to give the appearance of a monofilament fiber. The denier ranges from 70 to 1120, depending upon the number of multifilaments in the aggregate.

VYRENE ■ Vyrene is produced as a white, round monofilament in deniers ranging from 75 to 200.

GLOSPAN ■ Glospan is produced as fused multifilaments. They are white, irregular in shape, and arranged in an irregular pattern forming deniers ranging from 40 to 2920. Glospan is manufactured in two types: S-1 and S-5. The latter has greater stretch but lower holding power.

BLUE C ■ This fiber is also produced as fused multifilaments arranged in an irregular pattern. It is very white and comes in deniers ranging from 70 to 3360.

NUMA ■ Numa is another very white coalesced multifilament spandex of irregularly shaped fiber arranged in an irregular pattern. The deniers originally were in the medium range of 140 through 560, but the company has been working on the development of finer deniers.

FORMS OF SPANDEX YARNS

Spandex fibers are made into several forms of yarn depending upon the functions to be served. The factors that determine the selection of the form of yarn include the desired amount of elasticity, power, hand, fabric sheerness and styling, the yarn's resemblance to the other fibers in the fabric in which it will be used, and fabric end use.

BARE YARNS ■ The extruded, fused multifilaments and the monofilament spandex may be used without being covered. These bare yarns are utilized where lighter, sheerer, more supple, and more elastic fabrics are desired. Bare spandex yarns are more economical due to the elimination of the covering operation and the greater fabric yield that results from cutting smaller garments with a higher stretch level.

Bare yarns are incorporated into Raschel power-net and circular-knit fabrics for foundation garments and swimwear. They may also be used for support hosiery and sock tops.

COVERED YARNS ■ Spandex fiber is covered by wrapping yarn of any other fiber around it, which is the method originally used to cover rubber for apparel use. The stretch of spandex is limited by the extent to which the spiral of the cover yarn can be pulled. Covered spandex yarns also have the appearance and hand of the yarn used for covering. Covered yarns are used for Raschel power-net and circular-knit fabrics, as well as other fabrics that require stretch and good holding power, such as for foundation garments, swimwear, and support hose.

CORE-SPUN YARNS ■ The core-spun technique is somewhat similar to that for producing covered spandex yarn. By application of a conventional cotton or wool spinning system, a roving of covering fiber (or a blend of fibers) is twisted to form a sheath of staple fiber around the spandex core that is held under tension and subsequently relaxed. The hand and texture of the yarn is determined by the covering staple, and the elasticity is limited by the length to which the twisted sheath may be extended. The spandex core of such yarns may be as little as 5 to 15 percent of the total fiber content, but it will provide more stretch and holding power than thermoplastic stretch yarns of similar diameter.

Core-spun yarns are claimed to have greater versatility and application than the above-mentioned spandex yarns. Consequently, they are being utilized in a wide variety of woven as well as knitted fabrics including dresses, blouses, slacks, suits, sportswear, coats, uniforms, and raincoats.

INTIMATE BLEND SPUN YARNS ■ Much interest has been expressed regarding yarns spun of spandex fibers blended with inelastic fibers. As a textile fiber, spandex has many properties that make it suitable for blending. Its superior stretch characteristic has resulted in considerable experimentation in the development of blends of spandex staple with other fiber staple. These include promising blends of 4 to 30 percent spandex that is spun with other fibers into staple yarn. These blends provide sufficient elasticity and holding power for woven and knitted fabrics.

The most common finishes given to fabrics containing spandex fiber are as follows.

Bleaching—for whiteness
Semi-decating—for improved hand
Calendering and pressing—for smoothness
Dyeing and printing—for decorative effects
Heat setting—for dimensional stability
Water repellency—for rainwear

Spandex fibers are inherently white; bleaching is therefore done only when the other fibers used in the yarn or fabric require it. However, since spandex fibers are yellowed by chlorine, a reducing bleach that does not contain chlorine should be used. Optical whiteners may be used safely.

Semi-decating, calendering, and pressing are done under careful conditions without tension and at appropriately low temperatures to avoid possible loss of elasticity.

Heat setting is done under carefully controlled conditions to maintain the required degree of elasticity of the spandex fiber and to impart dimensional stability to the fabric. The degree of elasticity is reduced, but if properly done, it can maintain a level of elasticity appropriate for the particular end use of the fabric.

Spandex fibers have very low absorbency. However, blended fabrics containing other fibers that are absorbent may be treated with a water repellent.

EVALUATING FABRICS CONTAINING SPANDEX

Fabrics are never made entirely of spandex fiber. As has been indicated, spandex yarns are frequently made in combination with other fibers. These yarns are generally incorporated with other yarns in fabrics. When bare spandex yarns are used, they are always utilized in conjunction with other yarns in fabrics. The form, amount, and arrangement of spandex yarns used in fabrics depend upon the type and construction of the garment, the fabric weight, and the amount of stretch and holding power desired. In fact, the primary purpose of using spandex is to obtain elasticity with holding power.

When considering the performance and care of fabrics containing spandex, attention must be given to the fiber used with it as well as to the fabric's construction and finish. In addition, some consideration should be given to the particular spandex fiber used. While many of the properties of these fibers are similar, certain differences do exist among them.

Strength. Spandex fiber does not reach the breaking point until after the fiber has been stretched to its maximum length. This point is not usually reached in general use and wear. The strength of the various spandex fibers is quite adequate. The great flexibility of spandex fibers further adds to their serviceability and durability. In comparison to rubber, spandex is far superior in break strength and flex life. The abrasion resistance of the various spandex fibers is good, thereby contributing to their good wearing characteristics.

Elasticity. Elasticity is the prime characteristic of spandex along with its holding power. Spandex fibers may be stretched from 500 to above 700 percent—that is, five to over seven times the relaxed state before breaking. This is almost as much as rubber yarn, which may be stretched to a maximum of about 750 percent. Also, the restraining force, or power, of spandex is about twice that of rubber that has been stretched 100 percent (or twice its length). Spandex is almost twice as elastic as the stretch nylons and exceeds their holding power by about six times.

The most elastic spandex fiber is Glospan Type S-5, which has a maximum elongation of about 725 percent. However, its power is lower than the others. Vyrene may be stretched to about 700 percent, and Glospan Type S-1 may be stretched about 600 percent. Lycra, Blue C, and Numa spandex fibers are comparable with a stretchability of about 500 to 600 percent. All the spandex fibers have instant and almost complete elastic recovery that is substantially retained, along with their holding power, over extended periods of repeated washing and wearing.

The great elasticity of spandex far exceeds the requirements for comfort and power in apparel. As a base of reference, a study by the textile industry reveals that body movements require the following amounts of skin extension.

Back (across the shoulders)—13% to 16%   Knee (lengthwise)—35% to 45%
Elbow (lengthwise)—35% to 40%   Knee (circumference)—12% to 14%
Elbow (circumference)—15% to 22%   Buttock—4% to 6%

Standards of stretchability have been established from these figures. For stretch that is sufficient to provide comfort and freedom of body movement, stretchability of 25 to 30 percent with a recovery loss of no more than 2 to 5 percent is recommended. This amount of "comfort stretch" is suitable for a wide variety of apparel such as blouses, shirts, and jackets, as well as such home furnishings as slipcovers and upholstery.

For sufficient power to provide support, stretch of 30 to 50 percent with a recovery loss of no more than 5 to 6 percent is recommended. This amount of "power stretch" is suitable for support hose, foundation garments, skiwear, swimwear, and other athletic apparel, as well as for industrial uses. Depending upon the end use of the fabric the power stretch may be more than 50 percent, in which case a greater amount of spandex fiber must be incorporated into the fabric.

It is apparent that spandex fibers can readily satisfy many needs. Adequate and proper performance depends upon the yarn structure, fabric construction, and garment manufacture.

Resilience. Spandex fibers are highly flexible and resilient. This property of rapid shape recovery imparts a flat, neat appearance to fabrics.

Heat Conductivity. Spandex is not a good conductor of heat.

Drapability. The light weight and pliability of spandex fibers contribute good draping qualities to fabrics.

Absorbency. Spandex fibers have a very low absorbency—lower than even the polyester fibers. The least absorbent spandex is Vyrene, which is practically nonabsorbent. Glospan is slightly more absorbent, followed by Numa, Blue C, and then Lycra spandex, respectively. But this is relative. Therefore, for com-

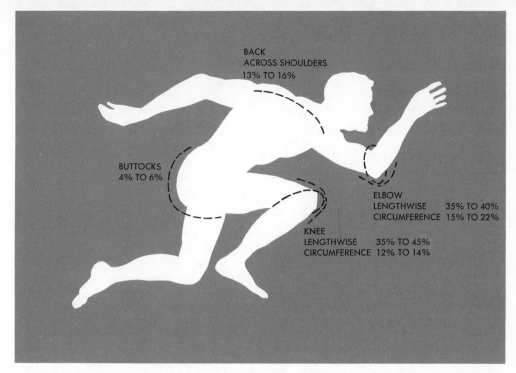

For comfort and freedom of body movement, stretch fabrics should provide for the amounts of skin extension shown in the drawing.

fort next to the skin, the spandex should be covered, core spun, or blended with fibers that will provide the desired absorbency.

Cleanliness and Washability. All spandex fibers are unaffected by dry-cleaning solvents. They are also machine washable with the usual household soaps and detergents, but the temperature of the water should be about 100 to 120 degrees Fahrenheit, depending upon the particular spandex fiber. Higher temperatures may reduce the elasticity of the spandex. Clothing containing spandex may be machine dried at temperatures usually between 140 to 160 degrees Fahrenheit. In general, these conditions are also satisfactory for the other fibers in the fabric. It is highly desirable to refer to the washing instructions that are frequently attached to the garments.

Effect of Bleaches. All of the spandex fibers are white, though the degree of whiteness varies. Under certain conditions, yellowing may occur. Fibers used in conjunction with spandex in the fabric may discolor and bleaching may be desired. However, the several spandex fibers differ in their reactions to bleaches and treatment must be given accordingly.

Lycra is yellowed by bleaches of calcium hypochlorite (also known as bleach powder), sodium hypochlorite, and hydrogen peroxide. Under certain conditions of concentration, these bleaches will also weaken the fiber. Sodium chlorite, a bleach used commercially, will degrade and discolor Lycra. A safe, effective bleach is one that contains sodium perborate, such as *Snowy*.

Vyrene may be safely bleached with a mild solution of hydrogen peroxide. Very weak solutions of sodium hypochlorite may be used with care, but yellow-

COMPARISON OF PROPERTIES—THE SPANDEX FIBERS

	LYCRA	VYRENE	GLOSPAN	BLUE C	NUMA
Strength	Satisfactory; excellent flex life	Satisfactory; excellent flex life	Satisfactory; excellent flex life	Satisfactory; excellent flex life	Satisfactory; excellent flex life
Abrasion resistance	Good	Good	Good	Good	Good
Elasticity (approximate)	520% to 600%; slight growth with use	700%; slight growth with use	S-1, 600%; S-5, 725%; slight growth with use	500% to 600%; slight growth with use	500% to 600%; slight growth with use
Resilience	Excellent	Excellent	Excellent	Excellent	Excellent
Absorbency	Practically none	Practically none	Practically none	Practically none	Practically none
Laundering care	Hand or machine washable with household soaps or detergents	Hand or machine washable with household soaps or detergents	Hand or machine washable with household soaps or detergents	Hand or machine washable with household soaps or detergents	Hand or machine washable with household soaps or detergents
Ironing temperature	Quickly with warm iron (low setting)	Quickly with warm iron (low setting)	Use warm iron	May be pressed with warmer iron than others	Use warm iron
Shrinkage	None to water below boiling point	None to water	None to water	None to water	None to water
Household bleaches	Sodium perborate; others may yellow and weaken	Mild solution of hydrogen peroxide, sodium perborate, or sodium hypochlorite with care and tepid water; others yellow and weaken	Any household bleach; sodium chlorite degrades	Hydrogen peroxide or mild solution of sodium perborate; chlorine bleaches will yellow	Chlorine bleaches will yellow

	LYCRA	VYRENE	GLOSPAN	BLUE C	NUMA
Effect of heat	Yellows and loses elasticity above 300°F; melts at 446°F	Shrinks at about 160°F; loses much strength above 380°F; heat-sets above 300°F	Good dimensional stability. Specific information not available	Very good stability. sticks at 534°F; melts at 554°F	Good dimensional stability. Sticks at 437°F; melts at 511°F
Resistance to light	Good, but loses some strength and yellows slightly after prolonged exposure	Good, but will slowly discolor	Very good, but will discolor slightly	Very good, but will discolor slightly	Very good, but will discolor slightly
Seawater	Not harmful	Not harmful	Not harmful	Not harmful	Not harmful
Resistance to mildew	Good	Good	Good	Good	Good
Reaction to alkalies	Good resistance to most alkalies	Rapidly deteriorated by hot alkalies	Rapidly deteriorated by hot alkalies	Good resistance to most alkalies	Good resistance to most alkalies
Reaction to acids	Good resistance to most acids; some discoloration may occur	Resistant to cold dilute acids	Resistant to cold dilute acids	Good resistance to most acids; some discoloration may occur	Unaffected by weak acids
Affinity for dyes	Good for wide variety; colorfastness poor to good, depending upon dye and technique	Good for wide variety; colorfastness poor to good, depending upon dye and technique	Good for wide variety; colorfastness poor to good, depending upon dye and technique	Good for wide variety; colorfastness poor to good, depending upon dye and technique	Good for wide variety; colorfastness poor to good, depending upon dye and technique
Resistance to perspiration	Good	Good	Good	Good	Good
Resistance to oils	Good	Good	Good	Good	Good

ing may occur if the water is too warm. Sodium perborate should also be used with care.

Glospan may be safely bleached with any household bleach. However, the commercially used sodium chlorite bleach will affect its properties.

Blue C spandex is bleached most effectively with hydrogen peroxide. A mild solution of sodium perborate bleach may also be used. Although Blue C spandex has good resistance to chlorine bleaches, it will be yellowed by them.

Numa has good property retention when bleached, but chlorine bleaches cause slight yellowing.

A question may arise concerning the ill effect of the chlorine in swimming pools on swimwear containing spandex. The answer is that pools are usually treated with calcium hypochlorite. If this solution is of a proper level, it is not likely to be strong enough to degrade the fiber performance, particularly if the water temperature is not above 80 degrees Fahrenheit. Furthermore, the fiber is usually well hidden or covered and possible yellowing is not likely to be noticeable.

Effect of Seawater. Since we are considering the important place that spandex fiber is taking in swimwear and related uses, it is important to emphasize that it is unaffected by seawater.

Shrinkage and Growth. Spandex fibers will not shrink from exposure to water, however, some do shrink upon exposure to certain temperatures (discussed below). On the other hand, a garment may have a small loss of elastic recovery as it is used. This gradual extension is known as "growth." The amount of growth may not be too significant, particularly if taken into consideration in garment construction.

Effect of Heat. Exposure to heat has varied effects on the spandex fibers. Generally, excessive exposure to heat should be avoided. As a rule, ironing should be done quickly and with a warm iron.

Lycra yellows and loses elasticity and strength at over 300 degrees Fahrenheit. It sticks at 347 degrees Fahrenheit and melts at 446 degrees Fahrenheit.

Vyrene begins to shrink at about 160 degrees Fahrenheit. Above 380 degrees Fahrenheit, its strength drops sharply; it becomes thermoplastic above 300 degrees Fahrenheit and may be heat-set in this range.

Glospan is claimed to have good dimensional stability when exposed to heat. However, its reactions at specific temperatures have not yet been reported.

Blue C spandex has very good stability against heat. It sticks at 534 degrees Fahrenheit and melts at 554 degrees Fahrenheit. Therefore, it can withstand higher temperatures than most other fibers.

Numa sticks at about 437 degrees Fahrenheit and melts at about 511 degrees Fahrenheit.

Effect of Light. Light and other atmospheric conditions have varying effects upon the several spandex fibers. However, no really serious damage may be expected to occur in the normal use of spandex for dress or sportswear.

Lycra has initial good resistance to light, but over a prolonged period of time, it will lose some strength and yellow slightly. Fumes of oxides of nitrogen will also cause yellowing.

Vyrene has good resistance to degradation by light but will slowly discolor.

Glospan, Numa, and Blue C spandex have very good resistance to degradation by sunlight. Although there is no loss of physical properties, they discolor slightly. They also have good resistance to gas fumes.

Resistance to Mildew. The spandex fibers have good to excellent resistance to damage by mildew.

Resistance to Moths. As may be expected, spandex fibers are unaffected by moths.

Reaction to Alkalies. Reactions of spandex fibers to alkalies vary, but all are affected.

Lycra, Numa, and Blue C spandex have good resistance to most alkalies. Vyrene and Glospan are rapidly deteriorated by hot alkali. Spandelle is readily deteriorated by a strong alkali such as sodium hydroxide.

Reaction to Acids. Reactions of spandex fibers to acids also vary. Lycra and Blue C spandex have good resistance to most acids, though some discoloration may occur. Vyrene and Glospan are resistant to cold dilute acids. Numa is unaffected by weak acids.

Affinity for Dyes. The spandex fibers have a good affinity for many classes of dyes, including disperse, acid, chrome, and other dyes. While the colors are good, colorfastness ranges from poor to fair on continued exposure to light, washing, and seawater. The degree of fastness depends upon the dye used and the technique of application.

Resistance to Perspiration. Indications are that all of the various spandex fibers have good resistance to degradation from perspiration.

Resistance to Oils. An important attribute of all of the spandex fibers is their high resistance to body oils, cosmetics, and suntan lotions. This is a particularly important advantage over rubber for use in such garments as girdles and swimwear.

COMPARISON OF SPANDEX FIBERS

The chart on pages 406–407 is for the reader's general guidance. It is a summary composite based on information supplied by the producers of these fibers and on evaluation of the performance of the fibers as described in the literature included in the bibliography. The reader is reminded that variations do exist in blend combinations, types of yarn, fabric weights, constructions, and finishes and that these factors will affect the performance. It is also possible that future changes in the chemical and physical compositions of these fibers may alter their performance.

REVIEW QUESTIONS

1 Name each of the spandex fibers and its manufacturer.

2 What is spandex fiber?

3 Compare the elastic properties of spandex to those of (a) stretch nylon, (b) rubber, (c) stretch cotton.

4 Explain what is meant by (a) "comfort stretch," (b) "power stretch."

5 How much stretch is needed for comfort over various parts of the body?

6 Describe the different forms of spandex yarns and indicate their characteristics and uses.

7 What finishes may be given to fabrics containing spandex fibers?

8 What limitations do you consider spandex fibers to have?

9 Describe and illustrate the appearance of each spandex fiber.

10 Compare the properties of the spandex fibers.

THE OLEFIN FIBER

22

POLYPROPYLENE

Olefins are a family of polymers that may be generally described as "paraffins," a group familiar to the consumer as wax. While it is possible to develop an infinite variety of fibers from this paraffin group, polypropylene has been developed furthest and has the greatest potential for consumer acceptance.

HISTORY OF POLYPROPYLENE

Research in polymer chemistry under high-pressure techniques in the 1930's led to the polymerization of a form of polyethylene in England. Ultimately, this led to the independent initial development of polymerization of polyethylene under low-pressure techniques in Germany, by Professor Ziegler (who won the Nobel Prize for scientific discoveries resulting from this research), and in the United States, by the Phillips Petroleum Company. This provided the basis for commercial production of another form of polyethylene plastic from which such flexible plastic products as the familiar squeeze bottle is now made.

Subsequent research led to the development of varieties of polyethylene and also revealed the possibility of a wide variety of related olefins. The basis for controlling the molecular arrangements of these olefins was established in Italy by Professor Giulio Natta who, with Ziegler, received the Nobel Prize in 1963 for his explanation of the polymerization of polypropylene. Professors Natta and Ziegler also filed the first patent applications for the manufacture of polypropylene fibers. Production was begun at the Montecatini Company in Italy, in 1951, under the trademark of *Meraklon*.

Meanwhile, several American companies engaged in research, development, and limited production of polyethylene monofilament. These fibers, however, had certain common disadvantages and greater attention was turned to the development and commercial production of polypropylene fiber, which has a higher melting point, greater resilience and strength, as well as a lighter weight. The first commercial production of polypropylene resin was done in the United States in 1957 by the Hercules Powder Company, Inc. This company later acquired facilities at Covington, Virginia, for the manufacture of its polypropylene fiber, *Herculon,* thus becoming the first completely integrated manufacturer in the United States from raw material to finished fiber.

Another company moving in this direction was Reeves Brothers, Inc., one of the first producers of polypropylene fiber under the trademark of *Reevon.* By a series of mergers and corporate reorganizations, this company became a part of the Alamo Industries, Inc., which announced in 1965, the new trademark of *Marvess* to identify its polypropylene fiber. This trademark is licensed by Alamo to other companies that meet certain quality standards.

By this time, these and other producers, such as U. S. Rubber Company, established plants capable of producing millions of pounds of polypropylene fiber. In an effort to compete with the other, better-established man-made fibers, producers began promoting polypropylene before certain of its limitations (subsequently to be resolved) were overcome. As a result, consumer reaction was skeptical and acceptance was slow. However, it is expected that, with continued improvements and sound consumer education, polypropylene fiber will find a good market for such diverse products as rope, rugs, sweaters, hosiery, slacks, and other apparel.

METHOD OF MANUFACTURE

The production of polypropylene fiber varies among the manufacturers. In fact, individual manufacturers have variations in their processes to achieve certain properties, such as dyeability, light stability, heat sensitivity, and shape of the filament cross section. The production of polypropylene fiber results in a relatively economical and inexpensive fiber because the basic substance from which it is made is propylene gas—a by-product of petroleum distillation. The most costly aspect is the manufacturer's initial investment in research and plant establishment.

The basic procedure is to polymerize propylene gas with the aid of an appropriate metal compound, such as titanium chloride, in a diluent. The polymer formed from the propylene is slurried in the diluent to decompose the catalyst, and is then filtered, purified, and reduced to powder form as polypropylene resin. The resin is melted and extruded through a spinneret in filament form. The filaments are then treated and drawn to get the proper crystallinity and molecular orientation in order to obtain such desired characteristics as strength, abrasion resistance, elasticity, resilience, and shrinkage.

FORMS AND TYPES OF POLYPROPYLENE YARNS

As has been stated, polypropylene fiber is produced in a variety of forms and in a wide range of deniers. Some are nondyeable white, some are nondyeable pigmented, others are completely dyeable. They are produced in bright and semibright forms. Some are highly stabilized to resist degradation by sunlight; some are highly heat stabilized. The fibers may be crimped or uncrimped. The texture and appearance may vary, depending upon the fiber cross section. Some of the fibers are designed to be suitable for specific products (such as rugs), others for wearing apparel, others for industrial purposes. Many of these characteristics are tentative as manufacturers improve their products and develop new types.

The polypropylene fibers are produced in monofilament, multifilament, tow, and staple form. These, in turn, are made into several forms of yarn.

MONOFILAMENT YARNS ■ The monofilament yarns are produced from individual filaments, and the range of denier is very wide. The yarns are used for such purposes as automobile seat covers, outdoor furniture webbing, and radio grille fabrics.

MULTIFILAMENT YARNS ■ Polypropylene multifilament may be produced as straight or bulked yarn of about 17 to 420 filaments, ranging from about 165 to 3750 denier. The straight multifilament yarn is used for both general apparel and industrial purposes, depending upon the type of polypropylene fiber.

SPUN YARNS ■ Polypropylene filaments may be cut into staple and subsequently spun on a conventional cotton or wool system with very slight modifica-

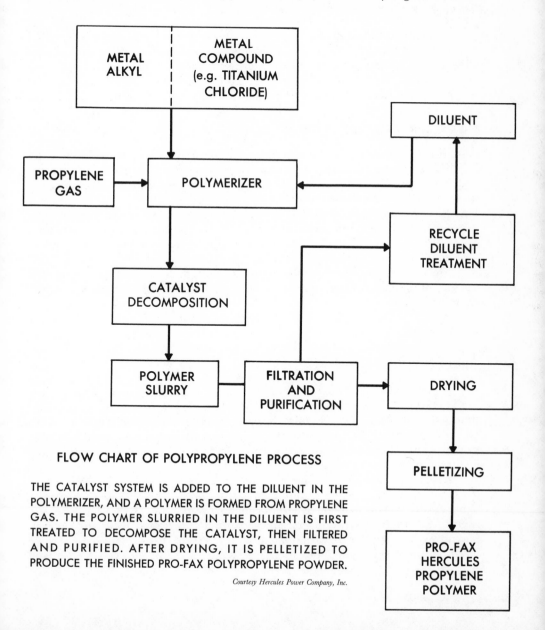

FLOW CHART OF POLYPROPYLENE PROCESS

THE CATALYST SYSTEM IS ADDED TO THE DILUENT IN THE POLYMERIZER, AND A POLYMER IS FORMED FROM PROPYLENE GAS. THE POLYMER SLURRIED IN THE DILUENT IS FIRST TREATED TO DECOMPOSE THE CATALYST, THEN FILTERED AND PURIFIED. AFTER DRYING, IT IS PELLETIZED TO PRODUCE THE FINISHED PRO-FAX POLYPROPYLENE POWDER.

Courtesy Hercules Power Company, Inc.

tion either into 100 percent polypropylene or blended with other fibers into spun yarn. Polypropylene tow may be processed on a Pacific converter into spun yarn. Yarns of spun polypropylene staple have been found to be relatively pill resistant and are being used for a wide variety of apparel.

BULK AND TEXTURED YARNS ■ Multifilament polypropylene fiber may be crimped or textured. The crimped multifilaments are thrown into yarn. This type of yarn is being used for carpets. It shows much promise for this purpose because polypropylene has good resistance to abrasion, soiling, staining, and pilling, as well as being virtually static free. The yarn is bulky and has a soft, pleasant hand.

TRADE NAMES OF POLYPROPYLENE YARN

To identify and promote their respective products, the manufacturers have given trademarks to their polypropylene yarns as shown in the chart on page 415. Although certain basic properties are similar, it is apparent from the foregoing discussion that the characteristics of the yarns differ insofar as the type of polypropylene fiber, its cross section, and the yarn construction are concerned.

FINISHING POLYPROPYLENE FABRICS

Much work remains to be done in developing finishing techniques for fabrics containing polypropylene fiber. Polypropylene is resistant to water and a wide variety of chemicals. Some finishes, such as water and stain repellents, are unnecessary. In blends with other fibers, such chemical finishes as mercerizing may be applied if heat conditions permit. Heat sensitivity is a problem because it is generally recommended that polypropylene not be subjected to temperatures above 250 degrees Fahrenheit. Also, many types of polypropylene are nondyeable and printing is also a problem.

Mechanical finishes, such as napping, will enhance the soft texture and warmth of the fabric. Other finishes, such as embossing and heat setting, require caution.

Producers are optimistic that these problems will ultimately be met satisfactorily.

EVALUATING POLYPROPYLENE FABRICS

A prime reason for the interest in polypropylene is its low cost, which is due to the abundance and cheapness of the propylene gas (a petroleum by-product) from which it is made. This makes it less expensive to produce than any of the other man-made fibers. It is also the lightest of all textile fibers and therefore provides more fiber per pound for greater area coverage, thereby contributing further to relatively low cost.

Along with the low-cost factor, polypropylene has many inherent properties that could also make it popular for fabrics. However, the fiber's heat and light sensitivity and its poor dyeability factor are handicaps that have not yet been overcome by the producers. Since manufacturers produce many types of polypropylene fibers with variations of characteristics to try to overcome these limitations and since developmental work continues, all-inclusive statements of

POLYPROPYLENE TRADE NAMES

TRADE NAME	MANUFACTURER	TYPE	SPECIAL CHARACTERISTICS
Amco Polypropylene	American Manufacturing Company, Inc.	Monofilament	Industrial use
Amerfil	American Thermoplastic Products Corp.	Monofilament	
ATCO	American Thermoplastic Products Corp.	Monofilament	
Beamette	Dawbarn Division W. R. Grace & Co.	Monofilament	
Diamond	Metlon Corporation	Monofilament	Flat
DLP	Dawbarn Division, W. R. Grace & Co.	Monofilament	Various forms: round, flat, high tenacity
Easthampton Polypropylene	Easthampton Rubber Thread Company	Monofilament	
Herculon	Hercules Powder Company, Inc.	Multifilament, staple, tow	Multifilament; straight, bulked
Lus-Trus	Southern Lus-Trus Corp.	Monofilament	
Marvess	Alamo Industries, Inc.	Monofilament	Various forms: round, flat, textured clear, solution-dyed, dyeable
Nypel	Nypel Corporation	Monofilament	
Polycrest	U. S. Rubber Company	Multifilament	Textured
Tuff-Lite	Industrial Plastics Co.	Monofilament	
Vectra E	The Vectra Company	Monofilament	
Voplex	Vogt Manufacturing Corp.	Monofilament	Round, flat
Wyomissing	Wyomissing Company	Monofilament	

performance are not possible. However, some generalities may be drawn from information provided by the producers based upon tests under laboratory conditions and from limited evaluations based on performance in daily consumer use and care.

Strength. The range of the strength of polypropylene fibers is quite wide, but in general, it is comparable to that of nylon and the polyesters. (There are indications that continued developmental research may result in types of polypropylene that would be stronger than any existing fiber.) The strength and generally good abrasion resistance of polypropylene fiber make it durable and serviceable for both consumer and industrial uses.

Elasticity. Polypropylene fibers are less elastic than nylon fibers. Over a period of time, constant stress on the yarn results in a certain amount of permanent elongation. It is interesting to note that the relative elasticity, strength, and smoothness of the fiber (said to provide a snag-free characteristic) are the basis for one company's promotion of *Vectra* polypropylene for women's sheer hosiery, which is in competition with nylon hosiery.

Resilience. Polypropylene fiber has good resilience. This property contributes to its suitability for rugs as well as apparel. However, it is a general characteristic that the greater the strength of polypropylene fibers, the less resilient they are.

Heat Conductivity. One of the great advantages of polypropylene is its superior light weight. This characteristic combined with its ability to be crimped and otherwise treated to form bulky, lightweight yarns gives polypropylene very good insulating qualities. Very comfortable and warm blankets and sweaters can be made of such yarn.

Drapability. No information is available regarding the drapability of polypropylene. However, since it can be produced in various cross sections and is lightweight and sufficiently pliable to be processed into a variety of yarns, it may be expected that fabrics of polypropylene will drape satisfactorily.

Absorbency. Polypropylene is practically nonabsorbent. While this presents severe limitations in terms of comfort when worn next to the skin, as well as for dyeing and printing, the lack of absorbency does provide certain advantages. Polypropylene cannot be saturated with water; consequently, it acts as its own water repellent. It also resists soiling and staining by such substances as grease, cosmetics, fruit juices, soft drinks, coffee, and eggs. These substances tend to stay on the surface of the fiber and can be readily removed with water and a detergent or other household cleaner.

Cleanliness and Washability. Polypropylene fabrics can be washed or drycleaned easily. Soil tends to remain on the surface and can be readily removed from fabrics. There is no loss of strength when wet and any soap, detergent, or cleaning agent may be safely used. However, since polypropylene is heat sensitive, warm rather than hot water is recommended. Fabrics of polypropylene are dimensionally stable, shape retentive, and quick drying. Again, when being washed or dried, the fibers should not be exposed to high temperatures.

Effect of Bleaches. Polypropylene has good resistance to degradation by various bleaches at temperatures below 150 degrees Fahrenheit. Loss of strength begins when the fabrics are subjected to bleaching solutions above that level. This is another reason why the water temperature should not be too high when laundering.

Shrinkage. Polypropylene is unaffected by water and will not shrink. However, depending upon the type, it does begin to shrink when subjected to temperatures of 212 degrees Fahrenheit (boiling) and above.

Effect of Heat. Reference has already been made to the heat sensitivity of polypropylene. Because it is thermoplastic, polypropylene fabrics can be heatset to a desired shape—in fact, they are moldable. However, depending upon the type of polypropylene, the fibers shrink and then soften at temperatures above 265 degrees Fahrenheit, and they melt at temperatures above 325 degrees Fahrenheit.

To overcome this handicap, some types of polypropylene have heat stabilizers to reduce their sensitivity. However, they have not been as successful as desired. They tend to break down when exposed to certain conditions and chemicals in finishes and certain other conditions in the use and care of the fabrics.

Effect of Light. Polypropylene is deteriorated by exposure to direct sunlight. The ultraviolet light causes the breakdown. To overcome this, light stabilizers have been added to certain types of polypropylene. This technique has had limited success because these stabilizers, like the others, tend to break down.

Resistance to Mildew. Polypropylene is wholly resistant to mildew.

Resistance to Moths. Polypropylene is not attacked by moths or similar insects.

Reaction to Alkalies. Polypropylene has excellent resistance to alkalies.

Reaction to Acids. Polypropylene has excellent resistance to most acids.

Affinity for Dyes. The greatest handicap of polypropylene fiber is its dyeing difficulty. To overcome this, some types are pigmented before extrusion; however, this method provides only limited colors. Some types are modified to take specific dyes; but, here, again, a complete color range is lacking. Attempts to vary conventional dyeing techniques have had some effect but the colors are generally not fast to washing, to dry cleaning, or to light. Surface pigment binders have provided some washable and dry-cleanable dark colors, but these tend to crock.

Continued research promises to overcome these difficulties. For instance, premetallized acid dyes and disperse dyes similar to those used for nylon show promise. Certain of the latter have shown good fastness to washing, to dry cleaning, and to light.

Resistance to Perspiration. Polypropylene is a relatively chemically inert fiber. It therefore will not be deteriorated by perspiration.

POLYPROPYLENE FIBER BLENDS

Polypropylene fiber has been successfully blended with cotton, wool, and rayon, but more evaluation is needed to determine the optimum blend proportions. The chief values of polypropylene in blends would be to lower the yarn cost, to reduce the yarn weight, to improve the yarn bulk and therefore warmth, to contribute strength and durability, as well as to add shape retention and enhance the cleaning and drying properties.

REVIEW QUESTIONS

1 What is meant by the designation, olefin?

2 Describe the basic procedure for producing polypropylene fiber.

3 Name five polypropylene trademarks and their manufacturers.

4 In what ways may the various types of polypropylene fibers differ?

5 Describe the characteristics that are generally common to all polypropylene fibers.

6 What limitations do the polypropylene fibers have?

7 What are the most favorable properties of polypropylene fibers?

8 What kinds of yarns can be made of polypropylene fibers?

9 What characteristics do polypropylene fibers contribute to blends?

SARAN

23 THE VINYLIDENE CHLORIDE

"Saran" is a generic term that refers to a particular type of plastic fiber that is a linear copolymer of vinylidene chloride and vinyl chloride. Some variation in its chemical composition is possible.

HISTORY OF SARAN

The chemical compound vinylidene chloride was discovered in 1840. It is a clear, colorless liquid that boils at 90 degrees Fahrenheit. Although chemists since 1920 had observed that it could easily polymerize, it was not until 1936 that further research was conducted. At that time The Dow Chemical Company began a research program, probably spurred by the successful results of other companies' research with polymers, which ultimately resulted in 1940 in the commercialization of its fiber, saran.

The relatively low cost of the raw materials from which this fiber was made and certain of its other desirable features attracted the attention of several companies. Since the designation saran had not been registered as a trademark, other companies also used the term, and it became recognized as a general identification for this fiber. Subsequently, each company registered its particular saran trade name.

METHOD OF MANUFACTURE

The raw materials used to produce vinylidene chloride are ethylene, which is derived by cracking natural petroleum, and chlorine, which is electrolyzed from seawater. Ethylene is treated with chlorine to produce trichlorethane, which in turn is treated with lime to produce unpolymerized vinylidene chloride. The vinylidene chloride is then copolymerized with a small quantity of vinyl chloride to produce a powdered resin. The resin is melted and extruded through a spinneret into a water-cooling bath. While still being cooled, it is drawn out 400 percent to improve its crystallinity and molecular orientation, thereby increasing its strength in a manner similar to nylon.

The fiber may be produced in different shapes. Some are round, some flat, others oval. One type, *Rovana,* appears to be flat. Under the microscope, it appears to be folded over on itself several times, giving added bulk with lighter weight than is generally available in saran fiber. (See page 14.)

The natural color of saran is pale gold or straw. It may be delustered to a translucent or to an opaque appearance by the addition of a delusterant such as titanium dioxide. The fiber may be solution-dyed, but the colors are not bright because the natural color of saran tones down the hue.

FORMS AND TYPES OF SARAN YARNS

Saran may be made in monofilament, multifilament, and staple forms, though its use as a monofilament predominates. Some manufacturers produce a few types frequently associated with the shape of the fiber.

MONOFILAMENT YARNS ■ These yarns are made in a wide variety of diameters. Some companies express the thickness of the yarns in denier, others in terms of a decimal part of the inch. In denier, monofilament saran yarn is produced in 70 to 1100; in inches, in a range of .005 to .05 inch diameters. It is used for a wide variety of purposes, such as window screens, handbags, millinery fabrics, and trimmings. Saran is also produced in rattanlike monofilament strips. This form is readily adapted to fabrics used for seat covers in automobiles, buses, and railroad cars, as well as for outdoor furniture.

MULTIFILAMENT YARNS ■ The production of saran multifilament yarns is more limited. They are used for brocades and other fabrics. The amount of twist given to each of the following yarns varies depending on the desired ultimate result. Examples of saran multifilament yarns are as follows.

750 denier, of 50 filaments
1200 denier, of 100 filaments
3000 denier, of 300 filaments

STAPLE ■ Saran staple fiber has been produced in 2- to 40-inch lengths in three forms: straight, crimped, and curled. The fiber deniers range from 10 to 70. Although saran staple may be used for a wide variety of purposes, including outerwear, rugs, and linings, it has not received much acceptance for consumer use, though it has been used for such industrial purposes as filter cloths.

TRADE NAMES OF SARAN YARNS

Several companies produce saran yarns. The basic quality of the yarns is the same, since they are all generally made of the same substances in the same way. The important differences among the yarns are dependent on whether they are monofilament, multifilament, or staple, and on the denier of the fibers and the amount of twist in the yarns.

It should be noted that the trademark *Rovana* may be used by the fabricator only when the fabrics meet the rigid specifications established by the manufacturer of the fiber, The Dow Badische Company (formerly The Dow Chemical Company).

Velon, produced by Firestone Plastics Company, Inc., is another trade name for saran. Velon is also made in plastic sheet form for plastic tablecloths and similar protective coverings. *Saran Wrap* is another trade name for a very thin, clear sheet form used for wrapping foods and other items. It is produced by The Dow Badische Company.

Except for the plastic sheets, these companies produce only the yarns. The ultimate fabrics are woven by other companies. The quality of saran fabric depends further on the construction as well as on the type of yarn used.

SARAN TRADE NAMES

TRADE NAME	MANUFACTURER	TYPE	SPECIAL CHARACTERISTICS
Anavor	Dow Badische Company	Multifilament	
Rovana	Dow Badische Company	Monofilament	Flat, folded
Vectra Saran	The Vectra Company	Multifilament, monofilament	

FINISHING SARAN FABRICS

Saran is a thermoplastic fiber and can be permanently shaped at relatively low temperatures. Saran fabrics can therefore be molded into any desired shape. They can also be embossed in both deep and shallow patterns. Lamination of saran fabrics to other substances, such as polyurethane foam, vinyl film, paper, rayon, or cotton can be accomplished by bonding the heat-sensitive saran. Another method of laminating is by using appropriate adhesives.

Saran fabrics can be dielectrically sealed, eliminating the need to stitch the fabrics together. This results in a stronger bond and less likelihood for tearing at these points as well as in greater impermeability.

Chemical finishes are generally not used for saran. It is inert to many chemicals, and it is inherently water repellent. It cannot be dyed by conventional means, and printing can be done only with pigment resins.

EVALUATING SARAN FABRICS

Saran has some valuable properties as a textile. It also has some definite limitations.

Strength. The strength of saran fiber varies with its diameter. Generally, the finer filaments are stronger than the coarser ones. Saran is weaker than any natural fiber except wool. It is weaker than most man-made fibers; it is stronger than regular viscose or cuprammonium rayon, acetate, and Arnel triacetate.

Elasticity. Saran has a fair degree of stretchability. Its return to original shape is more gradual as the amount of initial stretch is increased. The elasticity of saran has contributed to its use for seat covers and for upholstery used in outdoor furniture.

Resilience. Saran is a rather stiff fiber. While it is rather resistant to crushing, heavy compression could permanently deform the fiber and thereby reduce its resilience.

Heat Conductivity. Saran fabrics are not good conductors of heat but are easily affected by it. The heat conductivity of saran can be reduced by bulking the fiber.

Drapability. Saran is a rather stiff fiber. Finer diameters, of course, are more pliable, but saran is not generally considered to have a draping quality.

Absorbency. Saran is one of the least absorbent of all textiles, having virtually no absorbency. It is similar in this respect to polypropylene. Saran cannot be used for such garments as underwear, shirts, blouses, and dresses, since they would not absorb perspiration or atmospheric moisture and therefore would be uncomfortable. On the other hand, saran fabrics, being virtually waterproof, are suitable for outerwear, such as raincoats, and for outdoor furniture. Tablecloths are another use for saran.

Cleanliness and Washability. Saran fabrics may be easily cleaned by merely wiping them with a damp cloth. If desired, laundering or dry cleaning is safe. It must be remembered that saran fabrics should be kept away from heat when being dried because of their tendency to melt.

Effect of Bleaches. Saran has good resistance to staining. Therefore, it does not generally need bleaching, though saran has good resistance to damage by any of the usual bleaches.

Shrinkage. Saran is unaffected by water and will shrink only at temperatures above 168 degrees Fahrenheit.

Effect of Heat. Saran also loses strength at its shrinking temperature. It softens at 240 to 320 degrees Fahrenheit, depending upon the type. It melts at about 340 to 350 degrees Fahrenheit. This places a serious limitation on saran fabrics. They cannot be easily ironed, and cigarette sparks are dangerous because they will melt holes in the saran fabric.

Effect of Light. Exposure to sunlight over a long period of time will tend to darken saran fabrics slightly, but there is no appreciable loss of strength. This shows saran's value as an outdoor fabric.

Resistance to Mildew. Saran fabrics are wholly resistant to deterioration from mildew.

Resistance to Moths. Saran is unaffected by moths or other insects.

Reaction to Alkalies. Saran has good resistance to most alkalies; however, it is discolored by hot solutions of sodium hydroxide and ammonium hydroxide.

Reaction to Acids. Saran has good-to-excellent resistance to acids. This resistance to acids as well as alkalies makes saran very suitable for industrial filter cloths.

Affinity for Dyes. Saran cannot be dyed by the usual methods because it is nonabsorbent. However, by adding the desired color to the solution before the saran filaments are spun through the spinnerets, it is possible to obtain an extensive variety of colors. These colors, being inside the fibers, are very fast and will not wash out or fade.

Resistance to Perspiration. Saran is very resistant to perspiration.

1 What is saran? How is it produced?

2 What are the leading trade names and manufacturers of saran yarn?

3 What kind of yarns can be made of saran?

4 For what purpose is saran most suited? Why?

5 What are the chief advantages and limitations of saran?

Although ordinary glass is a hard and inflexible mineral substance, it can be made into fine, translucent textile fibers that have the appearance and feel of silk.

HISTORY OF GLASS FIBER

The idea of making yarns and fabrics from glass is hundreds of years old. During the Renaissance, artisans were drawing out a "spun glass" of fine glass strands or rods for decorative purposes on goblets and vases. In 1893, Edward Drummond Libbey exhibited a glass dress, lamp shades, and other articles of woven glass at the World's Columbian Exposition in Chicago. The fabric was made of bundles of glass fibers woven together with silk threads. The experiment was spectacular but of no practical value, since the fabric was too stiff to be creased, folded, or draped.

Some progress was made during the early 1900's when several patents were issued in Germany and in England on various processes for drawing glass fibers. These fibers were relatively coarse, and the cost was high. During World War I, however, Germany suffered a shortage of asbestos and developed a somewhat primitive method of producing filaments of glass fibers from heat-softened glass rods. These fibers were used for insulating purposes.

It was not until 1931 that experiments were started in the United States to produce glass fibers that were finer, more pliable, and lower in cost. At that time, the Owens-Illinois Glass Company and the Corning Glass Works started to develop a method of drawing out glass from the molten state through fine orifices into pliable filament form. For several years, work progressed in the development of filament and staple yarns. By 1938, sufficient progress was made to indicate a promising future for glass fiber for practical textile purposes. The two companies merged to form the Owens-Corning Fiberglas Corporation. Their textile product is registered under the trademark of *Fiberglas*.

Other companies became very much interested in this new product, particularly after World War II when competition began to develop in the promotion of what was, and is still, frequently referred to as "fiber glass." Of course, each company also attached its own trade name to the product.

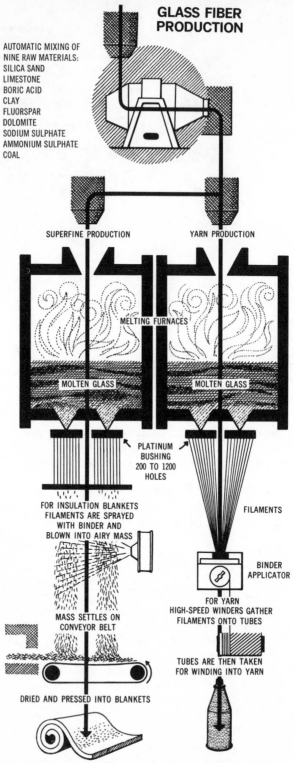

GLASS FIBER PRODUCTION

AUTOMATIC MIXING OF
NINE RAW MATERIALS:
SILICA SAND
LIMESTONE
BORIC ACID
CLAY
FLUORSPAR
DOLOMITE
SODIUM SULPHATE
AMMONIUM SULPHATE
COAL

SUPERFINE PRODUCTION

YARN PRODUCTION

MELTING FURNACES

MOLTEN GLASS

MOLTEN GLASS

PLATINUM
BUSHING
200 TO 1200
HOLES

FOR INSULATION BLANKETS
FILAMENTS ARE SPRAYED
WITH BINDER AND
BLOWN INTO AIRY MASS

FILAMENTS

BINDER
APPLICATOR

MASS SETTLES ON
CONVEYOR BELT

FOR YARN
HIGH-SPEED WINDERS GATHER
FILAMENTS ONTO TUBES

TUBES ARE THEN TAKEN
FOR WINDING INTO YARN

DRIED AND PRESSED INTO BLANKETS

Method of glass fiber production is dependent upon end use.   *Courtesy Pittsburgh Plate Glass*

There are two methods of producing glass fiber yarns. Both begin with accurate batch formulation of selected silica sand, limestone, soda ash, and borax (or other ingredients depending on the ultimate purpose of the fiber) in an electric furnace. From the precisely controlled furnace, the molten glass at a temperature of about 2,500 degrees Fahrenheit flows to marble-forming machines that turn out small glass marbles about five-eighths of an inch in diameter. These marbles permit visual inspection of the glass for the purpose of eliminating impurities that would interfere with subsequent operations or lower the desired uniform quality of the fibers. The marbles are then remelted in small electric furnaces and extruded through spinnerets.

Another method eliminates the marble operation but maintains quality control. The molten glass is extruded directly from the bottom of the furnace through spinnerets. The kind of fiber desired—continuous or staple—determines the process that will follow.

CONTINUOUS-FILAMENT PROCESS ■ This process produces continuous filaments of indefinite length having exceptional brilliance. Molten glass flows downward through temperature-resistant metal-alloy bushings (spinnerets) that have two hundred or more small openings. The strand of multiple filaments is

Raw materials are melted in a bucket to form molten glass, which is drawn through platinum bushings at the bottom of the furnace.

Courtesy Pittsburgh Plate Glass Co.

A typical platinum bushing has been highly magnified in the photo at left. It contains hundreds of tiny openings through which molten glass is drawn from the furnace to form filaments hundreds of times thinner than human hair.

Courtesy Pittsburgh Plate Glass Co.

carried to a high-speed winder. Since the winder revolves at a much faster rate (more than two miles a minute) than the stream flow from the melting chamber, the tension attenuates the glass while it is still molten, and thus draws out the fibers in parallel filaments to a fraction of the diameter of the openings. After winding, the filaments are twisted and plied to form yarns by methods similar to those used for making other continuous-filament yarns. These yarns are used for such fabrics as curtains and draperies.

STAPLE-FIBER PROCESS ■ The staple-fiber process produces fibers that have long-staple characteristics. As the molten glass flows through small holes in the temperature-resistant bushing, jets of compressed air literally jerk the thin stream of molten glass into fine fibers varying in length from 8 to 15 inches. The fibers fall through a spray of lubricant and a drying flame onto a revolving drum on which they form a thin web. This web of staple fibers is gathered from the drum into a sliver. The sliver is then made into yarn by methods similar to those used to make cotton or wool yarn. The yarn thus produced is used primarily for tapes and fabrics for industrial purposes where insulation is needed.

FORMS AND TYPES OF GLASS YARNS

Glass fiber is produced in a wide range of fine diameters. They can be so fine as to be seen only through an electron microscope. A more common diameter filament extruded from one cubic inch of molten glass could be so fine as to be drawn to a length of 380 miles.

The fineness of the fiber contributes greatly to its flexibility. One form, produced by Pittsburgh Plate Glass Company, is finer than human hair, and its hollow center provides lighter weight and greater insulative properties.

Manufacturers produce various types of glass fiber for different end uses. Some are for home furnishings, others are being developed for apparel. They vary in fineness and flexibility to provide a range of textures and styles. *Fiberglas*

Beta, Taj, and *Filo Diamente* are such fibers, which are produced by Owens-Corning Fiberglas Corporation.

Some types of glass fiber can resist heat up to 13,000 degrees Fahrenheit and withstand forces encountered at speeds of 15,000 miles per hour. These are used as filament windings around rocket cases, nose cones, exhaust nozzles, and heat shields for aerospace equipment.

Some types of glass fiber, such as *Avaton,* are impregnated into various plastics to contribute strength to the fiber. These are used for such diverse products as boat hulls and seats, fishing rods, and wall paneling. Other types of glass fiber are used for reinforcing electrical insulation. Some types are used as batting for heat insulation in refrigerators and stoves.

Glass fibers are made into three types of yarn: multifilament, spun, and textured.

MULTIFILAMENT YARNS ■ Continuous-filament yarns have numerous strands that are produced in a wide range of diameters. The individual strands may measure .00025 inches (about .25 denier) and may number as many as 1800. The yarn thickness generally ranges from about .0026 inches, or 26 denier, to over .055 inches, or 22320 denier. These yarns are used for a wide variety of purposes, from draperies to cord.

More than 200 fine, continuous glass fiber filaments are shown coming from the melting tank through white hot bushings (above the operator). These fibers are being guided together into a high-speed winder on the floor below, where they are twisted into a single thread.

Courtesy Pittsburgh Plate Glass Co.

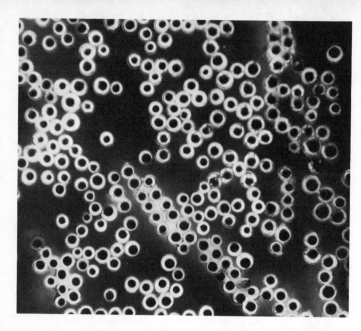

These unique *PPG* glass fiber filaments have been magnified several times to show the hollow cross section. These fibers give lighter weight and greater insulation to products in which they are used.

Courtesy Pittsburgh Plate Glass Co.

SPUN YARNS ■ Various diameters of glass fiber yarn is made from staple. These yarns are used for industrial purposes, such as conveyor belts and electrical-braid insulation.

TEXTURED YARNS ■ Different types of textured glass fiber yarns have been produced. An air-bulking process, similar to the technique used to make Taslan, disarranges and loops the filaments giving the yarn a rough texture. *Aerocor,* produced by Owens-Corning, is such a yarn. It looks and almost feels like wool or mohair. A process of expanding individual strands or groups of glass fibers permits the weaving of Aerocor into openwork casements, producing a fabric that looks like wool or linen. In flat weaves it looks like linen.

Novelty-structure yarns made of thick-and-thin and other types of uneven-surfaced filaments provide further textural effects. These are intended to offer additional styling effects at a lower production cost.

Textrafluff glass fiber is shown before being fed through a gun (left) and after (right). This fiber is used for insulating purposes.

Courtesy Pittsburgh Plate Glass Co.

Another type of textured, or bulky, glass yarn is *Textrafluff,* produced by Pittsburgh Plate Glass Company. The multifilament yarn is smooth when shipped. When it is to be used for insulating, it is fed through a gun that expands it into a fluffy yarn.

TRADE NAMES OF GLASS FIBER YARNS ■ Trade names of glass fibers that are produced by several companies for various purposes are presented on page 430.

FINISHING GLASS FIBER FABRICS

A basic finishing operation for all glass fiber fabrics is to subject the cloth to high temperatures. This releases the stresses that may be present in the yarns as a result of twisting and weaving. This treatment provides the fabrics with such desirable qualities as wrinkle resistance, greater durability, and good hand. They may then be treated in a number of ways. Color may be applied with the aid of a binder to hold the dye to the surface of the cloth. The fabric may be coated with a protective agent to improve its abrasion resistance. For marquisettes, the finish is regulated to produce a crisp yet flexible fabric.

A patented process called *Coronizing* is also available. This process combines a heat-setting treatment with the application of finishing resins. The heat setting relaxes the fibers, permanently crimps the yarns, and sets the weave, giving the fabric a soft hand, good drape, and wrinkleproof qualities. The finishing resins provide abrasion resistance, launderability, and water repellency. Better color retention and the use of pastel shades is possible with the aid of this process.

EVALUATING GLASS FIBER FABRICS

Most glass fiber fabrics for consumer purposes have been made of filament yarns. Since all glass fiber is produced in the same general manner from similar ingredients, the fiber used for similar purposes has similar properties. In fact, the designation of glass fiber is more frequently expressed as fiber glass. As has been mentioned, this term is often interchanged with the Owens-Corning trade name of *Fiberglas.*

Strength. Glass fiber is the strongest of all textiles. Some types are stronger than equivalent diameters of stainless steel. However, because glass cuts into glass as the yarns slide and rub over each other and are flexed, the filaments roughen and break and the fabric becomes hairy. This will also occur when glass fiber draperies, for example, rub against rough objects such as window sills or radiators. This poor abrasion resistance can be overcome to some extent by Coronizing.

Elasticity. Glass fiber is virtually inelastic. Being the least elastic of all textiles has obvious disadvantages for clothing; but when used for draperies and curtains, such fabrics will not stretch or sag out of shape.

Resilience. The lack of elasticity has no effect on the flexibility and wrinkle resistance of glass fiber fabrics. With the aid of certain finishes, glass fiber fabrics have good wrinkle-resistance qualities.

Heat Conductivity. As with ordinary glass, yarns made of glass fiber are good conductors of heat. Yet, when glass fiber is in staple form, the thousands of fibers form cells of trapped air. These dead air spaces act as excellent insulation and make glass fiber staple batting very effective as an interlining in jackets and coats. (The same principle is applied to insulate refrigerators and stoves.)

GLASS FIBER TRADE NAMES

TRADE NAME	MANUFACTURER	TYPE	SPECIAL CHARACTERISTICS
Aerocor	Owens-Corning Fiberglas Corporation	Multifilament	Textured
Avaton	Owens-Corning Fiberglas Corporation	Staple	Industrial applications
Famco-Fiber	Famco Company	Monofilament	
Fiberglas	Owens-Corning Fiberglas Corporation	Multifilament, staple	Roving, mat, chopped, milled
Fiberglas Beta	Owens-Corning Fiberglas Corporation	Multifilament	
Fiberglas Taj	Owens-Corning Fiberglas Corporation	Multifilament	
Fiberglas Filo Diamente	Owens-Corning Fiberglas Corporation	Multifilament	
Fiber Glass	Johns-Manville Company, Inc.	Multifilament	
PPG Fiber Glass	Pittsburgh Plate Glass Company, Inc.	Multifilament	
Textrafluff	Pittsburgh Plate Glass Company, Inc.	Multifilament	Bulk

Drapability. The fine glass fibers have excellent flexibility and pliability and can be woven into fabrics of excellent draping quality, particularly when given the proper finish. Consequently, they are excellent for curtains and draperies. Glass fiber fabrics can be easily sewed by hand or by machine with good-quality mercerized cotton thread, using a sharp needle and a long stitch under low tension.

Absorbency. Glass fiber is not absorbent—a property that represents both advantages and disadvantages. Being nonabsorbent, these fabrics are water repellent and, in general, unaffected by water. This quality makes glass fiber unsuitable for clothing worn next to the skin because perspiration and humidity make the fabric uncomfortable.

Cleanliness and Washability. The smoothness of glass fiber fabric makes it a clean fabric. Dirt and dust do not cling as readily to such fabrics as to rough materials. The cleaning of these fabrics is simple and quick. They may be wiped clean with a damp cloth. If complete immersion in water is desired, the temperature of the water and the soap or detergent used are immaterial, since these factors will not affect glass fiber fabrics. No strenuous agitation of the fabrics is necessary because the dirt comes off easily. The cloth will dry just as fast as the water will evaporate off the surface. If the fabrics are hung properly while wet, ironing is unnecessary.

Effect of Bleaches. Glass fiber is unaffected by bleaches; bleaching is in fact unnecessary since this fiber does not discolor.

Shrinkage. Glass fiber is dimensionally stable. It will not shrink because it is unaffected by water.

Effect of Heat. Glass fiber is highly resistant to heat and will not burn. The types available for general consumer use begin to lose strength at about 600 degrees Fahrenheit, and they soften above 1350 degrees Fahrenheit.

Effect of Light. Sunlight has no effect on glass fiber fabrics. This makes them useful for outdoor purposes, such as awnings, as well as for such decorative fabrics as curtains and draperies.

Resistance to Mildew. Glass fiber is unaffected by mildew, but the binder or resin used to finish or size such a fabric may be attacked by mildew.

Resistance to Moths. Moths and other insects do not attack glass fiber.

Reaction to Alkalies. Glass fiber is resistant to most alkalies.

Reaction to Acids. Glass fiber is damaged only by hydrofluoric and hot phosphoric acids.

Affinity for Dyes. Since glass fiber is not absorbent, it cannot takes dyes by ordinary methods. Special methods are used to bind the color to the surface of the fabric. Another procedure adds color to the molten glass before fibers are formed, providing a limited number of colors.

Resistance to Perspiration. Glass fiber is unaffected by perspiration.

REVIEW QUESTIONS

1 How are glass fiber yarns made?

2 Discuss the strength and abrasion-resistant qualities of glass fiber.

3 What desirable qualities does Coronizing give to Fiberglas fabrics?

4 Discuss the general care required for fabrics made of glass fiber.

5 How do the elasticity and resilience of glass fiber compare to those of other fibers?

6 How is glass fiber affected (a) by sunlight, (b) by heat?

7 How is glass fiber affected (a) by alkalies, (b) by acids, (c) by perspiration, (d) by mildew?

8 What are some of the uses (a) of glass fiber filaments, (b) of staple fibers?

9 Give the trade names of six glass fibers and indicate how these fibers differ.

COMPARATIVE CHARACTERISTICS

25 SUMMARY OF FIBER QUALITIES

To make a satisfactory textile choice for a particular use, one must understand not only the separate and combined properties of the various textile fibers but also their comparative merits.

The commercial value of any fiber depends largely on the extent to which it possesses certain characteristics, such as tensile strength, elasticity, fineness, cohesiveness, and sufficient length—all of which facilitate the process of spinning into yarn that will produce satisfactory fabrics for the consumer. The effectiveness of finishes and care of fabrics depend upon such properties as the effect of heat, reaction to alkalies and acids, and affinity for dyes. The consumer is also concerned with serviceability, performance, and ease of care. Therefore, consideration must be given to such factors as absorbency, cleanliness and washability, effect of bleaches, shrinkage, resilience, drapability, resistance to mildew and perspiration.

The choice, then, is a matter of selecting the fabric of the fiber or combination of fibers that offers the most desirable properties and will best satisfy the particular purpose for which the fabric or garment is intended. But this kind of determination has become increasingly difficult with the greater number of fiber groups and the variations within each group. Consideration is given here to the general properties of each group, classified by the Federal Trade Commission in accordance with the Textile Fiber Products Identification Act, such as acrylics, polyesters, spandex, and so on. The wide variations of properties existing within each group does indeed make specific and precise statements difficult, if not impossible. Reasonable comparisons among the groups are given here; for relative values of fibers within the group, refer to the chapter that pertains to them.

LENGTH

To form a yarn, fibers are made to lie parallel and are then twisted. If the fibers are long, there will be fewer ends protruding from the surface of the twisted yarn. Fewer surface ends result in a smoother fabric, which has less attraction for dirt particles. The smooth surface also helps to give an attractive luster to the finished cloth. Short fibers cause more surface ends and more points of potential separation, thus making a relatively weaker fabric.

The expression "The longer the fiber, the stronger the yarn" is true only when fibers within a single group are compared; for example, two or more wool fibers or two or more cotton fibers. Comparing wool with cotton reveals that wool fiber, though longer than cotton fiber, is not stronger.

Long-staple yarns within each group of fibers produce stronger, smoother, more serviceable fabrics that cost more than the less durable fabrics made from short-staple yarns. In wool, for example, the short-staple fiber is used in the manufacture of woolens, and the longer staple is reserved for worsteds. Worsteds are considered more serviceable. A similar distinction is found in every textile fiber.

The longer fibers produce the smoother yarns; the shorter fibers produce more surface ends, which results in fuzzier yarns.

Man-Made Fibers. The length is dependent on the ultimate use of the fiber, as well as on engineering problems in its production. The long, or continuous filament, fiber is used to produce smooth-surfaced fabrics. The staple, or short fiber filament, is used for soft, fuzzy fabrics.

Fortisan saponified rayon is the only man-made fiber made in filament form only. Viscose and cuprammonium rayon, acetate, Arnel triacetate, nylon, the polyesters (with the exception of Kodel), certain acrylics (Acrilan and Creslan), polypropylene, spandex, saran, and glass fiber are produced in both staple and continuous filament forms. The length is dependent on the ultimate use of the fibers and on the convenience of handling.

Silk. Raw silk fiber from cultivated cocoons is the longest of natural fibers. It consists of a continuous fiber that varies in length from 1,200 to 4,000 feet. It produces a smooth, lustrous fabric.

Shorter broken and cut silk fibers are also available. These are reduced to convenient staple length for spun silk yarns to produce coarser, rougher, and textured fabrics.

Linen. The flax fiber is longer than the cotton fiber and the wool fiber, ranging from 12 to 20 inches. This length accounts for the absence of lint in linen fabrics.

Wool. The length of the average woolen staple varies from 1 to 3 inches. Worsted yarns are made of 3- to 8-inch staple fibers.

Man-Made Fibers in Staple Form. The fibers in this group generally range from ½- to 6-inch lengths and are frequently made to resemble wool yarns. They are also sometimes spun to resemble cotton yarns and are sometimes blended to produce various effects and properties. The man-made fibers produced in staple form only are the high wet-modulus rayons, certain acrylics (Orlon, Zefran, and Zefkrome), and the modacrylics.

Cotton. Cotton fiber is the shortest of all fibers, varying from ½- to 2½-inch lengths. The bulk of the domestic cotton crop ranges from ¾- to 1½-inch lengths.

LUSTER

Luster is produced by the reflection of light from a smooth surface. A lustrous effect in fabrics adds to their attractiveness and, in some cases, may be absolutely necessary, depending on the purpose of the fabric. While luster may not be desired, as in napped or crepe surfaces, an appropriate lustrous effect is generally a desirable quality.

Degrees of luster are obtained in several ways. The use of long-staple yarns produces a smooth surface that has a natural luster. Caustic soda in the mercerizing process is a chemical method of producing luster. The satin weave and certain finishing processes also are used for this purpose.

The luster of a fiber has an important effect on its ultimate use. A fabric such as satin is expected to have a high luster and is therefore made of a highly lustrous fiber, while a fabric such as flannel is expected to be dull and is therefore made of a dull fiber. Here is the sequence of fibers according to luster.

Lustrous Man-Made Fibers. This group includes viscose, cuprammonium, and high wet-modulus rayons as well as acetate, Arnel triacetate, nylon, polyesters, acrylics, Verel modacrylic, polypropylene, and glass fiber. These fibers can be produced with a very high luster, which is referred to as "bright." However, luster can be controlled to a great extent, and some of these fibers are produced in lesser degrees of luster.

Silk. The luster of silk depends on the amount of surrounding sericin, or gum, that is removed from the surface of the filaments. The degree of luster is generally high.

Linen. The luster of the flax fiber is apparent at all times. This characteristic is helpful in identifying the fiber.

Semidull Man-Made Fibers. This group includes Zantrel high wet-modulus rayon, Fortisan saponified rayon, Dynel modacrylic, and saran. These fibers have a semidull or soft luster. When otherwise appropriate, the semidull appearance of these fibers makes for compatible blending with cotton, wool, or other staple fibers.

Cotton. Cotton generally does not have much natural luster. The degree of luster varies, however, with the type of cotton: the better the quality, the higher the luster.

Wool. Wool has crimp and a serrated, scaly surface. Better quality wool has more crimp and scales, which, in turn, reduces the amount of luster possible. The best wool, therefore, does not have natural luster.

Some fibers that belong to the wool group show some degree of luster; these are the hair fibers, such as mohair, vicuña, camel's hair, alpaca, and cashmere.

Spandex. Spandex is produced as a dull fiber so that it will become as inconspicuous a part of the fabric as possible.

Fibers differ in their resistance to tearing apart when subjected to tension. Therefore, the serviceability and durability of a fabric is not determined by the length of staple alone. Tensile strength is a prime necessity in fibers if the resultant fabric is to withstand the strain of wear. The ability of a fiber to resist wearing away by friction or rubbing, referred to as abrasion resistance, is another aspect of durability. Yet, it does not follow that tensile strength and abrasion resistance go together. The relative strengths of the fibers are as follows.

Glass Fiber. Glass is by far the strongest of all textile fibers. Its tensile strength exceeds that of stainless steel of an equivalent diameter, yet its abrasion resistance is not high.

Fortisan Saponified Rayon. With the exception of a special type of Fortrel polyester fiber, Fortisan saponified rayon is the next strongest fiber. It is about three times as strong as silk, which is the strongest natural fiber. However, Fortisan temporarily loses some strength when wet.

Nylon, Polyesters, Polypropylenes, and High Wet-Modulus Rayons. These textiles are all relatively strong. There is much overlapping of tensile strengths among the groups of fibers as well as among the fibers within these groups. Polypropylenes and polyesters do not lose strength when wet, and nylon weakens only about 10 percent when wet. The high wet-modulus rayons also have some temporary loss of strength when wet.

Abrasion resistance varies. For example, regular nylon staple has the highest abrasion resistance of all the fibers but does not possess the greatest tensile strength.

Silk. This fiber has long been known as the strongest of the natural fibers. Considering the extremely small diameter of the fiber (varying from .001 to .005 inch), silk is one of the strongest of textile fibers. The breaking strength of raw silk is equivalent to nearly one-third the breaking strength of the best iron wire of the same size.

Linen. Flax fiber, which is second in strength to silk, is especially durable. Linen gains strength when wet.

Cotton. This natural fiber has good strength. When wet, its strength may increase temporarily by as much as 30 percent. Cotton may be permanently strengthened by mercerization.

Acrylics. In general, the acrylics are weaker than cotton, though there is a fairly wide range of strengths among them. For instance, some types of Creslan, Zefran, and Zefkrome are stronger than the modacrylics, while the other acrylics are weaker. Acrylic fibers generally lose about 20 percent of their strength while wet and should therefore be treated with reasonable care. These fibers have good abrasion resistance.

Modacrylics. Dynel competes favorably with the stronger acrylics; Verel is generally stronger than the weaker Orlon and Acrilan acrylic fibers. The modacrylic fibers have the advantage of not losing any appreciable strength when wet. They also have good abrasion resistance.

Saran. The strength of saran has been demonstrated by a man standing on a suspended window screen made of this fiber. Since saran is virtually non-absorbent, it is not weakened by water.

Viscose Rayon. Viscose and cuprammonium rayons are approximately equal in strength; however, since it is possible to produce some varieties of viscose rayon of greater than usual strength (known as medium- and high-tenacity rayons), viscose rayon is rated above cuprammonium. The strength of rayon fiber is conditioned by its moisture content. When wet, viscose rayon loses from 40 to 70 percent of its natural strength; but this strength is completely regained when the fiber is dry. Viscose rayon is, therefore, not considered a weak fiber because it is judged by its natural strength when dry, which is one-half to one-third that of silk.

Cuprammonium Rayon. The strength characteristic of cuprammonium rayon, whether wet or dry, is similar to that of ordinary viscose rayon. Cuprammonium, however, is not produced in medium- or high-tenacity forms.

Acetate. Acetate is a relatively weak fiber. It has relatively low tensile strength as well as low abrasion resistance. Furthermore, acetate may temporarily lose up to 45 percent of its strength when wet.

Wool. Wool has the lowest tensile strength of the natural fibers; however, because its springness and resilience actually increase its wearing strength, it is rated above some of the other fibers. While wet, wool may temporarily lose as much as 25 percent of its strength.

Arnel Triacetate. The tensile strength of Arnel closely approximates that of wool. When wet, Arnel temporarily loses up to one-third of its strength. Arnel does not have good abrasion resistance.

Spandex. When compared to other fibers, spandex fibers have low tensile strength. However, the point of stress is reached only after the fiber exceeds its maximum point of elasticity. In normal use, this point is not readily reached; therefore, tensile strength is not usually a matter of concern. The abrasion resistance of spandex fibers is quite good.

ELASTICITY

Elasticity means that when the fiber is elongated or stretched, on release of tension, it will tend to return to its original length. Consequently, the less stress that is necessary to stretch the fiber and the more nearly it returns to its original length, the more elastic it is. The greater the elastic quality, the more the fiber will resist tearing. This elasticity contributes not only to the strength of a fiber but to the strength of a fabric as well. Elasticity permits materials to drape well on the body. Because elastic fibers do not break as easily as inelastic ones, this quality also facilitates the spinning process.

Spandex. Spandex fibers are by far the most elastic textile, being almost as elastic as rubber. They can be stretched from 500 to 700 percent, which is almost twice as much as that of the specially processed stretch nylons. Spandex returns to its original condition readily upon release of tension. Spandex also has the restraining or holding power so desirable for support and foundation purposes.

Nylon. Nylon has a high degree of elasticity. It has the ability to return readily to its original shape after a great deal of stretching. This is one of the characteristics that has made nylon an excellent fiber for women's hosiery.

Polypropylenes. Polypropylenes have fairly good elasticity, and one type of polyproylene, called *Vectra,* is being promoted to compete with nylon. However, polypropylenes generally tend to lose the ability to relax to their original length if the tension is retained too long.

Wool. Wool is one of the most elastic fibers, certainly the most elastic of the natural fibers. It can be stretched to about 30 percent of its original length without breaking.

Saran. Saran can stretch up to 30 percent of its original length before breaking, and it returns to its original size slowly.

Silk. Silk is the second most elastic of the natural fibers. With too much strain, however, it will never recover its original size.

Arnel Triacetate. Arnel triacetate is much less elastic than silk, yet it does have good recovery to its original dimension after tension is released.

Acetate. Acetate has about the same stretchability as triacetate but slightly less recovery.

Acrylics and Modacrylics. These fibers have relatively little elasticity. However, there are variations among them in the amount of stretchability and recovery that can be expected.

Polyesters. These fibers have even less elasticity than the acrylics and modacrylics.

Viscose Rayon. Rayons are not considered to be elastic fibers. Comparatively, however, viscose rayon is the most elastic of the rayons.

Cuprammonium Rayon. Cuprammonium has less stretchability and recovery than that of viscose rayon.

High Wet-Modulus Rayons. These rayons are even less elastic than cuprammonium rayon.

Fortisan Saponified Rayon. Fortisan has the least stretchability of the rayons. However, it has the best recovery of dimension when it is relaxed.

Cotton. Cotton has very little natural elasticity. The elasticity in certain cotton fabrics is added by special processing, such as slack mercerization.

Linen. Linen is the least elastic of the natural fibers.

Glass Fiber. Glass fiber is inelastic, but this should not be confused with flexibility. Glass fiber is quite pliable due to the fineness of the fiber.

RESILIENCE

Resiliency means that the fiber can be compressed or crushed and, on release of pressure, will tend to return to its original shape. When a fiber is resilient, it can be spun or twisted into springy yarns and the resultant fabric is also resilient. This quality causes the fabric to be wrinkle-resistant, with the resistance varying according to the degree of elasticity inherent in the fiber. Resilience also contributes to the abrasion resistance of a fabric. Some fibers have both elasticity and wrinkle resistance, but it is possible for a fiber to have none or little of either. It is also possible for a fiber not to have one quality, such as stretchability, but to have the other quality of wrinkle resistance.

Fibers that are not inherently resilient can be given a degree of resilience by reducing them to short staple. Short-staple yarns contribute softness to a fabric and help to make it somewhat crease-resistant, but some strength is sacrificed. A chemical finish can be used to obtain crease resistance, but this method may also affect the strength of the fiber.

While it is difficult to establish an absolute range for the fibers, the following generalities are adequate for average consumer needs.

Spandex. Spandex has excellent resilience, flexibility, and pliability. It is also very springy, reacting much like rubber.

Man-Made Polymer Fibers. Nylon, polyesters, acrylics, modacrylics, and polypropylenes have very good-to-excellent resilience that varies with the type of fiber in each group. The resilience can be enhanced by texturing or by crimping the fibers.

Saran. The polymer saran has very good resilience. However, it can be deformed by bending and by adding heavy pressure.

Arnel Triacetate. Arnel has a resilience rivaling that of nylon. Fabrics of Arnel hold their shape very well and resist wrinkling that normally occurs from much wear or packing. The wrinkles that might occur generally tend to hang out.

Acetate. Acetate has good resilience, though it is not equal to that of triacetate.

Glass Fiber. Glass fibers are surprisingly resilient, which is due to their extreme fineness and consequent flexibility. Excessive flexing or heavy creasing pressure will, however, cause the fibers to crack and break.

Wool and Silk. These are the most resilient natural fibers. The resilience of wool varies with its quality, and the better grades are very resilient. Pure silk is also very resilient, and the wrinkles that develop in silk fabrics tend to hang out. Weighted silks are much less resilient.

Rayons. These are the least resilient of the man-made fibers. Fortisan saponified rayon is the most resilient of the group. The high wet-modulus rayons are a little more resilient than cuprammonium rayon. The fineness to which cuprammonium rayon can be spun makes it possible to achieve more resilience than viscose rayon.

Cotton. Cotton lacks appreciable resilience. While special finishes reduce this disadvantage, the durability of the fabric is also reduced.

Linen. Linen is relatively brittle, and sharp creasing will crack the fibers. It is the least resilient of the major fibers and requires special finishes to improve its resilience.

HEAT CONDUCTIVITY

The ability of a fiber to conduct heat has great significance in textiles. The degree of heat conductivity determines whether fabrics are suitable for winter or for summer use.

In addition to the heat conductivity inherent in the fiber, the kind of yarn, fabric formation, and finish will also affect this quality. When a fabric is loosely constructed, for example, it has air spaces, which have an insulative property. The captive air pockets contained in a napped surface add warmth to a fabric. These are the more important considerations concerning the warmth or coolness of a fabric along with the following generalities about the heat conductivity of the fibers themselves.

Linen. The flax fiber is the best conductor of heat. Linen fabric is therefore most suitable for summer apparel, as it allows the heat of the body to escape easily and quickly.

Cotton. Cotton fiber is a good conductor of heat. Cotton fabrics are also suitable for summer clothing. The surface of the cloth has much to do with the degree of heat conductivity.

Rayons. Being cellulosic fibers, the rayons are also good conductors of heat.

Fortisan saponified rayon can be spun into very fine fibers that can produce fine yarns for sheer, cool fabrics. Cuprammonium rayon is not only an inherently good conductor of heat, it also lends itself to sheer and therefore cool fabrics because the yarn can be made extremely fine. High wet-modulus rayons are likewise good conductors, making cool, comfortable fabrics. Viscose rayon is a good conductor, but it may not be as cool as cuprammonium since the yarns produced may not be as fine.

Arnel Triacetate. The triacetate cellulose Arnel is not as good a conductor of heat as the pure cellulosic fibers. Also, being less absorbent, it feels warmer and is less comfortable in warm weather.

Acetate. Acetate is a poor conductor of heat. Because it does not absorb much moisture, it has a tendency to feel warm and clammy on warm, humid days.

Nylon. Nylon fabrics seem to have the peculiar property of being cold in winter and warm in summer. Actually, this is dependent on whether filament or staple is used and on the construction of the fabric. The spun staple nylon has thousands of air pockets that act as an excellent insulator; therefore, the staple nylon fabrics will be warm. The warmth or coolness of the filament fabrics is dependent on the porosity of the weave and on the amount of moisture in the air and on the body, for nylon reacts to moisture in the same way as acetate does.

Polyesters. The polyester fibers are promoted for summer-weight fabrics, particularly in blends with more absorbent fibers. While they are fair heat conductors, the polyesters can be crimped to add bulk and insulation to fabrics. They also have been found to provide excellent warmth as fiberfill for sleeping bags and quilts.

Silk. Silk is a natural protein fiber and therefore a nonconductor of heat. It may be used for winter clothing. Silk is generally thought of as a cool summer fabric; however, the coolness of a silk garment for summer wear is directly dependent on its lightness in weight and the sheerness of the fabric: the lighter and sheerer the fabric the cooler, the heavier the fabric the warmer.

Wool. Wool is very warm for two reasons: it has a scaly surface that provides air pockets for insulation, and it is composed of a protein, which is a nonconductor of heat.

Acrylics and Modacrylics. These fibers have a low rate of heat conductivity. They are also relatively lightweight and, when crimped, provide considerable insulation. This lightweight bulk produces very warm fabrics. The dog-bone shape of Orlon acrylic fiber and Dynel and Verel modacrylic fibers contribute additional bulk and insulation for their relatively light weight. Fabrics of these fibers are warmer than wool fabrics of equal weight.

Polypropylene. The polyproplenes are low conductors of heat and have the lightest weight of all textile fibers. When they are crimped, they provide excellent lightweight bulk for warm fabrics.

Glass Fiber. This fiber is unique in regard to heat conductivity. While glass filaments conduct heat, the staple acts as an excellent insulator because of the thousands of air pockets it traps. For this reason, glass staple batting is used for insulating refrigerators, stoves, and houses.

Spandex. Spandex is not a good conductor of heat. However, because it is usually blended in small amounts with other fibers, this does not become a significant factor.

Saran. Saran is also a low conductor of heat.

DRAPABILITY

The drapability of a fabric, or its ability to hang and fall into graceful shape and folds, is dependent upon the construction, the kind of yarn used, and the fibers in the yarn. The other factors being equal, the pliability and springiness of the various fibers will contribute different amounts of drapability.

Wool and Silk. These natural protein fibers have excellent draping qualities.

Cotton and Linen. These natural cellulosic fibers do not have good draping quality; linen, however, has the better drape of the two, which is partially due to its longer fibers and greater body.

Rayons. These fibers have only fair drapability, and the long, fine filament forms produce the most drapable fabrics. Fortisan saponified rayon, for example, provides good draping quality for curtains.

Acetate and Arnel Triacetate. These fibers generally have body and draping qualities that are better than the rayons.

Nylon. These fibers can produce fabrics of softness, body, and suppleness, which provide superior drape. The trilobal type of nylon, such as Antron, has excellent draping qualities.

Polyesters. The polyesters have fair drapability. Some types, such as the trilobal Dacron, are better in this respect than others.

Acrylics and Modacrylics. These fibers provide fair drapability, but this quality varies with the type.

Polypropylenes. These fibers are now considered to have only fair drapability. However, their stage of development is such that a further period of observation is required.

Spandex. Spandex fibers have excellent pliability and contribute to the drape of the fabric in which they are combined.

Saran. This is a relatively stiff fiber and therefore does not drape well. The fabric is used for upholstery, but it is not used for draperies or apparel.

Glass Fiber. Glass fibers can be produced in such fine diameters that they may be extremely flexible. Consequently, glass fiber can have very good draping quality. However, due to certain limitations (which may be ultimately overcome), glass fiber is not used for apparel, though it is quite well suited for curtains and draperies.

ABSORBENCY

The quickness with which a fabric absorbs moisture and gives it up again in evaporation has an important bearing on health and comfort. Textile fibers vary in their natural absorptive capacity, but absorbency may be increased by fabric construction or by a finishing process. A loosely constructed fabric or one with a napped surface, for example, is more absorptive than a smooth-surfaced fabric.

Wool. Wool fibers absorb moisture quickly and hold a large amount, allowing it to evaporate slowly. In fact, wool can absorb up to 20 percent of its weight in water without feeling damp, and 50 percent of its weight in water without dripping. When wet, wool does not stick to the body and is ideal for outerwear on cold, damp days.

Silk. Silk fiber absorbs moisture readily and, like wool, can hold much water without feeling wet.

Rayon. The absorbency and drying qualities of both viscose and cuprammonium rayons are closely akin to those of silk, and the high wet-modulus rayons fall into the same range of absorbency. Fortisan saponified rayon is the least absorbent of the rayons. Because rayons absorb moisture readily, they tend to feel wet and heavy when the air is humid.

Linen. Linen absorbs moisture more quickly and dries more quickly than cotton. For this reason, coupled with its strength and hygienic characteristics, it is excellent for towels and handkerchiefs.

Cotton. Cotton absorbs water rather well, but does not dry very quickly.

Acetate. Acetate does not absorb much moisture: only 14 percent of its weight at a 95 percent relative humidity. On warm humid days, the moisture therefore clings to the surface of acetate, and it feels uncomfortable. Although acetate clings to the body and feels warm and clammy, it dries quickly.

Arnel Triacetate. The absorbency of Arnel is slightly lower than that of acetate under normal temperatures and humid conditions. However, Arnel absorbs more moisture in higher humid conditions, which accounts for its somewhat greater comfort than acetate. Fabrics of Arnel also dry quickly.

Nylon. Nylon absorbs about half as much moisture as acetate. It also feels very clammy and uncomfortable on warm, humid days. Filament nylon garments dry very rapidly, often in one hour; staple nylon yarn dries more slowly. Water droplets cling to the surfaces of the short pieces of nylon fiber and have difficulty evaporating from within the central portion of the yarn. Garments made of spun nylon yarn may take twenty-four hours to dry.

Acrylics. While the acrylics are less absorbent than nylon, the range of their absorbency is quite close. Water does tend to cling to the surface of the acrylic fibers and this adsorbency results in water penetrating between the fibers of the yarn, causing such fabrics to dry slowly.

Modacrylics. There is a decided difference in absorbency between the Dynel and Verel modacrylic fibers. Verel is more absorbent than the acrylics, but Dynel is much less absorbent; in fact, Dynel has absorbency similar to that of the polyesters.

Polyesters. These fibers have very little absorbency. Therefore they do not stain easily and are relatively water repellent.

Spandex. Spandex fibers are even less absorbent than the polyesters.

Polypropylenes and Saran. These fibers are virtually nonabsorbent. Moisture tends to lie on the surface. They resist staining and may be considered to be water repellent.

Glass Fiber. Glass fiber is not absorbent.

CLEANLINESS AND WASHABILITY

The consumer is interested in knowing what textiles are hygienic, how long a garment may be expected to remain clean, and whether it will require special care when laundering or dry cleaning is necessary. The fibers that show smooth surfaces under the microscope produce fabrics that are easy to launder; thus garments made of linen, silk, and rayon wash easily. A napped surface on any one of these materials makes it necessary to give the garment more care in washing. The fact that a fiber does not absorb much water does not imply that the fiber is unhygienic. Actually, such fibers usually do not absorb dirt particles and have relatively smooth surfaces. The water then washes the dirt off the surface, and the fiber dries quickly.

Glass Fiber. A fabric made of glass filament yarn may be cleaned either by rinsing in water or by wiping with a damp cloth. Neither dirt nor water affects glass fiber because both remain on the surface.

Polypropylenes. Since polypropylene fibers are virtually nonabsorbent, they do not stain or attract dirt readily and surface soil may be easily wiped off. Fabrics may be washed in any household detergent or they may be dry-cleaned. However, because polypropylenes are generally heat sensitive, very hot water and other sources of heat must be avoided.

Spandex. Dirt and stains also tend not to soil spandex fibers easily. They are not harmed by the usual soaps, detergents, or dry-cleaning fluids. However, they are very heat sensitive and must be handled accordingly with care.

Saran. Saran may get dirtier a little more easily than the above-mentioned fibers because dirt can get imbedded into its slightly softer surface. However, it does wash easily, but the water should not be too hot.

Polyesters. The polyesters are smooth-surfaced fibers that do not get dirty easily. They may be dry-cleaned or laundered with a soap or a detergent. Most stains wash out readily. Heat-set garments made of polyesters do not lose their shape or permanent creases after washing. These garments also dry very quickly and do not shrink. Some types of polyesters have a tendency to pill.

Nylon. Nylon filament is also a smooth-surfaced fiber that does not get dirty readily. It may be laundered easily with a soap or a detergent. Fabrics made of nylon filament may be heat-set, so that they will retain their shape and creases or pleats after washing. Staple nylon launders easily also but takes longer to dry. Nylon staple pills very easily.

Acrylics and Modacrylics. All of the acrylic and modacrylic fibers have approximately equal degrees of cleanliness. Since they are usually made into fuzzy, soft yarns, they can get dirty easily; however, fabrics of these fibers wash readily and retain their shape, creases, and pleats. They all have good wash and wear characteristics and may also be readily dry-cleaned. Some types of these fibers pill badly, others pill moderately, and some special types have relatively good pill resistance.

Silk. Silk makes a hygienic material because of its smooth surface and absence of short fiber, which cause it to shed dust and to give up dirt readily. If handled properly, silk can be washed easily, unless it is given special finishes that require dry cleaning.

Acetate and Arnel Triacetate. These fibers are not as smooth as silk, but they can be easily dry-cleaned. They may also be laundered with a mild soap in warm water.

Linen. Because of the smooth surface of its fiber, linen gives up stains readily and affords little adhering surface for particles of dirt. Bacteria do not thrive on linen. Linen launders well, and its softness is enhanced by repeated washings.

Cotton. The short cotton fiber produces a fabric with a relatively rougher surface than that of linen, silk, or rayon, and therefore soils easily. Nevertheless, cotton fabric is considered a hygienic material because it can be cleaned easily. Since cotton is stronger when wet, it withstands rough handling and boiling temperatures.

High Wet-Modulus Rayons. These rayons do not soil as easily as cotton or the other rayons. They do lose some strength when wet and require more careful handling than cotton. However, they retain considerably more strength than the other rayons when wet. If desired, they can also be dry-cleaned.

Viscose and Cuprammonium Rayons. These rayons are dry-cleaned for the best results. Laundering must be done with care, particularly the spun rayons that have a shrinkage problem.

Fortisan Saponified Rayon. Fortisan saponified rayon should be dry-cleaned.

Wool. The scaly surface of the epidermis of wool fiber attracts dust, bacteria, and dirt particles. Consequently, wool fabric requires frequent dry cleaning, or washing if the nature of the fabric permits it. Felting occurs when wool is washed improperly. A wool garment should not be rubbed or handled like a cotton one.

REACTION TO BLEACHES

Sometimes fabrics are bleached to get them whiter or to remove stains. When a bleach is used, it should be put into the water and be thoroughly mixed before the garment is added. This will prevent the possibility of damaging the fabric with a bleach that is too concentrated.

Most white man-made fibers do not usually turn gray or yellow. Sometimes, however, the finish on the fabric may cause the discoloration. It is therefore a good idea to wash garments first without a bleach to determine whether one is necessary.

Cotton and Linen. The natural cellulosic fibers cotton and linen may be safely bleached by using normal care with the ordinary household bleaches containing sodium hypochlorite. For more careful treatments, sodium perborate and hydrogen peroxide bleaches may be used.

Wool and Silk. The natural protein fibers wool and silk must be bleached with care. Hydrogen peroxide is the safest bleach for them.

Viscose, Cuprammonium, and Fortisan Saponified Rayons. These man-made cellulosic fibers may be bleached with mild solutions of sodium hypochlorite. For safer results, hydrogen peroxide may be used.

High Wet-Modulus Rayons. Unlike the other rayons, the high wet-modulus rayons require individual treatments. Avril may be bleached with sodium hypochlorite. Lirelle may be safely bleached with hydrogen peroxide or sodium perborate. Zantrel should not be bleached with the usual household bleaches; it requires the commercial type of sodium chlorite or paracetic acid. Nupron can be bleached with sodium hypochlorite, sodium chlorite, or hydrogen peroxide. Xena is unaffected by bleaches.

Acetate and Arnel Triacetate. These fibers must be bleached with care in a mild solution of sodium hypochlorite or hydrogen peroxide.

Nylon, Polyesters, Saran, and Glass Fiber. These fibers must also be bleached with care, although most bleaching agents can be used. These include the household bleaches containing sodium hypochlorite, sodium perborate, or hydrogen peroxide.

Acrylics. With the exception of Creslan, the acrylics can also be safely bleached with any of the household bleaches. Creslan requires sodium chlorite.

Modacrylics. The modacrylics require individual, different treatments. Dynel may be bleached with any household bleach. On the other hand, bleaches cause the excellent whiteness of Verel to discolor.

Polypropylenes. These fibers may be bleached with the usual household bleaches, but their heat sensitivity require that the water temperature never be above 150 degrees Fahrenheit and preferably lower.

Spandex. The spandex fibers require various individual treatments. Hydrogen peroxide may be safely used for fabrics containing Blue C, Numa, or Vyrene spandex fibers. Any household bleach may be safely used for fabrics containing Glospan; sodium perborate bleach is safe for Lycra and Vyrene.

SHRINKAGE

Shrinkage caused by water varies from considerable to none, depending upon the fiber. Fibers that are susceptible to this shrinkage may be given special finishes, which significantly reduce the residual shrinkage that may occur from laundering or other exposure to water.

Wool. Wool shrinks more than any other fiber, though some finishes reduce its shrinkage potential and a few make it shrinkproof.

Cotton, Linen, and the Rayons. The cellulosic fibers cotton, linen, and all the rayons shrink considerably when wet. Shrink-resistant finishes are available to control this.

Silk and Acetate. Silk and acetate tend to shrink somewhat, though not as much as the fibers mentioned above.

Other Man-Made Fibers. Arnel triacetate, nylon, polyesters, the acrylics and modacrylics, spandex, polypropylene, saran, and glass fiber do not normally shrink when wet if the yarns and fabrics have been properly constructed and processed. Polypropylene, however, will shrink when it is exposed to moderately hot temperatures.

EFFECT OF HEAT

Heat affects different fibers in different ways and at different temperatures. Some fibers scorch and flame; others melt and flame or shrink. Some fibers are self-extinguishing, others are completely noncombustible. Some appropriate fire-retardant and protective finishes are available.

Cotton. Cotton is highly resistant to degradation by heat. It scorches at about 300 degrees Fahrenheit but does not burn until the temperature is 475 degrees Fahrenheit.

Linen. The reaction of linen to heat is similar to that of cotton. Because of the greater natural stiffness of linen, it should be very damp when ironed and the iron should be hotter than ordinarily used for cotton.

Wool. Although wool will start to decompose at 266 degrees Fahrenheit, it does not flame. It will support combustion at 572 degrees Fahrenheit. Wool should be pressed with a steam iron, or a very damp pressing cloth should be used with an ordinary iron.

Silk. Silk is less resistant to heat than wool. It will decompose at about 330 degrees Fahrenheit.

Rayons. All of the rayons decompose at temperatures of about 300 to 350 degrees Fahrenheit and then flame and burn in a manner similar to cotton. The lower scorching temperatures of the rayons require the use of a cooler iron than for cotton.

Acetate. Acetate will stick to the iron at about 350 degrees Fahrenheit. At

500 degrees Fahrenheit it will melt; then it will char, sputter, and flame. A cooler iron should be used for acetate than for rayon. Cigarette sparks and glowing embers falling on acetate fabrics will melt holes in the fabric on contact.

Arnel Triacetate. Arnel is a little more resistant to heat, melting at 572 degrees Fahrenheit. Heat-treated Arnel will stick to an iron at temperatures only above 482 degrees Fahrenheit. Arnel will also be damaged by glowing embers.

Nylon. Nylon is more sensitive to heat than triacetate. One of the major differences between nylon 6,6 and nylon 6 is their comparative heat sensitivity. Both yellow when exposed to a temperature of 300 degrees Fahrenheit, but nylon 6 melts at about 420 degrees Fahrenheit; nylon 6,6 sticks at 445 degrees Fahrenheit and melts at about 480 degrees Fahrenheit. For purposes of safety, it is advisable to iron nylon in the same manner as acetate. Nylon garments may be commercially heat-set to retain their shape after washing or dry cleaning without further pressing or ironing. As with acetate fabrics, cigarette sparks and glowing embers will melt holes on contact.

Polyesters. Each of the polyester fibers has a different sticking and melting temperature. Furthermore, variations exist among the types of each polyester. In general, they react at temperatures somewhat similar to nylon 6,6, with melting temperatures ranging from 455 to 500 degrees Fahrenheit. Being thermoplastic, these fibers can be heat-set.

Acrylics. The acrylic fibers also vary in the way they are affected by heat. Acrilan, for example, shrinks at 487 degrees Fahrenheit. Sticking temperatures for the acrylics range from 400 to 490 degrees Fahrenheit, and they melt at higher temperatures. These fibers can also be heat-set.

Modacrylics. The modacrylic fibers will not support combustion. However, Dynel will shrink considerably at 260 degrees Fahrenheit, and it will melt at higher temperatures. Verel is a little more heat resistant, but it will stick at about 390 degrees Fahrenheit and will melt above that temperature. Both fibers can be heat-set.

Spandex. There is wide variation in the effect of heat on spandex fibers. Vyrene is the most sensitive; it starts to shrink at 160 degrees Fahrenheit and loses strength rapidly above 250 degrees Fahrenheit. Lycra yellows and degrades above 300 degrees Fahrenheit and melts at 446 degrees Fahrenheit. Blue C spandex is much more resistant to heat; it melts at 554 degrees Fahrenheit. According to the producer of Glospan, it has good dimensional stability but reactions to specific temperatures have not been given. Numa sticks at about 437 degrees Fahrenheit and melts at about 511 degrees Fahrenheit. All spandex fibers can be heat-set.

Polypropylenes. Polypropylenes are among the most heat sensitive of all fibers, which is one of their major disadvantages. Added heat stabilizers have shown some limited success. In general, polypropylene fibers will shrink progressively at temperatures above 212 degrees Fahrenheit (boiling), and they melt above 325 degrees Fahrenheit. Polypropylene fibers can be heat-set.

Saran. Saran fibers are also heat sensitive. They stick at about 210 degrees Fahrenheit and melt above 340 degrees Fahrenheit. Saran is self-extinguishing when the flame is removed.

Glass Fiber. Temperatures must be extremely high to damage glass fiber. It begins to lose some strength at 600 degrees Fahrenheit and softens above 1350 degrees Fahrenheit. Obviously, ironing not only will not affect glass fiber, it is actually a waste of time and effort.

EFFECT OF MILDEW

Mildew often attacks textiles, particularly where there is dampness. Mildew stains and deteriorates fabrics and leaves a musty odor.

Nylon, Polyester, Acrylic, Modacrylic, Polypropylene, Saran, and Glass Fibers. These fibers are wholly resistant to mildew. If any of these fibers ever appear to get moldy, it is actually the finish on the fiber and not the fiber itself that is mildewing. Such mildew will wash off readily leaving no stains or damage.

Spandex. These fibers have good-to-excellent resistance to mildew.

Arnel Triacetate. Arnel is highly resistant to mildew.

Acetate. Acetate has good resistance to mildew, though discoloration will develop.

Wool. Wool has good resistance to mildew, but it will succumb after a period of time.

Silk. Silk has good resistance to mildew but eventually will be damaged under extreme conditions of dampness and darkness.

Cotton, Linen, and the Rayons. All of these fibers will definitely be attacked by mildew.

EFFECT OF SUNLIGHT

Textiles are constantly exposed to the outdoors and light. Some need to be very resistant to degradation by sunlight.

Cotton. Cotton loses strength in sunlight and has a tendency to yellow.

Linen. Linen is much more resistant to light than cotton.

Wool. Wool loses strength. Its dyeing properties, however, are improved on exposure of the fiber to sunlight.

Silk. Silk will be deteriorated more quickly than cotton or wool.

Rayons. Viscose, cuprammonium, and high wet-modulus rayons lose strength after a long period of exposure. On the other hand, the Fortisan saponified rayon has excellent resistance to deterioration by sunlight.

Acetate. Acetate will lose some strength, but it will not lose as much as viscose rayon.

Arnel Triacetate. Arnel also loses some strength from exposure to sunlight but less than acetate.

Nylon. Prolonged exposure to sunlight deteriorates nylon. Bright nylon is more resistant to sunlight than is the semidull or dull nylon. Ultraviolet absorbers may be incorporated during the production of nylon to overcome this problem.

Polyesters. While these fibers have good resistance to sunlight, they will lose strength after prolonged exposure.

Acrylics. The resistance to sunlight degradation varies from very good to excellent among the various types of acrylic fibers.

Modacrylics. Dynel has good resistance to sunlight but deteriorates from prolonged exposure. However, Verel has superior resistance.

Spandex. Some spandex fibers will discolor from exposure to sunlight, but their resistance in general is good to very good. They may, however, gradually lose elasticity and strength.

Polypropylenes. One of the disadvantages of these fibers is their susceptibility to deterioration by sunlight. To overcome this, light stabilizers are sometimes incorporated into the solution during production. However, these stabilizers may themselves break down under certain conditions.

Saran. Saran darkens slightly in sunlight, but it is not deteriorated. As a result, it is used a great deal for window screens and outdoor furniture.

Glass Fiber. Sunlight and outdoor exposure do not affect glass fiber.

REACTION TO ALKALIES AND ACIDS

A knowledge of the reaction of textile fibers to alkalies and acids is important, as alkalies destroy animal fibers; and acids, even in a weak solution, destroy vegetable fibers. For example, chemical tests for determining the fiber content of fabrics are made by noting the disintegration of wool and silk when exposed to a strong alkali, and there is a similar reaction when cotton and linen are exposed to acids. Good results in the bleaching, finishing, and dyeing processes depend on the reaction of the fibers to alkali or acid chemical agents. Not only is this reaction important in testing and manufacturing; it also closely touches the consumer when the care of fabrics is considered.

This reaction to alkalies and acids is most important to the consumer when fabrics are washed. Proper soaps and detergents should be selected for laundering the various kinds of textiles.

Cotton. Cotton is destroyed by concentrated inorganic acids—such as hydrochloric, hydrofluoric, sulfuric, and nitric—and is damaged when such acids are in dilute solutions. It is not injured by alkalies even in hot, strong solutions. Strong soap may be used for washing cotton.

Linen. The reaction of linen to acids is similar to that of cotton. Linen is not readily damaged by alkalies; however, strong soap should not be rubbed on the fabric as it will turn linen yellowish.

Wool. Dilute acids do not injure wool, but concentrated acids destroy it. Wool is quickly destroyed by strong alkalies. It dissolves if completely immersed in a boiling alkali. A neutral or mild soap must be used for wool.

Silk. The organic acids—acetic, tartaric, stearic, and formic—have little effect on silk. Weak inorganic acids also have little effect, but strong solutions injure silk. A dilute solution of nitric acid produces a bright yellow color in silk, and this reaction identifies silk from wool when testing.

Silk is destroyed by strong alkalies; strong soap should be avoided when washing silk. Compared with wool, silk is more resistant to alkalies but less resistant to strong acids.

Rayons. All the rayons react to acids in the same manner as cotton—they are disintegrated by hot dilute acids and cold concentrated acids. Viscose, cuprammonium, and Fortisan saponfied rayons are also weakened by alkalies, and strong solutions deteriorate them. However, high wet-modulus rayons have good resistance to alkalies, and they have the advantage over the other rayons in that they can be mercerized without serious deterioration.

Acetate. Strong acids will destroy acetate. Acetate will, however, withstand solutions of organic acids as strong as 28 percent. Acetate is easily affected by alkalies, especially if the water is very hot. Mild soaps and lukewarm water should, therefore, be used when laundering acetate.

Arnel Triacetate. Acids and alkalies have the same effect on Arnel that they have on acetate. Care should be taken to use mild soaps and lukewarm water when laundering fabrics of Arnel.

Nylon. Nylon is affected by concentrated solutions of the strong mineral and organic acids. Alkalies, however, have virtually no effect on nylon.

Polyesters. Polyesters have good resistance to most mineral acids, although a concentrated solution of sulfuric acid will decompose them. They also have good resistance to weak and strong alkalies; however, they will be disintegrated by strong alkalies at boiling temperatures.

Acrylics. The acrylic fibers have good-to-excellent resistance to mineral acids. They generally have fair-to-good resistance to weak alkalies but will be weakened by stronger alkali solutions.

Modacrylics. Dynel and Verel differ only slightly in their reactions. There is little or no effect of either the acids or the alkalies on Dynel. Verel has excellent resistance to acids, and although it is not weakened by alkalies, it may be discolored by them.

Spandex. There is a wide range of reactions of spandex fibers to alkalies and acids, depending upon the particular fiber, the kind of alkali or acid, as well as its strength and temperature. In general, the spandex fibers have poor-to-good resistance to most alkalies and acids.

Polypropylenes. The polypropylenes are among the most resistant textiles to alkalies and acids, being relatively inert.

Saran. Saran has fair resistance to concentrated sulfuric acid and good resistance to others. It is unaffected by most alkalies, but it is affected to a limited extent by sodium hydroxide and ammonium hydroxide.

Glass Fiber. The only acids to affect glass fiber are hydrofluoric and hot phosphoric acids. It is also damaged by hot solutions of weak alkalies and cold solutions of strong alkalies.

AFFINITY FOR DYES

The readiness with which a fiber absorbs and retains dye affects the appearance and serviceability of a fabric. Affinity for dyes is usually determined by the porosity of a fiber.

Cotton. Cotton has affinity for direct dyes, reactive dyes, certain azo dyes, and sulfur and vat dyes in a reduced state. The fastness of direct dyes is improved by the aftertreatments that are sometimes given. Mercerized cotton absorbs and retains dyes better than cottons that are not so treated.

Linen. Linen fibers have a poor affinity for dyes. The hard nonporous surface of the fiber and its natural gum content (pectin) do not allow even penetration of the dyestuff. A more favorable reaction can be induced by removing the pectin by a strong bleaching process, but this may entail some sacrifice in the durability of the fabric. For this reason, unbleached linens are preferable when extreme whiteness is not a primary consideration.

Wool. Wool has a very high affinity for dyes. Wool fabrics dye well and evenly.

Silk. Silk has excellent affinity for acid, basic, and some direct and reactive dyes.

Rayons. The several kinds of rayon have affinities for the same dyes as cotton, but they usually dye to a deeper shade. Dull rayon, however, does not pick up dye as readily as bright or semidull rayon. The dyestuff is absorbed evenly, and the material is consequently dyed successfully. Some rayons are solution-dyed and have excellent fastness.

Acetate. Acetate can be colored with disperse, acid, basic, and azoic dyes.

However, some colors, such as grays and blues, tend to gas-fade and turn red or purplish. Excellent fastness can be obtained by solution-dyeing.

Arnel Triacetate. Arnel has good affinity for the same dyes as used for acetate. Its resistance to gas-fading and crocking is generally somewhat better than that of acetate, if properly dyed. Black solution-dyed Arnel has excellent fastness.

Nylon. Nylon dyes fairly well when acetate dyes are used, and the colors are generally fast. It can also be solution-dyed.

Polyesters. These fibers can all be dyed with disperse and developed dyes at high temperatures. For some types, cationic dyes may be used.

Acrylics. A wide variety of dyes are used for acrylics depending upon the color, the kind of acrylic fiber, and the particular type. No single dye can be used for all acrylics. Zefkrome is produced in precolored form only and has superior fastness.

Modacrylics. The modacrylics can be colored with disperse and cationic dyes. Some vat dyes can be used on Dynel; Verel can be dyed with premetalized and basic dyes.

Spandex. The spandex fibers take a wide variety of dyes well. These include disperse, chrome, premetalized, and some selected acid and basic dyes. This is one of the great advantages of using spandex rather than rubber.

Polypropylenes. One of the major limitations of the polypropylenes has been their lack of affinity for dyes. Consequently, the fibers are frequently pigmented during manufacture. Some have dye receptors added during production to facilitate dying with disperse dyes and certain vat, sulfur, and azoic dyes.

Saran. Saran can be dyed only by including the color before the fiber is extruded.

Glass Fiber. A special technique is used that causes the dye to stick to the surface of glass fiber.

REVIEW QUESTIONS

1 How may a knowledge of textiles help the consumer?

2 What is the sequence of development of fiber into fabric?

3 What practical significance has the quality of absorbency in apparel?

4 Explain how length of staple affects the quality of a fabric.

5 What quality of acetate makes it desirable as a lining material?

6 What type of rayon would make the best-wearing coat lining? Why?

7 (a) Why is elasticity important in textiles? (b) How may elasticity in textile fabrics be improved?

8 What qualities of linen make it suitable for (a) towels and handkerchiefs, (b) summer apparel, (c) draperies?

9 What qualities of silk make it suitable for (a) women's dresses, (b) neckties, (c) ribbons?

10 Why is cotton used so extensively for infants' wear?

11 What qualities of rayon make it a poor fiber to use for (a) sewing thread, (b) stockings, (c) winter underwear?

12 What specific qualities do spun rayon fabrics have that are not found in filament rayon fabrics?

13 What properties may wool fabrics be expected to have?

14 How does a napped surface affect the hygienic quality of a fabric?

15 Why does a cotton bathing suit feel cooler than a woolen one?

16 Why does a fabric of nylon filament yarn dry faster than one of nylon spun yarn?

17 What single characteristic do all the acrylic fibers have that is of great advantage to the consumer and homemaker?

18 Why is the use of saran limited?

19 Which textiles will be damaged quickly by cigarette sparks?

20 Which textile would be considered best for curtains? Why?

21 Compare the warmth of wool, acrylic, and polypropylene fabrics.

22 Compare the elasticity of wool, silk, nylon, and spandex.

23 Compare the launderability of the various textiles.

SUGGESTED ACTIVITIES

1 Obtain as many samples of fabrics as you can, and cut them into small square pieces, three by three inches. Mount them on small cards. Determine the fiber content of each sample, and record your data on the card. Give all possible uses for each fabric. Give the reasons for your answers in terms of the basic qualities of the fibers.

2 Observe carefully the various contents of your home furnishings, and make a record of every item that uses any textile fibers. Add the name of the fiber used, indicating if this is a guess or the result of observation and analysis. Give reasons for each answer.

26 VEGETABLE AND MINERAL FIBERS

MINOR TEXTILES

The textile industry uses other fibers in addition to those already studied. Each has its field of usefulness. Some have qualities that make them suitable for purposes that none of the fibers previously discussed could fulfill satisfactorily. Others can be used as acceptable substitutes or even adulterants, as long as the finished goods fulfill the purpose for which they are intended, and the selling price is in line with the value of the product.

VEGETABLE FIBERS

JUTE ■ Jute is a natural fiber obtained from a tall plant of the same name. It is grown throughout tropical Asia, chiefly in India, for commercial uses. The plant is easy to cultivate and harvest. The fiber is obtained by retting, similarly to flax. The fine, silklike fiber is easy to spin but is not durable, as it deteriorates rapidly when exposed to moisture. Jute is the cheapest textile fiber and is used in great quantities. Because of its lack of strength, jute is difficult to bleach and can never be made pure white. It can be converted into a woollike fiber by treatment with a strong caustic soda.

Though jute is often used as an adulterant with other fibers, it can be easily recognized when tested for its marked sensitivity to mineral acids. Concentrated mineral acids readily dissolve jute. Dilute mineral acids rot it quickly. It is especially weak in salt water. Jute is used as a substitute for hemp, as binding threads for carpets and rugs, as rug cushions, as a filler with other fibers, and as a linoleum base. It is made into coarse, cheap fabrics, such as novelty dress goods and heavy cotton bagging.

KAPOK ■ Kapok is a natural fine, white hairlike fiber obtained from the seed capsules of plants and trees grown in Java, Borneo, Sumatra, and Central America. It is sometimes called "silk cotton" because its luster is almost equal to that of silk. Kapok resembles cotton in general appearance but is always of shorter average staple—less than one inch. Under the microscope, kapok can be easily distinguished from cotton, as it appears to be a hollow tube with very thin walls and frequent folds but no twist.

The smooth texture and weakness of kapok prevents its being spun into yarn, but it is felted for use in mattresses, cushions, upholstered furniture, and life preservers. Kapok is buoyant, but with continued use has a tendency to mat and become lumpy. This condition can be improved if bedding articles in which kapok has been used are aired and put in the sun at frequent intervals. Kapok is resistant to vermin and is especially resistant to moisture, drying quickly when wet. It is adaptable for articles that are constantly exposed to moisture. Kapok is also used for soundproofing in airplanes and for insulating material in refrigerator cars and trucks.

RAMIE ■ Ramie is a natural woody fiber resembling flax. Also known as *rhea* and *China grass,* it is obtained from a tall shrub grown in southeastern Asia, China, Japan, and southern Europe. The fiber is stiff, more brittle than linen, and highly lustrous. It can be bleached to extreme whiteness. Ramie lends itself to general processing for textile yarns, but its retting operation is difficult and costly, making the fiber unprofitable for general use. When combed, ramie is half the weight of linen, but much stronger, coarser, and more absorbent. It has permanent luster and good affinity for dyes; it is affected little by moisture. Ramie is used as filling yarn in mixed woolen fabrics, as adulteration with silk fibers, and as a substitute for flax. The China-grass cloth used by the Chinese is made of ramie. This fiber is also useful for rope, twine, and nets.

HEMP ■ Some thirty varieties of hemp, another tall plant with a natural woody fiber, are grown in nearly all the temperate and tropical countries of the world. All these varieties resemble one another in general appearance and properties, but only those having fibers of high tensile strength, fineness, and high luster have commercial value. Hemp must pass through a retting process and subsequent manufacturing operations similar to those used for flax. It resembles flax closely, and its fiber is easily mistaken for linen. Hemp is harsh and stiff and cannot be bleached without harm to the fiber. As hemp is not pliable and elastic, it cannot be woven into fine fabrics. Manila hemp, which is very strong, fine, white, and lustrous, though brittle, is adaptable for the weaving of coarse fabrics. Hemp is durable and is used in carpet and rug manufacturing. It is especially suitable for ship cordage and sailcloth as it is not weakened or rotted by water. Central American hemp is chiefly used for cordage.

SISAL ■ Sisal is a natural fiber obtained from the leaves of a plant that resembles cactus, grown in Africa, Central America, the West Indies, and Florida. The best supply is produced in Yucatan, where it is known as *henequen.* The smooth, straight fiber is light yellow in color. Sisal is used for the better grades of rope, for twine, for the bristles of inexpensive brushes, and as a substitute for horsehair in upholstering. Sisal may be mixed with hemp, but it should not be used for ship cordage because it disintegrates in salt water.

COIR ■ This natural coarse brown fiber is obtained from the husk of the coconut. It is stiff but elastic. Because of its resemblance to horsehair, it is used for stuffing upholstered furniture. Coir is also suitable for cordage, sailcloth, and coarse mattings.

PINA ■ Pina, or pineapple fiber, is obtained from the large leaves of the pineapple plant grown in tropical countries. This natural fiber is white and especially soft and lustrous. In the Philippine Islands, it is woven into pina cloth, which is soft, durable, and resistant to moisture. Pina is also used in making coarse grass cloth and for mats, bags, and clothing.

ALGINATE FIBERS ■ Interesting research has been conducted with seaweeds. British scientists at Leeds University have derived jellylike calcium alginate from certain forms and extruded it into multifilament fibers. They are flameproof and are used to some extent instead of asbestos for theater curtains in England.

The calcium alginate fibers have a dry strength comparable to that of viscose rayon. However, considerable strength is lost when wet, and the fibers could ultimately disintegrate if care is not exercised. This characteristic has resulted in some interesting applications. For instance, alginate yarns have been used as *scaffolding* to help support other yarns in the manufacture of lightweight, sheer, and lacey fabrics. After these fabrics have been constructed, they are washed with soap and water to disintegrate the alginate yarns, leaving the desired design or gossamer effect not attainable by the usual methods of fabric construction.

The alignate fibers have also been used in medical applications for dressings. They have been found to hasten blood coagulation and to facilitate healing when placed over wounds. Alginate fiber dressings have also been used by dentists as packing to stop bleeding; as healing progresses, they eventually break down and disappear.

The strong sisal fiber, obtained from the leaves of the agave, has long been used for rope. Now, however, it is receiving competition from polypropylene fiber.

Courtesy CIBA Review

MINERAL FIBERS

METAL THREADS AND TINSEL ■ Any of the ductile metals, such as gold, silver, copper and even the cheaper alloys, can be drawn out into fine filaments. These are used to ornament fabrics. Metallic threads are made round or flat and may be twisted with any of the major textile fibers. Sometimes, base metals are drawn out as fine wires and are covered with the more costly metals. Thus, silver thread may have a core of copper covered with a layer of silver; similarly, gold thread may consist of gold-plated copper wire. Recently, Brunswick Corporation introduced its *Brunsmet* stainless steel fiber.

When metal threads are elongated to an extremely fine diameter, they are usually known as *tinsel*. Among the many types are fine tinsel lamé, tinsel laminette, tinsel bullion, and tinsel braid. *Metal threads* are used in the millinery trade and as decoration in the form of fringe and braid, as well as for woven and embroidered patterns on tapestries, brocades, and upholstery fabrics. Fine tinsels are used in fabrics for evening dresses, handbags, and ecclesiastical robes.

These metal yarns, however, have many limitations. Some, such as gold or silver, are very expensive. All are heavy. Frequently they make the fabrics too stiff to drape well. Silver threads tarnish, and all fabrics containing metal threads pose a cleaning problem.

To overcome these disadvantages, special types of metallic yarns have been developed. One technique of producing these yarns is to sandwich a layer of metal (usually aluminum foil) between two extremely thin layers of clear polyester film called *Mylar*. When a silver color is desired, the adhesive holding the polyester film to the aluminum is clear; when gold or some other color is desired,

Asbestos rock (left) is manufactured into asbestos fiber (center). Note the similarity of asbestos fiber to cotton fiber (right).

Courtesy Johns-Manville Corporation

pigments are added to the adhesive or printed on the film before laminating. Such a thread not only can have a metallic gleam, but it can also be in any color. This foil type of metallic yarn woven into a fabric resists bleaching, mercerizing, vat-dyeing operations, and many other wet-finishing processes that are required to finish fabrics that also contain other fibers which may require such processing.

Another technique of producing metallic yarns is to expose a layer of Mylar polyester film to aluminum vapor under high vacuum, so that the layer of Mylar becomes coated with aluminum particles. This metallized film is then sandwiched between two layers of clear Mylar film. Color is imparted to the adhesive as described in the above-mentioned process. The metallized type of metallic yarn is, however, brighter and more lustrous. It also is better suited for some types of looms and offers a greater yield of yardage per pound because it is lighter in weight.

Some metallic yarns are made of aluminum foil bonded between two layers of cellulose acetate butyrate film. Others are made of aluminum covered with a polyolefin. The selection of metallic yarn used in combination with other textiles depends upon the economy involved as well as its compatability with the other textiles for general care purposes. Usually, these metallic yarns are very flexible, drape very well, and give good service.

These metallic yarns are produced by several companies. They employ essentially the same methods of production, using one of the two basic techniques described above. Each company produces the yarn under its own trade name. Some of the better known names are *Durastron, Lurex, Metlon,* and *Reymet.*

ASBESTOS ■ Asbestos is a natural fiber obtained from varieties of rocks found in Italy, South America, and Canada. It is a fibrous form of silicate of magnesium and calcium, containing iron, aluminum, and other minerals. The soft, long, glossy white fibers are pressed into sheets; and the best quality can be spun into yarn. Chrysolite asbestos is the most valuable for the latter purpose, as it has a fine, long staple that has strength and flexibility. Asbestos yarns are always made as ply yarns to increase their tensile strength. Asbestos will not burn, but it will melt at a sufficiently high temperature. It is acidproof and rustproof. Asbestos is now made in greatly advanced types of fire-fighting suits and fire-resistant fabrics, and in fireproof materials of many types—theater curtains, draperies, shingles, tiles, auto brake lining, andiron holders, and partitions. It is spun around copper wire and wrapped around pipes and joints of high-pressure steam engines. Inferior grades are used for soundproofing.

CERAMIC ■ Ceramics are a group of fibers introduced in 1966. An outstanding characteristic of ceramic fibers is high heat resistance, which makes them particularly well-suited for rocket applications. The American Viscose Division of F M C Corporation manufactures its ceramic filament fiber under the trade name of *Avceram;* the Carborundum Company introduced its ceramic filament fiber as *Fiberfrax.*

SLAG WOOL ■ Molten lead or iron can be processed into the form of fibers, which are used as felt and packing material for insulative purposes in the building trades. This by-product of the blast furnace is light in weight; it is fireproof, heatproof, soundproof, verminproof, moistureproof, and rotproof.

1 For what purposes are the minor natural fibers generally used?

2 Name five minor fibers, and give one use for each.

3 Why is jute never available in a pure-white color?

4 Why is kapok always felted, never woven?

5 How does kapok differ from cotton?

6 Compare ramie with linen.

7 Why is hemp especially suitable for sailcloth?

8 (a) How are metal threads and tinsel made? (b) For what purposes are they used?

9 Describe the qualities of asbestos and its uses.

10 (a) What by-product of the steel industry is used as insulative material? (b) Name four of its qualities.

11 (a) What is the source of alginate fibers? (b) What are they used for and why?

27

RUGS AND CARPETS

Floor coverings have been made from textile fibers for more than 5,000 years. Throughout civilization, rugs and carpets have formed a part of the history and culture of races and nations. Early kings and conquerors included valuable rugs among their treasures and trophies, and many of these famous pieces have retained values that in some cases are inestimable. Priceless handmade carpets and rugs woven hundreds of years ago in the Far East are exhibited today in museums as representative of the patient labor and creative art of weavers whose skills have passed on through many generations.

Well-chosen rugs or carpets serve as a colorful foundation for the decorative plan and color scheme of all rooms in the modern home. As floor coverings are among the most expensive items in a house-furnishings budget, careful consideration must be given to fiber, color, decorative character and design, size, and construction to obtain the best value for any price level.

RUG COMPOSITION

Floor coverings are made from various kinds of fibers—cotton, silk, wool, rayon, acetate, nylon, polyesters, acrylics, modacrylics, polypropylenes, and blends of these fibers, as well as from mohair, jute, hemp, or grass straw. The wool fiber has been the most popular natural fiber for rugs because wool has offered the advantages of extreme softness, resiliency, absorbency to shock and noise, and, particularly, resistance to wear when the right fibers and construction have been used. Wool rugs, however, can be attacked by moths and other insects.

Rugs of man-made fibers are not damaged by these insects. The nylon, polyester, acrylic, modacrylic, and polypropylene fibers have varying degrees of softness and resilience (as related earlier in the text). Nylon is extremely durable. The polyester and acrylic fibers wear rather well but there is some tendency to pill, though manufacturers claim to have minimized this problem. Indications are that polypropylene gives less pilling difficulty. Polypropylene also builds up much less static electricity; after standing or walking on polypropylene carpets, fewer irritating shocks will occur when metal objects are touched. These man-made fibers are not particularly absorbent, and polypropylene is the least absorbent. Rugs made of these fibers therefore resist staining. Spilled substances, such as ink, soda, mustard, and the like, can be wiped off readily without leaving a stain. One great disadvantage of rugs constructed of nylon, polyester, acrylic, modacrylic, and polypropylene fibers is that, since these fibers are thermoplastic, a burning cigarette or any other very hot object will melt a hole at the point of contact. Of all fibers used for rugs, rayon is the least durable and least resilient; and it had been the least expensive until the introduction of polypropylene.

Ultimately, the choice of a rug will depend on its attractiveness, its construction, its serviceability, and its cost. The consumer must weigh the relative merits of these factors in making his choice.

RUG CONSTRUCTION ■ The terms *rug* and *carpet* are used synonymously, but the form or the size in which these coverings are manufactured differs. Rugs may vary in shape as well as in width and length. In general, certain size standards are maintained that in the larger rugs have been adapted to standard sizes of rooms. The term *broadloom* does not refer to quality but describes a type of carpet woven all in one piece on a loom wide enough to produce the width desired.

The factors that account for differences in price are the type, quality, and quantity of fiber used, as well as the amount of twist, the number of plies in the yarns, and the basic method of construction. Carpets may be woven, tufted, or knitted. Weaving is the slowest and most expensive method of construction; tufting is the most rapid and least expensive.

Some rugs are coated on the back with a plastic binder, latex foam, or urethane foam. They are sometimes referred to as *patent-backed,* which is an inexpensive method of providing firmness, body, and resilience. This technique contributes flexibility in laying the rug because patent-back rugs can be cut in any direction without fraying the edges or unraveling the yarns, and the edges do not require binding. This feature permits the patent-back broadloom to be fitted easily to irregularly shaped areas. Also, holes caused by damage or wear can be cut out and matched pieces put in their places.

The surface appearance and texture of a rug is affected by its construction.

The roll of carpeting shown below has been coated on the back with latex.

Courtesy American Carpet Institute, Inc.

Cut Pile. When the pile is cut and the yarn is untwisted, a soft, plush effect is achieved. When the cut pile is made of tightly twisted yarns, the surface has a harder, friezé texture. Examples are Axminster, chenille, Oriental, velvet, Wilton, and tufted broadlooms.

Uncut Pile. When the pile is uncut to retain the loops, a pebbly, harder texture is obtained. Examples are Brussels, tapestry, and tufted broadlooms.

Combination Cut and Uncut Pile. Attractive surface-texture effects are obtained by combining cut and uncut pile in interesting patterns. This may be done on woven and tufted broadlooms.

Sculptured. The pile may be woven in different heights to form either a definite or a random pattern, which provides uneven but interesting and attractive patterns. This textural effect is also referred to as *carved* and *multilevel*. Combination cut and uncut pile may be utilized in this construction in woven and tufted broadlooms.

Flat. This construction exists in novelty and special-purpose rugs made from miscellaneous fibers. These rugs do not have any pile and, ordinarily, they can be used on either side. Examples are grass rugs and hooked rugs.

TERMS USED IN THE INDUSTRY ■ Judging a rug or carpet for quality of construction requires some understanding of certain terms used in the industry.

Tufts are the cut loops of surface yarns held in the small squares that are discernible on the reverse side of the rug. *Pitch* expresses the number of warp threads crosswise of the loom to each 27 inches of width. *Wires* refer to the number of tufts to the inch in the warp or lengthwise direction.

The construction of the rug is indicated by the closeness of the tufts in each direction—that is, by the pitch and wires. The number can usually be determined by counting the rows of tufts on the back of the rug. Compact construction of the tufts, represented by a high number of pitch and wires, indicates a dense pile, showing that a greater quantity of fiber has been used, resulting in a more durable product. Density of construction is considered the most important factor in determining the durability of floor coverings.

Additional crosswise yarns are used to bind the pile to the backing of the rug. The number of yarns used is indicated by the term *shot*. In a two-shot construction, one crosswise yarn can be seen between each row of tufts, the other crosswise yarn is behind the row. In the three-shot construction, there are two crosswise yarns between each row of tufts and a third yarn in back. The three-shot construction requires additional yarn and more loom operations. Though more expensive, it is more durable.

DOMESTIC RUGS

In the United States, floor coverings are often classified as domestic and imported. The *domestic* group includes all kinds of rugs made in this country regardless of the source of raw materials. The *imported* group includes Oriental, Chinese, Indian, and other foreign products. Today, these divisions and even specific types of rugs do not tell the consumer all that should be known because both good and poor qualities are found in all constructions.

AXMINSTER ■ The Axminster rug has been the most popular. There is no limit to the number of colors that may be used in its design. The colored yarns

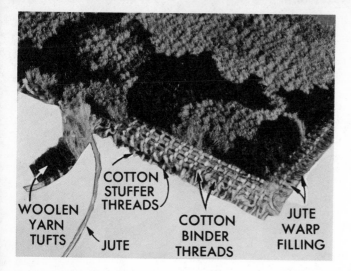

Axminster construction shown in detail.

Courtesy Mohawk Carpet Mills, Inc.

WOOLEN YARN TUFTS

COTTON STUFFER THREADS

JUTE

COTTON BINDER THREADS

JUTE WARP FILLING

are wound on separate loom spools in the weft direction. The spools are fitted in an overhead roller and produce an endless supply of surface yarn. Weeks are required to set the yarns for an Axminster design; but, once arranged, the 9 by 12 size may be woven in only an hour or two. Only soft-twisted yarn is used for the Axminster, as the weave is not tight enough to permit the use of hard-surfaced yarn. The surface closely resembles hand-knotted carpet, but the Axminster can be easily distinguished from any other type because it can be rolled only in its lengthwise direction. The stiff jute fibers used in the backing form pronounced ridges on the reverse side. The better quality Axminster has a deep pile, some flexibility in its backing, and as many as 70 tufts to the square inch. The less expensive grades have fewer tufts, a low pile, and a very rigid back.

BRUSSELS ■ The Brussels was the first type of carpet woven on a Jacquard loom. It is woven like a Wilton except that the wires used to make the surface loops do not have any cutting ends. As the wires are withdrawn, the pile is left as upright loops instead of cut pile. Hard-twisted yarns are used for the pile, producing a very durable product. The best quality Brussels is usually woven with five frames and has 9 wires to the inch and a pitch of 256.

Chenille construction shown in detail.

Courtesy Mohawk Carpet Mills, Inc.

WHITE LINES ARE WARP OF CHENILLE

LINEN BINDER THREADS

COTTON BINDER WARP

CHENILLE WARP

JUTE WARP

COTTON BINDER WARP

CHENILLE FUR OR CATERPILLAR

WOOD FILLING

THE WEFT BLANKET CLOTH
BEFORE BEING CUT

THE CHENILLE FUR OR
FURRY CATERPILLAR

THE WARP OF THE CHENILLE FUR

Photos Courtesy Mohawk Carpet Mills, Inc.

Hand tufting (left) is done in chenille weaving by using a steel comb. The comb brings up the surface yarns in the fur through strong cotton-catcher warp threads as four shuttle motions weave the heavy backing yarn to the base of the fabric. Chenille fur (right), or hairy caterpillar, is made from woolen blanket cloth. The cloth shown has been partly cut so that the warp of the caterpillar may be seen.

CHENILLE ■ Chenille is the most expensive of the domestic types, and it offers the widest range of possibilities with respect to depth of pile, design, colorings, and width. Chenille may be constructed as wide as 30 feet without a seam, and can be made as a single unit to fit irregularly shaped areas. It can be produced with a pile up to a full inch in height. This height, when supported by a heavy cushion back, gives a luxuriously soft and resilient quality and remarkable durability.

The woven chenille construction requires two separate loom operations. First, soft- or hard-twisted yarns are woven into a blanket containing cotton warp threads. Actually, this blanket is composed of vertical soft- or hard-twisted yarns bound together by the cotton warp. Another machine cuts this filling halfway, producing furry strips that are held together by the cotton yarns in the center. This strip, which resembles a caterpillar, is pressed into V-shaped form; and the separate ends are tied together, forming a continuous chain. This chain is subsequently used on the second loom as a filling for the final weaving of the chenille rug. A well-constructed chenille uses a fine quality wool and a densely packed high pile, which results in the durability characteristic of this weave.

Smyrna rugs resemble chenille, as they are made with a chenille fur. But the fur is twisted into a round yarn instead of the V shape of the chenille. A shot of fiber filling makes the Smyrna rug reversible—the pattern and pile are alike on both sides. It has a shorter pile than the chenille.

VELVET ■ The velvet construction is the simplest pile weave. Its pile is woven over wires having cutting ends that produce the cut tufts as the wires are withdrawn. All the fiber lies on the surface of velvet carpet, with no buried yarns in the backing. Only one yarn is used, and it must be uniform and

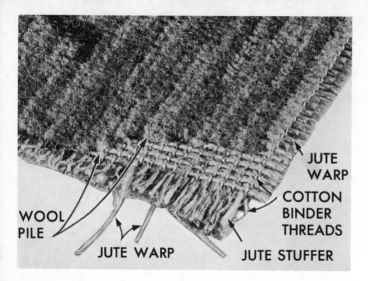

Velvet construction shown in detail.

Courtesy Mohawk Carpet Mills, Inc.

JUTE WARP

COTTON BINDER THREADS

WOOL PILE

JUTE WARP

JUTE STUFFER

of good quality throughout to absorb the dye evenly when printed. The common method of producing a pattern on velvet rugs is by printing the design after the rug has been constructed. Sometimes, yarns that have been printed before weaving are used. The velvet rug is inexpensive, as it is the fastest type to weave. It is made on an ordinary loom. Twisted yarns are used to produce what is known in the trade as hard-twisted velvets. For firmness, jute yarns, sized with glue, are used as stuffing warp yarns. The better-quality velvet rug has a deeper pile; its density should range from 56 to 80 tufts to the square inch.

WILTON ■ Wilton is an expensive weave to manufacture, ranking next to chenille. It is always woven on a Jacquard loom and is considered one of the best of all machine-made rugs. In weaving the Wilton, the surface yarn is held in trays called *frames*. Each frame holds spools wound with yarn of the same color. If there are six full colors in the pattern of a Wilton, there must be six frames. In a six-frame Wilton, only one of the six pile yarns appears on the surface at a time. The other five lie underneath, constituting hidden value in the form of added resiliency and quality. The number of frames in a Wilton varies from two to six, indicating the thickness of its fiber cushion and the number of separate colors in its design. A method known as *planting* makes it possible to add, in small areas, more colors than are indicated by the number of frames.

The pile effect of the Wilton is produced by looping the surface yarns over wires that have razor-sharp knives at the ends. When the wires are withdrawn, the knives cut the pile. The Wilton is made with soft- or hard-twisted yarns. When closely woven, the worsted Wilton offers maximum durability together with fineness of texture and delicacy of design even though it has a short pile. The finest grade of worsted Wilton is woven with six frames, with a three-ply yarn. It has 13 wires to the inch, a three-shot construction, and about 115 tufts to the square inch. Lower grades are woven with a smaller number of frames, have 10 wires to the inch, a two-shot construction, and as few as 60 tufts to the square inch.

The soft-twist Wilton has a more luxurious feel than the hard-twist Wilton because of its greater softness and depth of pile. It is made with at least two and a half frames and has 7½ to 9½ wires to the inch and a pitch of 214.

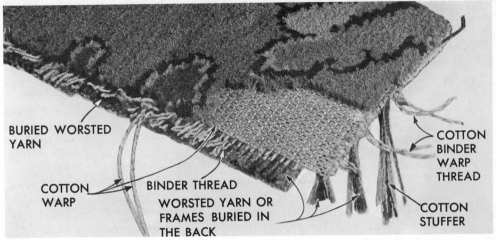

BURIED WORSTED YARN

COTTON WARP

BINDER THREAD WORSTED YARN OR FRAMES BURIED IN THE BACK

COTTON BINDER WARP THREAD

COTTON STUFFER

Courtesy Mohawk Carpet Mills, Inc.

Worsted Wilton construction shown in detail.

A better grade of woolen Wilton made from unusually heavily twisted woolen yarns with large and firm tufts is called "Saxony." These yarns produce a luxurious depth of pile with large, loose tufts and a coarse design. The rug is especially durable in spite of its extreme softness.

SHEEN-TYPE OR AMERICAN ORIENTAL ■ The name "American Oriental" is frequently used for the sheen-type or luster-type domestic rugs that are produced by the Wilton, Axminster, or velvet weave. The sheen in the domestic product is obtained by washing or brushing the wool rugs in a chlorine solution, which imparts the characteristic luster of the imported Oriental rug. The patterns are faithful reproductions and in many cases are woven through to the back, as in the genuine Oriental. When made of good-quality yarns, the American Oriental gives satisfactory wear and is very popular.

TAPESTRY ■ The construction of the tapestry rug is similar to that of the velvet except that the wires used to form the pile do not have any cutting ends.

Woolen Wilton construction shown in detail.

Courtesy Mohawk Carpet Mills, Inc.

JUTE WARP

COTTON WARP THREADS

COLORED WOOLEN YARN

JUTE WARP

THE VARIOUS COLORED WOOLEN YARN BURIED IN THE BACK WHEN NOT SHOWING IN THE PATTERN

COTTON WEFT THREADS

Thus an uncut pile is left when the wires are withdrawn. Because of its resemblance to the Brussels type, the tapestry rug is sometimes termed *tapestry Brussels*. This is a misnomer. The term attempts to attribute to the tapestry rug the superior construction of the Brussels, which is made on a Jacquard loom with a two- to five-frame construction. The tapestry rug is made on an ordinary loom and requires only one warp yarn. A good grade should have 8 wires and a pitch of 8. The tapestry rug is not intended for heavy or long wear. It does not have the softness of other rugs, nor does it have delicate or distinct designs. It is intended to satisfy the demand for an inexpensive yet sturdy product.

TUFTED ■ Tufted carpet represents a process of construction that can be utilized to simulate other types of rug construction at a much lower cost of production. The technique has become widely adopted by rug manufacturers, and over 85 percent of today's rugs are produced by this method.

The backing is constructed first. It is usually woven, generally of jute, kraftcord, or cotton. Recently, a woven nylon scrim with the yarn covered in polyurethane foam has been introduced under the trademark *Chemback*. (The backing may also be made of a nonwoven material, such as *Loktuft*, which is primarily composed of Marvess polypropylene fiber.) The newer backing media have added to the tufting technique such advantages as less dependence on uncertain foreign export conditions, reduction in manufacturing problems and costs, greater dimensional stability of the carpet, greater stability and inertness of the backing material during finishing operations, and greater resistance to bacteria and mildew.

The tufts are inserted in the interstices between the backing yarns by

Courtesy American Carpet Institute, Inc.

TUFTED CONSTRUCTION

TUFTS NEEDLED THROUGH WOVEN BACK

BACKING COMPOUND LOCKS TUFTS

Courtesy American Carpet Institute, Inc.

Creel rack shown above is used for carpet tufting machine.

a machine that simultaneously punches thousands of tufting needles through them. To secure the tufts permanently in place, the backing is then coated with a layer of latex. A second backing is sometimes added to enhance the body and hand as well as to improve the dimensional stability.

The tufting technique is extremely versatile. A wide variety of textures and patterns can be achieved with the tufting process. The pile can be cut, uncut, or sculptured, or it can be a combination of these. All kinds of color combinations and multicolor combinations are also possible.

KNITTED ■ Knitted carpets are made by using three sets of needles to loop together the backing yarn, the stitching yarn, and the pile yarn in a single operation similar to that of hand knitting. A coat of latex is applied to the back to give additional body. A second backing is often added for greater dimensional stability.

The pile is usually uncut, but cut pile can be obtained with modifications in the knitting machine. Sculptured surfaces are also possible. Solid, tweed, and multicolored patterns can also be achieved.

HOOKED ■ Hooked rugs from the Southern and New England states and from Canada are popular as throw rugs for bedrooms and halls. These are handmade of twisted rags sewed together, usually in Colonial patterns. They are also produced commercially in room and small sizes in cotton and in wool.

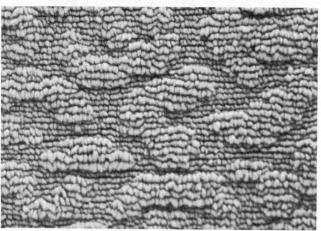

Above: Tufting machine in operation shows the tufting yarns at the top being guided down to be needle punched through the backing fabric coming off the roller at the front. The fabric is seen as it is fed off toward the rear of the machine.

Left: Variations in pile height give tufted carpeting a sculptured effect.

Photos Courtesy Allied Chemical Corporation

GRASS ■ A wirelike grass that grows wild in the northeastern section of the United States is used for grass rugs. They are woven with a plain weave that shows on one side. A pattern applied by stencil appears on the other side. Colored warp threads can be used to form geometric designs. Grass rugs are always varnished to preserve their surface.

SISAL ■ Sisal fiber imported from Central America and the West Indies can be made into rugs. The chief use of this fiber is for twine and rope, but its durability makes it adaptable for floor coverings. Sisal fiber is obtained from the leaf of a plant. It is twisted into strands and woven similarly to any of the fiber rugs.

IMPORTED RUGS

ORIENTAL ■ Very few of the Oriental rugs produced before 1795 are on the commercial market today, but many are displayed in museums. These older Orientals are valuable because of their age, beauty, and intricacy of design. Those made in the last ninety years are accepted as "old Orientals," and although scarce, are still obtainable.

Oriental rugs are classified according to the country and the section from which they originated. They are divided into six groups: Persian, Turkish, Caucasian, Turkoman, Indian, and Chinese. These groups can be subclassified according to their weave and also by the method of looping or knot tying that is characteristic of Oriental rug construction. Only two kinds of knots are used for the many kinds of Oriental rugs made throughout Europe and Asia. The Persian or Senna knot is more of a twist or wrapping; the Turkish or Ghiordes knot is a real knot as understood today.

The largest class of Oriental rugs has a pile surface composed of tufts. Each tuft is made separately by means of the knot formed by strands looped around the warp yarns. When the quality of an Oriental rug is being judged, consideration should be given to coloring, design, depth of pile, quality of the yarn, age, condition, and fineness of texture. The number of knots to the square inch may vary from 50 to 500.

The consumer may find it difficult to distinguish between the imported Oriental and the machine-made domestic product. It may be helpful to remember that the reverse side of the Oriental always shows the entire pattern in detail and that the pile is produced by rows of knots, which can be easily seen by separating the pile. The back should also be examined to see whether the entire pattern has the same colors on the reverse side as are on the face of the rug and to check the number of knots to the square inch.

In the genuine Oriental, the fringe of the rug is never sewed on; it is always an extension of the warp threads. In proportion to size the Oriental is always heavier than the domestic. Experienced rug merchants distinguish the two by examining the dyed portion of the pile nearest the knot. Oriental rugs use natural dyes, which usually fade to a lighter shade of the original color. The domestic rug uses aniline dyes, which fade to different hues.

CHINESE ■ Antique Chinese rugs were made with the Persian or Senna knot, making possible a large number of knots to the inch and a close shearing of the pile. Later, rugs were made with large coarse designs and a deep pile. In more recent years, Chinese rugs have been made in plain colors as well as in the floral and dragon patterns characteristic of Chinese design. The pile is unusually deep, making these rugs remarkably durable.

INDIAN ■ Small-sized rugs imported from India are made from felted goat's hair and embroidered by hand with bright wool threads similar to the work found in crewel fabrics. They are known as *Numdah rugs.* They are inexpensive and adaptable for general household use as they can be easily washed. Another rug imported from India, called a *drugget,* is woven with the wool of wire-haired sheep. Jute is used in its backing. It is usually highly colored and should be dry-cleaned instead of washed.

CARE OF RUGS

The appearance and the life of a rug depend on the amount and kind of attention it receives. Dirt and grit must be removed frequently; otherwise, dirt works into the recesses of the pile and into the backing, soon cutting the yarn fibers and finally producing worn areas. A carpet sweeper, or vacuum cleaner, should be used on carpets for a few minutes every day, surely twice a week, cleaning in the direction of the pile, not against it.

When sweeping a new pile-surfaced rug, loose pieces of the pile, or fuzz, are likely to come off. This is caused by the excess short fibers worked in during manufacturing operations. It does not necessarily indicate defects. When ends of tufts appear above the surface of a new rug, clip them level with the surface.

A new wool rug or one recently returned from storage should always be swept and brushed gently because the wool in the rug is in a dry condition, not having had sufficient opportunity to absorb its natural intake of moisture. The constant absorption of moisture from the atmosphere, so important for the healthful condition of a rug, keeps it resilient and resistant to wear.

Constant pressure on a rug flattens the tufts or slants them in one direction. The position of the rug or the furniture should be changed so that the wear may be distributed instead of concentrated in a particular area. This helps to prevent the uneven shading that occurs when sections of a rug show localized wear. An important safeguard in the care of a rug is to place a cushion backing under it to absorb the constant impact. Any stains should be removed promptly. Many spots can be easily removed when fresh. Removal is difficult when a stain has set. The rules for the removal of spots and stains from general textile fabrics apply as well to textile floor coverings. (See Chapter 28.)

Moths and carpet beetles may damage wool rugs. Keeping the rug clean and providing a healthful circulation of air reduces this danger. For this reason, some persons do not put their rugs away during the summer months, letting them remain on the floor for the frequent cleanings so essential for long and serviceable wear. Rugs that are cleaned frequently with a vacuum cleaner are never attacked by moths. If a damaged area is regular in form, this is an indication that the attacking insect is not the moth but the tow bug, which is likely to be found in overstuffed upholstered furniture.

Curling of the corner of a rug can be remedied by applying a hot iron on a damp cloth to both face and back of the corner. The curling is usually caused by constant tripping or by some similar unusual strain.

1 What basic properties of textile fibers are required for floor coverings?

2 What are the two main classifications of floor coverings?

3 What identifying characteristics distinguish Oriental and Chinese rugs?

4 How does the Brussels carpet differ from broadloom?

5 Describe the Wilton construction. How does a worsted Wilton differ from a woolen Wilton?

6 (a) How can humidity affect floor coverings? (b) How is this indicated to the owner? (c) What remedy is available?

7 Describe the Axminster carpet, indicating how to distinguish it from other carpets.

8 (a) What are the advantages of a chenille carpet? (b) What are the disadvantages?

9 Compare the imported Oriental with the domestic product.

10 Why is the patent-back construction important in carpet production?

11 What are some precautions to take in caring for floor coverings?

12 Under what conditions may a wool rug be left on the floor in summer?

13 Describe the tufting process.

14 Why have tufted carpets become the predominant type of rug?

15 Compare the attributes of the man-made fibers for rugs.

16 How do these characteristics compare with wool?

17 How are knitted rugs made?

18 What are hooked rugs?

19 What are sculptured carpets?

FABRIC CARE

28

SERVICE, ECONOMY, APPEARANCE

Fabrics should not only be carefully selected, they should be given proper care throughout their lives. This care includes: (1) frequent brushing and airing of garments, (2) clean storage when not in use, (3) immediate mending when damaged by tearing, (4) stain removal before washing or further use, (5) intelligent choice of cleaning method—washing or dry cleaning, (6) frequent laundering when the fabric is washable, (7) proper method of laundering for type of fabric, (8) proper ironing or pressing.

BRUSHING AND AIRING

The frequent brushing of garments, especially those having napped surfaces, removes the kind of dirt that starts as dust. The accumulation of dust particles soils the fabric (even when the soil is not readily discernible) and eventually causes deterioration.

When a garment is not washable, and does not require frequent dry cleaning, its life can be prolonged and its appearance kept bright and attractive by brushing. To offset the absorption of perspiration in such garments, they should be frequently aired, outdoors if possible. If this is not possible, hang clothes for a time outside the closet in a well-aired room. Frequent brushing with a clothes-brush that has soft but firm bristles is necessary to keep wool garments in good condition. Hang them on wide-shouldered hangers in a closet where clothes are not packed tightly together. Occasional airing is also necessary to prolong the life of wool fiber. Clothes hanging in a closet should always be buttoned, and zippers should be closed.

STORING

Clothing that is not in daily use should be protected from deterioration by storage in dustproof containers in which a moth preventive for wools is used. No useful purpose is served if the garment is stored without careful brushing and airing because the accumulated dirt damages the stored articles. For long storage, garments should be washed or dry-cleaned and stored immediately, preferably in sealed containers.

If newly purchased linens are to be stored for a while, they should be washed to remove any possible sizing. Any residue of starch in new or used stored linens may cause mildew. If white linens are wrapped in blue paper, and the ends of the package are sealed to exclude light and air, the linens will not turn yellow during storage.

MENDING

A torn fabric should be mended before further use. Makeshift repair with a pin tends to cause longer tears or frays that are more difficult to mend. The mended portion will be less noticeable if it is repaired before the surrounding yarns are further damaged.

METHODS OF STAIN REMOVAL

Successful removal of stains from fabrics depends on the basic principle of not allowing the spot or stain to become set. A stain should be removed at the first possible opportunity because it may be more easily dissolved when fresh. Different fibers require different methods and different stain removers. Use of an incorrect remover may damage or even destroy the fiber content of a fabric. Knowledge of the nature of the stain makes possible the immediate use of the appropriate method and removal agent. Hot water should never be used on an unknown stain. The heat will set the stain, making it more difficult to remove. If the stain is known to be of a nongreasy nature, sponging with cold water may be all that is necessary. On the other hand, a greasy stain requires the use of carbon tetrachloride or some other dry cleaner, such as benzine, gasoline, turpentine, or denatured alcohol. There are four effective methods for removing spots and stains.

DIP METHOD ■ When the entire fabric can be immersed in the stain remover, the best method is dipping. This is the most convenient method if the spot is large, or if there are many spots on an all-cotton or all-linen fabric.

STEAM METHOD ■ Stains on wool, silk, or any colored fabric may be removed by steaming. The stained area is saturated with steam by spreading the cloth over a bowl partly filled with hot water into which a small amount of the appropriate removal agent has been placed.

DROP METHOD ■ Small drops of a removal agent can be applied by means of a medicine dropper, glass rod, or orange stick.

SPONGE METHOD ■ Sponging is the most frequently used method of stain removal, but if it is not done with care, it will not be effective. An absorbent cloth or a blotter should be placed underneath the stain to absorb the removal agent as well as the stain. The blotter also prevents further spreading of the wet area. Both the sponging cloth and the absorbent material should be renewed whenever they show the slightest tinge of the stain. The stained portion of the fabric must not be soaked with the cleaning fluid, and the fabric must not be harshly rubbed. Apply small quantities of the fluid with a soft cloth using light strokes in a circular direction from the outer rim of the stain toward its center.

REMOVAL OF STAINS—FABRICS MADE OF NATURAL FIBERS

KIND OF STAIN	TYPE OF FABRIC	PROCEDURE AND REMOVAL
Acid	All	Neutralize with ammonia
Adhesive tape	All	Harden with ice cubes; rub off with fingers, then carbon tetrachloride or kerosene
Airplane glue	All	Apply acetone or nail polish remover followed by alcohol
Alcoholic beverages	All	Soak in cold water immediately followed by white vinegar, then rinse with cold water
Alkali	All	Neutralize with vinegar
Blood	Cotton, linen	Soak in cold water, then in dilute ammonia; wash
	Silk, wool	Sponge with cold water
Butter	All	Sponge with naphtha or carbon tetrachloride
Candle wax	All	Scrape away, then sponge with benzine
Chewing gum	All	Apply ice; soak in cold water; sponge with carbon tetrachloride or ether
Chocolate	Cotton, linen	Soak in cold water; wash with hypochlorite bleach
	Silk, wool	Soak in cold water; wash in hydrogen peroxide
Coffee	Cotton, linen	Soak in cold water; wash
	Silk, wool	Soak in cold water, then in hydrogen peroxide
Egg	Cotton, linen	Soak in cold water; wash
	Silk, wool	Soak in cold water; sponge with carbon tetrachloride
Fruit	All	If fresh, pour boiling water through stain; if stubborn, bleach with hypochlorite or hydrogen peroxide
Grass	All	Sponge with alcohol, then with soap and water
Ice cream	All	Sponge with gasoline or carbon tetrachloride
Iodine	All	Soak in alcohol or boil in solution of sodium thiosulfate (photographer's "hypo")
Ink (writing)	Cotton, linen	If fresh, soap and water. If dried, sponge with bleach, then sponge with oxalic acid, then wash; or put in sweet milk and let turn sour
	Silk, wool	Sponge with hydrogen peroxide, then with oxalic acid or skim milk
Ink (ball point)	All	Let stand 10–15 minutes in detergent suds, rinse. If stain remains, use vaseline or sodium hydrosulfite, then sponge with carbon tetrachloride. Some inks dissolve in glycerine followed by shampoo
Iron rust	Cotton, linen	Sponge with oxalic acid, rinse well; or spread with salt, moisten with lemon juice, and place in sun
Lipstick	Cotton, linen	Rub with lard until stain is soft, scrape off grease, wash in hot suds
	Silk, wool	Sponge with alcohol or carbon tetrachloride
Mildew	Cotton, linen	Sponge with hypochlorite bleach

KIND OF STAIN	TYPE OF FABRIC	PROCEDURE AND REMOVAL
Milk or cream	All	Sponge with benzine or carbon tetrachloride
Mustard	Cotton, linen	Apply warm glycerine; wash with suds and hydrosulfite bleach
Oil	All	Wash in soap and water or sponge with carbon tetrachloride
Paint	All	Wash in soap and water and sponge with carbon tetrachloride or with turpentine on wrong side of stain (latex and acrylic paints wash out if not dried)
Perspiration	All	Sponge with peroxide and ammonia
Rubber	All	Sponge with carbon tetrachloride
Rust	All	Sponge with lemon, vinegar, or oxalic acid
Shellac	All	Sponge with denatured alcohol
Scorch	All	If light, dampen and place in sunlight or sponge with hydrogen peroxide
Sugar	All	Sponge with hot water
Tar	All	Moisten with carbon tetrachloride or with benzine. Scrape off, then sponge residue with same solvent
Tea	Cotton, linen	Soak in borax solution, rinse; or keep stain moist with lemon juice, then expose to sun for day or two
Urine	All	Varies. Sponge with soap and water or with salt solution, then apply dilute ammonia or hydrogen peroxide briefly and rinse
Varnish	All	Sponge with equal parts alcohol and benzine
Vaseline	All	Sponge fresh stains with carbon tetrachloride, or spread talcum. Let stand; then brush
Water spot	Silk, wool	Hold in steam until damp, then iron damp

Feather the edges of the stain to prevent formation of a ring, which indicates an improper method of sponging, an excessive amount of cleaning fluid, or lack of sufficiently quick evaporation. Rapid evaporation can be obtained by blowing on the fabric or by placing it in front of an electric fan. To prevent a ring, hold the fabric over the spout of a steaming kettle until the area is damp. Then iron immediately.

KINDS OF STAIN REMOVERS

Acids, alkalies, and water are three main types of removal agents. No single chemical can be used to remove all spots from the many different kinds of fibers. For example, since acids destroy cotton and linen, they cannot be used to remove stains from these fibers. Similarly, alkalies cannot be used on silk and wool. Viscose or cuprammonium rayon can be treated like cotton. Acetate requires special care, as it dissolves in acetone, acetic acid, and chloroform, or when exposed to a hot iron.

Acids and alkalies should be used only as mild solutions. When using a mild acid such as vinegar, any possible damage that might occur to the fabric must be counteracted by applying a weak alkali, such as a solution of bicarbonate of soda or ammonia water to neutralize the acid. The fabric should be thoroughly rinsed in clear water. If an alkali solution is necessary, it should be followed immediately with a mild acid solution (such as lemon juice, vinegar, or a dilute solution of acetic acid) to neutralize the action of the alkali. The fabric should be well rinsed.

A general chemical stain remover has become available. One is sold under the trade name of *Texize K2r*. It comes both in a tube and an aerosol spray can, and it may be safely used on wool, silk, and various man-made fibers. However, it should not be used for the cellulosic fibers of cotton, linen, or rayon. Texize K2r will remove spots and stains made by most foods, beverages, grease, oil, alcohol, shoe polish, grass and cosmetics, as well as most ball-point and stamp pad inks. A thin layer of this remover should be worked into the dry stained area of the fabric, and after the substance has completely dried to a chalky white, it should be vigorously brushed away.

Many man-made fibers, such as the polyesters, acrylics, modacrylics, polypropylenes, and saran are not very absorbent, and fabrics of such fibers do not readily stain. Removal of stains generally requires merely wiping with a damp cloth or washing with a mild soap in warm water.

BLEACHING AGENTS AS STAIN REMOVERS

Various bleaching chemicals are commonly used to remove stains. But such chemicals must be used carefully because they extract color and weaken the cloth. Household bleaches of chlorine solutions (sodium hypochlorite) should be used only on cottons, linens, and rayons—never on silk or wool. If a stain is to be removed with a bleaching chemical, the fabric should be stretched over a bowl of hot water and fastened around the edge of the bowl. The bleaching agent should be dropped on the stained area with a medicine dropper. This application must be followed immediately with a thorough rinsing. The entire procedure must be done quickly so that the bleaching agent will not remain too long on the material and cause undue weakening of the fabric. To prevent weakening, a few drops of oxalic acid or sodium thiosulfate (photographer's hypo) will neutralize the action of any chlorine bleach that may remain in the fabric. If a bleaching agent is used on a colored fabric, the dipping method is advisable to avoid unequal distribution of any subsequent loss of color.

Sodium perborate and oxalic acid are effective in removing iron rust, metal stains, and some ink stains from all types of fabrics. These chemicals are the least harmful of all bleaches, but they must be used quickly to prevent abstraction of the dye. For white woolens, sodium perborate is particularly effective and harmless. For the removal of mildew, ink, iron rust, dye stains, iodine, grass stains, and fruit stains, a solution of one teaspoon of sodium hydrosulfite in a glass of water is one of the most effective bleaches. But the liquid must be used quickly, and the fabric should be well rinsed. Otherwise, the color is destroyed and the fabric is weakened.

Hydrogen peroxide may be used on all kinds of fabrics. It is a mild bleach, but it can be made more effective by the addition of a little ammonia. Oxalic acid and sodium hydrosulfite cannot be used on weighted silk.

Where a stain is known to be of a greasy nature, the use of a solvent alone is sufficient. Grease stains are easily removed by the following solvents: carbon tetrachloride, benzine, turpentine, Stoddard solvent, gasoline, ether, acetone, alcohol. With the exception of ether, acetone, alcohol, and colored gasoline, these solvents will not change the color of the material. Sponging is generally most effective. The solvent should be applied on the wrong side of the fabric. The absorbent cloth underneath the stain will draw the dissolved grease and solvent from the fabric.

For fresh grease spots or slight oil stains, a sprinkling of talcum, powdered chalk, or magnesium carbonate (magnesite) rubbed into the stained area and left for a while, will absorb the grease. When the absorbent powder is subsequently brushed off, the stain will be entirely removed. Butter stains can be removed in this manner, but they must first be heated to melt the butter before they can be fully absorbed.

DRY CLEANING

Many consumers make serious mistakes when deciding whether to wash or to dry-clean a fabric. In general, it is best to follow the advice of the salesperson or the information sometimes attached by label to a garment or fabric. Though dry cleaning is more expensive than washing, it pays to have a garment dry-cleaned rather than take a chance on washing and ruining the garment. If acetate is dry-cleaned at home, the cleaning fluid must not contain alcohol, chloroform, strong acetic acid, or acetone. Any of these destroy acetate—particularly acetone, which is the solvent used in the acetate process. The commercial dry cleaner identifies acetate by moistening a finger with acetone and rubbing it on some unexposed portion of the fabric. If the threads become hard and feel soap-like, the fabric is acetate.

LAUNDERING METHODS

When a fabric is known to be washable, frequent and prompt washing is desirable, particularly of clothing worn next to the skin. If such garments are not washed after each use, they are more difficult to clean, and the body perspiration that they have absorbed causes the fabric to deteriorate while awaiting cleaning. In general, fine underwear and brightly colored outer garments and household linens should be laundered at home. Knowledge of how to wash fragile and dainty white garments as well as dyed fabrics is essential for good results.

Just knowing that a fabric is washable is not enough information for good results in laundering. The consumer must be acquainted with the proper method for washing each type of garment and fabric. Some fabrics may be subjected to hard laundering, which includes boiling and the use of strong soaps, without too great a strain on their durability. It may be done at home as well as in commercial laundries, where it is customary to use strong substances for bleaching purposes and for sanitary reasons. Before any attempt is made to wash clothes, colored fabrics should be separated from white ones, and heavy work clothes from fine and delicate pieces, as different washing methods are necessary. Bad stains must be removed before the fabrics are immersed in hot water. Slightly soiled clothes that do not require soaking should be washed in water not over 115 degrees Fahrenheit. Extremely hot water tends to set dirt spots and minor spots or stains that may not have needed special treatment. Clothes that are very soiled should be soaked in warm, soapy water for about ten minutes.

A good quality of household soap or detergent should be dissolved in a washing machine or in a tub of hot water. Soft water will lather quickly, resulting in a more thorough cleaning. If the water is hard, the soap tends to curd because there is a high concentration of iron, calcium, magnesium, and aluminum salts in hard water. Any of the good commercial water softeners may be used to precipitate these soap-destroying metals in the water. Hard water can be softened by the use of washing soda, or sal soda (hydrated sodium carbonate). Some detergents already contain water softeners, which are described on the packages.

REVIEW QUESTIONS

1 In what way does the label on a garment help in caring for the garment?

2 (a) Why should most clothes be placed on hangers when not in use? (b) Why are knitted garments an exception? (c) How should knitted clothes be kept?

3 Why is a firm brush recommended for brushing clothing?

4 Why should garments not be crowded in a clothes closet?

5 Why should white garments be kept separate from colored ones?

6 Give illustrations of what is meant by "needed repairs." Give reasons for attending to these without delay.

7 (a) Why should clothes be given a rest? (b) How does this apply to wool clothes?

8 Why should a stain or spot be removed as soon as it is discovered?

SUGGESTED ACTIVITIES

1 For your next buying trip to a retail store, prepare a list of questions that you consider important enough to ask the salesperson to make certain that your selection of the clothing item is a prudent one.

2 Cut six advertisements from a newspaper, and circle all the textile terms that have taken on new meaning for you since studying textiles. Explain how familiarity with these textile terms has proved helpful to you recently.

BIBLIOGRAPHY AND INDEX

BIBLIOGRAPHY

REFERENCE TEXTS

For supplemental reading in specific and related areas:

American Fabrics Magazine: *Encyclopedia of Textiles,* Prentice-Hall, Inc., Englewood Cliffs, N. J., 1960.

Birrell, Verla: *The Textile Arts: A Handbook of Fabric Structure and Design Processes,* Harper & Row, Publishers, New York, 1960.

Buresh, Francis M.: *Nonwoven Fabrics,* Reinhold Publishing Corp., New York, 1962.

Chambers, Helen G., and Verna Moulton: *Clothing Selection,* J. B. Lippincott Co., Chicago, 1961.

Denny, Grace: *Fabrics,* J. B. Lippincott Co., Philadelphia, 1962.

Goldberg, J. B.: *Fabric Defects,* McGraw-Hill Book Company, New York, 1950.

Hathorne, Berkeley L.: *Woven, Stretch, and Textured Fabrics,* John Wiley & Sons, Inc., New York, 1964.

Hess, Katharine P.: *Textile Fibers and Their Use,* J. B. Lippincott Co., Chicago, 1958.

Hopkins, Giles E.: *Wool as An Apparel Fiber,* Holt, Rinehart & Winston, Inc., New York, 1953.

Labarthe, Jules: *Textiles: Origins to Usage,* The Macmillan Company, New York, 1964.

Lauterburg, Lotti: *Fabric Printing,* Reinhold Publishing Corp., New York, 1963.

Linton, George E.: *Applied Textiles,* 6th ed., Duell, Sloan & Pearce, Inc., New York, 1961.

————: *The Modern Textile Dictionary,* Duell, Sloan & Pearce, Inc., New York, 1962.

Mauersberger, Herbert Richard: *Matthews' Textile Fibers,* John Wiley & Sons, Inc., New York, 1954.

Merrill, Gilbert R., et al.: *American Cotton Handbook,* 2nd ed., Interscience Publishers, Inc., New York, 1949.

Moncrieff, R. W.: *Man-made Fibers,* John Wiley & Sons, Inc., New York, 1963.

Oelsner, Gustaf Hermann: *Handbook of Weaves,* Dover Publications, Inc., New York, 1951.

Picken, Mary B.: *The Fashion Dictionary,* Funk & Wagnalls Co., Inc., New York, 1957.

Pizzuto, Joseph James, and P. L. D'Alessandro: *101 Fabrics Analyses and Textile Dictionary,* Textile Press, New York, 1952.

Press, Jack J.: *Man-Made Textile Encyclopedia,* Textile Book Publishers, New York, 1959.

Stout, Evelyn E.: *Introduction to Textiles,* John Wiley & Sons, Inc., New York, 1965.

Textile Institute Staff: *Identification of Textile Materials,* Textile Institute, Manchester, England, 1951.

Von Bergen, Werner: *American Wool Handbook,* 2nd ed., John Wiley & Sons, Inc., New York, 1963.

PERIODICALS AND TRADE JOURNALS

For up-to-date information on developments and trends in fibers, fabrics, apparel, style, and fashion:

American Dyestuff Reporter: 44 East 23rd Street, New York, N. Y. 10010.

American Fabrics: 24 East 38th Street, New York, N. Y. 10016.

America's Textile Reporter: 286 Congress Street, Boston, Mass. 02210.

A.S.T.M. Standards on Textile Materials: American Society for Testing Materials, 1916 Race Street, Philadelphia, Pa. 19103.

Ciba Review: Ciba Limited, Basel, Switzerland.

Clothing Trade Journal: 300 Speedwell Avenue, Morris Plains, N. J. 07950.

Consumer Bulletin: Consumer's Research, Washington, N. J. 07882.

Consumer's Guide: U. S. Department of Agriculture, Washington, D.C. 20250.

Consumer Reports: Consumers Union of U. S., Inc., 256 Washington Street, Mt. Vernon, N. Y. 10553.

Corset and Underwear Review: 111 Fourth Avenue, New York, N. Y. 10003.

Curtain and Drapery Department Magazine: 230 Fifth Avenue, New York, N. Y. 10022.

Daily News Record: 7 East 12th Street, New York, N. Y. 10003.

Infants' and Children's Review: 111 Fourth Avenue, New York, N. Y. 10003.

Journal of the Textile Institute: 16 St. Mary's Parsonage, Manchester 3, England.

Knitted Outerwear Times: 386 Park Avenue South, New York, N. Y. 10016.

Linens and Domestics: Haire Publishing Co., 111 Fourth Avenue, New York, N. Y. 10003.

Men's Wear: 7 East 12th Street, New York, N. Y. 10003.

Millinery Weekly Inc.: 56 West 39th Street, New York, N. Y. 10018.

Papers of the A.A.T.T.: American Association of Textile Technologists, 7 East 12th Street, New York, N. Y. 10003.

Pepperell News Sheet: Pepperell Manufacturing Co., 111 West 40th Street, New York, N. Y. 10018.

Sportswear on Parade: 393 Fifth Avenue, New York, N. Y. 10016.

Testing League Bulletin: United States Testing Company, Inc., Hoboken, N. J. 07030.

Textile Age: 22 West Putnam Avenue, Greenwich, Conn. 06830.

Textile Industries: 1760 Peachtree Rd., N.W., Atlanta, Ga., 30309.

Textile Organon: 10 East 40th Street, New York, N. Y. 10016.

Textile World: 330 West 42nd Street, New York, N. Y. 10036.

The Boys' Outfitter: 175 Fifth Avenue, New York, N. Y. 10010.

Women's Wear Daily: 7 East 12th Street, New York, N. Y. 10003.

MISCELLANEOUS BROCHURES

For handy general textile references:

A Dictionary of Textile Terms: Dan River Mills, Inc., 111 West 40th Street, New York, N. Y. 10018 (Free).

Fiber Facts: FMC Corporation, American Viscose Division, 1617 John F. Kennedy Blvd., Philadelphia, Pa. 19103 (Free).

Index, Educational Material on Man-Made Fibers: Man-Made Fiber Producers Association, Inc., 350 Fifth Avenue, New York, N. Y. 10001 (Free).

Man-Made Fiber Industry Fact Book: Man-Made Fiber Producers Association, Inc., 350 Fifth Avenue, New York, N. Y. 10001 (Free).

U. S. Department of Agriculture, Office of Information, Catalogue of government bulletins on textiles, Washington, D. C. 20250 (Nominal charge).

U. S. Government Printing Office, Superintendent of Documents, Mailing list of all government bulletins, Washington, D. C. 20402 (Free).

University of Texas, Division of Extension, Bureau of Industrial and Business Training, Austin, Texas 78712.

TEXTILE COMPANIES AND ORGANIZATIONS

The following companies provide excellent samples, kits, literature, slides, and motion pictures. Some are available to individuals or groups under various arrangements ranging from none to nominal charges; others are offered on a loan basis only.

Natural Fibers

Cotton American Cotton Manufacturers Institute, 10 East 40th Street, New York, N. Y. 10016.

Cotton Council International, 1918 North Parkway, Box 12443, Memphis, Tenn. 38112.

Crompton-Richmond Company, 1071 Avenue of the Americas, New York, N. Y. 10018.

The National Cotton Council of America, 350 Fifth Avenue, New York, N. Y. 10001.

Linen The Irish Linen Guild, Educational Department, 1271 Avenue of the Americas, New York, N. Y. 10020.

York Street Flax Spinning Company, Belfast, Ireland.

Wool American Sheep Producers Council, Inc., 909 17th Street, Denver, Colo. 80202.

Botany Industries, Inc., 1290 Avenue of the Americas, New York, N. Y. 10020.

Burlington Industries, Inc., 1430 Broadway, New York, N. Y. 10010.

Forstmann Division, J. P. Stevens & Company, Inc., 1460 Broadway, New York, N. Y. 10036.

Silk International Silk Association, U.S.A., Inc., Educational Department, 185 Madison Avenue, New York, N. Y. 10016.

Kanebo New York Inc., 350 Fifth Avenue, New York, N. Y. 10001.

The Japan Silk Association, Inc., Public Relations Department, 285 Fifth Avenue, New York, N. Y. 10016.

Man-Made Fibers

Acetate American Viscose Corporation, Product Information, Public Relations Department, 1617 John F. Kennedy Boulevard, Philadelphia, Pa. 19103.

Celanese Fibers Company, Division of Celanese Corporation of America, Education Department, 522 Fifth Avenue, New York, N. Y. 10036.

E. I. du Pont de Nemours & Company, Inc., Product Information Section, Textile Fibers Department, Centre Road Bldg., Wilmington, Del. 19898.

Eastman Chemical Products, Inc., Educational Department, Fibers Division, 260 Madison Avenue, New York, N. Y. 10016.

Acrylics American Cyanamid Company, Fibers Division, Public Relations Department, 111 West 40th Street, New York, N. Y. 10018 (Creslan).

Chemstrand Company, Public Relations Department, 350 Fifth Avenue, New York, N. Y. 10001 (Acrilan).

E. I. du Pont de Nemours & Company, Inc., Textile Fibers Department, Product Information Section, Centre Road Bldg., Wilmington, Del. 19898 (Orlon).

The Dow Badische Company, Textile Fibers Department, 350 Fifth Avenue, New York, N. Y. 10001 (Zefran, Zefkrome).

Glass Fiber

Owens-Corning Fiberglas Corporation, National Bank Building, Toledo, Ohio 43601 (Fiberglas).

Pittsburgh Plate Glass Company, Fiber Glass Division, One Gateway Center, Pittsburgh, Pa. 15222 (PPG Fiber Glass).

Modacrylics

Eastman Chemical Products, Inc., Educational Department, Fibers Division, 260 Madison Avenue, New York, N. Y. 10016 (Verel).

Union Carbide Chemicals Co., Textile Fibers Dept., Advertising Manager, 270 Park Avenue, New York, N. Y. 10017 (Dynel).

Nylon

Allied Chemical Corporation, Product Information Section, Fiber Marketing Department, 261 Madison Avenue, New York, N. Y. 10016.

American Enka Corporation, Merchandising Department, 350 Fifth Avenue, New York, N. Y. 10001.

Chemstrand Company, Public Relations Department, 350 Fifth Avenue, New York, N. Y. 10001.

E. I. du Pont de Nemours & Company, Inc., Product Information Section, Textile Fibers Department, Centre Road Bldg., Wilmington, Del. 19898.

Polyesters

Celanese Fibers Company, Division of Celanese Corporation of America, Educational Department, 522 Fifth Avenue, New York, N. Y. 10036 (Fortrel).

E. I. du Pont de Nemours & Company, Inc., Product Information Section, Textile Fibers Department, Centre Road Bldg., Wilmington, Del. 19898 (Dacron).

Eastman Chemical Products, Inc., Educational Department, Fibers Division, 260 Madison Avenue, New York, N. Y. 10016 (Kodel).

Polypropylenes

Hercules Powder Company, Fiber Development Department, Wilmington, Del. 19899 (Herculon).

United States Rubber Company, Product Information, 1230 Avenue of the Americas, New York, N. Y. 10020 (Polycrest).

Rayons

American Enka Corporation, Merchandising Department, 350 Fifth Avenue, New York, N. Y. 10001.

American Viscose Corporation, Product Information, Public Relations Department, 1617 John F. Kennedy Boulevard, Philadelphia, Pa. 19103.

Celanese Fibers Company, Division of Celanese Corporation of America, Education Department, 522 Fifth Avenue, New York, N. Y. 10036.

Courtaulds North America, Inc., 600 Fifth Avenue, New York, N. Y. 10020.

Saran

The Dow Badische Company, Textile Fibers Department, 350 Fifth Avenue, New York, N. Y. 10001.

Spandex	American Cyanamid Company, 111 West 40th Street, New York, N. Y. 10018 (Numa).
	E. I. du Pont de Nemours & Company, Inc., Textile Fibers Department, Wilmington, Del. 19898 (Lycra).
	Globe Manufacturing Company, 456 Bedford Street, Fall River, Mass. 02722 (Glospan).
	United States Rubber Company, Textile Division, 1230 Avenue of the Americas, New York, N. Y. 10020 (Vyrene).
Triacetate	Celanese Fibers Company, Division of Celanese Corporation of America, Educational Department, 522 Fifth Avenue, New York, N. Y. 10036 (Arnel).

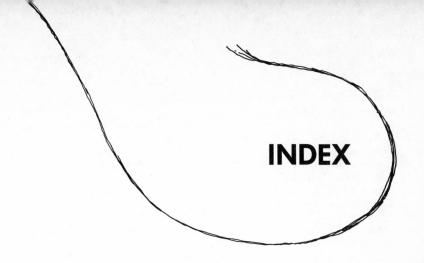

INDEX